*The Emerging States of
French Equatorial Africa*

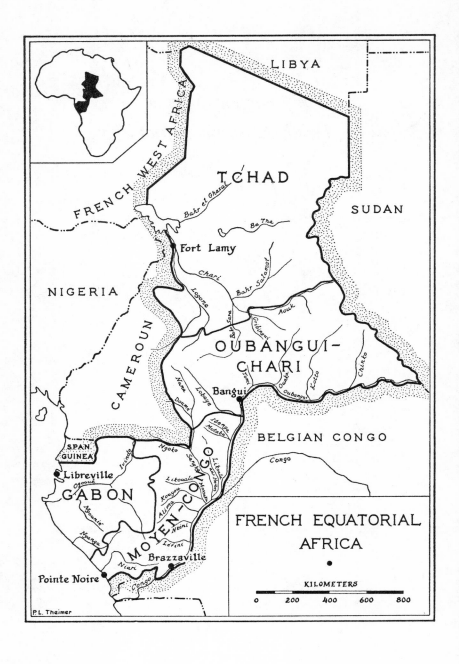

FRENCH EQUATORIAL
AFRICA

KILOMETERS

0   200   400   600   800

P.L. Theimer

The Emerging States of

French Equatorial

Africa

VIRGINIA THOMPSON
and
RICHARD ADLOFF

STANFORD UNIVERSITY PRESS, STANFORD, CALIFORNIA
LONDON: OXFORD UNIVERSITY PRESS

PREVIOUS BOOKS BY VIRGINIA THOMPSON AND RICHARD ADLOFF

The Left Wing in Southeast Asia
Minority Problems in Southeast Asia
French West Africa

Stanford University Press
Stanford, California
London: Oxford University Press
© 1960 by Virginia Thompson Adloff
All rights reserved
Library of Congress Catalog Card Number: 60-13871
Printed in the United States of America
Published with the assistance of the Ford Foundation

First published, 1960
Second printing, 1961

To
M. L. B. *and* V. E. B.

Preface

For nearly half a century the territories of Moyen-Congo (Middle Congo), Gabon, Oubangui-Chari, and Tchad constituted the administrative federation of French Equatorial Africa. Because of the cumbersomeness of the official title, the federation was commonly referred to by its initials, AEF (Afrique Equatoriale Française), and for convenience we shall use this abbreviation in the following pages.

Among the changes initiated by the *loi-cadre*—the "basic law"—of 1956 was that of referring to AEF somewhat vaguely as a Group of Territories, a term that took into account the unpopularity of the federation concept, but that designation survived for only a few months. By early 1959, the sweeping reforms in the structure of Overseas France which were wrought by General de Gaulle led to the disappearance of the Group as well as of AEF as governmental entities. Meanwhile, Moyen-Congo had become the Republic of the Congo, and Oubangui-Chari became the Republic of Central Africa; Gabon and Tchad were similarly transformed into republics but retained their old names.

Because the aim of this book is to provide a broad background, it is devoted in large part to the period in which French Equatorial Africa and its four territories existed as such; hence we have used the old names except in sections that concern the most recent political metamorphoses. As the book goes to press, no single name denoting the geographical group of the former AEF has yet been devised. Since the four new republics that have risen phoenixlike from the ashes of the old federation have entered into agreements that reestablish a few of their economic and financial ties, and since all are members of the new Community—the inheritor of the Fourth French Republic and its Overseas Territories—the title of this study attempts to reflect the old as well as the new order.

Our book *French West Africa* (published in 1958) deals, in a number of fields, with developments common to both federations; this volume does not repeat such data. The general pattern followed is that of *French West Africa,* but because of political developments in AEF since 1957, a fuller treatment has been given to the individual territories, which have now become autonomous republics. At the same time, the story of the former federation has been told in considerable detail because of our conviction that the evolution of the area can be fully understood only in the light of its past.

Besides printed materials available in France and the United States, sources include interviews accorded us during two trips in AEF in 1956 and 1958 and documents collected in the course of those trips. All students of AEF, however, are handicapped by the lack or incompleteness of source materials. In some fields, notably the economic, the documentation is relatively abundant, but in others it is spotty or even nonexistent. Such gaps are particularly conspicuous with respect to political and social developments that have taken place outside the main urban centers.

As was the case during our travels throughout French West Africa in 1953, we received in AEF invaluable aid and warm hospitality from both French and African officials, as well as from private individuals. And we were again so fortunate as to have the companionship and guidance of our friend Maurice Joriot, a long-time Africanist. We should also like to express our gratitude to John Ballard of Boston University for his helpful criticism of portions of the manuscript.

Since November 1959, when research for this book was completed, the internal political situation in the states of former AEF has unfolded without spectacular surprises, aside from Lisette's sudden elimination from the scene in Tchad. In May 1960, one month before the Belgian Congo's accession to independence, Fulbert Youlou induced the governments of Bangui and Fort Lamy to join with that of Brazzaville in a Union des Républiques d'Afrique Centrale (URAC), which would share a common nationality, diplomatic representation, and external defense system, and as independent states remain within the remodeled Franco-African Community. Gabon, also yielding to the prevailing trend toward independence but still insisting on separate ties with France, refused to join the URAC but agreed to remain within the existing customs union and cooperate in the economic, technical, and military fields. Though this was only a partial fulfillment of Youlou's ambitions, the URAC became by mid-1960 a potential pole of attraction for the Bakongo in former Belgian territory who followed the leadership of President Kasavubu in his power struggle with Premier Lumumba. The long-standing close relationship between the two Bakongo leaders, Kasavubu's presence at the ex–French Congo's independence celebration, and his subsequent use of Brazzaville radio added fuel to the flame of Lumumba's wrath. This had already been aroused by France's abstention in two Security Council votes against Belgium's policy, the presence of thousands of Belgian refugees in Brazzaville, and Lumumba's conviction that Youlou with French support was attempting to lure the dissident Bakongo of the Léopoldville region into some new form of union with their fellow tribesmen north of the Congo river. However, as this book goes to press, the situation in the former Belgian Congo—with all the international complications that it has caused—is so confused as to preclude any reasonable forecast as to its denouement.

V. T.

August 1960   R. A.

Contents

Illustrations

MAPS

PLATES

Photographs by Richard Adloff

(BETWEEN PAGES 276 AND 277)

1   *Distribution* of bulletins de vote, *Moyen-Congo.*
Government-built housing for Africans, Pointe Noire.

2   *Board posting official controlled prices, Pointe Noire market place.*
Palais de Justice, Brazzaville.

3   *Hotel Mayombé at Pointe Noire. Market in Brazzaville.*

4   *Nave of Ste. Anne-du-Congo Cathedral, Brazzaville.*

5   *Abbé Fulbert Youlou, President of the Congo Republic.*

6   *Diesel-engine train of the Congo-Ocean railroad.*
Schoolroom in Diosso, Moyen-Congo.

7   *Chief of the village of Diosso.*
Print shop of the Catholic Mission (built 1885), Loango, Moyen-Congo.

8   *Léon Mba, of Gabon.*

9   *The CGTA's boat* Fort-Archambault *on the Oubangui river.*
New hospital at Libreville.

10   *Approach to village on the Oubangui river.*
Mobile leprosy clinic, Oubangui-Chari.

11   *Cotton-textile mill, Oubangui-Chari. Fishermen's huts, Tchad.*

12   *Ahmed Koulamallah, of Tchad.*

13   *Market place at Largeau, Tchad. Cattle-training center, Tchad.*

14   *Market place arcade, Abéché, Tchad. A village of western Tchad.*

15   *Typical structures of a western Tchad village (Massa tribe).*

16   *Construction of a* case *(hut), western Tchad.*
Musician of the Massa tribe, Tchad.

PART I

The Federation

CHAPTER 1

The Colonial Background

The history of Afrique Equatoriale Française before its contact with Europeans remains largely unknown, although in recent years a little light has been thrown on it by archaeologists and anthropologists.[1] Guides in the form of written documents and monuments are lacking, and oral traditions—dating back at best only a few centuries—were not recorded in any lasting medium. The dense forest that covers much of central and coastal AEF was inimical to the development of large political entities such as existed for centuries in parts of French West Africa. Only in the equatorial stretches of the Congo basin and in the northern savannah regions did strong kingdoms arise and flourish.

On scanty evidence it is believed that the Negrillos were the first to populate the great forest and that they were later attacked and driven back by invaders coming from the north and northeast (Batéké, Boubangui, Bakalaï, and Fang) at about the same time as from the southeast (Mpongoué, Oroungou, Nkomi, Bavili, Bayaka, and Mba). The course of events in this area was characterized by obscure and confused struggles between many tribal groups.[2]

To the north, the savannah and semidesert zones seem to have been inhabited by populations of diverse origin, mainly Negroes crossbred with Arabs or Berbers. At the end of the eleventh century, Islam was introduced into the region now known as Kanem, which then and for hundreds of years thereafter was the scene of chronic warfare and a crossroads for caravan trade. In Borkou, traces have been found of a Hamitic people whose architecture resembled that of ancient Rome,[3] and recent archaeological discoveries in the Midigué butte near Fort Lamy disclose the former existence of a highly evolved fetishist people, the Sao.[4] But it was probably because of the dynamic pressure of Islam that most of the medieval political units were created in what is now Tchad, and these warred with each other, the indigenous populations, and their neighbors in Fezzan, Cameroun, and northern Nigeria. Despite this, and until the nineteenth century, the sultanates of Kanem, Borkou, Ouaddaï, Baguirmi, and Kouti prospered through raiding expeditions, while the countries on which they preyed were depopulated and laid waste to the point of becoming semideserts. Slaves and pillage formed the shaky economic basis of these states, whose survival was moreover internally menaced by an unending series of uprisings and palace revolutions.

3

The Coming of Europeans

In the Congo basin the historian is on the somewhat surer ground provided by the accounts of European travelers and missionaries from the late fifteenth century on. Here, as in so many other parts of the world, the Portuguese were the first comers, during the third quarter of that century. In 1484, Diego Cao explored the mouth of the river which was then called the Zaïre and later the Congo, the latter name being derived from that of a nearby Negro kingdom whose capital was at San Salvador in Angola. During most of the sixteenth century, three kingdoms existed in that area: the Loango or Brama, lying between the Ogooué river and the Congo; the Mani-Congo, or kingdom of the Congo, whose fluctuating boundaries included at their greatest extent the coast from Sette-Kama to Banguela; and, in the hinterland, the Batéké kingdom of Anzico, whose chief was called the Makoko. Yet in the era of the great explorations in the non-European world, the Congo-Gabon coast was less well known than that of west or south Africa, and only gradually was a mosaic of fragmentary knowledge built up.

During the sixteenth century the Portuguese were busily setting up trading posts that soon dotted the coast, and whose names have survived to this day. (For example, the name Gabon was first given to that river's estuary because its appearance suggested the outlines of a cloak with sleeves and a hood—in Portuguese, *gabão*.) Throughout the 1500's the Portuguese tried to develop trade, and in so doing introduced into the coastal lands corn, manioc, and some animal husbandry. In the early days, this trade was wholly barter: cloth, beads, hardware, tobacco, firearms, and liquor were exchanged for gold dust, ivory, palm oil, and precious woods. As this commerce yielded unsatisfactory profits, the Portuguese came to concentrate on a single product, the human slave, for whose detention and shipment abroad they constructed special entrepôts called barracoons. Slaves were brought to them from beyond the Anzico country. They were either sold by their own tribes or acquired through raids, and were sent to the coast via a long line of intermediaries. Apparently the coastal peoples suffered not at all from the slave trade, for when they were not rivals to the Portuguese in this domain, they collaborated with them.

Although the Portuguese did not long remain the only European traders in the area, throughout the seventeenth century—when the kingdoms of Loango and Congo were at their height—Portuguese influence continued to be paramount. In the sixteenth century, rivals appeared in the form of Dutch, English, and especially French merchants, whose ships traded along the Guinea and Angola coasts. By the seventeenth century, monopolistic chartered companies had largely replaced enterprising individuals in this trade. Financially, the results were mediocre. Nevertheless, by means of this commerce, fairly regular contacts were maintained between Europe and the equatorial regions of central Africa. On the eve of the French Revolution, some 70 French firms were trading with the coast of

Gabon and had acquired a lead there over their European rivals, who competed bitterly with each other to acquire the maximum of captives brought from the interior. The Europeans did not create this slave trade, for slavery was already a deep-rooted institution in central Africa, but they profited by it and played a large part in emptying equatorial Africa of its most robust men.

Fortunately, European contacts with this part of Africa were not confined to the slavers. To the coast, as early as 1470, came Portuguese priests whose establishments gradually built up a following of some 32,000 Africans, and in 1645 they were joined by Capuchins. In 1703 there was founded at Paris a missionary society of the Holy Spirit (les Pères du Saint-Esprit), which began to send members to central Africa as well as to the Far East. And it was a French priest who in 1760 was named Apostolic Vicar of the Loango mission. These missionaries recorded the first authentic data on the country and its peoples. In 1776, a French *abbé* named Proyart gathered together all the current knowledge of local history and customs and published a history of the Loango, Bakongo, and other kingdoms of central Africa. Since the missionaries of that period did not penetrate the hinterland, their studies were limited to the coastal peoples. Although these accounts largely coincided with the decline of the kingdoms of Loango and Congo, these kingdoms were shown to have been remarkable states. At its peak, the Loango kingdom stretched as far north as the Gabon estuary and had expanded to the south and east as far as the Mayombé, at the expense of the Congo kingdom. Its structure was that of a federated state; its capital was a thriving town, and its seven provinces were administered by chiefs chosen from certain leading families.

About 1830 new elements, both external and internal, gradually altered the situation. Shortly before this, the Batéké of Anzico had been driven north by warriors from the Congo kingdom and in this migration came into contact with a numerous and bellicose tribe, the Boubangui, who had penetrated as far south as what is now called the lower Oubangui river. The Batéké tried for 30 years—during the mid-nineteenth century—to contain the Boubangui, but not until 1875 were they finally successful. Thereafter the Boubangui did not dispute the Batéké's role as intermediaries between the coastal traders and the hinterland, and even paid tribute to the Batéké chief, the Makoko.

Concurrently, a marked change was taking place in European—particularly French—policy, the expansionist trend of which had been checked for many years by the Revolution and the Napoleonic Wars. The decision reached by the European powers during the first quarter of the nineteenth century to suppress the slave trade radically altered their relations with central Africa. Then, in July 1830, France decided to establish missionary, trading, and naval refueling posts along the Gabon coast. Lieutenant Bouët-Willaumez, who had already explored the Gabon estuary, was charged by the French navy in 1842 with carrying out this operation and also with suppressing the slave trade in that area. With the cooperation of French missionaries, he had already established friendly contacts with the local African chiefs. Indeed, in 1839 the chieftain called "King Denis" had ceded to France two small plots of land for the construction of fortifications and had signed an alliance with his French colleague, King Louis-Philippe.

Treaties with other chiefs followed, and these permitted French boats and also missionaries to penetrate inland beyond the estuary without the use of force. But progress was slow in this respect and virtually nil toward the accomplishment of Bouët-Willaumez' second task—suppression of the slave trade, which persisted clandestinely despite all efforts to check it. In 1849, the officers of a French ship, after capturing a boat carrying slaves, settled them on the right bank of the Gabon estuary in a place which was given the appropriate name of Libreville. Fortunately this site was propitious for trade, and after Gabon was freed from the jurisdiction of Dakar in 1881, Libreville became the center of French administration and influence along that coast. From 1849 until the outbreak of the Franco-Prussian War in 1870, it was also the point of departure for all French explorations of the great forest lying to the east.

Exploring the Interior

Between 1842 and 1862 the many treaties signed by French officers and Gabonese chiefs gave France "full and entire sovereignty" over the Gabon river and the lands that it bathed. During that period, a few venturesome individuals explored the Ogooué valley and some other parts of the interior, among them Paul du Chaillu, an American hunter of French descent.

The broad estuaries of the Gabon coast led the early comers to believe that these might be waterways leading far inland. The Gabon river appeared to be the most promising of them, but it was soon found to be little more than an arm of the sea. Then the Rio Muni was shown to be of only secondary importance. As for the Ogooué river, local tradition maintained that it divided Africa in two, and it was thought that those who controlled it could channel to the Atlantic coast the economic resources of all central Africa.[5] But a short-lived expedition by a French naval vessel in 1862 was inconclusive; and soon after, France was defeated in the war with Prussia. As a result, explorations in the area came to a standstill until the mid-1870's. In 1873 a French naturalist, Bouvier, at his own expense organized another expedition up the Ogooué, but after making more progress than his predecessors he abandoned the enterprise a year later. By this time English and Germans were competing with French explorers and the race for control of equatorial Africa was on.

At this point the tide was turned in France's favor by the initiative of a naturalized Frenchman, the Italian count Savorgnan de Brazza. Born in Rome in 1852, he studied at the French naval academy and entered the French navy in time to serve briefly in the Franco-Prussian War. This was followed by his participation in the Kabylie campaign of 1871 and in a voyage to the south Atlantic the year after. It was during a period of leave in Gabon that he began investigating the lower Ogooué. At the age of 20 he developed the project of exploring the Ogooué and the Congo, but not until three years later, in February 1875, did the Naval Ministry give its approval and name Brazza head of a small expeditionary force.

Brazza's first Ogooué venture, in 1875–78, proved disappointing, for he found that the river did not lead to the heart of Africa. During the next three years, however, he acquired new knowledge of the mysterious hinterland and made friendly contacts with chiefs along the way. Convinced that he could still reach the Congo by this route, and undaunted by illness, the rainy season, the loss of his baggage, and the hostility of some river tribes, Brazza left the Ogooué and struck out to the east overland, then descended the Alima river in a dugout. By August 1878, however, he was at the end of his strength and his provisions, and had to return to the coast. From there he went to Paris, where he readily won support for a second mission, of which he was appointed head.

In part, Brazza's facility in obtaining official sponsorship was the result of his own achievement, but he was also aided by the fact that King Leopold II of the Belgians had shortly before given his blessing to a Congo expedition led by the famous explorer Stanley. To Brazza's chagrin, Stanley reached the mouth of the great river in August 1879. Four months later, Brazza was once again off to Africa in the hope of gaining the upper reaches of the Congo before his rival. Taking the same route as on his first expedition, he founded Franceville on the upper Ogooué in 1880. Then, taking with him a Senegalese sergeant, Malamine, an interpreter, and a few Negro troops, he crossed the Batéké plateaus and reached the Léfini and the Congo. Here he received emissaries sent by the Batéké chief, the Makoko, whom he persuaded to sign a treaty on September 10, 1880, accepting a French protectorate. Three weeks later the Makoko ceded to France the territory of Ncouna, on the north bank of the Congo, for the purpose of establishing a post there. It was to this post that the Geographical Society of Paris later gave the name of Brazzaville.

Brazza's next goal was to link these new possessions with the coast by the shortest possible route. After leaving Malamine in charge of the Ncouna post, he followed the Niari valley and from the coast eventually reached Libreville by sea. From there, with only a brief pause, Brazza went up river again to Franceville and was well on his way back to the Congo when he learned, late in September 1881, that he had been replaced as head of the Congo mission by a former associate, Mizon. Puzzled and distraught, Brazza returned to the coast by still another route, the Niari-Kouilou, and embarked for France in June 1882. He had completed two and a half years of almost uninterrupted exploration, traveled more than 4,000 km., and gained for his adopted country, by wholly pacific means, a territory equivalent in area to about one-third of France. On his arrival in Paris, he was cheered to learn that his Senegalese sergeant Malamine, with a few *tirailleurs* and the Makoko's men, had foiled Stanley's attempt in July 1881 to take the embryonic Brazzaville. And the loyal Malamine had done this in defiance of the orders of Mizon to abandon the post and return to Franceville.

This episode did much to strengthen popular support for Brazza in Paris, where his position had been weakened by a wave of anticolonialism that swept France at that time. (Fears of overinvolvement in Indochina and of antagonizing Britain in Africa as well as in Asia brought about the downfall of Premier Jules Ferry, Brazza's backer, late in 1881.) But the checkmating of Stanley, then widely regarded as France's chief adversary, made a national hero of Brazza, and he added to his prestige by conducting a vigorous propaganda campaign in the press, by lectures, and by reports to the government. Through these means the French public acquired a concept of the Congo as the key to control of central Africa and to exploitation of ivory and wild rubber resources that would bring immense prosperity to their owners. On November 21, 1882, the Parliament, to which the Congo lands were pictured as a fertile field for trade and for France's civilizing influence, ratified Brazza's treaty with the Makoko by 444 votes to 3. Soon afterward, Brazza was appointed the head of a third and far better equipped official mission, given the title of Commissioner for the Republic in the French Congo, and provided with a fund of 2,275,000 francs. Specifically, he was instructed to take possession in the name of France of the territories that he had explored and to give them an administrative organization. By this time, even the anticolonials were pleased by the prospect of forestalling other European powers in the rubber-rich Congo and of transforming a handful of trading posts along the Gabon coast into a vast colony capable of further expansion to the north and east.

Brazza began his third mission in April 1883 by founding some 20 posts along the coast north of Loango and in the Ogooué valley. He then hurried on to Brazzaville, where he was able to present the Makoko with a ratified treaty and generally strengthen France's hold over that region. Leaving a trusted companion, Charles de Chavannes, at Brazzaville, he moved north to join another of his lieutenants, Dolisie, who had been busy making treaties with the tribes of the lower Oubangui. Returning to the coast, Brazza began organizing another exploration of the upper Congo. The climax to French expansion that year came with the signing of a treaty with the King of Loango, by which he placed his country under the protection of France; in return France confirmed that the chiefs and the people were to retain full property rights to all their lands except Pointe Indienne, which was ceded outright to the French government.

Division of the Spoils

A turning point in the destinies of Africa came in the year 1884, with the holding of an international congress at Berlin. By that time, the appearance of Germany in the African arena and the conflicting claims of the European governments already established there—particularly the differences between Portugal and Leopold II concerning claims to the Congo area—seemed to call for a general settlement. At the Berlin congress, the International Association of the Congo (later the Congo Free State) won recognition as a state, and the Act of Berlin signed February 26, 1885, laid down certain general rules governing European occupation and development of central Africa. Although the French Congo was not given direct access to the mouth of the Congo river, France retained possession of the lands explored by Brazza and of the Niari basin. To offset Britain's occupation of the Niger river's mouth and to acquire a share in the trade of that river, France agreed to internationalize the Congo as well as the Niger.

Aside from this example of what has been called a "curious colonial collectivism," the theory of zones of influence was accepted and the rights of the first occupant acquired legality, provided occupancy was effective. In practice the Act of Berlin settled far less than it seemed to at the time it was signed. International rivalries were accentuated rather than appeased, a series of bilateral treaties altered boundaries repeatedly, and direct sovereignty through military and economic occupation largely supplanted the former adherence to international free-trade doctrines. Nevertheless, the Act of Berlin marked the end of an era. As a result of the abolition of the slave trade and, later, the opening of the Suez Canal, the central African coast lost much of its importance as a site for trading posts and fueling stations for naval vessels en route to the Far East. What now aroused European interest and provoked a rush to stake claims far inland was the wealth of the interior, largely rubber and ivory.

A special agreement with Portugal (May 17, 1885) settled the French Congo's southeastern boundary; two treaties with the Congo Free State, in 1887 and 1892, recognized the Oubangui river as the boundary between it and French territory. The northeastern and northwestern frontiers, however, were defined with far more difficulty and generally to France's disadvantage. In 1887, Brazza claimed the region north of the Oubangui as a zone of French influence, for he wanted to unite French West Africa, Algeria, and his Congo into a vast empire of which Lake Tchad would be the center. French expeditions did occupy the territory later known as Oubangui-Chari and in 1889 founded the post of Bangui there. But the French push from that point to the northwest and northeast met with effective Anglo-German opposition. In 1890 Britain forced France to recognize Nigeria's boundaries as extending to Lake Tchad, and four years later Germany obliged France to agree to an extension of Kamerun's northern frontier also to that lake. Confined now to the eastern shore of Lake Tchad, the French turned eastward and there came up against two opponents of unequal strength, the British and a Sudanese adventurer named Rabah.

In the early 1890's, the surprising discovery that the upper Oubangui river ran east instead of north encouraged some Frenchmen to think that it opened their way to the Nile. For almost a decade this erroneous conviction diverted French expansionism fruitlessly toward the east. It led to the remarkable exploit of the Marchand Mission, in which 12 Europeans

and 150 *tirailleurs,* from December 1897 to July 1898, trekked across a vast
and uncharted territory from Libreville to the upper Nile, only to end in
the resounding French diplomatic defeat at Fashoda in 1899. The Anglo-
French agreement reached at that time excluded France from the Nile
valley and set as the eastern boundary of her African territories the Chari
and the Ouaddaï region. Fashoda had an enormous psychological impact
on French opinion of that period. The French were both proud of Marchand's exploit and chagrined by having had to withdraw ignominiously in
the face of English opposition, and for a time colonial expansion was discredited. Yet the setback at Fashoda did have one practical advantage—
that of channeling French expeditions to the north, in the region that
later became Tchad territory.

Even before the Fashoda incident, France had planned to occupy the
Baguirmi region, which was believed to be the gate to Ouaddaï and the
desert area. But both the Crampel Mission of 1890–91 and the Maistre
Mission of 1892–93 got this project off to a bad start, for they ran into the
active hostility of the Khartoum-born slave trader Rabah, who had carved
out for himself a vast "empire" in the Chari-Baguirmi region. After the
Fashoda checkmate and smaller defeats in Baguirmi, a vast converging
operation was organized, with the aim of linking together all France's possessions in northern, western, and central Africa. An expedition under
Foureau—who was later replaced by Lamy—marched down from the Algerian oases; another, under Voullet, moved eastward from Niger territory;
and a third, headed by Gentil, came up from the Congo region. Despite
incredible hardships and bungling, because of the indiscipline of both officers and troops, the hostility of tribes encountered along the way, and the
extremely rugged terrain through which the expeditions passed, the three
columns met on Lake Tchad at Kousseri, on April 21, 1900. The next day
a decisive battle took place, in which both Rabah and the French commandant Lamy were killed. This campaign, called "le rendez-vous du
Tchad," did succeed in fulfilling Brazza's dream of uniting all France's
African possessions and of expanding the Gabon-Congo territories even
beyond the shores of the great lake. By 1900 France had acquired, in addition to the original coastal forest region and the riverlands of the Oubangui
and Congo, a pastoral and desert area in Tchad. The whole was an enormous, amorphous mass made up of three distinct economic zones whose
only means of intercommunication was provided by a common river system.

Acquisition of this huge colony had taken only a few years and involved
merely minor military expeditions, for the great bulk of the new lands had
been annexed by wholly peaceful means. But the colony's lack of natural
frontiers and its general geographical situation were such that its political
boundaries underwent many changes. In some cases, such as the Franco-
Spanish agreement of January 27, 1900, and the Franco-Portuguese treaty
of January 25, 1901, only slight rectifications were involved. The boundary
with the Congo Free State remained fairly stable, and the Entente Cordiale
with Britain in 1904 largely ended Franco-British rivalry in this part of

Africa.[6] With Germany, however, the situation was very different, and the successive alterations in Kamerun's northeastern frontier reflected France's fluctuating diplomatic fortunes in Europe. A new Franco-German agreement of April 18, 1908, gave way in 1911 to another treaty, a result of the Moroccan crisis of that period, which cost AEF some 275,000 square kilometers. This loss was remedied a few years later, however, when Germany's defeat in World War I enabled France to retrieve more territory than it had lost.

The French Congo's Administrative Framework

Expansion of the French Congo colony had been so rapid and on such a large scale that its administrative structure had to be repeatedly revised. After Brazza had been named Commissioner of the French Congo in April 1886, difficulties arose from the multiplicity of Paris ministries on which he had been made dependent. He was responsible politically to the Ministry of Foreign Affairs and administratively to the Ministry of the Navy through its Under-secretary for the Colonies. Two and a half years later, a decree of December 11, 1888, linked his territories to France's West African possessions, but in a few months the earlier status of the French Congo was restored. As to internal administration, a decree of February 27, 1889, created a hierarchy of African personnel for the colony, including canton and post chiefs and *agents de culture,* the latter being assigned administrative duties in addition to those of developing agriculture and trade. In 1890 the French Congo acquired its own budget, amounting then to 1.5 million francs, and its revenues were made dependent mainly on customs duties and consumer taxes.

The next decade not only brought a tremendous territorial push to the north but also ushered in the reign of the big concessionary companies, which were given virtually sovereign powers over an enormous proportion of the colony's total area. (See below.) The sparse administrative posts that had been set up in Oubangui-Chari could not effectively control so large an area, and attempts to increase the zone of effective control from these posts met with more or less open opposition. In the forest region there were spasmodic outbreaks (although never in the form of a mass uprising) in such trouble spots as the Ngoko Sangha. In the upper Oubangui area the task was harder, for there the terrain required that insurgent bands be overcome one by one. Everywhere the regime installed by the concessionary companies not only complicated the government's task but was in itself a primary cause of widespread unrest.

The task of pacifying Tchad took even longer and required larger-scale military operations. First the resistance led by Rabah's two sons had to be quelled. Then Sultan Doumourah of Ouaddaï showed his hostility to French penetration by attacking some military posts in the south. This action did not immediately bring on open warfare, but in 1909 French troops occupied Abeché, and two years later Colonel Largeau finally established French control of Ouaddaï. His capture of Faya in 1913 confirmed France's sovereignty over Kanem and Borkou. Although Oubangui-Chari had been considered sufficiently pacified by 1911 to be turned over to a civilian administration, only part of Tchad was similarly transferred in 1915, and to this day military officers command the region of Borkou-Ennedi-Tibesti (often referred to as the BET).

Even before military operations ended in the north, an attempt was made under Martial Merlin to give unity to this sprawling area of disparate elements. In 1910 it was administratively welded into a federation modeled after that of French West Africa. Each of its four territories—Moyen-Congo, Oubangui-Chari, Gabon, and Tchad—was theoretically to retain economic and administrative autonomy, but a government-general, set up at Brazzaville and charged with guiding and giving coherence to local policies, soon developed a strong centralizing trend. Over the years the government-general of French Equatorial Africa underwent more of a metamorphosis than did its counterpart at Dakar, but the two federations met similar fates in the end, and melted from the scene early in 1959.

Rule by the Concessionary Companies

Deep disagreement in regard to the policy that should be followed in the French Congo persisted for 20 years before the creation of the AEF federation. The humanitarian school was led by Brazza, who energetically opposed turning the Congo into a field of economic exploitation. He believed that the colony should be a protectorate, dependent on the Ministry of Foreign Affairs, and that it should be developed in the interests of its African population. Specifically he opposed the decrees of 1898–99 which transferred ownership of the land and waterways from the Africans to the French state. He considered these decrees to be both illegitimate and impolitic. Furthermore, he felt that large-scale commerce should not be introduced until the government had organized a system of communications.

Unfortunately for the Congo, contemporary opinion in France favored dividing up the colony among big concessionary companies. The Third Republic had been sold the concept of a colonial empire in which expansion was the corollary of industrial growth. The Belgians' success in exploiting the ivory and rubber of their Congo lands and the prosperity of the British Niger and East Africa companies were attributed to two factors: the organization of large-scale capital on a company basis, and the fact that the exploiting companies were given a monopoly of trade and a measure of sovereignty over immense areas. This conviction was reinforced by one of the major principles embodied in the Act of Berlin, namely, that of economic nondiscrimination between its signatory nations in the Congo basin treaty area. Development by the French government of its Congo colony, it was feared, might lead to international protests; accordingly exploitation by private concessionaires of what were then thought to be the boundless riches of the Congo appeared to be the only viable solution.

Eugène Etienne, then a member of the French Cabinet, was the most persuasive exponent of this thesis. As early as 1880 he urged in Parliament the establishment of concessionary companies, and in 1891 he drafted a law that not only would permit the creation of such companies and grant them exclusive political and economic rights over the areas conceded, but would not require them to pay quit-rent to the state in return. Before this law could be submitted to Parliament, the government in which Etienne was Minister of Colonies fell. However, his successor, Théophile Delcassé, shared Etienne's views, and by simple decrees in 1893–94 he granted two individual entrepreneurs 30-year concessions that covered nearly 150,000 square kilometers. When news of this leaked out to the public it caused such a political furor that the decrees were annulled in 1895 by the Minister of Colonies. On the grounds that such action was illegal, Daumas, one of the concessionaires, attacked the government through the Council of State and eventually won a compromise settlement. Thus the issue was far from resolved, and three years later the partisans of the concessionary system returned to the charge.

Two events that had deplorable consequences for the Congo occurred in 1898. Because of his obstructionism, Brazza was dismissed from his post. Then a Commission of Colonial Concessions was set up in Paris, and its report led to the adoption of the concessionary system. Companies were to be given exclusive rights over all agricultural, forest, and industrial exploitation for 30 years, and after that period outright ownership of whatever land they had developed and any forests in which they had regularly collected rubber. In exchange, they were to pay the state a sum that varied with the size of their concessions, plus 15 per cent of their annual profits. They were also to build roads and maintain order, and to safeguard local Africans' rights by creating reserves for them and respecting the customary utilization of land and forests by villagers and tribes. A gesture of deference to the Act of Berlin was the proviso that some zones would be set apart for free trade.

The gates were now wide open, and as S. H. Roberts has summed up the situation:[7]

> Between March and July 1899 no less than 40 concessionaire companies obtained privileges in the Congo by decree. In all, monopolies were conferred over 650,000 sq. km., a little more than the whole area of France. All of the land from the coast to the Oubangui Bend, except for small areas around Libreville and Brazzaville, were claimed in this way. In addition, a huge patch on the Upper Oubangui—all of the immediately or distantly exploitable area of the Congo. In effect, the whole Congo was handed over to large companies with a registered capital of 59½ million francs. The government in practice abdicated its functions and limited itself to the imposition of taxes and the collection of quit-rents. It was in fact an amazing experiment in what might be termed a multiple delegation of sovereignty, although the actual text of the companies' concessions allowed no such right.

In two vital respects these monopolistic arrangements flouted the Berlin Act, and the first to react were some British traders long established in the

Gabon coastal zone.[8] Their protests at being forcibly ejected from the treaty-guaranteed free-trade zone were sufficiently effective for the case to be taken up eventually at the intergovernmental level. And in 1907 the French administration was compelled to pay them 1.5 million francs in indemnity and to cede them an area of 300 square kilometers. Far more serious in its long-term repercussions was the flagrant disregard of African rights as guaranteed by both the Act of Berlin and the companies' contracts, and the African victims had no means of obtaining redress.

The incredible abuses to which the concessionaire regime and the government's negligence gave rise were not known in France until a sensational article entitled "Les Bourreaux des Noirs" appeared in Le Matin on February 15, 1905. This story, which was reprinted in many other French newspapers, recounted the atrocities committed by two officials, Gaud and Toqué, against the helpless Africans in their charge. At their trial in Brazzaville that year, the excuses made for their brutality were, first, that the Africans would not work unless forced to do so, and second, that the French troops in Tchad were wholly dependent on supplies brought overland by porters from the south. Toqué, probably the less guilty of the two, claimed that he was required to find 3,000 porters a month to carry provisions hundreds of kilometers through a country without means of communication other than paths. The authorities seem not to have inquired as to the methods used by their officials provided that the indispensable supplies arrived for the troops, and the porters were neither paid nor fed by the government. Toqué pleaded that he had simply reinforced the pre-existing system of slavery by setting up "hostage camps" to retain the women and children of men recalcitrant to corvées and tax payments. The Brazzaville trial showed that such abuses were neither localized nor confined to two pathological individuals isolated in the bush. Punitive expeditions conducted by both officials and company agents led not infrequently to the destruction of farms, the burning of huts, and the massacre of women and children.

The furor aroused in France by the revelation of such cruelties in the Congo compelled the Paris government to make at least a show of investigating the situation. Brazza, who had been living in unhonored retirement at Algiers for the preceding seven years, was the obvious choice, and he gladly accepted the mission to "save" his Congo and its miserable population. But it soon became evident that he was up against the hostility not only of the French government and the concessionary companies but also of the Catholic missions established in the Congo.

A powerful opponent was the so-called Colonial Party in France, whose organ, La Dépêche Coloniale, defended the big companies that monopolized the Congo's ivory and rubber trade.[9] Largely because of that party's influence, Brazza received no cooperation from officials on the spot and even had trouble obtaining relevant documents and interviewing the Europeans and Africans who could supply him with the data he needed. Local civil servants were afraid that Brazza had come to displace them, and the only aid he received was from a few officials and army officers who were revolted by their task. Harder to account for was the hostility shown toward him by the Catholic bishop, Augouard,[10] and the Commissioner of the Republic, Gentil. Probably the contemporary wave of anticlericalism in France was responsible for their attitude. Bishop Augouard, although conceding that atrocities had been committed against Africans, contended that Brazza's aim was to "laicize" the French colonies.[11] Gentil, for his part, was a staunch enemy of freemasonry. Yet Brazza was able to unearth enough information to write a full report of the Congo's plight which was so damning that the government repeatedly refused to make it public. Crushed by what had happened to his beloved Congo, Brazza got no farther than Dakar on his way back to France. He died there on September 14, 1905. Fortunately, his faithful companion, Félicien Challaye, published in France[12] enough extracts from Brazza's report to support French liberal opinion in its insistence that the government radically alter its Congo policy.

The keynote of Challaye's report was the depopulation and misery of regions in central Africa that had formerly been populous and relatively flourishing. He held responsible for this decline the recruitment of porters, the forced collection of rubber to pay taxes, the absurdly low wages paid to laborers, and the hostage camps for women and children. Moreover, he asserted, these practices were the cause of sporadic revolts and the death or emigration of thousands of Africans. The clause in the concessions agreements which permitted the companies to employ armed guards had led to many of the worst abuses. A government that had ordered its officials on May 9, 1899, to regard company agents as their collaborators and had made tax receipts the yardstick for their promotion could not wash its hands of the results. However, in the three-day Parliamentary debate that led to the Clementel reforms of February 22, 1906, Jaurès and Caillaux stigmatized the concessionary system as the guiltier of the two. In part because of this, the government's main concern in the years that followed was less to strive directly to improve African well-being than to restore its own authority in the Congo at the companies' expense. But legally the companies could hold their concessions until 1929 unless they were persuaded to revise their contracts, and the government at that time could do little more than try to penalize the companies for their failure to respect the clauses of existing agreements.

The Clementel reforms, which were inspired by humanitarian indignation, were sustained also by the advent of an economic depression in the Congo. From 1898 to 1900, the influx of capital had produced budget surpluses in the Congo which many mistook at the time for genuine prosperity.[13] About 1900, however, there came a financial and economic crisis. For this the high cost of the Marchand Mission and the decline of the Kouilou ports after the opening of the Belgian Matadi railroad were held less responsible than the concessionary regime. More immediately influential was the fact that the companies were beginning to lose millions of francs, and the investors who had been led to expect huge and immediate dividends suffered a rude awakening. The French public began to realize that no inventory of the supposedly fabulous wealth of the Congo had ever been made, that many of the conceded areas were inundated for half the year and isolated by immense, trackless distances during the other half, and that manpower in the Congo not only was very limited but was being rapidly decimated by disease and forced labor. Worst of all, perhaps, in the eyes of that public, was the discovery that the local management of many companies had been inefficient as well as criminally negligent of African life.

By 1903, at least one-third of the actual, and one-fifth of the nominal, capital—that is, nearly 12 million francs—had been lost without a trace.[14] To be sure, some of the better-run companies had made profits aggregating about 10 million francs by 1906, but 9 others had disappeared and 21 had a total deficit of over 9 million francs. The fall in rubber prices that took place in 1907 was the final straw that led the companies to compromise with the government and with a public opinion now definitely hostile to the concessions regime.

Negotiations between the government and the surviving companies were based on a restriction of company operations, both geographically and administratively, in return for outright ownership of the most profitable portions of the area originally conceded to them. Beginning in 1910, companies in Gabon gave up nearly 6 million hectares in exchange for full title to 120,000 hectares. In the Sangha-Oubangui region, 11 companies organized themselves into the Compagnie Française du Sangha-Oubangui with a capital of 12 million francs; this new combine accepted a ten-year lease on a portion of their joint lands and the exclusive right to exploit only rubber thereon. (In 1920 this lease was renewed for only a part of this area and exploitation terms were made stricter.) All told, 20 companies accepted some compromise and 18 others were eliminated; the conceded area had shrunk to 3,800 square kilometers; and the government had resumed control over 300,000 square kilometers—an area that was added to in 1923.

In establishing a balance sheet for this period, one must note that the companies had spent some millions of francs on development works in their concessions, and the AEF treasury had received from them in rentals and taxes 3.5 million francs up until 1906 and 360,000 francs a year thereafter for the duration of the leases. But the debit against these revenues was crushing. Ivory had virtually disappeared from the conceded areas, and the rubber vines had been depleted owing to the companies' failure to replant; trade was stagnant and the population was decimated. Disillusionment regarding the Congo was almost total on the part of the French government and the French public alike. Not only was the colony considered a dismal economic failure, but, on humanitarian grounds, the exposure of brutalities there had dealt a shocking blow to French prestige in the world.

The Interwar Period

It would be pleasant to relate that the decline of the concessionary regime, which began in 1910, spelled the end of the sordid story of French colonization in the Congo. But abuses continued until the eve of World War II, mitigated at times by reforms that followed outbursts of French public indignation whenever scandalous conditions in AEF were brought to light. For this much-needed publicizing of the seamy side of AEF life, four French writers were mainly responsible.

René Maran's *Batouala* was awarded the famous Prix Goncourt, and this assured it of wide reading by the French intelligentsia of the early 1920's. Although the scene of this novel was laid in a corner of Oubangui-Chari and its author had no doctrinaire thesis to defend, the picture it drew of the brutish behavior of whites and Negroes alike and of their grimly hostile relationship was interpreted as a general condemnation of colonialism in AEF. Some settlers tried to discredit any generalizations based on Maran's particular experience, claiming that as a West Indian Negro he was no more qualified than were whites long resident in AEF to be spokesman for Africans of the federation.[15]

A few years later, similar testimony from so eminent a writer as André Gide could not be assailed on the same grounds. Gide's trip to AEF in 1925–26 was originally aimed at fulfilling his childhood longing to see the Congo; "I did not foresee," he wrote in *Voyage au Congo*,[16] "that the agonizing social questions raised by our relations with the natives would soon preoccupy me and become the *raison d'être* of my journey." In an article reminiscent of Zola's *J'Accuse,* published in the *Revue de Paris* of October 15, 1927, Gide lashed out against the concessionary regime in general and the Compagnie Forestière du Sangha-Oubangui in particular. In this and other writings, Gide told and retold the ghastly events that had transpired in the Boda region when he was there and of which he had sent a detailed account to the then governor-general of the federation. Gide described a local prison, half of whose inmates had been killed by physical punishment and poor food, the forcing of women and children to work under grim conditions to maintain a road used only for the company manager's and the administrator's weekly trips to market, and the evils of portage, which was hopelessly underpaid and which—along with the forced gathering of rubber—led to the neglect of food crops and the displacement of whole villages. Specifically he denounced the administrator of Boda, who had condemned defaulting rubber gatherers to run round and round the market place under a molten sky until they fell to the ground, where they were beaten by guards so that "the dance could go on." Said Gide:

> The evil with which I am here concerned inhibits the progress of a people and a country; it ruins both for the profit of a few individuals. I hasten to say that this is peculiar to our AEF and is especially true of Moyen-Congo and Gabon. It has disappeared in Oubangui-Chari since the concessionary companies in that colony have themselves given up their privileges.
>
> Through what lamentable weakness, despite the opposition of well-informed and competent people, was the regime of big concessions agreed to in 1899? But that is not what should surprise us, since after all such a regime in that period seemed useful. To develop a new country, one should not re-

ject the capital, energy, and good will that was being offered. The surprising thing is that this frightful regime, this shameless exploitation, still survives, after its harmfulness is recognized, after it has been denounced many times by governors of the colony on the grounds that it has in no way developed the country but rather has skimmed off the cream. The settlers of AEF have done very little; it is the big companies that are responsible. And because there is now a question of renewing their privileges, I take up my pen.

When one recognizes the occult powers of these companies, one is no longer surprised. It is in Paris that the first evil begins . . . the Congo is far away. It is better not to learn what it is more restful to ignore. And on the spot it is hard to get information even if one tries to: one can travel for months without seeing more than the décor. Traders report rumors, administrators can talk only to their superiors, chiefs have to be discreet, missionaries must stay silent so that they may remain in the country. . . . Despite what people may say, it is not against the administration that I am speaking. . . . I regret its impotence against evil and am trying to strengthen its hand.

If Gide's revelations had been confined to literary periodicals and two books, they might never have caused the stir that they did. It was thanks to Léon Blum, who published a résumé in *Le Populaire*,[17] that Gide's crusade was brought before a big public and that a controversy was aroused by it in the press. Weber, head of the Compagnie Forestière, felt called upon to refute the "hearsay testimony of a credulous poet."[18] He pictured his company as a constructive element working to develop a "regrettably barbarous country that vegetates." Far from growing rich on the blood of Africans, it had "never made its 6,000 shareholders happy," all of whom were described as *épargnants modestes* in France. As for "unfortunate excesses and repressions," he threw the blame for these onto the shoulders of the administration. A report at about this time from the head of the AEF judicial service and evidence supplied by some Catholic missionaries supported Gide's accusations, but his detractors continued to denounce him as insincere, gullible, or a communist sympathizer.

To get to the bottom of these charges and countercharges, a prominent daily newspaper, *Le Petit Parisien,* sent to Africa one of its best reporters, Albert Londres, who had considerable experience in the French colonies. In his subsequent book, *Terre d'Ebène,* Londres was far less gentle than Gide with the local administration. Gide had been careful to pinpoint his narrative geographically and to state repeatedly his conviction that AEF civil servants were too few in number and were left too much at the mercy of the company agents to intervene effectively. Londres, for his part, stressed the responsibility of the AEF government for the high mortality among African laborers that accompanied the building of the Congo-Ocean railroad from Brazzaville to Pointe Noire. By the contract made with the Compagnie des Batignolles, wrote Londres, the AEF government had agreed to supply workers for construction of that line, but it had totally failed to supply transportation, lodging, medical care, and food for them. Londres claimed that in order to lay 140 kilometers of track through very difficult jungle country without the aid of any modern machinery, the government had sacrificed the lives of some 17,000 Africans and had caused many others to flee to adjacent territories. Shocking as the facts in his case were, it was rather the ironic and sensational manner in which Londres wrote that caused his report to enjoy a *succès de scandale* in Paris. To check on Londres, whose assignment had been to verify Gide's charges, *Le Temps* in 1929 sent out a more moderate reporter, R. Poulaine, and *Le Matin* in turn dispatched its man Gerville Réache to AEF. These writers largely confirmed Londres' figures, denounced the administration as negligent, and reiterated the charge that forced labor was emptying many of the federation's villages. If Gide's writings were primarily instrumental in ending the concessionary regime, the reporting of Londres and Poulaine must be given much credit for the improved working conditions under which the rest of the Congo-Ocean railroad was constructed.

Londres' reproaches were not confined to the federal government but were also heaped upon the local settlers and the indifference of Metropolitan France:

> We work in a tunnel without any general plan, clear idea, or funds. . . . We have only one real port, poor roads, and a poor railroad. French Black Africa does not simply slumber—it snores . . . because of France's indifference and the colonies being forced to live off their own meager resources. We must spend money in our colonies and save the Negro by suppressing portage. What we practice is no longer thrift, it is stupidity.[19]

And in another vigorous passage, Londres denounced "the colonials who try to make everyone think that all is well" and resent anyone who "tries to raise the veil that they have drawn over events and peer behind the screen that they have set up."

Several vivid pictures of the settler element in the AEF of the 1930's were drawn by three other writers who followed Maran, Gide, and Londres. Pierre Fontaine's book[20] gave resounding praise to Governor-General Renard, whose life was deliberately sacrificed, he maintained, by the robber barons and monopolists whose wickedness he tried to control. One of these colorful and unscrupulous characters was described at length. This was a pioneer called "Le Barbu" (The Bearded One), who from modest beginnings as a provisioner of the French army grew enormously wealthy by trading in gold, ivory, and hides and eventually monopolized the coastal commerce of AEF. Benefiting by the indulgence of the administration, Le Barbu employed a small army, acquired a concession of several thousand hectares in the Loango region, ruined his rivals, and was able literally to get away with murder.

Far different was the story of a *petit colon,* Marcel Homet, whose *Congo, Terre de Souffrances* aroused widespread comment in France when it was published in 1934. It recounts a young agricultural engineer's unsuccessful fight against big business in AEF and against an administration subservient to it. Upon arriving in the federation in 1927, Homet was astonished to find that no soap was being manufactured from local fats. But when he tried to set up a small soap factory, he was told by an official to desist because the import duties on manufactured oleaginous products were a mainstay of the AEF budget. Homet persisted, and his plant was burned down. Next he tried processing manioc into tapioca, but suddenly his laborers left him without cause, and he could buy manioc in the local market only in small quantity and at exorbitant prices. Not only did several other such failures end by ruining him financially, but he was thrown into Brazzaville's unsavory jail "on the testimony of false witnesses." His wife escaped to Léopoldville, where she published an account of the injustices inflicted on her husband, and later he followed up this account with his autobiography. Another firsthand but more detached description of the *colons* of AEF was that of Marcel Sauvage, who, on the eve of World War II, wrote that they were "no worse than any other *métropolitains.* . . . Most of their principles seem to melt away under the tropical heat and their courage goes no farther than what is required for making money or satisfying their vanity. And the Africans naturally bear the consequences."[21]

Such were the portrayals of life in AEF that became common currency in France, for few Frenchmen ever visited the federation. Nor was the occasional foreign observer more flattering. Negley Farson wrote of this same period that "French Equatorial Africa is the most understaffed, underpaid and unpopular of all the French colonies, and it is hard to enlist French officials to go there."[22] The climate was notoriously unhealthy, living conditions were primitive, and the lack of opportunities for constructive work made most of the Frenchmen there yearn only for the day when they could retire to France. The little news that filtered out from, or about, AEF was invariably bad, and the French public preferred to ignore the federation's failures rather than try to remedy them. "Cinderella of the French Empire" was a term often applied to one or another of the poorer French colonies, but the glass slipper would probably have been most fittingly awarded to AEF above all the others.

AEF's Hour of Glory: World War II

In the years just before World War II there was no evidence of any radical change in this bleak picture. The slow progress accomplished under Governors-General Augagneur, Antonetti, Renard, and Reste had not been steadily maintained and passed generally unnoticed. Although there were fewer big companies in the federation than before World War I, those that had survived seemed all-powerful. They were said to be able to ruin at will the few small merchants operating there, count on the administration to carry out their orders, and even make a travesty of the justice dispensed in the courts of law. Opening of the Congo-Ocean railroad in 1935, made possible by a Metropolitan loan, had gone far to eliminate portage, but forced labor was still a widespread practice and took its toll of the African population. AEF lacked the necessary funds and qualified personnel to overcome its main handicaps—shortage of manpower and inadequate means of communication.

French and world opinion was therefore totally unprepared for AEF's reaction to the Franco-German armistice of June 1940. The federation's much-maligned officials suddenly proved willing to forgo the prospect of pensions by opting for Free France. And the Africans, who had been so brutally oppressed, not only remained loyal but volunteered in large numbers to join de Gaulle's armed forces. That this most wretched of French colonies should become the overseas cradle of the French resistance movement made AEF overnight, and for the first time in its history, popular in French eyes. Perhaps, after all, the federation had been misjudged. In fact, the pendulum now swung too far in the other direction, and again, as in the early days, AEF suffered from an exaggerated estimate of its potentialities.

To the Guyanese governor of Tchad, Félix Eboué, must go most of the credit for this wartime "miracle." But a group of men in the extreme south of AEF also deserve a large share. General Dr. Sicé, a main organizer of the resistance movement at Brazzaville, has given a dramatic account of its development during the hectic summer of 1940.[23] When it became apparent there in early July that the federation's highest official, Governor-General Boisson, and the Commander-in-Chief, General Husson, were, after some hesitation, going to obey orders from Vichy, a dissident group of civilians and army officers began clandestinely to organize a revolt. Here as elsewhere in French territory, emotions were deeply stirred and opinions were divided as to whether to follow Pétain's lead or join with Britain. Some months passed before an effective movement could be built up among the French and Africans, in collaboration both with adjacent British and Belgians and with Gaullist agents. Moyen-Congo and Tchad were the first to be won over, and after them, Oubangui-Chari, but Gabon was too divided to rely upon.

Brazzaville was electrified to learn, on August 25, that Tchad under Governor Eboué had re-entered the war, was in close contact with the Nigerian government, and was preparing to receive de Gaulle's delegate. Three days later the Free French of Brazzaville took over the local government in a few hours and without bloodshed, and on August 30 Oubangui-Chari followed suit. Now only Gabon remained in the Vichy camp, and all efforts to convince its governor, Masson, that he should follow the lead of the rest of AEF failed. Free French forces were compelled to besiege Libreville for six weeks before it surrendered on November 9, and its governor, torn by conflicting loyalties, committed suicide. Gabon was the sole territory on which the war left deep scars, for regrettable reprisals followed the capitulation of Libreville.

Now firmly in the saddle everywhere in the federation, the Free French laid down their war policy for AEF. They gave an assurance that the federation would not become a burden on Britain but, rather, would furnish the Allies with the maximum military and economic aid. Furthermore,

AEF was to evolve internally in such a way that it would be restored to France after her liberation in better political and economic condition than ever before. In all of those respects the federation succeeded far beyond expectations.

Two months after de Gaulle had toured AEF in October 1940 and had set up a High Commissariat of the Free French at Brazzaville, two African battalions began military operations against the Italians at Mourzouk. A little more than a year later, the Fezzan was conquered by Colonel Leclerc from a base in Tibesti, and his troops crossed the desert to win a spectacular victory at Bir Hakeim. In this campaign, only 555 of his 3,268 soldiers were European, all the troops were volunteers, and the majority came from the Sara tribes of Tchad. Also in the military domain, AEF served the Allied troops as a strategic base and point of transit. The port of Pointe Noire provisioned Allied ships plying between Freetown and South Africa, and Tchad's airfields were used as refueling points by Allied planes flying between Takoradi and the Middle East.

Although AEF's military contributions to the war were small in scale, they were at least gratifying to French pride. But its more considerable economic contributions were less widely heralded and also more difficult to make because they necessitated a reorientation of the federation's economy. In 1940 it looked as if AEF would become a dead weight on the Allies, for its imports and exports had always been tightly linked with Metropolitan France. Great Britain was in no position to replace the Metropolitan market because she could get everything that AEF produced from her own African dependencies. But soon outlets were found in some Commonwealth countries, and Britain contracted to purchase all the federation's output of cotton, coffee, wood, oleaginous products, wax, and gum copal. And to some extent the Belgian Congo replaced France as AEF's main provisioner.

The local Free French authorities applied themselves to the task of making AEF not only self-sufficient economically but also a supplier of strategic raw materials for the war effort. The gathering of wild rubber was revived on a big scale, cotton cultivation was intensified, and gold mining was encouraged. The Public Works Service built or improved roads and airfields and enlarged the port of Pointe Noire, and the Congo-Ocean railroad worked to capacity to provision Allied troops and to ship out AEF's produce. Creation of the Caisse Centrale de la France Libre (later transformed into the Caisse Centrale de la France d'Outre-Mer) and stabilization of the sterling–franc rate not only solved most of the immediate financial problems but permitted the federation to set up a reserve fund. In addition, a large sum was contributed by both Africans and Europeans toward the purchase of arms and airplanes. The presence of many officials and troops made the federation's merchants prosper, and this contributed to the illusion that AEF was now a rich country. Few noted that the intensified cultivation of cotton and collection of rubber had caused rural Africans' living standards, already very low, to decline still further. Indeed, the insistence that AEF should live off its own resources actively contributed to their impoverishment. After the war ended, AEF lapsed once more into penurious dependence on the Metropole, but a few years later it became apparent that the war had stimulated the federation's economy on the whole, and above all had boosted its inhabitants' morale.

Mainly responsible for the long-term improvement in AEF's status was the policy pursued by Eboué, whose incumbency as governor-general from November 8, 1941, until his death in 1944 marked an enormous step forward. Although his attention was given mainly to promoting the war effort, he regarded this as only an indispensable preliminary to the accomplishment of his major task—the betterment of the Africans' condition. In a series of circulars, Eboué set forth his ideas, which seemed revolutionary at the time, concerning native policy and administration.[24] Long study and experience in Africa had convinced him that France's predilection for Gallicizing a small minority of Africans to form an elite that would become assimilated to the French governing class had served mainly to detach that elite from the mass of the population. He also felt that the new economic enterprises introduced by Europeans, such as mines, factories, and plantations, had played a sinister part in the breakdown of tribal traditions among rural Africans. Hence his first decrees as governor-general had the aim of setting up a system in which African institutions, such as the *chefferie,* would be strengthened as a means of preserving vital cultural traditions. By seeking out the authentic traditional chiefs and notables, training them in modern methods, and restoring their external dignity in the eyes of their own people and the French administration, Eboué hoped to create an elite composed not simply of functionaries but rather of genuine leaders in close touch with the bulk of population. Thus the task of the French administrator would no longer be one of control, but instead one of guidance, designed to help the elite develop a sense of responsibility for increasing the welfare of their people.

To encourage the growth of an African bourgeoisie in the new urban centers, Eboué in 1942 laid the foundations for two African communes in the suburbs of Brazzaville. And to arrest the detribalization of the urban population, as well as to prepare them for their new responsibilities, he gave the *Notables évolués* a special status in the hope that they would become leaders in the self-governing institutions to come. In the legal sphere, African judges were to preside over criminal as well as civil cases in newly constituted customary courts, and they were to apply local laws modified by basic European concepts of justice. Mission schools "working in the common interest" were to be supported on the same basis as state schools. Also to be encouraged were any youth or cultural organizations that might develop in the Africans a sense of civic responsibility. With regard to the rural community, Eboué opposed the recruiting of Africans for work on European plantations or in industrial enterprises. Instead he favored the development of an indigenous peasantry for whom nearby European planters would serve as teachers. If the current war effort and, later, certain industries required a large labor force, he insisted that workers no longer be transplanted as individuals but be resettled with their families in new villages constructed for the purpose. Rising living standards, Eboué believed, would benefit the small African trading class and promote its growth. The role of European settlers, as Eboué conceived it, was to guide rural Africans or to direct enterprises that required large amounts of capital and technical knowledge.

As a result of the special conditions created in AEF by the war, together with support from the Free French government in London, Eboué had a unique opportunity to put his program into action. Considering that he headed the federation for only three years, the list of his accomplishments is impressive, and his influence on the policies evolved at the Brazzaville Conference of 1944 was preponderant. The political and economic reforms of the postwar years in Black Africa owe much to Eboué's initiative. At the time of his death in May 1944, Brazzaville possessed—thanks largely to his efforts—a *lycée,* a military school, a powerful radio broadcasting station, an African labor office, two African communes, and a housing bureau, and in the realm of intangibles he had laid the foundations for future advances in the fields of justice, education, agriculture, and industry.

AEF is unique in the annals of French colonial history in that the most constructive contributions to its evolution were those made by an Italian-born aristocrat and a Negro from the Western Hemisphere.

CHAPTER 2

The Administration

To the French Navy were entrusted the first posts that France acquired in Gabon, and in 1881 they were joined administratively with Guinea under a high-ranking naval officer. Five years later, Gabon was detached from France's Guinea Gulf possessions and put in the charge of a lieutenant-governor made responsible to Brazza, who that year was named General Commissioner for the French Congo.

In 1902, the French Congo itself was divided into two main regions. One of these, the lower Congo area plus Gabon, was effectively occupied by the French and given a fairly complete administrative network. The second region, to the north, had not been wholly pacified and was in part under the army's command. It soon became apparent that other changes must be made: Tchad needed a more military government, and because of the lack of communications in the southern region, administration of even that area from Libreville or Brazzaville was impractical. Greater decentralization was the aim of further modifications that took place between 1903 and 1905. All of French central Africa was placed under a commissioner-general stationed at Brazzaville, but it was divided into the four regions of Tchad, Gabon, Oubangui-Chari, and Moyen-Congo, each headed by its own administrator. Only the last two of those regions and a small portion of Gabon lay within the Conventional Basin of the Congo. (See p. 212.)

The hazards of history and geography were in part responsible for the confusion and instability that have marked the long evolution of AEF's administrative structure. But they also reflected France's vacillation between the theories of assimilation and association in respect to her colonial dependencies. When assimilationists predominated in the Metropolitan government—which was the case more often than not—centralization was the basis of French policy toward Black Africa. But partisans of the principle of association found their position inadvertently strengthened by the practical difficulties encountered in centralizing the administration of so distant and underdeveloped an area as AEF. Though the French tendency to centralize authority was strong, the local necessity to decentralize the federation's administration was deeply felt, so that the pendulum swung back and forth between those contradictory policies.

Because of France's indecision on so vital an issue, the decentralization of AEF's administration was not materially advanced by the successive re-organizations—all nominally made with that objective—which were carried out in 1910, 1934, 1937, 1941, 1944, and 1946. Despite frequent alterations in boundary lines, the progressive replacement of military by civilian administrators, and changes in the names and sizes of administrative units —not to mention the incessant rotation of the officials commanding them— the grip of Brazzaville was no more loosened locally than was that of Paris on the federation's government.

Stability was attained in this confusing period[1] only in the federal structure itself, modeled after that of French West Africa, and in the personnel of AEF's civilian high command. Except for the creation of Tchad colony in 1920, the basic structure of the federation remained the same from its creation in 1910 until 1959, and AEF had only seven governors-general from 1910 until the outbreak of World War II.[2]

The governor-general, or high commissioner (as he was usually called after 1947), was named by decree of the French government, and his headquarters were at Brazzaville. He was the depository of the powers of the Republic for the federation: he alone could correspond with the Minister of Colonies, and he controlled the local civilian, judicial, and military services. Specifically, he was responsible for the federation's internal and external defense, and for all the economic, financial, and technical directorates that constituted the government-general. Subordinate to him were the lieutenant-governors of Moyen-Congo, Gabon, Oubangui-Chari, and Tchad. Aiding him was an official holding the rank of colonial governor who was secretary-general for AEF, and an administrative council. The council was a purely advisory body named by the governor-general and made up of federal officials, four French citizens selected by the Chambers of Commerce,[3] and four French-speaking Africans chosen to represent the native population. The council elected a permanent committee of nine members which met regularly at Brazzaville throughout the year, and it handled much of the direct administration, particularly the civil and financial services.

Maintaining close relations with the Metropolitan government on the one hand, and with the four local colonial administrations on the other, was the chief task of a governor-general of AEF before World War II. In France the federation was represented by one delegate to the Conseil Supérieur des Colonies and by an economic agency in Paris. It was the governor-general, however, who was the principal liaison with the Metropole, and among his major duties was that of adapting instructions from Paris to the local situation and of keeping the Minister of Colonies informed of significant developments in AEF. The Minister of Colonies had the right to disapprove regulations issued by the governor-in-council and he held certain disciplinary powers that enabled him to impose his authority on a governor-general. But in practice a governor-general's independence of action was most effectively curtailed by the limitations inherent in the federation's underdevelopment. Perhaps because of the greater distance that separated AEF from Paris or because its first governors-general had especially strong personalities, the latter were left more on their own than were their counterparts at Dakar. In the 1930's, for example, a governor-general was able with impunity to refuse for eight years to promulgate locally a decree on education drawn up specifically for AEF by the Minister of Colonies.[4]

Not only did the governor-general of AEF have a relatively free hand in his dealings with the Paris Ministry, but he enjoyed almost unfettered control over the four colonial administrations, which were replicas of the government-general. Each of these colonies was headed by a lieutenant-governor, who was aided by a secretary-general and an appointed advisory council. This official framed the local budget, controlled the territorial civil service, and was alone empowered to correspond with the governor-general. Despite repeated attempts to gain greater independence of action, the lieutenant-governors were tightly controlled from Brazzaville. As Martial Merlin, the first governor-general of AEF and father of the federation, succinctly told these subordinates, "I govern, you administer." Indeed, the governors-general often did both, as was the case in Moyen-Congo for a brief period beginning in 1925. The climax to this centralizing tendency came in 1934 when Governor-General Renard, as an economy measure, suppressed the territorial budgets and made the lieutenant-governors merely his administrative delegates, although they retained their titles and the colonies continued to be recognized as separate units. As matters worked out, a single budget and a central secretariat for the whole federation complicated rather than simplified the administration.

If this centralization had been confined to the upper echelons it might have succeeded, but its extension in depth to the district level was certainly premature. For lack of sufficient administrative personnel, 20 provinces or departments, 42 circumscriptions, and 131 subdivisions were set up within the framework of the existing four colonies.[5] In area, the new provinces averaged 125,000 square kilometers, and the means of communication were not yet good enough to warrant the creation of such large entities. In 1936 there were created 14 more units, of which 11 were classed as departments and 2 as autonomous subdivisions, and the commune of Brazzaville was separated from its encircling province.[6] Governor-General Reste, responsible for these additions, made another gesture toward decentralization when he separated the budget estimates for the four colonies, but he also created two new federal services (agriculture and animal husbandry) and two inspectorates for AEF (general administration and labor conditions).[7]

By isolating AEF from the Metropole, World War II forced still another change in the federation's administrative structure, particularly in the financial domain. Decentralizing reforms initiated by Eboué in 1941 and 1944 culminated in the law of October 16, 1946, which restored budgetary autonomy to the four colonies and set up a separate federal budget. The smaller administrative units were once again divided up and reconstituted as 32 regions, 132 circumscriptions, 2 autonomous districts, and 6 mixed

communes. The extent and importance of these new units varied considerably. In some, the populations ranged from 3,000 to 10,000 inhabitants,
and only about 30 of the largest ones could be said to correspond to natural
regions.[8]

Largely responsible for these multiple transformations was the federation's dearth of men and resources. But there were other impediments in
the way of applying the admirable principle laid down as early as 1892
that the limits of administrative units should be determined by geographic
and ethnic considerations. In many parts of AEF there were no clear-cut
natural boundaries, and in others the population was partly or wholly nomadic. These conditions positively encouraged boundary alterations and
led Moyen-Congo and Gabon to dispute possession of the Haut-Ogooué
and the Haute-Nyanga; Moyen-Congo and Oubangui-Chari, that of Haute-
Sangha; and Oubangui-Chari and Tchad, that of Moyen-Logone, Mayo-
Kebbi, and Moyen-Chari. Boundary changes were also prompted by the
government's need to recruit labor from the more populous districts and
hence to alter arbitrarily certain territorial frontiers. After 1946, boundaries
became more stable because the constitution of the Fourth Republic required action by Parliament to effect such changes. It was not until the
spring of 1959 that another drastic revision took place in the local administrative setup of Moyen-Congo and Oubangui-Chari, mainly because of the
desire of their new African governments to ensure their parties' success in
the forthcoming elections.

Eboué's reforms in 1941 and 1944 were not dictated wholly by wartime
exigencies nor confined to the comparatively minor changes outlined above,
but were part of his then revolutionary theories about the governing of
French Africans (see pp. 23–24). To some extent his ideas were carried
out and developed in AEF by his friend and successor, Bayardelle, whose
career was strikingly similar to that of Eboué. Both were born in the
Antilles and had been among the earliest colonial administrators to join
the Free French—Eboué at Fort Lamy and Bayardelle at Nouméa. A brief
meeting at Brazzaville, following Bayardelle's transfer to Djibouti, ce-
mented a friendship between the two men, and Eboué invited Bayardelle
to become his secretary-general for the federation. Before the war ended,
however, Eboué died, and Bayardelle, appointed to succeed him at Brazzaville, was left alone to execute the policies in which they both believed.
Among the most important of these were the decentralizing of the AEF
administration and the bringing of democratic institutions to the federation.

In a speech at Brazzaville on December 19, 1945, Bayardelle forthrightly
stated that "our greatest enemy is the sclerosis of the administration, an
administration that lives of and by itself, and is blind to the living issues
and to the human materials with which it deals." But Bayardelle, worn
out like Eboué by the war, died on May 3, 1947, only a short time after
the new assemblies had been created (see pp. 37–38) and the man who
replaced him, Charles Luizet, likewise succumbed after serving only a

few weeks as governor-general of AEF. Thus three successive governors-general who had been able civil servants and outstanding members of the Resistance died prematurely in harness, leaving AEF bereft of their leadership on the threshold of a new era.

André Soucadaux, AEF's secretary-general, was twice called upon to take over the government of the federation—before and after Luizet's incumbency—and to guide through its formative year the Grand Council, which he described at its inaugural session as the "spiritual offspring of Eboué and Bayardelle."[9] In January 1948, Bernard Cornut-Gentille was named to succeed Luizet. Although he, too, was a career civil servant and a member of the Resistance, AEF found in Cornut-Gentille a new and different type of high commissioner, for he was younger than his predecessors and had never before served in Africa.[10] During his three and a half years at the helm in AEF, Cornut-Gentille managed to make himself popular with even the most outspoken young Africans,[11] and when he left Brazzaville in 1952 to become governor-general of French West Africa, his departure was deeply regretted in AEF.

Both Soucadaux and Cornut-Gentille were strongly in favor of decentralizing the AEF administration. In pushing this they were aided by the creation of the Grand Council and the territorial assemblies, which automatically accomplished a decentralization that none of the earlier reorganizations, nor the war itself, had brought about. But because any such fundamental reform could not take place without the assent of France's slow-moving Parliament, the measures taken subsequently by Soucadaux and Cornut-Gentille did not go far or fast enough to suit many of the African elite, for they concerned only the administration proper and even there they did not descend to the municipal level.

Europeans and Africans alike had long recognized that a devolution of authority from the Metropole to the government-general, and from the latter to the territories, was a practical necessity in so distant, vast, and understaffed a federation as that of AEF. President Flandre of the Grand Council, in replying to Soucadaux's pledge of greater decentralization, vividly described the plight of businessmen and officials isolated in the bush, who were compelled to refer matters of even minor importance to Brazzaville for a decision. To appreciate the need for decentralization, he said,

> . . . one would have had to live 1,200 kilometers from Brazzaville and have handled all questions in writing through the channel of the local administration—a letterbox from which correspondence is not collected every day—to get through eventually to headquarters. Brazzaville has always jealously guarded its monopoly of policy decisions and even the details of their execution. This procedure had to be repeated for every facet of industrial or commercial activity, and weeks—even months—passed before a reply was received. Then followed an exchange of letters containing requests for further information. A federal official, overwhelmed by the abundance of such correspondence, was unable to reach a decision, either because he lacked first-hand knowledge of local conditions or because the conditions had changed

since he knew them. Only those who have thus wasted time and energy can truly grasp the necessity for decentralization. Certainly operating conditions in this country could be made far easier by cutting down the delays in transmission, by lightening the load of paper work for responsible officials, and by undertaking a study of conditions on the spot. . . . In brief, we expect both an economy and a simplification to be achieved by this reform.

But the promised reform was so slow to materialize that the permanent committee of the Grand Council, in April 1948, accused the government-general of deliberately slowing it down and even of overstaffing the federal services to the point where Brazzaville had come to harbor an "army of functionaries."[12] The secretary-general protested that the federal administration was moving as fast as it could, and that the process could be speeded up only if AEF's parliamentarians succeeded in prying the government-general loose from the grip of the French Overseas Ministry. Overdecentralization, he added, could be quite as objectionable as overcentralization, for AEF lacked the resources needed to set up and equip separate services in each territory. When the government-general finally got around to publishing some decentralizing measures in the *Journal Officiel* of January 16, 1949, the Grand Council was not placated, because these steps had been taken without its formal approval and without taking into account the wishes it had expressed.

In regard to administrative decentralization, Cornut-Gentille went further than had any of his predecessors. He gave priority to the territories, especially Gabon and Tchad, in the recruitment of new personnel, and he appreciably strengthened the powers of the territorial governors. These officials were accorded wide authority over both the African chiefs and the European administrators in their respective areas. They were empowered to appoint, promote, penalize, and grant leaves of absence to local civil servants; to hire, by contract, agents whose annual salary did not exceed 400,000 CFA francs; and to supervise execution of the local programs drawn up by the federal public-works and forestry services. Federal directorates thenceforth had to confine themselves to general policy decisions and over-all programs, and for the first time the heads of those services were required to visit each territory so as to study problems on the spot and in consultation with the territorial governor.

These steps were applauded as being in the right direction, but they did not prove to be effective everywhere in eliminating the long-standing conflict between the territorial administrations and the federal services. Two years later a European assemblyman of Oubangui-Chari could still say:[13]

I have watched the ferocious struggle between all the services and the responsible governors for three decades. Each of those federal services—agriculture, public works, animal husbandry—has tried to extricate itself from the authority of the governor of Oubangui-Chari and place itself under that of a Brazzaville inspectorate or directorate. Each side has alternately scored a victory. At present a healthy understanding has been reached as regards the rural economy by the agricultural and animal-husbandry services working in col-laboration with the territorial governor. But the public-works service is still holding out, and it is playing its trump card with the Plan funds. If there is dirty linen to be washed, it tries to have this done at Brazzaville where all is soon forgotten.

To the African elite, however, this protracted tussle between the territorial administration and the federal services was of secondary interest, for it was an inter-French conflict. So far as the politically conscious Africans were concerned, the heart of the matter lay in the sharing of executive and legislative power with the French government, and their aspirations in this direction gave a new twist to the old issue of decentralization. All were agreed on the necessity for getting the administration to allocate more of its authority to the elected bodies, but differences of opinion arose on how this transferred power should be shared between the Grand Council and the territorial assemblies.

There were three issues on which all the elected assemblies locked horns with the French government, but they were more symptomatic and sym-bolic than crucial in themselves. These were, in chronological order as they arose, (1) the right of the assemblies to send their members off on "missions of information," (2) the initiative taken early in its history by the Grand Council in reapportioning financial resources between the fed-eral and territorial budgets, and (3) the overstaffing of the federal services with high-paid Metropolitan officials. Wherever these issues involved a flouting of the assembly's authority by the administration, it is interesting to note that European and African assemblymen presented a united front. On the third issue, they were even joined by the local administration in protesting this practice to the Metropolitan authorities.

In the matter of information missions, the local government maintained that the assemblies had no right to investigate the operations of the federal services or to question officials belonging to them unless they were expressly authorized to do so by the governor-general. The federal secretary-general told the Grand Council that it could dispatch members to obtain informa-tion only on subjects lying clearly within its legal attributes and that such missions must be defined precisely in time and area.[14] Furthermore, the Grand Council had no right at all to investigate private enterprises unless invited to do so, and even then it could not publicize its findings. To placate the councilors, the government-general offered them organized tours of certain federal establishments: in 1948 they were invited to visit the new port of Pointe Noire and the following year to study the forest industry of Gabon. Nevertheless, the assemblymen continued to insist on obtaining independently any data relevant to their work, and eventually the matter was referred to the Metropolitan authorities for a decision. While the Council of State then reproved some assemblies for overstepping bounds, it did confirm their legal right to send out information missions under specified conditions. Actually, under the thin disguise of information mis-sions, the issue here at stake was basic. The attitude of the local administration was inspired by its determination not to permit the assemblies to trespass on the domain of the executive or to allow their members to use such missions for political-party propaganda purposes. The assemblies, for their part, were equally determined not only to exercise their existing prerogatives but to stretch them in order to drain off to their own advantage some of the power long wielded by an autocratic administration.

While it could be said that this conflict ended in a draw, the dispute over allocating funds from the federal to the territorial budgets soon culminated in complete defeat for the assemblies. Because the federation was largely and chronically dependent upon subsidies from Metropolitan France, the French treasury kept a much closer grip on the disbursing of AEF's financial resources than it did on those of richer French West Africa. In February 1949 the Council of State, by a strict interpretation of the constitution, annulled without further explanation the Grand Council's decision of late 1948 to reallocate federal funds. At the time, the Grand Council could do nothing about so unequivocal a verdict except to complain that Metropolitan France was trying to sabotage its efforts to help carry out the officially approved policy of decentralization. This issue was revived later, after the passage of the *loi-cadre,* when it became a vital factor in determining the attitude of Gabon toward creation of a federal executive to replace the government-general.

On the third issue, that of overstaffing the federal services, the local administration was for once largely in accord with the assemblymen's protests. All resented France's dispatching to AEF high-ranking officials who were rarely the ones needed by the federation and who, as a rule, occupied desk jobs in the federal or territorial capitals. The whole administrative structure was obviously top-heavy and out of proportion to AEF's needs and resources; moreover, there was considerable duplication of jobs in the federal and territorial services. Every new appointment to the federal services evoked harsh criticisms from the Grand Councilors, and they reminded the government of its pledge to compress such expenditures and to decentralize. As the chairman of the Grand Council's Finance Committee put the problem on October 5, 1952, "AEF is like a simple unskilled laborer who has been given a golden shovel with which to dig in light and sandy soil."

By 1952 this question had become acute, for the passing by Parliament of a series of laws granting pay increases to civil servants and adding a new category eligible for family allowances coincided with a crisis in the federation's finances (see pp. 130–31). Early that year, Paul Chauvet, a high-ranking official previously posted in Indochina, became governor-general at a very difficult time in the federation's history, both financially and administratively. Such decentralization as had been accomplished by the laws of 1946 concerned mainly the administrative and budgetary functions, and had not altered the prewar relationship between the high commissioner and the Ministry of Overseas France. At the time, no one questioned the supreme authority of Parliament throughout the French Union, or that a major duty of the high commissioner was to coordinate and adapt to local conditions the laws laid down by that body in the form of general principles. But the high commissioner's dependence on the Rue Oudinot was less acceptable, especially as its means of control over him and the government-general had been reinforced by the great improvement in air services between Paris and Brazzaville. Since 1946, however, a new element had come into the picture. The high commissioner was no longer the sole medium for communicating with, or exercising pressure upon, the French government, for AEF now had 21 representatives in France's parliamentary bodies.

Thus, by 1952, when Chauvet took over, the three-cornered inter-French tug of war that had long gone on covertly between the government-general and Metropolitan France, and between the former and the territorial governments, had receded into the background. Its place had been taken largely by the struggle between the French government at the Metropolitan, federal, and territorial levels and the African representatives in Parliament, the Grand Council, and the local assemblies. Concurrently a minor and localized conflict had developed between the Grand Council and the territorial assemblies, mainly in regard to finances. All of these developments had altered the role of the high commissioner and had made it a more difficult one. Increasingly it fell to this official to encourage and guide the decentralization that was gathering momentum, so that it should not reach the point where AEF would secede from France or the federation dissolve into mutually independent units.

From 1947 to 1954, conservative governments were in control in Paris, and little progress was made toward delegating more authority to either the high commissioner or the elected assemblies, although "decentralization and deconcentration" remained the goal of official policy. What was then preoccupying the high commissioners was how to transfer more power to the territorial governors without at the same time jeopardizing the efficiency of the federal technical services. To be sure, this was also the period when left-wing African politicians were complaining about the government's interference in local elections, its refusal to share power with the elected assemblies, and the stiff-necked attitude of French administrators toward the new representative institutions. At that time, however, the African politicians were still inexperienced and little organized, and—with some notable exceptions—Europeans continued to dominate the local administrative bodies and even the political parties. More effective African opposition to the strong hand exercised by the local administration arose with, and was in part due to, the coming to power in France of the more liberal governments of Mendès-France, Faure, and Guy Mollet. Such advances as AEF made, beginning in 1954, were far more the sequel of the progressive views of five successive Ministers of Overseas France and the work of the French West African parliamentarians than of any efforts put forth by its own elected representatives.

Under the exceptional powers granted by Parliament to the Mendès-

France government on August 14, 1954, the French Overseas Minister, Louis Jacquinot, was able to act with more dispatch and authority than had his predecessors on several matters deeply affecting the administration of the African territories. The long-overdue bill reorganizing municipal government throughout French Black Africa was given its first reading in the National Assembly that month, and at about the same time, action was taken on a report submitted by a ministerial mission sent to Africa in 1952–53 to study ways and means of decentralizing the administrations there. On December 15, 1954, Jacquinot told the National Assembly that he was preparing a draft law for AEF distinct from that for French West Africa. Although he intended to give more freedom of action to the high commissioners of both federations, he planned to restrict the powers of Brazzaville's Grand Council more than those of the Dakar body in regard to the division of financial resources between the federal and territorial budgets. Because a sizable segment of AEF was still subject to the Congo Basin Convention of 1885 and also because of the conspicuously uneven distribution of wealth among the AEF territories, that federation was to be treated differently from French West Africa. It had been decided to guarantee a minimum percentage of the federal resources of AEF to each of the four territories and to take as the basis for dividing the remaining revenues the amounts produced in goods and taxes by each territory. Like the government-general itself, the federal budget would be restricted to maintaining only the technical services common to all the territories, such as mines, transport, and communications.

Before this draft law could even be debated, the Mendès-France government fell, and six more months passed before the subject was again taken up by Parliament, this time as a vital part of the *loi-cadre* of June 23, 1956. Besides providing a basis for the evolution of the French Union toward federalism, this "framework law" opened the way for all French Black Africa to take a big step toward internal autonomy, with no distinction drawn between the two federations. Later, decrees were to embody the specific measures required to carry out the general principles laid down in the *loi-cadre*. These included granting universal suffrage to all men and women over 21 years of age; establishment of executive councils (*conseils de gouvernement*) having a majority of elected members; creation of circumscription and rural councils; reorganization of the civil service; enlargement of the membership and powers of the territorial assemblies; and instituting of a single college for the election of their members. A seventh measure—the only one touching on economic aspects—concerned the modernization of rural production and the encouragement of private capital investment needed in the Overseas Territories.

Of the political innovations in the *loi-cadre,* the two most important were the creation of the councils that would share the executive power with the governor and in time develop into cabinets, and a marked extension of the competence of the territorial assemblies into the legislative domain. The powers to be acquired by the assemblies would diminish not only those of the local administration but those of the government-general and the Grand Council as well. As for the government-general, its role was reduced virtually to that of over-all coordination and arbitration, chiefly in the economic and technical domains. And the Grand Council lost a significant part of its financial powers to the territories, without receiving any compensation in the form of control over the high commissioner, who no longer had to consult the Council but was made responsible solely to the French government. Even at the time the *loi-cadre* was being debated, it was clear that it had grave flaws. Perhaps its two most notable drawbacks were its failure to establish clear-cut divisions between the territorial, the Group (as the federation was now called), and the ministerial spheres of action, and to replace the government-general by some workable but less cumbersome formula that would preserve the essentials of unity.

The AEF deputies took no outstanding part in the debates on the *loi-cadre* itself nor in those on the decrees applying its provisions; for the most part they let their colleagues from West Africa carry the ball. To some extent this was due to the difference in emphasis they respectively placed on various aspects of the law. The West Africans were aroused over the composition and responsibilities of the proposed executive councils and, above all, over whether a federal executive and parliament should replace the government-general. The Equatorial Africans, on the other hand, were more concerned with maintaining and increasing France's financial and economic aid to AEF and with the reorganization of the civil service. Both Grand Councils, however, showed an eagerness to retain their old powers, and to that end the AEF body stressed the need to maintain former interterritorial ties.[15]

On the whole, AEF was greatly pleased by the *loi-cadre,* which generated there none of the furor and heated dissidence that it provoked in French West Africa. To be sure, several formulas for achieving interterritorial unity were put forward by Boganda and Youlou (see pp. 49–50), but these were not aggressively pushed. Yet the general reluctance shown by all the territorial leaders, particularly those of Gabon, to commit themselves to any revival of the federal administrative structure did not preclude other forms of cooperation between them. In fact, their interdependence was generally recognized and even publicly stressed. As early as June 1957, the African heads of the newly constituted territorial governments met at Brazzaville under the chairmanship of Chauvet to decide which of the economic and technical services should be jointly administered. There it was decided to retain the existing taxes for the time being and in the future to consult one another regularly before submitting to their respective assemblies any project for fiscal changes.[16] A compromise was reached on the matter of tariffs, though again this was on a temporary basis. The Grand Council, it was tentatively decided, would continue to determine the export duties on cocoa, coffee, and cotton, while those on peanuts, vegetable oils, and forest products would be decided by the individual territorial assemblies.

After the referendum of September 28, 1958, had made the *loi-cadre* obsolete and confirmed the AEF territories' overwhelming desire to remain in the Franco-African community, and after their legal status had been determined two months later by the proclamation of four autonomous republics, a new series of conferences was held to map closer relations between them. The meeting that took place at Paris in mid-December was attended by the four premiers of the new republics, the presidents of their legislative assemblies, and the leaders of all the main political parties. These delegates definitely rejected the concept of a federal parliament and executive, but they eventually signed an agreement, on January 17, 1959, to establish a customs union and a common administration for transport and communications services. This was a far cry from the proposal for a strong federal executive, sponsored by Senghor and the Parti du Regroupement Africain (PRA), that had rent French West Africa asunder, for AEF was moving steadily toward a point midway between complete autonomy and federation. At that time it seemed that it was the AEF republics which were for once showing the West Africans a reasonable way of salvaging from the machinery of the former federation the elements indispensable for their joint survival.

As agreed upon at Paris, a committee on which each state was represented met at Brazzaville on March 26, 1959, having been convened by the new high commissioner, Yvon Bourges. (In July 1958, Bourges had succeeded Pierre Messmer, who had been high commissioner of AEF for only seven months.) Its task was to draw up an inventory of the states' common heritage from the federation and to formulate the principles according to which it would be liquidated and divided among the four republics. Details were to be worked out at another conference in June, on the eve of the date on which the Group of AEF would cease to exist legally. Despite the difficulties encountered at this June meeting, the expert chairmanship of Bourges and the behind-the-scenes guidance of Lisette succeeded in salvaging the essential economic and financial ties that had bound the federation together. The premiers also agreed to meet regularly, at least twice a year, for mutual consultation, and to set up coordinating machinery in the form of a permanent secretariat situated at Brazzaville.

While the June 1959 meeting promised to be more constructive than was anticipated at the time, the third premiers' conference, held at Libreville the following October, was a resounding failure. Internal political dissension in Oubangui prevented Premier Dacko from attending, and when Fulbert Youlou learned of Dacko's defection he, too, decided to remain at home. The only two prime ministers present at the Libreville meeting, Mba and Tombalbaye, thus had no choice but to adjourn, and the future course of such conferences was left open to doubt. Until greater internal stability is attained, the leaders of the four AEF republics will probably be able to give only minimal attention to their common problems, and consequently the pursuit of a united policy may go by default.

CHAPTER 3

Representative Institutions

A series of decrees in October 1946 allotted AEF six seats in the National Assembly, eight in the Senate, and seven in the French Union Assembly, and also gave each territory an elected representative assembly. (See Tables 1 and 2.) Both the electorate and the members of the territorial assemblies were divided into two colleges.[1] Metropolitan citizens composed almost the totality of the electorate and the assembly membership of the first college, whereas Africans who had retained their personal legal status[2]

TABLE 1.—AEF REPRESENTATION IN PARLIAMENTARY BODIES, AS OF NOVEMBER 1947

	National Assembly		Council of the Republic		French Union Assembly
Territory	First College	Second College	First College	Second College	
Gabon .... ⎫		1	1	1	1
Moyen-Congo .... ⎬ 1		1	1	1	1
Oubangui-Chari ...... ⎫ 1		1	1	1	2
Tchad .... ⎭		1	1	1	3
Total	6		8		7

Source: Grand Council, document annexed to minutes of session of November 24, 1947.

TABLE 2.—AEF PARLIAMENTARIANS AND THEIR PARTY AFFILIATIONS, 1954

Territory	National Assembly	Council of the Republic	French Union Assembly
Gabon	Aubame, IOM	Durand-Reville, RGR Gondjout, IOM	Boucavel, IOM
Moyen-Congo ..	Tchicaya, UDSR	Coupigny, ROM Malonga, ROM	Lounda, RGR
Oubangui-Chari	Boganda, Indépendant-Paysan	Aube, ROM	Lhuillier, RPF Darlan, A., RDA
Tchad	Béchir Sow, RPF Sou Quatre, RPF	Gautier, ROM Sahoulba, ROM	Laurin, RPF Djima Doumbaye, RPF Rogué, RPF

Source: Présidence du Conseil (La Documentation Française), *L'Evolution Récente des Institutions Politiques* (etc.), March 11, 1954.

37

made up the second college. In most of the territorial assemblies, the prevailing ratio was two representatives of the first college to three of the second college. (See Table 3.)

TABLE 3.—TERRITORIAL REPRESENTATION IN AEF ASSEMBLIES

Territory	Representation in 1946, by College		Total No. of Members		
	First College	Second College	1946	1952	1956
Gabon	12	18	30	37	40
Moyen-Congo	12	18	30	37	45
Oubangui-Chari	10	15	25	40	45
Tchad	10	20	30	45	60

Source: E. Trézenem and B. Lembezat, *La France Equatoriale* (Paris, 1950).

Almost a year later, a law of August 27, 1947, created a Grand Council of 20 members, each territorial assembly electing five and voting as a single college. These assemblies and the Grand Council were required to hold two regular sessions a year, for a specified number of days, but extraordinary sessions could also be called by the head of the local administration or by the high commissioner. Each body elected a permanent committee of three to five members to carry on its work between sessions.

Although the territorial assemblies acted as an electoral college in voting for AEF's representatives in the Senate, the French Union Assembly, and the Grand Council, their most important powers related to financial matters. Subject to cancellation by the Council of State at Paris if they should contravene or overstep the law, the decisions of the representative local assemblies were final in a number of fields. Foremost among these was the power to amend, reject, or approve the budgets submitted to them by their respective territorial governors. Furthermore, they were obligatorily consulted on such matters as local land concessions, loans, the organization of the administration, labor and social security, the *état civil,* public works, and the like. The governor could, and often did, submit many other questions to the assemblymen for their advice; the assemblymen were also permitted to pass resolutions and to address directly to the high commissioner or the Minister of Overseas France any observations in the general interests of their territory. However, they were forbidden to discuss political questions or other matters considered to be exclusively the province of the administration. On the federal level, the Grand Council had the same prerogatives as did the assemblies on the territorial level, and it had to be consulted on all questions affecting two or more territories. In addition, it set the fiscal duties for imports and exports, and it allocated subsidies and rebates to the territories from the federal budget.

The Electorate and Elections

In 1946, the franchise was extended to members of both sexes who were 21 years of age or over and belonged to one of the twelve categories specified by the law—civil servants, members of native courts, Notables, soldiers and veterans, heads of native collectivities, those holding honorary decorations, etc.

In 1946 the debates in the National Assembly on the question of whether the Overseas Territories should have a double or a single electoral college were long and heated. In April of that year, the political climate in Paris was favorable to instituting the single college, but six months later the attitude of the Metropolitan majority had changed to the point of passing a law setting up the double college in all the African territories except Senegal, over the strong protests of the African deputies.[3] The French West Africans waged a bitter fight against it, but to no avail. From AEF, only the voice of its sole African deputy, Tchicaya, was raised in the National Assembly to plead that his federation be given the single electoral college, on the ground that it had played a leading part in the Resistance movement. But even the French deputies who favored the single college for West Africa seem never to have seriously considered extending it to AEF, because of AEF's political inexperience and immaturity. Nor was AEF's small European population treated with much greater indulgence: the first colleges of Moyen-Congo and Gabon were to vote jointly for one deputy, while those of Tchad and Oubangui were to share another.

Actually, there was no strong current of opinion in AEF to back up Tchicaya's protests, and the following year the Africans in Tchad's territorial assembly even voted to maintain the double college there. Except in Oubangui, the first and second colleges worked together harmoniously during the early postwar years, and in the elections throughout the federation all the parties sponsored both European and African candidates. When the territorial assemblies elected AEF's first representatives to the Senate and French Union Assembly, in January 1947, more Europeans than Africans (eight to seven) were chosen, despite the fact that the majority of territorial assemblymen belonged to the second college. And the ratio of AEF's first Grand Councilors was much the same as that of the territorial assemblymen, as was the membership in its main committees, which usually had a European chairman and an African *rapporteur*. By and large, the African representatives looked upon their European colleagues as guides and mentors, and elected the most experienced among them to be presidents of the assemblies and chairmen of the technical committees. Even after Africans began replacing Europeans in such posts in 1950, there was a striking absence of racial antagonism in AEF's elected bodies. Cooperation was most conspicuous in Gabon's assembly and least evident in that of Oubangui-Chari.

Perhaps one reason for this era of good feeling in AEF was the small size of the electorate in the first postwar years. (See Table 4.) In fact, this was one of the arguments used by Malbrant against introducing the single college in AEF for the legislative elections of June 1951, when that question again came up for discussion in the National Assembly. Yet the percentage of votes actually cast by registered electors in AEF was com-

TABLE 4.—THE ELECTORATE IN AEF

Territory	Population (round numbers)	Registered Electors (Second College)				Percentage Voting
		Nov. 1946	June 1951	Mar. 1952	Mar. 1953	
Gabon	409,000	26,530	70,843	86,530	87,365	47.8 (1946) 41.7 (1951)
Moyen-Congo ...	684,000	23,119	118,523	176,711	186,509	67.7 (1946) 44.3 (1951)
Oubangui-Chari ..	1,072,000	32,716	111,204	187,908	192,891	70.1 (1946) 60.9 (1951)
Tchad	2,241,000	27,664	250,341	307,970	317,646	64.5 (1946) 66.2 (1951)
Total	4,406,000	110,029	550,911	759,119	784,411	

Source: Adapted from Présidence du Conseil (La Documentation Française), *L'Evolution Récente des Institutions Politiques* (etc.), March 11, 1954.

paratively high, ranging from 47.8 per cent in Gabon to 70.1 per cent in Oubangui. Among the deputies, advocates of the single college included not only the Africans and the "egalitarians," but also those who felt that the double college had led to an unfortunate aggravation of racialism by giving separate representation to African demands and grievances. On April 24, 1951, the National Assembly voted in favor of adopting the single college in Moyen-Congo and Oubangui and for an appreciable increase in the whole electorate of AEF. But the Senate rejected the principle of the single college for any of the AEF territories, and for the federation accepted only three new categories of voters—the mothers of two children, the heads of households, and the recipients of civil or military pensions. Although Tchicaya characterized the new electoral law as one "shameful to Parliament,"[4] it brought about a fivefold increase in the number of registered electors in AEF. The following November, Parliament also voted a substantial enlargement of the membership of the territorial assemblies. (See Table 3.)

Such a large and sudden increase in AEF's electorate probably accounted for the decline in voter participation in the June 1951 elections to the National Assembly. The percentage fell everywhere except in Tchad, where it increased by nearly 2 per cent, perhaps as the result of the local administration's determined efforts to bring out the anti-RDA vote. In 1952 came another, although not so imposing, enlargement of the AEF electorate and, proportionately, of the number of candidates running for election to the territorial assemblies. (By that time, the pay of parliamentarians had risen to about 300,000 CFA (Colonies Françaises d'Afrique) francs a year and the daily stipend of territorial assemblymen to 800 CFA francs during sessions. In 1954 the latter was raised to 1,326 CFA francs a day, but the assemblymen still claimed that it was insufficient and asked for 2,000 CFA francs.) The year 1952 also marked the comeback of the Rassemblement

Démocratique Africain (RDA) in AEF, under various territorial party labels, and saw the first of a series of outbreaks that threatened to jeopardize the tranquility of European-African relations.[5]

Nevertheless, Governor-General Chauvet, in his speech to the Grand Council on September 30, 1953, was pleased to stress the political calm that pervaded AEF, despite an increase in unemployment and the federation's worsening financial situation. In 1954 the atmosphere was still generally peaceful, but President Flandre of the Grand Council commented in his address of May 29 to that body that "a malaise has been created here . . . by quarrels carried on in the press and by speeches which through a chain reaction have led to heated altercations in the Grand Council." The following year, the question of the single college again came to the fore in connection with the Municipal Reform Bill, then being debated in Parliament. This time there was no doubt as to the sentiments of AEF's elected representatives concerning the matter. A resolution passed on November 16, 1955, stated that "the Grand Councillors, considering that maintenance of the double college is a discriminatory measure taken against AEF, which is an integral part of the French Republic, have decided not to attend the extraordinary session called by the governor-general." But after a reassurance by cable from Minister Teitgen, they changed their minds a few days later and proceeded to vote the federal budget without further ado. Yet during that same month the two European representatives from AEF in the French Union Assembly continued to assure their colleagues that the "Africans in AEF want to be represented by Europeans, albeit Europeans of their own choosing."[6]

This statement was not disproved by the elections of January 2, 1956, to the National Assembly; only the unexpected dissolution of Parliament late in 1955 delayed final passage of a bill that would have instituted the single college throughout AEF. Thus, the fact that these elections were the first to be troubled by violence (at Brazzaville) could not be attributed to elimination of the restraining influence exerted by the double electoral college. As a matter of fact, when the single electoral college and universal suffrage were instituted and when membership in the territorial assemblies was increased by application of the *loi-cadre* of June 23, 1956, these changes did not greatly alter the political situation in the federation. Party alignments, which were basically tribal or simply represented the following of an individual leader, remained proportionately much the same as before, although by 1957 the electorate had grown to well over two and a half million.[7]

What had been markedly changed by the *loi-cadre* was the role of Europeans in AEF politics. For the past several years, the European residents of the federation had shown a growing indifference to exercising their franchise or running for elective office. Some veteran parliamentarians such as Bayrou and Durand-Reville began to stress the view that local politics should be left exclusively to the Africans, and that Europeans should intervene only in the economic and technical spheres without becoming embroiled in AEF party politics or tribal quarrels. On the other hand, some Frenchmen living in AEF continued to seek election, although in smaller numbers than before, and all of the big parties carried a few Europeans on their lists of candidates. Now, however, it was no longer a question of membership in Metropolitan parties or of furthering specifically European interests. Such men as Vial and Jayle in Moyen-Congo and Guérillot in Oubangui, who remain a political force in their territories, have placed themselves at the service of African politicians, as advisers or backers, and in so doing have acquired for themselves the dubious label of *éminences blanches.*

CHAPTER 4

Political Organizations

The Brazzaville conference of 1944 awakened AEF's political consciousness and, it is sometimes said, provided the federation with a political birth
certificate. Before World War II, AEF had no elected bodies and no political life, properly speaking. Only Gabon—and for some of the same reasons
as Senegal—had evolved somewhat less slowly than had the other territories. There in the 1920's and 1930's a few small parties developed, but
they proved to be ephemeral. To a limited extent their place was taken in
Gabon and Moyen-Congo by the syncretic religious sects, which usually
acquired a marked political coloring (see pp. 308–14), but Islamized Tchad
never developed even such substitutes as these.

To be sure, among the Negroes of central Africa there existed innumerable associations of one sort or another, but all were cast in the mold of
traditional African society. Almost without exception they were limited in
area and membership, were confined to tribal and religious groups, and
were of the mutual-aid type.[1] Nevertheless, these associations permitted a
handful of Africans to gain an apprenticeship in organized secular activity,
which produced indigenous leaders for many of the parties that sprang up
in AEF during 1945–46. However, because these men generally lacked
training and experience, European and Negro outsiders dominated the
political scene in the federation for some years.

Metropolitan Parties

It was inevitable that the first to enter the AEF political vacuum would
be branches or affiliates of the big Metropolitan parties. Because the federation had served as headquarters for the overseas Resistance movement,
Gaullism was both a sentiment and an organized force in AEF; it accounted for the rapid growth among Africans and Europeans alike of the
Rassemblement du Peuple Français (RPF) in all the territories except
Gabon, and particularly in Moyen-Congo and Tchad. An outstanding record in the Resistance was for years a *sine qua non* for candidates running
for elective office. The RPF long profited by the loyalty evoked by de
Gaulle's name, and in ways that increasingly exasperated its political opponents (see p. 560, n. 15). And when that party tried to make political
capital out of a marriage fund which the general himself had given to

44

THE FEDERATION

enable young Africans to pay the bride price, the African Grand Councilors refused to let de Gaulle's name be used any longer in connection with it.[2]

Until late 1953, the RPF remained predominant in Tchad, but by 1949 in Moyen-Congo it no longer had many African members and had become almost exclusively a European party. In Oubangui the RPF was never anything but the party of the government and the French residents, and in that territory the long association of the administration with the rule of the concessionary companies automatically alienated Africans from the RPF. Generally speaking, the pressure exerted by the RPF-oriented administration throughout AEF during almost all of the federation's electoral campaigns until 1956, as well as the survival of the dual college there until that year, enabled RPF candidates and policies to exert political force long after they had ceased to express the views of a majority of the electorate. To the foregoing factors, Bayrou and Malbrant in the National Assembly, Durand-Reville[3] in the Senate, and Laurin in the French Union Assembly owed their exceptional parliamentary longevity despite their inflexibly conservative views. But gradually Gaullism as a *mystique* was divorced from the RPF as a political party, so that de Gaulle himself emerged undiminished in popularity and prestige. The spread of a religio-political cult, Ngol (named for the general), and the spontaneously enthusiastic welcome given de Gaulle in August 1958 by the populations of Fort Lamy and Brazzaville testified to the vitality of the loyalty that he continued to inspire in all strata of the African population.

The Section Française de l'Internationale Ouvrière (SFIO) was the second big Metropolitan party to found branches in AEF, but the socialists never enjoyed there the popularity that they had in French West Africa. In the first place, the Popular Front government of 1936 did not provide the same stimulus to the African elite as it had to the African liberals of Senegal, where its program met with a warmer response. Though the SFIO founded a branch at Brazzaville as early as January 1946, membership was for some time confined largely to minor European functionaries and failed to spread to the African electorate. The trade unions—normally a source of socialist strength—resisted the SFIO's attempts to organize them in Moyen-Congo, the only territory that possessed enough concentrations of wage earners to be effectively unionized. Reportedly, the Balali even threw stones at the postwar socialist organizers because the word *syndicat* had unfortunate associations for them.[4] During the 1930's the only *syndicats* known in the Balali region were those of merchants, some of whom had allegedly denounced the Matsouanists to the government. In Moyen-Congo, only Jacques Opangault and the M'Bochi tribe were responsive to the SFIO program and propaganda, and this still further alienated the Balali from the socialist party.

For many years, in fact, the SFIO was a party of minor importance; it had a following only in Moyen-Congo and Tchad, and even in those territories its membership long remained stationary. It was not until socialism there took on an indigenous, even ethnic, coloring that the party forged ahead. In the process, Opangault emerged less as a socialist than as a tribal leader, and Koulamallah gave socialism in Tchad a strongly localized orientation. Although the Congolese and Tchadian socialists later changed the name of their organization to the Mouvement Socialiste Africain (MSA), it is noteworthy that their respective leaders have continued to stress close ties with the Metropolitan SFIO and not with the counterpart movement in French West Africa. In September 1957, the refusal of its European members to run for office in the Moyen-Congo branch of the MSA as a matter of principle left the socialist movement there wholly in the hands of Africans, which furthered good Franco-African relations inside that party.

The third Metropolitan party to gain a toehold in AEF was that of the communists, but its success was shorter-lived than that of the RPF or even the SFIO. On February 26, 1946, the government-general permitted the organizing of a Groupe d'Etudes Communistes de l'AEF,[5] and similar "study groups" were set up in all the territorial capitals except Libreville. In conformity with their policy in French West Africa, the French communists preferred operating indirectly in AEF by creating local unions of the Confédération Générale du Travail (CGT) and later by helping to establish and promote local branches of the RDA after that movement was initiated at Bamako in October 1946.

To no small extent, the early unpopularity of the communists and of the RDA in AEF stemmed from a series of six trips made there by leaders of the French communist party and their parliamentary allies in 1948–49. The federation received more communist attention than did any other part of the French Union—the party sent only two delegations to French West Africa—because the local sections of the RDA were in trouble and called on the Metropolitan leaders for aid.[6] This was particularly true in Moyen-Congo, where some of its territorial assemblymen, French Union Councilors, and senators suddenly resigned from the RDA. Charged with an "information mission," Raymond Barbé and his colleagues visited Brazzaville, Pointe Noire, Bangui, Fort Archambault, and other cities, calling for disobedience to the colonialist administration and to the traditional chiefs, "who have sold out to the French government." Not appreciating the strength of pro-Gaullist sentiment in AEF, the communist spokesmen made the mistake of attacking both de Gaulle and local Resistance leaders, and this tactic alienated an important segment of the African as well as the European population. Their visits did the RDA in AEF more harm than good, and were in part responsible for a stiffening of the administration's attitude toward that party's leaders.

African Parties

By far the strongest African party in AEF during the early postwar years was the RDA, but it was well organized only in Tchad and western Moyen-Congo, relatively weak in Oubangui-Chari, and virtually nonexistent in Gabon.[7] (See also Chapters 22–25 on the individual territories.)

In 1946 the Tchad branch of the RDA, the Parti Progressiste Tchadien (PPT), was organized by a thoroughly Gallicized, 25-year-old Negro from the French Antilles named Gabriel Lisette. After graduating from the Ecole Coloniale in Paris, he occupied an administrative post in the Logone region, where he built up a strong following among the Sara population. It was both the strength and the weakness of Lisette that no other Tchadian leader could compare with him in intelligence, training, and organizing ability. Since the RDA, from its inception, aimed to spread its organization far beyond the confines of French West Africa, it was consistent with that policy that a nonindigenous Negro should become its party leader in Tchad. His very ability, however, made him both feared and opposed by the local pro-RPF administration, after he left its ranks to head a radical African party. Then, too, the fact that he had not been born in Tchad, as well as that he was supported by the Sara, made him doubly alien in the eyes of many Tchadians, especially those from the northern and eastern parts of the territory. Partly because Lisette was preoccupied by his duties in Paris as a National Assemblyman, his career in Tchad has alternated between victory and defeat. Despite his remarkable political resilience the day must soon come when indigenous Tchad politicians will eliminate and replace him. There is little doubt that the RDA can and will use Lisette elsewhere, but more uncertain is the fate of the RDA in Tchad without his leadership.

Quite different from Lisette is the RDA's first leader in Moyen-Congo, Jean-Félix Tchicaya. Born in Gabon in 1903, he was nevertheless recognized as an authentic leader of the Vili tribe in the Pointe Noire region. Though he was a signatory of the original RDA manifesto at Bamako in September 1946 and was consistently re-elected deputy for Moyen-Congo with over-all RDA support, he never rose to eminence in the councils of that movement to the same extent as did Lisette. So long as the M'Bochi socialists were Tchicaya's main adversaries, Tchicaya's career ran smoothly. But when Opangault joined with the Balali leader, Fulbert Youlou, to oppose him, Tchicaya's following shrank to the point where he became almost a political cipher in Moyen-Congo. To salvage the party in that territory, the RDA top brass realistically—if cruelly—dropped Tchicaya and allied themselves with the Congolese man of the hour, Fulbert Youlou.

In Gabon the RDA failed to get an early footing. That territory's perennial deputy, Jean Aubame, was an independent in local politics until he founded the Union Démocratique et Sociale Gabonaise (UDSG); in the National Assembly he followed Senghor's leadership, adhering successively to the Indépendants d'Outre-Mer, the Convention Africaine, and the PRA. His rival, Léon Mba, likewise a Fang and the founder of a local party, the Bloc Démocratique Gabonais (BDG), did not become a prominent political figure throughout the territory until 1956. Then he joined the RDA and later attended congresses of that party in Bamako and Paris. But both the UDSG and the BDG are wholly territorial parties, and their connection with the French West African PRA and RDA, respectively, is largely confined to the top-leadership level.

The course followed by the Union Oubanguienne, the RDA branch in Oubangui-Chari, was somewhat different from that in the other territories. Its founder, Antoine Darlan, was for some years criticized for running the party as a one-man show. Darlan's early career resembled that of Gabriel d'Arboussier: both men were mulattoes, had attended communist congresses in Europe after the war, were comparative late-comers to the RDA, and were then elected to the French Union Assembly. But Darlan lacked d'Arboussier's finesse and intelligence, and he never played an analogous role in the French Union Assembly or in the upper echelons of the RDA. His aggressive nature, as well as the violence with which he expressed his views, aroused not only the hostility of the local administration and European members of the territorial assembly, but the dissent of his African colleagues there as well. Moreover, beginning in 1952, he found himself competing for political popularity with Barthélemy Boganda, a far more magnetic and more authentically African leader than himself. Although Darlan later joined the MESAN party, founded in 1952 by Boganda, he continued to belong to the RDA and occasionally attended its big congresses. It is possible, however, that Boganda's sudden death in March 1959 may enable Darlan to rise once more to the surface and revitalize the Oubanguian branch of the RDA.

Neither the RDA nor the Metropolitan parties have played the role in AEF that they have in French West Africa. Although it could be said that the organization and platforms of the Metropolitan parties were no better suited to West Africa than to AEF, the leaders of AEF were even less well prepared to adapt them to their needs or even to understand their policies. Only the RPF took root in AEF, and this occurred in but two of its territories and only for so long as Gaullism was identified with it and Europeans dominated local politics. The SFIO, too, acquired a foothold in only two territories, and it languished in both until African leaders applied the socialist party label to what were really ethnic groups. Similarly, the French communists could build up no more than a tiny following in AEF so long as they operated as an alien party, and were more successful only when they effaced themselves in order to promote the RDA more effectively.

Theoretically, the RDA stood a much better chance than the Metropolitan parties of becoming the outstanding interterritorial movement in AEF. It was led by French African Negroes and had a platform that, by and large, expressed the main aspirations of both the African elite and the masses. Yet the RDA in AEF suffered from two grave handicaps. One was a lack of qualified indigenous leadership capable of organizing the movement on a federal basis; it even had trouble finding suitable territorial leaders to head its local branches. The second was that it appeared in AEF eyes to be "made in French West Africa." For years AEF has been saddled with an inferiority complex toward its western neighbor, not only because French West Africa was larger, better equipped, and more accessible to outside influences but also because its more numerous population had greater opportunities for education and economic advancement.

Until 1956, the RDA high command paid little attention to its branches in AEF. It seemed not to take their leadership very seriously, with the exception of Lisette, who operated in the National Assembly more as the RDA spokesman than as deputy for Tchad. But the rift that became obvious in the RDA's West African ranks after the *loi-cadre* was adopted in June 1956 aroused the interest of Houphouet and his lieutenants in gaining additional support in AEF for their policies. Furthermore, a propitious moment for an RDA offensive there seemed to be at hand. In Tchad, Lisette had returned to power and the PPT's victory in the March 1957 territorial elections assured his becoming the first vice-president of its government council. In Gabon, Léon Mba—whose BDG was now allied with the RDA—was also due to head the new local government, although without such strong support in the territorial assembly as Lisette's. The outlook for the RDA in Oubangui seemed hopeless, for the grip of Boganda and his MESAN on the population of that territory was unshaken. Moyen-Congo was the area that most urgently required RDA intervention, since Tchicaya's popularity among the local electorate was obviously waning fast, and the transfer of RDA support to Youlou became imperative after the March 1957 elections. Immediately after the results of the elections became known, Houphouet sent to Brazzaville three of his ablest assistants—Lisette, Ouezzin Coulibaly, and Dr. Sylla. Prolonged negotiations led, late in May, to an RDA-UDDIA alliance, which became an influential factor in the contest that was shaping up for control of the AEF Grand Council.

The main contender for the presidency of that body was Boganda, so it was to the interest of the RDA to win him over if possible. Talks between Boganda and Lisette, which took place during the same months as the RDA-UDDIA negotiations, seemingly failed in their chief objective. Indeed, Boganda came out ahead in these negotiations, for he acquired a toehold in Tchad through the permission granted him by Lisette to organize a branch of the MESAN there.[8] This concession, followed by the RDA's support of Boganda's candidacy as president of the Grand Council in June 1957, was granted in the evident hope of persuading Boganda to enter the RDA fold, but it was soon obvious that the intense personal ambition of the MESAN leader had not been sufficiently taken into account. The only *quid pro quo* that the RDA received was the election of two members of its group to the posts of first and second vice-president of the Grand Council. Moreover, the RDA's support in those elections of its new ally, the UDDIA, earned it the enmity of the three Moyen-Congo MSA Grand Councilors. This development ended any chance of carrying out another of Lisette's projects—that of effecting a reconciliation between Youlou and Opangault.[9]

Boganda's popularity with the Grand Councilors reached its peak in

October 1957 when he vigorously denounced the French officials who were covertly hostile to the *loi-cadre* and who were resisting transfer of the executive power to African hands (see p. 394), but thereafter his popularity waned. In any case, by that time the RDA must have lost hope of persuading Boganda to stop playing a lone hand and apparently decided to close its ranks in AEF. To bolster the loyalty of those local leaders who had given proof of their willingness to follow Houphouet's lead, a pressing invitation was extended to them to attend the Bamako RDA congress in September 1957; and for the first time at such a gathering, AEF was represented by a strong delegation numbering 20 members.[10] These AEF delegates, especially Léon Mba, gratifyingly rallied to Houphouet's position, and none showed any inclination to join the faction that favored a strong federal executive.

In AEF itself the strengthening of the RDA's organization ties during the winter of 1957–58 paid off—and at Boganda's expense. The candidate put up by the RDA to compete with him in the elections for presidency of the Grand Council, held on March 24, 1958, lost by the narrow margin of one vote. Though party lines were drawn more sharply than before, the struggle between the RDA and its opponents during the summer of 1958 did not center on the major issues facing the federation but was almost wholly a personal contest for power between Boganda and Youlou. Three delegates from AEF—Goumba from Oubangui and Aubame and Ekoh from Gabon—did attend the Parti du Regroupement Africain (PRA) congress held at Cotonou in July; of these, two were leaders of the anti-RDA forces in Gabon, and the other was head of the MESAN government of Oubangui. But they took no outstanding part in its debates, and on their return to AEF they declared that they were not advocating secession from France. The freedom allowed by both the PRA and the RDA to their territorial branches to vote as they pleased in the September 28 referendum was used in AEF to turn in a unanimous vote in favor of joining the Franco-African Community. In the following November, all the territories—though not by unanimous votes—decided to become autonomous republics and member states of that Community. Moreover, they were generally in agreement as to the undesirability of setting up a strong federal executive to replace the defunct government-general.

The Africans newly come to power had no intention of surrendering any of the many well-paid posts (40 ministerial portfolios and 200 seats for deputies) that would automatically vanish if a unitary government were created for all of AEF. Moreover, each territory had its own reasons for rejecting such a step. Both of Gabon's main political parties were determined, for both sentimental and financial reasons, to cling to that territory's direct ties with France and to cut loose from the grip of Brazzaville. In Tchad, Lisette naturally reflected the views of his chief, Houphouet; his rival, Koulamallah, was no more eager than was Lisette for the territory to be controlled from distant Brazzaville, and for some time he even favored retaining Tchad's status as an Overseas Territory. There remained Moyen-

Congo and Oubangui, each headed by a man anxious to assert his leadership not only over the other territories of the former federation but over related tribes in the Belgian Congo and Portuguese Angola as well. During the summer of 1958, Boganda and Youlou each worked hard to line up the other territories behind his particular scheme, and both failed. The only encouragement that Boganda received came from the leaders opposed to the RDA—Aubame, Opangault, and Tchicaya. As for Youlou, the most favorable response to his proposal came, apparently, from his fellow Bakongo south of the Congo river. Boganda's sudden death in March 1959 eliminated Youlou's main rival in this field, but the future of Youlou's plans for the Bakongo of the Belgian Congo and Angola depends upon the fate of the Abako party in the Belgian colony and the reaction of the Angolese Bakongo.

Among the many causes of the rejection of the proposal of a unitary state for AEF, in general, and of the Boganda-Youlou proposals for hegemony, in particular, probably the most fundamental was the strength of regionalism and tribalism, only thinly disguised by political-party labels. Although some farsighted leaders in the former federation recognized the need for retaining certain economic and social ties, not only with France but among themselves, the greater part of the unity that had been built up by the French in AEF seemed to dissolve with the liquidation of the government-general. In fact, so strong was the centrifugal tendency that it caused disparate elements to join together, at least temporarily, to resist anything that might be interpreted as an attempt to force unity upon them, particularly if it originated outside of AEF. Such was the case with the RDA, whose West African leaders were believed by many of the AEF elite to aim at swallowing up their new republics.

This fear was openly expressed after the announcement was made that Houphouet planned to tour AEF and to hold the next meeting of the RDA coordinating committee at Brazzaville in November 1958. Already, during the preceding summer, the three adroit and sophisticated envoys sent to AEF by Houphouet to cement the RDA-UDDIA alliance had provided a contrast to the provincial and naïve local politicians that proved embarrassing to the latter's parties. The defection of Guinea and the growing strength of the PRA in Senegal, Niger, and Dahomey, it was rumored, had made the West African leadership of the RDA more determined than ever to establish itself firmly in AEF. Moreover, the anti-Togolese and anti-Dahomean riots at Abidjan in the fall of 1958 further convinced the forces opposed to the RDA in AEF that the Houphouet faction was losing out in West Africa and must at all costs be prevented from finding compensation in AEF. Whether it was because of the strength of this opposition or simply because of the RDA's habit of postponing or canceling congresses, the scheduled meeting of its coordinating committee at Brazzaville did not take place. It was reported[11] that the MSA of Tchad and Moyen-Congo and the PRA of Gabon, as well as Boganda and Tchicaya, believed that by jointly exerting pressure they had gained this victory and that for the time being they had averted any danger of AEF's being "colonized by French West Africa. This is what they tell their militants, to whom the rivalry between Sekou Touré and Houphouet is presented as the struggle of the African people against the African bourgeoisie."

The crystallization of this sentiment among the leaders of the opposition parties makes the future of the RDA in the AEF republics difficult to predict. So long as the RDA leadership and directives appear to come from West Africa, the forces resisting that movement may remain united and sufficiently strong to check any further RDA inroads. But if the RDA can convince the electorate of AEF that it has become an indigenous local movement, its superior organization and political know-how should enable it to win out easily over its disparate and basically disunited opponents. A possible straw in the wind was the presence of delegates from all four AEF republics at the RDA congress held at Abidjan in September 1959, whereas the Parti de la Fédération Africaine (formed at Dakar in July 1959 as the result of a merger between Senghor's PRA and the anti-Houphouet faction of the RDA in French West Africa) did not attempt to form any branches in AEF, and AEF sent neither delegates nor observers to that party's inaugural congress.

If the AEF states are ever to enter into a lasting union, this will have to be accomplished from within and by their own peoples. Thus far, all outside political organizations, whether Metropolitan or African, have failed to put down deep roots in AEF. So strong is local feeling—especially tribal and regional—that leaders and parties have remained vital forces only for so long and in so far as they have operated within a particular traditional context. The European parties have disappeared from the political scene, along with the Africans who belonged to them. Only the authentic tribal leaders, such as Léon Mba, Youlou, and Koulamallah, have retained a firm hold on their following. The electorate's dependence on leadership and the dearth of able and enlightened leaders in AEF constitute one of the greatest handicaps to the political evolution of its new countries. The death of a Boganda jeopardizes the future of even so strong a party as the MESAN, and only a few of the tribes—possibly the Fang and Bakongo—would have enough vitality and cohesion to weather such a loss politically. The Brazzaville massacres of February 1959 showed that the temptation to appeal to tribal animosities as a means of keeping or extending political power is almost as irresistible to an AEF leader as is that of replacing uncooperative civil servants by loyal members of his party.

Parliamentary democracy and the party system, as these are understood in countries of Western European tradition, remain alien forms of political self-expression in AEF. A more typical and perhaps more enduring form is that which has been evolved in the southern territories of the former federation by the politico-religious sects (see pp. 308–14).

CHAPTER 5

Municipal Government
and Rural Councils

A decree of March 14, 1911, empowered the governor-general in council to transform the principal European settlements of AEF into mixed communes, subject to approval by the Minister of Colonies. (In this context, the word "mixed" indicates that the councils of such communes included both African and European members.) Accordingly, in October of the following year the mixed communes of Brazzaville, Libreville, and Bangui were created, and for each of these an official of the general cadre was named by the respective territorial governor as administrator-mayor. He was aided by a municipal council composed of four nominated members, chosen by him, of whom one was an African. This was a purely advisory body and could make recommendations only on such subjects as municipal finances, public property, and the judicial administration.[1]

In 1919 Fort Lamy was made a mixed commune, and in 1936 Port Gentil was likewise promoted, but not until October 1950 was a seventh, Dolisie, added to the list. In the meantime some minor changes were made in the organization of these communes, notably an increase in the size of their councils (from 8 to 12 members) but not of their powers. The last reorganization before World War II was that of December 28, 1936, and it set a pattern for AEF's limited form of municipal government that was to remain essentially unchanged until 1955.

An interesting development in the field of municipal government, initiated by Eboué during the war, had no parallel in French West Africa. To carry out his policy of giving more prominence to the traditional elite[2] and of training its members for future self-government, Eboué gave legal status to a new category of Africans—that of the *Notables évolués*. With the aim of enabling them to serve an apprenticeship in the management of public affairs, he created, on July 29, 1942, native communes in Brazzaville's African suburbs of Poto-Poto and Bacongo. In Eboué's master plan these two bodies were to serve as liaisons between the African population of their communes and the administrator-mayor of Brazzaville, and they were placed in charge of wholly African councils disposing of their own separate budgets. Unfortunately this project was in effect stillborn, for neither the Africans nor the Europeans of Brazzaville showed any interest in carrying forward the experiment after Eboué's death in 1944.

It was Eboué's ambition to bestow on the most progressive of the African Notables (the majority of whom were chiefs) a legal status midway between that of French subject and citizen. A first group of 11 Notables was accorded this status on April 1, 1943, and a second group numbering 93 was similarly designated on August 23, 1943, but there the matter ended. The only eligible Africans who showed any enthusiasm for this improved legal status were some subaltern civil servants who hoped to derive material advantages thereby.[3] Almost no interest at all was shown by the chiefs, small merchants, artisans, and planters, who apparently failed to grasp the purport of this reform. Nor did the European officialdom of the federal capital display any greater understanding of its potentialities, for they saw no point in creating an elite class whose evolution was to continue along traditional, not French, lines. Until 1955 the native communes continued to function, but ineffectually because of their lack of financial independence and the poor caliber of many of their appointed councilors. Two African members of the French Union Assembly even proposed on March 17, 1948, that these "caricatures of municipal government" be totally suppressed.

In the early postwar years, much the same criticism was leveled by the African elite against the federation's six mixed communes, though each of those organizations had its own budget. According to such critics, only illiterate and docile Africans were selected by the administrator-mayor to serve on these councils, and their European members easily dominated all of their activities.[4] In this connection Bangui was usually pointed to as the outstanding example of municipal self-misgovernment in AEF. In 1948, eight of its 12 municipal councilors were Frenchmen, representing some 1,200 European residents, whereas the nearly 40,000 Africans of Bangui had as their spokesmen only four councilors. Aside from this numerically disproportionate representation, 98 per cent of the town's budgetary resources, it was said, was spent on the European quarter, and a mere 2 per cent on improving living conditions for the African urban population, which supplied two-thirds of the revenues Bangui derived from taxation.[5] Specifically, it was charged that the administrator-mayor had done nothing to help the African residents during the severe floods and fire of 1946–47, but that he had concerned himself solely with rescuing some equipment belonging to the municipality. It is small wonder that one of the first acts of Oubangui's territorial assembly was to ask urgently for a reform of the town council's membership.[6] The main grievance harbored by this and other territorial assemblies against the administrator-mayors was the arbitrary way in which they exercised their right to expropriate the property of urban Africans. Legally, this could be done only for the execution of town improvement programs or in the "general interest." Yet some mayors were accused of having forced African town dwellers to move to unhealthy and peripheral areas simply to make room for expansion of the European quarter.

At various times, beginning in 1946, municipal reform projects for AEF were debated in the parliamentary bodies and in the local assemblies. In Paris it was proposed that the decree of November 26, 1947, which had reorganized some municipalities in French West Africa and created *communes de moyen exercice,* be extended to AEF.[7] In some ways the new communes resembled the mixed communes, but their councils were elected and they were saddled with heavier financial responsibilities. This was thought by some to be a desirable intermediate step for some of AEF's towns, which in no case could hope to become full communes in the near future. To qualify for the status of full commune, a municipality had to be able to meet all its expenditures from its own resources, and not one of the federation's towns was in a sufficiently prosperous condition to assume such a responsibility. Although the advancement to *communes de moyen exercice* would represent only a slight step toward municipal self-government on the part of mixed communes, it would nevertheless permit the Africans of small towns to serve their apprenticeship in the management of urban affairs during the five-year period required for those towns to rise to the status of full communes.

Some African councilors favored not only turning the existing mixed communes into *communes de moyen exercice* but also immediately establishing such governmental structures at Pointe Noire, Lambaréné, Bambari, Bangassou, Fort Archambault, and Abéché. In sparsely populated AEF, all of these towns were important and none had any form of municipal self-government. Other councilors, however, preferred starting afresh and giving municipal reforms in AEF a different turn from those in French West Africa. Although the elite of both federations wanted their towns to have elected mayors and councils holding real powers, especially over the disposal of urban property and over taxation, the AEF Africans were primarily concerned that their territorial assemblies should acquire control of the municipal governments. Perhaps because local African opinion on this subject remained divided and because the French government gradually gave in to some of the assemblies' demands, no drastic changes were made for many years in the existing situation except to add fast-growing Dolisie to the roster of mixed communes in October 1950. At all events, no AEF town had the political or economic importance of a Dakar or an Abidjan; hence, the urge to reform the municipal machinery was correspondingly slighter.

In practice, the administrative division of the African towns of AEF into ethnic groups, each under its own *chef de quartier,* worked well enough until the great influx of newcomers to the towns in the postwar years created some difficulties by partially obliterating tribal lines. In time and under pressure from the territorial assemblies, the government to some extent coped with this problem by enlarging the town councils and appointing more Africans to represent not only the minority ethnic groups but the political parties according to the relative strength shown in the most recent local elections.[8] That African demands for municipal reforms were less clamorous in the AEF towns than in those of French West Africa is also traceable in part to the former's record of greater financial stability.

About 95 per cent of the communes' ordinary revenues consisted of rebates on the taxes collected within their areas, the amount of which was fixed each year by the government; in addition, there were annual subsidies from the territorial budgets and loans. Their obligatory expenditures, such as those entailed in the collection of taxes and maintenance of the municipal police, roads, markets, etc., absorbed most of their ordinary revenues; any development works had to be financed by loans.[9] Even though it was in vain that the Grand Councilors sought control over disposal of the loans they granted, the fact that almost all of such sums was being used for the improvement of African housing tempered the ardor of their demands. Similarly, the control exercised by the territorial assemblies through the granting or withholding of subsidies to the municipalities stopped short at that point, and the administrator-mayor was free to manage the town's revenues pretty much as he liked. Moreover, not all of AEF's municipalities required such subsidies. In the period from 1950 to 1954, neither of Gabon's communes was subsidized by the territorial budget, nor did Pointe Noire or Dolisie ever show a deficit from the time they were organized as communes. Then, too, the subsidies allocated to Brazzaville, Fort Lamy, and Bangui over that same five-year period were not large, aggregating no more than 228.8 million CFA francs.[10] Thus, although the territorial assemblymen would have liked to maintain a more effective control over the municipal councils and their budgets,[11] and periodically grumbled about the government's delay in modernizing the municipalities' "obsolete decrees," they did not regard this as an issue of prime urgency. In general they were willing to wait until Parliament got around to accomplishing the long-promised reform of municipal government throughout French Black Africa.

The history of the municipal reorganization bill, which finally became law on November 15, 1955, was an outstanding example of the cumbersomeness of the French parliamentary process. Eight years in the drafting and debated several times during that period by the French Union Assembly, this bill did not reach the floor of the National Assembly until August 1954. After its passage there by the big majority of 433 to 62 votes, it was held up for more than a year by the Senators' fears lest its provision for the single college for electing the municipal governments in specified towns of French Black Africa should serve as an opening wedge for the extension of this system to the territorial elections. When this hurdle had been successfully taken, six of AEF's mixed communes—Dolisie was promoted later—were transformed overnight into full communes without passing through any intermediate stage. And because this bill also provided facilities for the creation of other types of communal organization, the Oubanguian towns of Berbérati and Bambari early in 1957 became the first *communes de moyen exercice* in AEF. The next year, the four Gabon towns of Bitam, Oyem, Lambaréné, and Mouila, which had been organized as mixed communes in August 1957, were also moved up to the status of *communes de moyen exercice,* and at about the same time Dolisie became a full commune.

All of these transformations took place amid greater calm than did similar changes in French West Africa; in part this was due to the foresight of AEF officials in smoothing the path well in advance. At a meeting held at Brazzaville on August 30, 1956, they proposed a new division of revenues between the municipalities and the regions that proved generally acceptable to the territorial assemblies. The reduction involved in the municipalities' revenues was regarded as just, for it was widely recognized that more of an effort had been made to improve the towns than the countryside and that the communes were relatively more prosperous than were the territories. Another helpful proposal made well in advance of the first municipal elections was that of creating territorial *bureaux des communes* within the framework of the local administration. The task assigned them was to study where and how new communes should be created; in Moyen-Congo such a bureau was set up in 1955, and in Tchad the territorial assembly has been seriously considering organizing one in preparation for promoting Moundou and Fort Archambault to the status of communes. Other centers will probably undergo a similar evolution.

The accuracy with which the first municipal elections on November 18, 1956, reflected the existing political situation in their respective territories distinguished AEF from, for example, Senegal, where one political party dominated the capital's administration while its rival controlled that of the territory. In Moyen-Congo, the UDDIA won a majority of the council seats in each of its three communes; in Oubangui, the MESAN triumphed first in Bangui and later (April 7, 1957) in Berbérati and Bambari; at Fort Lamy in Tchad, the RDA and its allies captured 18 of the 33 seats on the municipal council; and at Libreville and Port Gentil the honors were divided, as in Gabon's territorial government, between the BDG and the UDSG.[12] Moreover, the mayors of Brazzaville (Youlou), Bangui (Boganda), Libreville (Mba), and Fort Lamy (Lisette) were the very men who later came to head the new government councils of their respective territories.

At the outset, this harmony of municipal and territorial administration made for good working relations between the assemblies and the municipalities, but as time went on it proved to have grave drawbacks. Some of the mayors had so many other duties that they tended to neglect that of administering their municipality. More ominous has been the spread of political party strife to the conduct of municipal affairs. In the fall of 1958 the authors were told by some municipal councilors of Fort Lamy that their meetings sometimes became so turbulent that the police had to be called in to separate the warring factions. This transfer of party politics to the level of the municipal government has had unfortunate repercussions on the revenues of some towns. In July 1958, the failure of Bangui's population to pay taxes as they had done in the days before Bangui became a full commune was attributed by Mayor Boganda to the "lying propaganda" of some anti-MESAN forces.[13]

The story of AEF's rural councils resembles that of its municipalities, but in even slower motion and with virtually no positive accomplishments to record.

As part of the general program of administrative decentralization initiated during the decade preceding World War II, a regulation of January 7, 1936, authorized the establishment of Councils of Notables under the chairmanship of each *chef de région*. A few such councils were set up in each territory, but the law was never systematically applied to all of rural AEF. Since there was no precise definition of the term "Notable," the choice of council members was left to the individual regional officer, and he usually selected the local chiefs. They were charged with giving their advice on local taxes and public works but were never empowered to carry out their decisions. Being both illiterate and administratively dependent on the chairman, the councilors offered little but tacit acquiescence to the chairman's proposals. In the eyes of the African peasantry, the Councils of Notables became almost indistinguishable from the *Sociétés de Prévoyance* (see pp. 168–69). With the passage of time, the futility of consulting the Councils became so obvious that they were convened less and less frequently and in some areas simply disappeared altogether.

The creation of regional and district councils, each with its own budget, had been recommended by the Brazzaville Conference in 1944, but years went by and nothing was done to bring them into being. Tired of waiting for Parliament to act in what seemed to him so vital a matter, Governor-General Chauvet in 1952 proposed to the Grand Council that AEF provisionally set up regional councils in anticipation of a more general measure.[14] He thought it highly desirable for the rural elite to be more closely associated with the management of local affairs and to be given enough financial independence to carry out schemes of their own devising. As a nucleus for these councils he suggested utilizing the Councils of Notables but enlarging their membership to include "all valid elements of the rural population." In Chauvet's view, this meant combining on the same council the region's territorial assemblymen with the traditional chiefs and perhaps a few representatives of local private interests. To provide the funds needed for the council budgets, he asked the territorial assemblies to institute a *taxe vicinale,* of which the proceeds would be used exclusively for the building of village paths, markets, and some small engineering works.

If this proposal had not envisaged reviving the ineffectual and unpopular Councils of Notables and also adding to the population's tax burdens, the territorial assemblies might have responded more favorably. In 1952 Gabon was the only territory to create a *taxe vicinale* and to set up special committees to handle its proceeds in the areas where it was collected. It was not until the end of 1954 that Moyen-Congo followed suit, and Oubangui did not do so for still another year. Although Chauvet told the Grand Council on October 24, 1955, that the results already obtained in Gabon were "excellent" and those in Moyen-Congo "encouraging," not all of the African elite shared his opinion. Gabon's assemblymen noted that the new councils worked well in some regions but poorly in others.[15] In Moyen-

Congo only the administration's insistence had overcome the "reluctance and hesitation of the assembly members, who feared lest the government's proposal be simply a form of disguised fiscality that could be deflected from its alleged purpose by the administration."[16] But the strongest resistance of all came from Tchad, which Chauvet described as "the only territory that has refused to democratize its basic administrative unit." The members of its assembly preferred creation of a wholly new regional organization to any revival of the "feudal" Councils of Notables, were wary about imposing any fresh taxation, feared the repercussion on the territory's limited financial and personnel resources, and showed themselves generally hostile to a measure that might detract from their own authority.[17]

In 1955 the long-awaited law drafted by the Metropolitan government was submitted to the French Union Assembly and debate on it occupied three whole sessions. All the members were in accord with the government's aim to give the rural populations the same chance to serve their political apprenticeship as the town dwellers, but the terms on which this was offered were far less precise and liberal than were those of the municipal reorganization bill. The assemblymen felt that too wide discretionary powers had been left to the local administration in regard to where, when, and how rural councils were to be created; that the potential resources for their budgets had been too loosely defined; and that, in the case of AEF, it would be redundant to institute councils at both the regional and district levels.[18] Inasmuch as neither the parliamentary bodies nor the territorial assemblies, to whom the same draft law was also submitted, put forward constructive alternatives that were generally acceptable, the matter was shelved until passage of the loi-cadre on June 23, 1956. But the decree providing for "councils for rural collectivities," issued under the terms of that law, was even vaguer and more elastic than the draft proposal debated in 1955. Even more latitude was left to the territorial authorities to determine the geographical area, composition, powers, and budgetary resources of such councils. Moreover, the only general principles laid down were that the "collectivity should be conscious of its interests as a group" and that its resources be sufficient to balance its budget.

Thus, the initiative in regard to rural councils passed to AEF's African-dominated government councils, and the French could now only indirectly "urge the territories to take the steps necessary for setting them up."[19] The new governments of AEF showed no more zeal in seizing this opportunity than before, though all were agreed on the theoretical desirability of establishing democratic institutions at the village level. The situation was further complicated by the intention of each of the new republics to revise the regional and district units for electoral purposes and by the lack of qualified African personnel to staff them. As of mid-1959, no rural councils had been added to those already in existence.

CHAPTER 6

The Civil Service

A theme stressed by all observers of the AEF scene before World War II was the numerical inadequacy and the instability of the federation's administrative (and technical) personnel. This shortage was the direct result of the exceptionally low pay of officials assigned to this isolated country, where the climate was rigorous, comfort and diversions almost nil, and the cost of living high. In the years since World War II, the main target of criticism has been the plethora of European officials, as well as their heavy cost to the local budgets, uneven distribution throughout the federation, and uncooperative attitude toward the new democratic institutions. During both periods, however, a perennial cause of complaint has been the too frequent rotation of officials.

In view of the mounting objections from Equatorial Africans since 1946 that their country is being "over-administered," it is interesting to recall the preceding years when an administrative void existed. Until 1908, government posts administered only 26 per cent of AEF and the civilian staff commanding them numbered a mere 107.[1] Thanks to a loan granted by Paris in 1909, the government was able to strengthen and expand its network of posts. The device of entrusting distant or unpacified regions to military officers was resorted to partly because of the economy thus effected, for they were paid from the Metropolitan treasury whereas the pay of civilian officials came from the colonial budget. But as the Third Republic generally frowned on such practices and as the country was becoming pacified, these military units were progressively eliminated. At the same time, because of World War I, the number of civilian functionaries also decreased.

Between 1914 and 1923 the ranks of civilian functionaries were reduced from 495 to 395, a decrease of 20 per cent, and this trend continued unchecked. As of 1928, only 250 of the 366 existing administrative posts were filled[2]—in Tchad alone, 42 per cent of the subdivisions had no official in charge—and the understaffing of the customs department and land office meant a large loss in revenue to the colony.[3] For lack of such personnel, there was little or no development of resources that might have brought in the funds required to hire more and better qualified officials and technical agents.

In 1927, the French government, recognizing that a higher pay scale might make service in AEF more attractive, offered a local monetary supplement equivalent to an official's base salary. Soon this bonus was increased to 120 per cent, but the world depression of the early 1930's forced a return to the 100 per cent level in 1933. Simultaneously, all base salaries were reduced by 10 per cent and the total number of civil servants in AEF was cut to 211. (At the time, the technical departments had only 175 agents, including 69 in the health service.) The following year, a policy of filling administrative posts as soon as possible by Africans was officially announced, but because of the then low standards of AEF education this long remained a dead letter. For some time thereafter, vacancies in the upper echelons were filled simply by moving up Europeans from the lower ranks.

Poor pay and unattractive living conditions were not the sole reason for AEF's shortage of skilled administrative personnel; other reasons were the subordination of officials to the concessionary companies (see pp. 15–20) and their frequent transfers from one post to another. In his *Voyage au Congo,* Gide drew a vivid and touching picture of the overworked, underpaid, and often sick civil servant, isolated in the bush and usually lacking competent assistants. He was rarely left long enough in one place to make it worth his while to learn the local languages and customs or to carry out conscientiously a well-planned program. The undersupply of competent officials and the lagging development of the means of communication were the major causes that led to the creation of overlarge administrative units in 1934 and again during World War II.

After the war there began a marked expansion of the administration, chiefly through the creation of new services, and with it of the European personnel. This increase was especially notable in the technical federal services charged with execution of the Plan (see pp. 110–11), and was much less evident in the corps of administrators, who were still scarce and subject to frequent transfers. Although the number of Europeans employed in the federation trebled between 1939 and 1948, most of the newcomers were concentrated in the towns, particularly in Brazzaville. As of August 1948, Oubangui-Chari lacked the officials to staff five districts.[4] Other territories—especially Tchad—wanted to break up oversized units because "they no longer correspond to economic and social realities," but they had to ask the Metropole to provide the extra funds required to staff the new posts.[5] An over-all shortage of administrators because of poor pay could no longer be invoked as an excuse for transfers, yet the postwar European personnel were shunted about as often as before. In 1951 the president of the Grand Council[6] noted that Oubangui-Chari had had nine governors over the preceding five years and Tchad three governors during the preceding two years, and that Gabon in the course of its 100 or more years of French occupation had been ruled by 110 governors. When these gubernatorial migrants moved, a flock of lesser officials accompanied them, with the result that the whole territorial administration was upset. As a by-product of these frequent changes in command, many areas were left at the mercy of venal and incompetent interpreters.[7]

AEF's territorial assemblymen often asked that an end be put to this practice and that greater stability be attained at all echelons of the civil service. A resolution to this effect voted by the Grand Council in 1949 had to be revised three times so as not to offend the government-general, which regarded intervention in this domain as impinging on the executive's authority. In the final version, the Councilors asked that home furloughs thenceforth be granted to top officials once every three (not two) years; that an administrator about to go on leave provide training for younger men to take over; and that, when the question arose of reposting a civil servant to an area where he had previously served, the wishes of the population there be taken into consideration. The last-mentioned point was pressed by some African Councilors who feared frequent transfers less than they did being saddled with unpopular officials. In the Oubangui territorial assembly, one of its members, Yetina, read aloud a petition from the inhabitants of the Berbérati region begging that they be delivered from an autocratic administrator. Said Yetina:[8]

> These officials get funds for road maintenance but they don't always pay their laborers, giving them, perhaps, only some cloth, salt, or a medal. A few even imprison villagers for two weeks to a month for having failed to salute them; others they arrest on the pretext that they are vagabonds.

In March 1948, Gabon's territorial assemblymen unanimously requested the governor to circularize his subordinates, asking them to be more courteous in their dealings both with the public in general and with those whom they administered in particular.[9]

The general unpopularity among Africans of European officials in AEF —except, often, the governors-general—could be ascribed in the main to the arrogance of these Europeans (sometimes combined with incompetence), to their playing politics, and to their pay. Of these factors, the most long-standing was the supercilious, even hostile, attitude adopted by some French administrators (particularly in the regions) toward the rising generation of African politicians. These administrators were inclined to be high-handed not only in their dealings with the rank and file of the population, but even toward African parliamentarians and assemblymen. Some, it was said, could hardly wait for the assembly sessions to end so that they could revert to their old authoritarian practices. Between sessions, the assemblymen going to the districts on information missions or to study some proposed land concession often ran afoul of "obstructionist officials." The collecting of data by African councilors was regarded by some Metropolitan civil servants as an unwarranted interference in their work, whereas the former claimed that they had the right to be present at palavers between the administrator and local chiefs so as to be sure that the people's rights were respected.

In regard to their presence at discussions relating to land concessions, the government gave satisfaction to such demands and so instructed its rural officials. Besides being anxious to have such controversial matters amicably settled, the government-general wanted to discipline, even to weed out, the incompetent and anachronistic officials, many of whom had been sent to AEF by Metropolitan France against its wishes. Cornut-Gentille was quoted[10] as having said in 1949:

> This federation has an administration which has understood nothing and
> learned nothing since the Brazzaville Conference. It is formed of over-age
> functionaries who have clung to a "policy of authority" but who know very
> thoroughly the human milieu in which they live. . . . The young ones are
> full of good will but they have no knowledge at all of the real needs of the
> populations among which they work.

And his successor, Chauvet, while defending the "many good, devoted,
and conscientious workers" among his officials, made this telling comment
in a speech to the Grand Council on September 30, 1953:

> Better than anyone else I know that the administration shelters a number—
> fortunately very limited—of persons who have neither the physical nor the
> intellectual aptitudes, nor even the professional conscience, required to fulfil
> their tasks. I have asked, and in part obtained, permission to eliminate them,
> and in time I hope to get complete satisfaction in this respect.

Yet if France was guilty of having imposed incompetent or inappropriate officials upon the government-general, Brazzaville was similarly
guilty in relation to the territorial governments. President Tardrew of
the Tchad assembly complained of the "army of colonels" sent to Fort
Lamy by the Brazzaville authorities, for whom the territory had no posts
corresponding to their rank. Not only were they a burden on the territorial budget but they took the place of younger, less expensive, and more
active men.[11]

That some highly placed administrators, either from personal conviction or on orders from their superiors, played politics in the local elections
still further alienated the African elite against the whole corps. Intervention of this sort by certain administrators could hardly be open to doubt,
since two AEF parliamentarians of such diverse views as René Malbrant
and Antoine Darlan publicly voiced almost identical complaints on the
subject, albeit for different reasons. Darlan told his colleagues in the
French Union Assembly that he had many documents in his possession
proving that local officials had used their powers in Oubangui to favor one
party (the RPF) at the expense of its rival (the RDA),[12] despite orders
from the French government to observe a "total neutrality." In the National
Assembly, Malbrant, in speaking of the forthcoming elections of June 1951,
complained of the "abusive and costly" transfer of officials in Tchad for
political reasons.[13] To this the spokesman for the Queille administration
frankly replied that he could not be expected to keep in key overseas posts
officials "whose attitude and policy is formally opposed to that of the government to which I belong."

Although such charges of undue official interference in AEF politics
subsided somewhat after the June 1951 elections, the functionaries of the
federation were not to be left in political peace. This much maligned corps,
after having been subjected to successive pressures by the concessionary

companies and the French government, was, after 1957, also to feel the weight of the new African authorities. Lisette, the premier of Tchad who had himself suffered from the administration's political opposition in 1951, was accused seven years later by his African opponents of shifting officials about in the Borkou-Ennedi-Tibesti region (BET) simply to further the interests of his own party there (see p. 436). In the Congo, Fulbert Youlou, who had also complained of French officialdom's support for his opponent Tchicaya in the 1956 elections, was himself guilty in January 1959 of sending officials from his own party to administer the M'Bochi fief of his socialist rivals.

The third significant reason for the resentment aroused in AEF by some French administrators and technical personnel was their excessive cost to the federation's budget. Even as early as December 1947, the federal expenditures for personnel alone were larger than the total budget of a single territory,[14] and the territories were faced with a similar problem. At about that time, Oubangui had on its territorial payroll some 170 Europeans and 2,185 Africans, of whom one Metropolitan assemblyman said:[15]

> These functionaries use up nearly half of our budget and we can pay them only at the expense of more necessary items. We have tried to reduce their number, but the director of each service has courteously explained to us that he has already reduced his needs to the strict minimum. . . . Such an enormous staff is due to the unbelievable amount of paper work, which is steadily increasing and will soon occupy all the Metropolitan officials simply to keep the administrative machinery functioning. And we cannot tamper with their salaries . . . which amount to double or triple those prevailing in private industry. Functionaries who don't do their work satisfactorily—and I maintain that such exist in some of the services—cannot be dismissed or replaced, yet they are still called "indispensable." All of this requires a vast reorganization which unfortunately is beyond our competence and should be undertaken by our parliamentarians and even by the officials themselves.

As of 1950, the four-million-odd inhabitants of AEF were being administered by an ensemble that comprised 1,700 Europeans and 11,000 Africans officials, of whom a few were officials but the great majority were auxiliary personnel. Not only had the European staff trebled between 1939 and 1950, but it had received several appreciable salary increases, largely as the result of laws passed by Parliament. In 1947 these personnel absorbed 36.4 per cent of AEF's revenues (314 million CFA francs); in 1948, 39.2 per cent (414 million); and in 1949, 44.4 per cent (835 million), despite the fact that Metropolitan France in 1948 agreed to pay the highest-ranking civil servants, magistrates, and gendarmes serving overseas. This rapid rise in the pay scale, a European Grand Councilor asserted, had reversed the prewar situation, when employees in private enterprises were better paid than were civil servants; he also expressed doubt that the government's efficiency had increased proportionately to the growth in the number and pay of its officials.[16] To this his African colleagues retorted that none of their compatriots had ever left private employment to enter government service, because African civil servants had not received similar salary increases.

In 1947 Soucadaux had drafted a project reforming the civil service, which he based on two main principles.[17] The first was that of automatic salary increases geared to the local cost of living so as to protect AEF from an inflation that he feared might ensue from the extension overseas of the increases voted by Parliament in the Metropolitan officials' pay scale. The second was that of creating a common cadre for the federation in which "all discrimination based on race and religion would be eliminated."[18] France was slow to act on this proposal, and a general reform of the AEF civil service did not get under way for another five years. Meanwhile, a reclassification effected locally had, according to some members of the Grand Council, simply made the situation of three-fourths of the African personnel worse than it had been before.

From 1889 to 1938, the few Africans who had been admitted to the upper cadre enjoyed the same pay and privileges as did Europeans doing equivalent work. But a regulation of March 5, 1938, initiating an expatriation bonus for Europeans changed this situation and, combined with a subsequent salary reduction of about 25 per cent applied to Africans, brought strong protests from the latter.[19] Further discrimination was instituted in regard to housing and leaves, and the gulf between the white and Negro civil servants was widened still more by the postwar pay increases for Metropolitan officials. While the African civil servant did not begrudge the special privileges accorded to such of the Metropolitan officials as merited them, Aubame told the National Assembly, he did resent the principle of unequal treatment, and Aubame's stand in this matter was supported by his compatriots in the Grand Council and territorial assemblies.

Passage of the Lamine-Gueye law of June 30, 1950 (which guaranteed identical conditions of recruitment, pay, and promotion between Metropolitan and overseas functionaries), was regarded as a great victory by the Africans, but it did not bring about the big pay rises they had anticipated. Considerable resistance was displayed by the AEF administration and European councilors to applying to African functionaries some of its provisions, notably those relating to family allowances and to bonuses for officials living away from home.[20] The African members of the Grand Council insisted on applying the letter of the law, while the government claimed that there simply was not enough money to do so. In the course of two long and heated debates, old grievances were aired about the advantages enjoyed by Metropolitan officials over their African counterparts in such matters as free housing and transportation and expatriation bonuses. The African councilors were determined not only that their compatriots in the civil service should get a fair deal but also that the birthrate should be increased by means of substantial family allowances. The administration, for its part, was concerned primarily about the financial repercussions on all of the AEF budgets.

A little more than a year later, the Finance Committee of the Grand Council reported[21] that the spirit of the Lamine-Gueye law had been completely distorted in its application to AEF. Although the status of the higher and middle categories of African civil servants had been improved, the lowest class was worse off than before. Moreover, the overwhelming financial burden that this law had imposed on the federation had been accompanied by "monstrous abuses" in the allocation of family allowances.

Application of the Lamine-Gueye law certainly caused the expenditures for personnel to increase in 1951 by 30 to 32 per cent over those in 1949, but 3 per cent of this rise was caused by the recruitment of additional staff.[22] The Grand Councilors protested against this steady increase in personnel but finally agreed to accept 20 Europeans and 192 Africans of the 42 European and 304 African candidates proposed by the government. Actually the year 1951 witnessed the first decline since the war in the number of administrative officials recruited, but this was financially offset by a concurrent increase in the technical services. In the budgetary session held in the fall of that year the government was told by the Grand Councilors that AEF's worsening financial situation dictated that an end be put to further increases in the number and pay of its employees. Not only was the size of this personnel out of line with the federation's resources but its numerical relationship to the total population was more disproportionate than in any other part of the French Union.

The economic depression of 1952 in AEF was more effective in stopping further recruiting of personnel than were all the criticisms voiced in the Grand Council, and it gave added weight to the perennial demand for a profound reorganization of the administrative structure. The federal services, particularly the Postes-Télégraphes-Téléphones (PTT),[23] were the prime target of attacks. Undoubtedly there were competent government employees, but there was too much duplication of jobs, dead wood, and downright malingering. President Flandre told the Grand Council on September 30, 1952, that some of the highest-paid officials stayed only a few months of the year in AEF and then got themselves repatriated for "reasons of health," and that once back in France they overstayed their leave—for which well-known and oft-repeated offense the Rue Oudinot would not let the government-general dismiss them.[24]

The abnormal rise, amounting to 24 per cent, in AEF's expenditures for personnel between 1953 and 1955 was not due to new recruits—on the contrary, the total number of government employees had shrunk—but to laws passed by Parliament raising the pay and increasing the emoluments of a certain category of functionaries. In 1954 this item in the federal budget totaled 1,437 million CFA francs and in 1956 it rose to 1,771 million. A similar financial hemorrhage afflicted the territories, and it would have been less resented had it not benefited chiefly the European personnel. Ahmed Kotoko told Tchad's territorial assemblymen in 1952 that its 380 European officials cost, on the average, 700,000 CFA francs apiece annually, whereas its 2,243 African employees received salaries averaging only about one-tenth of that amount.[25] No serious effort had been made, he went on to say, to reduce the number of territorial personnel, and on the rare occasions when the ax fell it was always on an African victim. He and his compatriots in the assembly were especially bitter about the employment of European women at approximately four times the salary of an African performing the same work, and about the rehiring of dismissed African functionaries on a daily basis, which meant not only a lower income for them but the loss of all the privileges that went with a civil service status.

Much the same grievances were voiced in the Oubangui assembly on September 6, 1950, particularly in regard to the dismissal of those long in service and their replacement by younger men at a lower salary. To this the administration responded by saying that the assemblymen could not have it both ways: they complained that there were too many inefficient officials and then criticized dismissal of the incompetent. (On this occasion the government spokesman cited the cases of African functionaries who were never at their desks on time, would not go to work if it rained, and could not lay their hands on data asked for by their superiors.[26]) Even rich Gabon bewailed the fact that the humblest of its European employees cost the budget a million francs a year, and charged that, at the same time, Africans were being pushed out of government service to make way for the *petites amies* of Metropolitan functionaries.[27]

Although the cost of unwanted and unloved Metropolitan officials remained a collective thorn in the flesh of all the African and many of the European assemblymen, relations between them and French officialdom generally improved over the years. Some of the diehard old-timers had been replaced by younger men with more egalitarian ideas, and the administration was observing far more neutrality in local politics. In his speech to the Grand Council on October 24, 1955, Chauvet mentioned this improvement but maintained that relations were not yet all that they should be, and for this he divided the blame between the two elements. In regard to certain officials he spoke of the residue of—

> detestable habits left over from another era, the feeling of false dignity and superiority generally based on a lack of intelligence and of heart. These are reflected in inadmissible attitudes and words, a paternalistic *tutoiement,* and a refusal to comprehend. . . . Some are prejudiced against their African collaborators because of isolated and unfortunate experiences. . . . On the other hand, some young Africans are reserved and distrustful, exhibit a surly touchiness, and refuse to accept proffered friendships. Some even practice a "reverse racialism" and would like to seal off their country from outside contacts, or wall themselves up in sterile isolation. . . . And there are also those who feel that a diploma automatically entitles its holder to a job and should open every door.

Six months later, and again in June and October 1957, the high commissioner warned against undue speed in Africanizing the cadres. With the best will in the world, he said, the training required would take a long time; the new African governments should guard against the temptation to set up an overgenerous pay scale. For many years to come, he added, most of AEF and particularly Tchad would require the services of Metropolitan functionaries. This warning and perspective, coming at a time when application of the *loi-cadre* was already giving rise to some friction and when the African politicians were just beginning to exercise power, provoked a vehement reaction. Jacques Opangault, the socialist leader of Moyen-Congo, expressed his disapproval of "certain supercilious officials whose retrogressive attitude has caused them to give a restrictive interpretation to the *loi-cadre*."[28] But it was Boganda who rose to sudden federation-wide popularity by his attacks on Metropolitan officials in Oubangui and in Brazzaville.

In a stormy session of the Oubangui assembly on October 19, 1957, Boganda castigated the Rue Oudinot as that "citadel of colonialism" responsible for the behavior of those "rebellious state officials who are saboteurs of the *loi-cadre*," and he asked for the recall of three French administrators. To the applause of the assembly he told them to get out of the territory and "let our wives and children throw after them the *tison ardent,* the symbol of final departure and a reminder of the shameful and accursed memories that we will keep of them." This denunciation was such a success that Boganda repeated it with embellishments in the Grand Council two days later. Already, in November 1956, he had called for the suppression of the administrative services of the government-general, but this time demagoguery impelled him to go further. His unrestrained language provoked almost equally furious protests from the Intersyndicat des Fonctionnaires, which included most of the Metropolitan members of the general cadre. Eventually this was smoothed over in both Oubangui and Brazzaville, but it did not improve relations between the African politicians and the Metropolitan officials, some of whom asked to be transferred to other areas.

Even though Boganda's outburst expressed a widely felt reaction, this reaction sprang from pent-up resentments rather than from any general desire on the part of Africans to see Metropolitan officials depart *en masse.* The politically conscious elite are only too aware of their own inadequacies and of their need for further training and guidance. At the time of the Brazzaville riots of February 1959, tribute was paid by all strata of the local population to the French functionaries who had managed to get the situation under control, and the administration was even reproached for not having acted sooner and more forcefully. In certain regions of AEF, notably in the BET, European officials are the only ones acceptable as arbiters between mutually hostile ethnic groups, and they alone have the experience and the authority necessary to get their orders obeyed. As yet the Africans are not strong enough, either in number or in training, to replace them to any appreciable extent.

Though there have always been far more African than European government employees in AEF,[29] few of them have occupied high posts, so that salaries of the Africans have been proportionately less expensive budget items. In 1954 there were six times as many Africans as Europeans in AEF government service, but only 88 of them were in the "upper" cadre, whose members totaled 1,327.[30] By then, all of the territorial cadres were wholly Africanized, but it was in the most lowly category that their number was the largest. The main reason for this poor showing was the inadequacy of the educational facilities in AEF before World War II, when no complete cycle of secondary studies was locally available. In the early 1930's the French authorities had become concerned about this lack, and in February 1935 they set up at Brazzaville the Ecole Edouard Renard to prepare African agents to enter the territorial cadres or commercial employment.[31]

In 1946 this school was transformed into a federal establishment and was renamed the Ecole des Cadres Supérieurs. The majority of its pupils came from the urban primary schools of Brazzaville, Dolisie, Libreville, and Bangui, and they were all given free board and tuition. The general education offered in the school resembled, but was inferior to, that of a Metropolitan modern *collège,* in that its three-year course did not go beyond preparation for the first part of the baccalaureate. However, there was also special instruction in accountancy, stenography, and administrative law. Because the Ecole des Cadres Supérieurs failed to prepare students for a specific career, its diploma proved to have little practical value, and most of its graduates simply chose the profession most immediately remunerative.[32]

For this reason a new orientation was given to the school in 1949–50 and the selection of candidates for admission was made stricter. When it opened in revised form, 16 students were enrolled in its section on administration, 16 in that of the PTT, 10 in that of meteorology, and 11 in education. It was planned the following year to add still another section, for the training of sanitary agents, and eventually to transform the whole school into a technical institute that would train engineers. At about the same time, the federal government proposed following the example already set by Oubangui and establishing a center that would enable African functionaries from all parts of AEF to compete more effectively in the examinations for admission to a higher cadre. All of these projects were slow in materializing, and in 1951 some Grand Councilors expressed their dissatisfaction with the results obtained and their preference for sending Africans to France for training.[33]

In 1953 the government-general made still another attempt to solve the problem of preparing Africans locally for better careers in the administrative service, and this time it followed the advice of the Grand Council and of the functionaries' unions—all of whom wanted to eliminate the recruitment of agents under contract. That year a Centre de Préparation des Concours Administratifs was founded at Brazzaville, at which a group of 12 Africans holding the elementary *brevêt* were given a one-year course designed to facilitate their entry into the upper cadre. The handful of Africans who possessed a B.A. degree were not required to take such an entrance examination, but those who had obtained this diploma in France showed little inclination to return to the federation as civil servants. Some of them had proved highly responsive to the wooing of extreme left-wing organizations in Metropolitan France and so had no desire to serve under the current African politicians, whom they regarded as ignorant and reactionary. Others had married French wives and preferred to stay on in France, and still others had chosen professions for which there were few openings in AEF. This state of things led the federal government in 1955 to lay down a new policy on the granting of scholarships—that of allocating them only for studies directly related to AEF's needs, particularly for training in the technical field.[34]

In the spring of 1956, on the eve of passage of the *loi-cadre,* the AEF Information Service published a report on the progress already made in Africanizing the federation's cadres.[35] Aside from daily workers, there were at that time 9,000 Africans employed in the upper and territorial cadres: the technical services were still staffed predominantly by Europeans and it was into the upper cadre that Africans had chiefly penetrated during the preceding three years.[36] Since it was primarily for this cadre that the preparatory center had been established in 1953, the government was pleased at the good showing made by its graduates. Yet this success did not affect the stagnation of the African component in the technical departments and the highest administrative cadre. No advanced technical training was available nearer than that given in the specialized schools of French West Africa, and AEF's scholarship holders in France continued to prefer degrees in law or literature to those in science.

One of the main principles laid down by the *loi-cadre* was that of drawing a clear-cut distinction between the state and territorial services. Unfortunately the language in which this provision of the law was couched was vague and hence was open to various interpretations. In any case, Parliament obviously meant to territorialize as many of the existing services as possible and to reserve the largest number of posts therein to local talent. Members of a territorial service were placed under the local assembly and paid by it, whereas officials of the state services were responsible to the high commissioner (and ultimately to the Minister of Overseas France and to Parliament) and were paid in large part by the French treasury.[37]

Metropolitan officials were solemnly promised that the new regulations would in no way adversely affect their pre-existing status, so that it was in the psychological domain and in day-to-day work, rather than in their material well-being, that difficulties arose in carrying out this provision of the *loi-cadre.* Psychologically it was hard for many of the high-ranking French officials, accustomed to being obeyed, to take orders from younger, less experienced, and comparatively untrained African politicians. Moreover, there was confusion in regard to overlapping responsibilities, for some officials were placed under the federal as well as the territorial government. In some instances it was certainly ill-will, but in others it was the law's failure to define duties more precisely, that created friction and led to Boganda's attack on the corps of Metropolitan officials in October

1957. Although the Grand Councilors on November 16 adopted a compromise resolution to the effect that they had not meant to condemn the whole general cadre, and members of the Intersyndicat des Fonctionnaires also gave assurances of their loyalty to the local governments and to the spirit of the *loi-cadre,* the basic problem remained unsolved. On the whole, European officials inclined toward a solution that would reintegrate them into a wholly Metropolitan cadre, from which they could be assigned overseas—but only at the express request of a territorial government. It was also proposed that French functionaries no longer serve anywhere as direct administrators but confine themselves to the role of advisers. At all events, it was generally agreed that in the years to come, no more French students should be recruited for the Ecole Nationale de la France d'Outre-Mer at Paris. From May 1955 on, this school had been undergoing a progressive Africanization, and by the end of 1958 two-thirds of its pupils were from overseas and its name had been changed to that of Institut des Hautes Etudes d'Outre-Mer.

During that interval, the territorial assemblies of AEF had been discussing a new statute for African civil servants, which was imperative because of the imminent transfer of many former federal services to their jurisdiction.[38] As early as May 1957 the government-general proposed to the new African governments that they use as the basis for study the laws in force for Metropolitan functionaries, which divided civil servants into five categories and specified how each was to be recruited, paid, promoted, and penalized. The government-general also stressed the need to maintain uniform regulations between the territories so that functionaries would not be tempted to move from one to another in the hope of improving their status, and for the same reason to maintain parity with conditions in private employment. After three revisions, involving mainly adaptations of the Metropolitan code to local conditions, an identical draft proposal was submitted to the four territorial assemblies.

The long debates in those assemblies on the functionaries statute were most instructive, for they reflected the particular experience and attitudes of each one. Moyen-Congo's assemblymen, for example, wanted certain posts reserved for men, whereas those of Oubangui thought that all jobs should be open to women as well, yet both groups felt that no discrimination should be made in regard to an official's family status (polygamous or monogamous). The debate in Tchad's assembly took another tack. At first its members were eager to give territorial functionaries every possible advantage and to suppress almost all former disciplinary measures, because many assemblymen had themselves been penalized in years past because of their political activities. Later, however, they partly reversed this stand, for they realized that they must not make civil servants a superprivileged corps.[39]

To some extent all of the AEF assemblies were now reaping the whirlwind. Composed in large measure of civil servants, they had sought over the years to improve the position of the African functionary, downtrodden as compared with his Metropolitan colleagues. Thus by the time that the African politicians came into control of the local governments, the unions of African civil servants had developed aspirations of pay scales so high that, if they had been granted, the territories would have been bankrupted. Matters came to a head in July 1957, when the syndicates of African functionaries demanded equality of treatment with the Metropolitan civil servants, whose salaries had been raised by Parliament earlier that month. In November the Oubangui unions struck, and the next month those of Moyen-Congo followed suit. At Bangui, Premier Goumba assured the strikers that he sympathized with their grievances but that he could not meet demands that would have the effect of making them in the eyes of the Oubangui peasants an unduly privileged minority.

Even without giving the African functionaries full satisfaction, the territories were already running into heavy weather in financing the transformation of their governments. To be sure, in January 1958 France promised them aid in meeting most of the expenditures this would involve, and it soon became obvious that the bills would be enormous. Each territory had now about ten ministers, not to mention their *chefs* and *directeurs de cabinet,* and to maintain the dignity of their office, free lodging and transport as well as a roster of subordinate functionaries seemed to them indispensable. Furthermore, all the territories wanted to create new administrative units, and additional personnel would be required to staff them. Criticism was voiced in French parliamentary bodies about the "sumptuary expenditures" involved, and the high commissioner repeatedly warned against any further increase in the number of officials or of their salaries.

Yet in January 1958 Gabon's assembly voted to increase its corps of civil servants and to give them a general pay rise of 10 per cent. It should be noted that Gabon had a special reason for this move: ever since oil had been discovered at Port Gentil there had been a steady flow of the territory's civil servants to employment in private enterprise.[40] Officials in Tchad were exposed to no such temptation and that territory was far from being as prosperous as Gabon, yet its executive council demanded that the assembly give it the "means to work"—in other words, 70 new officials whose salaries and emoluments would cost the territorial budget some 50 million CFA francs.[41]

CHAPTER 7

The Status of the Chiefs

In AEF the status of chiefs varies so widely, both in the eyes of the local population and of the French administration, that it is virtually impossible to make any valid generalizations about it. Even in pre-European days, no common denominator apparently existed among them except the exercise of undivided administrative, religious, and judicial powers by chiefs of all ranks. Despite the French addiction to centralized authority, France never worked out any consistent policy toward the chiefs, although the system of government that it set up and the mere presence of Europeans in AEF tended directly and indirectly to undermine the chiefs' position. By the partial transformation of chiefs into functionaries, their religious authority was sapped; with the creation of a higher network of law courts, their judicial powers were restricted; and because of the grant of freedom to former slaves, their social and economic influence waned. Yet no positive action was taken to train the chiefs as administrators or to give them a secure legal status based on some general principle—in fact, so pragmatic was the treatment accorded them that it varied with the area and even with the individual case. The regulation of December 23, 1936, which organized the chieftaincy in AEF, conformed to the then-prevalent trend toward decentralization.

It was in the forest region that the classical French policy toward native chiefs, like that applied throughout most of French West Africa, found its fullest expression. Here the terrain was not conducive to large concentrations of population and there existed a multitude of petty chiefs whose authority was very limited in area, often confined to a single family, and generally depended on the strength of the individual chief's personality. Moreover, in Gabon a characteristic of the dominant Fang peoples was their egalitarianism and their tendency to break up into small units. Furthermore, their pursuit of warfare and commerce gradually led to greater mobility and independence for the young men of the tribe at the expense of the power formerly wielded by their elders and chiefs.

To give some cohesion to this mosaic of scattered tribes, the French set up a hierarchy of land, village, and canton chiefs, which, in most cases, corresponded to no recognized traditional authority. And to facilitate their administration, villages in the forest regions of Gabon and Moyen-Congo were regrouped and placed under a chief nominated by the French, who was assigned the task of collecting taxes, keeping order, and settling as many disputes as he could by conciliation. Since the chiefs so selected were rarely those who had been consecrated by custom, they exercised little moral influence and proved to be, on the whole, unsatisfactory intermediaries between the government and the population. Most of the resettled populations disappeared from the artificial villages created by the French and withdrew into more inaccessible parts of the forest. This failure, along with the chronic shortage of French administrative personnel, induced the administration in Gabon to try the experiment of having canton chiefs elected by the chiefs of the villages included in their area.

In other parts of AEF, such as western Oubangui, the practice of imposing chiefs on the cantons with the acquiescence of local Notables continued to prevail. There "straw men" were often put forward by the traditional chiefs to serve as a screen between themselves and the government. These "straw men" were apparently accepted as genuine chiefs by the district or regional administrator, who frequently had little knowledge of, or concern for, those exercising real power by virtue of customary law. Yet in AEF, because practical necessity made for a looser administrative network and because tribal sentiments remained generally stronger, there did not develop in that federation the same resentment toward the chieftaincy that was to be found in the western and coastal regions of French West Africa.

In northern Tchad and eastern Oubangui the sultanates remained strong until recent years. Geographical and economic conditions in those areas, as well as the Islamic religion and the feudal institutions brought probably from East Africa, had led to the establishment of large, strictly hierarchized units headed by autocratic rulers. Incessant warfare and slave raids certainly decimated the northeastern populations, but at the same time they reinforced the power of the chiefs, who had long been deeply entrenched in Ouaddaï, Kanem, and the BET region when the French first appeared in Tchad. The military officers who governed that territory until 1920 ruled through these chiefs, and even after civilians took over control of most of Tchad the lack of the substitute personnel and of the means of communication required the perpetuation of indirect administration. In the desert areas farther to the north, the tribal chiefs maintained for many years virtually untrammeled authority over their nomadic peoples in what Eboué described as "a regime of organized anarchy."

The introduction of democratic institutions in 1946 and the change in economic conditions brought about first by the war and then by the Plan undermined the position of the chiefs everywhere in the federation, though more gradually in the north than in the south. Their revenues were shrinking as the populations became progressively disinclined to pay them the traditional tribute, and the administration did not raise the chiefs' income to keep pace with the ever-higher cost of living. More and more young men were deserting the countryside for the towns, where they found greater freedom and opportunities for gainful employment. This development constituted a double threat to the chieftaincy—a shrinkage of the population under their control and the rise of a youthful elite, whose superior education enabled its members to acquire posts in the administration and power through election to the territorial assemblies.

This situation became most acute in Tchad, where the southern Negroes —erstwhile slaves of the "white" chiefs in the north and east—formed the backbone of a new and radical political party (see p. 431). To be sure, this development was partly offset by the fact that some of the new African politicians, such as Koulamallah and Sahoulba, were members of the chief class, that the administration continued to support the chieftaincy, and that a few of the paramount chiefs became members of the assembly and later even formed a chiefs' party, the GIRT. In some regions, the choice of assemblymen depended wholly on the sultan's wishes, which were followed blindly by the electorate, so that the elite in general took care not to antagonize these potentates. By 1952, it could be said that tension in the purely political sphere between the chiefs and the new elite had largely died down,[1] but it persisted and grew in the economic and juridical domains.

The need to establish some order in the inchoate chieftaincies of Black Africa and to bolster their position had been insistently brought to the attention of the French government by Eboué during the war.[2] In 1946 Parliament began consideration of a draft statute for those chiefs, but it was soon realized that the position of chiefs was in no two places the same and was changing so rapidly everywhere that the legislators hesitated to intervene at any given point to crystallize their statutory position.[3] On the one hand, it was necessary to support chiefs who had been loyal auxiliaries to the administration, still retained influence over their people, and checked the further disintegration of African society. On the other hand, the risk run in such an over-all policy was the maintaining in power of feudal aristocrats who opposed the rise of a younger, better-educated, and more democratic generation, and also of chiefs who had been appointed without consideration of the degree to which they possessed authority consecrated by tradition. Years passed while the Parliament struggled vainly with this problem, and meanwhile it decided that something must be done to improve the worsening material situation of the chiefs.

As to the principle of raising chiefs' salaries and of giving them secretarial help, the French government and the African elite were in agreement, but not as to the details or the means of doing so. Here the long-standing disparities in the chiefs' pay scale were a major ground of disagreement, as was the capacity of each territory to finance any salary increases. In Oubangui and Tchad villages, for example, chiefs received a rebate ranging from 5 to 3 per cent on the taxes they collected, the percentage depending on the promptness with which the sums due were remitted to the territorial treasury. In Gabon, during the first post–World War II years, village chiefs received 10 per cent of the taxes they collected, though this was later reduced to the same percentage as elsewhere.[4] Naturally the income derived by chiefs from this source varied sharply within a given territory, but all of them reportedly supplemented it by various legal and illicit means. The chief of an Oubangui village of some 400 inhabitants got from taxes only around 600 CFA francs a year, whereas his colleague in a larger community might receive annually as much as 12,000 CFA francs.[5] Then, too, the chiefs of sedentary populations had much less trouble in collecting taxes than those in the north who had to deal with nomads and seminomads, and so by prompt remittance the former could earn a larger rebate percentage.[6]

Although the income derived from taxation by village chiefs was small considering their manifold and onerous duties, their plight was not deemed as crucial as that of canton chiefs, for the successive increases in head taxation that occurred in each territory after the war automatically swelled the revenues of village chiefs whereas the canton chiefs were paid a fixed salary. In 1948, canton chiefs were granted a pay rise of 2½ per cent, the first such increase in four years. Yet the increments neither erased the conspicuous inequalities among them nor gave most of the canton chiefs enough income to live on independently. At the same time these salary increases constituted a growing burden for the straitened territorial finances. In 1953–54 the average salary of a canton chief in Gabon was about 1,500 francs a month; in Oubangui the lowest-paid canton chief received 1,800 francs monthly; and in Tchad, where the highest salary earned by a canton chief was 5,000 francs a month, the average pay was between 2,000 and 3,000 francs. The territorial assemblies also acted to provide more secretaries for canton chiefs, the great majority of whom were illiterate. By 1950, 34 Oubangui chiefs had been assigned secretaries; in 1953 Gabon followed suit for 27 of its 57 canton chiefs; and in 1956 Moyen-Congo sent out 64 secretaries to its district chiefs.

Despite these successive improvements in their pay and staff, it was said that the chiefs still exacted from the population more taxes and services than were owed either by law or by custom, and demanded "gifts" up to 1,000 francs from litigants for rendering a favorable judgment.[7] In Tchad and Oubangui, canton chiefs were further reproached with having aggravated the compulsory nature of cotton cultivation there, because of the bonuses they received for producing exceptional crops in the areas under their control. Yet most assemblymen continued to show indulgence toward such abuses, on the ground that the salaries of canton chiefs were still insufficient, and even so left-wing a politician as Antoine Darlan showed a surprising solicitude for them as a group.[8]

In this connection, it is worth noting that the assemblymen eagerly seized on any opportunity to discuss the status of chiefs. Not only was it a subject dear to the African heart but it gave the assemblies one of their rare opportunities to side-step the administration's interdiction on their debating political questions. By and large, the cause of the canton chiefs was supported by the African elite, as in Oubangui, whenever the government seemed to discriminate against them in favor of Metropolitan officials.

This was also the case in Tchad, where a traditional chief whose authority had been undermined by the government was apt suddenly to find himself popular as a sort of martyr. Conversely, wherever chiefs were regarded as docile agents of the administration, as in some parts of eastern Moyen-Congo, they became proportionately unpopular. Nevertheless, the African assemblymen, by and large, recognized the "eminent role" played by chiefs in African society and their usefulness as intermediaries between the administration and the population, and for the time being at least were willing to strengthen their hand. In 1950 the assemblies of Moyen-Congo, Gabon, and Oubangui all voted to provide chiefs with insignia denoting their rank, so as to enhance their prestige and authority.[9]

Even though the average pay of canton chiefs remained inadequate after three postwar increases, their salaries aggregated a sum that few of the AEF territories could afford to pay.[10] An obvious remedy was to reduce the number of chiefs, particularly of African *chefs de quartier* in towns, and to improve the salary and training of those retained.[11] This was the substance of a proposal made by Chauvet to the Grand Council on September 30, 1954,[12] but for years the territorial administrators continued to insist that many chiefs were required because the people would not obey one who did not belong to the same ethnic group. In some places the population actually asked for additional chiefs. In Gabon, for example, the residents of Haut-Ogooué requested the appointment of two provincial chiefs to control "the innumerable small chiefs who are apt to render judgments on the basis of old feuds."[13] As was the case with the French administrators, the main difficulty was not so much the superfluity of chiefs as it was their uneven distribution and their total cost to the local budgets.

Broadly speaking, the problem of paramount chiefs was acute only in Tchad, where they were more powerful than in other parts of AEF and where the abuses they committed were not always known to the administration. There the Bébalem incident (see pp. 432–33) and later the refusal of peasants in the Batha region to pay tribute to the chiefs impelled the government to undertake a long study of the chiefs' status. Governor Colombani assured the Tchad territorial assembly on November 26, 1954, that the reorganization he was proposing in consequence of this study constituted no threat whatsoever to the traditional chieftaincy, whose members would be supported by the government in proportion to the efforts they made to adapt their traditional role to the social changes now taking place. Inasmuch as the official labels of district and region had usually been given to the over-large historic sultanates, he suggested breaking them up into more ethnically homogeneous units. In addition the governor proposed as an experiment to reclassify the chieftaincies and revise their pay scale in one area.

As matters worked out, both the study undertaken by the government and the action taken on its derivative proposals by the Tchad assembly went much farther than the administration had originally intended. In carrying out this official inquiry it had been found necessary to include also the question of the customary dues owed to traditional chiefs. The assembly showed its dissatisfaction with both the scope and some details of the government's proposal. Certain chiefs, it was claimed, had been erroneously included in the same category as sultans or heads of tribes;[14] others were already overpaid because their inefficiency and exactions were actually harmful to the administration that they were supposed to assist. Many chiefs, an assemblyman asserted, not only were directly abusing their powers but were giving their armed retainers (*goumiers*) such a pittance as salary that the latter preyed upon the defenseless population.[15] Then, too, southern members of the assembly were up in arms against the payment of higher salaries to northern chiefs than to those in the south (the discrepancy being officially justified by the greater wealth of the cotton-growing regions and the comparative ease of collecting taxes there).

There seems little doubt that, comparatively speaking, certain northern potentates were too highly paid—the sultan of Ouaddaï and the Alifa of Mao reportedly received monthly salaries of nearly 400,000 CFA francs—while others less fortunate were allotted no more than 36,000 francs a year. Moreover, some of the chiefs getting the highest salaries were among those who committed the worst abuses in regard to exacting forced labor and collecting more than was their rightful tribute. What had brought the matter of chiefs' salaries to a head was the refusal of the peasantry of Batha to pay such tribute any longer and the clashes in Kanem over division of the date harvest (see p. 455). Not a single traditional chief in Tchad, it was said in the assembly, had voluntarily given up or even reduced the tribute to which he was entitled by custom, and more often than not the chiefs collected more than their due.

At the assembly's insistence the administration agreed to pay the sultans' retainers directly and to apply throughout the territory the reclassification of the chieftaincy, without, however, revising the chiefs' base pay or interfering with their right to collect religious tithes. Tchad's assemblymen were even willing to increase the head tax so as to get the funds necessary to raise the salaries of chiefs, in the hope that the latter would no longer collect—at least by force—their customary dues. In practice, however, it was found difficult to draw the line clearly between customary dues and religious tithes. (The latter amounted in Muslim regions to 10 per cent of the harvest and to one animal out of every 30 to 40.) Then, too, the direct payment of *goumiers* by the administration resulted in a loss of authority over them by their overlord, and reforms appropriate to one part of the territory miscarried in others. Confusion existed in the minds of even the most cooperative chiefs as to what dues were to be suppressed and where, and the need both for more elasticity in application and for greater precision in wording of the law became so obvious that the whole reform was submitted to the government for revision in 1958.

The government of Tchad is indeed on the horns of a dilemma. It is pledged to respect indigenous custom and cannot afford to alienate the chiefs who have been loyal or helpful and still retain influence, especially in a sensitive frontier region. (The example of Sudan, which since attaining independence has suppressed a large proportion of the chiefs' dues, religious as well as customary, has not been lost on the population in nearby regions of Tchad.) Yet the survival of a feudal chieftaincy in the northeast is a dangerous anachronism, for the exactions of the more autocratic chiefs there have been largely to blame for the exodus every year of thousands of young Tchadians to Sudan. Many observers believe that the Tchad chieftaincy, even modified as it has recently been, must be radically altered unless it is to disappear entirely. The main hope of peaceably transforming the feudal sultans into constitutional monarchs is thought to lie in the creation of regional councils.

CHAPTER 8

Justice and Courts of Law

Gabon was a juridical appendage of Senegal until nearly the end of the nineteenth century, and the only judicial institution that it possessed was a court of arbitration at Libreville. In 1878 this was replaced by a first-degree court, but appeals from its decisions still had to be carried to St. Louis-du-Sénégal until a *conseil d'appel* and a criminal court were established 19 years later at Libreville for the colony of Gabon-Congo. No change, however, was made in the personnel rendering justice, and all judicial functions in AEF continued to be exercised by administrators.

A decree of March 17, 1903, ruled that thereafter career magistrates should preside over the Higher Tribunal, which was now to replace the *conseil d'appel*, and over the first-degree courts that were to be set up at Libreville and Brazzaville. But the separation of judicial and executive powers, laid down as a principle in this decree, remained largely theoretical, and civil servants continued to fill the posts of *juges de paix* (conciliation or police magistrates) of wide competence. The birth of the federation in 1910 necessitated a further reorganization as well as an expansion of the judicial system. It was now decided that *juges de paix* must also be career magistrates, despite the obvious shortage of such personnel, and that the Higher Tribunal should be replaced by a court of appeal for the four colonies, to be installed at the new federal capital of Brazzaville. At the same time Native Courts were created, whose competence included all civil and commercial cases between Africans and certain criminal cases as well. In this way a sharp line was drawn between two categories of justice in AEF. One was for French subjects, who were to be judged by native judges in accordance with local customs; the other was for French citizens, in great majority Europeans, who were to be judged by French magistrates and according to the Metropolitan codes.

Native Courts, as organized by four successive decrees (April 27, 1927; May 16, 1928; January 10, 1930; and July 8, 1943), fell into one or another of three categories—first degree, second degree, and customary. Courts of the first degree were set up in each district and chaired by the local administrator. Similarly, a second-degree court was established in each region under the presidency of the *chef de région*. Although these courts had competence in all types of cases, and two assessors aided the chairman in each, in practice only the second-degree courts judged criminal cases, and one of its two assessors was a European. Litigants were required to submit all civil and commercial lawsuits to conciliation before going before the first-degree courts. Appeals from judgments by second-degree courts could be carried to the *Chambre d'Homologation*,[1] attached to the Brazzaville court of appeals. On the other hand, decisions by the first-degree courts in civil and commercial suits were final if Africans alone were involved and if the customary law applied were not "contrary to the principles of French civilization." As of 1939, AEF had 141 *correctionnel* (minor-offenses) tribunals and 34 courts of the second degree. In July 1943, Eboué added another category, the customary courts, to this group, and a year later the Free French government instituted a native penal code for Black Africa—both destined to be short-lived.

The virtue of the prewar system was that its stress on African customs and on informal procedure made for rapidity in the rendering of justice. Furthermore, the French intervened merely to mitigate the harshness of certain African penalties and to keep order. Its drawbacks were the failure to separate judicial from executive powers and the lack of any guaranty of the rights and freedom of the individual. Moreover, the development of a consistent local jurisprudence was hampered because the judgments given in the prewar courts were contradictory, being based on widely divergent customs. The reform of 1946 corrected some of these defects, but at the same time the functioning of the courts was slowed down by a more cumbersome procedure and in penal cases justice at times miscarried because Metropolitan laws often inappropriate to AEF were applied instead of African customs.

Abolition of the *indigénat*[2] and of the native courts for criminal cases was aimed at giving Africans a juridical status and security in keeping with their newly acquired French citizenship, and at the same time safeguarding the structure of African society. The latter goal was to be achieved by permitting African French citizens to retain their civil legal status unless they specifically renounced it, and to continue to be judged by native courts in civil and commercial cases.[3] Yet the very principle of the separation of powers and that of equality before the law were in themselves revolutionary for a society in which the chiefs traditionally exercised undivided powers and the social hierarchy was based on the inequality of individuals and their subordination to the group.

This radical change in French Black Africa's judicial system was motivated by the generous sentiments felt in postwar France toward the peoples in its overseas dependencies, and the reforms themselves were at once accepted enthusiastically by the African elite. Abolition of the *indigénat* and the separation of judicial from executive powers through the establishment of French criminal courts staffed by career magistrates were welcomed as spelling the end of the local administration's arbitrary hold on the dispensing of justice. Furthermore, application of the Metropolitan penal code, which was based on the equality of individuals before the law, was highly acceptable to the youthful African intelligentsia, eager to undermine the authority of the chiefs. But as time went on, their enthusiasm waned, mainly because of the difficulties encountered in applying the new reforms.

The decree of November 27, 1947, was the most important of a series of steps taken in the first postwar years to reorganize the federation's system of justice. By it the judicial service of AEF was placed simultaneously under the French Ministries of Justice and Overseas France and, for personnel, under the Metropolitan Conseil Supérieur de la Magistrature. As to its organization and the law which was to be applied except in native courts, these were based on Metropolitan models somewhat adapted to AEF's special geographic and demographic conditions. The Brazzaville court of appeals still topped the whole system, but because of the immense distance that separated it from the northern regions, an annex was set up at Fort Lamy to handle appeals from the second-degree courts of Tchad and Oubangui. Commercial cases were not to be tried in separate courts but in first- and second-degree tribunals by *juges de paix* of wide competence. Though the number of *correctionnel* courts was to be increased to 84, there would thenceforth be only a single criminal court, with headquarters at Brazzaville. To counter overcentralization, this court was empowered to hold sessions anywhere in the federation as required. As to the law applied in penal courts, only a few modifications were made in the Metropolitan code, and the main changes introduced were procedural —the juries required in the Metropolitan system and the African assessors in that of AEF were now both eliminated.

The first and most obvious effect of these changes was an almost catastrophic slowing down of the processes of justice. Despite its new mobility, the single criminal court proved to be the worst bottleneck of all, and this became especially serious in certain regions where the administration was concerned that crime be swiftly suppressed.[4] Then the civil courts, too, had a heavy backlog of cases, for the amount of litigation before them had grown by leaps and bounds in the first postwar years. At first this was regarded as a hopeful development, in that it was thought to reflect a more widespread confidence in the new system of justice and also to make the courts more accessible to the population. But as time went on it was realized that the Africans were becoming disillusioned with the established courts and were returning more and more to their traditional judges—the chiefs, fetishers, and sorcerers—and this, from the administration's viewpoint, was an ominous development.

Apparently the rural population had grown impatient with the dilatory handling of civil suits and had been disoriented because of being no longer judged according to custom in the criminal courts. Moreover, many of the judgments rendered were inequitable, either because of the judges' ignorance or because of the pressure exercised on them by the administration. Close observers of the African Negro have noted his willingness to accept punishment if convinced of his guilt but also his acute sensitivity to the slightest injustice.[5] As for the African elite, they were particularly incensed by the "political" verdicts handed down in the Bébalem and Berbérati cases (see pp. 432, 392), which, Boganda frankly told the Grand Council in November 1955, "do not do honor to the cause of French justice." To the elite, who had been banking on the 1946 reforms to extricate Africans from the grip of the administration in the judicial domain, the results seemed a snare and a delusion. They openly attributed this prolongation of the *status quo ante bellum* to a deliberate distortion of the reforms by ill-willed local officials. In part this was probably true, but it was primarily practical difficulties—the shortage of qualified personnel and funds—that prevented an effective separation of the judicial from the administrative services and caused the interminable delays in court action, and it was the inappropriateness of the Metropolitan codes that was responsible for many of the miscarriages of justice.

Long before World War II, AEF had been plagued by a dearth of career magistrates. According to a report made to the French Senate in 1924,[6] AEF then had only one-third of the magistrates it needed, and some of the posts of *juges de paix* had never been filled. Nor was the situation improved in June 1935 with the innovation of *juges de paix* having *correctionnel* competence, for such posts had to be filled by local administrators, of whom there was also a shortage. As of 1939 the federation had only 15 magistrates in active service and about 170 civil servants functioning as judges. After the war, an appreciable effort was made to send more magistrates to AEF, recruiting them from among graduates of the legal section of the Ecole Nationale de la France d'Outre-Mer or the holders of a *licence en droit* who had passed a special competitive examination. By the end of 1946 the number of magistrates serving in AEF had risen to 24, but at that time the number of those placed under their jurisdiction (in penal suits) had risen very suddenly from about 10,000 to more than 4 million. Although the authorities tried earnestly during the next seven years to recruit more magistrates for the federation, they found little desire on the part of promising law students in France to serve in so backward an area as AEF, especially as the conditions of their promotion and pay were less favorable overseas than in Metropolitan France. At the end of 1951, by which time, it had been overoptimistically estimated, AEF would have its full complement of 137 magistrates, they numbered only 65 and were, moreover, ill prepared for their work there. Maître Rolland, an eminent Paris lawyer who toured AEF that year, observed[7] that the AEF magistrates had little knowledge of local customs and languages, a very small and poorly trained auxiliary staff, not even elementary documentation, and virtually no supervision by the attorney general.

In the parliamentary bodies as well as the territorial assemblies the French government was reproached with its failure to carry out the separation of powers overseas. To such criticism the government spokesmen usually replied that so vast and underpopulated a federation as AEF must be viewed realistically and that reforms so radical as those of 1946 could not be carried out overnight. Not only did the government have to cope with a shortage of qualified personnel but it also lacked the funds to provide courthouses, lodgings, and transport for magistrates. In 1947, as a temporary measure, *juges de paix* with limited *correctionnel* powers had been installed to supplement the handful of existing French courts. At the same time, the number of administrators serving as judges had been greatly reduced, and many motor vehicles belonging to other government services had been lent to the magistrates to enhance their mobility.[8] Such excuses and explanations did not wholly placate the African elite, and on September 10, 1949, the Grand Council passed the first of a series of resolutions asking the government to accelerate the separation of powers. One reason for their intransigence in this matter was the widely held belief that some local civil servants were deliberately hindering the process. To be sure, some administrators—especially the younger generation—regarded their magisterial duties as time-consuming work for which they lacked the proper training, but others reportedly clung to their judicial duties and to the bonuses they received for performing them.[9] Rogué, a former governor of Tchad, even admitted to the French Union Assembly as recently as July 10, 1956, that he knew "local administrators who saw in the arrival of a magistrate a loss to their own authority."

By 1954 the transfer to Black Africa of many magistrates who had until then been serving in Indochina ended the long-standing shortage in that category, but it increased local anxiety concerning another aspect of the 1946 reforms—that of their cost. Although France in 1948 took over the payment of the salaries of overseas magistrates, the federation found it increasingly difficult to defray the expenses involved in building courthouses and lodgings and in providing the magistrates with transportation. In 1949 the National Assembly rejected AEF's plea for financial aid in these respects, and the Fonds d'Investissement pour le Développement Economique et Social (FIDES) likewise turned a deaf ear. But in 1951, when the French government urged AEF to speed up application of the 1946 reforms and at the same time reduced to 100 the number of magistrates to be allotted that federation, it also allocated 130 million Metro. francs to help meet the expenditures involved in installing them.[10] From 1947 to 1952 the cost of the 1946 reforms, in building alone, came to 140 million CFA francs, nine new jurisdictions that had been created could not function for lack of personnel and equipment, and, to complete the reform—particularly in rural areas—it was calculated that a total of 350 to 400 million more CFA francs would be needed.[11] The cost factor, as well as the requirement to set up labor courts (in conformity with the provisions of the Overseas Labor Code of November 1952), led the federal government to propose in 1953 a centralization of the judicial services.[12]

Surprisingly enough, the territorial assemblies which had voted only the year before to decentralize the judicial services now agreed to this proposal without any debate.[13] A decree of January 5, 1954, expanded the jurisdiction of the Brazzaville court of appeals to include Oubangui, which had been placed under that of Fort Lamy in 1947. In the interval it had been found that there were more appeals from verdicts of the second-degree courts of Oubangui than from those of Moyen-Congo and Gabon together, with the result that the well-staffed Brazzaville court of appeals was handling only one-fourth of all such cases throughout the federation.[14] The reorganization aimed to permit the three magistrates of the Fort Lamy Chamber to concentrate on the territory of Tchad, where distances were enormous, evidence hard to collect, and the crime rate particularly high.[15]

For some years thereafter, the reorganization effected in 1954, along with the concurrent influx of magistrates from Indochina, stabilized the situation of the courts applying French law throughout AEF. At that time the federation had 25 *juges de paix* of wide competence (of whom six were in Moyen-Congo, six in Gabon, six in Oubangui, and seven in Tchad) and eight first-degree courts located in the main towns (Brazzaville, Pointe Noire, Libreville, Port Gentil, Bangui, Fort Lamy, Fort Archambault, and Abéché). In 1955 the attorney general felt warranted in congratulating himself upon the efficiency and celerity with which his services operated.[16] It was a remarkable achievement, he claimed, that the magistracy of a country five times the size of France could deal with cases twice as rapidly as in Metropolitan France, and for this reason he did not envisage any appreciable enlargement of it except in the auxiliary personnel of *greffiers* and the police.

As to the *greffiers*, the assemblymen had no objection to training more Africans in this branch of the judicial service, but they were of two minds about the police force, *gendarmes*, and *sûreté*. In so far as those forces dealt with the crime rampant in many AEF cities, checked the illegal immigration and contraband trade across the federal frontiers, detected frauds in mining enterprises, and controlled the black markets, the assemblies were willing to support them. On the other hand, the assemblymen were outspoken in regard to the ignorance of the law shown by the African police and *gendarmes*, their brutality toward their own compatriots, and their slothfulness and inefficiency. The members of Tchad's assembly were particularly bitter on the cost of the territorial security forces, especially as they had failed to stop the growth of crime in Fort Lamy. This had become the second biggest expenditure of the territory's budget in 1955 despite the fact that Metropolitan France had been paying the *gendarmes* since 1948.[17] Dissatisfaction with the disproportionately small return in terms of general security for the large outlay involved in maintaining the so-called "forces of order" made the Grand Council hesitate to grant the government's request to vote the funds required to establish a federal police school. Yet the need to strengthen the security forces was so evident that in May 1950 the Grand Council acceded, on the understanding that the *sûreté* would train 40 African recruits a year.[18]

In two other domains, both related to the administration of justice— that of prisons and that of the legal profession—the Grand Council and the government did not so easily come to terms. For many years the bad state of the federation's prisons had been deplored by all concerned.[19] As always, and with reason, the government claimed that it lacked the funds to prevent overcrowding and to give prisoners the individualized treatment that they needed. The assemblymen agreed that there was not enough money to build new prisons but insisted that the government could and should improve the food of inmates, punish guards who maltreated their prisoners, and prevent the illegal detention in up-country jails of men awaiting trial simply to make use of them as a cheap labor force.[20] (Such labor was normally though not always used for public works, and the work was always collectively performed outside the prison walls.) To such charges the government spokesman invariably replied that he immediately took punitive action whenever specific instances of abuses were brought to his attention. And with time, conditions in the federation's prisons apparently have improved, although those in the territorial capitals are the only ones having a specialized staff and that of Brazzaville alone has been described as a model penitentiary.[21]

Another stock answer given by the government to the allegations by assemblymen that abuses on the part of those in authority often went unpunished was that everyone in AEF could always have recourse to the law. To this the usual reply was that the procedure of the courts was incomprehensible to the great majority of illiterate Africans[22] and that there were too few defense lawyers available to them. To be sure, defense lawyers had no role to play in the African customary courts, and the commercial cases that required legal advice were almost invariably transferred to the French tribunals.[23] Nevertheless, the African elite regarded with suspicion the government's attempt to limit membership in the Ordre des Avocats en AEF (organized in April 1947) to locally experienced holders of a *licence en droit*. As of 1949 there were only eight defense lawyers established in the federation (two each at Brazzaville and Fort Lamy, and one each at Bangui, Libreville, Port Gentil, and Pointe Noire) and the government showed no inclination to increase their number. Not only was this complement considered by the African assemblymen to be too small for a population of over four million, but the conditions imposed by the government for practicing law in the federation would be discouraging to the AEF scholarship holders who were then preparing in French universities for a legal career. In 1954 the government somewhat eased those conditions[24] but it did not yield in the matter of organizing a bar association in AEF.

On the foregoing subjects, the forces of government found themselves in total or partial dissension with the African elite. But in the matter of the customary courts and of the law to be applied in them, there were contradictions both in French policy and in the Africans' reaction to it. The French, on the one hand, desired to safeguard African civilization as the unique product of its environment and traditions and the equal of other cultures. At the same time, however, there was an underlying assumption of the superiority of French civilization and a corresponding ignorance of African customs, which were felt to be inferior and only transiently to be tolerated until the population had evolved to the point where it would be ruled wholly by French law. In post-Liberation France, AEF was considered fortunate to have escaped application of the Vichy regime's racially discriminatory laws, which had been imposed in French West Africa, but this did not prevent a general return to the prewar assimilationist policy. The governor-general was still allowed considerable latitude about applying all or part of Metropolitan legislation to the federation, and some modifications were made in legal procedures, but the newly constituted territorial assemblies were not consulted on this vital subject.[25] On May 20, 1948, the French Union Assembly debated at length the advisability of codifying custom in Black Africa. Some thought such a code would be helpful; others feared that it would crystallize custom and thus prevent its further evolution; and a minority wanted special courts for Christians and for Muslims to be set up. But all were convinced that sooner or later the customary courts were bound to disappear and that all the inhabitants of AEF would be judged by French civil as well as criminal law.

As time went on, however, it became increasingly obvious that many Metropolitan laws were totally inappropriate to AEF and also that they contained conspicuous loopholes which should be eliminated. The existence of criminal secret societies of leopard-men,[26] discovered as early as 1916 in AEF, had long before pointed up the not-unnatural lacunae in French law on the punishment of cannibalism. And later, the failure of legal deterrents to check the power of village sorcerers—often exercised in collaboration with a local chief anxious to get rid of dissident elements—was recognized as being partly responsible for the migration of many rural youths to the towns.[27] Sins of legal omission and commission in French Black Africa became so apparent that the National Assembly, on October 27, 1950, voted without debate an essentially antiassimilationist resolution. On the proposal of AEF's European deputies, Malbrant and Bayrou, that body decreed that thenceforth the Metropolitan penal code be better adapted to local African conditions and customs (when the latter were not in contradiction to the principles of French law) and that the penalties inflicted by French overseas courts conform more closely to those conditions and customs. To carry out this resolution, more precise data on laws actually in force and a greater knowledge of the many local customs of AEF were required. So the government-general at Brazzaville began to gather together in a *recueil législatif* all of the existing laws, decrees, and regulations throughout the federation, as well as the relevant decisions made by the territorial assemblies—a work that was finally completed in 1954.[28] And to amass more information about existing customs, *comités coutumiers* were set up in the regions under the chairmanship of the local magistrate or administrator.[29]

The Africans of AEF agreed with the French government on the need for reforming civil justice in general and the customary courts in particular. In 1952 the attorney general went so far as to ask for suppression of the latter, but he lacked the funds needed to set up substitute tribunals. He was also deterred by the Africans' divided views on the subject, for the controversial question of the chiefs' powers was involved. Wherever the assessors were reputedly venal or the chiefs were government appointees, the African elite favored abolition of the courts over which they presided. Such men, it was claimed, were not true representatives of their people, did not know local customs, and illegally inflicted penalties with the sole aim of reinforcing their abusive authority.[30] Much less unanimity was shown by the African assemblymen in regard to the courts chaired by the traditional, especially the paramount, chiefs. Some felt that because such chiefs were authentic indigenous leaders the suppression of their judicial powers would disastrously lessen their prestige. Others criticized their judgments as arbitrary and self-interested, claiming that in the northern sultanates certain minor misdemeanors were illegally punished by imprisonment in clandestine jails whose very existence was unknown to the administration.[31] The most radical of these critics favored having both judges and assessors elected, if customary courts were to be retained at all.[32]

Naturally the government denied that it chose only docile servitors for such posts, claiming that its appointments as judge or assessor were made only after an extensive examination of candidates' qualifications, and it was firmly opposed to making the native magistracy elective. Yet it recognized that many of the criticisms of the courts were justified, and in 1954 began a detailed study of their functioning with a view to reorganizing them within the framework of existing laws. By a federal circular of November 16, 1955, the government-general abolished the customary courts and replaced them by first-degree courts. Many of the former judges and assessors in the customary courts were retained to staff the new tribunals, and beginning in January 1957 they were to be paid from the territorial budgets. By integrating them into the organization set up for the French law courts, the federal judicial service hoped to exercise a stricter control over their functioning. And by publishing their verdicts in the *Journal Officiel*, it was anticipated that the judgments pronounced by the African judicial personnel would become legally more valid and precise. So as to avoid a sharp break with the past, these courts still were not allowed to impose fines, their decisions could be appealed, and the law that they were to apply remained that of local customs. By imposing a uniformity of structure and a federal control over the courts' functioning, it was hoped to modernize the whole judicial structure of AEF without concurrently disorienting its African populations, who would continue to be judged in civil cases by their compatriots and according to their traditional customs.

Passage of the *loi-cadre* six months later might well have invalidated the reform of 1955 by turning back to each of the territories authority that could have been used to establish different judicial systems. But the compromise between the old and the new, as embodied in the 1955 reform, seems to have been successful enough to have averted the danger of such fragmentation. The pre-existing administration of justice is among the few services of the former government-general that has been retained by the new republics of AEF on a uniform basis.

CHAPTER 9

The Armed Forces and Veterans

From the standpoint of military expenditures, the cost of acquiring and defending AEF has probably been among the lowest in any of France's overseas dependencies. For the occupation period, it has been estimated that, in terms of manpower, at most 700 soldiers were killed and 1,200 to 1,500 wounded, of whom about four-fifths were Africans.[1] France took control of all of southern AEF without having to fire a shot, and only in the north did anything resembling an active military campaign take place. As to monetary expenditures, they too have been comparatively slight: the initial cost was not great, and even that of maintenance declined steadily as more and more areas under military command were turned over to civilian administrators. By 1928 the French government was paying only about 14½ million francs a year for its military establishment in AEF, nor did it ever require that federation to contribute financially toward the costs of imperial defense as it did French West Africa, Madagascar, North Africa, and Indochina. Moreover, Senegalese troops recruited and trained in French West Africa sometimes served in AEF without this entailing any expense whatsoever for the latter federation.

Beginning in 1940, military expenditures in AEF by both France and the federal government rose appreciably, as the result first of Resistance operations centered there and much later of France's evacuation of the Fezzan. Not only did Leclerc's march from Tchad across the eastern Sahara to Bir Hakeim entail a large outlay, but very considerable sums have been and are still being paid out to veterans of that campaign in the form of pensions. In recent years, the evacuation of French troops from the Fezzan, under terms of the Franco-Libyan treaty initialed August 10, 1955, caused a big increase in military expenditures beginning in 1957, for the defenses of the eastern Sahara had to be reorganized and reinforced. Until their repatriation in November 1956, not more than 500 French troops had been stationed in the Fezzan, chiefly at Sebha, and this small and inexpensive expeditionary force had been sufficient to control almost all of the *pistes* (tracks) in that area. Loss of the use of strategic centers in the Fezzan meant that France had to build new airfields and *pistes* inside French territory so as to maintain contacts between central and north Africa and to provision French garrisons in northern Tchad and the southeastern Sahara. Moreover, France's evacuation of the Fezzan also stimulated the

Algerian FLN to step up their use of Libya as a base for troop training and for smuggling arms across the frontier, so that the French had to reinforce the military units in that area and improve their equipment. While Metropolitan authorities continued to defray almost all of the increased military expenditures involved in this operation, AEF for the first time in its history was required to make a substantial monetary contribution toward its own defense, which amounted to about 400 million CFA francs in 1957.[2] As of late 1958 a great deal of work was still being done on military installations in northern AEF, particularly the airfields of Fort Lamy and Bouar.

It was not until 1919, seven years after a similar policy was carried out in French West Africa, that compulsory military service was instituted in AEF. According to the law, French subjects were conscripted for a three-year term while French citizens were required to serve only two years. But because of the sparseness of AEF's population and its generally poor physical condition, only a small proportion of those eligible to serve were actually inducted.[3] In fact there was no necessity for conscription, because certain regions of Tchad spontaneously supplied the army with numerous volunteers who proved to be excellent soldiers.

Until recent years the training given to these troops was very scanty. "How long does it take you to make an African into a soldier?" asked a British writer who toured AEF on the eve of World War II. A French official replied, "Twenty-eight days. Even if we catch them wild, we can teach them to obey commands and carry a rifle in that time. Anyway, they are not supposed to know much . . ."[4] Under the pressures created by the Free French Resistance in AEF, better training facilities were developed at Brazzaville, but these were both temporary and limited and did little to help African soldiers to obtain commissions. As of 1948 there were only six Africans among the 321 commissioned officers stationed in AEF. In the National Assembly on July 16, 1948, Communist party spokesmen accused the government of deliberately placing obstacles in the path of Africans who aspired to become army officers. This the government of course denied, claiming that the proportion of African officers and noncommissioned officers was growing steadily, but it insisted that more rapid progress depended upon an improvement in AEF's generally low educational standards. It was not until 1956 that official plans were announced for opening a training school for African officers in Tchad, to be called the Ecole Général Leclerc.[5]

There will certainly be no dearth of Tchadian candidates for admission to this school. For many years the Sara tribes in the southwest have shown such an aptitude and liking for the military life that they are often called "the Senegalese *tirailleurs* of AEF." During World War II the Free French army in the federation numbered at its peak some 10,000 men, of whom the very great majority were Sara. After the decree of November 18, 1947, laid down the principle of equal pay for Metropolitan and overseas troops, the attraction long felt by the Sara for the army uniform and life of adventure and travel was heightened by the prospect of an income vastly superior to that of most of their compatriots. The Sara volunteered in such numbers for the Indochina war that a large number of applicants had to be turned away.[6] Those who served in the Far East were said to have been much taken with *les belles vietnamiennes,* and the survivors returned to their home territory rich men by local standards. After Dien-Bien-Phu, some of the Sara volunteered again to fight in North Africa, for in early 1954 army rolls in AEF had been cut to 7,000.[7]

For both economic and political reasons the existence of three sets of veterans living in AEF has become a problem to the French. Their pensions amount to a sum that not only is a drain on the French treasury but is also an inflationary factor particularly affecting Tchad's economy. In the first two postwar years, the Metropolitan authorities had been negligent toward the Black African veterans. The situation of those veterans, though unfortunate, was never so bad in AEF as in French West Africa, for more of the French officers who had served with Negro troops continued to live in the former federation and to give help to individual needy cases as they came to their attention.[8] The *mystique* of the Resistance remained a vital force in AEF far longer than elsewhere in Africa. Moreover, in 1947, the French army sent a military mission under Henri Ligier to study the situation of veterans in AEF before making a similar investigation in French West Africa. To the members of this mission, who went from village to village in their zeal to interview as many individuals as possible, the government was indebted for its first valid data on the plight of AEF's African veterans. Their dossiers were examined and brought up to date; the arrears in their pensions, amounting to 13 million CFA francs in 1947, were paid up; the parents of those killed in combat were aided and their orphans officially recognized as "wards of the nation"; and, in general, the "scandalous inequalities" from which they had suffered were rectified.[9]

Under the impetus provided by the accomplishments of the Ligier mission, the Office des Anciens Combattants at Brazzaville was reorganized and enlarged, and territorial branches were created. The scope of the work accomplished by Ligier and his colleagues can be better appreciated when it is realized that at the time there were nearly 15,000 veterans living in AEF.[10] All of AEF's assemblymen were willing to support the work being done by territorial Offices on behalf of the veterans, but many of them resented the attempts made by the Rassemblement du Peuple Français to make use of those organizations for political propaganda purposes. For a few years after the war, the RPF in Oubangui and Tchad sometimes held party meetings in the territorial Offices, and was reported to have claimed credit for such benefits as the distribution to veterans of clothing which, in fact, had been paid for by the local budget.

The admixture of party politics to the general problems posed by veterans in AEF was apparently not taken very seriously by the French authorities so long as it remained on a minor and strictly local scale. African veterans of World War II were steadfastly loyal to France, and all they humbly asked was that they be given their just due. By the end of 1954, however, this situation had begun to change, for some veterans of the Indochina war who had returned to their native villages were giving vent to criticism of their traditional chiefs and of the French administration.[11] This was true in particular of the men who had been prisoners of the Vietminh, and it was feared that they had been ideologically contaminated by political agitators, although there was no reported evidence of the participation of veterans—either as individuals or as a group—in the founding of political parties.

To offset such subversive influences, two experiments were successfully tried out in the Sara regions. One was to select, as administrators of those areas, officials who had formerly been officers with Negro troops, and the other was to set up in the Logone region *villages de 15 ans* in which veterans who had served for that length of time in the French army were grouped together in a semimilitary environment. Presumably similar measures will be taken in dealing with the African veterans who have been serving in Algeria. On June 2, 1956, Lisette told the National Assembly that letters from Negro soldiers fighting there to their friends and relatives in Black Africa indicated that the morale of some of them had been badly shaken. Ever since 1954, left-wing Negroes have been denouncing the use of their compatriots as soldiers in the North African war. But because the Sara are not Muslims and hence are less susceptible to pan-Arab propaganda, the situation has never been thought to be so dangerous for AEF troops in Algeria as for the Islamic soldiers of French West Africa serving there.

CHAPTER 10

Foreign Contacts

Except for France and possibly Egypt, the only foreign countries that have markedly influenced AEF have been its immediate neighbors, and to widely varying degrees. The federation has been too isolated and too poor to be coveted by any other world power, and, moreover, its inhabitants are too limited in their outlook and education to show much interest in the East-West struggle.

Until 1957 the United States had no consular representation in AEF, and the American consul stationed at Léopoldville simply crossed the river to Brazzaville whenever he had business there. Nor did the USSR maintain any such officials in the federation: on December 4, 1950, in the National Assembly, the Minister of Overseas France denied rumors then circulating in the foreign press to the effect that seven Soviet agents had been disseminating propaganda in AEF. A handful of political and labor leaders, such as Antoine Darlan and Jean Charlot, did attend a few communist congresses in Europe, but the AEF Africans were never courted as assiduously by the European communists as were those from French West Africa. Clearly it was not the lure of communism for the federation's inhabitants that the French government feared, but rather the admixture of fanatical Islam with the nationalism of former colonial peoples. It was against this danger that Governor-General Chauvet warned in a speech to the Grand Council on May 23, 1956. He spoke then of the "lesson of Bandung,[1] which clearly designates Africa as the area of expansion for certain overpopulated countries of Asia, allied to the fanaticism of some Arab nations, more racialist than religious, from whose raids and oppression Black Africa suffered for centuries."

The lack of a long seacoast and of natural barriers along its land frontiers has made all of AEF exceptionally vulnerable to outside influences emanating from neighboring countries. Political boundaries hamper but do not obliterate tribal and family ties, and the formalities involved in crossing such boundaries have only slightly impeded the flow of persons and goods. Relations of a nonpersonal order between AEF and adjacent territories have been motivated very largely by price and wage considerations—the purchase or sale of merchandise and the pay scale for laborers—though occasionally Spanish Guinea and Portuguese Angola have served as permanent places of refuge for dissidents from AEF seeking to escape from oppressive chiefs or the exactions of the French administration. In addition, the ports of Nigeria and Cameroun are important in the provisioning of Oubangui and Tchad as well as in their export trade, and the Nigerian and Camerounian systems of rail and road communications are vital lifelines for those two landlocked territories. Official relations have been particularly amicable between AEF and adjacent British and Belgian territories, and information on a wide variety of subjects is regularly exchanged between the three governments. As for the great majority of AEF Africans, they have thus far seemed largely indifferent to what is going on politically among their neighbors, although in recent years increasing interest has been shown by the Gabonese Fang in their confreres living in Cameroun and Spanish Guinea, and by the Bakongo in their relatives in the Belgian Congo and Portuguese Angola. Until early 1959 the European governments of those territories seemed little concerned about such developments, and the French authorities in AEF were preoccupied mainly with the federation's relations with the Arab countries to the north and east.

The Arab Countries

In northern and eastern AEF the normal transfrontier interchanges were reinforced in the west-easterly direction by the influence exerted upon the Muslim populations of Tchad (and to a lesser extent those of Oubangui) by the religious and cultural leadership of the eastern Arabs. Demographic and geographic factors have made this interchange strongest between Tchad and Sudan; the desert progressively diminishes the impact on Tchad of events in Libya and North Africa; and because of the vast distance that separates AEF from Saudi Arabia and Egypt, those two countries have, for the most part, influenced only the individuals who have made the Mecca pilgrimage or studied in the universities of Cairo. Sand, as a highly placed French official told the authors in 1958, has been the salvation of Tchad as a barrier to its Arab neighbors.

Although northern AEF, unlike the corresponding region in French West Africa, was Arabized before it was Islamized, the Muslim religion has proved to be the most powerful magnet drawing the peoples of that area toward the east. About 1,600,000 Muslims live in AEF, mainly in the north, but everywhere their number is growing (see p. 308). Because Tchad possesses the largest concentration of Muslims in the federation and lies athwart the overland pilgrim route to Mecca from West Africa, that territory has been longest in contact with the holy cities of Arabia and with Al Azhar University at Cairo. Much of the growing pilgrim traffic since World War II has moved by plane or ship to Mecca and Djidda, yet thousands of pilgrims—particularly the poorest ones—continue to cross Tchad on foot or by motor truck on their way to Khartoum and the Red Sea ports. Just what proportion of these pilgrims originates in AEF itself is unknown, but their number is sufficiently large to entail considerable expenditures by the federation in their behalf. Despite the official French policy of maintaining neutrality in religious matters, each year since the war the federal budget has paid for the pilgrimage transport of outstanding local Muslims, as well as of an official specialized in Arabic affairs and an African doctor to accompany the AEF pilgrims going in official convoys. In addition it has provided, through the French consuls in the Middle East, an annual subsidy of about 100,000 CFA francs for the relief of destitute AEF pilgrims stranded there.[2] By organizing and facilitating the material side of the Mecca pilgrimage, the French government has been able to supervise the activities of those included in the officially chaperoned groups, but it has been unable to exercise any control whatsoever over the far larger number who make the pilgrimage on their own.

The unabashed fleecing of the Mecca pilgrims and the existence of a Negro slave trade in Saudi Arabia have not endeared the Arabs of that country to the Muslims of AEF. The French government is said to have proof of at least one attempt on the part of the Saudi Arabs to subvert pilgrims from its African dependencies.[3] But as these pilgrims are with few exceptions both poor and illiterate, speaking only a rudimentary Arabic, they have not proved a fertile field for either pan-Arab or anti-French propaganda. Naturally those who remain longest in the Arab countries are the most susceptible, and some pilgrims take several years to work their way across Africa to the Muslim shrines. On the whole, however, the influence of their sojourn in Saudi Arabia on AEF pilgrims seems to be almost wholly a religious one. They are happy to perform a major Islamic duty, but the cost to them in energy and money is so great that they are eager to return home, and the French government has every interest in accelerating their round trip.

Egyptian influence on AEF is quite different from that of Saudi Arabia, though in both cases it is based on the brotherhood of Islam. For many years it was the superior learning of Egypt's religious teachers that attracted the few AEF Muslims able to study in its theological schools. More recently, Nasser has been making a bid for the leadership of Africa in other fields, both economic and political, and to accomplish his aim he must eliminate both European and African competitors. He would like to have Egypt provide the cotton cloth which the majority of Africans wear, but has found European textiles firmly entrenched in the sub-Saharan markets. And in offering his leadership to his "Negro brothers still oppressed by colonialism," he has encountered not only European opposition but ambitions similar to his own on the part of such Negro nationalists as Nkrumah. Though Nasser's appeal as a "liberator" of African colonial peoples has been undeniable, particularly since the abortive Suez invasion of 1956, the new Egyptian imperialism has labored under various internal as well as external handicaps.[4] Egypt's interests and energies are already dissipated in three directions—Europe and the Near and Middle East—and its leaders lack the time, energy, and knowledge required to master the complex and varied situations in each African territory. Specifically in regard to AEF, Egyptian Wahabism has little appeal for the local Muslims, who are almost all members of the Tidjaniya sect, and the Egyptians living in AEF (who numbered only about 20 in 1958) are too few to serve as a fifth column for Nasser's infiltration. In operating there, Nasser perforce relies on propaganda carried on by means of tracts, radio broadcasts, and individual agents. Probably far more effective is the time-honored practice of extending facilities to Negro students in Egyptian universities and hospitality to African politicians out of favor with the governments in their home countries.

Few Egyptian publications circulate in AEF, and in any case the printed word is hardly an ideal medium for propaganda among a population with so low a literacy rate as that of Tchad. Yet some evidence has come to light that Arab League literature has been mailed to some of the elite of Fort Lamy and Brazzaville.[5] A wider audience is reached by the anti-French broadcasts from Cairo radio, first in a program called "La Voix des Arabes" and more recently in one entitled "La Voix des Africains." The tone of these broadcasts is vehement and they are beamed mainly to the peoples of East Africa. In Tchad, few Muslims own a radio receiving set and even fewer understand the pure Arabic of North Africa. Probably Egyptian films reach a larger part of the population, but very few of these carry a political message. In all these media—literature, radio, and film— Western output is more copious and more skillfully presented in AEF than is that of the Egyptians.

There remain the *agents provocateurs,* who are said to infiltrate Tchad with ease and in considerable numbers. Tchad is not important enough, however, to be their main target—it is principally a place of transit on their way to bigger game in Nigeria and northern Cameroun. Actually the best agents of Egyptian propaganda are the AEF graduates of Cairo universities, and it is believed that some 100 Tchad students are now studying at Al Azhar.[6] In that milieu they absorb pan-Arab as well as pan-Islamic ideology at the same time as theology, and they spread these ideas upon their return home. Tchad students have reportedly participated in anti-French demonstrations at Cairo, and press dispatches have mentioned—though without particulars as to his name or program—a "representative of the Tchad Independence Movement" at the various conferences held at Accra and Cairo in 1957–58. Although few Tchadian students in Egypt have proved to be either serious scholars or able propagandists, many of them working at menial jobs to earn a living and only occasionally attending classes, they enjoy considerable prestige after their return to Tchad. Shortly after the war, the Faqi Ouellech, after studying at Al Azhar, went back to Abéché, where he founded a school. He soon became so embroiled in local intrigues against the sultan, however, that the government expelled him from the territory. Although this incident had no widespread local repercussions, it served to awaken the French administration to the political dangers of an Egyptian religious education. It also led to the founding of the Franco-Arabic College at Abéché and of a local newspaper in Arabic, the *Etoile du Tchad* (see pp. 321–22).[7]

In the mid-1950's, the attainment of independence by Libya and the

Anglo-Egyptian Sudan, as well as the outbreak of the Algerian revolt, alerted Paris to the ease with which AEF might be converted to pan-Arabism. Alarmist articles, with a mystery-story flavor, began appearing in the press, and parliamentary bodies hastily appointed committees to study the federation's defenses. The experts did not deny that the proximity of two independent states belonging to the Arab League might be contagious for AEF and create there a situation that should be "watched and weighed," but they were inclined to think that it was not crucial. Governor-General Chauvet, at a press conference on June 1, 1956, said:

> . . . to state that foreign agitators do not constitute a danger for the future would be as inaccurate as to assert that they have already deeply penetrated the territory. . . . Those who might enter our northern territories would find that 60 per cent of the population is not Muslim. . . . The wholly or seminomadic tribes are scattered over a wide area, largely preoccupied with their own daily problems, and jealous about keeping their own way of life. . . . By living in close contact with the Negroes, Islam has lost there much of the purity and fanaticism that it retains in Arab countries. One could say at present that while the Tchad Muslims are conscious of belonging to a vaster Islamic world, they do not yet look far beyond their horizon.

The lack of data makes it hard to know whether the Africans of AEF shared this viewpoint or, indeed, what their general reactions to pan-Arabism may be. The thousands of Muslim travelers who have been shuttling across Tchad in recent years—in 1956 about 25,000 crossed in the west-east direction and 18,000 in the east-west direction—cannot have failed to leave some ideological residue among the local population. Yet in three tours of French Black Africa the authors found far more interest in what was going on in neighboring Arab countries, including Algeria, among West Africans than among the closer Equatorial Africans. A few relevant statements have been issued by AEF Muslim organizations, but they are mainly expressions of loyalty to France, and their accuracy in reflecting local public opinion is doubtful. In this category was the open letter addressed to Nasser by the Muslim Cultural Center of Poto-Poto, in which its signatories asked why he should think French Black Africa would prefer to ally itself with the Arab bloc rather than with the Western bloc, and they claimed the right to develop a Muslim-African civilization without outside interference.[8] This Center, founded in August 1953 by a French convert to Islam, has raised sufficient funds to build a meeting place, house a small library, conduct adult education classes, and issue irregularly a periodical entitled *Islam-AEF*. When the writers visited the Center three years after it was created, they learned that it was run by French West African Muslims, had a membership of only about 1,200, and was split into mutually antagonistic factions. Similar Muslim organizations exist in other AEF towns, but even that of Fort Lamy, with some 4,000 members, could scarcely be termed dynamic or flourishing.[9] No specifically Muslim political party exists as yet in AEF.

In the northern territories both the terrain and the inhabitants' strong sense of regionalism and tribalism inhibit organized Muslim activity there, either local or foreign. Memories of the Arab slave traders, along with evidences of the Arabs' feeling of superiority to Negro Muslims, undoubtedly have conditioned the response of Islamic Tchad to the siren call coming from the east. In this respect the question reportedly posed by Koulamallah (long regarded by the French as dangerously pro-Egyptian) to one of his Sudanese cousins is significant:[10]

> I asked him, Why do you Negro Africans want to ally yourselves with the Arabs? The color of your skin will always be against you. . . . The great danger for Sudan is Egypt, as it is for Tchad. For some time the Egyptians have been trying to conceal the fact that they have black slaves, but we all know that they have them.

The religious bond between AEF Muslims and the eastern Arabs is undoubtedly a strong one, as are the family ties with the inhabitants of neighboring countries. The animist Sara, who are fighting in Algeria, have probably been touched by nationalist propaganda but they can hardly be receptive to pan-Arabism. The Tchad territorial assembly has been the only representative body in the Saharan regions of French Black Africa except Niger to have welcomed inclusion of its desert area in the French-sponsored OCRS (see pp. 436, 466). Thus it appears that local interests still remain paramount in northern AEF, and that such repercussions as the ferment in North Africa and the Middle East may have had on the federation's Islamic population have been felt more indirectly than directly. In the near future, the Algerian situation cannot but affect Tchad more deeply than at present, for its outcome may well determine the Arab League's next moves in AEF. Some believe that if the Algerian war is settled in a sense favorable to the French, Nasser will seek compensation in Tchad for his failure in North Africa, and that if the FLN is victorious in Algeria, Tchad will be divided between that country, Libya, and Sudan.

Of all the Arab League countries, Sudan is the one closest to AEF in every sense. The volume of transfrontier traffic is the largest in the neighborhood of Adré and Abéché and is far smaller along Oubangui's boundary with Sudan. A considerable number of Sudanese traders live permanently in Tchad, having established themselves along the road from Abéché to Fort Lamy, whence they have spread out to the south. An appreciable proportion of what is called the Sudanese colony in Tchad is made up of merchants whose ancestors migrated there several centuries ago and who therefore cannot properly be termed foreigners. The Sudanese residents, though not greatly liked by the indigenous population, have considerable influence on them, but the political and religious ideas that they propagate are personal and have never been traced to directives from Khartoum.[11]

Similarly, it is by contagion rather than by any official stratagem that the new egalitarian ideas of the Sudanese, since they acquired independence, have spread among the populations of eastern Tchad. It is believed that the abolition of religious tithes and customary dues in Sudan was largely responsible for the refusal of the peasantry in the Tchad sultanates to submit any longer to such exactions (see pp. 76–78), and also for the attempt by some recently impoverished Sudanese chiefs to make common cause with their counterparts in Tchad for the purpose of offering joint resistance to this democratic trend. Pressures from those diehard chiefs, as well as from the new Sudanese leaders, caused several hundred Sudanese to seek refuge in Oubangui and Tchad in 1954–55, but they soon returned to Sudan. Good relations between the Tchadian and Sudanese governments were troubled neither by such episodes nor by the expulsion from Tchad of several Sudanese merchants found guilty of engaging in illicit currency operations or of intriguing against the sultan of Ouaddaï, despite the fact that they occurred at a time when tension was increasing in the Muslim world.

When the last British administrator of Darfour came to Abéché in June 1954 to announce the imminent departure of British civil servants from Sudan, "the French officers grouped around the governor of Tchad listened in silence, full of foreboding for the future."[12] They feared that this would mean the end of the mutually helpful relations they had long enjoyed with Sudan, and that the British would be replaced by young pro-Egyptian Sudanese officials. Yet as it turned out, their anxiety—at least on the administrative level—proved to be unfounded. Sudanese politics developed in such a way that the men who in 1953 had been partisans of union with Egypt soon realized, after they came to power, that there was an incompatibility of interests between the two countries. Subsequently, Sudanese officials welcomed the French technicians who came to demarcate a new frontier between the two countries, as they did the members of a French information mission visiting Sudan, and they were pleased to exchange diplomatic envoys with France.

The French Senators who were sent in the spring of 1956 to make an on-the-spot study of the clandestine arms traffic supposedly going on between Sudan and north Cameroun via Abéché were able later to report to their colleagues that it did not exist on any large scale or in organized form.[13] Even more reassuring was the refusal, later in the year, of the Sudanese government to break off diplomatic relations with France because of the Suez invasion. In fact, throughout 1957 economic missions were exchanged and other steps were taken to promote closer relations between Sudan and Tchad. Early in 1958, Air-France opened a weekly service between Fort Lamy and Khartoum, and a few weeks later a trade agreement was announced, by the terms of which France agreed to take more Sudanese cotton and Sudan to buy more French manufactured goods.[14]

During the past few years French policy makers have observed uneasily the instability of Sudan's governments, for they realize that the existing good relations with that country might be upset by a coup d'état that could bring to power a pro-Egyptian government at Khartoum. The French authorities have striven to lessen the economic and cultural attraction of Sudan for the Tchadian population, and in the former field have been aided by the fact that there has been a decline in the prosperity of the Sudanese regions adjoining Ouaddaï. Goods are now less abundant and cheap there than they were during the British regime, hence the *chekalla* (migrant workers) are today less tempted to emigrate to the area. To compensate for the loss of the money income derived from seasonal work in Sudan, the government of Tchad has been encouraging the cultivation of cash crops in Ouaddaï, such as cotton, peanuts, and gum arabic. To put a stop to the pressure exerted on the peasantry by Tchad chiefs—another main cause of the migrations—efforts have been made to check their abuses of authority. Finally, to offset the attraction of the Sudanese schools of Arabic and Koranic learning, the French have built and equipped a modern Franco-Arabic college at Abéché. And in pursuing these policies, the new African government of the Tchad Republic is as eager as were its French predecessors to stay on good terms with Sudan but at the same time prevent it from developing into a pole of attraction that might eventually depopulate or subvert the populations in its eastern regions.

With regard to Libya, lying athwart the northern border of Tchad, the attitude of France in recent years has been determined, successively, by political considerations having to do with the French Saharan regions; by sentimental ones associated with Leclerc's conquest of the Fezzan during World War II; by strategic ones bearing specifically upon the Algerian revolt and generally upon communications between north Africa and French Black Africa; and by economic ones related to the planned development of the eastern Sahara's petroleum resources.

After Rabah's defeat by the French in 1900 on the shores of Lake Tchad (see pp. 10, 429), the Senoussi brotherhood, operating from its Libyan stronghold, was free to pillage Borkou, Ennedi, Kanem, and Ouaddaï.[15] It took 15 years of almost ceaseless campaigning by the French army to wipe out the centers of Senoussi power in what later became the colony of Tchad. During World War II, the Senoussi penetrated the French Sahara as far as Tamanrasset and, with their local nomad allies, tried to wage the "holy war" instigated by the Turkish government of Libya against the French and British empires in west and central Africa. Later the Senoussi became increasingly involved in the campaigns that culminated in the Italian conquest of Libya. They were driven out of Tibesti by 1919 but it was not until three years later that peace was fully restored in the French areas. After their defeat by the Italians, some of the Senoussi chiefs and merchants sought refuge in Tchad and Oubangui, where a considerable number of them still remain. When Italy finally established her sovereignty over Libya, she sought to revise the Franco-Italian treaties of 1902 and 1919 regarding AEF and French West Africa respectively. On January 7, 1935, Mussolini and French Premier Laval initialed a treaty that delimited a portion of Libya's western frontier, but it was never ratified, and on December 17, 1938, the Italian government announced that its terms were no longer acceptable.

In 1943, Leclerc and the Free French forces conquered the Fezzan on their way north to Bir Hakeim, and at once the British announced their intention of sending in officers to take over the administration of that area. But de Gaulle insisted that by right of conquest his delegates should govern the region, and he succeeded—at least temporarily—in attaching the Fezzan administratively to the Algerian Territoires du Sud.[16] In northern Libya, the Senoussi leader Idriss, who had never acknowledged the Italian conquest and had lived in exile for 20 years in Egypt, remained unswervingly loyal to the British cause throughout World War II. After the armistice he was rewarded by Britain by being recognized as king of Cyrenaica.

As soon as the war ended, the Soviet Union let it be known that she would like to administer Tripolitania as a trust territory. Disturbed by such a prospect, Britain hastily negotiated an agreement with Count Sforza by which for ten years Tripolitania would be placed under the trusteeship of Italy, Cyrenaica under that of the British, and the Fezzan under France as the administering power. In the United Nations this agreement was defeated by the narrow margin of one vote, so Britain on November 18, 1949, joined the majority which favored making Libya an independent state, in which the three provinces of Tripolitania, Cyrenaica, and the Fezzan were to be united under the rule of King Idriss.

French diplomacy at this time was singularly maladroit. France made no determined effort either to win Libyan gratitude by wholeheartedly supporting the cause of independence or to defend her own interests in the Fezzan. To be sure, there was then every reason to regard that province as an economic liability. In area the Fezzan was about the size of France, but its population was estimated to number at most 54,000 and the average annual cash income of its inhabitants was only about 6,000 francs.[17] However, the Fezzan's misery was not due to its lack of water and of fertile soil —archaeological remains indicate the former existence of a flourishing civilization there—but to the incessant raids of the nomadic Touareg, Toubou, and Arabs, which had bled the country white. Its capital, Sebha, was no more than a wretched oversize village. Its only areas of relative prosperity were the three fertile oases of Sebha, Ghat, and Ghadames, which produced dates, cereals, and natron, but they were lost in the immense dunes and rocky summits of the surrounding desert. Petroleum had not yet been discovered in the Fezzan, and French interest in the area at that time centered chiefly on its strategic location in relation to French dependencies in north, west, and central Africa.

From ancient times the Fezzan has been one of the keys to central Africa. It is the avenue of overland communication between the Mediterranean and Negro worlds and between Egypt and the Sahara. It was the invasion route used by both the Arabs and Leclerc, and formerly the merchant caravans passed through it carrying slaves, gold, and ivory. Though its usefulness to traders has declined sharply in recent years, its strategic importance is still great, particularly for France, since it borders on the French Sahara, AEF, and French West Africa, and lies directly on the axis of communication between Paris, Brazzaville, and Madagascar.

In the hope of retaining the Fezzan after the war, the French maintained a garrison there, poured in considerable amounts of money, and assigned administrators and technicians to develop the region. Land was given to the inhabitants, artesian wells were dug, a health service was created, and schools were started.[18] After the United Nations decided to grant independence to Libya, the French agreed to continue subsidizing the Fezzan each year to the amount of about 800 million Metro. francs, but they showed no enthusiasm about helping to underwrite the far larger deficit of the new Libyan state. At the outset this was met by the British, who granted Libya 3.75 million pounds sterling a year; after 1954 the United States agreed to contribute $4 millions annually until 1960, and $1 million in each of the following 11 years. The *quid pro quo* for all of these subsidies was the granting by the Libyan government of permission to station troops and use airfields in the country. For the British and Americans this concession was confirmed by treaties made in July 1953 and September 1954 respectively, whereas the French military occupation of the Fezzan rested simply on a temporary agreement of December 1951 between France and Libya, renewable every six months.

If it had been obvious from the beginning that the sovereign state of Libya was not viable economically without considerable outside help, it was equally evident that it lacked basic unity. Although King Idriss was powerful as head of the Senoussi sect, he was opposed by some of the youthful intelligentsia of Tripoli, and, not having a direct heir, he had to cope with intrigues over the succession, which divided his family and court into rival factions.[19] In 1957 Thomas Hodgkin summed up the situation thus:[20]

> Libya is extremely dependent on British and, more recently, American aid. All these factors—the lack of a well-developed national consciousness, the absence of constitutional channels for expressing popular opinion, a monarchy that hovers between autocracy and constitutionalism, a Parliament with few roots in the electorate, a situation of continuing military and economic dependence upon the West—combine to produce a political void which has to be filled. Perhaps Nasserism will prove to be the liberating force. . . .

Libya indeed seemed to be an ideal instrument for Nasser's new policy of imperialism in Africa, and though he had no funds to bestow there, he lavished advisers and teachers on the Libyan government. King Idriss, by virtue of past loyalty and current subsidies, was bound up with the West, but the youthful elite of Tripoli regarded Egypt as the most dynamic of the Arab nations and the one most likely to oppose effectively Western ascendancy in Libya. This element was undoubtedly responsible for the agitation in Tripoli to get rid of the British occupation troops, for the government's active sponsorship of Algerian independence, and for Libya's joining the Arab League in March 1953. Despite the discovery of several Nasser-inspired plots against the Libyan government, which caused the expulsion between 1955 and 1958 of at least six Egyptian diplomats and military attachés[21] and reinforced the king's allegiance to his Anglo-American supporters, pro-Arab League sentiments were strong enough to impel the Libyans to take a strong stand against the French, to whom they felt no corresponding obligation. Shortly after the Algerian revolt broke out in November 1954, King Idriss informed Paris that he would not again renew the temporary agreement of 1951 nor would he sign a treaty of alliance with France similar to those he had made with Britain and the United States. Moreover, he insisted that all French troops be immediately evacuated from the Fezzan.

The existence of an independent state adjacent to French territories in north, central, and west Africa had never been relished by France, but the threatened occupation of the Fezzan by Libyan troops was even more distasteful, for it would trouble the allegiance of the nomadic tribes astride the frontier, bring the Arab League to the threshold of Tchad and the French Sahara, and jeopardize the defense of Algeria. It would also necessitate a costly rebuilding of the *piste* between north Africa and Tchad, which then passed through the Fezzan, as well as the reinforcing of the French military units that policed the eastern Sahara. The indignation aroused among the French by the king's move was directed not only against the Libyan government but also against the British and their own diplomats. The fact that Libya allowed some 20,000 Anglo-American troops to remain in the country but claimed that the presence of fewer than 500 French soldiers in the Fezzan was a menace to her sovereignty seemed patently unjust. The old wounds caused by British policy in Syria were reopened, for the French saw behind the king's intransigence the hand of some of his British civil servants who had served in the Near East during the war. And they alternately blamed their own diplomats either for letting themselves be duped by their so-called British allies or for failing to follow Britain's lead. By the end of 1954 France was indeed on the horns of a dilemma: if she yielded to Libyan pressure, the defense of Algeria would be impaired, yet she hardly dared to risk maintaining her troops by force in a country whose sovereignty she had formally recognized.

Long and delicate negotiations between the French and Libyan governments began at Paris on January 2, 1955, and were continued there and at Tripoli during the ensuing seven months; their course was not made smooth by a series of incidents that occurred during that period. In the same month that negotiations were opened, the Libyans, over the protest of the French Minister at Tripoli, sent a military mission from Koufra to occupy the oasis of Aouzou in Tibesti, nearly 100 kilometers inside French territory. This mission was stopped by a *méhariste* patrol and the Libyans had to turn back, but the discovery of potentially valuable mineral resources in Tibesti at about that time naturally strengthened Libya's irredentism in respect to this area. The whole question of the AEF-Libyan frontier was next brought to international attention by a resolution (No. 392-V) introduced in the United Nations proposing that the issue be submitted to the arbitration of a third party chosen by France and Libya or by the UN Secretary-General. A few weeks later the French had to exert pressure in both London and Tripoli to prevent the dispatch of a Libyan military column with a British escort to Tibesti,[22] and France firmly refused to withdraw her troops from the Fezzan while the Franco-Libyan negotiations were going on. So an agreement was finally reached and a draft treaty initialed on August 10, 1955, in which both parties pledged "peace, good relations, and the security of the frontier regions."

By its terms France agreed to remove her troops from the Fezzan in return for Libya's pledge that their place would be taken exclusively by Libyan forces, that facilities would be granted for the passage through the Fezzan of a specified number of French military convoys, that French technicians would continue to service the airports of Ghat and Ghadames, and that French planes could freely land there for five years and at Sebha for two years, after which these airfields and their equipment would become Libyan property. In case of aggression by any third party there was to be mutual consultation in regard to the defense of the Fezzan. As to the economic aspects of this treaty, France promised to help Libya technically to develop its agricultural and industrial resources, and in the cultural domain undertook to provide scholarships for Libyans in French educational institutions and French teachers for Libyan schools. Annexed to the treaty was a subsidiary agreement regulating the transfrontier caravan and animal traffic and also the policing of the region. In Libyan eyes the main virtue of this treaty was France's recognition in fact and in law of their government's sovereignty over the Fezzan. From the French viewpoint the major advantages were Libya's abandonment of her designs on Tibesti and her willingness to accept a rectification of the frontier southward from the Ghat-Ghadames area by a joint Franco-Libyan commission.

In France the treaty aroused opposition both in Parliament and outside. It was said that France had got very little in return for abandoning the Fezzanese oases, which had made it possible for a handful of French troops easily and economically to guard all the *pistes* in that sensitive region. Libya had refused not only to let France reoccupy the Fezzan in case of war and to suppress the anti-French activities of Algerian rebels in the country, but even to sign a treaty of alliance. French public opinion was irked by the Libyan press, which played up the treaty as indicating France's capitulation to the Arab League, and was alarmed by the establishment of a heavily staffed Soviet Embassy at Tripoli in 1956 by invitation of the Libyan government. But it was above all the Libyans' active championing of Algerian independence and the evidence of increasing arms-smuggling by the FLN from Libyan bases that gave pause to the French government and general staff. Ben Bella, it was reported, intended with the Libyans' consent to establish bases at Ghat and Ghadames, and other stories had it that Algerian cadres were being trained at a military school set up at Marsa-Matrouk and that the Ajjer nomads were being propagandized and armed by emissaries sent to Tibesti from Tripoli. Outstanding French diplomats and politicians urged Parliament to reject the Libyan treaty "as spectacularly as possible," yet on the eve of the date set by the treaty for the French withdrawal from the Fezzan, Parliament ratified it by a large majority after a short and calm debate.[23] The difficult position internationally in which the abortive Suez invasion earlier that month had placed France was largely responsible for this outcome: the government pressed Parliament to accept the treaty as offering the best terms that could be hoped for under the circumstances.

Without waiting for ratification of the treaty, the French military authorities began to carry out a program revising the defense system in the eastern Sahara, the cost of which, it was estimated in 1956, would come to some 600 million francs. In a speech to the French Union Assembly on December 10, 1957, the Minister for the Sahara, Max Lejeune, was able to report that old *pistes* in the region had been improved, a new one was being built across the Tassili des Ajjers wholly in French territory, work had been completed on demarcating the new frontier between Ghat and Ghadames, new units had been sent to Saharan posts, and old ones— especially at Djanet and Fort Flatters—had been strengthened and equipped with more motor vehicles and planes. The tempo at which these measures were carried out had been accelerated by a series of incidents that occurred during 1957. Not only had the flow of arms and money from Benghazi and Tripoli to Algeria been stepped up, but two raids in the Ghat area from the Libyan side of the frontier, in September and October, showed that the FLN was trying to open a new theater of operations in the south Sahara.

These incidents not only alarmed the French authorities but began to disturb the British as well, for their agents had begun prospecting for oil in the Libyan Sahara. Britain's counsels of moderation were apparently heeded by the Libyan government, already alarmed by Egyptian intrigues in the country. By the end of November the Algerians had reportedly left the Fezzan at the insistence of the Libyan authorities,[24] and their departure had a calming effect on the frontier tribes. Caïd Brahim, chief of the Tassili Touareg, reiterated his loyalty to France, and the hundred or more members of his tribe who had been placed at the disposal of the FLN by the mayor of Ghat asked the French for forgiveness.[25] Thereafter relations with the Libyans improved to the point where, in December 1957, the French government could begin negotiations for the evacuation of Saharan oil through their territory.[26]

Though undoubtedly Libya remained as opposed as ever to France's exerting any influence in the Fezzan, its government was subjected to too many internal strains and was too weak economically to give active support to the Algerians against the French in the Sahara. Moreover, the French had an effective means of retaliation in the control they exercised over the Fezzani living in Tchad, though this was to some extent a two-edged weapon. Libyans own a majority of the palm groves in Tibesti, and the heir to the aged Touareg caïd Brahim lives in the Fezzan. However, the chief of the Chorfa tribe, pious Senoussi who have been living at Ati in Tchad since the Italian conquest of Libya, is next in line to suceed King Idriss.[27]

Furthermore, several thousand members of the Ouled Suliman, the tribe whose chief is *wali* (governor) of the Fezzan, are residents of Tchad, and as one of its members told Thomas Hodgkin, "if our government makes things too difficult for the French, the French can always make things difficult for the Ouled Suliman."[28] Most of the Libyan merchants living at Fort Lamy are peaceable citizens anxious that no incident should lead to their expulsion from French territory. The French refused the Libyans' requests in 1956 and 1957 to permit them to establish a consulate in Tchad to look after the interests of their nationals. As one French Union Assemblyman for Tchad said bluntly: "The Fezzani in Tchad don't need such protection. If they do not return to Libya it is simply because they prefer to remain in Tchad."[29]

For the present the Fezzani of Tchad are certainly better off economically than are their compatriots in Libya, but the situation may change radically if the Fezzan proves to be as oil-rich as many anticipate. This possibility has not escaped the attention of some Negro nationalists in French territory, a few of whom seem to be developing counterirredentist aspirations in regard to the Fezzan. Cheikh Anta Diop, the scholarly West African exponent of *négritude*, writing in *Présence Africaine* (December 1956–January 1957) stated that he did not believe in the existence of a Libyan national consciousness and expressed the hope that Libya would turn toward Black Africa. In his eyes this would have the advantage of splitting the Arab world and of giving Negro Africa the outlet to the Mediterranean that it badly needs.

The Belgian Congo

To those who visit both banks of the Congo, the contrast between the prosperity of the Belgian side and the poverty of AEF is strikingly symbolized by the skyscrapers of dynamic Léopoldville situated only four kilometers across Stanley Pool from Brazzaville. Because of the sharing of an easily traversed water frontier over a great distance, and of the French language spoken on both sides of the river, relations have tended to be closer between these two territories than between AEF and any other nearby European dependency.

For many years the Belgian Congo has provided employment for several thousand Brazzaville workers and has been a paradise for smugglers; for the French of the federation it has been an object of envy, emulation, and competition. To offset the feeling of inferiority caused by the Belgian Congo's wealth, the French have attributed to the Belgians all the faults of the *nouveaux riches*. As to the Belgians, when they thought about AEF at all, it was with the patronizing condescension reserved for poor relations whom they were willing to help out from time to time but who could easily become—in the political sphere—a dangerous nuisance. While economic exchanges predominated before World War II and have remained important since that time, Franco-Belgian relations in recent years have been increasingly influenced by political developments on the French side since 1946.

Contacts between AEF and the Congo have been most constructive in the technico-economic domains, though occasionally they have been fool-ishly competitive. The results of long-term scientific experimentation in such matters as the cultivation of crops and of animal husbandry have been generously shared by the Belgians with their trans-Congo neighbors, and Belgian skills and capital have greatly aided AEF's cotton industry. On the whole, the French have been grateful for this aid, though during the 1930's voices were occasionally raised against the "foreign interests" that were "taking over AEF." Concrete evidences of French chauvinism that have been generally more harmful are the wasteful duplication of certain facilities along both banks of the Congo, though the policy adopted in recent years by the responsible authorities in both territories has aimed at complementary rather than competitive public works. But for many years, the mere fact that one of these colonial powers launched an enterprise was seemingly enough to impel the other to do likewise. Thus parallel railroad lines run along both banks of the Congo, river ports have been built op-posite each other on the shores of Stanley Pool, two large airfields have been constructed to serve Léopoldville and Brazzaville respectively, and now the Belgians and French propose to build costly hydroelectric dams not far apart at Inga and Kouilou, each of which will be capable of generating more electricity than can conceivably be used in the whole region.

Nevertheless, there has been considerable cooperation between the two territories in some economic sectors. For a few years the inhabitants of Léopoldville bought electric current from the generating plant at Djoué, near Brazzaville; in 1952 the French began negotiating with the Belgians for use of the Léopoldville-Matadi pipeline to bring fuel in from the coast to provision AEF; and in 1953 the Belgians agreed to permit the federation's railroad to transport the copper ores purchased in the Congo for French industries. Belgian and French technicians have cooperated in marking the channel of the Congo River and in destroying growths of the water hyacinth that has become a menace to river navigation. Steps have been taken jointly to suppress the contraband trade that has developed because of the ease with which the Congo can be crossed in most places where it forms the common frontier and of the abundance of comparatively cheap consumer goods available in Belgian territory. In regard to regular com-mercial exchanges, AEF has always had an unfavorable balance of trade with its Belgian neighbor,[30] for meat is the only product of the federation that is readily salable in the Congo. Even that export has not been a pay-ing proposition, since the transport of meat by plane is very costly and the Belgians prefer to ship, as cargo for the return flight, Kivu tea rather than the textiles and bicycles that the populations of Tchad and Oubangui want to buy. Indeed, the trade deficit for AEF is so chronic that each year the Paris Office des Changes must allocate 130 million Belgian Congo francs to finance the transfrontier trade.

Aside from the importation of some Congolese politico-religious sects, relations in the political sphere have been just as lopsided, though in the direction opposite to that taken by commercial exchanges. During the two world wars the Belgians were actively helpful to the French in fighting their common European enemy. In 1915 Belgian troops joined those of Britain and France in ousting the Germans from the Cameroons and Togo. In the summer of 1940, Belgium was the first government to recognize the Free French and to offer refuge and aid at Léopoldville to the Frenchmen conspiring against the Vichy-dominated regime at Brazzaville. But when it came to their dealings with the African populations, the Belgians pursued a policy sharply divergent from that of the French. If Belgium has enabled the Congolese Africans to attain the highest living standards on the dark continent, the French have offered their Africans the dignity of citizenship, the right to organize political parties and labor unions, and increasing participation in the government of their country. The Belgians were indifferent to this French policy but at the same time alarmed by it. According to the able French correspondent, André Blanchet,[31] no Belgian official has ever dreamed of applying such a policy to the Congo or has had enough curiosity about its functioning to cross Stanley Pool and attend a session of the AEF Grand Council. Until the January 1959 riots broke out at Léopoldville, the Belgian residents of that town apparently believed that political ferment would never develop from inside the Congo but only through contagion from the French side of the river. In fact, whenever disturbances occurred in AEF, they tried to seal off their territory from such political infection by simply stopping the Congo ferry services.

During the fall of 1958 the Belgians in the Congo were reportedly anxious and reassured by turns. De Gaulle's speech at Brazzaville in August, in which independence for French Africa was mentioned officially for the first time, aroused the fears of Belgian conservatives. These were somewhat calmed by AEF's virtually unanimous vote in favor of joining the Franco-African Community in the September 28 referendum, but exactly two months later the Belgians were once again alarmed by the transformation of the territory of the Moyen-Congo into the Republic of the Congo. Its premier, Fulbert Youlou, was known to be on friendly terms with Kasavubu, leader of the most important Léopoldville political organization, the Abako (Association du Bas-Congo), and to share with him the ambition to reunite in one group the Bakongo living in AEF, the Congo, and Angola.[32]

CHAPTER 11

Finances

Public Investment and the Plan

AEF's basic equipment, or infrastructure, has been built up almost wholly by the use of French public money, whereas private capital—in much smaller amounts—has been invested primarily in commercial and secondarily in production and transportation enterprises.

Before World War II, the aid supplied to AEF by France took the form of loans (see p. 123) for public works and of subsidies to meet the federation's budgetary deficits and even interest payments on its public debt. Since 1947 this situation has not fundamentally changed, though the form taken by public investments has been altered and the sums involved have greatly increased, and Metropolitan France has felt impelled to take over an ever-larger share in the financing of all types of investment except in the commercial and mining spheres. In place of the haphazard and grudging grant of successive loans to finance isolated public works in AEF, that federation was thenceforth to be developed systematically and substantially within the framework of the overseas section of the Monnet Plan for Modernization and Equipment (usually referred to simply as the Plan). By a law passed on April 30, 1946, there came into being a fund called FIDES (Fonds d'Investissement pour le Développement Economique et Social), to be financed by annual subsidies from the Metropolitan budgets and contributions from the territories concerned. An organization entitled the CCOM (Caisse Centrale de la France d'Outre-Mer), a wartime creation, was at the same time empowered to handle the FIDES accounts and also to grant long-term loans at low interest rates from other funds given it directly by the French government. Such loans were to be made to public bodies and enterprises or for specific projects designed, like FIDES itself, to transform the Overseas Territories into modern countries.

In AEF, as elsewhere in French Africa, FIDES provided an unprecedented stimulus to development in both the social and economic domains, but its impact was felt less strongly and less immediately there than in French West Africa. For one thing, smaller and less populous AEF naturally received a more modest share of FIDES funds than did its western neighbor. More important, FIDES found there an even less developed economic base on which to operate than in French West Africa. Pre-World War II loans had been used almost wholly in the southern territories, mainly for the construction of a single railroad and two ports, and the economy of the rest of the federation remained almost devoid of infrastructure. Unexpectedly, however, World War II temporarily brought a financial ease to the federation that enabled it for the first time not only to get rid of almost all its back debt but even to undertake some construction works financed from its own resources.

During the war, AEF set up a Supporting Fund for Agricultural Products that helped crop expansion; a Rubber Bonus Account that aided in building roads, schools, and dispensaries in the rubber-producing regions; and a War Profits Fund that was used to improve the ports of Pointe Noire and Owendo.[1] After the Liberation, liquidation of the wartime Caisse de Péréquation made it possible to build some local airfields. Then, beginning in 1948, a Cotton Supporting Fund, financed largely through local contributions, was diverted to the construction of roads and works of general usefulness in Oubangui and Tchad—regions that until then had not benefited by any development program. But by this time AEF was beginning to be submerged once more in debt and, in any case, its wartime spurt of auto-financed equipment works had been not only short-lived but spotty. Moreover, its inadequate prewar infrastructure had been subjected to exceptionally heavy pressure and was worn out, and what had been constructed during the war suffered from having been jerry-built with such few and scanty materials as were then available. Thus AEF, always far behind French West Africa in regard to infrastructure and skilled manpower, had on hand neither the equipment, the building enterprises, nor the labor force required to carry out the Plan. Until these could be set up, a large portion of the credits allotted to the federation by FIDES went unused and were either blocked in Paris or simply turned over to the federal or territorial reserve funds.

Delay in carrying out the Plan was naturally longest in the backward northern territories, but even in the south, work on it did not really get under way until about 1950. By that time it had become obvious that grave mistakes had been made as to both the Plan's program and its execution, for which the FIDES directorate and the AEF authorities blamed each other. Since there was no shortage of public investment money at this time, these mutual recriminations centered on the choice of projects and of organizations or persons to handle the funds involved in executing them. In the early stages the Plan had aroused so much enthusiasm and gratitude in AEF that over-high hopes were placed on the benefits it would soon bring to the federation. Then delays occurred that could be attributed not only to practical difficulties but to "procedural obstruction" on the part of the Paris authorities. Besides the uncertainty as to the global sum that might be voted each year by Parliament for carrying out the Plan in the Overseas Territories, there was the additional unknown factor of the time required for the directorate of FIDES to make up its mind as to how much money would be available and for what projects in AEF. In view of the general ignorance about AEF's resources and their lack of development, it was inevitable that much time and energy should be wasted, but the

federation's newly elected assemblymen came increasingly to resent what
they felt to be the FIDES directorate's ill-informed and arbitrary decisions.
After 1952, when AEF had to begin paying interest on CCOM loans and
for the upkeep of FIDES local operations, and the funds available to the
federation shrank, an increasingly sharp struggle developed between Brazzaville and Paris for control over the orientation and execution of the Plan.

It was not until half a year after passage of the law creating FIDES
that the government-general of AEF was asked to draw up a ten-year
development project under the Plan—and within two months' time. Fortunately, the federal economic services had already been reorganized on
March 1, 1946, with the establishment of an over-all Directorate of Economic Services charged with the study and handling of all economic questions affecting AEF. On the following December 12, at Brazzaville, a
special committee comprising the heads of all relevant services approved
the hastily drawn-up program for AEF and also created a permanent secretariat for the Plan. Despite the speed with which AEF acted, the FIDES
directorate claimed that the federation's program had been submitted too
late to be included in its current budget and had also failed to follow the
directives it had issued. A revised edition was approved by the government-
general in May 1947, but the next month the Paris authorities proposed
further modifications. In fact, the Plan for 1947 had to be revised seven
times before it was finally accepted by FIDES. And when the program
for 1948 began to meet with the same alterations and delays, the Grand
Councilors unanimously passed a resolution asking that no further changes
be made in it by FIDES except for "urgent reasons," that the original time
schedule be adhered to, and that the territorial assemblies be given the
opportunity to express their views on the programs for their respective areas.
President Flandre expressed himself even more freely:[2]

> Paris has tried to regulate every detail of our utilization of the Plan credits
> and so has made us lose precious time. We have been treated as if we were
> minor children, unworthy of having confidence placed in us.

As finally approved in October 1948, AEF's ten-year Plan for the 1947–
56 period totaled 51 billion CFA francs. Of this sum, 61.4 per cent was
to be allotted to the infrastructure, 14.3 per cent to production, and 24.3
per cent to social enterprises. By administrative areas, the federation (including the railroad and the port of Pointe Noire) were to get 7,866,300,000
francs; Gabon, 10,437,730,000 francs; Moyen-Congo, 10,026,750,000 francs;
Oubangui, 10,221,450,000 francs; and Tchad, 12,972,750,000 francs. As to the
specific programs approved, the FIDES directorate had turned down a
number of the projects submitted by AEF on the ground that they had not
been sufficiently studied or their cost not accurately estimated. The Grand
Council, for its part, claimed that some of the schemes approved by FIDES
did not correspond to the federation's real or greatest needs, and began
to show concern as to how far the whole Plan was going to affect adversely
AEF's financial position. According to the Paris planners, FIDES was

to provide money for construction, but it was up to the overseas beneficiaries to supply the sums required for the maintenance of what FIDES had built and for the lodging and salaries of the new personnel involved. It was also at this time that AEF was experiencing its worst practical difficulties in carrying out the Plan's first projects. Equipment and material ordered from abroad were slow in being delivered, and it was also found that the work projected for AEF was on too small a scale to attract big Metropolitan building companies to the federation unless they were guaranteed against financial loss.[3] Moreover, it was now realized that execution of the Plan required spending more time and money in research and detailed studies of the projects approved. Pending solution of these various problems, FIDES blocked a large portion of the credits allocated to AEF, and this so aroused the Grand Councilors' resentment that they decided to send a delegation of protest to Paris in the late fall of 1949.

Early in 1950 the Grand Councilors were further disconcerted to learn not only that smaller funds would be made available to AEF that year but that the whole ten-year Plan had now been reorganized into a series of four-year Plans. In the heated debates that ensued as to the territorial division of the depleted FIDES credits, the spirit of federal solidarity wore thin and the Grand Council came within an ace of voting to refuse acceptance of the Plan in its existing form.[4] High Commissioner Cornut-Gentille, after admitting that perhaps AEF had drawn up "too grandiose" an initial program, himself went to Paris, where he spent four months working out a new arrangement. Not only did he obtain an increase of a billion CFA francs in AEF's current allocation, but he persuaded some French companies to continue working in the federation despite little prospect of their being paid in the near future. Though somewhat mollified by his success, the Grand Councilors insisted that henceforth they and not the FIDES directorate must decide what projects should be carried out in AEF. They also pleaded that an end be put to the uncertainties surrounding both the program and its financing that were making long-term planning impossible, halting work on new projects, and even leading to the repatriation of some technicians who had been brought out to the federation at great expense.[5] Obviously the Plan for AEF required drastic revision, particularly its road program, which, if it were carried out as originally planned, would absorb almost all the money currently available. Thus far the Africans' living standards had not been appreciably raised, production had not been increased to the point where it could pay maintenance costs, and the main beneficiaries in AEF appeared to be the big Metropolitan construction firms, which were making profits without commensurate accomplishments in terms of new building.[6] Just at the time when the practical and technical difficulties that had slowed down execution of the Plan seemed on the point of being solved, the funds to carry it out were cut and the FIDES directorate radically revised its orientation without taking into account the criticisms and pleas of the federation's elected representatives. Thus by late 1951 a general feeling of disillusionment about the Plan began to pervade AEF, and it was shared by Metropolitan France, though for different reasons.

From 1947 through June 1950, FIDES had placed at the disposal of the federation over 16 billion CFA francs, in addition to which it had allocated large subsidies to the local branches of various research organizations. Of these credits France was to contribute 55 per cent and the territories concerned 45 per cent, but in reality France supplied almost the total amount of long-term low-interest loans (20–25 years, at 2 per cent) granted to AEF public bodies through the CCOM. The federation not only had made almost no financial contributions toward its own equipment but was hard pressed to begin paying in 1952 the interest on such loans and the upkeep charges on such projects as had been completed. As matters had turned out, a larger proportion of the available FIDES funds than originally intended had been spent on the means of communication and less on the development of production. Indeed, the term "Plan of Development" as applied to a country so devoid of basic equipment as AEF was a misnomer, and it should, rather, have been called a "Plan of Creation." So the FIDES directorate decided that for the sake of both the Metropolitan and the African taxpayers it must place more stress on increasing overseas production as the only possible hope of enabling the enterprises financed by the Plan eventually to pay their own way.

Yet a backward glance, rather than contemplation of the immense task that lay ahead, might have heartened the planners of both France and the federation. Progress, though uneven, had been real and AEF's economy was now more vigorous than before the war. FIDES had so improved AEF's infrastructure that it had attracted investments by private capital, though perhaps not on such a scale as had been hoped for. Though no precise data were as yet established regarding the federation's mineral wealth, maps had been drawn and an inventory taken of its other resources, more credit facilities had been made available, labor was being trained and building enterprises were under way, a beginning had been made on public housing and urbanization plans, and new schools and hospitals had been built. Living conditions for Europeans had been markedly improved, those for Africans less so, but the increasing sale of consumer goods to the native population showed a slow but undeniable rise in their purchasing power. On the debit side of the ledger, the rural economy had been neglected in favor of the urban centers, social expenditures had too rapidly outdistanced those devoted to economic improvements, the distribution of credits among the four territories had proved to be inequitable, and some of the main accomplishments of FIDES were out of line with the federation's development and needs. The execution of Tchad's projects, for example, lagged far behind those of the southern territories, and Gabon rightly complained of the slowness and costliness of the work done on its roads and ports. That AEF's infrastructure had been strengthened beyond its productive capacity was shown by the fact that the railroad was unable to find the freight it could now carry and that the port of Pointe Noire did not receive the tonnages it was already equipped to handle.

When the second four-year Plan (1952–56) was drawn up, it was hoped that the experience gained over the past years might serve as lessons to the Paris authorities, but once again they failed to see eye to eye with AEF's elected assemblymen. The Plan's new aim was to increase both agricultural and industrial production in the perspective of a European community, and its authors failed to mention the Africans' main aspiration that the Plan should raise the level of living of the overseas population. AEF's new High Commissioner, Paul Chauvet, felt compelled to follow his predecessor's path to Paris in order to persuade the FIDES directorate that the position of his federation differed from that of other overseas territories. He stressed AEF's dangerous dependence on wood and cotton exports and the small scale of all its output. The federation's list of exports might look varied and impressive, but even the most substantial of them could never loom large in the French market, let alone the world market.[7] To be sure, transportation charges, both internal and external, accounted for a good part of its high production costs, but even if AEF were fully equipped and its economy further diversified, it probably could never expect a brilliant economic future. In return for the federation's pledge to increase the tonnage of its exportable products and lower their cost, it was to be permitted to go on with such projects as those of the Niari and Logone valleys (see pp. 500, 458), initiate the building of some schools and health centers, particularly in rural areas, and continue its experiments with *paysannats* and the regrouping of villages (see pp. 171–73). The year 1952 was to mark a transition between the first and second Plans, during which the Overseas Ministry would send a mission to AEF to study and discuss on the spot just which projects should be most stressed during the ensuing four years. For that whole period AEF was to be allocated 17.5 billion CFA francs, of which 45 per cent would go to production, 34 per cent to basic equipment, and 21 per cent to social works.[8] As to the territorial division of FIDES credits, Gabon and Moyen-Congo each would receive 16 per cent, Oubangui 20 per cent, Tchad 34 per cent, and the federation itself 13 per cent.

On the whole, the Grand Council was gratified by these concessions. Some members, however, complained that the new Plan sacrificed the human to the economic element, while others still criticized the procedure of "financing the Plan each year at imprecise dates with variable sums for changing objectives."[9] The change in the Plan's orientation coincided with the beginning of the severe financial crisis through which AEF passed in 1952 and 1953. Because the laws passed by Parliament during this period increased AEF's obligatory expenditures to the point where they were absorbing virtually all of the territorial and federal revenues, criticism of basic French policies was revived and intensified. This gave cogency to the argument that Metropolitan France should assume responsibility for some of the secondary projects (such as the improvement of regional airfields) that were normally financed from local resources. Furthermore, since "AEF was a generation behind other French Black African areas," the FIDES directorate was urged to make need, rather than economic

importance, the criterion for its division of funds among the various overseas territories.

To some of these pleas France proved responsive, in view of the worsening financial position of all the French Black African dependencies. On
July 1, 1953, she agreed to increase from 55 per cent to 75 per cent her subsidies for the overseas equipment program; in mid-1955 she raised this to
100 per cent on certain grants for social and production enterprises; and
by January 1, 1956, she had assumed financial responsibility, without prospect of reimbursement, for 90 per cent of the Plan's total expenditures.
In the meantime, the federation's budgets were showing signs of recovery,
thanks to both a revival of its foreign trade and increased production—
the latter being a long-term consequence of works initiated under the first
Plan. After several years during which it could not afford any such largesse,
AEF was able in 1955 to allocate from its own resources modest sums
toward its own equipment. In 1955 also the Grand Councilors made some
progress in the matter of procedure and control over the Plan, though they
continued to complain of the steady shrinkage in the funds allocated to
AEF by FIDES. On May 1, 1955, Parliament agreed to vote FIDES
credits for a period covering a number of years and to make more lenient
terms on loans granted to its Black African territories. This put an end
to a long-standing grievance of the Grand Councilors, to the effect that
each year FIDES submitted to them at the last possible moment a program
for the federation that had to be accepted virtually *in toto* under pain of
indefinitely delaying its execution because of the time required to get
FIDES approval of any changes they proposed. Then a decree of December 1, 1955, reorganized the structure of FIDES so that not only were
African representatives given more voice and responsibility for determining
what local works should be carried out under the Plan but local funds
were channeled into developing the production and social equipment of
their respective territories.[10]

Consequently, when FIDES not unexpectedly reduced the total sum
available to AEF under the third four-year Plan, this cut was largely
offset by France's assumption of some of the expenditures formerly financed
from local resources. The new division of operations as well as of FIDES
credits, as between the *section commune* and the territorial sections, gave
rise to criticism and disputes, and this breach in federal solidarity naturally
was widened by passage of the *loi-cadre* in June 1956. In fact, some of the
assemblies had already asked that the *section commune* take over several
of the projects assigned to their territorial sections, yet refused to hand
over to the *section commune* the corresponding credits, voting to use them
instead for other local purposes.[11] In 1957 and again in 1958, the Plan
credits originally allocated to the territorial sections were reduced, to the
benefit of the *section commune,* though each assembly still had more funds
at its disposal than formerly. While some assemblymen claimed that this
transfer had been made because France still exercised control over the
section commune, the FIDES directorate said that it had been due to the

need to allocate more funds to such schemes as the Kouilou dam, whose execution would be of benefit to several territories.[12]

In 1959 FIDES became the Fonds d'Aide et de Coopération (FAC) so as to make its name conform more clearly to the new political realities, and also in that year the first funds were allocated to the four republics by the Common Market countries. A third source of public money recently invested in the area was an initial grant made to Tchad by the OCRS in pursuance of an agreement signed on August 3, 1959.

Private Investments

Only for a few years and in certain enterprises have investments made by private capital in AEF matched those made from French public funds. The same situation has prevailed in French West Africa, but the total of both types of investments there was larger and foreign capital did not play so important a role as in AEF, particularly in the period before World War I. The special international status accorded AEF by the Act of Berlin and the privileges granted to concessionary companies in the late nineteenth and early twentieth centuries attracted private foreign capitalists, particularly from nearby Belgian Congo, where somewhat analogous conditions prevailed. The decline of the concessionary regime curtailed the interest of private foreign investors in AEF, and it was not revived to any marked degree until the discovery of Gabon's mineral wealth reawakened it in the late 1950's.

According to a British estimate made in 1936, private investments in AEF then totaled about £15 million, or only a fourth the sum of public investments. Other experts have disputed these figures, but all are agreed that proportionately they are fairly accurate and that private investments were mainly concentrated in trading firms.[13] Foreign capital, chiefly Belgian, dominated AEF's cotton companies and its lone mining enterprise in the Niari region, Dutch capitalists controlled transportation in Tchad and northern Oubangui, and the British invested mainly in such commercial enterprises as Patterson-Ziconis and Unilever's Société Commerciale du Kouilou-Niari. The scale of such foreign holdings, particularly when compared with the meager sums invested by Metropolitan capitalists, alarmed some patriots in France and angered French settlers in AEF. "The foreign trusts," wrote Homet in 1934,[14] "are masters of our colony and that is why everything is done to prevent French colonists from going there." That same year Susset, head of a Parliamentary mission to AEF, came to the same conclusion:[15]

> I am convinced that we will never get out of our colonies what we have the right to expect so long as we let all those organizations which have foreign capital as their base install themselves there and virtually take over the soil and its products. These foreign companies profit handsomely from our hospitality and efforts to improve the infrastructure, and drain our wealth.

Actually there was no cause for alarm, for AEF was too poor and too undeveloped to yield to any investors profits large enough to arouse covetous designs that might endanger France's sovereignty over the federation.

One of the main motives behind the great increase in French public investments in AEF after 1946 was to encourage private capital to follow in its wake. It was realized that this would not occur unless the state first undertook the research and experimentation required to show which enterprises were likely to become profitable. Hence France accepted the burden of setting up a costly infrastructure, research stations, and credit institutions so as to create conditions favorable for private investors to enter the field. For a few years it looked as if this policy had borne fruit. During the first four-year Plan, FIDES invested in AEF an average of 3.5 billion CFA francs annually. In 1950, private investments totaled 3 billion CFA francs and in 1951 and 1952 they came to 3.5 billion, thus about equalling those made from public funds. In that period private capital was attracted to building enterprises and the purchase of equipment materials in approximately equal parts. Aside from the state companies and those in which private as well as public funds were involved (called companies of "mixed economy"), 348 new firms were founded in AEF between 1947 and 1950, of which by far the largest number and the most heavily capitalized were in the commercial field.[16] The capital of the 162 companies already in existence before 1947 was increased during that period by a total of 2,646 million CFA francs. It should be noted, however, that a considerable portion of these so-called "private" capital funds was derived from loans granted by the CCOM to help launch new enterprises or to enlarge those already operating in AEF.

From 1952 on, the situation changed markedly. Credit became much tighter in France, and there was a shrinkage in both public and private investments in AEF just at the time when the federation itself was undergoing a trade recession. In that year the sums invested by private capital came to only a little more than one-third of the total of public investments.[17] Moreover, French investors were becoming worried at that time by the large proportion of public funds going into financially unproductive social works. The federation's Chambers of Commerce and its employers' organization (COLPAEF, or Comité de Liaison du Patronat de l'AEF) warned that neither Metropolitan France nor AEF could afford to sustain the tempo of such investments or to pay for the upkeep of the works being financed by them, and the years that followed confirmed their worst fears.[18] A few new industries, such as the Niari sugar mill, were indeed started, but their financial success was dubious, and in the meantime many of the small enterprises initiated in AEF after the war failed. The total of private investments in the federation was shrinking each year, and in any case they were not serving appreciably to increase AEF's production. Some of the larger established enterprises continued in existence, but their field of operations tended to contract rather than to expand.

In 1956 the total of private investments in AEF came to 2,100 million CFA francs, but of this only 500 million went toward the creation of new companies.[19] By far the largest single sum (over 1,642 million) represented an increase in the capital of a single firm, the Société des Pétroles d'AEF (SPAEF); 256 million were invested in agricultural and animal husbandry enterprises, 149 million in construction companies, 129 million in the wood industries, and 265 million in mining. The year 1957 saw a sharp upturn in the investment picture because of a rekindling of interest in AEF's mineral resources, and also a concurrent lowering of the fiscal charges imposed by the federation and territories on certain types of enterprises whose activities were expected to benefit the federation's economy. Private investments in AEF that year rose to 8 billion CFA francs, but once again SPAEF was responsible for the major share of this increase (6 billion); about a half-billion represented the capital of 50 new companies, and the balance came from capital increases by 34 existing firms, notably the Compagnie Cotonnière Equatoriale Française (COTONFRAN). In 1958, 79 established companies added nearly 4 billion CFA francs to their capital funds, and 57 new firms with a total of more than 754 million CFA francs of capital entered the AEF scene. Reinvested profits accounted for a goodly proportion of these capital growths, and it looked as if the political uncertainties of that year had slowed down investments from both public and private sources.[20]

Nevertheless, the mineral deposits of Gabon are likely to attract annual increments in the amount of capital invested in AEF's mining industries; the progress made by the Common Market organization probably will be accompanied by larger investments in the federation by France's European partners; and completion of the Kouilou dam is expected to draw a big influx of capital from various sources to the Pointe Noire region. Propitious to this development is the recent change in attitude toward foreign capital investments on the part of many of the African elite. Unhappy memories of the concessionary-regime period made them suspicious of such investments for many years as "politically dangerous."[21] Although it cannot be said that the majority of AEF's assemblymen are as yet enthusiastic about investments other than those coming from the franc zone, Gabon's political leaders are eager to attract foreign private capital to their territory.[22] Most of the governments of AEF's new republics seem willing to lower further the duties on imported equipment and materials and to give long-term fiscal guarantees to foreign investors on two conditions. One is that the enterprise concerned must be likely to benefit the local populations, and the other, that the indigenous materials utilized be processed so far as possible on the spot.

Currency and Banking

Until 1941, the monetary system of France was in use in AEF, as in French West Africa, although the local franc that circulated in both federations was issued by the Banque de l'Afrique Occidentale Française (BAO). As a result of AEF's opting for Free France during World War II, its credit system and banknote issue were completely revised. The severing of its ties with France and with Vichy-dominated French West Africa led to the creation of a new bank of issue for AEF and Cameroun. This privilege was accorded in July 1942 to the Caisse Centrale de la France

Libre, which had been established in December 1941 and which, after the war, was renamed the Caisse Centrale de la France d'Outre-Mer (CCOM). The Free French authorities felt that AEF's strategic position and backward economy called for the installation of a public monetary organization that would not only issue banknotes but would be in a position to help finance an equipment program and transform the federation's *économie de traite*—the exchange of raw materials against manufactured goods.

By a law of September 26, 1948, the CCOM's statutes were somewhat modified and its management placed under an 18-man committee, and it was empowered not only to handle the FIDES accounts but also to grant long-term loans at low interest rates from other funds given it directly by the French government. Branches of the CCOM were set up in all of AEF's territorial capitals, later including Pointe Noire after that town replaced Brazzaville as the capital of Moyen-Congo. From the outset, the CCOM was well received in AEF,[23] though this was due in part to a fear that if it were suppressed AEF might be made directly dependent on the French Ministry of Finance. Throughout French Black Africa that Ministry was blamed as being mainly responsible for successive currency devaluations that gravely harmed the economy of both federations and was scored for the parsimony with which it allocated credits for the Overseas Territories.

On December 25, 1945, the CFA (Colonies Françaises d'Afrique) franc was created for France's tropical African dependencies and Madagascar. AEF's currency thus underwent a devaluation, though the measure had been designed to protect colonial money from the decline in value which the Metropolitan franc had suffered as a result of the war. This move, which had been secretly and unilaterally decided upon in Paris, aroused a great outcry in French West Africa. In AEF, on the other hand, it was accepted in relative calm as simply "one among a number of postwar measures."[24] Quite different was the reception given there to the devaluation of January 26, 1948, and to the decree of October 17 of the same year, which made a single CFA franc equivalent to two Metro. francs. One of its deputies[25] claimed that the harm done to AEF's economy would be far greater than that to French West Africa: the latter federation had undergone only two postwar devaluations whereas AEF had been subjected to three since February 1944 and was, moreover, generally more vulnerable because a large part of AEF was under the "open-door" regime. For a short time, devaluation might help AEF's exports, but it would certainly increase vastly the cost of the imports on which it was dependent. A 1947 study of family budgets in that federation had shown that 67 per cent of expenditures was for merchandise of foreign origin, for France at that time was in no position to supply the consumer or equipment goods that AEF vitally needed. Now AEF would be compelled to pay far higher prices for the articles of prime necessity that were available only in hard-currency markets.

The sense of having been unfairly treated by Metropolitan France that pervaded AEF throughout 1948 might not have become so acute had France been more generous in the first postwar years about returning to the federation a larger share of its sterling and dollar earnings. AEF was required to send to France such of its exports as France wanted—cotton and gold; in return it received "foreign currency dispensed with an eye-dropper" and luxury goods that were either unneeded (such as perfumes) or downright harmful to the African population (alcoholic beverages). Never before, it was said, had AEF's trading posts diplayed such an array of bottled liquor, while the few piece goods the federation received immediately found their way into the black market, where they were resold at exorbitant prices. During the years 1945 through 1947, an AEF deputy claimed that the federation had exported to France merchandise that brought in $68 million, of which only $18 million had been returned to AEF.[26] The government disputed these figures,[27] but agreed to soften the blow dealt by devaluation to AEF's economy by giving back in the future a much larger share of its hard-currency earnings and increasing French shipments of essential goods to the federation.

France kept its word on its currency pledge and also allocated AEF about $10.5 million of its Marshall Plan funds.[28] Only gradually, however, was French industry able to expand and diversify its exports to AEF, and their price rose faster and higher than did those of similar goods available outside the franc zone. Thanks to the Act of Berlin, AEF was technically freer to trade than was French West Africa, but in practice both federations were closely tied to France's economy. Both were burdened by the expensive CFA franc and both were handicapped by the shortage of hard-currency reserves. In fact, because of AEF's greater distance from French markets, the cost of living soared even higher that it did in French West Africa. An American journalist who visited AEF in the spring of 1959 observed that the CFA franc's purchasing power there was about equivalent to that of a single Metro. franc in France, making AEF one of the most expensive places in the world.[29] Frenchmen as well as Africans recognized that the CFA franc was stifling French Black Africa's economy, but all were equally adamant against another devaluation because of the tremendous monetary difficulties it would create. "The fundamental dislocation produced by the high-priced colonial franc," this journalist concluded, "remains a major problem for the new Community."

Before World War II, AEF's meager credit facilities were handled by three private banks, the BAO, the Banque Commerciale Africaine (BCA), and the Banque Belge d'Afrique. They concentrated on financing the *économie de traite* through short-term loans, and the only form of "social credit" dispensed in the federation was that provided on a small scale by the Crédit Agricole. Since the Liberation, credit facilities have been expanded and become more diversified: the range of short-term loans has greatly increased, and medium- and long-term loans have begun to play an important part in the development of AEF's economy.

The oldest of AEF's six deposit banks is the BAO, which in 1924 opened a branch at Brazzaville 23 years after it had been founded at Dakar. Gradually it installed agencies throughout the federation, at Port Gentil (1928), Libreville (1930), Pointe Noire (1936), Bangui (1946), and Fort Lamy (1950). Despite the loss in 1941 of its note-issue privilege for AEF, this bank—in which the federation has remained a stockholder—is still the most important in the country in the sum total of its deposits and the scope of its loans. It has done much to finance AEF's wood industry and cotton crop, as well as the big trading firms and public-works enterprises. Among its multiple local interests is a large share in the Industrie Cotonnière de l'Oubangui et du Tchad.

AEF's second prewar bank, the Banque Belge d'Afrique, plays a special role in the federation's banking system. A year after it was founded at Léopoldville in 1929, it expanded to AEF, where it set up branches at Brazzaville, Bangui, and Pointe Noire. It helped to create AEF's cotton companies in the early 1930's, and ever since then has played a preponderant role in financing the local cotton crop, as well as participating in the export of timber and coffee. Since the war it has maintained close and cordial relations with the CCOM. The third oldest of AEF's banks, the Banque Commerciale Africaine (BCA), has branches in all the territorial capitals. The BCA differs from its colleagues in being not only a deposit institution but also a business bank through its subsidiary, the SIFA. It has special interests in the Compagnie des Plantations de l'Ogooué and the Compagnie Sangha-Likouala, and it has helped to create other enterprises and to orient their development. In 1953 it increased its capital from 300 to 500 million CFA francs.

Of the banks that began operating in AEF after the war, the most important is the Banque Nationale pour le Commerce et l'Industrie (BNCI). Within five years after its establishment there in 1945, it had formed the most complete network of any bank in the federation, with agencies at Dolisie, Port Gentil, and Lambaréné as well as in the territorial capitals. With equal speed and efficiency, the BNCI attained an outstanding position as a deposit bank and source of short-term loans. The Société Générale was the second nationalized French bank to be introduced in AEF after the war. In 1948 it opened branches at Brazzaville and Bangui, and soon afterward expanded to Libreville, Port Gentil, and Pointe Noire. The latest comer to the federation is the Crédit Lyonnais. It has established agencies in all the capitals except Libreville and helps to finance certain export crops, but the scope of its activities in AEF cannot compare with that of its operations in north and west Africa.

All the banks mentioned have played a very active part in developing AEF's economy, and the scale as well as the orientation of their short-term loans have reflected the steady rise in their deposits. Details of their operations have been made public only since 1944, at which time the deposits of the three banks then in existence aggregated only 566 million francs.[80] The growth in deposits and loan operations by both old and new banks in the postwar period has been remarkably rapid, and by 1954 they were granting loans at the rate of over 10 billion CFA francs a year.[31] While AEF's banks should be given full credit for the remarkable activity they have shown over the past 15 years, much of this expansion was made possible by the aid given them by the CCOM.

Aside from its functions as accountant for FIDES and as a bank of issue,[32] the CCOM was charged after the war with dispensing credit to AEF's banks and coordinating their short-term loan activities. Organizationally, the CCOM has completely separated its function as a credit institution, granting mainly medium- and long-term loans, from that of bank of issue, in which respect it acts almost exclusively as a banks' bank. Only on very rare occasions has the CCOM itself entered the short-term-loan field, deliberately refraining from competing there with the deposit banks to which it has granted abundant facilities with the aim of developing AEF's economy. In AEF the CCOM's normal rediscount rate is 3 per cent, but this has been lowered to 2.5 per cent in the case of loans to finance agricultural cooperatives and wood and cotton exports. So liberal, in fact, was the CCOM's policy toward the deposit banks that the number of those banks' agencies tripled between 1945 and 1953, at which point some felt that it was time to slow down their expansion.[33]

With regard to medium- and long-term loans, the CCOM has operated directly, for this has always been a field in which the deposit banks have been either unable or unwilling to assume the risks involved. Here the CCOM has intervened either through the handling of FIDES funds or directly by loans granted to public collectivities, to companies of "mixed economy," or to private enterprises whose activities fitted in with those of the Plan. By the end of 1954, the CCOM had granted medium- and long-term loans aggregating 6,502 million CFA francs, of which 795 million had gone to state companies or companies of "mixed economy," and 1,707 million to private firms.[34] In 1955 the amount of public funds available for investment in AEF shrank noticeably. This was due not only to a tightening of credit in France but to completion of much of the Plan's public-works program and to the enhanced responsibilities assigned to the Cotton Supporting Fund in AEF.[35] Also, in the federation, some of the CCOM's medium- and long-term loan operations were being taken over by a local organization which it had helped to found and develop, the Crédit de l'AEF.

In 1948 the governor-general of AEF with some difficulty persuaded the authorities in Paris that the federation should have its own medium- and long-term loan organization, which he proposed to call the Crédit de l'AEF. Its aims were to help finance cooperative societies, approved agricultural associations, and handicraft enterprises, and, above all, to aid Africans who wanted to acquire small plots of land for the purpose of building homes. In October of that year the Grand Councilors accepted with pleasure the statutes drawn up for the Crédit de l'AEF, but within six months they were quarreling with the administration over the composition of its directorate and the ceiling to be placed on the amount of loans granted

to certain enterprises.[36] They were so insistent that the new organization
not become a purely governmental agency, and that they have some control over its operations, that the draft statutes had to be returned to Paris
for revision. Eventually the Grand Councilors won their main point, and
two of them (Europeans) were duly elected to the Crédit's permanent
committee at Brazzaville. The CCOM increased its share in the Crédit's
capital funds to 27 out of a total of 60 million CFA francs, and by means of
a loan covering the balance enabled the federation to acquire complete
control of the new organization.

After a difficult *accouchement*, the Crédit de l'AEF was born on May
9, 1949, and trouble continued to haunt its infant years. From the outset
it was criticized for allegedly favoring European enterprises and for refusing or ignoring the requests for loans made by Africans.[37] The European
directors of the Crédit naturally denied this charge, claiming that most
African applicants simply could not provide the loan guarantees that the
institution was legally required to demand. As of September 30, 1950, the
Crédit had received over a thousand requests for loans; of these, 500 had
been examined and 285 granted to 101 Europeans and 184 Africans.[38] Because the funds at its disposal were very limited and the interest it charged
on medium- and long-term loans was low (5½ per cent), it must pursue
a prudent policy. By so doing and by keeping down its operating costs,
the Crédit had even managed to end its first year with a small profit. The
Grand Counsilors acknowledged the need for caution, but felt that the
procedure followed by the Crédit was too slow and cumbersome, for approval by both the permanent committee and the relevant territorial committee was required for granting loans outside Moyen-Congo. They asked
for a greater decentralization of the Crédit's operations and for a new loan
from the CCOM. By the end of 1950 the Grand Council had succeeded
in getting a grant of 60 million CFA francs from the CCOM and in replacing the two Europeans by Africans on the Crédit's permanent committee, but it had to wait until 1957 to receive satisfaction in regard to
decentralizing the Crédit's administrative machinery.

By 1952, the experience gained during the preceding three years indicated the desirability of orienting the Crédit's loans to the rural areas
and away from the towns, especially those of Moyen-Congo.[39] Because the
need to improve African housing had been paramount at the time when the
Crédit was established and because functionaries were the safest credit
risks, two of that organization's original goals—aid to peasants and artisans
—had been neglected. If the Crédit was to satisfy the continuing demand for
housing loans and also extend its operations to the countryside, funds in
addition to the 91.5 million currently available would be required—but
it seemed unlikely that the Paris authorities would grant them. In 1951
the CCOM had turned down the Crédit's request for a fresh capital infusion on the ground that some of its outstanding loans had been inadequately guaranteed or had been used by their recipients to make usurious
profits. Eventually the CCOM granted the Crédit another 100 million, in

the belief that its past mistakes could be corrected and that it was an experiment worth continuing.

Time has proved that the CCOM's faith was justified, for the scope of the Crédit's operations and the percentage of its loan recoveries have steadily increased. The Crédit has not attempted to help finance AEF's two main industries, wood and cotton. The former is almost wholly in the hands of powerful European companies and the latter is financed by a banking consortium and a Supporting Fund. Rather, it has dispersed its loans among a wide variety of small enterprises. Of its loans, 80 per cent are of the medium- and long-term type in about equal proportions; while those for housing and property improvements still predominate, loans to agricultural cooperatives and the Sociétés Indigènes de Prévoyance (SIP) and also to handicraft industries have increased. In May 1955 the Crédit launched still another category of loan, which rapidly became very popular. This is the *crédit au petit équipement,* which enables individuals who meet specified residential or employment conditions to purchase furniture, refrigerators, bicycles, and the like.

The greater political autonomy acquired by the territories through application of the *loi-cadre* was paralleled by a decentralization of the Crédit's administration and operations. In 1957, branches were inaugurated in each of their capitals and placed in the charge of a technical director who was made responsible to a local committee.[40] These territorial committees were empowered to grant loans of up to 5 million CFA francs; requests for loans above that amount had to be referred to the directorate at Brazzaville, which was also given the task of centralizing the branches' accounts and of laying down general policy.

During the 1957–58 fiscal year, the Crédit granted 4,000 new loans totaling 500 million CFA francs, of which 150 million went to the agricultural sector (chiefly in Moyen-Congo and Oubangui), 26.5 million to the craft industries, 270 million to housing, and 49.25 million to "small equipment." From its inception in May 1949 through June 1958, the Crédit loaned 2,158 million CFA francs to more than 10,000 individuals or enterprises.[41]

The Federal Budget

Financial autonomy was accorded AEF, as well as French West Africa, by a law of April 13, 1900, France taking responsibility only for the federation's military expenditures and a few loans guaranteed in time of economic crisis.[42]

In 1903, Gabon and Moyen-Congo were each given a budget, while the expenditures for the French Congo's General Commissariat and for Oubangui and Tchad territories were grouped together in a special section of Moyen-Congo's budget. This was frankly a temporary expedient, corresponding to the existing stage of French penetration of the hinterland, and three years later, on February 11, 1906, two new budgets were

set up. One combined separate sections for Oubangui and Tchad, while
the other was a general budget for the area then included in the French
Congo. This change required a redistribution of revenues and expenditures which worked out mainly to the benefit of the general budget. Although the latter took over the expenses involved in the services of the
treasury, education, public works, the PTT, native administration, and
customs, it was allocated all the revenues from import and export duties
and from the public domain. In practice, such an abrupt centralization
proved premature because of the inadequacy of the means of communication. In those days, for example, it took six months for letters to be
exchanged between Brazzaville and Fort Lamy. Each year the general
budget incurred a deficit, which in 1909—when the budget totaled about 5
million francs—came to 402,000 francs.

Establishment of the government-general in 1910 necessitated another
financial reorganization, based on two principles. One was that all purely
administrative expenditures must be borne by the budget of the colony
where they were incurred, and the other, that the general or federal budget
should take over both the revenues and expenditures of the services common to all of the colonies. By far the largest source of income for the
federal budget was indirect taxes, specifically customs duties. Each year
the French Parliament was to decide what sum, if any, it would allocate
to the federation, and the federal budget was likewise to determine annually what subsidies it would grant to the colonial budgets. It was also
provided that a special section could be annexed to the federal budget for
such loans as the government-general might be authorized to raise. Besides the subsidies received from the federal budget, the colonial budgets
were to be financed by purely local revenues, mainly from direct taxes.
They were to be drawn up by their respective lieutenant-governors, but
had to be approved by the governor-general.

This was the financial regime under which AEF lived for the next 25
years. During that period the volume of its budgets apparently grew slowly,
though successive currency devaluations make them difficult to appraise.
At the outset, the federation's entire revenues amounted to little more than
15 million francs, and of this sum only 6,900,000 francs derived from local
resources, the balance being supplied by Metropolitan France in one form
or another. By 1934, when the federal budget came to little more than
100 million francs, France was even compelled to advance the money
needed to pay interest (amounting to 63.5 million francs that year) on the
loans which AEF had contracted. All the colonies except Tchad (which
was partially still under military government), as well as the federation
itself, had growing deficits, mainly because of AEF's heavy operating expenses. That year their combined deficits were equivalent to one-third of
their total revenues, reserve funds had practically vanished, and fresh loans
had to be granted by the French treasury.

To be sure, the practice of granting special funds to AEF antedated
creation of the government-general, but most of them were for the purpose

of covering the military occupation of the northern territories. The cost
to France of administering Gabon and the French Congo from 1871 to
1906 was far smaller, amounting to only 55 million francs.[43] But the establishment of a government-general, superimposed on four colonial administrations, increased appreciably the burden of Metropolitan France, and in
addition France financed AEF's medical service, the building of a radio
station at Brazzaville, and other works. In the years between 1910 and 1934
such exceptional grants to the federal budget for civil expenditures
amounted to 56,577,888 francs; moreover, AEF was permitted to contract
four loans—some of which were interest-free for a specified period—from
the French treasury, totaling 1,612 million francs.[44] Such financial benevolence on the part of France toward one of its dependencies was unusual,
and has been variously explained as compassion for AEF's exceptional
poverty, expiation for the sins of the concessionary-company period, and
compensation for the territory taken from AEF in 1911 and handed over
to Germany in return for a free hand in Morocco.

Yet with all this financial bolstering, AEF's financial situation failed
to improve fundamentally. Consequently, on June 30, 1934, there came
another financial reorganization whereby the four colonies lost their financial autonomy and AEF was given a reserve fund and a single budget,
to which that of the railroad was annexed. Soon, however, much the same
difficulties arose as in 1906, when a similar centralization had been attempted, though the means of communication had greatly improved in
the interval. On December 31, 1937, therefore, it was found advisable to
set up separate sections for each of the colonies, though they remained
within the framework of a single budget. As these changes were made when
the world economic depression was ending, AEF's budgetary situation
improved. Between 1935 and 1940 the volume of the federal budget
doubled, reflecting a financial amelioration that could not be wholly
attributed to continued subsidies from France or to the franc's devaluation
in 1936. Yet the fear of increasing the already heavy public debt, on which
charges at that time amounted to 40 per cent of the federation's ordinary
expenditures, prevented AEF from contracting further loans to carry out
a development program, and the result was economic stagnation. The
situation of AEF on the eve of World War II has been summed up by
Lord Hailey as follows:[45]

> Ordinary receipts, including the subvention, were estimated (in 1937) to
> amount to 196 million francs, railroad receipts were estimated similarly to
> cover only the bare operating costs, making no contribution to interest charges
> or a renewals fund. Of a total ordinary expenditure, including debt service,
> of 198 million francs, about 48 millions represented the cost of the adminis-
> trative and financial services; about 12 millions provided for public works;
> and 19 millions for social services, chiefly medical and education. . . .

Before World War II, taxes were the main source of the federation's
own revenues, and their structure was similar to that prevailing in French

West Africa. Initially taxes were paid in kind, usually in rubber, to the value of 3 francs annually per person. Obviously the form taken by this tax had been devised for the benefit of the concessionary companies, and their abuse of this system led in 1909 to its replacement by a head tax paid in cash by both sexes, which varied from district to district. As of 1932 the head tax ranged from 5 to 40 francs in Gabon, 10 to 30 in Moyen-Congo, 4 to 30 in Oubangui, and 5 to 20 in Tchad. Three years later the minimum had been raised to 15 francs and the average was about 30 francs. The objective of this increase during the depths of the depression was both to obviate larger subsidies from France and to offset a decline in customs revenues. Until that time the rate of such taxation had been lower in AEF than in French West Africa or the Belgian Congo and, even according to such a severe critic of the local administration as André Gide, it did not weigh over-heavily on the African population:[46]

> Africans accept without difficulty the head tax, which they regard as a ransom paid by the conquered to the conqueror, and this means that they do not contest it. I have never encountered a single case in which an African protested against a tax which is not excessive, or would not be if the census was accurately taken. Sometimes, however, the head tax of several persons who have died or emigrated falls on a single individual.

The chronic shortage of supervisory administrative personnel (as well as the fact that often an official's promotion depended on his tax-collecting capacities) led to abuses that spelled disaster in certain regions,[47] and this situation was aggravated in the 1930's by depression-inspired economies. Except in the towns—where a nominal tax roll was kept—no tax receipts were issued, and the chiefs, who were entitled to keep a percentage of the taxes they collected, naturally put pressure on the population to pay them more than was legitimately due. In addition to the head tax, always the mainstay of the colonial budgets, there were other direct taxes that fell mainly on Europeans. These included taxes levied on all land held on individual tenure, and on income beginning with 15,000 francs for single and 20,000 for married persons.

World War II sharply altered AEF's simple tax structure. Existing rates, with the exception of income taxes, did not undergo much change, but a series of wholly new taxes[48] was set up to finance the Free French war effort. Direct taxes, however, were no longer the federation's main source of income, for AEF's isolation from France was followed by an unexpected rise in its foreign trade and consequently in customs revenues. The year 1941 closed with a surplus of 22,600,000 francs, that of 1942 with 34,300,000, and that of 1943 with about the same amount. AEF's debt load was cut down at the same time from 80 to 15 million francs, and the reserve fund, whose deficit amounted to 7 million in 1940, had 94 million in its coffers by 1945. Moreover, all this was accomplished despite the federation's assumption of "expenditures of sovereignty" formerly paid by France and despite contributions to support the Free French forces. In 1946, the last year in which AEF had a single budget, there was a marked upturn both in customs revenues and in expenditures, chiefly in the cost of personnel because of France's upward revision of official salary scales. The federal budget rose from 625,415,000 francs in 1945 to 1,029,858,000 the following year.

This sensational improvement in the finances of AEF, together with the postwar stress on economic as well as political decentralization, led to the decree of October 16, 1946, which restored financial autonomy to the territories and   generally revived the budgetary structure of 1910. The laws of 1946 and 1947 that created the territorial assemblies and Grand Council did not affect this basic division but did introduce the concept of obligatory and optional expenditures in all of the new budgets. Obligatory expenditures included payments on the public debt, contributions to the Colonial Officials Retirement Fund, and the cost of specified public services (justice, finance, health, education, mines, public works, meteorological, and the PTT). Generally speaking, expenditures of interest to all the territories were to fall within the federal budget and to be met by indirect taxes, while those of local interest were to be assumed by the territory concerned and to be covered by the revenues from its direct taxes. Since such revenues would not normally be sufficient to meet the territories' expenditures, the federal budget was to pay over each year a large proportion of its income to help balance the local budgets. But because the basis for these annual federal subsidies and rebates was not precisely laid down by the law, such allocations became the subject of incessant and acrimonious controversy among the four territories. As matters worked out, the federal budget usually divided up among the territories the totality of its revenues from export duties and a varying percentage of its much larger income from import duties.

The war had wrought a profound change in the relative importance of AEF's sources of revenue, which no longer consisted mainly of taxes but rather of customs duties. In the first postwar years, 54.6 per cent of the federation's income came from import and export duties, 11.2 per cent from the head tax, and 8.1 per cent from income tax.[49] Its population was too small and too poor to pay more than minimal personal taxes. AEF's internal trade was too limited to make the imposition of a *taxe de transaction* (such as existed in French West Africa and Madagascar) worth the difficulties of collection. The Congo Basin Convention had made much of AEF an "open-door" area in which the government could not protect infant industries by a tariff wall. Local production remained so small in scale that this further curtailed the federation's tax potential. In order to produce more, AEF needed large amounts of outside capital, and it was essential not to frighten away possible private investors by heavy fiscal demands. So its tax system has been constructed more in the light of economic than of financial considerations, and perforce foreign trade has continued to be the major source of its income.

Customs duties have been assessed on almost all merchandise entering and leaving AEF, which until May 30, 1947, formed a tariff union with Cameroun. All imported goods paid ad valorem duties averaging 12 per cent, but certain products such as tobacco, alcohol, and fuel paid a specific duty. Imports were also subject to another tax of 6 per cent, called *taxe sur le chiffre d'affaires*. Hence imported merchandise normally yielded 18 per cent of its value in duties, though the rate on some produce was lower and certain items were wholly exempt. Ad valorem duties were also collected on exports, but these varied widely according to the product exported. Except for gold shipments, they also were subject to a tax on the *chiffre d'affaires*, which in the early postwar years amounted to 3 to 4 per cent. Furthermore, a very small impost was collected on most raw-material exports to defray the expense of maintaining relevant research institutions and the export-standardization service. Added to the foregoing were other miscellaneous indirect taxes, such as those on the internal sale of tobacco, soap, and alcoholic beverages and of all local forest and mineral products; on exploitation of the public domain (permits for wood-cutting, ore extracting, and mineral prospecting), on registration and stamp duties, and on property sales and transfers. But of all the indirect taxes, those on imports and exports were by far the most important. Customs revenues rose from 225 million francs in 1945 to 2,221 million in 1949, reflecting not only the currency devaluations of 1945 and 1948 but also a general rise in the price of imports, a growth in their tonnage, and an increase in the tariff rates.

Direct taxes were of four main categories—head, commercial, *cédulaire*, and income—and a small impost called the *centimes additionnels* was collected for the benefit of the Chambers of Commerce and Agriculture. The head tax was paid by all persons 18 years of age and over except those included in one of ten groups (wounded war veterans, paupers, students up to 21 years old, mothers of at least three living children, etc.), and in the early postwar years it ranged between 40 and 1,500 francs. Traders paid for their patents and licenses and a percentage of the *chiffre d'affaires* for certain merchandise. The *taxe cédulaire* on wages and salaries varied between 11 and 21 per cent, and persons with an income of 100,000 CFA francs and over paid according to a sliding scale, the maximum being 40 per cent on incomes of more than 700,000 CFA francs. The pastoral population in Oubangui and Tchad were taxed in proportion to the size of their herds and did not pay a head tax. Everywhere property was subject to taxation that varied with the degree of its development, the terms of its concession, and the like. The basis for assessing direct taxes was laid down by the Grand Council, but the rates were established locally by each territorial assembly and therefore varied widely in time and space.[50] In 1955, for example, income tax was said to be largest in Moyen-Congo, where it accounted for three-fifths of all the taxes paid, and Oubangui was then believed to be subjected to the highest taxes of all types.[51]

The income from direct taxation rose sharply from 228 million francs in 1946 to over 773 million in 1949, but it was not increasing as fast as that derived from indirect taxes, and an AEF deputy to the National Assembly claimed that direct taxes were almost nonexistent in his federation.[52] It being evident that the territorial budgets, into which most of the direct taxes were paid, were in increasing difficulties, the administration announced in 1949 that it would undertake a revision of the direct-tax system. But the federal budget, too, was encountering difficulties and had to draw on the reserve fund in 1945 to the extent of 33 million francs and in 1946, of 126 million. The rapid growth in the volume of the budget continued in 1947, by which time there had been an over-all increase of 39 per cent compared with the federation's single budget a decade earlier. The currency devaluation of October 1948 worsened the situation despite the assumption that year by France of the payment of salaries for some high officials and all the magistrates and *gendarmes* in AEF. This eased somewhat the position of the federal budget but failed to check the growing deficits of the territories.

To bring relief to their budgets and to promote the territories' financial autonomy, the Grand Council voted in its November 1948 session to suppress the subsidy system and to hand over some of the most considerable federal revenues directly to territorial collection and management. Three months later, however, this decision was annulled by the Council of State, presumably on the ground that such a move threatened the disruption of AEF's fiscal homogeneity. Yet something drastic had to be done to cope with the territories' growing deficits, so the government promised to revise by 1950 the basis on which the federal revenues were allocated.[53] In the meantime another call was made on the reserve fund and eventually the federal budget for 1950 was balanced at 3,267,700,000 CFA francs, about the same total as for the preceding year.

As of 1950, about one-third of the federation's total revenues were turned over to the local budgets as rebates and the balance was used to pay for the federation's general expenditures. These rebates varied considerably because they were based on the individual territory's economic activity but were usually larger than the revenues realized from its own direct taxes. But if revenues from imports—the federal budget's mainstay —did not come in as anticipated, the federation could not pay its own expenses and had to seek compensation in taking what it needed from the export duties on which the territories counted to balance their budgets. Not only was there uncertainty until the end of each year as to what surplus would be available, but in some territories the budgetary session of their assemblies was held prior to that of the Grand Council, which determined the amount of the allocation to be divided among the territories. The system by which the government-general collected certain revenues from the territories and then turned back a proportion to them was both costly and cumbersome. Worse still, however, in the eyes of many assemblymen, was the very structure of the federal government, which was so top-heavy that it absorbed a disproportionate amount of the resources that the territories had earned and wanted to use for themselves.

If there was prolonged uncertainty each year as to the size of the rebate that each territory could dispose of, there was no doubt at all as to the steady rise in territorial as well as federal expenditures owing to the successive increases in personnel costs. Although a good year for foreign trade could rapidly swell the revenues of the federal budget, there was little or no elasticity in the income from direct taxes collected by the territories. Because of the poverty of the population and the small scale of internal trade, the territories' own revenues remained virtually unexpandable, while their expenditures rose with each increase in the number and pay of officials. The territorial budgets for 1950, even before the Lamine-Gueye law of that year forced another and enormous increase in personnel expenditures, showed deficits totaling 501 million francs. Since the indebtedness of the territories varied considerably, the government decided that it must radically change the principle on which federal grants to them had been made. Beginning in 1951, therefore, such allocations were no longer based solely on the concept of rebates but took on the character of subsidies and were determined primarily by the individual territory's need. At the same time, the administration and the Grand Council cast about for means of acquiring additional revenues for both the federal and territorial budgets.

Study of the tax structure, begun in 1949, was long delayed by the lack of accurate statistics, and the conclusions drawn from it as to the federation's financial predicament were often contradictory. Direct taxation of all types, it appeared, provided nearly 20 per cent of the total revenues[54] and indirect taxes supplied the balance, of which imports brought in twice as much as exports. But there was little agreement as to what proportion of direct taxes was supplied by which element of the population (since the situation varied widely with each territory), or as to whether AEF was lightly or heavily taxed compared to other countries of the French Union. The government was inclined to believe that without undue hardship for the population direct taxes could be increased and the revenues therefrom augmented by a better assessment and collection of income tax. The Grand Council and territorial assemblies, on the other hand, early took a firm stand against any rise in the head tax. More unanimity existed on the subject of indirect taxation, and several proposals to reduce its rates were for the most part acceptable to all parties. Here the government was concerned mainly with lightening fiscal obligations in order to attract capital investment, and the representative assemblies were primarily anxious to check the fast-rising local cost of living, for which they blamed largely the high import duties.

The prolonged and often heated debates to which revision of the tax system gave rise from 1950 on lost their somewhat academic character in 1952. By that time not only had all of AEF's budgets risen tremendously but the federation's rapidly worsening economic and financial position made the preceding years now appear in retrospect as a "period of euphoria." Not only did the revenues from AEF's foreign trade fall sharply, but by the end of 1952 three new elements had entered the picture that threatened to bankrupt the federation. One was passage by Parliament of the Overseas Labor Code, which eventually would bring new financial burdens in the form of family allowances for wage earners. Then AEF had to begin payments for its equipment program under the Plan just at a time when FIDES was reducing its investments there. Finally, and of more immediate concern, was the huge bill amounting to nearly 3 billion francs suddenly presented by Metropolitan France for loans and supplies granted AEF during and after the war.

In fact the crisis of 1952 was so severe that the government-general at long last made a big effort to cut down its expenditures, and the Grand Council and some of the territorial assemblies were finally induced to vote appreciable tax rises. To swell the federal revenues, taxes were raised on certain luxury imports (tobacco and alcoholic beverages), on the *chiffre d'affaires* on imported goods (from 6 per cent to 7 per cent), and on fuel purchases. At the same time, export duties on cotton, oleaginous products, and sisal were reduced, the railroad was persuaded to lower freight rates on products for exportation, and special aid was granted to the forest industry, particularly hard hit by the 1952 recession. The government-general, which in 1951 had slightly reduced its allocations to the territories in an attempt to force them to economize, was now determined not to cut down subsidies any further, and even proposed that special grants be made to those in most acute financial distress. By emptying the reserve fund the federation managed to balance its budget but not to pay its back debts.

Financially the year 1953 proved to be even worse than anticipated, though the lumber industry staged a comeback and the territories tried with more effectiveness to cope with their financial difficulties. The federation was increasing and diversifying its production and exports but naturally had no control over world markets, in which the prices they fetched continued to decline. The result was a 25 per cent drop in the federation's estimated revenues, and its budget had to be revised radically several times. Nevertheless, it did not reduce its subsidies to the territories and it absorbed the totality of the current deficit. While this helped the territories to diminish their indebtedness, it still totaled in round figures some 180 million francs, and the more prosperous territories—though their relative status changed from one year to another—resented having to come to the rescue of their poorer colleagues and urged a return to the rebate system. All, however, blamed the federal government for not distributing to them a larger proportion of its revenues because of the extravagant scale of its administration and the inefficiency of its finance services. The government-general, for its part, claimed that it had pared the federal budget to the bone: if it had to maintain a plethora of high-ranking officials this was the responsibility of Metropolitan authorities, as was also the belated presentation without prior warning of a huge bill for past expenditures. Since there was general agreement that the debt ceiling had been reached and that AEF could do nothing to improve the prices paid for its exports, to lower the cost of its imports in the French market, or to reform the administrative structure without the consent of Parliament, France must come generously to the aid of the stricken federation.

In the fall of 1953, Metropolitan France—recognizing the great gap between the federation's needs and resources—offered AEF an exceptional subsidy of 400 million francs, but on conditions that were considered unacceptable by the federation's elected representatives because they would infringe on the powers of the Grand Council and territorial assemblies. Finally this was ironed out to AEF's satisfaction and the 1953 budget was balanced. France granted the subsidy and raised the guaranteed price for locally produced cotton, and FIDES took over some of the equipment charges formerly assumed by the federal budget, in return for which the federation promised to effect certain economies and to try to raise some tax rates. The administration was pruned of a number of officials, the Grand Council agreed to raise duties on imported alcoholic beverages, perfumes, and shoes, but the territorial assemblies held out against increasing the head tax or altering the assessment and rates of the income tax to bring in a greater yield. On October 21, 1953, the Grand Council finally accepted the budget proposed for 1954, whose total was estimated to be 12 per cent lower than that for the current year.

During the first months of 1954 the economic situation unexpectedly began to improve, in part because investments made under the Plan were at long last giving results. Exports continued to rise and brought higher prices, imports revived, and the note circulation increased.[55] Duties were even lowered on some exports and imports, supporting funds for certain products were either established or reinforced, merchants were offered a 10 per cent rebate on AEF goods sold in non-franc markets, and there was a gain in the yield of direct taxes. Aid from France that year in various forms totaled over one billion CFA francs, larger subsidies (which came to over 45 per cent of the federal income) were granted to the neediest territories (Oubangui and Tchad), and the federation liquidated the greater part of its past debts and even ended 1954 with a surplus of 385 million francs. On the debit side was the steady rise in the local cost of living and the ever-heavier burden represented by growing personnel charges and payments under the equipment Plan. Over 83 per cent of total expenditures were operating costs, and of this one-quarter was incurred by the social services (11 per cent to education, 13.4 per cent to health, and 0.8 per cent to labor),[56] which, while vital for the population's evolution, were consumers, not producers, of revenue. The federation's financial dependence on France had increased, and it was feared, alternately, that the French taxpayer would either tire of subsidizing AEF or exact as its price the imposition of rigid controls.[57] Moreover, the relative prosperity which the improved foreign trade situation had brought to the federal budget might well be temporary and was only indirectly shared with the territories, whose own revenues remained almost stationary while their expenditures continued to mount.

Nevertheless, AEF in 1955 faced the future with "reasonable optimism." For the first time in its history, the federation's accounts were up to date and the Grand Council knew exactly where it stood financially.[58] No tax increases were in prospect, and the government even proposed further lowering some customs duties. The volume of the budget that year exceeded its predecessor by 278 million francs, but France agreed to grant AEF a subsidy almost as large as that of 1954. And with the continued improvement in the foreign trade situation, the federation, by the end of the year, was able to liquidate its past indebtedness and build up its reserve fund to the legal minimum of 100 million francs. The budgets of Oubangui and Tchad were comparatively healthy, Gabon seemed disposed to wipe out its past debts by practicing greater austerity than theretofore, and only Moyen-Congo's finances continued to be deficitary. Yet the whole picture retained its fundamentally somber aspect. Almost all of AEF's revenues still had to be devoted to covering operating costs. France's subsidies would certainly decline as the federation's financial situation improved, and that improvement continued to depend on getting good prices in external markets for two of its products—timber and cotton. The revenues of the territorial budgets were increasingly absorbed by operating expenses, of which the percentage devoted to paying personnel had risen from about one-third in the first postwar years to over one-half.

The year of the *loi-cadre*, 1956, brought that "fundamental reform of AEF's structure" long demanded by its elected representatives. Though the decrees embodying its basic principles were not to be applied to the federation until 1957, it was already obvious that they would drastically alter the financial relations not only between Metropolitan France and all the Overseas Territories but between the AEF government-general and its component parts. With the dissolution of the federation and the creation of elected territorial governments, the local assemblies would receive a far larger share of the revenues that had formerly fed the federal budget and would also gain direct control over more taxes. At the same time the territories would incur heavier expenses, although France had agreed to pay state officials and to help with the cost of setting up the new governments. In the interval before this transformation could take place, AEF had both to prepare for the future and to cope with its current financial difficulties.

As a transition measure to prepare the way for greater territorial independence, the government-general proposed a return to the rebate system. Not only would this meet Gabon's long-standing complaints about the inequity of rich territories' chronically supporting poor ones but it would also promote greater territorial economic activity and put an end to the annual bargaining and bitterness that accompanied each allocation of the federal budget's surplus.[59] Despite the improved trade position, AEF's financial situation, the High Commissioner warned, was still tight.[60] Even without any numerical growth in the civil service of the federation, a 4 per cent annual increase in the expenditures for personnel could be expected owing to the regular rises in salaries voted each year by Parliament. An augmentation in other expenditures, notably those required for the Plan, the reorganization of FERDES, the setting up of more supporting funds, and the liberalization of family allowances must also be foreseen. And at the same time a shrinkage must be anticipated in France's subsidies and FIDES investments, as well as a decline in the income derived from certain taxes. AEF's efforts to attract foreign capital by reducing imposts on production and exports between 1952 and 1955 had already cost the federation about one billion CFA francs in revenues.[61] So the government proposed and the Grand Council accepted a significant change in the basis of taxation, the rates of which were thenceforth to be set by the four territorial assemblies.

Beginning January 1, 1957, fiscal burdens were to be lightened and long-term tax concessions accorded enterprises deemed likely to contribute to the economic development of AEF, such as the Compagnie Minière de l'Ogooué (COMILOG), and no longer to companies or individuals simply and normally reinvesting their profits in the country. Thus the rate of the industrial- and commercial-profits tax was reduced, but fewer concerns and persons were exempted from paying it. Then the tax on the *chiffre d'affaires*, which had formerly fallen mainly on consumers, was now transferred—with some notable exceptions—to producers and was to be applied even to companies operating in AEF but not incorporated there. Furthermore, import duties, rises in which had until then affected mainly luxury items, were to be slightly increased on such consumer goods as clothing, soap, and foodstuffs. As to income tax, the exemption allowance for individuals was raised to 180,000 CFA francs and the highest rate was to be applied to incomes of 6 million.[62] With all these revisions AEF still depended for its financial salvation on Metropolitan subsidies and on foreign trade, and in 1957 the volume of both was smaller than in the preceeding year. Whereas 1956 had ended with a surplus of 120 million (paid into the reserve fund), the balance of trade in 1957 was unfavorable: exports had grown but imports had increased even more rapidly.

In its spring session of 1957, the Grand Council formally voted to transfer to the territories the financial powers assigned to them under the decrees applying the *loi-cadre*. And on June 10, the High Commissioner convened a conference of the heads of the new territorial governments for the purpose of salvaging the maximum possible unity of fiscal and tariff regimes among the members of the Group, as AEF was now called. Thanks largely to the able chairmanship of Governor-General Chauvet, federalism triumphed over regionalism in the fiscal domain. It was agreed that for the time being the existing tax system would be retained and that there would be mutual consultation among the territories in regard to any proposed changes in their fiscal structure or rates. As to tariffs, a compromise was reached: the Grand Council was to establish the duties on cocoa, coffee, and cotton exports, while those on oleaginous products and timber were to be determined by the territorial assemblies after taking into consideration the recommendations of the conference and of the Grand Council.[63] A second interterritorial conference was held at Brazzaville in October, which confirmed the willingness of all the territories to coordinate their fiscal and tariff policies through negotiated agreements, provided the Group would not have imposed on it a federal executive, and a convention to this effect was signed at Paris the following January and ratified by the territorial assemblies in June and July 1958.

In the meantime, the decentralization moves undertaken in 1957 had reduced the Group budget for 1958 (amounting to 6,826,215,000 CFA francs) by 30 per cent compared with that of the previous year. The surplus from the 1957 budget totaled about 475 million, and though the territories had larger revenues at their disposal, they had even heavier operating expenditures than before. Their respective financial situations continued to vary markedly, and it appeared that if the principle of federal solidarity was to survive, the rebate system, based on a purely economic accounting, would have to be tempered by charity toward the territories in need. Gabon, with its new mining and petroleum industries in addition to those deriving from its timber, had a bright future, and one in which Moyen-Congo would share, but the outlook for Oubangui and Tchad was uncertain and far less rosy. To forestall a resurgence of interterritorial dissension in regard to division of the Group surplus, the governor-general proposed in October 1958 that an agreement be reached as soon as possible on a fixed percentage basis similar to that accepted by the Grand Council in 1956. The Group budget for 1959 (estimated at 6,604,400,000 CFA francs) provided for rebates to the new republics of AEF 20 per cent larger than the territories had received in 1958, when Gabon got 100,210,000 CFA francs, Moyen-Congo 155,230,000, Oubangui 122,760,000, and Tchad 171,-700,000.

CHAPTER 12

Transportation

In the heart of Africa, AEF forms a north-south corridor of irregular shape. It possesses neither economic nor geographic unity, and its 800-kilometer coastline is disproportionate to the vastness of its area. Political frontiers notwithstanding, eastern Tchad economically and geographically merges with Sudan, just as southwestern Tchad and northwestern Oubangui merge into northern Cameroun and Nigeria. Gabon is a maritime province apart, separated by almost impenetrable forest from its neighbors to the south and east. Only parts of Moyen-Congo and Oubangui have an authentic unity—that given them by the great river system that forms their eastern boundaries.

During the late nineteenth century, AEF was thought to possess a magnificent system of interconnecting rivers. Explorers of the hinterland gradually dispelled this illusion, but they did find one bright spot in an otherwise discouraging picture. This was the continuously navigable stretch of over 1,000 kilometers formed by the Congo river and its tributary the Oubangui, which linked Brazzaville to a point just south of Bangui. Beyond those two towns, the waterway was cut by rapids which, in the south, made navigation as far as the sea impossible. AEF did possess a network of rivers totaling over 5,000 kilometers in length, but they were only intermittently navigable, either because of shoals and waterfalls or because their flow was seasonal and very irregular. Tsetse-fly infestation made much of AEF uninhabitable by cattle or horses, hence throughout much of the federation human portage was the only means of carrying provisions to the settlements and garrisons of the north, and merchandise to the markets or shipping centers.

Portage took such a toll of the populations of AEF and gave such meager returns that both humanitarian and economic reasons dictated its suppression. The nature of the soil in Oubangui and a few parts of Tchad made road-building there possible, and in the 1920's Governor Lamblin endowed the former territory with a road system that is still the best in the federation. But this was not feasible in the great forest or in the many areas that the rivers inundated each year for months at a time. In any case, AEF's great distances, low productivity, sparse population, and shortage of labor made the construction of an extensive system of communications too costly and difficult for so poor a federation to undertake. Indeed it was

the unlikelihood of its ever becoming a paying proposition that delayed
for 36 years the building of a railroad from Brazzaville to the ocean, aside
from the difficulties of financing its construction. Yet something drastic
had to be done to break the vicious circle: so long as its means of communication remained primitive or nonexistent, the federation would never
increase its production nor would its populations be released from the de-
structive servitude of portage. Therefore, in 1922 work began on the Congo-
Ocean railroad, which was completed after 12 years at an immense cost
in manpower and money. The fact that thousands of laborers died during
its construction and that it operated at a loss until World War II aroused
great indignation among French idealists and confirmed the misgivings
of the French businessmen who had originally opposed the undertaking.
Yet this railroad saved thousands of other Africans from the degradation of
portage and at long last gave a large portion of the hinterland an outlet
to the sea.

The Federal Artery (*Voie Fédérale*), as the combined river and rail
route between Bangui and Pointe Noire has been called, still has its detractors as well as its partisans. The latter contend that it provides relatively
cheap transport, considering the distance traversed, and that it has given
economic unity to at least three territories of the federation. Those opposed to the Federal Artery, on the other hand, claim that it can be fully
used for only six months of the year and that it is an expensive route, if the
time and expenditures involved in the transshipment and storage of freight
are taken into consideration. They also point out that Gabon makes almost
no use of the Federal Artery, for the products of its hinterland are carried
to its own seaports by way of the territory's navigable waterways. Moreover, Tchad, according to this same school of thought, has actually been
a victim of the Federal Artery, which has done little to lessen its isolation
and much to increase the cost and delays in the transport of its imports and
exports.

While everyone agrees that something must be done to improve Tchad's
communications with the outside world, sharp differences of opinion have
arisen as to what that something should be. Supporters of the Federal
Artery and of federal solidarity in general, and Oubangui businessmen in
particular, want a railroad to be built into Tchad north from Bangui.
Others, and these include members of the Douala Chamber of Commerce
and many merchants of Fort Lamy, favor building a railway that would
connect western Tchad and Oubangui with the Cameroun rail system. In
recent years two more possible solutions have been mooted, but both depend
on forces outside Tchad's control. One is a link to the Nigerian network's
railhead, which will soon be located at Maiduguri. The other is a more
nebulous project—that of building a railroad from the Red Sea to Nigeria
that would cross Sudan and Tchad in an east-westerly direction.

The ten-year Plan, as conceived in 1946, expressed France's long-standing ambition to build AEF's economy into an integrated whole by means
of an improved infrastructure. In broad outlines it was proposed that

Tchad should supply meat, textiles, and rice to the other three territories, and that the wood and mineral exports of Gabon, Moyen-Congo, and Oubangui would pay for all the federation's imports. To be sure, this dream of pseudo-autarky might run afoul of the international agreements involving AEF, or prove not economically feasible. But those were the days of grandiose visions and euphoria in Paris, and there very little was known exactly of the problems involved. One thing seemed obvious to the master planners—the highest priority must be given to improving AEF's means of communication, external and internal, and so 52 per cent of FIDES funds for the federation were allocated for this purpose. Cornut-Gentille echoed this viewpoint when he told the Grand Council that "transport is AEF's no. 1 problem."[1]

First place on the communications agenda was given to the Federal Artery; hence large sums were spent on making the Oubangui and Congo navigable over a longer stretch and for more weeks of the year, on enlarging the ports of Pointe Noire, Brazzaville, and Bangui, and on relaying some of the Congo-Ocean's trackage and acquiring more rolling stock for that railroad line. As to Gabon, its ports' equipment was to be modernized and a road linking Dolisie to Cameroun would cross the territory and give access to some of its isolated regions. Elsewhere roads were to be built as feeders to the railroad or to the rivers at points where they were navigable. The most costly part of this last-mentioned program would be the construction of a network of roads linking Oubangui with Tchad and both their systems with the Benoué at Garoua. A decision about giving Tchad a more permanent and adequate outlet was relegated to the future. Airfields were to be built for each of the capital cities and some secondary centers, but only a small portion of the Plan funds were to be involved, as Metropolitan France was taking over the bulk of such expenditures as part of its imperial defense program.

When the time came for drawing up AEF's Plan for 1952–56, stock was taken of FIDES' accomplishments to date. While its expenditures in the field of communications had visibly aided AEF's economy, there was a great deal of unfinished business left over from the first Plan, a general lack of balance in what was completed, and a few costly failures. The road program was badly bogged down: vast sums had been spent in bringing machinery and technicians to AEF, yet in terms of actual construction the results were minimal, particularly in Gabon. Then it was found that the Federal Artery had been overequipped and that to make it work to capacity and also pay its way, the federation's production must be increased. Consequently the communications sector was demoted to second place: the stress was now placed on the internal network, and it was to be developed primarily for serving the federation's main producing centers—Brazzaville and the Niari valley; Bangui, Boali, and Oubangui's coffee plantations; the Logone; and the animal-husbandry and cotton zones of Tchad. Traffic was to be concentrated along a few main itineraries, notably the Federal Artery. In keeping with this policy, the road program was cut back, the techniques of road-building were changed so as to better suit local conditions, and a tighter control over the construction companies was established. Financial encouragement was given to the principal navigation companies on the Oubangui, Sangha, Congo, and Benoué rivers to enlarge their fleets and speed up their services. Negotiations were entered into with the Belgian Congo to procure some of its ore shipments for the Congo-Ocean railroad, and their success brought about a better balance between the volume of the freight it carried to and from the Atlantic.

On the debit side must be chalked up some omissions or shortcomings, which, however, may be remedied in the not-distant future. The government's attempts to achieve better coordination among all the services operating on the Federal Artery not only encountered the difficulties inseparable from any such effort to combine public with private enterprises, but also reawakened the hostility of those perennially opposed to according further favors to that itinerary at the expense of other routes. When in 1954 the government insisted on a reduction in the rates for transporting cotton, coffee, and certain imports along the Federal Artery, cries of protest arose from the private navigation companies, traders, and truckers' associations. They claimed that the authorities were trying to force exporters to use this route at their expense, in an indirect attempt to justify the vast expenditures that had been made and were still being made on its improvement.[2] That same year the government did succeed in the easier task of placing the three public organizations that managed the railroad and ports of Brazzaville and Pointe Noire under a single directorate, and moved ahead with its plans to amalgamate their accounts into a single budget. Progress toward the government's more difficult goal of setting up a comprehensive organization that would embrace all the transport services in the federation went much more slowly. Although a study committee was formed in 1955, it was not until three years later that an Association of AEF Transporters was set up at Brazzaville.

Among the major omissions of the second and third Plans was the continued neglect of Gabon's communications system. Little progress was made on its road program, and only slightly more on the improvement of its ports. In late 1959, however, it seemed likely that private enterprise would step in and accomplish what public funds had failed to achieve. The discovery of petroleum along the coast and of big manganese and iron deposits in the interior should make a reality of the long-discussed plan to expand Port Gentil's loading and unloading facilities and also should give rail access to a sizable segment of Gabon's isolated hinterland. Ore shipments from Franceville to Dolisie should also make an appreciable contribution to the paying traffic carried on the Congo-Ocean railroad.

But there still remains Tchad, for no decision has yet been reached as to which of its three possible outlets will be selected for construction or expansion. In 1957 and again in 1958 both the Grand Council and the Tchad territorial assembly took a stand against building the proposed

Port Sudan–Nigeria railroad across French territory. Political considerations also lie behind the disfavor with which possible rail links with Nigeria and Cameroun have been regarded by the assemblies of Tchad and Oubangui, for their members feel no assurance about the policies that those countries may adopt after they become independent states. Another factor that entered the picture in December 1958 was the French currency devaluation, which increased the rates for Tchad exporters and truckers and thereby lessened the attraction of the Nigerian route. Two studies undertaken by the Fort Lamy Chamber of Commerce (at the request of the Tchad government) of the relative costs of basic imports along Tchad's three outlets showed that the franc's devaluation had made the Federal Artery competitive with the Nigerian route, at least for southern Tchad.

As this book is being written, it appears that the odds now favor construction of the Bangui-Tchad railroad, with a possible extension as far as Abéché. One of the decisions reached at the four premiers' conference held at Brazzaville on June 23–25, 1959, was to entrust management of the whole Federal Artery to a new Agence Transéquatoriale de Transports, and to support the project to build the Bangui–Tchad railroad. It may well be the French taxpayer who will support the cost of such a railroad's construction, but it is hard now to see how the new republics of AEF could pay even for its operating expenses. They remain on the horns of the federation's chronic dilemma—the concentration of four-fifths of its population in areas 1,000 to 2,000 kilometers from the sea, and the poor returns received from bulky exports which cannot pay for needed imports or even for the cost of transporting them.

The Congo–Ocean Railroad

Originally conceived as but one section—albeit the most important—of a rail network throughout the federation, the Congo–Ocean is the only railroad so far built in AEF, except for small branch lines connecting it with the port of Brazzaville, the sugar mill of the Société Industrielle et Agricole du Niari (SIAN), and the copper mines of Mindouli. Though it runs only through the extreme south of Moyen-Congo and lacks important feeder tracks, the Congo-Ocean serves all four territories, to widely varying degrees, and is thus a truly federal enterprise.

As long ago as 1886 Brazza envisaged a comprehensive rail system for AEF, and stressed that the sector most urgently needed was a line that would link Brazzaville, terminus of the navigable stretch of the Congo, with the sea. But he wanted the track to be built wholly in French territory so as to serve the north bank of the Congo. And his view prevailed, when in 1890 King Leopold proposed to the French government the building of a railroad that would link the two sides of the river as a joint Franco-Belgian enterprise.[3] So the Belgians went ahead alone, and by 1898 had constructed a 386-kilometer rail line between Léopoldville and Matadi port. Though ten years earlier the French had started making the first of a series of studies for their railroad, actual construction did not begin until 1922, and it took 12 years to complete. In the meantime AEF perforce used the Belgian line (to the very limited degree which its capacity permitted) and human portage, and the results were highly unsatisfactory. Not only was Matadi port frequently congested,[4] but the French disliked having the whole economic life of AEF dependent on a foreign railroad over which they had no control.

These considerations moved Parliament to grant on June 12, 1909, the first of a series of loans for further study of a Brazzaville-to-ocean railroad and later for its construction. Millions of francs were spent by ten successive study missions, whose members submitted contradictory reports as to where the track should be laid and where its terminal seaport should be located. During this period World War I intervened, and when the surveys were resumed in 1919 the franc's value had so declined that more funds were necessary. Another delaying element was the pressure exerted by private interests to have the railroad pass through property they owned.[5] Finally, in 1922, Pointe Noire was selected as the railroad's western terminus, a contract for construction of the line was signed with the Parisian Société des Batignolles, and Governor-General Augagneur gave orders to start work on the only sector of "undeniable utility"—that between Brazzaville and the Mayombé. In February 1923 the Belgian government proposed to France that she give up the enterprise as "unnecessarily expensive" and proposed instead enlarging the capacity of the Matadi line.[6] The French, however, were at long last committed to construction of the Congo-Ocean line, although subsequent events made some of them regret that the Belgian suggestion had been rejected.

From the outset the Congo-Ocean railroad ran into such grave difficulties that several times it was on the point of being abandoned. Building a roadbed over the mountainous Mayombé jungle presented almost insuperable technical difficulties; then it proved very hard to recruit and keep an adequate labor force; and the construction took much longer and cost far more than had been originally estimated. Only the determination of Governor-General Antonetti (who succeeded Augagneur in 1924) kept the project going, and for his tenacity he barely escaped being dismissed from his post. Reports of horrifying conditions in the railroad's labor camps were printed in the Metropolitan press and repeated in Parliament, and Antonetti was reviled by the representatives of local interests on whose toes he had trod. Parliamentary missions were sent out in 1926 and 1929 to investigate the situation, and Antonetti himself was twice recalled to Paris for an accounting. Though he was not completely exonerated, Antonetti was nevertheless not held primarily responsible for the waste of human life and money entailed by the railroad's construction.

Actually it was the system of forced labor and the lack of preparedness and supervision on the part of both the construction company and the public authorities that were basically at fault. The Société des Batignolles brought virtually no machinery or equipment to AEF, so that it had to depend on African manual labor.[7] Remembrance of the conditions under which the Matadi railroad had been built caused the countryside on both banks of the Congo to be deserted. A brief experiment in using imported Chinese labor was a dismal failure, and laborers had to be recruited in the more populous countries to the north. Thousands of men rounded up there and brought by force to the humid jungles from the dry savannah zone could not adjust themselves to the climate or the local food, and either deserted in droves or died for want of proper care and nourishment. In 1924 special regulations had been issued in regard to the housing, medical treatment, and rations for African railway laborers, but officials were lacking to enforce them. Conditions in the Congo-Ocean labor camps were certainly very bad, but Georges Boussenot, who headed the Parliamentary inquiry commission in 1929, concluded that reports had exaggerated them.

He found that between the years 1921 and 1929 the loss of laborers, including those dismissed for incapacity or medical reasons, came to 11 per cent of the number recruited, rather than the 40 per cent reported in the press.[8] Many recruits had run away the first night, taking their provisions and blankets with them, and the French public had erroneously been informed that these deserters numbered among the camp casualties. It was a current saying in AEF at that time that for every kilometer of track built, one European had died, and that an African life was lost for every tie laid. During the four years preceding completion of the line, the mortality rate was sharply reduced as a result of improved working and living conditions. In all, out of a total of about 120,000 workers, probably 15,000 to 18,000 persons (almost all Africans) perished in the construction of the Congo-Ocean railroad—a horrifying total, but one not unique in the annals of colonial railroad building.[9] Time has given a new perspective on Antonetti's life work, and made him almost a hero in African eyes. Aside from its economic aspects, the Congo-Ocean railroad played such a determining role in suppressing human portage in Moyen-Congo that the territory's assemblymen have on several occasions paid warm tribute to the man chiefly responsible for its construction.

In money terms, this railroad's 511 kilometers of 1.06-meter-gauge track cost France 231 million gold francs, and it was opened to traffic on July 10, 1934. For many years thereafter the controversy raged as to whether it would ever economically justify its construction. In his zeal to win support for this line, Antonetti had certainly exaggerated its potential, even claiming that it would become one of the greatest railroads in the world[10] and be able to carry 600,000 tons of merchandise a year. Actually its capacity was 455,000 tons, and 13 years passed before it ever carried so large a load. Clients and merchandise failed to materialize on a large scale, including sizable tonnages of the Mindouli copper ore on which high hopes had been placed. Rates on the Matadi railroad were lower, and it carried five times as much traffic as the Congo-Ocean. In 1937 the latter's special budget showed that its receipts barely covered operating expenses and could make no contribution to interest charges or a renewals fund. On the eve of World War II there were many in France and AEF who agreed with Susset's condemnation of the railroad as "an absurdity and a disaster."[11]

Almost overnight, in 1941, the Congo-Ocean's economic position changed radically, and with it the strategic role it played in AEF's war effort. During the rest of the war, 70 trains a week ran on its tracks, its workshops helped to repair military equipment, and it carried troops and matériel to the desert front.[12] At the same time, however, it was noted that there was no increase in its regular passenger or merchandise traffic. Moreover, when the war ended, the Congo-Ocean's locomotives and cars were worn out, and in many places the track needed re-laying. Economies practiced at the time of its construction were reflected in sharp curves and steep grades, and the train service was further slowed down by occasional landslides and the use of wood as fuel. When AEF's imports mounted after the war, the Congo-Ocean was unable to handle the increase, and the congestion at Pointe Noire port in 1946 and 1947 took on formidable proportions.[13] It was not until 1948 that FIDES came to its rescue by ordering diesel locomotives and modern rolling stock from the United States and enlarging its workshops. By 1950 the Congo-Ocean technically was rejuvenated beyond recognition, but problems of a different type had arisen in the interval—those of administration, personnel, and the irregularity and imbalance of its freight traffic.

By a law passed on February 28, 1944, management of the Congo-Ocean railroad was slated to be transferred from the Public Works Department to a commercial, financially autonomous Régie. But this was not accomplished before creation of the Grand Council, whose members from the outset opposed such a transfer, being influenced in this matter by the attitude adopted by the African employees (*cheminots*) of the Congo-Ocean. The latter had been convinced, by the failure in 1947 of the prolonged strike conducted by their French West African colleagues against the Régie recently instituted in that federation, that they were more likely to better their status and working conditions under a public administration than under a semiprivate one. In this they were counting on the greater security of wages, promotion, and pensions that derived from their current position as government employees, and also on the benevolent intervention of the Grand Council in labor disputes. This view was confirmed in September 1949 when their threat of a strike won them pay concessions from the railroad authorities. The Grand Councilors, for their part, were reluctant to give up the control they possessed over the railroad's policies and rates that would have resulted from the change-over to a Régie.[14] In vain the government spokesman argued that the *cheminots'* status would not be adversely affected by the change and that the railroad under a commercial management was less likely to become an annual burden on the federal budget: in 1952 and again in 1953 the Grand Council refused to vote in favor of a Régie.[15] By this time an improvement in the Congo-Ocean's financial position had removed one of the major arguments in favor of a Régie, so the government then accepted prolongation of the status quo.

In 1947, the Grand·Council, supported by the federation's Chambers of Commerce, refused to accept a proposed 50 per cent rise in the railroad's rates, claiming that the increase in its European personnel had been unjustified.[16] This rebuke was effective, and gradually the railroad staff was reduced from a peak of 3,424 in 1950 to 2,725 in 1954: of those only 143 were Europeans and they were retained in the key technical and administrative posts. But this numerical reduction had been more than offset by wage and salary rises—such expenditures by 1954 formed 51.1 per cent of the total—and by an increase in annual payments into the renewals fund from 128 to 138 million CFA francs.[17] Moreover, to palliate the effects of the trade recession of 1952, the railroad that year had reduced its rates on the transport of wood and oleaginous exports. Yet at the same time an efficient management, an increase and a better balance in the freight it carried, and above all the economies effected in its operating expenditures that resulted from the Plan's improvement in its equipment gave ground for hope that soon the Congo-Ocean might be paying its own way.

In 1948 the Congo-Ocean transported 252,588 travelers and 278,647 tons of freight, and its revenues amounted to 241,300,000 francs.[18] Re-equipment and improvements of the line were largely completed by 1950, but it was still far from carrying its capacity load and the freight was, moreover, unbalanced and irregular in its distribution. On the up-run to Brazzaville it carried 170,000 tons of imports, but in the other direction only 100,000 tons of local products:[19] the seasonal character of AEF's exports meant that the Congo-Ocean worked to capacity in September and October but had a minimal load in March and April. The year 1952 marked a setback for the railroad, reflecting the shrinkage in AEF's foreign trade. Passenger traffic declined by 10 per cent, freight transport by 15 per cent, and revenues by 5.7 per cent.[20] Early in 1953, however, there entered into the picture a new element that promised to redress partially the lack of balance between the up- and down-traffic. After prolonged intergovernmental negotiations, the Belgian Congo agreed to let the Congo-Ocean transport some of its raw-material exports purchased by Metropolitan industries, of which the most important item was 20,000 to 30,000 tons of copper ore and palm oil. This windfall, together with an austerity budget, permitted the Congo-Ocean railroad to end 1953 with a small surplus of 4,500,000 CFA francs. In fact the Congo-Ocean was now so well and economically run that in 1954 there was restored to its management control over the budgets for the ports of Brazzaville and Pointe Noire, which had been made autonomous six years before. And in October of that year, the railroad was even able to reduce its rates for transporting a wide range of exports.[21]

In 1955 the Congo-Ocean's traffic increased to 370,000 tons and its revenues to 696,741,000 CFA francs, and its budget even showed a surplus although the cost of personnel was absorbing 54.9 per cent of its total expenditures. Its position had become so strong that it received two unexpected tributes that year: the government definitely renounced its plan to set up a Régie, and this youngest of French Black African railroads was cited in an official Metropolitan report as a model for railroad régies elsewhere in the French Union.[22] A breakdown of its major items of freight showed that on the down-run it was carrying in 1954 about 30,000 tons of wood, 14,000 tons of cotton, 10,000 tons of palm kernels, 10,000 tons of lead ore, and 20,000 tons of copper ore, and that on the up-run it was transporting some 50,000 tons of building materials, 10,000 tons of fuel and lubricants, and 30,000 tons of general merchandise and beverages. In 1955 there was an impressive increase in the tonnages transported, especially on the down-run, and Governor Rouys confidently predicted that with additional equipment the Congo-Ocean's capacity could be boosted to 800,000 tons.[23] Its staff had been further reduced to 2,588, and been given a "legal status of a commercial type, which along with a wage increase has improved labor relations and also the line's efficiency."

However, there were a few dark spots in this optimistic appraisal. Passenger traffic was declining steadily. The Congo-Ocean still depended overmuch on the transportation of lumber, for which world market conditions fluctuated widely. Despite successive tariff cuts, rates on the Congo-Ocean were still nearly double those on the Matadi line. Finally, and most serious of all, the growth in AEF's exports and shrinkage of its imports under the Plan had reversed the previous situation and brought about an equally undesirable lack of balance in the freight carried on its up- and down-runs. All the foregoing phenomena were accentuated in the years that followed. In 1958 the Congo-Ocean's income rose to 1,047,600,000 CFA francs compared with 904,000,000 in 1957; its passenger traffic declined to 833,400 from 879,300; and the tonnage of freight transport increased to 534,806 from 497,720 tons.[24] The same year, personnel costs had so sharply increased and the gap between the up- and down-traffic had so widened that the government proposed the first rate rise (averaging about 11 per cent) since 1952, particularly on wood and coffee transport.[25] But here, as in so many other aspects of AEF's economy, the government is counting mainly on the Kouilou project to restore the Congo-Ocean's equilibrium, through an increase in the up-traffic to be supplied by COMILOG's purchases.

Roads

At the end of World War I, AEF's "road system" consisted merely of an assortment of *pistes* (tracks), two of which were suitable for motor traffic. The combined length of these two was less than 40 kilometers, and both had been built to connect the navigable portions of two rivers. The Gabonese road linked Fougamou and Cindara on the N'Gounié, while the other connected the capital of Oubangui to Zinga, the northern outpost for navigation on the Federal Artery.

Oubangui was the first colony to be given even the semblance of a road network by army engineers. Its lateritic soil lent itself to road building, and after World War I it had the good fortune to be administered by an enterprising governor who was determined to eliminate so far as possible human portage. In the 1920's Oubangui's capital was progressively provided with overland communications to the northern, eastern, and western parts of the territory, and was also linked by road to Tchad. In 1931 a road between Bangui and Yaoundé in Cameroun was completed, and thereafter the tempo of road-building activity was increased and it was extended to the other colonies of the federation. A second AEF-Cameroun link was supplied by a small road built between Mitzic and Ebolowa, and construction of the Congo-Ocean railroad necessitated paralleling the rail line by a road on which supplies could be brought in.

Almost all of these roads were broken by unbridged streams or rivers which had to be crossed by means of primitive ferries. The task of road-building was assigned to administrators whose main concern was to give access to district headquarters or sizable markets. They were men technically unqualified for such work, who lacked adequate maps and money and had only a small unskilled labor force at their disposal. Naturally the colonies best served by waterways had the fewest roads, and only the cotton zones had anything resembling a true road network. On the eve of World War II, Oubangui had 7,000 kilometers of roads, most of them usable throughout the year; Tchad's roads totaled 4,600 kilometers, but very few of them were usable during the rainy season; Moyen-Congo possessed 3,200 kilometers of *pistes*, of which only 500 were motorable; and Gabon had a mere 1,000 kilometers of so-called roads.[26]

World War II brought some improvement in this situation, especially in the northern territories, which by 1946 possessed 26,000 of the federation's total of 37,000 kilometers of roads and tracks. However, the construction undertaken at that time was not determined by economic but by military considerations. Some machinery was brought in and a few permanent bridges were built, but the great majority of roads and wooden bridges were still constructed and maintained by forced labor, and "one could hardly drive 100 kilometers without getting bogged down."[27] It is no wonder that the planners of 1946 decided that road-building was the *sine qua non* for AEF's economic advancement, and for this purpose they allocated one-third of the funds available under the Plan.

With one major exception, the basic policy laid down by this Plan was that all of AEF's roads should serve as links between seaports and the main points on its navigable waterways. The exception was a trans-Gabon route running north from Dolisie on the Congo-Ocean railroad and connected with the Cameroun road system. The main effort was to be concentrated in the northern territories, where the Oubangui river was to be linked with the Benoué in Cameroun by an elaborate network that would give access to the main producing centers and settlements.[28] Of the four categories of roads set up, the most important were the federal highways that were to unite AEF's territories; they were to be made motorable for heavy traffic throughout the year and maintained by federal funds. In all, about 13,500 kilometers of roads were to be built or improved, but of these priority was given to 5,000 kilometers divided about equally among the four territories.[29]

This program failed so dismally in execution that the soundness of the basic principle on which it rested has often been overlooked. Its scope was simply too vast for the means available to carry it out. If the Paris planners had had at their disposal more exact data as to the climatic, topographic, demographic, and other conditions in AEF, and if the local governments had been less anxious to get the Plan started lest the credits allotted to it go unused, many bad mistakes might have been avoided. The general approach to the problem was much the same as if it had been a question of building highways in Europe. Machinery, of which the ECA supplied over half, was to be used, rather than manual labor, and contracts were signed for each of the territories with five big Metropolitan construction companies,[30] on a general cost-plus basis. In mid-1951, when the time came to draw up the second Plan, it was found that three years after these companies had brought their machinery and technicians to AEF, there was very little indeed to show in the line of actual accomplishments. In Tchad 175 kilometers of road had been built, in Oubangui 80, in Moyen-Congo 50, and in Gabon only 40.[31]

Obviously, Paris had grossly miscalculated the amount of time and money required to carry out the first segment of the Plan. It took longer than anticipated to get delivery in AEF of the machinery ordered, to lodge technicians, and to bring together a local labor force. Then, too, it had been estimated that a kilometer of road in the federation could be built for 2.4 million francs, whereas the actual cost proved to be from 4 to 20 million a kilometer, depending on the territory—a total outlay of 43,400 million instead of 14,527 million if the original program had been carried out. Some of the delays were unavoidable, and the degree to which prices rose after 1948 could not have been clearly foreseen, but better preparation of the program would surely have revealed more of the margin of error. Fundamentally at fault was the attitude of the Paris planners, who had ignored local economic realities and been seemingly indifferent as to whether or not the roads they decided to build would ever justify their cost.[32] Little account had been taken of the production factor or of the differing needs and conditions prevailing in each of the territories. Contracts with the construction companies had been carelessly and, in some cases, irregularly drawn up.[33]

The FIDES directorate was largely to blame for permitting the lure of spectacular and grandiose achievements to dominate more mundane and practical considerations, but the Grand Council, which had approved the first road program, also had to share in the responsibility. Its resounding failure naturally demanded a scapegoat, and mutual recriminations alternated with *mea culpas*. A major reorientation of the road program would in any case have been in order, but this became a downright necessity by mid-1951, when it was apparent that there would be a notable shrinkage in all the Plan funds. In August the Grand Council sent out a mission of inquiry to appraise what had been accomplished in each of the territories and to make suggestions for the future.

According to the report of this mission, debated on September 11, 1951, the situation of the territories varied markedly, being good in Oubangui, fair in Tchad, average in Moyen-Congo, and bad in Gabon. The soil and climate of Oubangui made the building and upkeep of roads there relatively easy, whereas in Gabon the prolonged rains, the terrain, and the lack of labor all conspired to yield uniformly poor results. One of Moyen-Congo's main roads was said to be motorable throughout the year, but the other was described as "very difficult." Tchad's roads were reported to be "acceptable" in the dry season but impassable for six consecutive months. In one area (the Bangui-Damara road, for example) an *autostrade* had been built, whereas the great majority of existing roads had been neglected and were now in even worse condition than at the end of the war. One striking conclusion that could be drawn from the mission's report was that, aside from the variations in local conditions, the differing degrees of competence, common sense, and over-all planning displayed by the individual construction companies accounted for the unevenness of the results obtained.

In Paris the keynotes sounded for the second Plan were austerity, production, and *rentabilité*, and in AEF the task of adapting this policy to the federation's road program was entrusted to its Public Works Department. The funds available were cut by nearly half, and over the next four years they would amount annually to only about 1.5 billion CFA francs. A distinction was drawn between the main axes—some of which had to be abandoned—and secondary roads, and in the allocation of new kilometrage to be undertaken, Gabon was assigned 608 kilometers, Moyen-Congo 635, Oubangui 1,670, and Tchad 1,265. In so far as possible the Public Works Department and local construction firms were to be used. The contracts with the Metropolitan building companies were rescinded and new agreements with some of them were made on terms that tightened the government's control of their expenditures.

Government spokesmen in AEF tried to present this transformation of AEF's road program in the best possible light. No more public money would be wasted on the building and upkeep of uneconomic highways— only those really essential to the federation would be retained, and such funds as were available would be devoted to bettering the existing network by utilizing the machinery and materials at hand. Each year the governor-general duly reported in detail to the Grand Council on the progress made. But in early 1955 the announcement of a new cut in FIDES appropriations for AEF's roads under the third Plan reopened old wounds. On two occasions President Flandre of the Grand Council analyzed the situation and expressed his colleagues' reactions:[34]

> It is vital to build more roads, for on them hinges the success of the whole Plan. There is no use in increasing production if there is no way of shipping it out, and funds for road-building have been steadily whittled down. . . . More than half of the federation's road network is nothing more than tracks.

Some of those that were usable 15 years ago are now almost impassable. All of Tchad's roads are seasonal, yet that territory is dependent on selling its agricultural output. Libreville is now practically cut off from the rest of Gabon, whereas about a decade ago it was linked to its northern and eastern regions. Ninety per cent of all our budgets are given to paying the administration's operating expenses, and we have no funds even for our secondary roads.

The first Plan gave top priority to road-building . . . but what is left of all this fine program? 100 to 200 kilometers of modern roads which cost a fantastic price. So it was decided to improve the existing network by replacing wooden by permanent bridges, widening roads, and using local materials to give them a harder surface. Yet even this kind of work is costing from 5 to 7 million CFA francs a kilometer. The total of our annual credits (in recent years) has permitted the construction throughout all the federation of only 100 to 150 kilometers of new roads annually. At that rate it would take many years to provide AEF with the minimal road network it needs. It is true that a big effort has been made in regard to secondary airfields. But the economic life of the federation is not limited to the 20 or 30 localities that are served by airplanes, particularly in view of the lack of feeder roads whereby the articles brought in by air can be distributed. . . . And now we are being granted the smallest sum yet—325 millions for 1955–56.

If AEF's road situation in 1955 was far inferior to that envisaged by the authors of the ten-year Plan and in no way commensurate with AEF's current needs, it nevertheless indicated that real progress had been made. An appreciable portion of the old roads had been improved to the point of being capable during much of the year of carrying a reasonable amount of traffic, and in consequence the cost of truck transport had been driven down. This was particularly true in the cotton zones and especially for the roads linking Bangui to Tchad. In the south, work had concentrated on the branch roads leading to the ports of Libreville and Pointe Noire, the stations of the Congo-Ocean railroad, and the loading points on navigable streams.

After completion of the second Plan, progress continued at the same unspectacular but steady pace, as indicated by the growth in numbers of the federation's motor vehicles. In 1924 there was hardly one to be found throughout the whole federation, but on the eve of World War II they numbered about 2,000, and ten years later that figure had doubled. As of January 1, 1958, Moyen-Congo had 10,326 motor vehicles of all types, Oubangui 5,585, Tchad 4,863, and Gabon 3,800.[35] Thus far the only territory that has set up a Special Road fund, following the example of French West Africa, is Moyen-Congo.

Waterways and Shipping

The importance of AEF's 5,000 kilometers or more of navigable waterways can be better appreciated when it is realized that its seacoast is only 800 kilometers in length, that for many years the federation had virtually no roads, and that it did not possess a single railroad (510 kilometers) until 1934.

AEF's navigable network is made up of three main parts—the great axis of the Oubangui and Congo rivers and two territorial systems, the Chari-Logone for Tchad and the Ogooué-N'Gounié for Gabon. Smaller rivers exist elsewhere in various parts of the federation, but their navigability is even more limited than is that of the three major systems.

The 1,200-kilometer stretch between Brazzaville and Bangui is lengthened by the Congo-Ocean railroad at its southern extremity to Pointe Noire on the Atlantic, and to the north by roads and tracks leading from Bangui to western Oubangui and southern Tchad. Considering that its economic importance to the whole federation is far greater than its location on AEF's eastern boundary might indicate, it seems strange that for many years little was done to increase its navigability or improve the craft it carried. To be sure, an official mission studied this waterway in 1911, but its main accomplishment was a map that is still being used, naturally supplemented by data acquired over the years. The mission also drew up a project for future improvements but at the same time warned of the difficulties to be expected in carrying it out—the enormous length of this river system, the impossibility of approaching river banks in many places, the constant shifting not only of its sandbanks but of its bed as well, the backwardness of the river population, who carried off such markers as were set up, and the need for specialized and expensive equipment to cope with each river's varying conditions. Moreover, AEF's economy, stagnant for many years, offered little incentive for so vast and costly an undertaking, and the result was a few short-lived efforts followed by long periods of apathy.

In 1924 an agreement was signed whereby France pledged to mark the channel of the Oubangui and Belgium that of the Congo. The Belgians used special equipment and two engineers to carry out their part of the bargain efficiently. But the French, after a year's delay, sent only a naval captain to the Oubangui, with inadequate equipment and funds, and soon after he had done what little he could, the sandbars shifted and the buoys he had placed disappeared. Similarly ineffectual was the attempt at about the same time to remove the rocky reef of Zinga, which prevented all but small boats reaching Bangui.[36]

The ten-year Plan of 1946 took up more or less where the 1911 mission had left off, and it concentrated exclusively on the Oubangui-Congo axis. At this time the main stress was placed on road transportation, and even on the Oubangui-Congo, work was not begun until April 1949. There were valid reasons for this delay—the time required to conduct preliminary studies, get delivery of equipment ordered from abroad, and train a local labor force. But there was also an underestimation of the import needs of the northern territories and of the expense of overland as compared with water transport.[37] Then it was also thought that the cost of the work to be done on the Oubangui far exceeded the value of the traffic it would ever carry (then about 30,000 tons a year).

The Congo river presented no problems at all, for its flow was remarkably regular and it was open throughout the year to steamers up to 800 tons drawing two meters of water. The Oubangui, however, was fully navigable only from July to December and, at low water, not beyond Dongou, 320 kilometers upstream from its juncture with the Congo. Moreover, it was encumbered with sandbanks, islands, and rocky ledges, of which the most dangerous was that of Zinga, 100 kilometers downstream from Bangui. To eliminate the costly and time-consuming transshipments of freight at Zinga, FIDES undertook first of all to remove that reef. It has required a decade to accomplish this task, but the removal of thousands of tons of rocks annually has permitted larger boats to go farther upstream for more weeks of each successive year. In 1952 there appeared a new menace to navigation on the Congo portion of this artery—the water hyacinth, which, by its rapid and prolific growth, has covered buoys and markers and periodically clogged up the river. Three years later it began to appear on the Sangha, and to prevent its contaminating the Oubangui the federal government rapidly took action patterned after the effective methods used by the Belgians on the Congo.

Slow and difficult as was the task of improving navigation on the Oubangui, it was simply a matter of finances and techniques. Quite different were the problems involved in dealing with the private company which held a quasi-monopoly of transport over this route—the Compagnie Générale des Transports en Afrique (CGTA). In 1947 the boats and barges plying between Brazzaville and Bangui, like those used in 1905, were fueled by wood deposited at various points along their route. Still operating on the principle that the tonnage carried downstream determined the load to be taken up-river, this company's business in 1947 had increased by only 3 per cent compared with prewar years, and the CGTA gave no indication that it intended to modernize its equipment or speed up its service. In 1948 the federal government asked the CGTA to do both, and it gradually acceded to this request, buying diesel-motored tugs and bigger barges.

Inevitably it took time for these changes to become effective and for the federation's foreign trade generally to pick up. In the meantime the Grand Council and the territorial assemblies of Oubangui and Tchad grew increasingly irritated with the CGTA, which was accused of "monopolistic practices" and of deliberately limiting the transportation of imports direly needed in the north. In its sessions of April 27, 1949, and May 10, 1950, the Grand Council passed resolutions asking the government to replace the CGTA by a company of "mixed economy" and to prevent it from putting into effect a proposed 10 per cent rise in its rates. To this the government replied that setting up a navigation company of "mixed economy" would be a long and difficult task, and that it had no jurisdiction over the tariff that could be charged by a private company. This storm blew over, however, with the gradual improvement in the federation's imports and the equipment and service of the CGTA. By 1955 the CGTA's administration had been reorganized, its obsolete equipment replaced by 20 diesel units and 100 barges, and the more efficient method of pushing barges substituted for that of towing them.[38] Furthermore, the tonnage carried by this company had risen to 104,000 tons from 39,500 tons in 1949; under government pressure it had lowered its transport rates for cotton and coffee; and it had acquired a monopoly of the traffic on the Sangha river. In 1956 it declared a 10 per cent dividend, and the following year announced an increase in its capital from 982 million CFA francs to 1,179,000,000. The CGTA is one of the rare companies in AEF whose activities and profits have been steadily increasing over the postwar years.

Through the port of Pointe Noire, at the western extremity of the Federal Artery, pass almost all of AEF's imports and a majority of its exports. Pointe Noire has had a checkered career, but with the passage of years its position as the Federation's primary port became ever more assured. It has not yet been used to capacity, but the probable rise in mineral exports and development of an industrial combine in the Pointe Noire region now belie the pessimism of those who opposed its construction on a large scale.

Because of the absence of a maritime bar at Pointe Noire, the slave-trading ships were early attracted to this port, as later were French naval officers. They set up an administrative post there but it was abolished in 1889, owing to the unhealthy proximity of its mosquito-breeding lagoon. The decision to make Pointe Noire the western terminus of the Congo-Ocean railroad was not made until 1932, after successive study missions had examined many possible sites. The cost of the port's construction was then estimated at 190 million francs, and two years later the contract to build it was awarded to the Société des Batignolles. A major handicap under which this company labored was the lack of local stone. The nearest available supplies had to be brought from a distance of over 100 kilometers, and for some years their transport formed the essential traffic carried on the railroad. Financial difficulties further slowed down the port's construction, and in 1938 the whole project had to be revised. It was hastily completed in 1942 in order to permit Pointe Noire to play a vital role in AEF's war effort. Additional work on it was accomplished under the Plan, and the port was equipped to handle 500,000 tons of merchandise annually.

Technically this port has proved satisfactory, and the chaotic conditions that prevailed there in 1946–47 were due to factors outside its control— the deficiencies of the railroad at that period and the great distance that separates Pointe Noire from world markets and provisioning centers. The committee of inquiry which investigated the port's situation in 1947 laid most of the blame on the railroad. But it also held partly responsible the inadequacy of the port's equipment in storage space and cranes, and the lack of supervision over its unskilled and undisciplined labor force.[39] To give the railroad enough time to move out the 30,000 tons or so of imports that were cluttering up the port, the committee's report proposed that ships be prevented from calling at Pointe Noire for three months. By 1950, improvements in the Congo-Ocean railroad had cleared up that bottleneck, but only a sharp increase in AEF's foreign trade could remedy the irregularity and costliness of the port's ocean-freight services.[40]

During the first postwar years, Pointe Noire's traffic consisted mainly of items imported into AEF under the Plan, and they greatly exceeded the federation's exports. The latter had not yet returned to the prewar level, and some of the most valuable of them—wood and cotton—were in part exported from Gabonese, Camerounian, and Nigerian ports. In 1952 AEF's foreign trade markedly declined, and in the succeeding years the imports financed by FIDES continued to shrink. In 1953, however, exports through Pointe Noire began to pick up. Initially this was due to the first copper-ore shipments from the Belgian Congo, but increasingly the growth in exports derived from AEF's expanded production. In 1954 Pointe Noire handled a record movement of 291,000 tons, of which the share of exports was 137,000 tons and that of imports had fallen to the 1949 level—154,000 tons. In the following year there was an over-all increase in AEF's foreign trade, but for the first time since the war, exports (187,690 tons) exceeded imports (165,370 tons), and there was also a rise in the number of ships touching at Pointe Noire (521 compared with 441 in 1954).[41] This increase in the tonnage passing through Pointe Noire continued, with exports progressively outdistancing imports. The port's capacity was almost reached in 1957 with a record traffic of 490,000 tons (compared with 425,000 tons in 1956), and of these, 285,000 tons represented exports. Cement and fuel were the staples of the import traffic, and timber that of export shipments. This trade expansion was naturally reflected in the port's budget (combined with that of Brazzaville's port), which rose from 119,363,354 CFA francs in 1956 to 195,760,000 in 1957, and Pointe Noire was able to transfer 32 per cent of its ordinary revenues to the renewals fund.[42]

The marked growth in the port's budgets was traceable in part also to changes in its administrative and fiscal regime. Until 1948 Pointe Noire's port was under the same management as the Congo-Ocean railroad; the next year it was placed under a newly created Maritime Subdivision of Pointe Noire; and in 1951 it was transferred to the Public Works Department and its budget combined with that of Brazzaville's port.[43] In 1952 the administration of the two ports was entrusted to a semiautonomous economic council, in an attempt to coordinate transport along the Federal Artery. A second step in the same direction was taken two years later when both ports and the railroad were placed under the same directorate, which it was hoped would eventually exercise control as well over Bangui port and the CGTA. In 1957 improvements were made in the port's equipment and fiscal regime preparatory to the increase in Pointe Noire's traffic anticipated after completion of the Kouilou dam.

Air-Transport Facilities

Before World War II, AEF had so few and such primitive airfields that passengers bound for Brazzaville had to fly in Sabena planes to Léopoldville and then take the ferry across Stanley Pool. (A Franco–Belgian agreement in the early 1930's providing for reciprocal privileges in the use of airfields aroused sardonic amusement among AEF's French residents.) Two French companies, Air-France and Aéro-Maritime (a subsidiary of the shipping firm Chargeurs Réunis), served AEF fitfully on their way to and from adjacent countries. Private flying, on the other hand, was comparatively well developed, especially in Gabon, where foresters were pioneers in building landing fields near their camps in the mid-1930's.[44] In a few of AEF's main towns, flying clubs had been organized, and they received a small grant from the government in return for their services in evacuating the sick from isolated up-country posts.

World War II greatly promoted the development of aviation in AEF. The federation's strategic location as a midway point between France and Madagascar and between the west and east African coasts was put to good use. From September 1940 through July 1943, AEF served as a transit point for more than 25,000 planes en route to the Near East, the Soviet Union, and India.[45] When the war ended, AEF possessed six airfields with hard-surfaced runways, and many smaller ones. Unfortunately they were hastily and poorly built, and some of them were located too near to towns. Under the ten-year Plan, 3,280 million Francs were to be spent on AEF's smaller airfields, not including the cost of improving its six principal ones, which was to be borne by France as part of her imperial defense system. Of the latter group only Brazzaville's airfield, Maya-Maya, was placed in the class A (international) category; the five others (Libreville, Pointe Noire, Bangui, Fort Archambault, and Fort Lamy), assigned to class B, were to be modernized by FIDES but maintained by the federal budget. The 31 airfields rated in class C were also to be reconstructed by FIDES, but their operating expenses were to be paid from the territorial budgets. The remaining 30 fields were to be built and maintained by the territory in which they were located.

The incongruity and extravagance of suddenly equipping with 67 airfields an underpopulated and underdeveloped federation that had had virtually no aviation facilities before the war did not escape the notice of the French communist party. Its spokesman in the National Assembly asserted on December 16, 1954, that the move was obviously a Western-inspired military conspiracy. Such criticism did not deter the French army from building its own airfields in the northern territories, nor did it interfere with the execution of FIDES' separate program, though as time went on several changes were made in the classification of AEF's airfields. The upkeep of the four described as of "general interest" (Maya-Maya, Bangui, Pointe Noire, and Fort Lamy) was taken over by Metropolitan France, and that of the 12 called federal,[46] by the federal budget. The 113 territorial fields (56 in Gabon, 13 in Moyen-Congo, 23 in Oubangui, and 21 in Tchad) were to be maintained and built from territorial funds.[47] Another reorganization took place after the political changes effected in 1957. The federal category was suppressed, and 2 of the airfields formerly included therein (Fort Archambault and Libreville) were reclassified as of "general interest," while the remaining 10 became territorial.

AEF's two major airlines, Air-France and Union Aéromaritime de Transports (the UAT, which was formerly called Aéro-Maritime), have greatly added to their equipment and services since the war. Both maintain regular flights between AEF and France and adjacent African countries, and have also developed a coordinated network. A few smaller companies also coexist, the outstanding of them being Air-Gabon and its subsidiaries Air-Congo and Air-Mayombé. In its first years the Grand Council was resentful of Air-France, which it accused of giving poor service and of demanding ever-larger subsidies instead of trying to reduce its operating expenses. Members of the Council further asserted that Air-France was preventing rivals from doing business in AEF, and proposed that the federation break this monopoly by setting up its own aviation company.[48] Nevertheless, in 1949 the Grand Council voted Air-France a subsidy of 20 million CFA francs in return for that company's pledge to enlarge its internal network. Air-France lived up to its word, but in 1951 asked for a 50-million-franc subsidy on the ground that the increase in its local services had led to a serious deficit.[49] The Grand Council did not accede fully to this request, but its hostility toward Air-France declined in proportion as the services offered by that company and the UAT grew in scope and regularity. Whereas in 1949 Air-France served only 10 localities in AEF, by 1955 this number had risen to 41, and all but 10 of them received an Air-France or UAT plane once a week. The Grand Council also continued to subsidize private flying clubs and to grant them special funds for the training of African pilots.

Airplanes in AEF are playing a vital role in the transport of persons, for there is almost no competition from other means of transport in the areas they serve. Air travel has become very popular with Africans as well as Europeans, and there has been a steady rise in the number of passengers. In 1950 a total of 42,414 passengers arrived at or departed from the federation's six main airports; five years later this had increased to 125,000. Less rapid and successful has been the development of AEF's air-freight service. Between 1950 and 1954, airborne cargo rose from 8,475 to 19,290 tons, and of these Fort Lamy's airport alone accounted for 7,838.[50] The two main axes of this traffic are between Douala and Bangui and Fort Lamy, and between Pointe Noire and Fort Lamy via Brazzaville and Bangui. The former is the better balanced and more prosperous of the two—on the run up from Douala, planes carry perishable, fragile, and expensive manufactured goods, and on the return they take cotton, meat, peanuts, and rice. On the second axis, planes carry on the down-run almost exclusively meat destined for the urban populations of Brazzaville, Léopoldville, and Pointe Noire, but they can find little remunerative cargo to transport northward. The announcement in April 1959 by Air-France and UAT of a 10 per cent increase in their air-cargo rates makes the survival of the freight service between Fort Lamy and Pointe Noire open to doubt. Later the same year, however, a regular weekly all-freight, nonstop plane service from Paris to the capital of Tchad was inaugurated.

An interesting aspect of the repercussions of AEF's changed political status on the development of aviation there is implied in an announcement made by the French government in October 1959. This authorized the UAT to aid in the training of African pilots and technicians for such of the new republics as wanted to found their own airlines. As a private company the UAT was obviously thought to be more acceptable than the semi-official Air-France to the nationalist susceptibilities now more evident among local African leaders. Currently, about one-third of the personnel serving on the internal AEF air network is African.[51]

CHAPTER 13

Land Tenure

Recognition of the land rights of Africans in general and of the local chiefs in particular was embodied in the treaties made by France with the indigenous potentates in the middle and late nineteenth century. However, the application to AEF of the Metropolitan law of 1898 and the subsequent cession of nearly two-thirds of the federation's entire surface to big companies (see pp. 12–16) whittled away the Africans' customary ownership of lands. Theoretically, African collectivities (the family, clan, or tribe) were still entitled to use what land they needed for growing food crops, and reserves were to be created for them amounting to one-tenth of the total ceded area.[1] But in practice the local French law courts, in cases involving land disputes between Africans and Europeans, invariably favored the concessionary companies, and as a result of the latter's pressure and of the lack of any geodetic survey the native reserves were never established.

As time went on and the concessionary-company regime proved to be an economic failure, most of the areas that had been ceded to the companies reverted not to the Africans but to the French state. Under the 1898 law, all "vacant and ownerless lands" were declared to form part of the public domain and were therefore regarded officially as the property of the government, either to keep for purposes of public utility or to cede as it saw fit. Gradually the granting of land concessions was hedged about with more and more conditions designed to safeguard the interests of both the state and the Africans by preventing would-be concessionnaires from acquiring land for purely speculative purposes. In 1926 the government's power to grant concessions up to 10,000 hectares was made subject to the condition that land over which Africans held customary rights could be alienated only upon the concessionnaire's payment of a compensation, the rate of which was to be fixed by the administration. Then in 1937 the government-general's right to grant concessions was limited in each case to an area of 5,000 hectares—beyond that amount the decision lay with the Minister of Colonies—and even then the concessionnaire received only temporary title until he had wholly fulfilled the development conditions laid down in his particular *cahier de charges*.

In the interwar period, steps also were taken to promote among Africans the, to them, novel concept of private property. Under the Torrens system, which was then applied to AEF, two classes of property rights were recognized—customary rights under tribal laws and full title to ownership acquired through a registration of lands granted, conceded, or purchased—and Africans were thenceforward able to obtain title to land up to ten hectares without the payment of any fee. These privileges were very little utilized, however, and then only in urban centers. The Torrens system was not adapted to African traditions regarding customary rights, the procedure involved was cumbersome and expensive, and it had the further disadvantage in African eyes of placing property so registered under the jurisdiction of French civil tribunals and not of the customary courts. By the end of World War II there were only 2,000 properties officially registered, including those owned by Europeans, covering a total of 451,222 hectares,[2] but it should be noted that many large private properties had never been properly registered, because of the lack of a land survey and because of the negligence of their owners.

During the debates on the proposed rights for the new federal councils and territorial assemblies in the National Assembly, the African deputies made impassioned pleas for a revision of the 1898 land law. They asserted that it had been a "disastrous myth" to claim that there existed anywhere in Black Africa "vacant and ownerless land"—there was not one inch of ground or waterway over which some African collectivity did not possess customary rights—and they denounced the state's haphazard grants of huge areas from which, in consequence, whole families and even tribes had been displaced without compensation.[3] If it should be impossible to abrogate the 1898 law, in view of the multiple problems then facing the French government, they wanted more power to be given AEF's elected representatives over future land grants. The African deputies stressed that they were not against the principle of granting concessions, for so vast and poor a federation as AEF badly needed private capital investments, but they wanted the Grand Councils to have a decisive vote in regard to their alienation. Finally a compromise was worked out whereby the governor-in-council was empowered to grant temporary title to agricultural and forest concessions of less than 200 hectares, but the approval of the territorial assembly was required for an area exceeding that size. Disagreements between the assemblies and the local administration were to be submitted to the Minister of Overseas France or the French Cabinet, whose decision would be final after consultation with the French Union Assembly. Much stricter conditions were imposed for the cession of urban than for rural property, but in both cases final title was granted only after all the developmental requirements specified in the *cahier de charges* had been fulfilled and the property duly registered.

In the ensuing years, the territorial assemblies managed to tighten their grip on the granting of landed property, not so much because there were many individual candidates seeking large concessions[4] as because the Plan's

urbanization and mechanized-cultivation programs called for the displacement of Africans from the center of towns and from parts of the Niari
valley. Oubangui's assemblymen were particularly resentful of the expro-
priation of African property in the capital city and the forced resettlement
of its owners in inaccessible villages ten kilometers from the heart of
Bangui.[5] Moreover, the granting of land to Metropolitan research organizations and companies (such as the IRHO, CGOT, and SIAN) for experimentation with mechanized cultivation led to endless disputes between
them, the African villagers whom they displaced, and the Moyen-Congo
territorial assembly. In some cases a concession of only 40 hectares provoked
a trial of strength between an assembly and the local administration that
could be settled only at the highest Metropolitan level.[6] It was in Moyen-
Congo that the largest number of concessions was sought, and every session
of its territorial assembly was largely given over to the consideration of such
requests. Eventually its members laid down certain rules that were generally followed by the other territorial assemblies—to wit, that it would never
grant concessions near an African village, or to any person or company
already settled on land for which even a provisional title had not yet been
granted, nor would it accept the administration's word that the local chiefs
and notables had given their consent to the ceding of an area against compensation unless this was done in the presence of a member of the local
assembly.[7]

During this period the government made a greater effort than ever
before to safeguard African urban property, because this was the only form
of land whose individual ownership had begun to be of value in the eyes
of the indigenous population, and because it had become the object of
speculation on the part of alien residents. For this reason and for carrying
out the FIDES urbanization plans, the government at long last undertook
a land survey in the main towns. To obtain title to their urban holdings
the Africans were simply required to erect some kind of permanent structure thereon and to register their ownership with a minimum of formalities. In regard to rural concessions, the government adopted two basic principles in the postwar era: candidates must propose to carry out an economically viable project and one that would also promote the development of
the country, and they must get the wholehearted consent of the population
concerned to the compensation offered for the waiving of its customary
rights.

While all of these measures were considered by the African elite as steps
in the right direction, they felt that the root of the trouble had not yet been
attacked—the French state's claim to ownership over all so-called "vacant
and ownerless lands." For years Parliament had had under consideration
a fundamental draft law designed to safeguard native land rights throughout the French Union, but it was not until the Paris government received
wide powers from the legislature on August 14, 1954, that decisive action
was finally taken. This took the form of a very precise and detailed decree
law, promulgated on May 18, 1955, which abrogated the law of 1898 and

gave satisfaction to the essential demands of the African populations. African customary rights over the land were confirmed and the machinery for transforming them into individual property was simplified; concessions could thenceforth be granted only after a formal renunciation of customary rights over the land in question; the territorial assemblies were given more authority in conceding land and in organizing a land survey; the government would be responsible for execution of the terms under which a concession was granted; and the state's right to own or expropriate property was restricted to land the "vacancy" of which could be effectively proved or that was indisputably necessary for works of public utility.

This very important reform aimed not only to put an end to long-standing abuses but to help develop the concept of private property among rural Africans, toward which the *paysannat* program was already tending by encouraging individual farmers to own the land they cultivated. Logically the next step to be taken was for the local governments to recover land that had been ceded years before but never developed. This was a delicate operation, for it was essential not to discourage the investment of private capital or to penalize unjustly concessionnaires who for valid reasons, such as the lack of labor, had been unable to develop their properties and who were not holding onto them simply for speculative purposes. In Tchad and Oubangui this was not a real problem. In Tchad there were virtually no concessions and the only land disputes that arose were connected with urban property and the ownership of date harvests in the Kanem oases (see p. 455). In Oubangui, almost all of the current concessions were being developed, and the main problem there was to prevent urban properties from passing into the hands of Haoussa speculators. It was only in the forest regions of Gabon and Moyen-Congo that the government felt it must assert its control over undeveloped concessions covering several thousand square kilometers that were the remnants of big grants made to companies 50 years earlier. After stormy debates in the Metropolitan parliamentary bodies, a law was passed on February 24, 1957, by the National Assembly empowering the overseas administrations, under certain conditions, to expropriate properties whose concessionnaires had failed for five years to carry out the terms under which they had originally received land grants.

CHAPTER 14

The Rural Economy

Agriculture

Until the end of World War II the overwhelmingly rural character of AEF was not reflected in its agricultural production. A glance at the list of exports for this period shows the predominance of uncultivated produce —ivory, wild rubber, palm kernels, wax, sesame seed, and the like. The only cultivated or semiprocessed exports were cotton, palm oil, and very small tonnages of cocoa and coffee. With the exception of the two last-mentioned crops, exports were produced by Africans working for the big concessionary companies or for a few European planters. The companies benefited by more government support than did the individual planters, in the form of premiums for production and aid in getting laborers,[1] but cotton provided the sole export that might be described as large-scale. The only Africans who could be termed peasants were the cocoa and coffee farmers of Gabon, for they had settled on the land and had taken an interest in growing those crops after they realized good cash returns from their output.

Elsewhere, such farming as was done had a seminomadic character. Ashes left after the bush was burned over were the only fertilizer used; holes were then dug in the ground and the seed planted by hand; and the soil was cultivated several times with a few primitive tools. Such work was hard, the yields poor, and the soil's fertility soon exhausted, so the farmer moved on to a fresh piece of land and started the process all over again. Manioc was the main crop planted in the south and millet in the north, and in the African diet these cereal foods were supplemented by a few vegetables and fruits, and occasionally wild game and fish. Some tribes, such as the Sara of Tchad and the mountain dwellers of the Congo basin, had an aptitude for farming and grew fairly large crops wherever it was possible to do so. But the men of other groups, such as the Fang of Gabon and the Oubanguians, much preferred trade or hunting and regarded farming as demeaning for themselves though not for their women and children. Tradition assigned agricultural tasks to slaves, and after the French imposed forced labor for the concessionary companies and for cotton production the African estrangement from farming occupations was accentuated.[2]

In the early years of the French occupation, the population of AEF was so small and its pressure on the land so slight that famine rarely occurred, though undernourishment was chronic and widespread. To increase and regularize local food supplies the French administration instituted compulsory village granaries and farms (which came to be called *plantations-commandant*) in the early 1920's, but these were unpopular with the Africans and ineffectual in attaining their objective. Little was done to improve indigenous farming techniques except in the cultivation of cotton, cocoa, and coffee. During World War II the only new crop introduced into AEF was hevea, and to meet the Allies' requirements for strategic materials (wild rubber and palm kernels) severe demands were made upon the federation's rural populations. The abolition of forced labor in April 1946 was immediately followed by a slump in agricultural production, and the food provisioning of AEF's towns—whose population had grown markedly during the war—became increasingly difficult.

In 1946 the architects of AEF's ten-year Plan tackled the agricultural problem from several angles, but they showed less concern for developing indigenous food crops than those for export, particularly textile plants, oleaginous produce, coffee, and hevea. To be sure, 57 million CFA francs were allotted to African agricultural education and a station was set up at Botouali, Moyen-Congo, for the mechanical cultivation of rice, which the authorities hoped would eventually replace manioc and millet in the local diet. But most of the FIDES funds went to developing the federation's infrastructure, and almost all of the 3,953 million CFA francs allotted to agriculture were devoted to raising export production from 41,000 tons in 1947 to 287,000 tons ten years later.[3]

To carry on the research work and popularization of farming techniques for export crops, initiated by the federal agricultural service upon its creation in 1936, 480 million CFA francs were earmarked for setting up ten research stations and laboratories, most of which were placed under the management or supervision of relevant Metropolitan scientific organizations (see pp. 166–68). Cotton was to be developed by the Institut de Recherches du Coton et des Textiles Exotiques (IRCT) at three stations in Oubangui (Bambari, Gambo, and Bossango) and two in Tchad (Tikem and Bebedjia), and jute-type fiber plants, urena and punga, at another in Moyen-Congo (Madingou). Oil palms and peanuts were to be the specialty of two stations in Moyen-Congo (Sibiti and Loudima), first under the management of IRHO and later with the collaboration of CGOT, which in 1953 started its own experimental plantation in Gabon, near Lambaréné. A small station for hevea cultivation, set up during the war at Oyem, Gabon, was taken over with its annex at Kango by the Institut Français du Caoutchouc. And research and experimentation with coffee was to be centered at Boukoko, Oubangui-Chari. At some of these stations the development of local food crops was to be an auxiliary activity, but only three of them were to have that as their main preoccupation—Botouali for rice experimentation, Bailli for Tchad's millet and sorghums, and Grimari for Oubangui's manioc—and these were placed under the control of the federal or territorial agricultural services. Mechanized cultivation was the aim for all of AEF's export crops except cotton, and Moyen-Congo was the region chosen for almost all such experiments because it had the smallest labor force and the largest uninhabited areas suitable for large-scale agricultural production.

To help the Metropolitan organizations carry out this ambitious program, the federal and territorial agricultural services were reorganized and enlarged. The over-all service was the General Inspectorate of Agriculture, which had charge of the two federal stations at Loudima and Boukoko, supervised the territorial service, and controlled the operations of the Bureaus of Agronomic Research, Agricultural Education, Rural Engineering, Soil and Crop Protection, and Standardization of Exports. Each year there were submitted to the General Inspectorate for its approval the programs drawn up by the territorial services, which played the same role as the federal body in their respective territories. Coordination and supervision were the main tasks of the Agronomic Research and Soil and Crop Protection Bureaus, as well as keeping abreast of analogous work being done in adjacent countries. The Standardization Service, set up in 1947 and financed by a small tax on exports, succeeded in raising the quality of AEF's coffee and cocoa exports to a point where they were fairly satisfactory to Metropolitan importers, but its regulations were considered unnecessarily strict by most of the federation's producers. Probably the most constructive work done by any of these bureaus was that of Rural Engineering, which carried out a well-digging program in the pastoral regions and gave technical advice to the irrigation projects of the Logone and Lake Tchad.

The weakest of the five bureaus was certainly that of Agricultural Education, and it was the one most sharply criticized by the African elite. At each budgetary session of the Grand Council and territorial assemblies, the African councilors complained that the agricultural services were absorbing ever-larger funds and doing nothing to improve African food production or farming techniques. The services' technicians, it was said, were engaged either in futile research at the agricultural stations or in promoting export crops.[4] What the African councilors chiefly wanted from the agricultural services was an inventory of the federation's soils to determine which were the best suited to growing food crops by mechanical means. Their dual aim was to improve the diet of the population and to release African farmers from the back-breaking toil which gave such poor yields and cash returns that they had been alienated from agricultural occupations. To these criticisms the government spokesman as regularly replied that not all of AEF's soils lent themselves to mechanical cultivation, that more time was required for research and experimentation, and that as funds became available more tchnicians were being trained and employed in popularizing modern agricultural practices among African farmers. These debates usually ended by the assemblies' voting the credits asked for by the agricultural services, after their members had registered strong protests against the slow rate at which Africans were being trained as agricultural technicians and against the tardiness with which the government was developing food crops in general.

No technical agricultural training at all was given in AEF until World War II, during which apprenticeship centers were successively established at the agricultural stations of Grimari and Sibiti and gradually transformed into territorial schools. In 1945 a third center was annexed to the rubber station at Oyem, and three years later one was established at Tikem. As soon as the war ended, agricultural education was formally organized in AEF at three levels—elementary instruction was to be given at the apprenticeship centers installed at the territorial agricultural stations, a higher form of education was to be available at the main research station of each territory, and the apex of the network was to be a federal school situated at the Boukoko station. Apprenticeship centers were to recruit students among holders of the CEP (certificat d'études primaires); the territorial schools would receive the best graduates from the apprenticeship centers and also those possessing higher general-education certificates; and candidates for the three-year course at the federal school were required not only to have a secondary education but to pass a competitive examination and to pledge that they would remain in the federal service for ten years after graduation. From this system it was hoped that the agricultural services would acquire three grades of African technicians—monitors, agents, and conducteurs.

During their early years the apprenticeship centers and territorial schools received a fairly large number of pupils, and by 1949 they had graduated over 200 monitors and agents. But when the federal school opened its doors in 1949, not one candidate passed the entrance examination, and it had to be closed in 1951 without ever having trained a single pupil.[5] In fact, the number of students at the territorial schools so declined that that of Oyem was shut down in 1952 and its three students were transferred to the training center annexed to the Sibiti station in Moyen-Congo.[6] By that time it had become clear that formal agricultural education was a failure in AEF, and that the only hope of recruiting and training African technicians lay in the experimental farms attached to the research stations. This realization coincided with the reorientation toward increased production given by the second Plan late in 1951, and provoked a drastic revision of the government-general's agricultural policy.

The authorities were now able to appraise the achievements of the first Plan in the light of the growing discredit into which agriculture was falling in three of AEF's four territories. Only in southern Tchad could it be said that farming had made progress, both in export and food crops, that its population was relatively well nourished, and that the towns—though growing—had not depopulated the countryside. Northern Gabon perhaps provided another such exceptional area, but the rest of that territory and particularly the cities were in a precarious position regarding food supplies.

Bangui was still short of manioc but the situation was not so acute as in 1949. Brazzaville and Pointe Noire, however, had grown so rapidly that they had to import food from outside the territory, whose rural population was flocking in steadily growing numbers to the urban centers. Between 1938 and 1952 the production of certain key crops in the territories south of Tchad had declined by about 800 tons a year.[7] Rice production, on the other hand, was increasing throughout the federation, but in contrast to Tchad and Oubangui, where paddy farmers consumed what they grew, the populations of Gabon and Moyen-Congo continued to prefer manioc as their basic food and the government met with increasing difficulties in marketing the rice output. Little further was heard of the mechanical rice-cultivation experiments at Botouali, and indeed the whole scheme of mechanized agricultural production which had aroused general enthusiasm in the first postwar years was now considered of dubious benefit to AEF.

By the end of 1951, some 40,000 hectares of crops were under cultivation by machinery, chiefly in the Niari valley. Peanut, sugar cane, and urena harvests had certainly been increased in consequence, and the specialized stations had ironed out most of the technical difficulties involved in mechanized cultivation. But in certain regions it was noted that the soil was rapidly losing its fertility, and agricultural experts began to stress the need for teaching Africans about the dangers of erosion before they were taught how to run tractors. Undiscouraged, the African elite continued to demand mechanization of the production of indigenous food crops, and now the government became more responsive in its consideration of such requests. In Gabon, where the food situation was particularly critical, where farmers were too few, and where the village women were crushed under the burden of agricultural labors, the government undertook limited experiments in the mechanical cultivation of food crops. Even in the Niari valley the wholly mechanized European production of crops for export was giving way to a closer association between machinery and African labor.

Nevertheless, there was no abrupt revolution in AEF's agricultural policy but rather a change in emphasis, beginning in 1952. The government had cause to be pleased with the development of the new export crops of tobacco, peanuts, sisal, and hevea, and with the increase of traditional exports such as cotton, cocoa, and coffee. And it was not pessimistic about the future of urena, palm oil, and rice. It continued to push the expansion of all those export crops even after the price for nearly all of them began to drop sharply with the end of the Korean war boom and after the Metropolitan market had become saturated with oleaginous produce and coffee. A new export, bananas, was encouraged, though there was already a glut of Antilles and Guinean bananas, which far exceeded France's ability to absorb. To win a place for AEF's exports in markets outside the franc zone their high production costs had to be brought down, and to this end the Grand Council voted to lower the export duties on certain agricultural products and transporters agreed to reduce their rates.

These and other measures, in conjunction with the benefits accruing from the Plan's operations[8] and the monetary devaluations of August 1957 and December 1958, have led to a marked rise in AEF's agricultural exports. But they have not brought to the federation's farmers cash returns commensurate with their increased efforts, for AEF's exports are particularly vulnerable to the wide fluctuations in the world market for raw materials. If the sale abroad of the federation's agricultural exports is vital to its economic prosperity, the payment of a remunerative price to their producers is equally essential in order to increase or even maintain their output. By 1951 the importance of paying an adequate price to cotton farmers had been recognized, but it has been only within the past few years that federal price-supporting funds have been established for cocoa, coffee, and jute fibers.

This improvement in the farmers' cash income has affected only those who grow crops for export, and it is but one facet of a fundamental change that has been taking place in the government's agricultural policy since 1952. That year the high commissioner circularized a directive in which he assigned first place to improving the population's well-being by better nutrition, higher living standards, and greater monetary resources. In the agricultural domain the agencies through which these goals were to be achieved were the technical services, the SIP and cooperatives, credit facilities, and a comparatively new institution called the *paysannat*.

It is not easy to give a clear picture of the research organizations and agricultural stations operating in AEF, because of their large number, multiple and changing activities, interlocking administrative dependence on various public bodies, and occasional association with private enterprises. The French taxpayer has financed almost all the scientific agricultural work done in the federation, and the activity of private enterprise in this field has been minimal.

Before World War II, scientific research in AEF was very limited in scope and sporadic in accomplishment, being confined to five experimental farms (four for cotton and one for coffee). At first a handful of experts had charge of them, but after 1936 they were placed under the supervision of the newly created federal agricultural service. Wartime exigencies led to the creation of a hevea experimental farm at Oyem, Gabon, and after the Liberation the government-general took over the existing coffee station at Boukoko, Oubangui-Chari, and set up a second federal station for experimentation with mechanical cultivation at Loudima, Moyen-Congo. In the early postwar years, more and more stations were built, either for a particular vegetation zone or for a specific crop, but as time went on, many of them changed their specialty or added new crops to their field of activity, and all of them were dependent concurrently on one or more Metropolitan scientific organizations and on the agricultural service of the territory in which they were located. To complicate further an already confusing situation, local branches of international organizations such as the locust-control service and the soils bureau have functioned in the federation.

ATTTHE RURAL ECONOMY 167

Only a passing interest in AEF has been shown by some of the Metropolitan organizations, such as the Conseil Supérieur des Recherches Sociologiques, which dispatched a mission in 1953 to study the land tenure system, agricultural activities, and ethnic structure of the peoples of the Logone valley.[9] The Institut des Fruits et Agrumes Coloniaux (IFAC), too, did not start developing banana and citrus-fruit cultivation in AEF until 1952, and then this formed only a minor sector at the Loudima station. Others took over the management of the specialized crop stations in the federation shortly after the war. In 1946 the Institut de Recherches pour les Huiles et les Oléagineux (IRHO) assumed responsibility for the development of oil palms at Sibiti, Moyen-Congo, and of oleaginous produce generally until the Compagnie Générale des Oléagineux Tropicaux (CGOT) took over experimentation with mechanized peanut cultivation at the Loudima station in 1950 and later started its own oil-palm plantation near Lambaréné, Gabon. Still another Metropolitan postwar scientific body, the Institut de Recherches du Coton et des Textiles Exotiques (IRCT), whose field of operations included all French Black Africa, began in 1946 the most extensive of its activities in AEF. Gradually it came to manage two cotton stations in Tchad (Tikem and Bebedjia) and three in Oubangui (Bambari, Bossangoa and Gambo), as well as the urena experimental farm at Madingou, Moyen-Congo.

The Office de la Recherche Scientifique des Territoires d'Outre-Mer (ORSTOM), however, is by far the most important and all-embracing Metropolitan scientific institution functioning in AEF. Created in 1943 to direct and coordinate scientific work on socio-economic problems in Overseas France, ORSTOM not only has a deciding voice in the directorates of all the above-mentioned organizations but also its own Institut d'Etudes Centrafricaines (IEC) founded at Brazzaville in 1947. This institute has a geophysical research center at Bangui, an oceanographic annex at Pointe Noire, and territorial branches at Fort Lamy and at Libreville, and it publishes the findings of its staff either as monographs or in its Bulletin and Memoranda. Eminent scholars on its staff have undertaken some strictly research studies, such as those made by the musicologist Herbert Pepper, for the IEC is heir to the Centre des Recherches Ethnologiques founded by Eboué in 1943, but most of its work has a practical orientation. In the latter category are the sociological surveys that were made preliminary to the regrouping of Gabon villages (by Pauvert and Balandier) and to urbanization projects in Moyen-Congo (by Soret); oceanographic research designed to aid the fishing industry of Pointe Noire; studies of the timing and intensity of river inundations; soil studies of the Niari farming zone, potential coffee-growing lands of Gabon, and the cotton belt of Oubangui; a survey of the land-tenure system and ownership of date palms in the Kanem oases; and the like. Many of the IEC's projects have been aimed at remedying a fundamental weakness of the first Plan for AEF—the lack of adequate preliminary scientific studies—and during the past few years they have been closely geared to the federation's development program.

Valuable as is the work completed or in progress by the IEC, the African elite have not always been sufficiently convinced of its usefulness to be willing to underwrite a part of its cost.[10] Some of the Grand Councilors seemed only to see the IEC's expanding staff and elaborate network of laboratories and houses for its personnel, and were unwilling to share with Metropolitan France even half of the expenditures involved.[11] However, a reorganization of ORSTOM's administration, whereby AEF was given a larger representation on its directorate, helped to change their attitude. In 1958 and 1959 the governments of Tchad and Gabon asked ORSTOM for the IEC's services in making scientific studies for certain projects which their leaders wanted carried out in those republics.

Until 1952 AEF had only agricultural research stations and the experimental plantations attached to them, but it then started seed-multiplication farms and nurseries for food as well as for export crops. By 1956 the federation had one such farm per region and several nurseries in each district, some of which also operated fish hatcheries and raised poultry besides distributing fruit trees, cocoa and coffee bushes, selected oil palms, and the like.[12] Also by that year the territorial agricultural services had been reorganized according to the administrative divisions and modeled after those set up by the cotton companies in Tchad and Oubangui. A trained agronomist was named technical adviser to the *chef de région* and drew up the yearly agricultural program for his area, and *conducteurs* and monitors fulfilled the same functions respectively for the district and canton chiefs. As of 1956 there was one European expert for every 14,000 farmers and one African technician for every 7,000, and the *boys-coton* (see pp. 177–78) had been reduced to a very small number. Most remarkable of all, more Africans were taking up agriculture as a profession, and four of them were engaged in higher agronomic studies in France.

The Sociétés Indigènes de Prévoyance (SIP)[13] were organized in AEF on January 14, 1937, and in general followed the pattern of those that had been created in French West Africa 27 years earlier. They were organized according to the existing administrative divisions, membership in them was compulsory on the part of all African farmers and herders, and strict control was exercised over each society by the local administrator as its ex officio chairman. Another official, usually a member of the Bureau of Economic Affairs, was placed in charge of all the societies in a territory, and a common fund for all of them was inaugurated at Brazzaville under the control of the government-general. A slight decentralization was accomplished through their reorganization in 1940 and 1946, largely because of Eboué's criticism of the SIP's poor management. However, they retained the very comprehensive objectives originally assigned them—the development of local production and the improvement of the living and working conditions of their members. The SIP were empowered to stock and market the produce of their members, help them with the acquisition of farming equipment, and even lend them money to build houses. At the end of World War II, there existed in AEF 128 SIP with a total membership of

2,218,526, more than half of whom were Tchadians. Dues varied from one territory to another, ranging between 5 and 15 CFA francs in 1947. Because of their compulsory nature and the arbitrary utilization of their funds by the local administrator, they were commonly called *le petit impôt du commandant*. And because the small total of their dues was the SIP's sole financial resource, very little constructive work was accomplished by any of them and some were totally inactive.

When the birth of political institutions in 1946 gave French Black Africans their first chance to express their views, the SIP were among the local organizations most vehemently criticized by them. European merchants in AEF were also hostile to the SIP, because of the latter's alleged interference in normal trading operations. Consequently the Council of the Republic, in August 1947, recommended that the SIP be superseded by cooperative societies, following an inquiry into the current operations of the SIP to be made by the heads of the two federations. Unanimously the Grand Council and territorial assemblies of AEF asked that the SIP be suppressed and be replaced at once by cooperatives. The government-general complied to the extent of drawing up regulations governing the establishment of cooperative societies, but begged the councilors to reconsider their vote to suppress the SIP, claiming that the latter had performed useful functions, were the only African economic organization operating at the village level, and could not be replaced by cooperatives in the immediate future.[14] The government also promised to curtail the trading activities of the SIP, to abolish the common fund, transferring financial control of the SIP to the individual territories, and to give the African members more of a voice in the management of their particular society. A few steps were taken toward making the SIP more democratic institutions and integrating them into the federation's development plans, but for some years the government was scored by the African representatives for the slow pace at which it was carrying out the promised reorganization of the SIP. It was, in fact, not until July 6, 1954, that a circular issued by the high commissioner spelled out the reforms to be accomplished, and these were to be undertaken only step by step. By this time, however, the hostility of the African assemblymen toward the SIP had somewhat abated owing to the failure of the cooperative societies that had been set up in AEF during the interval.

Between 1948 and 1952, 15 cooperatives had been formed in the federation, five of which were in Gabon, four in Oubangui, and three each in Moyen-Congo and Tchad. Of the total, only three were production cooperatives, nine were of the consumer type, and four were described as "mixed."[15] The local regulations concerning the establishment and functioning of cooperatives in AEF were based on the very liberal Metropolitan law of September 10, 1947. Because this law envisaged very loose administrative control and few penalties for mismanagement, cooperatives were enthusiastically hailed by AEF Africans, who saw in such societies an unparalleled opportunity to escape from the grip of local officialdom and of the European companies' control of their economy. Although cooperatives were organized forthwith in all of the territories, it is their history in Oubangui that is the most instructive as to the general trend. All of the Oubanguian cooperatives were formed and chaired by African politicians, who succeeded in getting the territorial assembly either to grant them large subsidies or to guarantee loans made to them. Their management was inexperienced and lax, not to say dishonest in some cases, and at least two cooperatives were used to promote the political careers of their founders. By 1954 all had either gone bankrupt or were in such dire financial straits that the territorial budget had to support their losses.

Not all of AEF's cooperative societies followed such a disappointing course as those of Oubangui, and a few were reasonably successful. But the movement as a whole lacked cohesion, showed an almost total ignorance of the basic principles of cooperation, was inefficiently or dishonestly managed, and lent itself to political agitation.[16] In 1952 the government clamped down on the existing cooperatives in so far as the current law permitted, and began drafting new legislation better adapted to AEF's particular situation. It also decided to send some Africans to France for training in the management of cooperatives, beginning in 1954. French officials repeatedly stressed their belief in the cooperative movement as a sound long-run solution for the African segment of AEF's economy. In the interval they proposed that to instill the principles of cooperation among African producers there be set up an intermediate stage as an indispensable preparatory step. This was to be the transformation of the SIP into what were called Sociétés Mutuelles de Production Rurale (SMPR), membership in which was still to be compulsory but the management of which would be elected by their African members and placed under the administration's technical guidance and financial control. This proposal was obviously a compromise between the reorganization of the SIP long advocated by the government and the immediate establishment of cooperatives, which the African elite had for years been demanding but were now less certain about. Actually the cooperatives were by now almost as discredited as the SIP, though for different reasons. In 1958 all of the territorial assemblies were considering favorably the establishment of SMPR, but only that of Moyen-Congo had actually voted to accept them.

In a field closely allied to the activities of the SIP and cooperatives, that of agricultural credit, the administration also took steps to enlarge such resources, so as to make them more readily available to African farmers and herders, and, indirectly, to bolster the SIP by channeling some of these loans through that organization. A bank known as the Crédit Agricole, set up in 1931, still theoretically exists, though since World War II it has been moribund. Unadapted legally to AEF's needs and plagued by declining resources, the Crédit Agricole never played a very constructive role in the federation's economy, for it confined its few loans almost exclusively to European planters and companies. The African elite hoped that the Crédit de l'AEF (see pp. 121–23), founded in 1949, would fill the void resulting from the limited and dwindling operations of the Crédit Agricole. But it soon became apparent that the former was as rigorous in its procedures and as demanding of guarantees from African applicants and, moreover, was concentrating on housing loans, mainly to indigenous urban civil servants. It was next to impossible for the vast majority of African farmers to get loans from either of the existing institutions because as individuals they were unable to offer the necessary guarantees.

In casting about for ways of remedying this situation the government decided that it would take too many years to accomplish the needed reform of the Crédit Agricole, because it was a state institution, financed by public funds, and therefore dependent upon Parliament for any drastic change in its statutes. So in early 1954 the governor-general created in the Crédit de l'AEF a special agricultural section which was to operate with a minimum of formalities and offer low interest rates to borrowers intending to start new agricultural and pastoral enterprises[17] or to add to existing ones. Then in 1956 (after a false start in 1950) another department within the Crédit de l'AEF was formed—the Section des Aménagements Ruraux, which was the equivalent of FERDES in French West Africa and the Petit Equipement Rural du Cameroun. Its function was to grant loans or subsidies for small-scale rural equipment works proposed by a recognized group which, itself, had to participate either by work or funds in carrying out the program it had drawn up. Since the SIP were virtually the only rural collectivity recognized by the government, that organization now received more funds than it had ever before possessed. Through this enlargement of its activities the Crédit de l'AEF quickly increased the volume of its loans for the enlargement of small plantations, harvesting and processing of crops, and the like, to a total of 150 million CFA francs by mid-1958, the greater part of which went into Moyen-Congo enterprises. In 1957 its administration was decentralized in conformity with the provisions of the loi-cadre.

Of all the attempts made thus far to devise an agricultural policy for AEF as a whole, the most recent, comprehensive, and successful has been that embodied in the paysannat. This is the term used for the series of experiments, started in 1952, to transform the seminomadic farmers of the federation into peasants by altering the physical environment in which they live. The orientation given to the second Plan at that time coincided with the AEF government's concern to increase locally grown food as well as export crops and to check the emigration of farmers to the urban centers. In formulating the policy to be applied in setting up the federation's paysannats, the administration drew upon the lessons learned from past experience. The attempt to regroup villages in Gabon had shown the necessity for getting the local population's cooperation in so drastic a change in their physical environment; the first Plan had exposed the basic error of launching large-scale projects that were poorly prepared; the stress on mechanized cultivation had pointed up the danger of soil erosion and the social disadvantages of fostering purely European enterprises devoted to the expansion of export crops; and, after forced labor was abolished, the abandonment of farming generally wherever it was not sufficiently remunerative underscored the need to make living conditions for Africans in the countryside more favorable to compete with those in the towns.

At Kohiri, in eastern Oubangui, circumstances peculiar to that area in 1950 induced the local administration prematurely to start an embryonic *paysannat* there. From the semifailure of this experiment the authorities learned that the allocation of individual plots of ground tended to break down group life in that area, that soil conservation was too long-term an objective to be of any interest to the population concerned, and that cotton cultivation required some supplementary novelty such as a new crop, small-scale mechanization, or the use of draught animals to attract the farmers' cooperation.[18] If AEF's rural populations were to be persuaded to give up wasteful shifting agriculture and learn to farm intensively the land on which they would settle permanently, the site of the future *paysannat* had to be carefully chosen and prepared. It must be selected in relation to the soil's suitability for growing specific crops, concurrently for food and for export, and to the means of communications and markets. To make the new *paysannats* attractive and raise their members' living standards, adequate housing, schools, and dispensaries had to be built, as well as, in some regions, kilometers of roads and tracks. In order to modernize the farmers' archaic methods of cultivation, it was necessary that their equipment be improved and that technicians closely supervise the planting and care of crops. No longer were villages to be forcibly regrouped for the convenience of the administrator, doctor, or schoolteacher. The new *paysannats* were to be populated by specific groups of volunteers who would be technically aided in their efforts to achieve a better economic and social life.

The application of so supple a formula required long physical and psychological preparatory work for each *paysannat*, not to mention the creating of a network of seed-multiplication farms and a sizable staff of technicians. The first *paysannat* was started in the forest region of Moyen-Congo at Divénié in November 1952. By mid-1954 their number had grown to 21, they had been set up in all the territories but Tchad, and they comprised a total of 65,000 persons. All of these *paysannats* grew food crops: those situated in the forest zones of Gabon, Oubangui, and Moyen-Congo produced them in conjunction with cocoa, oil palms, or peanuts, while those in the savannah country usually cultivated coffee as their cash crop. Depending upon the population density and tribal traditions of the particular region, a *paysannat* might group 200 or 10,000 persons either practicing collective cultivation or farming individual plots of ground. Some had evolved much faster than others, such as the well-established cocoa *paysannats* of Woleu-N'Tem, whereas others that involved a reforestation as well as a crop program, such as the Moulenda *paysannat* of Moyen-Congo, were still in the experimental stage. Tchad's *paysannats* did not start functioning until 1956, for the problem there differed from that in the southern territories. Instead of bringing together small scattered groups and teaching them to cultivate one or more "rich" crops along with manioc, the densely populated villages of Tchad had to be broken up because they were exhausting the soil around them. But before the Tchadian farmers could be persuaded to add new food crops such as rice or peanuts to their cultivation of cotton, their water resources had to be increased either through irrigation or well-digging. This required an even longer preparatory period than in the south, and it was not until 1956 that five *paysannats* were founded in that territory.

Every year since 1952 the number of *paysannats* and of their inhabitants has grown, and with them thousands of hectares have been brought under cultivation. It now appears that a formula satisfactory to both the French and African authorities has been found for stabilizing and improving the well-being of the rural populations and for increasing the production of food and export crops. What remains to be seen is whether or not the new African governments will want or be able to carry out a policy whose success depends upon meticulous preparation and large amounts of money and technical skill.

Rice

Paddy is one of the few crops that is grown in all four territories of AEF and whose mounting production has created grave local marketing problems. Introduced comparatively recently into the federation, paddy can be called a "traditional crop" only in the Mossendjo district of Moyen-Congo, the Tchibanga region of Gabon, and the Logone valley of Tchad. Almost all of the rice grown in AEF is of the dry variety, though in the humid lowlands and inundated river valleys a marsh type is cultivated. There is some small-scale cultivation of paddy by mechanical means and some cultivation by Europeans in parts of the Niari valley.

Before World War II, AEF satisfied its small needs in rice by imports from Indochina and the Belgian Congo, which ranged annually between 2,700 and 3,800 tons a year during the last interwar decade. This rice was consumed solely by the southern urban populations and laborers in European-owned agricultural, forestry, and mining enterprises. For the rural Africans of AEF the basic food was and still is manioc in the Congolese basin and millet in that of Tchad. The interruption or irregularity of rice imports from the Far East during the war and early postwar years made the authors of the ten-year Plan decide to increase vastly AEF's paddy production. Missions were dispatched to study mechanical rice cultivation in the United States and to study the potential of the Logone valley for irrigated paddy development. The goal subsequently set for 1956 was 70,000 tons of paddy, of which 20,000 were to be exported to neighboring countries. The task of developing and distributing seed suitable to the various regions selected for the introduction or expansion of paddy cultivation was assigned to four agricultural stations, the most important of which were those of Boumi (in the Logone valley) and Botouali (on the Likouala-aux-Herbes). Propaganda was aimed at the African farmers to popularize paddy as a cash crop and one whose by-products could be used as animal fodder, and among town dwellers as a food that was more nutritious than manioc or millet.

As a result of these efforts, the area planted to paddy grew from about 16,000 hectares in 1948 to over 25,000 in 1954, and rice production during that period rose from around 3,500 to more than 8,000 tons, three-quarters of this being grown in one region of Tchad. Though these increases did not come up to the Plan's anticipations and the total amount of rice sold throughout AEF did not exceed 5,700 tons, the output proved to be embarrassingly large, at least in the southern territories. Whereas in Oubangui and Tchad production was balanced by consumption, in Gabon and Moyen-Congo transport difficulties, high production and sales prices, poor marketing organization, and inferior quality made the disposal of locally grown rice an ever-heavier burden for the administration. Only in the towns was rice as a food making any headway among the African populations, and they continued to prefer imported rice to the home-grown product because it was cheaper and of better quality. After considerable hesitation the government and elected representatives decided in 1955 to limit rice production to current consumption levels and to impose a duty on imported rice. As a corollary move, the local authorities have been trying to bring down rice-production costs and improve the quality of Gabon's and Moyen-Congo's output. They recognize that for the time being the increased local output of rice cannot provide the solution for the chronic undernourishment of AEF's population, nor can the Logone's immense potential for growing rice for export be utilized until Tchad's external transport problem is solved.

Cotton

It is difficult to reconcile the chronic unpopularity of AEF's cotton both in the federation and in France with its importance to the local budgets and to the Metropolitan textile industry. Its value in recent years has approximated 6,500 million CFA francs annually and it has accounted for over 43 per cent by value of all AEF's exports, besides which it has brought into the federation's coffers each year some 750 million CFA francs in duties. Of the total cotton production in French dependencies, AEF has supplied over 80 per cent. The federation's 40,000-odd tons of fiber has met about 11 per cent of France's needs in raw cotton and has saved her some $30 million annually that would otherwise have had to be spent for such purchases in the dollar zone. Technically successful, too, has been AEF's production of commercialized cotton. Although large-scale cotton culture started only in the mid-1920's, output grew to 118,000 tons in 1957-58, worth nearly 6,000 million CFA francs; yields have risen from about 100 kilograms per hectare to an average of nearly 300; and the quality of AEF's cotton has been pronounced competitive with that from foreign sources. At least 1.5 million Africans, or approximately two-thirds of the adult population of Oubangui and Tchad, are wholly or partly dependent upon cotton sales to supply their cash income, and in 1958 they received a total of 3 billion CFA francs from sales and 300 million more in the form of planting bonuses.

To all outward appearances AEF's cotton culture has been very successful and now it may be so appraised, but it has had its somber aspects. For Metropolitan France, cotton has been a costly luxury which since 1951 has with considerable regularity required subsidies, the amount of which has varied depending upon the world price for that commodity. To many French administrators and African chiefs—in the past far more than today —cotton has been a nightmare, for their salaries and in some cases their posts depended upon increasing its production. Even the four companies which from the beginning have held the monopoly of purchasing, processing, and exporting AEF's cotton crop did not become prosperous until recent years. And for nearly three decades the African farmer in northern AEF was more a victim than a beneficiary of the official pressure exerted on him to grow ever-larger quantities of cotton.

It was with the best of motives that the policy of growing cotton for export in AEF was launched, though some embittered enemies of the local administration claimed that its aim was to divert Metropolitan public opinion from dwelling on the "murderous and useless" Congo-Ocean railroad scandal.[19] For some years after World War I, it was evident that AEF could no longer count as in the past on two staples of its trade—ivory was fast disappearing and the price for wild rubber was falling fast. As a substitute source of cash income, cotton seemed to offer undeniable advantages. It was indigenous to the northern colonies, where both the soil and climate were propitious; its cultivation promised to stabilize the Africans of that area who practiced shifting agriculture; it could be grown in rotation with food crops; and finally, the output would find a ready market in France. Furthermore, success attained after long experimentation with imported varieties (first Triumph, then Allan) coincided with the trade depression of the early 1920's, and this was the determining factor that led the government to push cotton cultivation in Oubangui and Tchad.[20]

After trying in vain to interest French industrialists and bankers in promoting this crop in the federation, the government turned in 1924 to some Belgian and Dutch companies which had pioneered cotton farming in the Congo, where conditions were similar to those in northern AEF. Three of the four companies with which it made successive agreements and which were duly incorporated according to French law have survived to this day. These were the Compagnie Cotonnière Equatoriale Française (COTONFRAN), a subsidiary of the Société des Cotons du Congo; the Société Française de Cotons Africains (COTONAF); and the Compagnie Commerciale et Cotonnière de l'Ouham-Nana (COMOUNA). The fourth and only French company, the Société de la Kotta, established itself in Oubangui in 1930 but a few years later ceded its rights to the Société Cotonnière du Haut-Oubangui (COTOUBANGUI).

By the terms of its contracts with these companies, the government was to supply them within five years a minimum tonnage of cottonseed, grant them a ten-year monopoly of the purchase of cotton within a defined area, assure them a fixed percentage of profit over and above their operating costs, and recruit technical agents for the cotton farmers. The companies, for their part, guaranteed to collect, process, transport, and export all the cotton harvested in their respective zones, and to accept the purchase price and percentage of profits to be set each year by the government. To COTONFRAN in 1926–27 the largest zones were awarded—the Logone-Chari, Mayo-Kebbi, and Baguirmi regions of Tchad and the Batangafo district of Oubangui; COTONAF came next in importance, being assigned the cotton-growing areas of central and western Oubangui; then COMOUNA installed itself in 1930 in the easternmost Oubangui regions of M'Bomou and Haute-Kotto; and finally COTOUBANGUI in the intermediate area of Basse-Kotto. Despite the advantages they enjoyed and a steady expansion of the cotton belt and of production, these companies had a hard time getting under way. In 1930, three of them were virtually bankrupt and survived only through aid from the federal government and large-scale reductions of capital, and it was not until about 1936 that they began to make profits.[21] On the eve of World War II their privileges were renewed for another ten years.

From 1930 to 1938 the production of cotton more than tripled, reaching nearly 10,000 tons, almost all of which was exported to France after processing at the 30 gins built by the companies in the producing zones. At first cotton cultivation was simply spread to new areas as gins were constructed, but by 1933 the arrival of seven technicians from France permitted undertaking more research and developing of selected varieties. Early that year the government set up the Service Agronomique du Comité Cotonnière de l'AEF, and it established an experimental station for Tchad at Fort Archambault and another at Grimari for Oubangui. Thereafter substations were opened at Fianga, Tchad, and at Gambo and Ouham for eastern and western Oubangui respectively; although these had almost no staff and very limited funds, they experimented with some imported seed and successfully adapted the Triumph variety to Oubangui and an improved type of Allan (called N'Kourala) to Tchad. In 1937 the Service Agronomique was taken over by the federal agricultural service created the previous year, and became known first as the Service du Coton et des Textiles and later as the Service de la Sélection Cotonnière. During World War II, funds placed at its disposal enabled it to enlarge the existing experimental stations and start another at Tikem, but in 1945 its functions were handed over to the Institut de Recherches du Coton et des Textiles (IRCT), organized in Paris on a French-Union-wide basis.

Less successful were the efforts made at the same time to induce the African cotton farmers to employ better cultivation methods. The European technicians, known locally as *conducteurs*, were theoretically responsible to the local administrator, but as they were few in number and isolated, they perforce acted independently. Each was assigned so enormous an area to supervise that he recruited African assistants, beguilingly called *boys-coton*, and to train them started small experimental farms near his house. Inevitably the results were unsatisfactory and in time they became actively harmful. Not only were these so-called assistants poorly paid and ignorant, but they were entrusted with so much authority that they became the scourge of the populations placed under their supervision. A decree of November 2, 1935, enabled them—in theory under the control of their superiors—to impose fines and even imprison cultivators who "failed to protect and improve their crops" according to the directives issued by the experimental stations. Forced labor was abolished throughout the French Union after the war, but a local regulation of June 12, 1945, prolonged this regime in AEF, although a limit of 100 francs was placed on the fines and a month on the terms of imprisonment that could be imposed on negligent farmers.

The 700,000 or so cotton farmers of Oubangui and Tchad cultivate their fields on a family basis, and so far as possible their farms are grouped together in order to facilitate the struggle against the spread of plant diseases and parasitic insects. The ground is prepared in April, the sowing takes place in June and July, and the crop is harvested about mid-November. After the land is jointly cleared, the *boys-coton* assign each farmer an individual plot, the extent of which is set each year by the administration but usually varies between 30 and 40 *ares* (¾ acre to 1 acre). To avoid soil exhaustion and to assure the farmer of food crops, a three- or four-year cycle has been imposed in which cotton is rotated with peanuts, millet, corn, sesame, and green fertilizer. A number of times, experiments with mechanized cultivation have been undertaken and then discontinued for various economic and sociological reasons. Reportedly, the soils under such cultivation have been more rapidly impoverished, the cost of fuel and the difficulties of machinery maintenance make it uneconomic, and "depriving thousands of Africans of their land without associating them with its cultivation" is naturally considered undesirable.[22] Improving their traditional methods of farming is a worth-while aim, but only in very recent years has appreciable progress been made in this direction.

After harvesting his crop, the farmer carries it to the nearest purchasing center, whose location has been selected by the company controlling the relevant cotton area but whose date is fixed each year by the government. He is paid either individually or by village (the price also being set annually by the administration), in the presence of the district chief or the agricultural agent and of local Notables. This price has fluctuated but has generally risen from its very low prewar levels, especially since 1951, and now an appreciable difference exists between that paid for first-quality (white) and that for inferior (yellow) cotton. Initially, in 1925–26 cotton was bought from the farmer at 1 franc a kilogram; the world depression caused the price to fall to 60 centimes in 1933–34, with such bad psychological and other effects on the farmer that special sums were set aside in 1935 to raise it to 1.25 francs. In 1943–44 the price rose to 1.50 francs, in 1945–46 to 2 francs, and in 1947 to 5 francs, at which time a bonus of 3 francs per hectare was added for planting. In October 1946 a Supporting Fund was created, with two objectives. One was to mitigate the effects of

a fall in the world cotton market on the purchase price paid to AEF farmers, and the second was to aid them indirectly by building roads, schools,
dispensaries, and the like in the cotton zones.

During the war, the slightly higher price paid to the producer and,
above all, increased pressure from the administration swelled output of
cotton from 53,000 tons in 1943–44 to nearly 76,000 in 1945–46, but these
harvests were followed by a drop of some 20,000 tons the next season. This
was due in part to adverse climatic conditions but even more to the new
freedoms granted to Africans in the spring of 1946. Moreover, the latter
enabled the native elite for the first time to express their views on government policy, and toward the policy on cotton they were uniformly hostile.
Minutes of the elected assemblies of this period were filled with reproaches
to the administration for having "sold its soul to the cotton companies," and
with criticism of the latter for having failed to live up to their agreements
and for making huge profits at the expense of the downtrodden farmers.

There was little doubt that the government had been lax in its control
over both its own agents and the companies' operations. Many of the *boys-
coton* were brutal overseers, and in their coercive measures they were
abetted by some of the local chiefs, who received a cash premium based on
the size of the crop. Purchasing centers which, according to the companies'
contracts, should have been set up every 12 to 15 kilometers throughout
the producing zones were, more often than not, spaced at intervals of 18
to 20 kilometers. And after carrying his cotton to these distant centers
the farmer was not always paid even the full pittance due him, for no
regular accounts were kept of the exact amount that each brought in to
market. Though admittedly famine no longer stalked the cotton belt, the
administration's "obsession with cotton" had led to the neglect of food
crops. Food shortages were far more acute in Oubangui than in Tchad,
but everywhere the African elite blamed the government's cotton policy
for having turned the villagers against agricultural pursuits and caused
them to desert the countryside for the towns. On numerous occasions
Boganda denounced cotton cultivation as practiced in Oubangui as "the
great plague that has depopulated our territory,"[23] and in the French
Union Assembly it was claimed that AEF's "cotton farmers die of hunger
on a pile of gold."[24]

The latter metaphor dramatically expressed the dissatisfaction generally
felt by all of AEF's representatives and some of its officials with the policy
being pursued in the first postwar years by the cotton companies and the
management of the Supporting Fund. There is no doubt that from 1943
to mid-1946 the companies realized "considerable profits" averaging perhaps 13 per cent annually, but the exact figures are not known. (In the
Grand Council it was said on November 21, 1950, that the four companies
had made a net profit of 10 per cent since the war on operations totaling
about 2,000 million CFA francs, but this amount was challenged as an
underestimate.) Nor did anyone know precisely what their operating
costs came to, for the companies had every reason to pad these figures since

they were the basis used for calculating the percentage of profit guaranteed them by the government.[25] There was no doubt, however, that the companies had been able to pay off their back debts and between 1935 and 1945 to increase their total capital from 400 to 500 million CFA francs. In view of their undeniably flourishing financial position, the companies' opposition to raising the purchase price for cotton angered Tchad's and Oubangui's assemblymen as well as the Grand Councilors, and strengthened their conviction that the only way to overcome the African farmers' growing disaffection for that crop was to make its cultivation a remunerative occupation.

Partisans of the status quo claimed that cotton, albeit a "poor crop" and one whose transport was difficult and costly, was the best possible one for the "disinherited northern territories." Farmers who added cotton to their food crops increased their income by one-fifth, for in 1949 a total of 900 million CFA francs was earned by AEF's cotton growers, many of whom had no other cash resource.[26] Advocates of a higher cotton-purchase price, on the other hand, argued that not only was the current amount a poor recompense for three months of hard toil in the fields but barely enough to pay the farmer's taxes and customary dues and to cover other necessities such as a few meters of cloth. They pointed, too, to the large sums accumulated by the Supporting Fund, which they claimed should be distributed to the farmers who had earned them rather than be dissipated on a multitude of projects that bore little or no relation to the cotton growers' welfare. This last-mentioned phenomenon was due partly to the mechanism by which the Supporting Fund was financed and partly to the policy pursued by the officials who in large measure controlled its operations.

After the war a new Metropolitan organization called the Groupement d'Importation et de Répartition du Coton (GIRC) came to play an important role in AEF's cotton picture. To it the federal government sold at cost price the cotton crop bought from the four companies. The GIRC took over the bales at their loading points in AEF and exported them to France, where it divided them among French industrialist purchasers. The GIRC turned over to the Supporting Fund the difference between the purchase and sales price for AEF's cotton but not the 50 million francs or more that it realized from the successive currency devaluations of the first postwar years.[27] At the Brazzaville cotton conference of June 1948 the French government was urgently asked to dissolve the GIRC, but that organization was not liquidated until November 1950. Despite the GIRC's manipulations, the growth in AEF's cotton exports and the concurrent rise in the world market price had brought 790 million CFA francs to the Supporting Fund's coffers by mid-1947. The purchase price to cotton farmers was then raised to 5 francs per kilogram and a small planting bonus instituted, but half of the Fund's resources were allocated to such irrelevant projects as the Franco-Arabic school in Abéché, the port of Bangui, and vehicles for the use of the administration.[28] Despite sharp criticism of such a misuse

of its resources, the Fund's managing committee persisted in this policy
until the new agreements signed between the government and the cotton
companies in December 1949 radically altered its position.

During the prolonged negotiations for renewal of the cotton companies'
contracts, the Grand Councilors were aided by fortuitous circumstances in
their determination to get more advantageous terms for the federation in
general and the cotton farmers in particular. One was the government-
general's willingness to consult with them and the northern territorial
assemblymen and get their consent to the terms negotiated. Another was
the desire of the companies, which recently had been realizing big profits, to
continue operating in AEF, as was indicated by the zeal with which they
had been modernizing their ginning equipment throughout 1949. But
they remained adamant against raising the purchase price for cotton, and
they laid down very stringent conditions for construction of the textile
factory which the government insisted on their building in AEF. It was
indeed ironical that the cotton farmers of AEF were among the most
wretchedly clothed Africans in the federation, for the cost of imported
textiles had risen so high since the war that they were unable to pay the
price asked to supply their minimal needs of about ten meters of cloth a
year.[29]

While the conditions posed by the companies were still under consideration, two newcomers appeared on the AEF scene whose competitive
offers greatly improved the government's bargaining position. One was
the powerful Metropolitan firm Comptoir de l'Industrie Cotonnière, belonging to Boussac, which offered to build a textile plant if given the
monopoly of purchase in a cotton-growing region that until then had been
the preserve of COTONFRAN and COTONAF. The Grand Council
countered this proposal with the unacceptable offer of potential but not
actual cotton-producing land in Tchad's fifth zone. In time the Grand
Council came to regret its loyalty to the two long-established cotton companies, though it had the immediate effect of making the latter more
amenable to compromise.[30] If Boussac had been induced to invest heavily
in the federation, this would have associated a major French industrial
firm for the first time with AEF's cotton production, and perhaps have
made France less reluctant than it was to subsidize AEF's cotton output
during the critical years from 1951 to 1958.[31]

More successful than Boussac in its negotiations with the Grand Council
but also far less important for the future of AEF was TEFRACO (Compagnie Française des Textiles), the second group of French industrialists
interested in the federation's textile potential. This company was willing
to set up a textile plant at Brazzaville without demanding the same fiscal
and other concessions as the cotton firms. An arrangement was finally
worked out whereby TEFRACO was granted permission to build its plant
in Brazzaville, and the four cotton companies agreed to organize the Société d'Industrie Cotonnière de l'Oubangui et du Tchad (ICOT). This new
firm was to construct and operate a much larger textile factory at Boali

(in Oubangui) on condition that the government supply it with cheap current from a hydroelectric dam to be built with public funds over the waterfalls nearby. After a long delay both plants were built in 1952–53, but they have neither greatly affected AEF's cotton exports nor improved its textile supplies. Together they consume about 500 tons of fiber a year and turn out some 400,000 meters of cloth a month. Both are capable of considerable expansion, and in 1958 ICOT obtained a loan of 30 million CFA francs from CCOM to double its output. But TEFRACO from the outset ran into labor and financial difficulties, and to save this industry as well as the jobs for its 300 to 400 African employees, Moyen-Congo's territorial assembly was forced to grant it several fiscal concessions and lower the cost of the electrical current it used.[32]

This textile-plant issue was the most long-drawn-out and vexatious aspect of the 1949 agreements. In the matter of capital ownership and investments, reorganization of the Supporting Fund, and even the purchase price to be paid cotton farmers, the cotton companies not only proved amenable but even volunteered important concessions. In return for a ten-year renewal of their monopolistic privileges, the companies agreed that a 51 per cent majority of their stockholders be French citizens; that their capital be increased and 10 per cent of the total and of their profits be turned over immediately to the Supporting Fund and eventually to the cooperatives of African producers; and that representatives of the cotton farmers and the elected assemblies be given more of a voice in the management of the companies and of the Supporting Fund. Unfortunately AEF's cotton farmers were so unorganized that they could take almost no advantage of these new opportunities for policy making, which by default fell into the hands of the administration.[33] Nor was there any imminent prospect of creating cooperatives among African producers, and the only one then in existence, the COTONCOOP of Bangui, with a claimed membership of 24,500, was not represented either on the boards of the companies or on the Supporting Fund's committee.

Nevertheless, the 1949 agreements proved beneficial to both the federation and the companies. Investments in the companies have risen to over 2,000 million CFA francs, they have spent about 1 billion CFA francs in modernizing their equipment, and they now operate 46 wholly mechanized gins, whose capacity can be much enlarged. They have also built three mills to extract oil from some of the seed produced by the federation's gins, of which theretofore about 10,000 tons had been used for planting purposes and the rest (some 40,000 tons) had served as fuel for the gins or had been simply burned as refuse.[34] COTONFRAN remains by far the most important of the companies, handling 82,000 of a total of 118,000 tons of cotton in 1958, and it also has lower operating costs than its colleagues because of the concentration of its holdings in Tchad and one district in Oubangui. Owing to this compactness, COTONFRAN needs only 25 gins to process the totality of its tonnages, whereas the other three companies, with more dispersed holdings, have had to construct relatively more gins (21), each of which processes much smaller amounts and is far from being worked to capacity. Together the four companies employ about 175 Europeans and 4,000 to 8,000 African laborers, depending on the season of the year.

Conclusion of the agreements of December 1949 antedated a sharp rise in the world price for cotton. The Grand Council was now in a position to press effectively for a higher purchase price to be paid the cotton growers. In 1950 this was raised to 14 francs per kilogram and in 1951 to 25 francs, plus a planting bonus awarded to conscientious farmers in July and a rise in the premiums paid to chiefs from 0.25 to 0.30 francs per kilogram for cotton grown in their zones. This meant that a farming family which cultivated a hectare that produced 300 kilograms of cotton received 7,500 CFA francs a year, and for the first time, as Cornut-Gentille told the Grand Council on August 20, 1951, cotton growers were receiving a decent reward for their labors. At the same time the research stations under the IRCT and the farms sponsored by the companies were staffed by an increasing corps of technicians and were turning out larger amounts of selected high-yield seed. These were distributed widely and gratuitously, and the most meritorious farmers also received as premiums imported hoes, axes, and knives which could not be locally manufactured because of the lack of iron and blacksmiths.

The response to these stimuli was immediate, and a record crop of nearly 100,000 tons was harvested in 1951–52. Unfortunately there began at about the same time a sharp fall in the world price for cotton. In 1951 the Supporting Fund was rich, having 3 billion CFA francs in its coffers, but by the following year it was threatened with a big deficit,[35] for all were then agreed that no reduction must be made in the price of 25 francs per kilogram paid to the grower. At this time it was repeatedly stressed that the African farmer could not understand why fluctuations in the world cotton price should affect his income, and that another cut in the purchase price or elimination of the planting bonus might wholly alienate him from a crop that he had never liked anyway. To maintain it the companies were asked to compress their production costs, the truckers and services of the Federal Artery to lower their rates for cotton transport, and the federation to sacrifice some of its revenues derived from the export tax on cotton.

Transport has certainly been one of the factors chiefly responsible for the high production cost of AEF's cotton, especially that from Tchad, estimates ranging widely from 13 to 40 per cent of the total. Not only were the distances great between the 1,500 or so purchasing centers and the 46 gins and between the gins and the embarkation ports, but because of climatic conditions in the north, transportation had to be concentrated in a few months of the year (see p. 448). Moreover, transportation in a multitude of small trucks was uneconomic, but AEF's roads and bridges could not support 15-ton trucks. Fuel was expensive and the taxes on imported vehicles high, but it was felt that the big trucking companies like Uniroute and STOC (which had a quasi-monopoly of cotton transport in

Tchad and Oubangui) were exaggerating their costs in order to provide cheap rates for carrying merchandise on the return trip to the north. So official pressure was put on them and in 1954 and 1955 they protestingly accepted reductions in their transport tariffs for cotton. Cotton-export duties were uniformly very high but fluctuated widely, in conformity with the anticipated size of the federation's budgetary deficit. In 1948 they were raised from 18 to 35 per cent, then in 1950 lowered to 24 per cent. In a successful plea in 1954 to decrease this duty to 12 per cent, one of Tchad's Grand Councilors said:[36] "Cotton has the dangerous honor of being AEF's primary export both from the angle of the export duties it brings in and from that of the other taxes it supports." And he further pointed out that whereas cotton was then supplying 58 per cent of the federation's revenues, its share in AEF's total exports was only 35 per cent in terms of value. Since that time the export duty on cotton has hovered between 10 and 12 per cent.

By mid-1953, when the world cotton price was still very low and when both the government and private industry in AEF felt that they could make no further sacrifices to maintain the purchase price to farmers, a plea for help was sent to France. In the summer of that year Governor-General Chauvet made two trips to Paris to explore possible sources of aid. It was natural that he should first turn to FIDES, for under the Plan almost nothing had been done to promote cotton production beyond setting a goal of 42,000 tons of fiber by 1956.[37] Chauvet pointed out that even without FIDES' support, AEF had almost achieved that goal and that without any tariff protection in the Metropolitan market the federation's cotton now represented 80 per cent of all the French Union's output and was keeping the wheels of the French textile industry turning for two months of the year. He succeeded in getting FIDES to finance construction of the Boali hydroelectric dam (essential for Oubangui's new textile factory) and salaries for AEF's cotton technicians. From another new source, the Fonds d'Encouragement à la Production Textile, he got funds to maintain some of the experimental farms and part of the bonus for planting.[38] Yet with all these additional resources AEF's cotton deficit was not wholly covered, and in 1954 the authorities very reluctantly reduced the purchase price for white cotton to 24 francs a kilogram and for yellow cotton to 20 francs.

Contrary to the fears expressed at that time, AEF's cotton production continued to grow. After a stationary period in which the area planted to cotton in Tchad remained at about 210,000 hectares and that in Oubangui at around 140,000 hectares, this crop began to spread to the Salamat region of eastern Tchad (called the fifth zone) and to contract in Oubangui. The area planted to cotton was less influential in causing this expansion of AEF's output than the greater interest shown in this crop by Tchad's farmers and the improved yields from planting and ginning.[39] Even in Oubangui, where cotton harvests were shrinking, the output of fiber was maintained (see p. 409). Though cotton production has been subject to considerable variation, much of this can be attributed to climatic conditions, and on the whole, exports have markedly increased.

In one year of the late 1920's, AEF exported 242 tons of cotton; 30 years later it exported over 40,000 tons, the rate of increase having been most rapid since 1951. By the eve of World War II, cotton already held second place among the federation's total shipments, and since then it has been able to maintain that position despite rapid rises in the production of AEF's other export commodities and a fairly steady fall in the price of cotton in the world market. Nor has cotton since 1954 been able to benefit by the 20 per cent rebate granted to AEF products sold outside the franc zone, because virtually all of AEF's output is sent to Metropolitan France. With a rising local consumption of the federation's cotton, exports may decline in the future, but the amount of fiber absorbed by the AEF textile industry has made no appreciable dent on exports.

The arduous period of AEF's cotton is undoubtedly now over, and while some technical and financial difficulties remain, the long and difficult task of plant selection and propagation and of farmer training is already paying off. Reorganization of the Supporting Fund into a Price Stabilization Fund on May 1, 1955, gave AEF's cultivators and elected representatives a greater share in its management and definitely oriented the Fund away from projects not directly related to the producers' welfare, but its resources are still dependent upon the world price for cotton and on France's benevolence. The latter for some time has been wearing thin, and only a rise in world prices and the bumper crop of 1958 saved AEF's cotton growers from another crisis. The governments of the new Central African and Tchad republics have on several occasions voiced their determination to increase cotton production, for their leaders recognize that that crop has become indispensable to their respective economies. They hope to do this by persuasion and by making cotton-growing more remunerative—in 1958 the price for white cotton was raised to 26 francs a kilogram—but their ability to do so depends largely on factors beyond their control. In 1959 an agreement was negotiated by the governments of Tchad and Oubangui whereby those two republics would determine each year the rate of cotton export duties. In case of disagreement between them, the conference of the four premiers would make the final decision.

Secondary fiber plants

Except in the case of cotton, the production of fiber in AEF for export has thus far been a failure, mainly because the world price for such products has not been profitable in relation to production costs in the federation. For that reason the sisal grown in Oubangui and the punga and urena (indigenous jute-type fiber plants) of Moyen-Congo have suffered much the same fate, though in other respects their history has not followed the same course.

Optimum natural conditions exist for the propagation of sisal in the forest region of Oubangui, but the export trade is weighed down by transport costs and cultivation suffers from a shortage of labor. Private initiative and capital developed this crop on a plantation basis over a 25-year period, with minimal aid from a nearby federal agricultural station. Just at the time when plantations were coming into bearing and exports were approaching the 2,000-ton mark annually, and when a factory had been built and equipped to turn out 1,500 tons of finished products, the sisal market collapsed and no public funds were available to come to the rescue of this crop. Varying tonnages of sisal continue to be exported from Oubangui, but there is no further talk of large-scale production of that crop or of any increase in the local industrialization of its output.

In Moyen-Congo, on the other hand, both private and public capital have been poured into the purchase of wild punga and the cultivation and processing of urena, and though both suffer somewhat from a shortage of labor, transport to the coast for export has been easy and relatively cheap. Because some 18,000 tons of urena had been harvested yearly in the Belgian Congo, Metropolitan industrialists were persuaded that they could do likewise in AEF. To free themselves from dependence on 90,000 to 100,000 tons a year of Indian jute imports, they spent a billion francs between 1947 and 1953 in financing a company formed expressly to encourage the cultivation of jute substitutes inside the franc zone. And in AEF this company also benefited by the technical aid given it by experts of the IRCT and agricultural services. Urena, unlike sisal, did run into technical difficulties, both in cultivation and processing, which in time might have been resolved. Beginning in 1952, however, the bottom fell out of the market for tropical fiber products, and after four years of very low prices, urena's Metropolitan sponsors were no longer willing to throw good money after bad and liquidated their company in AEF.

In the cultivation of urena the federal government has shown a dogged determination that it never displayed toward the production of sisal. But unless the authorities find some way of maintaing a remunerative price to the grower, the future for all of AEF's fiber exports is very dubious.

Oil palms

Spontaneous growths of oil palms are to be found throughout the central Congolese basin. For the most part they are scattered among other trees in the great forest, and only in three areas do they constitute relatively dense groves—near Moabi in Gabon, south of Ouesso in Moyen-Congo, and in the Lobaye region of Oubangui. With the exception of the Moabi grove, the oil palm occurs in lightly populated zones, in which shifting agriculture is practiced and the palm tree is never cultivated. Only when the price for palm products is high are the local Africans willing to gather and crush the nuts. But so much labor is involved and the oil obtained—80 to 100 kilograms to the hectare—is so small in yield and so acid that the Africans have tended increasingly to neglect the natural growths. To improve the quality of the oil produced, nuts would have to be crushed by modern methods soon after they have been gathered, but the palm growths are so widely dispersed that the construction of a series of oil mills would not be economically worth while. Therefore, before World War II the government began distributing small portable presses to the SIP, with a resulting improvement in the quantity and quality of AEF's production. In 1925 AEF exported only about 595 tons of palm oil, but in 1938 it shipped out 6,500 tons of oil and 15,000 tons of kernels—a record tonnage that has never since been equaled.[40]

During World War II, African production declined but a few European individuals and companies became interested in starting oil-palm plantations. Some foresters, whose timber could no longer reach external markets, turned to planting small groves of selected oil palms developed at the federal experimental station set up at Sibiti in 1941. Then the Compagnie Française du Haut et Bas Congo (CFHBC), long established in AEF, started a big plantation near Ouesso, while another French firm, the Compagnie Commerciale de l'AEF (CCAEF)began a smaller one at Kango in the Gabon estuary. Also in 1941 the British and Free French governments concluded an agreement whereby the former would buy AEF's entire output in kernels, but shipping shortages interfered with execution of this agreement and only a few thousand tons were exported during the course of the war. Additional factors reducing the federation's shipments were the rural exodus to the towns and the founding of a soap factory at Bangui which absorbed a large share of local oil production.

The ten-year Plan set as AEF's goal the production of 20,000 tons of oil (to be derived from 10,000 to 12,000 hectares of improved palms) by 1956 through the improvement of the federation's natural growths and the development of plantations by private industry with government aid. In 1946 the Sibiti station was taken over by IRHO, and three years later it had 240 hectares planted to selected palms. By 1949, too, a large oil-storage plant had been built at Pointe Noire and secondary ones at Bangui and Brazzaville, and the Federal Artery had been supplied with special tanker cars and barges. By this time, IRHO had started improving 420 hectares of African family plantations near Sibiti and the Gabon agricultural service had founded an African cooperative society to develop the Moabi grove and had improved 600 hectares of natural growths in the Fernan Vaz area.

However, it was in the extension of plantations growing selected palms and using mechanical means for planting and processing that the authors of the Plan placed their main hopes for increasing AEF's output of palm products. The role of the Sibiti station and of the federal agricultural service, aside from improving natural groves and developing selected palms, was to conduct experiments in mechanized cultivation and milling on 24,000 hectares nearby. The requirement of 380 days of manual labor to plant one hectare with selected palms and of 80 to 100 days to gather and crush the kernels was far too much for the small labor force available in the palm-growing regions. By 1953 the Sibiti experiment had proved that within five years and with 400 laborers using seven tractors and two motorized winches a plantation of 2,500 hectares could be created, and that with 100 additional workers the kernels could be gathered and an oil mill operated.[41] In still another way the government tried to encourage the development of plantations: the Compagnie Générale des Oléagineux Tropicaux (CGOT) sent a mission to AEF in 1950 to select the best possible sites from the standpoint not only of soil and climatic conditions but also of the available labor supply and means of transport. Operating for three years from a base near Lambaréné, the CGOT finally approved five sites along the Oubangui and Likouala rivers in Oubangui-Chari, the Sangha near Ouesso in Moyen-Congo, the Ogooué near Lambaréné, and in the Gabon estuary.

Inevitably these helpful pioneering efforts by the government did not wholly solve the problems encountered by private companies in creating plantations in AEF. Planting companies had to employ a sizable staff of qualified technicians and possess enough capital not only to create a plantation but to wait 11 years for the palms to come into full bearing. Naturally there were few candidates able and willing to take such risks, and for a decade after the war the 3,000 or so hectares belonging to the established CFHBC and CCAEF and to a few smaller companies constituted the totality of AEF's oil-palm plantations. Now those of the CFHBC are being considerably enlarged, but the most hopeful development in recent years was the acquisition in 1956 of an area of some 1,500 hectares on the Ogooué river by an offshoot of Unilever, the Société des Palmiers et Hevéas du Gabon.

The slowness with which plantation output has developed is not the only reason why AEF's exports of kernels and oil have failed to return to the prewar tonnages. Other causes are world price levels and the increasing domestic consumption of palm oil. Because the shortage of fats was so acute during the early postwar years, the local authorities were misled into believing that the federation's oil-palm products would continue to find a ready sale at relatively high prices. In 1948 Metropolitan France absorbed AEF's shipments of 2,389 tons of oil and 7,563 tons of kernels, but the following year it stopped buying such products from French Black Africa because of market saturation. Although French Union purchases were resumed in 1950, the end of the Korean war boom early in 1952 led to a sharp fall in the price paid for oil-palm products in France as well as in world markets. In 1954 AEF was granted some protection for its kernels in the Metropolitan market and a high guaranteed price for a quota of 6,000 tons of oil shipments.[42] Actually neither these fluctuations nor concessions were very important to AEF's foreign trade, in which the export of palm products held a poor fourth or fifth place, for it was not until about 1957 that the improvements stemming from plantation cultivation and modern oil extraction were beginning to show in its output. By 1958 AEF's exports of kernels were still under 8,000 tons (valued at nearly 206 million CFA francs) and those of oil around 3,000 tons (worth over 134 million CFA francs).

It should be noted, however, that the federation's palm-oil shipments do not reflect its total production, for an increasing proportion of the output is being consumed by Africans and used by the local soap factories, especially in Oubangui. Some 13 such factories are operating in AEF and produce about 3,000 tons of crude soap annually. As this comes nowhere near meeting the local demand, more than 1,000 tons of soap are imported annually into the federation. An attempt has been made to increase and improve the domestic output, and in the future these factories may be expected to use ever-larger amounts of AEF's palm oil.

Peanuts

Peanuts have long been grown throughout the savannah zone of AEF for family consumption, but only in comparatively recent years have they been cultivated for sale locally and for export. The main obstacle to widening their cultivation has been the shortage of farmers in the appropriate region that has shipping facilities (Moyen-Congo) and, conversely the lack of cheap means of transport in the zones where the population density as well as natural conditions make large-scale cultivation possible (Oubangui and Tchad). For this reason the evolution of peanut production, which has been officially encouraged since World War II, has been different in the northern and southern territories, but everywhere it has increased, as have local sales and exports.

In 1938 only 1,260 tons of nuts were exported from AEF, the balance produced—the exact amount of which was never known—being consumed by the growers of the crop. The immensity of the areas suited to peanut cultivation in AEF, as well as the widespread postwar shortage of vegetable fats, incited the planners of 1946 to promote the development of this crop for export. But seeing the difficulties of selling Senegal's vast output in Metropolitan France and the failure of the British experiment in east Africa, they approached the problems posed by AEF with caution. Study missions traveled through France, the United States, and AEF, and their reports eventually recommended undertaking intensive peanut cultivation in the three areas where that crop was a traditional one and transport was easy. These were, in order of importance, the Niari valley and the Batéké plateaus in Moyen-Congo, and the Haute-Sangha in Oubangui. Priority was given to the Niari valley not only because it had suitable soil and access to the Congo-Ocean railroad, but also because the sparsity of the indigenous population and the presence of European planters there made possible experimentation with mechanized cultivation over a large area.

Loudima, a station on the railroad, became the federal center for these experiments and also for the development of selected seed, and in 1949 mechanized peanut cultivation was started on 2,000 hectares nearby. In 1951 the CGOT, by agreement with the government-general, took over management of this station, and for the next few years devoted itself to encouraging the European colonists of the Niari, both by example and by direct aid, to grow peanuts among other crops. Its efforts were rewarded, for it was mainly due to the European planters and companies of the Niari that the amount of shelled nuts sold in AEF rose from 1,400 tons in 1950 to 3,500 in 1953. And in the latter year the Société Industrielle et Agricole du Niari (SIAN)—the outstanding French agricultural company there— completed a modern mill which pressed over half of the 1,000 or more tons of oil produced in the federation. In 1953, also, exports rose to over 2,000 tons, compared with 380 the preceding year, largely owing to the higher prices paid for them in the Metropolitan market. Peanut shipments now occupied eleventh place in AEF's exports, and of these Moyen-Congo exported 1,740 tons, Tchad 230, Oubangui 90, and Gabon 80.[43]

By that time the CGOT had solved most of the technical problems posed by mechanized peanut cultivation in the Niari and had greatly increased yields per hectare, but it had yet to prove that such cultivation would be profitable.[44] To be sure, none of the Europeans grew peanuts exclusively, but they showed increasing reluctance to devote themselves to the mechanized cultivation for export of a crop of which Metropolitan France would guarantee a high price in the French market for only limited and fluctuating amounts. Although in the years since 1953 both the CGOT and the Europeans of Niari have persevered and even have increased their output, the center of AEF's peanut production has shifted to the northern territories, where peanut cultivation by African farmers has become more widespread and exportation has begun.

With the possible exception of Moyen-Congo, exports and local sales of nuts and oil have never reflected current production. This is true even in Gabon, where both are produced on a very small, though rising, scale, and it is particularly so in Oubangui and Tchad, where about 90 per cent of the peanuts produced—estimated at well over 100,000 tons—are consumed by their cultivators. In the early 1950's peanut planting began spreading beyond southern Tchad, where, as in Oubangui, the crop was grown in rotation with cotton. This development was aided in 1955 by the government's initiating the distribution of selected seed in the northern territories, which even began exporting small quantities of shelled nuts. The difficulties and cost of transporting peanuts to Nigeria are so great as to limit any appreciable growth of this export trade, but local consumption and sales are mounting rapidly. Peanut oil was exported from AEF for the first time in 1956. Oil production has taken hold with particular rapidity in Oubangui, where two newly constructed oil mills (with a total capacity of 2,700 tons of oil) and Bangui's soap factories absorb an ever-larger proportion of the nuts sold in the domestic market.

All of the new governments of AEF, particularly those of the northern territories, are eager to encourage greater peanut production both for domestic consumption and for export. In most areas two crops a year can be harvested, and the cash returns from their sale are proportionately higher and more easily earned than are those for a single crop of cotton. The stress is no longer placed primarily on mechanized peanut cultivation by Europeans but on African production in conjunction with other agricultural and herding activities. To awaken and maintain the African farmers' interest in peanuts, Tchad has set up a Price Supporting Fund, and recently it has been proposed that it be organized on an interterritorial basis. Tchad has also been a pioneer in establishing a standardization service to assure the high quality of nuts sold in controlled markets for export and in organizing a local commercial network.

These measures may raise the generally low level of prices that have been paid to African peanut farmers, which was probably responsible in large part for the decline in the quantity of nuts and oil shipped out of the federation in 1958–59. Despite greater peanut production, the amount of nuts in shell exported that year dropped to 2,600 tons compared with 3,700 in 1957–58, that of shelled nuts from 7,900 to 6,000 tons, and that of oil from 3,800 to 2,900 tons.[45] Furthermore, no way has yet been found to improve the peanut transportation situation, which remains the thorniest of all the problems that confront any appreciable increase in the federation's peanut exportation. As of the present writing it appears that the future of AEF's peanuts lies far more in the domestic than in the foreign market.

Coffee

During the late nineteenth century, explorers of AEF's hinterland found eight indigenous varieties of coffee bushes between the Mayombé and sahel regions. Two of these, the *arabica* and *liberica,* were cultivated for a short time by early colonists, while the *nana* variety (named for the river of the Haute-Sangha) was grown by African farmers in Oubangui for their own consumption.[46]

In 1925 the government began to encourage the planting of *kouilou* and *robusta* coffee in Gabon and Moyen-Congo, and that of *nana* and *excelsa* in Oubangui. For the rest of the interwar period a certain amount of official coercion was employed to push coffee planting so as to check the practice of shifting agriculture and to give the African farmers of those territories a cash income. Though for a few years coffee growing contributed to the prosperity of Woleu-N'Tem and Ogooué-Ivindo in Gabon, the Kouilou region of Moyen-Congo, and the Sangha and Kotto areas of Oubangui, the results of this effort were on the whole mediocre. It was not until about 1929, when European planters took up coffee growing in Oubangui, that that crop began to make appreciable headway. Exports rose from 100 tons in 1925 to over 1,400 tons ten years later. Then in 1936, when nearly 20,000 hectares in Oubangui had been planted to coffee, a blight suddenly struck the *excelsa* bushes—the main variety grown there. Consequently African farmers of the region almost totally abandoned coffee growing and turned to cotton cultivation, while the European planters replaced many of their *excelsa* bushes with the hardier *robusta* variety.

Though coffee production continued to increase moderately, both planters and administration had misgivings in the late 1930's as to the future of that crop in AEF. Aside from the blight's ravages of *excelsa* bushes, which apparently could not be brought under control, AEF's coffee could not compete as to quality or price with that grown in Ivory Coast and Cameroun. Governor-General Reste was one of the few high officials of that period who expressed his belief that "if high quality standards are maintained, coffee will certainly become one of AEF's chief resources."[47] When World War II broke out, the government urged coffee growers to devote themselves to oleaginous crops, with the result that many coffee plantations in Moyen-Congo and Gabon were abandoned. Yet despite the appearance of new plant diseases and labor shortages, Oubangui's European coffee planters persevered, and by the end of the war they were exporting slightly more coffee (2,416 tons in 1946) than in the last year of peace (2,236 tons in 1938).

Between 1946 and 1951 production continued to increase, attaining over 4,000 tons in 1949, but during that period exports rapidly declined and in 1950 they reached the low point of 1,600 tons. These were the years when all of AEF's coffee exports to Metropolitan France were perforce channeled through a French government purchasing monopoly called Groupement National d'Achat des Cafés (GNACA), which paid prices lower than those prevailing in the world market. So AEF's coffee planters held back a large part of their production and did not liquidate their stocks until the GNACA was abolished in 1950. In that year AEF exported a record 4,678 tons, which promoted coffee to eighth place in terms of value among the federation's total foreign shipments. This achievement can be better appreciated when it is realized that FIDES had done little to aid coffee production, that planters continued to be plagued by plant diseases and labor shortages, and that the duty on coffee exports amounted to 12 per cent.[48] Virtually all of these exports came from Oubangui, where, because of the above-mentioned adverse conditions inhibiting production by the European planters of that territory, they remained for some years thereafter stabilized at about 4,000 tons annually.

The increase in AEF's coffee production from 1952 on was the result of a marked extension of the area planted to coffee by African farmers, not only in Oubangui but also in Moyen-Congo and Gabon. The high prices paid for exports between 1950 and 1954 reawakened African interest in this crop, and plantations were started or revived in the forest regions of Gabon and Moyen-Congo, as well as in the Lobaye, M'Bomou, and Haute-Sangha areas of Oubangui. The *robusta* variety accounted for 88 per cent of AEF's total production, *nana* for 10 per cent, and *excelsa* for only 2 per cent.[49] The Boukoko coffee experimental station, founded in Oubangui during the war, was working to develop insecticides and disease-resistant varieties of bushes. Until an improved species of *excelsa* was perfected at that station in 1954, the government did not encourage the increase of coffee-growing areas and confined its work in this domain to supervising the quality of exports and the upkeep of existing plantations. Yet even without official encouragement the surface planted to coffee had grown by 1954 to cover 12,430 hectares in Oubangui (of which all but about 1,000 hectares were European-owned), 970 in Moyen-Congo, and 1,352 in Gabon.

Unfortunately for AEF's coffee planters, the development of a disease-resistant type of *excelsa* and the governmental blessing now given to enlargement of the area planted to coffee coincided with the beginning of a sharp fall in the world price for coffee. This blow was only slightly softened by France's raising of the duty on foreign coffee imported into the Metropolitan area, and so the government-general proposed setting up a Price Supporting Fund for AEF's coffee. At first the Grand Council turned down this proposal, not only because its members were congenitally opposed to the reinstitution of government controls but because the export duty on coffee would have to be raised to 15 per cent in order to finance the new fund. Eventually the Grand Council, seeing no prospect of an imminent rise in the world price for coffee, approved the principle of creating such a fund. But then new difficulties arose as to what the contribution of each producing territory should be and how the territories should be represented on the Fund's managing committee. Furthermore, agreement could not be reached on the price level at which the fund would come into operation. It was not until 1957 that these differences of opinion were ironed out and the Fund could begin functioning.

During the 1950 decade, coffee came to occupy an important place in AEF's economy in general and in that of Oubangui in particular, but this has been reflected more in the sizable increase in the areas planted to coffee than in any sensational volume of exports. Virtually all of AEF's coffee exports go to France and North Africa. Coffee shipments reached their highest point in 1956 with 5,900 tons, falling to 4,500 tons the following year, and rising only to 5,400 in 1958. Yet in 1958 coffee exports ranked third in the federation's total exports and were valued at 910 million CFA francs, and three-fourths of them were classed as of superior quality. In the next few years the large areas planted in the mid-1950's should come into bearing, and there is fair hope that by 1965 AEF's European and African planters will be producing 15,000 tons a year of superior-grade coffee.[50]

Cocoa

The story of AEF's cocoa is almost solely that of its development in Gabon. Though the tonnages exported are small (2,400 in 1957 and 2,800 in 1958), cocoa ranks third in terms of value among the federation's agricultural exports (over 452 million CFA francs in 1958). All of the output from the main producing region—north Gabon—is sent to Cameroun ports for processing and export.

In 1925 the establishment of road communications between AEF and the French mandate of Cameroun, where German colonists before World War I had successfully cultivated cocoa, made the Gabonese administration decide to promote the planting of that crop in the adjacent region of Woleu-N'Tem. Only by coercion were the local Fang induced to grow cocoa, for they were not farmers by inclination, and because of the isolation of that region there was a lack of imported goods that might have provided an incentive for cultivation of an export crop. In 1930 the world depression inspired the government to regroup and modernize the villages of Woleu-N'Tem and to create there a cocoa-producing *paysannat*. These measures also met with Fang resistance, but by 1936 the revival of world trade and the improvement in cocoa prices brought to the cocoa growers of that region a cash income far higher than that in any other part of northern Gabon, and from then on they grew cocoa voluntarily and in increasing quantities. Because their farming methods were defective and yields were poor, and because the cocoa trade was controlled by alien merchants, the Fang cocoa growers did not gain the profits they might otherwise have got, but they were sufficient for young men to pay the bride price and for families to raise their living standards appreciably. Villages in Woleu-N'Tem became stabilized, housing and clothing were more Europeanized, and the Fang developed a sense of individual property and a genuine attachment to the land.[51]

World War II, by interfering with exports, dealt a blow to Gabon's cocoa farmers, for they could not stock their perishable output against a future bettering of the shipping situation as could the producers of coffee. Nevertheless, cocoa exports rose steadily after the war to 2,709 tons in 1952, or more than double the 1,041 exported in 1938. The high prices paid after the war for cocoa caused a revival of cocoa planting in lower Gabon, where it had been abandoned in favor of forestry during the interwar period, and also led to the spread of cocoa cultivation to the region of Ogooué-Ivindo in northern Gabon. At about the same time the high prevailing prices induced farmers in the Sangha region of Moyen-Congo to start cocoa plantations there despite the difficulties of shipping out the harvest. By the end of 1954 Gabon's cocoa plantations totaled 15,138 hectares (of which 12,370 were in Woleu-N'Tem and 2,768 in Ogooué-Ivindo) and Moyen-Congo's totaled 720 hectares (645 near Souanké and 75 in the environs of Ouesso).[52]

The growth of AEF's cocoa-producing areas apparently was not affected by the sharp fall in cocoa prices that began in June 1954. Fortunately for Gabon, a territorial cocoa-supporting fund had been set up in 1948, and for a year and a half it was able to maintain the purchase price to farmers at a relatively favorable level. Meanwhile, both the local and federal governments encouraged the planting of new areas to cocoa. Old cocoa plantations were rehabilitated, and between 1953 and 1956 some 4,000 new hectares were planted to this crop.[53] But as the world price for cocoa continued to decline throughout 1955, the government-general decided to relieve the pressure on Gabon's budgetary resources and to reorganize the supporting fund on a federal basis. Initially this fund was to be financed by half of the proceeds derived from the 22 per cent duty on cocoa exports, and this proportion was maintained even after the Grand Council with many misgivings decided to lower the rate of that duty in November 1955.[54] Gabon's territorial assemblymen at first were displeased by the reorganization of the supporting fund. They became reconciled to it, however, when they learned that Gabon would be almost its sole beneficiary, would have a decisive vote on its managing committee, and would be able to dispose of 18 of the 20 million CFA francs that had been accumulated in the territorial supporting fund.[55]

Although the new federal fund was slow in getting into operation, cocoa production and exports continued to increase at a satisfactory rate both in Gabon and in Moyen-Congo. By 1959, exports had almost reached the 3,000-ton mark, and though the crop is still subject to varying climatic conditions it should in the near future show bigger returns when the recently planted areas come into full bearing.

Tobacco

Both as an import and as a local crop tobacco has long enjoyed great popularity in AEF. Besides the many indigenous varieties cultivated, the federation has imported large tonnages of tobacco leaf from the Western Hemisphere. Even as recently as the mid-1920's, this leaf served as small change in isolated areas, and could be bartered for food by Europeans traveling in the hinterland.[56] Since World War II, leaf-tobacco imports have declined as the production of Maryland tobacco developed in Moyen-Congo and Oubangui and as the cheap cigarettes manufactured at Brazzaville won a fast-growing clientèle.

Tobacco, though still a very secondary crop in AEF, is an important one for the economy of certain regions of Moyen-Congo and, to a lesser extent, parts of Oubangui, and it is regarded as a success by the administration and Africans alike. A family crop that can be cultivated by the village women and children, leaving the young men free to pursue other activities, tobacco is remunerative to the producer. Its cultivation is especially important in distant regions where it is often the sole cash crop and one whose high value offsets its transport costs. Chiefly responsible for its success has been the close collaboration between the public authorities in France and the federation, and the efficiency and continuity of operations by the Metropolitan Régie SEITA, which has a monopoly of purchases and exports. SEITA has been careful to see that Maryland tobacco is not cultivated in unsuitable regions. Furthermore, it has placed a ceiling on AEF's production that is strictly related to the needs of the Metropolitan cigarette industry, which absorbs four-fifths of the federation's output, amounting in recent years to between 600 and 850 tons. SEITA has also organized a purchasing system that is satisfactory to the growers, including the payment of premiums for quality output. The Grand Council has tried to encourage tobacco shipments by reducing the export duty from 12 to 10 per cent in 1955.

It seems likely that tobacco production will increase in AEF during the next few years. The cigarette factory at Brazzaville, which takes about one-fifth of the present crop, is not yet working to capacity (500 tons), and the local market for its output is steadily widening. Exports, too, may soon rise, for with the development of the Common Market, AEF's tobacco may find outlets in Europe beyond those it already possesses in France.

Rubber

Rubber was formerly a very important export of AEF and may in the future again play an outstanding role in the federation's foreign trade.

Wild rubber grows abundantly in the forest regions of Gabon, Moyen-Congo, and Oubangui. After the turn of the century, this product began to replace ivory as AEF's main export, and in 1911 it represented 62 per cent of the federation's total shipments and amounted to 1,697 tons.[57] This tonnage rose to 2,700 on the eve of World War I, only to recede to an annual average of about 1,400 tons between 1918 and 1930, when competition from plantation-produced hevea greatly reduced the market for the uncultivated variety. This was the period when the French public was becoming aware of the sordid story of forced rubber collecting by the Africans subjected to the control of the concessionary companies, and both economic and human considerations were combining to make the local government reconsider its policy toward rubber. It was now apparent that many of the rubber-producing regions had been bled white and that no effort had been made to reconstitute the natural growths. Moreover, the need to penetrate ever deeper into the forest to find rubber was producing harmful physical and psychological effects on the African laborers, and was also leading to their neglect of food crops. In 1937 Governor-General Reste denounced the collecting of wild rubber as both uneconomic and antisocial.[58]

Unfortunately, just at the time when this viewpoint had been adopted by both the government and local traders, World War II began and the Allies were cut off from their Far Eastern supplies of rubber. To help meet their needs for this commodity, the Free French authorities in AEF reinstituted the forced collection of wild rubber. Production reached the record amount of over 3,500 tons in 1944, and the high price at which AEF's rubber was purchased by the British contributed not a little to the federation's financial prosperity during the war. French officials regretted this "unfortunate retrogression" and, fearing that it might have "disastrous social and demographic repercussions should the war continue many more years," started among Africans a program of planting hevea to replace the gathering of wild rubber.[59]

High-yielding clones were imported from Cameroun and developed at Oyem in Gabon to such good effect that in 1942 Governor-General Eboué made that center into a federal hevea experimental station. By the end of the war the Oyem station had 15 hectares planted to hevea and an annex at Kango to develop rubber planting in the Gabon estuary, and these together were able to provide enough clones so that African farmers could start planting on 200 hectares around Minvoul in the Woleu-N'Tem and a French Société Industrielle et Agricole de la N'Gounié (SIANG) could plant 250 hectares near Lambaréné. In Oubangui another private company, the Société Africaine Agricole et Forestière (SAFA), whose parent organization, the Plantations des Terres Rouges, already had large rubber holdings in Indochina and Cameroun, was given a 3,000-hectare concession for planting hevea near Mbaiki in Oubangui. As of 1948, when the federation's exports of wild rubber had fallen to 325 tons, the area planted to hevea in AEF covered 1,000 hectares, and was increasing. By this time, too, the agricultural service of Moyen-Congo had experimentally planted 300 hectares to hevea near Komono, and was trying to popularize the crop among African farmers in the forest zone of that territory. For the first time, in 1951, hevea was exported from AEF.

The course of the war in Indochina further boosted rubber planting in AEF, but by big French companies rather than by African farmers, whose small-scale cultivation of hevea tended to disappear, notably in Gabon. Aside from suitable soil and climate, which existed throughout much of the forest zone, four additional elements were required for the success of such an enterprise—adequate financial, labor, and water resources as well as the means of communication. To be profitable, hevea had to be planted on a minimal area of 1,000 hectares, requiring an initial investment of 350 million CFA francs, and after that a 15-year period must pass before the plantation would come into full bearing. Then, to work these 1,000 hectares, a labor force of 700 to 1,000 men was needed, some of whom had to be skilled as tappers. In addition, considerable amounts of water were required to operate processing plants. Finally, planters had to be prosperous enough to support a 4 per cent export duty, a 2 per cent tax on the *chiffre d'affaires,* and a 0.5 per cent impost for the standardization service.[60]

Inevitably few companies and fewer individuals were able to bear such expenditures over a long period. Gabon could provide only a very small and unskilled labor supply, and the poor means of communication and inadequate water resources were lesser but still formidable handicaps. By 1957, only three hevea plantations had survived, one each in Oubangui, Moyen-Congo, and Gabon, and that in the last-mentioned territory (which had been bought from SIANG by a Dutch company) was in financial difficulties. However, in 1956 the Unilever subsidiary, Société des Palmiers et Hevéas du Gabon, was—as its name suggests—planning to plant rubber interspersed with oil palms on its newly acquired plantation along the Ogooué. As yet it is too soon to foresee the future of this crop in AEF, but if hevea planting succeeds there it will probably be the result of the enterprise of large and heavily capitalized companies and not that of individual African farmers.

Animal Husbandry

Until World War II, animal husbandry in AEF was determined wholly by natural climatic and geographic conditions and by the varying herding aptitudes of its inhabitants. It was above all the depredations of the tsetse fly that barred the pastoral Arab nomads from penetrating south of 10° N. latitude and that were responsible for the failure of animal husbandry to develop in Gabon, southern Oubangui, and Moyen-Congo. Probably for the same reason the Negroes of AEF have concentrated on farming and neglected herding, and nowhere in the federation has the rearing of animals been associated with agriculture. The great contributions made by the French administration, particularly since the war, have been the introduction of animal husbandry among Africans in zones where it never before existed and the creation of a meat-export trade. The spread of mixed farming, which is still confined to a few of the *paysannats,* should in time also bring about a revolutionary change in AEF's rural economy.

Nine-tenths of all the federation's livestock are to be found in Tchad, and almost all of the remaining tenth in Oubangui. In Tchad, animal husbandry absorbs the activities of more than half of the population, whereas in Oubangui it is only a secondary occupation. The use of Tchad's vast and generally excellent pasturelands is sharply restricted by the shortage of surface water, and the ceaseless migrations which this imposes on its herds are highly detrimental to their well-being and to the relations between their nomadic owners and the sedentary farming population. Oubangui has two favorable zones of animal husbandry, the one in the west being larger than that created just before the war in the east, but for the same reasons as in Tchad its herds, too, are destructively mobile.

In Gabon and Moyen-Congo no animal husbandry, properly speaking, existed until the 1950's, though villagers have long kept a few pigs, chickens, sheep, and goats. The Negroes of those territories have never been herders but simply owners of a few animals that are left to fend for themselves and that represent a supplementary source of income and very occasionally of meat. Only the Arabs of Tchad and the Peulh Bororos of Oubangui are professional herders for whom animal husbandry is their main resource. Yet even they practice almost no selective breeding, take little care of their animals, and utilize only a very small proportion of their cattle in the form of meat, hides, milk, and butter. In their eyes, cattle are a form of capital cherished for their number, not their quality, though increasingly their owners appreciate the income they derive from selling the young bulls for fetishist sacrifices and the cows in the markets of Nigeria and Sudan. Horses, camels, hides, and butter are also exported, but cattle constitute the main object of a growing and largely illicit trade with neighboring territories. Sheep and goats supply almost all of the meat consumed by the Arab and Peulh herders, except in the few areas where only cattle can be reared.

Indigenous cattle are of two main species. The *taurin* or *kouri* breed of the Lake Tchad region number only some 50,000, zebus forming the bulk of the cattle herds, which total perhaps 4 million head. Nigeria is by far AEF's most important market for live cattle. Officially about 65,000 head are exported there each year, but at least three times that number are annually smuggled across the border and exchanged for imported merchandise or Nigerian pounds. Sudan is a much smaller market for both legal and illicit cattle exports, and Oubangui takes from Tchad about 17,000 head a year, of which some 2,000 are re-exported to Moyen-Congo and the balance used locally to supplement that territory's inadequate production of beef. Gabon is irregularly and insufficiently provisioned from Cameroun, which is curiously both an exporter of cattle and an importer of Tchad's livestock. In Tchad and to a lesser extent in Oubangui there is a considerable internal trade in hides, milk, and butter, and also an export trade in hides and butter. Only about one-fifth of the hides and skins produced in Tchad are exported, and almost all go to Nigeria where they are re-exported as of Kano or Maiduguri origin. Oubangui's output goes to France and to Moyen-Congo, which has two tanneries. Created to meet wartime needs, these tanneries represent the first attempt in AEF to industrialize a product of animal origin. They absorb, however, at most only 10 per cent of the hide and skin exports, which vary considerably but rarely exceed 1,000 tons a year. Butter in liquid form is exported exclusively from Tchad and now only to Nigeria and Sudan. During the war, when this trade was encouraged for shipment to North Africa, exports rose to 2,000 tons, but they have now fallen to average only a few hundred tons a year. As is true of the products of Tchad's animal husbandry, the export of butter, hides, and skins could be vastly increased were it not for the high cost and other difficulties involved in their collection, processing, and transport.

Sheep, of which there are three main breeds in AEF, are reared in all of the territories, but they are exported only from Tchad. Of an estimated total of some 3 million head, about 60,000 are officially exported each year to Sudan where they are often exchanged for young camels, most of the remainder being consumed as meat by their owners. An attempt after the war to crossbreed the native sheep with astrakhan rams at the Abougoudam husbandry station near Abéché turned out to be one of FIDES' most costly failures. Horses, to the number of about 120,000 are reared mainly in northern and eastern Tchad and always in association with cattle. Some care is taken in the breeding of horses destined for the Arab chiefs or for export to Kano, but the great majority are left to browse where they may and are weaned and broken in at an unduly young age. Some selection is also practiced in the reproduction of camels, of which there are some 250,000 in Tchad. Some young breeding stock is imported from Sudan, adults are regularly exported to Nigeria where they serve for the transport of peanuts, and over-age camels are shipped to Fezzan where they are slaughtered for meat. Donkeys, like camels, are to be found almost exclusively in Tchad, where they number under 200,000 and are used mostly for carrying water. Pigs, on the other hand, are reared only in the fetishist south, where some millions of them are allowed to grow, without care, for the purpose of supplying meat to their owners. The same could be said of the innumerable chickens that roam about in the southern villages, and their eggs are rarely consumed or sold.

The French government has been encouraging the husbandry of all these breeds of animals in order to increase both local meat consumption and their owners' cash income. Under the first Plan, 234 million CFA francs were allocated to the animal-husbandry services for general equipment and 437 million to build centers for the production of vaccines and for the breeding and treatment of herds. Obviously the first move was toward strengthening the veterinary staff, which on January 1, 1946, consisted of only seven veterinaries and five assistants. This was slowly and effectively enlarged by the recruitment of European personnel, but little headway was made in persuading Africans to take up this career despite the provision of scholarships in France and at the Bamako interfederal school. Few of the indigenous population had even the simple educational background required and even fewer any inclination to become veterinaries.[61] A handful of African assistants were trained in AEF, but it was not until the end of 1956 that the Tchad assembly voted to establish a school for veterinaries in that territory. The animal-husbandry service was placed under a General Inspectorate at Brazzaville which supervised the territorial branches and sectors, of which there were 17 in Tchad, three in Oubangui, and two in Moyen-Congo.

Among the duties assigned to the animal-husbandry service, priority was given to the protection of herds against rinderpest, trypanosomiasis, and other contagious diseases which the local herders were powerless to combat. Two small vaccine-producing centers at Fort Lamy enabled the veterinaries to give mass inoculations that succeeded in holding rinderpest in check, and with the opening of a large federal vaccine-manufacturing center and research station at Farcha in 1954, they were able to attack other diseases, notably sleeping sickness, which was increasing its inroads on Tchad's herds. Nowadays the Farcha laboratory turns out enough vaccines for Cameroun as well as all of AEF, and its operations and research program have been taken over by a Metropolitan organization.

Second priority was assigned to the enlargement and improvement of the federation's herds, and 366 million CFA francs were allocated by FIDES for the construction of experimental breeding stations and 500 million for digging wells in the sahel zone. A main station for poultry and pig breeding was set up at Kilometer 17 outside of Brazzaville for the distribution of selected animals to substations at Owendo in Gabon and at Bambari, Bangui, and Bouar in Oubangui. The importation and acclimatization of trypanosomiasis-resistant N'dama cattle was the task of the Dolisie, Mindouli, and Banza Gounga stations in Moyen-Congo. In Tchad a horse stud was created at N'Gouri in Kanem, and an existing center for the improvement of local cattle by crossbreeding with N'dama was enlarged at Fianga. Abougoudam near Abéché was the point chosen for the ill-fated venture to rear astrakhan sheep, of which a smaller herd was located at Arada. It took so long for these stations to be established and to conduct their initial experiments that all of AEF's African assemblymen became very critical of the animal-husbandry service.[62] But their attitude changed to one of support when the stations began distributing selected animals to African farmers and creating new sources of meat and of income in places where such husbandry had never before existed. The most outstanding success in this field was the introduction of cattle husbandry in southeastern Moyen-Congo and in southern Gabon. The sensational development of ranching in the Niari filled them with less enthusiasm, for this was due mainly to the enterprise of a private French company and involved a 50,000-hectare concession. (The more recent creation of ranches in the Massakory region has not aroused the same interest because Tchad is par excellence the country of animal husbandry.)

The well-digging program, confined wholly to Tchad, was welcomed by the Africans, first in the cotton belt and later in the nomadic areas, for it was expected to sedentarize herds that were decimated by constant migration and to put an end to the seasonal destruction of crops by the migratory animals. But the increase in watering points attracted numerous herders who settled permanently in the south, where their presence was actively resented by the farmers already established there. In the northern trek areas the nomadic herders were unwilling to help amortize the expense of well-digging and upkeep by paying for the water used by their animals. In both cases traditional societies were faced with *faits accomplis* that involved a transformation of their perennial customs and social organization without adequate preparation. And throughout AEF, technical successes that were the pride of the French administration, such as the introduction of ranching and the export of frozen meat by plane, failed to arouse much interest on the part of the Africans, either the masses or the elite. They were the result of long-term experimentation by trained experts, and were considered to be primarily for Europeans and of little immediate benefit to the local population. To be sure, most of the meat shipped by plane from Tchad to the coastal cities has been consumed by Africans despite its high price. Even if the modern abattoir completed at Farcha in 1958 is ever able to work to capacity and export cheaper frozen meat in quantity to the south, this will still affect scarcely any but the urban populations. In the view of Africans of all categories, the only effective way of immediately increasing the meat consumption of the rural populations is by unrestricted hunting.

A regulation of November 18, 1947, sharply curtailed the number of firearms and hunting licenses distributed to Africans, as well as the amount of meat obtained through their use that could be sold in the federation's markets. The area covered by reserves on which hunting is forbidden amounts to almost 10 million hectares. These restrictions gave rise to an incredible volume of criticism in almost every session of the Grand Council and territorial assemblies. Again and again the administration was accused of unjustly favoring Europeans in the distribution of firearms and hunting permits out of fear lest the Africans stage an uprising if they were given permission to own guns. The government claimed that it was simply trying to protect the federation's wildlife and to create a tourist attraction that would bring in appreciable revenues. Returning to the charge, the African spokesmen claimed that the Europeans hunted for sport whereas their compatriots needed to protect their crops from the depredations of wild animals and also to get meat that was available from almost no other source in three out of AEF's four territories.[63] The government, too, was concerned about increasing the meat ration of rural as well as urban Africans, but it preferred the slower but surer method of creating animal husbandry in new regions and of developing it where it already existed. Thus official efforts were concentrated on the importation and distribution of trypanosomiasis-resistant cattle and other breeding stock, and in deflecting Tchad's livestock exports to foreign countries toward the south in the form of frozen meat. Secondarily, the government aimed to develop mixed farming, which would have the double advantage of supplementing manual labor by that of draught animals and of providing natural fertilizer for crops.

Technically, the administration's program has been proved feasible. Mass production of vaccines, digging of deep wells, acclimatization of cattle to tsetse-infested regions, creation of ranch-type husbandry, crossbreeding with imported stock, air transport of sizable tonnages of frozen meat— these measures have notably increased the size and health of herds and also the amount of meat supplies available in the south. From the financial angle, none of these projects has paid off, and thus far only the French government can afford to persevere in their execution. Despite undeniable successes the adequate provisioning of the southern territories in meat is far from assured, and the continued large-scale illicit export of livestock to neighboring countries remains a weakening hemorrhage not only for Tchad's finances and animal resources but for the welfare of the federation as a whole. The problem is now wholly a psychological and financial one, and on the solution of the latter aspect depends that of the former. If the new African governments of AEF can be convinced that it will pay them in the long run to develop animal husbandry and the wholesale export of meat, they may be willing to carry forward the French official program. But if they become discouraged by the time and money that this policy requires, they will probably accede to the wishes of their impatient electorate and revert to traditional practices, including that of unrestricted hunting.

Forests and Forest Products

On both sides of the equator in AEF, from the Atlantic coast to the frontier of the Belgian Congo, forest covers some 30 million hectares, and it can be roughly divided into the dense forest, the inundated forest, and mangrove swamps.

Mangroves abound in the estuaries and mouths of rivers along the coasts of Moyen-Congo and Gabon, and the total area they cover is considerable. To utilize these growths a larger labor force would be required than is available in the coastal regions. For some years the possibility of using mangroves for the manufacture of paper pulp has been under study in AEF, but the failure of an analogous experiment in Ivory Coast, where the labor supply is more abundant, has been an effective deterrent to embarking on a similar undertaking in the federation. The inundated forest stretches over a surface of some 10,000 square kilometers, chiefly in the Sangha region of Moyen-Congo. Since World War II a small forest industry has developed there, whose output is either exported to the Belgian Congo or sent to Brazzaville's sawmills. The only forest industries worthy of the name in AEF, however, are those of the dense forest in Gabon and, to a lesser extent, in western Moyen-Congo.

In those territories the secondary forest has encroached widely on the primary forest, for despite the small size of the Gabonese and Congolese populations, their practice of shifting agriculture and of starting bush fires has caused the disappearance of most of the primeval growths. Yet the area covered by the dense forest is still so vast and probably capable of producing annually about 50 million cubic meters of timber that the current output of some 400,000 to 500,000 tons seems surprisingly small. One reason is the very limited labor supply and internal market in AEF; another is the lack of well-equipped loading ports and the costly maritime freight rates for exports; still another is the absence of adequate means of internal transportation; and, finally, there is the handicap of the foresters' exceptionally high production costs, chiefly caused by the wide dispersal of valuable trees. Although mahogany, iroko, and other marketable trees are to be found in AEF's dense forest, the only two species that have been utilized on an industrial scale are okoumé and limba, not only because AEF possesses a quasi-monopoly of both but also because they grow in relatively compact stands and find a ready market abroad. Many others of AEF's tree species could be utilized, but there is little local demand for them and their value is not great enough to stand the transport costs entailed in exporting them.

The beginnings of the forest industry in AEF are obscure, but it is known that merchants trading in the *bois des îles*—mainly mahogany and ebony—were operating in Gabon during the last years of the nineteenth century and that they shipped timber out of the ports of Mayumba and Sette-Cama. By 1902, exports of timber amounted to about 11,000 tons, of which nearly half consisted of okoumé. When European industrialists, at about that time, came to recognize the exceptional suitability of okoumé for the manufacture of plywood, exports of that species from AEF grew rapidly until they reached 134,000 tons on the eve of World War I. Shipments were not resumed until 1920, after which they increased steadily throughout the interwar period, with only a brief decline during the world depression of the early 1930's, till they reached a record volume of 407,000 tons in 1937. By that time, wood exports had outdistanced all the federation's other raw material shipments in both volume and value. Okoumé exports were far larger than those of limba, and Gabon supplied four-fifths of them and Moyen-Congo the rest. Sawn wood appeared in the federation's exports for the first time in 1927, in the form of ties for the Metropolitan railroads, and 7,500 cubic meters of peeled wood were shipped out the last year before World War II, but the great bulk of AEF's wood exports were undressed timber.

Until the 1930's all of AEF's timber came from the coastal regions, was felled by Africans using only primitive implements, and was floated down the nearest waterways to the seaports. In such operations, labor was naturally the primary factor, and the scarcity, indolence, unreliability, and lack of skills of the workers were the recurrent complaint of all AEF's European foresters of this period. Gradually some of the big French companies began to mechanize their operations, and the retrenchment necessitated by the world trade depression strengthened this trend by eliminating poorly equipped foresters. In 1931 the first caterpillar tractors were imported into Gabon, and during the ensuing eight years more than 1,000 kilometers of Decauville tracks were built in the forest region for the transport of logs. Furthermore, as the areas near the water courses began to be worked out, the government made the granting of concessions and of cutting permits in the less accessible hinterland contingent upon an applicant's possession of a minimal amount of mechanical equipment. When large-scale production was resumed after the war and labor had become both scarcer and more costly, AEF's foresters bought as much machinery as they could afford, and the production of wood became one of the most completely mechanized industries of any in the federation. Inevitably this gave the big companies predominance in the industry and led to a decline of small enterprises, both European and African.

Mechanization was but one of several major changes that have transformed AEF's forest industry since World War II. Of equal importance have been the various types of controls exercised by the government over an industry that had theretofore operated independently of any law other than that of supply and demand. A beginning had been made in 1936 with the creation of a federal forestry service, but it was given neither the means nor the staff to carry out its assigned tasks of creating forest reserves, reforesting the most denuded areas to arrest soil erosion, and enforcing the forest regulations. These decrees (particularly those of 1927) deriving from the basic Metropolitan law of March 28, 1899, were so unsuited to AEF's forest industry that even a well-staffed forestry service would have found them hard to enforce. In the 1930's the government tried to offset the wide fluctuations in the world wood market by reducing cutting permits and imposing a quota on production, but it never succeeded either in getting the foresters to gear their output to the market's needs or in disciplining the host of intermediaries who acquired a grip on the export trade by advancing loans to small producers at high interest rates.[64] During the war, exports declined sharply (to 45,000 tons in 1943–44) but did not wholly cease, for Britain, then the sole buyer of AEF's timber, needed okoumé badly enough to allot it a limited amount of shipping space. But the industry's greatly diminished activity and the concurrent proliferation of state controls of all sorts permitted the AEF government to intervene effectively for the first time in regulating timber production and sales.

Administrative intervention first took the form of creating an organization called the Office des Bois d'AEF (OBAEF) on February 24, 1944, which was given a monopoly of the sale abroad of the federation's woods and of supplying timber to the local processing plants. At the outset the government-general participated in financing the newborn agency only to the extent of guaranteeing a loan made to it by the Banque de l'Afrique Occidentale Française. In its first operating year OBAEF ran a deficit of 9 million francs, largely because it had inherited a stock of unsalable wood left over from 1943 when the government had granted permission for the cutting of 62,000 tons of wood at a time when no shipping space was available. Recognizing its responsibility in this matter, the government gave OBAEF 3 million francs, but it insisted that the rest of the deficit be met by a levy of 10 per cent on the sales made by producers to the Office. This aroused the hostility of the foresters, who demanded a return to free trading through their prewar intermediaries. Their protests led to successive modifications of the Office's directorate and functions, so that it eventually became a cooperative of producers operating under official controls. But the government insisted upon retaining the right to limit the production of okoumé, either for technical or for economic reasons, and to grant cutting permits at public auction or on temporarily ceded areas, and also to bring in greater revenues to the producing territories by raising the taxes on wood production and sales.[65] It also laid down the policy of protecting AEF's forest resources by progressive increases in the area of the forest reserves and of the reforested surfaces. In carrying out this program the federal and territorial forestry services, particularly that of Gabon, were aided by a grant of 89.5 million francs from FIDES, which financed aerial prospecting of the forest zones, the taking of an inventory of valuable species, and the operating of two research stations.

In consolidating its control over the forest industry the government had an effective weapon in its power to allocate hard currency, which in the early postwar years was indispensable for the purchase of mechanized equipment. On the constructive side, it used the Office to finance loans at low interest rates to producers, to repair their machinery at its workshop, and to pioneer the mechanization of sawmilling. While admitting the usefulness of these functions, the various producers' organizations throughout AEF—and especially the Syndicat Forestier du Gabon, which was the one most affected—continued to protest against the sales monopoly held by the Office, its domination by "nonqualified" officials, its high running expenses, and its forced constitution of a reserve fund through the withholding of 10 per cent of the proceeds received from its wood sales abroad. Actually, the principal cause of the Office's unpopularity with the big producers was that for the first time it "permitted the government to acquire exact information about the foresters' operations and hence to apply strictly to them the financial and forest regulations."[66]

The producers' opposition might have been unavailing had it not been for the discovery in 1947 of "serious errors" in the Office's accounts,[67] which led to a notable reduction in its powers. By a decree of August 17, 1948, its monopoly was restricted to the sale of undressed okoumé in foreign markets and to the provisioning of local processing plants with but half of their timber supplies. The other half could be acquired through direct contacts between the plants and the producers, and industrialists located in France could also get their wood provisions from AEF independently of the Office. The directorate of the Office was also reorganized so as to make its operations more flexible and to give greater representation to the producers and a larger place to some of the prewar traders.[68] While a few of the die-hard producers continued to demand suppression of the Office, most of the foresters became reconciled to its standardization and control of okoumé exports to foreign markets, particularly after the Office had been instrumental in pulling the forest industry through the trade depression of 1952.

After okoumé exports had fallen that year by 23 per cent in tonnage and by 1,200 million CFA francs in value, the Office raised a loan of 250 million CFA francs from the Caisse Centrale de la France d'Outre-Mer (guaranteed by the federal budget) and lowered the price for its okoumé sold in foreign markets. This led to a rapid revival of okoumé sales, and within two years the Office had wiped out its debts, but this experience shook the local producing companies to their foundations. Not only did they have to take a big financial loss, but they found that their best foreign clients were beginning to substitute cheaper woods for okoumé and that even the Metropolitan market was starting to buy competitive timber from non-French African sources. Since the Office refused to buy any but first-quality okoumé—its purchases were restricted by law to its sales contracts —the foresters were left with stocks of inferior wood on their hands which the domestic market could not absorb. At the same time their production costs were rising, not only because of the need to penetrate ever deeper into the forest to find okoumé but also as a result of a rise in maritime freight rates which hit okoumé harder than other AEF woods.

Despite these unfavorable developments, AEF's producers in 1954 entered upon a period of unprecedented prosperity which was broken only briefly in early 1956 when adverse market conditions necessitated a 20 per cent cut in production. In 1954 the industry was aided by a premium (half of which was paid by the Metropolitan treasury and half by the federal budget) on AEF exports to non-French Union markets. At the same time, a reduction in the rates for wood transport by the Compagnie Générale des Transports en Afrique (CGTA) and the Congo-Ocean railroad helped Oubangui producers, and for the first time the Lobaye foresters began to export their output. Then, too, the currency devaluations of 1957 and 1958 were especially helpful to the wood industry, which sold much of its output outside the franc zone. While West Germany remained AEF's best customer, new markets were opened up in Italy, Holland, Israel, and Switzerland, all of which showed an increasing interest in the federation's limba and second-quality okoumé exports.

From 1954 on, all of AEF's wood exports increased, and although those of undressed okoumé remained in the forefront, shipments of sawn wood, veneer, and plywood also multiplied steadily. For all but okoumé the local producers had to find their own markets: the heavy shipping rates for AEF's output automatically limited the amount of such sales abroad, while domestic consumption has tended to decline since completion of the Plan's big public-works program and the substitution of other fuel for wood by the railroad and CGTA. The federation's 63 sawmills, which are capable of producing about 127,000 cubic meters of sawn wood a year, have never turned out as much as 100,000 a year, and its two plywood factories still operate far below capacity despite a steady increase in output. In very recent years the great plywood factory of the Compagnie Française du Gabon at Port Gentil has extended its markets outside of Europe and is operating at about 75 per cent of its annual capacity of 50,000 cubic meters. That of Plexafric at Pointe Noire had to close down in 1955, but was reopened the following year by Plywoods Ltd.,[69] which subsequently has been exporting its yearly production of about 1,000 cubic meters to South Africa. The main hope now for expanding the domestic market for AEF's processing plants lies in the industrialization of the Pointe Noire region, which is expected to take place after completion of the Kouilou dam. At present, however, wood exports closely approximate production, and as of 1958 nearly 2 million cubic meters of timber were cut down in AEF, of which 1,150,000 were okoumé and 330,000 limba.[70] This is considered to be about the maximum yield that AEF's forests can support in their present stage of development. Wood remains AEF's premier export, amounting in 1958 to 824,000 tons, valued at 7,780 million CFA francs. Of this total, France took shipments valued at 2 billion and West Germany 300 million, almost all of which consisted of okoumé logs. Okoumé alone accounted for 666,621 tons and its production in 1959 is expected to exceed that record figure.

The area over which temporary concessions and cutting permits extend now covers some 2.5 million hectares, well over half of these being for okoumé. Any further appreciable increase in this area must await the development of Gabon's second zone and, in the distant future, the opening up of the reforested areas, particularly those of the Mayombé which have been planted to limba under the sylvo-banana contracts (see pp. 503–504). Although the conceded area has steadily increased, so have the zones classified as forest reserves, which currently also cover some 2.5 million hectares. The activities of the forestry services are now aimed less at increasing production than at assuring its continuity by the transformation of the forest into accessible stands of valuable species.

Whether or not the new African governments of AEF will continue this policy is a moot question. They are certainly eager to maintain the considerable revenues brought in by wood production, but they are also determined to control the operations of the Office des Bois and to increase the participation by African foresters in the industry. As the great majority of Africans are congenitally even less disposed than are the European companies to accept any control over their use of natural resources, it remains to be seen whether the more enlightened elite will be able to withstand the pressure that will doubtless be brought to bear by the electorate for permission to cut down trees where and when they please. Yet if for political reasons or the lack of qualified technicians the forest reserves cannot be kept intact, the future of AEF's wood industry is dim. The big companies, despite their huge investment in the federation, particularly in Gabon, cannot be expected to remain there after their operations cease to be profitable.

Thus the hazards of a pseudo-nationalization of the wood industry and a prospective shrinkage in the producing area are added to the dangers arising from the chronic instability of the world wood market. Yet optimism as to the future of Gabon's okoumé was shown by the establishment there in 1958 of 15 new forest companies having a total capital of 250 million francs. Another hopeful sign in 1959 was the creation of a reforestation fund and the building of new roads in the forest zone.

Fisheries

In view of the great popularity of fish as a food among the populations of AEF, and the existence of about 150 species of edible fish off the Atlantic coast of the federation, it is curious that there are few professional fishermen among the maritime tribes. Though fishing is practiced by the villagers living on the coast and around the lagoons and estuaries, the only tribe whose sole occupation is fishing is one living at Fernan Vaz on the Ogooué, and even their boats are ill suited to venturing far out into the Atlantic. It has been chiefly foreigners—Africans from Dahomey or Europeans—who have been responsible for such small development of AEF's maritime fishing as has taken place.

Whaling off the Gabonese coast is the oldest of the European fishing operations in AEF. Since 1912, whalers belonging to French, Norwegian, and British companies have periodically operated intensively in Gabon's territorial waters in cycles of approximately four years. After World War II, the most stable of these companies, the Franco-Norwegian Société des Pêcheries Coloniales à la Baleine (SOPECOBA), bought elaborate equipment, employed a large staff, and built a processing plant at Cap Lopez. But a series of good seasons alternated with disastrous ones, and in 1953 it suspended operations off the Gabonese coast, to the detriment of the territory's budget.

The two other European maritime fishing concerns of AEF are located at Pointe Noire, and they have done much to supply Moyen-Congo's main towns with fresh, dried, and smoked fish and to train Africans in modern fishing and processing techniques.[71] Their catch is shipped in refrigerated cars on the Congo-Ocean railroad and even by plane, and they are responsible for almost all of the 1,000 tons of fresh fish sold annually in the Brazzaville market. These companies work in collaboration with the oceanographic research station of the Institut d'Etudes Centrafricaines (IEC) set up at Pointe Noire, and their efforts are now jointly directed toward the development of a tinned-fish industry that may include sardines, oysters, and tuna. However, any large-scale utilization of the federation's vast maritime fish resources must await construction of a big ice factory at Pointe Noire and the introduction of better fishing boats and equipment for the African coastal tribes. In recent years, about 2,000 tons of fish have been brought in annually at Pointe Noire, and of the total catch, African fishermen account for only about one-fourth.

Fishing in its rivers, lakes, and ponds has always been far more important in AEF than maritime fishing, and has been associated with an internal trade that antedated the European occupation. Remnants of this trade have

survived in the provisiöning of the Pool region with fish caught along the
two Likouala rivers, and during two months of the year the small cod of
Gabon are sold in the hinterland settlements.[72] Some of the river tribes
living along the Ogooué, Oubangui, Chari, and Logone are professional
fishermen, and their varied equipment and techniques are ingeniously
adapted to the particular conditions under which they carry on their work.
The catch of fresh-water fish throughout AEF is thought to be in the
neighborhood of 100,000 tons a year, nearly three-fourths of which comes
from Tchad.[73] Some 10,000 tons of Tchad's annual output is exported
clandestinely to northern Cameroun and Nigeria, while an unknown percentage of the catch along the Oubangui river is bartered for merchandise
in the Belgian Congo. The only outstanding scientific study as yet made of
fresh-water fishing production and techniques in AEF is that being done
in the Tchad basin by the Centre d'Etudes de la Pêche that was set up at
Fort Lamy in 1953.

For a few years after the war, the government-general showed little
interest in the output of the territories other than Tchad, taking the stand
that the development of fresh-water fishing in them was the concern of
the local territorial or municipal administrations.[74] Fishing was a form
of production almost totally neglected by the first Plan, although the federation was then importing each year over 3,000 tons of fish and part of its
own output was being smuggled into neighboring countries. By 1950 the
federal government awoke to the importance of promoting production of
fish both as an item in the local African diet and as a source of cash income.
Consequently an expert of the Water and Forestry Service was sent to study
the breeding of tilapia in the Belgian Congo with a view to its popularization among the hinterland tribes of AEF. A tilapia research and reproduction station was built at Djoumouna, near Brazzaville, and since its completion in 1953–54 it has shipped thousands of pairs of tilapia to family
ponds built under its supervision in the three southern territories of AEF.
Indeed it has now become the main tilapia station for central Africa, and
the published results of its experimentation circulate beyond the confines
of the federation.[75] It has also set up three fish stations in Oubangui and
trained more than 50 African monitors, who tour the rural areas of that
territory, Moyen-Congo, and Gabon teaching the population to construct
fish ponds and to care for and feed tilapia.

As of 1958, more than 25,000 family ponds had been installed in AEF,
mostly in Moyen-Congo and Oubangui, and their output was estimated
at about 250 tons of tilapia a year. FIDES has been financing this operation
at the rate of 35 million CFA francs annually, and the goal set for the
federation is 2,000 tons of fish a year. Inevitably some of the ponds have
been poorly maintained and utilized and a few have been wholly abandoned; perhaps only a third of those constructed are producing to capacity.
The official policy trend appears at present to be to lay less stress on the
family-type pond and more on the creation of small-scale industrial ponds
as a "method better adapted to the mentality of most of AEF's populations."[76]

CHAPTER 15

Trade

The most striking and also the most disturbing characteristic of AEF's foreign trade is the regularity with which the federation's expenditures for imports have exceeded the revenues realized from its exports (see Table 5).

TABLE 5.—FOREIGN TRADE OF AEF, 1950–55

Year	Tonnage (thousand metric tons)		Value (millions of CFA francs)		
	Imports	Exports	Imports	Exports	Excess of Imports over Exports
1950	306	343	13,393.6	7,253.8	6,139.8
1951	363	387	18,243.2	10,996.2	7,247.0
1952	356	356	20,129.6	10,227.4	9,902.2
1953	293	487	14,799.9	10,042.9	4,757.0
1954	299	613	16,681.8	12,794.9	3,892.9
1955	311	756	18,349.2	13,688.6	4,660.6

Source: J. Sentenac, "Le Commerce Extérieur de l'AEF en 1955," *Marchés Tropicaux,* December 1, 1956.

Except in a few isolated years and in regard to two countries, AEF's commercial exchanges have been deficitary, and to a generally increasing degree.

These deficits are not due to a decline in the production of exportable items. On the contrary, the volume of AEF's exports has grown steadily except during world economic depressions and wars. Their value has also regularly increased, though not in proportion to the size of the federation's export tonnages, for over three-fourths of AEF's shipments consist of wood and cotton, which are subject to wide fluctuations in the world market. The main cause of AEF's trade deficits is the fast-rising cost of its imports, which, however, have remained fairly stable as regards tonnages after a sudden spurt following World War II. AEF has had favorable trade balances only at times when there has been a dearth either of shipping or of manufactured goods available for import into the federation. When the local government or traders have tried to retrench, the deficit has been reduced, but since 1947 it has never been eliminated. To varying degrees the federation's commerce is deficitary in relation to all the currency blocs with which it trades except that of the West German mark, and it is normally largest with the franc zone.

This last-mentioned feature is mainly a postwar phenomenon, for French currency devaluations (in 1945, 1948, 1957, and 1958), as well as the control which Paris has exercised over the French Union's dollar and sterling reserves since 1944, have virtually nullified the open-door policy in trade sanctioned by the Act of Berlin. (World War II caused only a temporary, albeit radical change in AEF's external markets and suppliers.) Such monetary manipulations have enabled Metropolitan France to become AEF's main provisioner, as well as to retain its traditional position as the federation's best customer. With the strengthening of commercial ties between countries of the franc zone, particularly conspicuous in the postwar years, AEF has been virtually compelled either to do without imports or to buy simply what is available in the ever-more-expensive French market. To justify such a discriminatory policy, the French government has been paying higher than world prices for some of AEF's exports and has also regularly made up its budgetary deficits. It has, in addition, subsidized the exportation of certain goods to Black Africa and, since 1954, has offered rebates on the shipment to foreign markets of such of the federation's products as were no longer needed or wanted in Metropolitan France.

Official controls have been less operative in determining the nature of AEF's exports and imports than in shaping the course which the federation's commercial exchanges would follow. To be sure, from the first years of the French occupation, the production in AEF of produce needed in France was encouraged, but the changes that took place in its exports during the interwar period were mainly the result of purely economic forces. Like all undeveloped countries, AEF has consistently shipped out raw materials and has imported manufactured goods. But within this general framework, the nature of the raw materials exported has evolved, as has the type of manufactured articles that AEF buys abroad. From being an exporter of uncultivated produce such as ivory, ores, wild rubber, and undressed timber, the federation has gradually become an exporter of cultivated crops, and to an increasing extent its wood and mineral exports have been processed on the spot before being shipped to markets abroad.

The nature of AEF's imports, too, has undergone a transformation over the years. Before World War II, consumer goods—notably cotton textiles—predominated, though during the few years when the railroad and the port of Pointe Noire were being built, considerable amounts of equipment goods were also brought in. As a result of the ten-year Plan, equipment goods came to occupy first place among the categories of AEF's imports during the late 1940's and early 1950's. With the shrinkage in FIDES investment funds from 1952 on, consumer imports once again came to the forefront, but by then their structure, too, had somewhat altered. Because of the local development of some consumer-goods industries and because of rising African living standards, food imports have tended to become more important than those of cotton piece goods.

One of the outstanding developments in AEF since the war has been the growth of the internal market. This was made possible by the FIDES-financed improvement in the federation's means of communication and by the higher incomes of both African and European residents. Not only did the number of wage earners of both groups increase, but the Europeans' exceptionally high salaries in AEF enabled them to maintain a more luxurious way of life than in France, while the larger incomes of African functionaries, producers, and laborers permitted them to buy Western-type consumer goods and in this respect approximate to a greater degree than ever before European living standards. In view of the fact that these developments have been accompanied by a steady rise in living costs and by mounting inflation, protection of the African consumer and of his purchasing power has become, since 1954, a major concern of the local administration.

France's imports of AEF's cotton, wood, petroleum, and a few other items have enabled her either to earn or save hard currency. But the main beneficiaries of the postwar expansion of the federation's trade have been French industrialists and exporters, and their profits have been gained largely at the expense of the Metropolitan taxpayer and of consumers in AEF. Some local merchants have also made money, but more have gone bankrupt or merely kept their heads above water. When AEF has experienced a trade recession, it has been immediately reflected in the shrinkage of federal revenues (which depend very largely on customs duties), and the Metropolitan treasury has had to make good the ensuing budgetary deficits. The loss of AEF's trade would make only the slightest dent on France's economy, for the federation's purchases are believed to total less than a third of the annual business done by one of France's department-store chains, the Prisunic. The conviction that France was paying too heavy a price for its sovereignty over AEF and other countries of Black Africa gained ground in 1956 and undoubtedly facilitated the two federations' acquisition of political autonomy.

If purely economic considerations on the part of France were the only ones involved, France would be well out of tropical Africa. But AEF's financial structure and the welfare of its African populations would be adversely affected by such an abrupt withdrawal, for AEF's trade has long been integrated into the close-knit franc zone and shaped by its relations with France. Even with protected markets in Metropolitan France and French price supports and premiums for the production of exportable produce, its trading position has not been fundamentally improved, for the prices received for its main products are beyond control either by itself or by France and can be improved only by action on an international level. AEF has been producing more and more for export, and getting proportionately ever-smaller monetary returns for this increasing effort. Indeed, the plight of the federation, in regard to its trade position, resembles that of Alice in Looking-Glass Land, who had to run ever faster just to stay where she was.

The continuing rise of AEF's large deficitary trade balance has been a cause of concern for French officials and the African elite. They cannot see how imports can be appreciably reduced, except those of alcoholic beverages and luxury goods, and an all-around reduction is not considered to be desirable. But AEF will have to export much greater quantities than heretofore if it is to earn enough to pay for even its present imports, though it will certainly get more for its money when it can buy freely in the Common Market countries. The chief obstacles to any vast increase in exports, however, remain the perennial handicaps of the federation's vast distances and poor soil, and above all the sparseness and dispersion of its population.

Tariff

AEF's tariff has had so complicated a history and its evolution is so likely to be altered by the political developments of 1958–59 that only a cursory outline will be given here in order to provide the background needed to understand its influence on the federation's trade.[1]

In 1885 the Act of Berlin placed the southern portion of AEF under the regime of the open door. This meant that within the Congo conventional basin only fiscal duties, limited to 10 per cent, could be imposed and that no preferential tariff could be applied to merchandise coming from countries signatory to that treaty. In AEF the conventional basin included roughly all of Moyen-Congo except the Haut-Ogooué circumscription, that part of Gabon lying south of the 2° 50′ parallel, and the southern half of Oubangui, through which flowed the tributaries of the Oubangui river. Northern Gabon and all of the Ogooué basin shared the tariff regime of Metropolitan France until 1928, when a preferential tariff for this area was adopted. From 1898 to 1937, Tchad and the Chari basin were regulated according to a special agreement by which British subjects were placed on the same footing as French citizens there. In actual practice all the federation aside from most of Gabon was gradually included in the conventional basin zone.

In the light of the special economic position in which AEF found itself after the outbreak of World War II, a uniform tariff was initiated on September 21, 1940, that included all of Gabon, and at the same time a customs union was formed with Cameroun, itself placed under the open-door regime by a decree of December 27, 1941. After the Liberation, the Grand Council voted on May 8, 1947, to revert to the *status quo ante bellum,* but as matters worked out, Gabon remained within the Congo conventional basin and trade between AEF and Cameroun was regulated by a series of very liberal agreements negotiated annually. Similarly the international agreements governing AEF's trade have remained largely a dead letter since 1945. In practice, imports have been strictly limited by the amount of hard currency placed at the federation's disposal, and fiscal duties along with export taxes have been indispensable for the revenues of the federal budget.

Until 1949, an ad valorem duty averaging 12 per cent was applied to merchandise of whatever origin entering AEF, except for certain luxury goods (tobacco and alcoholic beverages) and fuel, which paid higher specific duties and formed about one-third of all the federation's imports from outside the franc zone. After imports financed by FIDES began arriving in quantity, the duty on equipment goods was reduced by 1 to 5 per cent, and certain types of imports (livestock, some foodstuffs, seed, fertilizer, and the like) were admitted duty-free. With some exceptions, imports also were subject to a tax on the *chiffre d'affaires,* which was generally at the rate of 5 per cent. The general policy adopted by the government at this time was to favor imports that would help develop the federation's economy and to place high duties on luxury goods and particularly on alcoholic beverages.

Export duties underwent a more marked change as the result of a regulation of July 12, 1950. Until then they had been generally on an ad valorem basis, ranging from 3 per cent on certain oleaginous produce to 18 per cent on cotton fibers. In addition, they were subject to a special tax for research and standardization control (from 0.50 to 1.50 per cent), a *taxe additionelle* that replaced the tax on the *chiffre d'affaires* (2 per cent), and in the case of wood a cutting tax (from 0.1 to 10 per cent). Beginning in 1950 these rates were revised with the double objective of "adapting their scale to the current economic situation" and of making their classification conform more closely to international usage. Duties now ranged from 1 to 22 per cent, and included taxes to finance price-supporting funds and research and standardization, but they did not include a tax on the *chiffre d'affaires,* the rate of which was 2 per cent on all exported commodities. Moreover, all articles shipped to Metropolitan France were thenceforth free of duty excepting cotton, tobacco, certain ores, and diamonds, for which a special export license was required.

To avoid a tariff chaos that might ensue from the imminent break-up of the federation into four republics, the government-general called together at Brazzaville in June 1957 the territorial governors and the new heads of the councils of government. At this conference—the first of its kind held in AEF—it was decided that the Grand Council would thereafter fix the export duties on cotton, cocoa, and coffee, but that the territorial assemblies would set those for peanut and wood exports. Despite a strong current of opinion favoring tariff autonomy in some territories, the new African premiers agreed at Paris on January 17, 1959, to re-establish the customs union that had formerly prevailed for AEF, and the following September they met again to work out the details of this agreement. At the latter meeting it was decided that all four republics would have the same import-duty rates, of which 20 per cent would be paid into a common solidarity fund and the balance be allocated to each state according to consumption.

Official Controls

Government intervention in the foreign and domestic trade of AEF has taken both direct and indirect forms. Generally speaking, the latter implement long-range policies which benefit only Metropolitan France. Direct controls, on the other hand, except those that prevailed during World War II, have been imposed as a rule only at certain times and places or for specific commodities, and they have been devised largely in the interests of local consumers and producers.

Application of the Act of Berlin to the Congo basin meant that the French authorities must respect freedom of trade in that area. To avoid contravening this provision, the Paris government of that time instituted the regime of concessionary companies, which were able to maintain a *de facto* trade monopoly despite the protests of British and other foreign traders already installed in the colony. Though non-French merchants, both European and African, continued to do business in AEF, the French were able to keep a dominant position in the federation's commerce even after the companies were liquidated. Another indirect method used to assure French primacy was that of orienting AEF's output to products that were needed by Metropolitan industries, the outstanding example of this being the forced cultivation of cotton. France in consequence has always been the best market for AEF's exports, but the open-door policy applied to much of the federation prevented France from becoming also its main provisioner until after World War II. Premiums for production and price supports for some of AEF's exports were virtually the sole instances of direct official intervention in the federation's trade until 1940, and these were in operation only temporarily during the depression of the early 1930's. The successive devaluations of the franc perhaps could not be properly termed intervention in AEF's commerce, but they illustrated the French propensity for taking steps in the interest of France without apparent concern for their repercussions on Black Africa's economy.

When AEF cast its lot with Free France in mid-1940, its trade patterns changed abruptly, thus giving the government-general its first chance to exercise control over the colony's commerce. In fact, this was forced on the local administration by the Allies' insistence that AEF's exports and imports be channeled through a government agency rather than be handled by private traders. Moreover, officially determined prices were imposed on goods sold in the domestic market. These controls were not lifted after the war, but rather were reinforced and were supplemented by others imposed directly and indirectly by Metropolitan France, again to its own benefit.

It was through this device of currency allocations that AEF was practically compelled to buy in the increasingly expensive franc zone and to reduce to very small proportions its purchases from the cheaper and better-provisioned hard-currency sources. The devaluations of the franc in 1945 and 1948 were, as always, steps in the interests of France's economy, taken without consultation with her dependencies. This time, however, AEF had elected spokesmen who could make their protests heard in Metropolitan as well as in local bodies. To offset the harm done to AEF's trade by these devaluations, the French government promised to turn back to the federation all the hard currency its exports earned, but the system of licenses for exports to and purchases in foreign markets instituted in 1948 by the government-general gave its officials the decisive voice as to what merchandise should be imported and by whom and at what prices it was to be sold locally. Thus the charges of favoring certain trading firms and merchants at the expense of others added to the general resentment expressed by mercantile organizations against the strait jacket in which the country's economy had been placed. What is more, the government did not have the means of enforcing respect for the prices it had fixed for locally sold merchandise. Consumer goods needed by the population were so scarce that inflation threatened and a large-scale contraband trade with neighboring countries inevitably developed.

The years 1949 and 1950 saw an easing of this situation. In 1949 most of the controls imposed on AEF's trade were lifted, and freedom was theoretically restored to private merchants, but a regulation of September 1, 1949, limited the profits they were allowed to make on imported goods and price controls were maintained on a few items of prime necessity. By the following year, French industry had begun to produce more goods for shipment to AEF and shortages were gradually eliminated even in the northern territories. But the control of foreign-currency allocations still remained with the Paris Office des Changes, and by reason of the parsimony with which dollars and sterling were doled out to AEF, the federation's purchases were perforce largely confined to the franc zone, where prices were becoming ever higher.

The trade recession of 1952, coinciding with the curtailment of the Plan and its reorientation toward increased production, led the government-general to take stock of AEF's trade position. Obviously the big growth in the federation's trade deficit that year was due less to deficient production than to the sharp drop in world prices for AEF's exports and to the expansion in the volume and value of imports. Equally obvious was AEF's overdependence on two commodities, wood and cotton, which were subject to wide price fluctuations in the world market. True, prices for AEF's exports were higher than before the war but not so high as during the early postwar years, equipment goods were forming a larger proportion of imports than before 1939, and the proliferation of small plants producing certain consumer goods had reduced imports of such commodities. But the basic weaknesses remained—the small volume and low value, as well as the poor quality and high production costs, of most of AEF's exports. At the same time, the price of French goods, and hence of AEF's imports, was steadily rising while that of the federation's exports was generally declining, and with it African purchasing power. Nothing could be done in the immediate future to remedy some of these fundamental defects, but the government-general did set about trying to improve the quality along with the quantity of AEF's production, reduce the impact of the distance factor on transport costs, diversify the economy, start more processing industries, spur the exportation of items of small volume and high value, and develop the internal market so that the consumer would be protected against sudden and unjustified price rises. The aid of the French government was needed to help AEF find new markets for some of its exports and to set up funds to cushion producers against sharp falls in the world prices for their output.

Though French policy was still mainly motivated by considerations of France's welfare, the year 1954 marked a departure from established practices in that AEF's trading interests were also taken into account in formulating measures both at Paris and at Brazzaville. That year the French government offered a premium of 20 per cent on some AEF exports sold in non-franc markets, and it also began paying subsidies to certain Metropolitan industrialists who would ship to Black Africa goods needed by consumers there. Price-supporting funds, theretofore confined to cotton, were now established for others of the federation's exports—sisal in 1953, oleaginous products in 1954, cocoa in 1955, and coffee in 1957. The government-general also took action aimed at assuring uniformity in prices and weights and measures throughout AEF, standardizing exports to improve the quality of the federation's goods sold abroad, reducing the cost of rail and river transport for both exports and imports, and negotiating lower prices for the water and electrical current sold in the main urban centers. Laws were drafted to enable the local administration to clamp down on rising prices in the domestic market, but these powers were not used until the devaluations of 1957 and 1958 had provoked a rapid rise in the cost of living and incited the new African republics to freeze prices in January 1959.

Purchasers and Provisioners

Before World War II, deficits with the dollar and sterling zones were chronic and showed little variation, even during the world depression, for imports into the Congo conventional basin were not subject to protectionist duties. In trade with France, AEF's exports did not exceed imports until 1934, and in that year as well as in 1935 and 1937 AEF had a favorable trade balance in that quarter.

Annually, during the interwar period, France supplied AEF with an average of only 35 per cent of its imports but took some 70 per cent of its exports. On the eve of World War II, the federation's chief foreign provisioners, in the order of their importance, were the United States (for fuel, machinery, motor vehicles, and flour), Portugal (for dried fish and wine), Germany (for coal), Belgium (for sugar and tobacco), and Japan (for cotton piece goods).[2] Its main clients were Germany and Holland (wood), Belgium (cotton, palm kernels and oil, and wax), and adjacent British colonies (cattle).

Inevitably World War II, particularly after AEF's rupture with the Vichy regime in August 1940, dealt a blow to the federation's exports, but it was responsible for pushing imports above the 1938 level. The greatest change brought about by the war, however, was in AEF's provisioners and purchasers, but, aside from increased trade with its African neighbors, this alteration in the federation's markets and sources of supply did not long survive the Liberation. In 1941, Great Britain and British dependencies came to occupy first rank among AEF's suppliers and customers. Initially Britain bought up all the stocks of AEF goods that could not be sold elsewhere and then, by an agreement signed in May 1941, took all the federation's oleaginous produce, rubber, and diamonds, and a large share of its coffee, wood, and livestock. This agreement remained in force until the last three months of 1944, and during its life Britain and British dependencies shipped to AEF cement, coal, and especially textiles. Beginning in 1942, the United States became one of AEF's main provisioners, supplying about 25 per cent of its imports, and also bought a larger share than before the war of its exportable output. Neighboring countries came to play a bigger role in AEF's foreign trade: the Belgian Congo supplied AEF with sugar, beer, construction materials, and some consumer goods; Portuguese Cabinda and Angola increased their shipments of dried fish and wine, and added textiles. For the first time in its history, the Belgian Congo became an important market for AEF goods, buying wood, hides and skins, and coffee. After 1944, north Africa entered the scene as both a provisioner and a purchaser of AEF.

Exports as well as imports rose phenomenally in value during the war, though the tonnages involved were in both cases far smaller than in 1938. After AEF lost its strategic importance to the Allies in 1944, it ceased to have any privileged position in the allocation of shipping for its trade. The regime of import and export quotas created during the war was progressively tightened in the first postwar years, and only trading in secondary products was freed of controls.

In exports, Metropolitan needs were given priority; France absorbed all of AEF's cotton, palm oil, coffee, and cocoa and also took much of its wood exports. Whereas in 1945 France bought about 47 per cent of AEF's exports but supplied it with only 4.2 per cent of its imports, and Britain and her dependencies were the source of up to 40 per cent of AEF's total imports, in 1946 France took 82.5 per cent of the federation's shipments. The following year France attained a more important rank among AEF's provisioners while retaining her position as its chief client. As of 1948, France took 72.8 per cent of its export shipments and supplied 50.4 per cent of its imports. During most of the first postwar decade, three-fourths of AEF's shipments went to the franc zone and two-thirds of its purchases were bought in the countries of the French Union. France took virtually all of AEF's exports of cotton, gold, and coffee, and much of its wood, cocoa, and diamonds; she also supplied practically the totality of the federation's imports of flour, tobacco, hardware, and textiles. By procuring from AEF some of the fiber needed for the Metropolitan cotton industry, France saved between $30 and $40 millions a year, and by re-exporting AEF's diamonds to the United States she was able to add to her dollar reserves.

The peak year for the franc zone in AEF's foreign trade was 1952, when that zone absorbed 83 per cent of the federation's exports. After that, the

French Union, especially Metropolitan France, slowly but steadily lost ground, though it continued to be AEF's principal provisioner and purchaser, accounting for about 63 per cent of the federation's total trade. Devaluations of the franc in 1957 and 1958 were responsible for a slight upturn in these exchanges. AEF's trade balance with the sterling zone was favorable from 1947 through 1951 and again in 1953. This is noteworthy, for AEF was one of the few countries of the French Union to have had a credit in sterling during the first postwar decade. The federation's British neighbors imported more from AEF than they exported to it, Nigeria taking most of Tchad's livestock and hides and skins exports. This situation was reversed in 1952 when the share of the sterling zone in AEF's export trade shrank from 14.5 per cent to 7.3 per cent. After a brief spurt in 1953, AEF's shipments to the sterling zone again declined, and in 1955 they amounted to 9 per cent and in 1956 to 6.1 per cent of its total exports. By 1957 the federation's exchanges with Britain and her dependencies had become deficitary, and after the devaluation of the franc, imports from those countries increased by nearly 30 per cent in value, thus sharply aggravating AEF's unfavorable trade balance with the sterling bloc.

After 1946, when the United States had supplied AEF with over 19 per cent of its imports, the purchases of the federation in the dollar zone lapsed to their small prewar proportions. By 1953 only 2 per cent of AEF's exports went to that zone, which, however, slightly improved its position as a supplier of the federation's imports. By 1956 the share of the dollar zone in AEF's foreign trade was clearly increasing, but again more as a provisioner than as a purchaser. That year the United States supplied AEF with 9.1 per cent of its imports but took only 3.3 per cent of its exports. After the franc devaluations of 1957–58, imports from the dollar zone were sharply curtailed.

In recent years the most conspicuous turn in the currents of AEF's foreign trade has been the rise of West Germany to the rank of the federation's main foreign customer. Before the war Germany had been a major purchaser of AEF's okoumé wood, but for obvious reasons that market vanished from the outbreak of the war until 1949. In 1950, Germany bought 200 million francs' worth of AEF's exports and six years later its purchases there had increased to 2,500 million CFA francs. Partly because of the undeveloped state of AEF's economy and partly because of exchange restrictions, the federation has not taken large quantities of Germany's industrial products, so its trade balance with that country has been consistently favorble to the federation. In 1956 AEF bought only 4 per cent of its imports from Germany, chiefly cement, machinery, and tools, but sold to that country 39 per cent of its okoumé exports and sizable quantities of limba. In 1958 the franc's devaluation caused a slight decline in these exchanges.

AEF's increased trade with its neighbors has been the only durable change wrought by the war in its foreign-trade currents. The real extent of this exchange is unknown because in large part it is clandestine in nature. AEF is mainly interested in obtaining textiles and bicycles from the

Congo, where they are far cheaper than in the federation, and it can sell to that neighbor, in quantity, only meat. Trade with the Belgian Congo is regularly deficitary, while with equal consistency the balance is favorable to AEF in its exchanges with Nigeria, which remains its best market for exports of livestock. The Sudan is also a larger purchaser of AEF's cattle than it is a supplier of imports to the federation, but this trade—both licit and illicit—is on a much smaller scale than are AEF's exchanges with Nigeria.

Exports

It is believed that, in early times, slaves were the single most important commodity in central Africa's trade, both foreign and domestic. When this commerce was prohibited in the Western world, European merchants trading along the Gabon coast turned to ivory, timber, and, later, rubber. Inland, the transfrontier trade in slaves survived much longer, and it also dealt in ivory and ostrich plumes.

Until 1937 the uncultivated produce of AEF's tropical forest dominated its export trade, the main items being wild rubber, ivory, logs, and oleaginous produce. As of 1929, six products accounted for 85.3 per cent of the federation's exports, and of these, two (wood and livestock) constituted 71.4 per cent of the total. The other four (palm kernels, rubber, ivory, and cotton) were, with one exception, uncultivated produce. Yet in the same year there were indications that the federation's exports were becoming more diversified. By the eve of World War II, rubber, ivory, and whale-oil shipments had dwindled to unimportance, and they were being replaced or supplemented by gold, palm oil, and coffee. These newcomers, along with the longer-established exports of wood and cotton, formed 90 per cent of AEF's total shipments. But, as had been the case a decade before, three of them made up 69.8 per cent of the whole; cotton was replacing livestock in importance but as yet it accounted for only 15 per cent of all exports. Wood, then as now, played the major role in both volume and value of the federation's exports.

During World War II, wood and oleaginous exports declined and those of cotton, gold, and rubber increased. Throughout the first postwar decade, AEF's export structure was evolving. Some products, such as wild rubber, disappeared entirely; others, notably gold, palm products, lead and zinc ores, and wax lost their relative importance; and shipments of some products such as cotton, coffee, diamonds, cocoa, and cattle were either maintained or increased. All the territories except Moyen-Congo supplied one or more major exports. Those from Gabon were wood, cocoa, and gold; from Tchad, livestock, animal-husbandry products, and cotton; and from Oubangui, cotton, coffee, and diamonds. Moyen-Congo's exports, however, were made up of small quantities of various commodities—timber, palm products, and lead and zinc ores, in that order of importance.

In 1945-46, exports included wartime stocks of nonperishable goods and hence did not reflect production, which had fallen greatly below prewar levels owing to the abolition of forced labor and the dearth of shipping and of inducement imports. By 1947 both production and exports began to revive, and this trend was confirmed in the following year. Exports doubled between 1946 and 1951, and they even exceeded the best annual prewar tonnages. Moreover, new export products—sisal, urena, meat, and peanuts—were now added to staples of wood, cotton, livestock, and mineral ores. Though a decline in the volume of some commodities was apparent (animal-husbandry products, whale oil, and mineral ores), the boom caused by the Korean war in the prices of some of AEF's output more than compensated for it. In 1952 the drastic collapse of prices for tropical produce was reflected in a marked drop in the volume and value of all AEF's exports except livestock. Above all it was the spectacular fall in wood prices that had the worst repercussions on the federation's revenues that year.

With 1953 came signs of recovery for all of AEF's exports except cotton, the country's single most important commodity from the viewpoint of the effect of its sales price on local African purchasing power. From the budgetary angle, the fall in cotton prices was offset by the rapid and re-assuring comeback made by wood shipments. On a much smaller scale, the improvement that took place in the sale of AEF's cocoa compensated for the decline in that of coffee. Exports totaled 487,000 tons, or 131,000 tons more than were exported in 1952; their value amounted to some 10,000 million CFA francs, or about the same as in 1950. Raw materials accounted for 84 per cent of exports by value, and okoumé alone made up 22 per cent of the total. Export tonnages in 1954 set a record (613,000 tons worth 12,800 million CFA francs), being greater by 26 per cent in volume and 27 per cent in value than those of the preceding year. In 1955 the record for ton-nages shipped out of the federation was again broken, the most notable increase being that of wood exports. Marked advances were also made in the export of cotton, meat, peanuts, and tobacco. Mineral production re-mained stable, and the output of coffee, palm kernels and oil, lead, hides, and sisal was discouraged by declining world prices. Wax, gum copal, and ivory shipments declined; those of whale oil disappeared. In the scale of value of territorial exports, Gabon held first rank, and was followed by Tchad, Oubangui, and Moyen-Congo in that order. Although Oubangui still occupied third place, its production had declined, and in 1955 it fur-nished only 20.7 per cent of AEF's total exports, by value, compared with 26.8 per cent in the preceding year.

In 1956 exports totaled 772,215 tons, valued at 14,134,600,000 CFA francs, as against 755,897 tons, valued at 13,688,000,000 in 1955. The composition of the export movement underwent little change, for wood and cotton to-gether represented 70 per cent of the volume, compared with 72.7 per cent in 1955.[8] Furthermore, the territorial division of exports also remained approximately the same. On a commodity basis, wood came mainly from Gabon and to a much lesser extent from Moyen-Congo and Oubangui; cotton wholly from Tchad and Oubangui; coffee principally from Ouban-gui with smaller quantities from Moyen-Congo and Gabon; gold from

Oubangui, Moyen-Congo, and Gabon; diamonds from Oubangui and Gabon; and sisal only from Oubangui. In terms of value, Gabon in 1956 supplied 32.7 per cent of the total (compared with 35.7 per cent in 1955 and 32.8 per cent in 1954); Tchad, 26.6 per cent (26.5 per cent in 1955, 25.3 per cent in 1954); Oubangui, 21.9 per cent (20.7 per cent in 1955, 26.8 per cent in 1954); and Moyen-Congo, 14.5 per cent (13.4 per cent in 1955, 11.1 per cent in 1954). Despite world price declines for most tropical produce, AEF was making an ever-greater effort to augment the volume of its exports.

Sales to non-franc countries were given a boost by the 20 per cent devaluation measures of August 10, 1957. In that year as a whole, exports duly expanded to 1,029,000 tons, marking an increase of 33 per cent in volume and 8 per cent in value over 1956. Wood alone accounted for 43 per cent of the total value, reinforcing Gabon's primary position among the exporting territories. Cocoa, coffee, cotton, and mineral-ores shipments were all less; as for other stable exports, their output remained virtually stationary though their sales prices continued to shrink. In Table 6, which indicates the growth in the volume and value of AEF's main exports in 1957 and 1958, it will be noted that wood and cotton were still in the first and second positions, just as they had been for more than a quarter of a century; a newcomer, petroleum, had taken third place; and coffee and cocoa held fourth and fifth ranks respectively.

TABLE 6.—PRINCIPAL EXPORTS OF AEF, 1957 AND 1958

Category	Quantity		Value (millions of CFA francs)	
	1957	1958	1957	1958
Thousand metric tons				
Livestock	24.9	26.5	316.6	350.0
Coffee	4.5	5.4	610.4	909.8
Peanuts:				
In the shell.............	3.7	2.6	148.3	101.9
Shelled	7.9	6.0	294.9	223.8
Peanut oil	0.5	0.1	42.9	9.1
Palm kernels	7.3	7.9	163.7	205.8
Palm oil	3.8	2.9	162.8	134.3
Cocoa	2.4	2.7	260.9	452.6
Wood	788.8	824.6	6,591.3	7,780.7
Cotton	33.9	39.1	4,391.1	5,918.5
Sisal	0.5	1.5	17.0	52.0
Crude oil	143.3	450.4	479.9	1,556.0
Thousands of carats				
Diamonds	110.6	104.9	423.7	350.9
Kilograms				
Gold	942.4	737.4	192.1	179.7

Source: *Marchés Tropicaux*, April 11, 1959.

Imports

Until World War II, imports into AEF were generally small in volume and consisted mainly of consumer goods, and their value only slightly exceeded that of exports. AEF's chief imports were cotton cloth, machinery, fuel, motor vehicles, wines, dried fish, rice, coal, and miscellaneous minor commodities. Many complaints were voiced at that time in regard to the poor quality, high cost, and scarcity of these imported goods, as well as the damaged condition in which most of them arrived in AEF.

After the first year of World War II, the volume and value of AEF's imports increased, particularly those of equipment materials and fuel. In 1940 the tonnage of the federation's imports had amounted to only 75 per cent of the 1938 volume, when they came to no more than 76,000 tons. After that, however, the Allies and neighboring countries became AEF's main provisioners, and the quantity of imports rapidly increased. By 1942 AEF was importing a fourth as much again as it had in 1938, though in 1943 this fell to about the prewar level. In general, imports were geared to the needs of the Free French army and of port construction, and consumer-goods imports were reduced to the minimum required to encourage Africans to produce rubber and cotton. Between 1941 and 1944 the value of AEF's imports increased by an impressive 256 per cent.

In 1945–46 the federation bought about the same amount as in 1938 but at prices four and a half times higher. In the interim, the purchasing power and desires of the population had grown, especially in the cotton belt. Unfortunately for them, the AEF Africans had developed a taste for textiles, hardware, and other merchandise just at the time when imports were restricted in quantity and variety to the few and costly commodities then available in the French market. In 1946 AEF's textile imports amounted to only 1,197 tons compared with 1,426 tons in 1938.[4] AEF was allocated by the Office des Changes $48 million in 1946, and in 1947 only a little over $11 million, and it was fast losing its power to buy in hard-currency markets. As a consequence a brisk contraband trade with Nigeria and the Belgian Congo came into being.

To offset the harmful effects on AEF's domestic market of the January 1948 devaluation of the franc, the French government promised that it would thenceforth turn back to the federation its dollar earnings, but for some years there was little improvement in the situation. Goods ordered in 1945–46 were not delivered to AEF until 1948–49, and even in 1949 Governor-General Cornut-Gentille, after touring the federation, reported that he found shops, especially in the north, devoid of imported goods except alcoholic beverages.[5] The enlargement in quotas that had been pledged by the French government turned out to be mainly theoretical, and AEF was able to buy only such surplus articles as were then available in Metropolitan France. Most of these were not only very costly but of the nonessential type, and for the average African consumer they did not replace the far cheaper and more suitable goods that had been obtained before the war from Japan, China, and Czechoslovakia.

By 1950–51, French industry had revived to the point where it could provision AEF more adequately, and the concurrent lifting of many official controls on trade soon improved the internal AEF market. By this time, too, the type as well as the quantity of imports had undergone a change. In 1951 the volume of AEF's imports was five times greater than it had been in 1937 (356,000 as against 76,000 tons), and equipment-goods imports were nearly eight times as large in 1951 as in 1937, while the arrivals of durable consumer goods had merely doubled.[6] Cotton cloth had fallen to second place (11.4 per cent of the total), and machinery, spare parts, and other materials needed for execution of the Plan now made up 14 per cent of all imports in terms of value. At the same time there was also an increase in the items imported for immediate consumption, such as sugar, flour, and dried fish. The high returns being realized by the federation for its exports during the Korean war boom induced traders to place large orders for delivery in 1952.

The arrival of this merchandise coincided with the general and severe fall in prices for AEF's exports and with the completion of the major public works undertaken by the Plan. Together they were responsible for the huge deficit in the federation's trade balance that year and for the decline in the proportion of equipment-goods imports as compared with those of consumer goods. Overstocking by traders, together with the government's retrenchment policy in 1953, accounted for the cutback of 25 per cent that year in the federation's imports, which chiefly affected cotton piece goods and corrugated iron. Imports fell in total value from 20 billion CFA francs to about 14.5 billion, but among them durable consumer goods yielded precedence to equipment materials, fuel, and foodstuffs. Little change occurred during 1954 in the volume of AEF's imports (299,000 tons compared with 293,000), but their value rose by 11 per cent (16,681 million CFA francs from 14,799 million). This increase was largely confined to a few products and did not affect such widely consumed items as flour, sugar, cotton cloth, and fuel, for which the prices even declined slightly. Yet the average value of 20 of AEF's principal imports, which represented 56 per cent of the total, increased by 2.5 per cent.[7]

In 1955 the exhaustion of stocks, record export tonnages, and another rise in the cost of French manufactures resulted in a 3.8 per cent increase in tonnage and a 10 per cent growth in the value of imports.[8] The disparity between comparatively stable tonnages and rapidly rising values, already evident in 1954, became more pronounced the following year, and stemmed from the same main cause—the rising cost of French-made consumer goods, which once again took precedence over equipment materials. Food and cotton-textile imports showed major increases, those of machinery and spare parts remained about the same, and those of fuel, cement, iron, and steel dwindled. The most conspicuous rise in import shipments involved articles for African consumption. Imports in 1956 exceeded those of 1955 by 15.7 per cent in tonnage and by 11.8 per cent in value. Equipment goods represented 28.4 per cent of the total in value, marking an upturn of about

TABLE 7.—PRINCIPAL IMPORTS OF AEF, 1957 AND 1958

Category	Quantity		Value (millions of CFA francs)	
	1957	1958	1957	1958
	Thousand metric tons			
Wheat flour	11.8	12.6	359	424
Sugar	11.3	8.0	603	517
Beer	7.6	10.6	332	552
Wine	14.5	13.1	573	774
Cotton textiles	2.8	3.8	1,094	1,704
Household goods	2.2	1.1	397	334
Siderurgical products	26.9	28.9	1,020	1,254
Metal items	14.4	8.8	1,085	827
Cement	91.9	72.1	709	533
Machinery	15.8	6.7	3,522	2,908
Petroleum products	128.0	149.0	1,733	2,200
	Number			
Trucks	1,709	1,951	1,016	1,220
Other automotive vehicles...	1,623	1,627	506	521

Source: *Marchés Tropicaux*, April 11, 1959.

3 per cent over the 1955 figure for such articles; merchandise for immediate consumption made up 42 per cent (compared with 50.5 per cent in 1955), and fuel imports accounted for 8.4 per cent, or slightly over 1 per cent more than they had in the previous year. Still higher levels in the prices of imports were mainly responsible for the more unfavorable trade balance, but the expansion of durable consumer-goods imports to the detriment of those of articles for immediate consumption was considered by the authorities to be an encouraging development.

The currency devaluation of mid-1957 automatically pushed up by 20 per cent the cost of the 35 per cent of its imports which the federation bought outside the franc zone. Imports rose in value by 27 per cent, and tonnages also increased, from 363,500 to 436,000 tons. Equipment-goods arrivals were mainly responsible for this, but food imports also rose, though to a lesser degree. The development of local industries producing beer, textiles, and cigarettes was beginning to reduce purchases of such items abroad. In 1958, the volume of imports was approximately the same as in 1957, but their value climbed still further, this time by 11 per cent (see Table 7). The share of food items remained constant at 18 per cent; equipment goods declined from 35 per cent to 28 per cent, and raw materials fell slightly, from 16 per cent to 15 per cent; fuel rose from 6 per cent to 8 per cent, and consumer goods from 25 per cent to 31 per cent. Altogether that year AEF imported 432,000 tons valued at 29,459 million CFA francs, compared with 436,000 tons worth 26,116 millions in 1957.

The Internal Market and African Purchasing Power

In the area later known as AEF, internal trading long antedated the

French occupation, but it was very limited in scope and volume, sometimes being confined to a single region or group of villages. The low density of the population, as well as the limitation placed by nature on its resources, largely accounted for the minuscule dimensions of such commerce. Transport was difficult because of the vast distances and natural obstacles involved, and also because it was carried on almost wholly by small boats (*pirogues*) and human portage, animal transport being impossible in the huge tsetse-infested regions. Another deterrent to trade was the clearly defined and zealously defended rights of the tribes, which controlled the merchandise sold in, or passing through, their domains.[9] Along the main rivers, tolls were collected at certain transit points, by the Batéké and Boubangui on the Congo and by the Fang on the middle Ogooué, and trading was perforce restricted to markets located as a rule 15 to 20 kilometers apart. Insecurity of life and property added to the merchants' hazards.

Nevertheless, there existed a certain amount of interregional or even external commercial exchanges. Slaves, ostrich plumes, wood, and ivory were in fairly steady demand; salt was brought to the hinterland from the coast or from the Saharan mines; dates from the northern oases were exchanged for millet in the savannah; and fish from the Congo were bartered for manioc in the forest zone. Africans long in contact with Europeans had become used to dealing by means of escudos in the south and thalers in the north. Elsewhere, bent copper wire, strips of cotton cloth, or cowrie shells were used as money substitutes.

The French occupation undermined the strict procedures that had governed intertribal and interregional trading. After a central authority assumed responsibility for the maintenance of law and order, European and alien African traders were able to break down the long chain of established intermediaries, and agents of the concessionary companies succeeded in creating their own localized trading monopolies. Improvement in the means of internal communication and the introduction of transport by steamers, trucks, and the railway helped to expand AEF's internal trade. Urban growth necessitated bringing food to the towns from the rural regions, and the installation of forest and mining camps led to a countercurrent of trade to provision their labor forces. Territorial interdependence in commerce grew proportionately. Tchad, for example, shipped livestock to Oubangui and Moyen-Congo, and in return bought wood and soap from those two colonies.

The evolution of trading in indigenous articles was accompanied by a less welcome stagnation in the sale of imported goods. Gide, on his famous journey through the northern colonies of AEF in 1925, noted there the dearth of suitable and good-quality merchandise, the staggering prices asked for imported goods, the long delays in filling orders placed abroad, and the lamentable condition in which three-fourths of the imports reached AEF as a result of careless packing. No wonder, he wrote, that Africans were reluctant to work when merchants provided no goods they wanted or could buy. He also denounced the youthful European traders who, irresponsible and unscrupulous, had come to AEF to make their fortunes as rapidly as possible "to the detriment of the country's resources and of the Africans."[10] Governor-General Eboué, writing in 1941,[11] spoke of—

> the hideous sun helmets, shorts that do not survive the first washing, knives that bend but do not cut. All are present here to show that the native clientele is not respected and that the idea is still current (in Europe) that Africa is a place where anything can be sold.

During World War II and the years immediately after its end, consumer goods were very scarce, and their distribution was taken over by government agencies. One such group was the semiofficial Chambers of Commerce, of which five already existed in the federation's main towns.[12] These organizations played a very active role in handling much of AEF's internal trade during the war and the four succeeding years, when the shortage of imported goods was most acute and official controls were tightest. After representative institutions were introduced in 1946, the territorial assemblies disputed the powers of the Chambers and strongly criticized their operations. In 1947 the Council of State had to intervene and define the rights of each, and it confirmed to the Chambers their prerogative of allocating imported goods and hard currency for any purchases made in non-franc markets.

This intervention, however, did not stop AEF's African assemblymen from reproaching the Chambers with favoring the big trading firms and discriminating against the small merchants, particularly the Africans.[13] Some went so far as to propose withholding the public funds that partly financed the Chambers, unless the latter's European members mended their ways and performed more conscientiously their task of helping to provision the rural African populations. Growth in the volume of imports, beginning in 1950, and the establishment in AEF of a larger number of commercial firms helped to ease the shortages, but the hinterland villages and the smaller towns in the north were still poorly supplied with imported goods. As recently as October 24, 1955, Governor-General Chauvet told the Grand Council that the federation's commercial network must be improved: the few firms that did business in the northern territories enjoyed a quasi-monopoly of imported merchandise, whereas in the south, particularly in the towns, there was a plethora of merchants. In the latter area they were not protected by tariffs, and the overkeen competition led to numerous bankruptcies.

Despite the above-described situation in the south, the prices charged for imported goods in Moyen-Congo tended to rise to heights that were considered by both administration and consumers to be unjustified. (An official study made in 1955 reported that the profit margin was too large, except on fuel, bread, and flour, prices of which were still controlled, and on construction materials, which were then selling poorly. Each time new taxes were imposed or the cost of imported French goods rose, the merchants put excessive mark-ups on their wares.) From the end of the war through 1948, the cost of living rose steadily—by 29 per cent in 1947 and 45 per cent in 1948. The next year the arrival of larger quantities of consumer goods, the comparative stability of salaries and wages, and the return to free trading in all but a very few articles brought about a revival of competition and a slight decline in prices. At the same time, however, the infusion of FIDES investment funds without a corresponding volume of consumer goods spelled inflation, and Chauvet complained to the Grand Council on September 30, 1952, that AEF had the highest living costs of any of the French African territories. He urged all traders to lower their prices and warned that if they did not do so voluntarily he was legally empowered to impose price controls anew.

This gubernatorial warning, along with the trade depression of that year, chastened AEF's merchants, and 1953 proved to be a year of remarkably stable prices in the internal market. The slight rise that occurred early in 1954 elicited another similar threat from Chauvet, which was effective enough for him to be able to report to the Grand Council on October 30 of that year that the cost of living had shown a "remarkable stability over the past 18 months" and that price declines had even been registered on such widely consumed items as rice, sugar, flour, soap, and fuel. During the year he took steps that led to reductions in internal transport tariffs and in the rates for public utilities in Moyen-Congo's main towns.

In 1956 and to a greater extent in 1957, living costs again rose, especially for foodstuffs. To offset the devaluation of August 10, 1957, the government blocked prices in all four territories and ordered merchants to declare their stocks of imported non-French goods. These measures proved to be too sweeping for officials to enforce, and prices climbed sharply in 1958, and again in early 1959, under the spur of the next currency devaluation on the preceding December 28. The increases in wages, salaries, and family allowances voted by the assemblies of the new republics further accentuated the inflationary trend.

The question naturally arises as to how the AEF Africans were able to increase their consumption of the exceptionally expensive imported goods on sale in the federation. Before World War II their purchasing power was reputed to be the lowest in all the French Empire,[14] and in 1944 it sank to an even lower level. After the war it was further endangered by inflation resulting from the volume of unproductive expenditures, particularly for military purposes, which were then higher than in any other French area except Indochina. From 1946 on it was threatened anew when FIDES funds were creating a disparity between supplies and needs and when black markets with their hosts of middlemen were rampant in the main towns. The dangers inherent in this situation were largely eliminated by 1949, and AEF may have owed its salvation principally to the fact that the great majority of its inhabitants lived and still live in the stage of subsistence economy. Except for a few widely used industrial products such as cloth, lamps, knives, and enamelware, most rural Africans seem scarcely touched by modern influences.

At the same time, it is clear that the economic expansion of the postwar decade has given birth, particularly in the towns, to a small African bourgeoisie composed of merchants, transporters, and some planters, whose purchasing power has been steadily rising. The growth in AEF's import tonnages cannot be wholly attributed to the large increase in the number of prosperous Europeans living in the federation since the war. The rise in note circulation and in African savings accounts also confirms the birth of an African bourgeois element, though this is still a very small group numerically.

Africans are by far the biggest users of AEF's paper money, so the increase in the circulation of banknotes is considered to be a reasonably accurate index to their prosperity, though the successive currency devaluations must also be taken into consideration. Because of fluctuations in the federation's foreign trade and the financing of crop harvests, note circulation in AEF has always been subject to seasonal fluctuations, of which February regularly marks the high point. After 1950 there was a steady growth in AEF's note circulation, owing mainly to the investments made by FIDES and also to private capital there, and in part to the successive rises in wages and salaries. In mid-summer 1949 the note circulation came to about 2,982 million CFA francs, and eight years later it amounted to 8,419 million, those two periods marking the lowest point in their respective years.

Savings accounts are thought to be a less reliable reflection of African purchasing power than is note circulation, for local custom militates against them. The lack of facilities further hampers use of them throughout much of the country. AEF's Caisse d'Epargne was set up in 1939, but for many years both the number of accounts and the amount of savings placed in them were insignificant. The management of savings accounts was entrusted as in Metropolitan France to the Services des Postes-Télégraphes-Téléphones as "the best way to reach the masses," but at the time the savings system was created in AEF there were only 21 PTT offices in the whole federation. Handling savings accounts was considered to be so complex and the opportunities for fraud so great that the government long hesitated to increase their number, and only town dwellers had access to them. In the rural areas, not only were tribal traditions not conducive to savings, but termites and other insects destroyed banknotes, whose owners were prone to exchange them as soon as possible for merchandise. Gradually the government opened more post offices with savings-account facilities, and it embarked on a minor propaganda campaign to promote African savings. In 1956, over 3,000 new accounts were opened in the 46 post offices then possessing facilities for handling them, and the funds deposited grew by over 36.5 million CFA francs. Yet even with that expansion, there were in mid-1957 only 15,636 accounts in all AEF and deposits totaled not quite 222 million CFA francs.[15]

No accurate figures have yet been published on the income or budget of an average AEF African. Only fragmentary data are available and these do not always come from unbiased or well-informed sources. On January

30, 1948, Antoine Darlan told the French Union Assembly that the cash revenues of his compatriots averaged between 700 and 1,200 CFA francs. A month later, René Pleven, speaking in the National Assembly (February 10, 1948) on the disastrous impact of a new currency devaluation in Black Africa, said that a study of AEF family budgets indicated that 67 per cent of their monetary income was spent on goods of foreign origin.[16] The author of a report on conditions in 1950[17] estimated that buyers of imported goods consisted largely of the federation's 500,000 or so wage earners and their families, to whom must be added another 800,000 producers of export crops. Nearly one-third of the total population, according to this same source, bought imported goods in shops, but in fact the diffusion of manufactured articles was much wider because barter was the means by which they were acquired by many rural Africans. The foregoing sampling and opinions are, at best, informed guesses, and none casts much light on the extent or diffusion of African monetary resources in AEF. All authorities, however, are agreed that indigenous purchasing power, though growing, remains very small, and that the single most important influence on it is the sales price obtained for the cotton harvest.

CHAPTER 16

Industry

The inadequacy of transport facilities and their high cost, the scarcity and lack of skills of AEF's labor, and the smallness of the internal market have all served to retard the federation's industrialization as they have its development in other economic fields. In addition, there are two obstacles in particular that have hampered AEF's industrial evolution—the lack of local power and the active opposition of certain Metropolitan industries. Now it appears that the former handicap is about to be eliminated, and in the more distant future, when the European Common Market comes into full play, the latter may also be overcome.

Even taking into consideration these grave problems, the rudimentary condition of AEF's industries on the eve of World War II was striking, especially in comparison with the more advanced status of neighboring countries. AEF possessed only a few primitive plants processing wood, palm kernels, and cotton, which made no more than minor contributions to the federation's external trade and even smaller ones to provisioning the hinterland populations. Of these enterprises the most important were the sawmills and wood-peeling factories of Gabon. Some cotton was ginned in Oubangui and lesser amounts in Tchad. In Moyen-Congo, after completion of the railroad, a dual-purpose factory was built to manufacture tapioca and also to extract oil from locally grown peanuts. To supply power to the workshops of the railroad and to the main river-navigation company, as well as to a few individuals and factories, small electrical generating plants were built at Brazzaville, Pointe Noire, and Libreville.

By cutting AEF off from France, World War II forced the federation to live more from its own resources, and so a small number of industries were set up, almost all of which were located in Moyen-Congo. There and in Oubangui soap factories were built that utilized the local palm oil; tanneries that processed Tchad's hides were constructed at Brazzaville and Dolisie, to the former of which was attached a shoe factory whose maximum output reached about 400 pairs a day; and a match factory was constructed in the Brazzaville area, as well as a foundry that used scrap metals. Lime furnaces multiplied in the region traversed by the railroad, a small cement factory was started near Bouenza, and at Pointe Noire a plant was built to treat coffee beans. Only the tanneries and soap factories survived the end of the war, and all subsequent plans to revive the cement industry and to launch a paper-pulp industry have failed to materialize.

In 1946, with the start of the ten-year Plan, a trend began toward industrialization. Some of the established industries mechanized their operations and a number of new companies built factories in AEF. But many investors who came to the federation to study its industrial potential went away discouraged by the difficulties. They foresaw that the importation of machinery and technicians and the training and lodging of local laborers would make the cost of setting up an industry in AEF double that of establishing a smiliar one in France.[1] Later, some of those who persisted in trying had to acknowledge defeat. Even a number of the big Metropolitan companies, which created branches in AEF at great expense to themselves and to the federation for the purpose of executing the infrastructure projects financed by the Plan, did not find it worth their while to remain there after 1952, when the funds of FIDES had begun to shrink.

A number of the industries—mainly oil-seed crushing, wood processing, cotton ginning, fisheries, and meat—that processed local products for the domestic market as well as for export were able to take root and even to expand. Certain others, such as cigarette factories and breweries, which utilized a combination of local and imported products, also succeeded. Almost without exception, however, their survival would not have been possible had it not been for the governmental aid they received in various forms. Both the administration and, to a lesser extent, the African elite have realized that in most cases private capital could not afford to take many of the risks involved. Official assistance, direct and indirect, has been forthcoming for industries regarded as useful to the country, and it has taken the form of subsidies, fiscal concessions, reductions in transport costs, research, and guaranteed markets and prices. In some domains, notably that of electrical energy, the government has itself built generating plants wholly or largely with public funds. As regards handicrafts, which were dying out in some regions because of competition from European manufactured goods, state artisan schools have been created to revive and improve local output and to find a market for it.

Yet in some domains the French government has failed to help newly established industries in AEF. Periodically the administration has been reproached for using its own technical services rather than private companies to carry out various public works.[2] This sort of complaint has usually been voiced by Europeans who have a direct interest in promoting the private industries concerned, but some French assemblymen and almost all of the African elite realize that by using its own technicians the government economizes public funds to the benefit of the precariously balanced federal budget.

More controversial has been the government-general's failure to oppose private Metropolitan interests which attack a nascent AEF industry that threatens to compete with them. An outstanding case in point is that of the Compagnie Française du Gabon, which built the world's largest plywood factory in AEF after the war. Wood manufacturers in France had for many years imported logs and sawn wood from Gabon, but they promptly strove to prevent the launching of a competitive plywood industry at Port Gentil. In 1952 they succeeded in barring the Western European market to its output, with the result that the Port Gentil factory has never been able to operate to capacity.[3] In other ways, too, the French government, by its negative attitude or by inaction, has prevented the establishment of certain new industries in AEF. Usually the government is aware of a firm's intention to install itself in the federation, because almost invariably it makes an appeal for public funds, Metropolitan capitalists being traditionally reluctant to invest in AEF. The federal government can simply refuse to help or, in the case of foreign capital, the Minister of Finance is able merely to withhold his permission. In some cases, to be sure, the government's passive opposition may be based on valid economic motives. But in others, notably that of the Compagnie Française du Gabon, its failure to stand up for a promising local industry not only smacks of collusion but is strongly reminiscent of the French policy known as the Colonial Pact.

The 1950's have marked what is probably a turning point in the history of AEF's industrialization. It has been shown by data gathered during that decade that Gabon possesses mineral resources promising to rank it in future among the world's principal producers of manganese and iron, and the extent of its wealth in ores is not yet fully known. Such deposits as have already been explored have justified a vast hydroelectric project that may make of the Pointe Noire region one of the most industrialized areas in Black Africa. For this reason AEF's electrical-energy sources and its mining industry deserve special scrutiny.

Electrical Energy

AEF's lack of coal deposits and the high cost of imported fuel were long recognized as mainly to blame for its industrial underdevelopment, and the search for compensatory hydroelectrical sources of energy dates back to the early twentieth century. Three missions, beginning in 1911, studied the basins of the Congo and of Tchad as well as the coastal regions, with a view to harnessing the power latent in the federation's numerous waterfalls. Their reports confirmed the abundance of such resources, particularly in Gabon and western Moyen-Congo. Though the work of these missions led to no actual hydroelectrical projects, it proved useful during the construction of the Congo-Ocean railroad. Utilizing AEF's water power seemed at the time too costly an enterprise in view of the dubious industrial future of a country so sparsely populated and so apparently lacking in appropriate raw materials. Even in the three main towns, where there was public distribution of current, there was little demand for it. World War II, however, created new power needs: Bangui was provided with a public distribution system made of makeshift materials, and after the Liberation a small municipal generating plant was built at Fort Lamy.

The orientation given to industrialization by the ten-year Plan required not only the rejuvenation of AEF's urban electrical equipment but also the development of new and bigger sources of power. In 1947 a mission sent to the federation by Electricité de France recommended an expansion of existing power systems and selected three sites for hydroelectrical development —Djoué and Loémé in Moyen-Congo, and Boali in Oubangui. The total cost of these projects was then estimated at 2.3 billion Metro. francs, and a company of "mixed economy" called the Energie Electrique d'AEF (EEAEF) was founded in 1948 to bring them into being. The construction undertaken by this company was to be financed by FIDES; it was to receive contributions from the federal government and technical aid from Electricité de France; and it was empowered either to sell current directly to consumers or to work through the existing concessionary companies. These were the Union Electrique Coloniale (UNELCO) which held a monopoly in Moyen-Congo and Oubangui, the Compagnie Générale de Distribution d'Energie Electrique in Libreville, and the municipal *régie* in Fort Lamy.

The EEAEF's first big project was started at Djoué, near Brazzaville, in 1949. In 1950 it began working on Fort Lamy's municipal system and drew up a program for lighting Tchad's secondary centers, the same year it founded a subsidiary company to undertake a public distribution scheme for Port Gentil, in 1952 it began construction of the Boali plant, and in 1954 its first detailed studies of the Kouilou falls got under way. Each territorial program had its individual method of financing, and only that of Djoué required that the federal budget underwrite its operating expenditures. The French treasury bore all the costs of installing Port Gentil's system, the cotton companies shared in the expense of installing the Boali plant, and European private capital is expected to help finance the Kouilou project.

Neither the Djoué nor the Boali plant is yet working to capacity, though the consumption of electrical current more than doubled in the decade between 1943 and 1953, rising from 1,091,000 kwh to 3,151,000. As of 1949, five towns had public distribution systems supplying 250,000 persons, including 9,500 Europeans, the generators of these systems being powered by diesel motors of only 5,000 horsepower. A considerable number of small industries and individuals had to supply their own current. Electricity was virtually nonexistent in rural areas, and even in the towns it was not dependable. By and large, the supply was adequate to the demand for lighting but not for the needs of any large-scale industry.

A main obstacle in the way of expanding the urban systems lay in the terms by which the government was tied to the major private concessionary company in AEF, the UNELCO. The basic contracts under which the UNELCO operated antedated formation of the representative assemblies, and the latter resented their inability to curtail the privileges and control the operations of that company. AEF's assemblymen frequently gave vent to complaints that the UNELCO unilaterally enjoyed the right to use the federation's wood for fuel, its penal labor, and its public funds in the form of loans without being under any obligation to alter the company's policy of charging high rates. Even after the construction of the Djoué and Boali plants provided Brazzaville and Bangui with surplus current, UNELCO made no effort to widen its service by lowering its rates to consumers.

To be sure, construction of those two hydroelectrical plants by the EE-AEF somewhat altered the picture, but because of UNELCO's long-term contracts with the government, it remained the chief distributing agency for electrical current in AEF. Under pressure by Governor-General Chauvet and the assemblies, the UNELCO did extend its network somewhat and, after 1954, lower its charges, but the cost of current still averages over 21 CFA francs per kwh in AEF's main towns. Domestic consumption has increased, as has that of local industries to an even greater degree, but neither has attained the level anticipated when the Djoué and Boali projects were undertaken. The industrial development of AEF has been and still is hampered by the inadequacy of power or by the very high price at which the available current is sold, and at the same time the power which the two existing hydroelectrical plants are capable of generating is far from being utilized. Hope of breaking this vicious circle is now being placed in the Kouilou dam, which, it is believed, could supply very cheap current to the Pointe Noire region and transform it into an industrial complex processing local and imported raw materials.

Political and economic developments in nearby African countries, as well as in AEF itself, brought so many new elements into the situation during 1959 that it is difficult to forecast the industrial future of the former federation's two southern republics. It seems probable that the Kouilou dam will be built, and if it is constructed well ahead of the Inga project in nearby Belgian Congo, the economy of Moyen-Congo and also of Gabon should in consequence be radically transformed.

Mining

Before Europeans came to AEF, its inhabitants apparently mined only iron, copper, and lead. In the Saharan and sahel regions of Tchad, the northern tribes extracted natron, which was carried by caravans to the saltless areas of the south. The indigenous population seems to have been unaware of the existence of gold and diamonds, which during many years were to figure as the most valuable output of European mining companies operating in AEF.

Copper was the first of the federation's ores to be mined on an industrial scale. From 1905 to 1935, a Franco-Belgian company extracted some 15,000 tons of rich ore from a single deposit in the Niari valley. Beginning in 1936, however, it ceased to mine copper and transferred its operations to a lead and zinc mine discovered in the early 1930's at nearby M'Fouati. Further prospecting, which continues to this day, has brought to light no new, sizable deposits of copper, and now only lead and, periodically, zinc, are mined by that company in the region. In the late 1920's French interest in AEF's mineral resources shifted to Oubangui, where gold and diamonds had just been discovered, and a few years later they were also found in Gabon and Moyen-Congo.

Though at about the same time prospecting for petroleum was begun, and traces of iron, manganese, tin, corindon, and colombo-tantalite were found by the federation's geologists during the interwar period, no profound study of their extent or quality was made. Indeed, such data as existed in regard to AEF's mineral resources before World War II were very fragmentary and spotty. They were not sufficiently impressive to persuade French capitalists to risk money in developing these deposits or to warrant providing the federal mines service with adequate public funds and a staff of competent technicians. AEF's mining industry was at least 20 years behind that of neighboring British and Belgian colonies, and was even less developed than its counterpart in French West Africa. Nevertheless, before World War II, the output of AEF's mines, particularly of gold, made the federation the foremost producer of metals in French Black Africa, and among local industries mining ranked second after that of wood.

Mineral prospecting and extraction, albeit on a reduced scale, were carried on during World War II because of the Allies' need for AEF's gold, lead, and diamonds. After 1946, under the spur of the ten-year Plan, prospecting was undertaken more widely and on a more scientific basis, and the extraction methods of existing mining enterprises were gradually improved. The official program formulated at that time required the Metropolitan and local governments, which had theretofore neglected this field, to take the initiative in prospecting for minerals and to encourage private investments through a revision of AEF's obsolete mining legislation and over-heavy taxation. These principles conformed with the general objective of encouraging the industrialization of Overseas France. Though it was realized that even with regard to AEF's known ore deposits no exhaustive study had been made, there was little expectation in the late 1940's that the federation might become a second Katanga. A well-known authority on AEF, Zieglé, wrote as recently as 1952:[4]

> AEF possesses mineral wealth that will help it to survive, but it cannot be classed among the great mineral producers of the world nor is its output essential to Metropolitan France. It involves only a few tons of lead, zinc, copper and gold, and some kilograms of diamonds . . .

Prospecting and research

Under the Plan, the public authorities were assigned the threefold task of making a detailed study of the ores already known to exist, compiling an inventory of all AEF's mineral resources, and aiding private industry to increase its productivity. For these purposes FIDES allocated 67 million CFA francs to improve the equipment of the federal mines service, 170 million to make a geological map of AEF, and 553 million to enable the federal government to share in the operations of the sole company then engaged in petroleum research. Aside from these grants, two newly created Metropolitan organizations established branches in the federation. Chronologically the first of these was the French Atomic Energy Commissariat, which began in 1947 to seek minerals relevant to its activities, first in Moyen-Congo and later in Gabon and Tchad. The second and more comprehensive of these Metropolitan bodies was the Bureau Minier de la France d'Outre-Mer, which was founded at Paris in 1948 and soon became active in all the French overseas areas. Its mission was not to compete with private mining enterprises operating there but to supplement their prospecting activities, to aid them with technical advice, and to share in the capitalization of any companies of "mixed economy" that might be formed to search for or extract AEF's ores. As matters worked out, the Bureau Minier concentrated on prospecting minerals that had never previously been extracted in AEF and in assessing the feasibility of working those that were either too expensive or too technically complicated for private industry to tackle.

From the funds provided by FIDES, two modern mineralogical and petrographical laboratories were built at Brazzaville and the federal mines service was reorganized and enlarged. This service, whose headquarters were in the federal capital, was made directly responsible to the government-general. It was divided into two operating sections, one for Gabon and Moyen-Congo and the other for Oubangui and Tchad, and in 1951 a directorate of mines was added to advise the government on mining policy and legislation. Its itinerant engineers visited the various mining camps to give technical advice, gather scientific data on the deposits being worked, and see that AEF's mining laws were observed. The federal service's geologists were given the task of drawing up a geological map for the federation in collaboration with such territorial mines services as then existed. By 1954 this map covered about three-fourths of Gabon, two-thirds of Moyen-Congo, half of Oubangui, and one-fifth of Tchad. In that year the federal mines service had a total staff of 81, including 13 mining engineers, 27 geologists, 5 chemical engineers, and their aides. The following year 7 more geologists were added and a federal Chamber of Mines was organized.

In July 1949, the first mining conference ever held in AEF had recommended the establishment of such a Chamber and this proposal was approved by the Minister for Overseas France, the four territorial assemblies, and all of the Chambers of Commerce except that of Brazzaville, which feared to lose such control over AEF's mining industry as it then possessed. Since 1944 there had existed a local branch of the Paris Chambre Syndicale des Mines, financed by the dues of its members. Now the question of providing support for a federal body from public funds delayed the creation of AEF's Chamber of Mines, but it finally came into being in 1955. The work done by this Chamber, and particularly that accomplished by the federal mines service, has been judged sufficiently valuable for the new republics of AEF to favor their perpetuation after the federation ceased to exist. On June 23, 1959, the premiers of the four new states decided to create an Interstate Mining Institute that would continue the research, analysis, and other activities that previously had been carried out on a federal basis.

Production

Four major changes have become apparent in AEF's mining production since World War II. These are the stagnation of the established mining industry; the virtual elimination of individual prospectors and small concerns and their absorption or replacement by a handful of large firms which have benefited by the technical and financial aid of the government; the discovery, largely through government initiative, of petroleum and massive quantities of ores that have attracted French private and foreign capital on a large scale; and the prospect of metallurgical industries in western Moyen-Congo, through an abundant supply of cheap electrical current.

The first two of the foregoing changes resulted in part from a situation that antedated the war—the exhaustion of easily worked deposits of copper, gold, diamonds, lead, and zinc. They were also caused in part, however, by postwar developments, notably the generally low and declining world prices for those metals, the rise in production costs, and the failure of further prospecting to disclose any sizable deposits of those ores. The disappearance of easily worked deposits and the growing scarcity of labor forced AEF miners to mechanize their operations as much as possible and to make living and working conditions more attractive to African laborers.

Against a background of falling prices, these developments necessitated expenditures on a scale possible only for heavily capitalized companies. As a matter of fact, even the biggest of these firms experienced difficulties in obtaining the foreign currency required to purchase machinery abroad and also in retaining their labor forces. Government aid enabled them to cope with the former obstacle to a considerable extent, but proved of no avail in respect to the latter. The British authorities could not be persuaded by the AEF government to permit Nigerian emigrants to work in the federation's mines, and the abolition of forced labor in 1946 prevented French officials from using coercion on AEF Africans. Mining was never a popular occupation among the indigenous population, who found the work too hard and living conditions in the camps too regimented and monotonous. Only a steady rise in wages and a marked improvement in the miners' housing, food, and recreational facilities prevented mass desertions, and even under better conditions the number of Africans employed in mining dwindled. As of 1950 the industry's labor force totaled about 25,000, but four years later it had declined to some 12,000, of whom 4,430 were working in gold mines, 7,480 in diamond mines, and 509 in the federation's sole lead mine.[5] Only the most mechanized and efficient firms were able to survive, and in this way the mining of gold has come to be dominated by the Compagnie Equatoriale des Mines and the Compagnie des Mines d'Or du Gabon; almost all of AEF's diamonds are now extracted by the Compagnie Minière de l'Oubangui Oriental and the Société Minière Intercoloniale and their subsidiaries; and the production of lead and zinc has long been the monopoly of the Compagnie Minière du Congo Français.

The major role of big companies in AEF's mining industry has been accentuated by the discovery of new minerals, though their evolution has differed from that of the older-established firms. The Compagnie Minière de l'Ogooué (COMILOG) controls production from the great manganese mines of Franceville, the Société des Mines de Fer de Mékambo will dominate that of iron ore, the Compagnie des Mines d'Uranium de Franceville is preparing to mine the only known sizable deposit of that mineral in AEF, and the Société des Pétroles d'AEF (SPAEF) for 23 years held the sole prospecting permit for petroleum in the federation. Although official organizations, notably the Bureau Minier, the federal mines service, and the Atomic Energy Commissariat have provided technical aid to one or another of these enterprises, the only large amounts of public funds invested in them have gone to the petroleum and uranium companies. Discoveries of the extent of AEF's mineral wealth during the past decade have led to such an influx of private French and foreign capital that the government was able to withdraw from the financing of most prospecting and extracting operations, though it retained control over the most strategic minerals (uranium and petroleum) and continued to aid private industries in other ways.

The contribution made by the public powers to AEF's mining industry, though of short duration, has been decisive. Before World War II the government contented itself with legislation confirming its ownership of the federation's subsoil and did virtually nothing to survey the possibilities of AEF's mineral resources or aid in their development even after the minuscule federal mines service pointed out the existence of deposits. The few mining companies that were operating in AEF did some prospecting in proportion as their mines became exhausted, but these were small-scale and highly localized operations. French financiers were not disposed to invest large sums in so distant, inaccessible, and poorly known a country as AEF. This state of things changed radically as a result of the methodical prospecting and research financed by the Plan beginning in 1946, which for the first time provided extensive scientific data on the federation's resources. By the mid-1950's petroleum had been discovered in Gabon and Moyen-Congo; Franceville's manganese deposits were estimated to be the second-largest known in the world, and those of its uranium to be the largest in the French Union; and the extent of the iron-ore reserves of Mékambo was believed to offset the transport difficulties created by their inaccessibility. Minor finds of potash and phosphates have been made in the southern territories, and although prospecting in Tchad is still only in its infancy, uranium and thorium deposits have already been found there.

The inventory of AEF's resources is far from complete, but owing to the government's pioneering efforts enough has already been discovered to arouse world-wide interest in their development. American capital, until recently confined to small official loans to two AEF diamond companies, has now heavily invested in the federation's manganese, iron, and petroleum prospecting and extracting. German, Italian, and Swiss bankers and industrialists are planning to participate in the processing of AEF's minerals that is to be made possible by construction of the Kouilou hydroelectric plant. Of the big new mining companies, only that of uranium remains a wholly French enterprise.

Legislative and fiscal reforms

The influx of such quantities of French and foreign private capital has prompted changes in AEF's mining laws and taxation, which are still being worked out. Aside from some modifications in procedure and controls, the federation's basic mining legislation dates back to a decree of October 13, 1933. With the advent of new mining companies to AEF and the control over permits vested in the elected assemblies after the war, it seemed to the members of the mining conference held at Brazzaville in July 1949 that a fundamental revision of the 1933 decree was in order. Typically, however, the French Parliament delayed indefinitely consideration of a new mining code for all Overseas France, and in the interval AEF perforce was limited to making only minor changes in the application of existing laws.

The principle on which this legislation rested was that of the state's control over the ownership and extraction of minerals. Before any prospecting could be undertaken, the government's authorization must be obtained; all mining rights were limited in area and duration; and prospecting permits could be transformed into extraction rights only if the permit holder had fulfilled the conditions laid down in the *cahier de charges* drawn up by the government and if the mines service considered that his deposit justified further development. Apart from certain "reserved" zones and minerals, over which the government retained full control, prospecting permits of either the A or B type could be granted to individuals or companies. Permits of the latter type were issued for areas under 400 square kilometers by the governor-general upon recommendation of the mines service and with the agreement of the assembly of the territory concerned: they were valid for two years and could not be renewed. Type A permits covered areas of 400 square kilometers or more, and were granted by decree if they received the prior approval of the governor-general, the relevant elected assembly, and the Comité des Mines de la France d'Outre-Mer. The holder of a type A permit was required to sign a contract whose terms he agreed to carry out. If his performance was satisfactory and the mines service approved, his permit could be transformed into one conferring extraction rights for a period of four years and renewable four times.

As of 1950, the total areas for which permits had been granted was large —it amounted to 76,000 square kilometers for holders of type B prospecting permits and 120,000 square kilometers for those of the A type. In addition, some 60,000 square kilometers had been allocated in the form of extraction rights or of concessions that antedated the 1933 legislation.[6] Moreover, requests for prospecting permits covering 120,000 more square kilometers were under consideration. In the National Assembly, Communist Party spokesmen in 1953 reproached the government with having granted an abnormally large number of permits to big companies in recent years.[7] To this the government replied that of the 78 individuals or companies to whom permits had been issued as of October 1, 1949, only 37 were engaged in extracting operations and 18 in prospecting, while 28 permits were either pending or had been allowed to lapse by their holders. It had to admit, however, that subsequent to that date the number of permits granted had rapidly increased and that currently some 250,000 square kilometers, or about one-tenth of AEF's total surface, had been or were about to be committed to one or another type of mining operation.

As for AEF's elected assemblies, their attitude toward the mining industry varied from one territory to another, ranging from the liberal policy adopted by that of Moyen-Congo to the more conservative approach of Oubangui's. As a rule, however, it differed from that taken toward other types of land concessions and underwent a swift change as the federation's mineral potential was shown to be exceptionally promising. Earlier, the Africans' misgivings had their origin in the inconvenience caused to nearby villagers by prospecting or extracting operations. To be sure, the proved abuse of a permit by its holder entailed its cancellation, but the great majority of rural Africans were too timid or too ignorant of their rights to take such cases before a court of law.[8] Then, too, some assemblymen feared that subversive political influences might be operating under guise of acquiring mining permits. A more fundamental uneasiness was also expressed in regard to alienation of the Africans' irreplaceable heritage if outsiders were permitted to extract this wasting asset. Admittedly the indigenous population was now in no position to take over the industry, but given time, capital, and the acquisition of technical skills they would be able to profit directly from their subsoil resources. Yet the African elite were also eager to acquire as rapidly as possible the revenues which only foreign capital and technicians could then procure for the country from its mineral deposits, and the sole condition they came to stipulate was that prospecting and extracting should not be undertaken near an African village.

Indeed, with the announcement of each new and sizable discovery of ores and petroleum, the attitude of African politicians in regard to Western mining companies moved further from latent suspicion toward amiability. In the years just after World War II the assemblies favored taxing the industry heavily, and were most reluctant to grant them any fiscal concessions. The issue, transfer, and renewal of permits were all subject to taxation, and companies had to pay a royalty (5 per cent ad valorem) on all ores they extracted as well as the tax on industrial and commercial profits. The industry also had to support export duties, which varied with the mineral concerned, as well as a tax on the *chiffre d'affaires,* and imports of mining machinery and equipment were subject to duties. In 1949 the government began a campaign to revise the fiscal system in accordance with the change that was taking place in AEF's mining industry. Claiming that AEF had now passed beyond the stage when mining required little machinery and labor was cheap to one in which large investments and elaborate equipment were indispensable, it urged the elimination of import duties on materials required for prospecting and extracting, and a reduction of the tax on the *chiffre d'affaires*. The Grand Councilors reluctantly accepted the former proposal, but asserted that they had already sufficiently aided an industry which benefited only big European companies that repeatedly asked for fiscal favors and in return produced less and less.[9] Six months later the government returned to the charge, and despite the councilors' continued reluctance to see the federal revenues suffer a further decline, they agreed to lower the export duties on gold from 6 to 2 per cent, on diamonds from 6 to 4 per cent, and on lead from 2 to 1 per cent.[10] The territorial assemblies were more amenable to such proposals, for their budgets were less directly affected by customs duties.

The discovery of new minerals that promised to attract French and foreign private capital to the federation on an unprecedented scale resulted in a rapid alteration of the African politicians' attitude toward the mining industry. Gabon, the territory richest in known deposits, took the lead in welcoming such investments. Not only did its assembly lower existing taxation on the industry, but it pledged to such companies as the Compagnie Minière de l'Ogooué (COMILOG) fiscal stability for a 25-year period. The other republics have followed suit, for their leaders now are more conscious than before of what the revenues brought in by industrial mining can mean for the development of their countries.

Copper

Illusions about Mindouli's copper deposits in the Niari valley have been blamed by some for the mistaken orientation initially given to AEF's mining industry.[11] Not only were these deposits mined by local Africans long before the French occupation, but as long ago as 1877 a German geologist published a study of them in Europe. Brazza, on his first journey to the Pool region, visited the Mindouli mines, and their eventual ownership was a main source of conflict between him and the Belgians in the Congo. Since that time many explorers and scientists have examined the Mindouli deposits, extraction on a small scale was begun there in 1900, and small quantities of ores were carried by human portage as far as Loango for shipment to Europe.

In 1903 there was formed a Syndicat Minier du Congo Français, in which Belgian and French financial interests were associated. After prospecting in the Mindouli region and obtaining a mining concession there, this Syndicat was transformed in 1905 into the Compagnie Minière du Congo Français (CMCF) with a capital of 6 million francs. Its activities for the next five years were wholly devoted to building a narrow-gauge railroad 160 kilometers long to Brazzaville. From 1911, when this line was opened, to 1914, 7,000 tons of ore were shipped over it for export via the Belgian railroad to Matadi. World War I, as well as exhaustion of the deposit, greatly slowed down the CMCF's operations, but they revived somewhat after 1925 when a processing plant was built at the mine site, to which a larger one was added in 1930. To ship out Mindouli's copper by means of an all-French route was one of the main arguments used in favor of constructing the Congo-Ocean railroad, but no sooner had that controversial line been completed than copper mining at Mindouli was suspended.

The reasons given for this stoppage by the CMCF's directors were the world trade depression, the exhaustion of Mindouli's rich deposits, and the mediocre results given by the processing plants, and they claimed it was more profitable for them to work the recently prospected lead and zinc mine at nearby M'Fouati. But a few French journalists and patriots saw in this the sinister hand of the Belgian shareholders, who were suspected of thus preventing Mindouli's copper from competing with that of Katanga.[12] Some of them even intimated that the Belgian shareholders were responsible for the "mysterious death" of Governor-General Renard because of his insistence that copper mining be resumed at Mindouli. Be that as it may, prospecting for copper was resumed in 1939, only to be interrupted a few months later by the outbreak of World War II. Under the stimulus of the Plan, it was taken up once more on a much larger scale after 1946, not only by the CMCF but also by the Bureau Minier and two Franco-American companies.[13]

For the second time, French hopes of finding another Katanga in the Niari valley were dashed. Though the Hapilo lead deposit was discovered, as well as a few small copper deposits, no large and rich finds were made. Early in 1954 the two Franco-American companies withdrew from the search, but the CMCF, the Bureau Minier, and the federal mines service have continued prospecting in the regions of Kibangou in Moyen-Congo and Mouila and Fougamou in Gabon, as well as in the Niari basin. Difficulties of transportation and of obtaining the large amounts of capital needed to work the newly discovered copper deposits have thus far discouraged would-be extractors. When the Kouilou dam is built, however, the problem of cheap power will have been solved and then the working of these deposits as a whole may be thought worth undertaking.

Lead and zinc

In the Lutété valley of the Niari basin, Africans knew of the existence of lead and zinc, as well as copper, before the coming of Europeans. At the end of the nineteenth century, a little mining was done there, but these deposits were not thoroughly studied until the 1930's. In 1935 the Compagnie Minière du Congo Français (CMCF) turned to lead and zinc mining at M'Fouati as the copper deposits of nearby Mindouli were becoming exhausted, and that company has continued to this day to be the sole producer and exporter of lead and zinc concentrates from AEF.

Extraction at M'Fouati is easy, for the deposits are situated mostly at surface level, but processing of the ores, especially those of zinc, is difficult.

M'Fouati's lead ores have a 53 per cent metal content; those of zinc contain no more than 43 per cent. From 1937 through 1945, the company turned out 51,665 tons of lead concentrates and 21,411 of zinc. Lead output reached a peak of 8,622 tons in 1940–41, but fell to about 4,000 tons between 1946 and 1948, and in 1949 extraction stopped for a year because of technical difficulties. Production was resumed in 1950 with 3,490 tons and rose to 6,400 tons in 1955, owing to improvements made by the company in its equipment beginning in 1951. By 1955, however, the M'Fouati mine showed signs of exhaustion and the company turned to a new deposit located at Hapilo, five kilometers away. There unexpected obstacles were encountered and output fell sharply, to the point where lead was no longer listed in 1958 as one of AEF's main exports.

While the output of lead has tended to increase and was periodically halted only by dwindling resources and technical difficulties, that of zinc has been much more irregular. Not only is its processing more onerous, but the world market for the ore fluctuates more widely. Maximum production was reached in 1940–41 with 2,737 tons of metal, in 1946–48 it disappeared altogether from the federation's exports, and it revived in 1949 with a mere 111 tons. In 1950, output rose to 1,552 tons, only to slip back to 838 tons two years later. Extraction ceased altogether in 1953.

All of M'Fouati's lead and zinc concentrates are shipped 20 kilometers to the Congo-Ocean railroad by road or by narrow-gauge rail line. During the war some of AEF's lead was sent to the United States, but since 1946 all such production has been reserved for the Metropolitan market. In 1956, lead ranked tenth in terms of value among AEF's exports, but zinc shipments have been irregular and never have attained such a position. Because of the wartime accumulation of stocks, exports reached their highest point in 1948 with the shipment of 10,173 tons of lead and 12,000 of zinc.

Since 1946, prospecting for lead and zinc has been done by the CMCF in other parts of the Niari valley, and since 1950 the Bureau Minier has participated in this work. Some small deposits have been found in the Mindouli area, and their development now seems likely, not because of their volume but because of their proximity to the Congo-Ocean railroad.

Gold

AEF is the main gold producer of the French Union and for many years that metal was the federation's chief mineral resource. But since the end of World War II, its production there has declined markedly, and gold now accounts for considerably less than half of the federation's mineral exports, in terms of value.

AEF's gold deposits were not known to the local Africans but were discovered by Europeans about 1885. Prospecting began in 1921 but production did not become appreciable until 1933. Gold was first sought in eastern Oubangui, near the Anglo-Egyptian Sudan frontier, by scientific missions and individual prospectors. In 1928 the first gold-mining company in the field appeared, the Compagnie Equatoriale des Mines, which made a series of strikes in the Berbérati region during the early 1930's. About the same time the Compagnie des Mines d'Or du Gabon (ORGA-BON) and the Exploitations Rainal (later transformed into the Société Minière de Micounzou) began operations in Gabon, where they worked rich deposits in the N'Djolé region. Gold was also found on the right bank of the Kouilou river and north of Mossendjo, in Moyen-Congo. Even in Tchad, gold was panned in the Mayo-Kebbi region, but on a very small scale. Thus, by the eve of World War II, this metal was being mined in every colony of the federation and in increasing amounts. The producing regions, in order of their importance, were the basin of the N'Gounié, central and western Oubangui, Ouesso, the lower Ogooué, the Niari, the basins of the Ivindo and Lobaye, and the upper Ogooué.

During World War II, gold mining was encouraged by the authorities, and 1941 saw a record output of around three tons. Gold was probably AEF's greatest contribution to the war effort and was responsible for the comparative independence of its currency policy during those years. From 1946 on, however, AEF's gold industry was beset with difficulties, and its situation has worsened with each successive year. Its two major handicaps have been the falling purchase price for gold and the scarcity and high cost of labor. The government has given aid to this industry only in the form of a few loans, a lightening of taxes, and the technical and financial aid provided by the Bureau Minier.

In 1946 the abolition of forced labor resulted in the desertion of the gold-mining camps by many African workers, who had never cared for that type of occupation. Some thousands of laborers are still so employed, but the companies must contend with growing difficulties in keeping them on the job, despite steadily rising wages. Repression of thefts and the sale of stolen gold to the black market have led to a regimentation of the gold-mining camps that has not made mining more attractive to the Africans. The obvious remedy is to mechanize gold-mining operations, and an ever-greater incentive for this has been the progressive exhaustion of the alluvion deposits, which are virtually the only ones ever worked in AEF. But the shortage of foreign currency with which to buy machinery, which plagued all of AEF's industries, was especially troublesome in the case of gold because of the sharp decline in the profits of the gold-mining companies. Until 1949 they were forced to sell all their output to the Caisse Centrale de la France d'Outre-Mer (CCOM) at a lower price than that prevailing in the world market, and after that date the price they received in the Paris free market fell to a point below production costs in the case of all but the biggest AEF companies. Despite increased prospecting by the companies themselves and the Bureau Minier, no new rich strikes have been made, and the cost of finding and extracting gold from rock veins has been considered prohibitive under present market conditions. Even officials of the Bureau Minier, who had been studying the type of machinery suitable for gold mining in AEF, came to the conclusion in 1955 that mechanization of the federation's gold mines would be economically worth while only under very special conditions.[14] Many of the small enterprises have gone under, suspended operations, or merged, and even the largest firms have been experiencing very hard times since the end of 1956.[15]

Before World War II, exports were tantamount to production, but for 1946 and subsequent years it is difficult to estimate the amount actually mined each year because of the shipment of accumulated stocks and the fraudulent sales of gold. For example, it is believed that in 1948 only 1.9 tons were mined, but exports that year amounted to 4.1 tons. Since then the output of gold has apparently gone steadily downhill, dropping to 1.5 tons in 1950 and leveling off at about 1.4 tons a year in the following five years. In 1956 production declined by nearly 30 per cent, in 1957 there occurred another shrinkage in the output from the main producing area, that of N'Gounié, and total exports in the latter year amounted to less than a ton. Gabon is still the main producer, output in Moyen-Congo being small and in Oubangui virtually nil.

In AEF it is anticipated that in all probability the output of gold will continue to dwindle, unless there is a sharp improvement in the world price for gold. There is no doubt that the federation has extensive untapped gold resources, but little chance exists that they will be worked if the present unfavorable economic conditions continue to prevail.

Diamonds

Except for a short interlude, AEF has been the main diamond-producing country of the French Union, and in 1952 it became the eighth-ranking producer in the world. Though its output is still far below that of the Belgian Congo and Ghana, there has been a fairly steady rise in exports, which have averaged about 5 per cent in value of AEF's total exports during recent years. All the output originates at present in Oubangui, for Gabon and Moyen-Congo produced diamonds only for a short period and never on more than a very minor scale. It is probable that important diamond deposits as yet unknown exist throughout the southern territories of the federation, but further prospecting and extracting demand more capital and laborers than are currently available there.

Diamonds were first discovered by a French engineer in the Bria region of Oubangui in 1913, but prospecting was not undertaken in earnest until 1927, at the same time as for gold. The gold-mining Compagnie Equatoriale des Mines was the pioneer in the industrial extraction of the stones, and it worked the Bria area for a few years prior to the world depression of the early 1930's. Diamond mining there lapsed from 1933 until World War II, when it became the object of considerable official encouragement. In 1936 the Compagnie Minière de l'Oubangui Oriental (CMOO) began working deposits in the Nola region of Oubangui, and it has continued to lead that industry in AEF up to the present time. From 1938 to 1945 it methodically prospected western Oubangui, and not until 1947 were prospecting and mining revived in the eastern part of the territory. At about the same time the

CMOO's subsidiary, the Société de Recherches et d'Exploitation Dia-mantifère (SOREDIA) undertook prospecting and small-scale extraction in Gabon and Moyen-Congo, but by the end of 1957, declining yields caused it to cease operations in those two territories, which in their peak years never supplied more than 10 per cent of AEF's total diamond exports. Currently the biggest producing region is that of the Haute-Sangha in Oubangui.

Output in 1938 came to 30,000 carats and ten years later it reached 120,000. Since 1952, production has hovered around 150,000 carats a year, of which nearly all is supplied by the CMOO and lesser amounts by the So-ciété Minière Coloniale, the Société Minière de l'Est Oubangui, the So-ciété Africaine des Mines, the Société Minière de Carnot, and the Sangha-mine, all operating in Oubangui. Since the end of the war many diamond-prospecting permits have been granted, but the big companies have been the only large-scale producers because they alone are financially able to buy the machinery needed in replacing hand-labor methods. All of AEF's diamond miners have been beset by labor shortages, but the CMOO and SMI were the sole recipients of sizable loans from the ECA and CCOM that enabled them to undertake prospecting over a large area and to find and work new deposits as the older and more accessible ones became exhausted.

These loans were made conditional upon repayment in diamonds over a long period of years to the Diamond Distributors of New York, Inc., where-as the rest of AEF's diamond exports were required to go first to Paris for appraisal before they could be sold in the European market. Because of the prevalence of thefts, the diamond trade in AEF is strictly controlled through the issue of special permits, and the miners—as well as the villagers living near the mines—are subjected to severe police supervision that has done much to make mining unpopular with the Africans. The inability of the diamond companies to recruit additional workers or even hold onto their present labor forces, which number about 10,000, is one of the major ob-stacles to expanding production. The government has aided the industry by arranging for loans and reducing export duties from 5 to 3 per cent ad valorem.

AEF has never met with difficulty in marketing its diamond output, of which nearly half is classified as jewelers' stones, and the prices received for them have been considered on the whole satisfactory. The future of the big companies, at least, is regarded locally with reasonable optimism, provided producers are able to increase their investments for prospecting and mechanization and can count on a continued labor supply.

Petroleum

At long last the story of petroleum in AEF has taken a happy turn. After 22 years of intermittent prospecting, oil in commercial quantity was found in the coastal region of Gabon in 1956, and since that date a succession of additional discoveries has been made nearby and also in the Pointe Noire area of Moyen-Congo. Probably no vast reserves of petroleum exist in AEF, but they are sufficiently large to justify the 20 billion Metro. francs that have been spent in discovering them, to save France annually about 4 billion francs in foreign currency, and to attract international capital to share in their development.

In the nineteenth century the first European explorers in Gabon noted that the Ogooué boatmen were using asphalt found around Lake N'Kogho to make their dugouts watertight, and subsequently numerous traces of petroleum were found in that general area. Yet no scientists attempted to investigate Gabon's resources until three geologists of the Standard Oil Company came to Gabon in 1925. Three more years were to elapse before Governor-General Antonetti sent a geological mission to Pointe Noire, where work on the Congo-Ocean railroad had uncovered traces of petroleum. This led to still further study in 1931–34 by the Mission de Prospection des Pétroles du Gabon, formed by the government-general and the Metropolitan Office National des Combustibles Liquides. Its report was sufficiently encouraging that this mission was transformed in 1934 into the Syndicat d'Etudes et de Recherches Pétrolières en AEF (SERP), which for the next five years prospected in Gabon, drew up a geological map of part of its sedimentary basin, and drilled seven small holes without success. In 1938 the SERP was enlarged by the participation of the Compagnie Française des Pétroles (CFP) and the Compagnie de Pechelbronn, and it was preparing to drill in the Mabara region of Gabon when World War II broke out.

Throughout the war, geological research, map making, and drilling were continued, though on a greatly reduced scale, by a staff of 17 Europeans and 1,000 Africans. By 1945, sufficient preparatory work had been done to show the need for more capital and better equipment if oil was ever to be found in AEF. For this purpose the Bureau de Recherches des Pétroles (BRP) was organized on October 1, 1946, the government-general, Gabon territory, and the CFP contributed money for the purchase of new machinery in the United States, and a bigger prospecting and drilling program was drawn up. Three years later the SERP was reorganized as the Société des Pétroles de l'AEF (SPAEF), in which French public funds supplied 65 per cent of the capital. It was granted a prospecting permit that covered 50,000 square kilometers in the coastal area of Gabon and Moyen-Congo, and it once again concentrated on prospecting in the region between Lake Azingo and the ocean. Even with its increased capital (1,200 million CFA francs), enlarged staff (100 Europeans and 1,000 Africans) and improved machinery, the SPAEF had no better luck than its predecessor, and in September 1950 decided to dismiss 40 per cent of its personnel, put its biggest drills into storage, and concentrate on further prospecting.

This decision brought protests from the Grand Councilors,[16] who had placed great hopes in SPAEF, and from AEF's parliamentarians.[17] In Paris both Durand-Reville and Bayrou urged the government to persevere. If oil had not been discovered in AEF where it was known to exist, they said, it was because too little money had been spent on finding it. Fortunately for AEF, these pleas were made only a few weeks before an oil strike was made by SPAEF in June 1951 on the banks of the Ogooué, about 50 kilometers upstream from Lambaréné. Though Gabon's hopes of finding oil there in commercial quantity were soon dashed, the discovery was sufficient to encourage SPAEF to continue its prospecting and revive its drilling operations. In 1954, this company turned from the hinterland to the coast, and began to explore the region from the estuary to the lagoon of Fernan Vaz. It was not until early in 1956, however, that the first considerable deposit of petroleum was struck—at a distance of about 700 meters from the desk of the director of the SPAEF at Port Gentil. Happily for France, this occurred six months before the abortive invasion of Suez.

More capital, of course, was then required, but by that time French private interests had shaken off their apathy about Gabon's petroleum. Two new companies, the COFIREP and FINAREP, supplied considerable funds, bringing SPAEF's total capital to 10 billion Metro. francs. Concurrently, because of the federation's shaky financial position, which had been worsened by the losses incurred by SPAEF over the preceding seven years, the government-general had to reduce its share from 20 to 6.7 per cent. Private capital, however, was forthcoming in such amounts that it could not be fully utilized in 1957. By that year, SPAEF was employing 300 Europeans and over 2,000 Africans, and "providing a livelihood for at least 10,000 persons altogether."[18] In May, the first shipment of a few thousand tons of Gabon's oil to reach Le Havre was received with ceremonies and publicity that reflected French relief at being liberated from complete dependence on the oil of the Middle East and American producers. Though Gabon's oil reserves probably did not amount to more than 5 million tons and it could never become a major source of supply for Metropolitan France, its petroleum was accessibly located near the sea and of a quality that made it easily marketable.[19] More important, perhaps, was the lesson that it had taught French private capital—that many years and very large investments were indipensable for prospecting and drilling even in regions where oil was known to exist.

In 1958 about 475,000 tons of crude oil were exported from four oilfields in Gabon (Pointe Clairette, Ozouri, M'Baga, and Alewana) and a few more finds were made in the nearby regions. More significant was the discovery of fairly extensive deposits in the Pointe Noire area at Pointe Indienne, where oil had first been struck in October 1957. Two months later, the Gabon assembly agreed to grant a "25-year period of fiscal stability" to SPAEF, whose prospecting permit was not due to expire for another 40 years. At about the same time Royal Dutch Shell and Mobiloil began negotiations with SPAEF for a share in the development of AEF's oil resources. In 1958 agreements were reached with those two foreign companies, SPAEF's capital was increased to 30 billion Metro. francs, and AEF's oil industry thus ceased to be a wholly French enterprise.

By the end of 1957, SPAEF had paid in taxes and royalties to the federal and Gabonese governments some 700 million francs, and such payments promise to be appreciably larger in the future. In 1959 SPAEF's petroleum exports were far greater than anticipated, and the extent of AEF's reserves is not yet known. "Petroleum fever," which struck the Gabonese in 1957, is now beginning to affect the inhabitants of Moyen-Congo, and along with the big development of the Pointe Noire region, petroleum may play no small part in the expected transformation of the economy of the two southern republics.

Manganese

On the eve of World War II, geologists of the federal mines service discovered in the Haut-Ogooué region of Gabon sizable manganese deposits. Their location 45 kilometers northwest of Franceville, in an inaccessible region 350 kilometers from the sea by direct line, discouraged would-be producers for the next ten years. It was not until 1948, when the Soviet Union, the biggest manganese producer in the world, virtually shut off sales of that ore, that American steel companies became interested in the Franceville deposits. At that time the largest American manganese consumer, U.S. Steel, was absorbing about a third of the 1.5 million tons of manganese imported into the country each year from varied sources. This company naturally became interested in the Franceville deposits and in 1949 sent an expert to investigate. His report was so encouraging that in 1951 a mission was jointly dispatched by U.S. Steel and the Bureau Minier to make a study of the region, and the following year a second mission was sent there to examine further the areas cited by its predecessor as being the most favorable. At that time it was thought that the deposits covered an area of about 50 square kilometers and amounted to perhaps 75 million tons of ore.[20]

These reports aroused great hopes in AEF and considerable controversy both there and in France. In France, concern was expressed over the likelihood that foreign interests would predominate in the company that was proposed for the exploitation of a resource located in a French dependency. And when sufficient capital from private sources was obviously not forthcoming, the deputies insisted that public funds be drawn upon so that France would hold a majority of the stock.[21] This stand threatened to disrupt the negotiations then being carried on in Paris between French government officials and representatives of U.S. Steel, but eventually a compromise was worked out whereby the company held 49 per cent of the stock and French interests—the Bureau Minier, Mokta el-Hadid, and CMOO—a 51 per cent majority. In September 1953 the Compagnie Minière de l'Ogooué (COMILOG) was formed, with an initial capital of 300 million Metro. francs, to make a further study of the deposits and of eventual methods of extraction, evacuation, and financing.

Quite different from the reaction of Paris to the formation of COMILOG was that of the Gabon territorial assembly. The major concern of its members was that the interests of the territory should not be sacrificed to those of its perennial rival, Moyen-Congo. They wanted COMILOG to be incorporated as a Gabonese company with headquarters at Libreville, Gabon to acquire a share in its capital and a seat on its board of directors, and a railroad for the transportation of the ores mined at Franceville to be built as far as possible inside the boundaries of their territory. At the same time, however, the African elite of Gabon were torn between their desire to see the long-neglected Haut-Ogooué region developed and fear lest their demands alienate private capitalists from undertaking the enterprise at all.

As to developing the region, the assemblymen received satisfaction. It took a long time, however, to reach a decision as to the means of shipping out COMILOG's manganese ores, and eventually there had to be a compromise between the most economical method—that advocated by U.S. Steel —and the developmental project favored by the Gabonese. An aerial cableway (*téléférique*) some 85 kilometers in length (the second-longest in the world),with a capacity for transporting 850,000 tons of ore annually, was to be installed over the most mountainous terrain. It was to be prolonged by a 285-kilometer railroad which would connect it with the Congo-Ocean railroad between Dolisie and Loudima and which would carry passengers and general traffic as well as the output of COMILOG. The total cost of creating these transport facilities was expected to amount to 24 billion Metro. francs, one-third of which would be supplied by French public funds, $35 million by a World Bank loan,[22] and the balance by COMILOG's shareholders. Transportation would be the major cost item involved, as extraction from the shallow deposits was expected to be easy, and the labor force of 4,000 to 5,000 men required at the outset would probably dwindle to 400 Africans when the mine entered production.

Thorough prospecting of the deposits, and the studies required to solve the transport, marketing, and financial aspects of the enterprise, occupied three years. In the interval the impatience of the AEF Africans threatened to get out of hand as they became more aware of the new and exciting vistas opened up by COMILOG's future operations. Reports made by experts showed that the Franceville deposits were concentrated in an area of 20 square kilometers and were among the richest in the world, containing reserves probably amounting to 150 million tons of ore of 50 per cent grade. Production was expected to begin in 1962, reaching 500,000 tons the first year and a million tons annually thereafter. Little difficulty was anticipated in marketing COMILOG's output—it was to be allocated to the shareholders in proportion to the capital they had invested, which meant that the American market would take 49 per cent and that of Western Europe 35 per cent, while the remainder would be made available to outside purchasers.

Before making their final decision to move forward with the project, the directors of COMILOG asked for fiscal concessions from the Gabon assembly and the Grand Council. These bodies duly granted fiscal stability for a 25-year period and a reduction in the current export duty on manganese ores. In addition the Grand Council accorded a diminution of the company's future tax on the *chiffre d'affaires* and of duties on all materials imported by COMILOG for its operations in the federation during the next 15 years. These concessions were considered satisfactory by COMILOG and on October 9, 1956, the decision was made by the shareholders to mine Franceville's ores and to build the cable-way and connecting railroad.

At various times, estimates have been made as to how much COMILOG's activities will mean to AEF's economy, aside from the jobs it will provide for local Africans. According to a statement made in 1957 by AEF's Director of Finance, the federal budget should receive in the form of duties and taxes 2 billion CFA francs for every million tons of ore extracted, provided the current price of 7,000 francs per ton is maintained.[23] The importance of such a sum is evident when it is realized that it represents four times the amount that France paid in 1957 to help balance the federal budget and is equivalent to nearly one-third of AEF's ordinary revenues that year. In December 1957 COMILOG increased its capital to 2,500 million CFA francs. Early in 1959 it was reported that the company planned to invest in its AEF operations a total of 17.5 billion CFA francs in the course of the following four years.

When the French government decided to build the Kouilou dam, a new element entered this picture which had aspects both favorable and unfavorable to COMILOG. The most unfavorable was the increased cost that this would entail for the company's railroad, since its tracks would have to be lengthened in order to avoid the region that will be inundated after the dam is built. Offsetting this, however, was the prospect of cheap electrical current that Kouilou could provide for the creation of a ferro-manganese industry at Pointe Noire. Such utilization of some of COMILOG's output locally would also satisfy a long-standing African aspiration for the setting up in AEF of processing industries and would add to the revenues of the southern republics.

Uranium

One of the most recent additions to the list of Gabon's known mineral resources is uranium, discovered at Mounana, 25 kilometers from the manganese deposit at Franceville, on December 21, 1956. For ten years the Atomic Energy Commissariat had been hunting for uranium in the Niari valley, and in 1955 it had transferred its prospecting operations to Gabon.

To gain a thorough knowledge of the extent and nature of this deposit, the Commissariat and some mining and financial groups, notably Mokta el-Hadid, formed the Compagnie des Mines d'Uranium de Franceville, and by mid-1957 it had 12 Europeans and 250 African laborers working there. Capitalized at the outset at 400 million CFA francs, this company reached an agreement with the Gabon territorial assembly on December 13, 1958, whereby it promised to invest in its mines 2,500 million Metro. francs and to build a plant in Gabon to process the ore. The amount of ore contained in the Mounana mine is not yet accurately known, but it is hoped that reserves are large enough to permit the extraction of 200 tons a year of 12 to 14 per cent uranium concentrates. In October 1959, after visiting the site, the head of the Atomic Energy Commissariat stated that the Mounana deposits were among the largest in the world, and certainly the biggest in the French Community.[24] It is expected that production will begin in 1961.

Iron

Though iron had been extracted by African blacksmiths in both the northern and southern regions of AEF long before the French occupation, it was not until 1955 that the deposits of the Bokaboka mountain at Mékambo in Gabon began to interest Western industrialists. French geologists who had been prospecting in that area since 1934 found evidences of the existence of massive quantities of iron ore, and the samples they brought back indicated that it was of excellent quality (63 per cent grade). Because these deposits were located in a mountainous region some 500 kilometers from the sea, the Metropolitan steel industry made no move toward developing them. But the picture changed when the Bethlehem Steel Corporation bcame interested in the Mékambo deposits and in December 1955 formed a company with the Bureau Minier to study them further and also to survey the possibilities for shipping their ores to the coast.

Throughout 1956 and 1957 these deposits were prospected intensively by the Franco-American syndicate, as were smaller ones in the Tchibanga area by the federal mines service. Several more years were required to complete this work at Mékambo, but the outlook was considered sufficiently promising for the syndicate to be transformed in early 1958 into the Société des Mines de Fer de Mékambo, in which Bethlehem Steel holds 50 per cent of the capital, French interests (mainly the Bureau Minier and Banque de Paris et des Pays-Bas) 34 per cent, and private German, Dutch, Belgian, and Italian companies 16 per cent. Preliminary studies alone were expected to cost 600 million CFA francs, and extraction and shipment of the ore perhaps 80 billion. At the time the company was formed, Mékambo's reserves were thought to contain some 500 million tons, and their development would be profitable only if extraction could be done at the rate of 10 million tons a year. The Tchibanga deposits were estimated at around 150 million tons and were of inferior quality, but they had the advantage of being located nearer to shipping ports. To export Mékambo's output, a railroad would have to be built across mountainous terrain over a distance of 500 kilometers, and 10 to 15 years would probably pass before Mékambo's iron exports could begin to pay off.

The immense amount of capital and the time lag would make necessary a gigantic financial and technical effort on the part of international steel interests, and it is not yet wholly certain that the enterprise will be launched, though its sponsors anticipate no marketing difficulties. To the Gabonese, the prospect of construction of a railroad through a region heretofore isolated and undeveloped is of far greater interest than the mining enterprise itself.

Phosphates

Extensive deposits of phosphates were found in 1938 in the Hollé region north of Pointe Noire, but their quality was so mediocre that for many years they were not thought worth mining. With the prospect that the Kouilou dam would be built and would supply enormous amounts of cheap current for the region, the question of phosphate extraction was revived, and the Bureau Minier intensified its search for additional deposits throughout the whole coastal area of Moyen-Congo and Gabon.

In 1955 the Bureau Minier took the initiative in forming with three north African phosphate companies the Société des Phosphates du Congo, which took over the mining permit granted some years before to the Société Minérais et Engrais. The new company prospected in different areas and found several new deposits in Moyen-Congo, the most promising of which was located at Tchivoula. Several hundred thousand tons were believed to exist there, and while they too were of inferior grade it was believed they would be worth extracting for local use within the context of the industrial combine to be created at Pointe Noire. Compared with the more dazzling vistas opened up by the Kouilou dam, the extraction of Moyen-Congo's phosphates seems a minor operation and one of dubious worth, but in the eyes of the local Africans, it is of much greater importance because it is linked to the manufacture of fertilizers for the country's farmers.[25]

Potash

While prospecting for oil in the Lake Azingo district of Gabon in 1953, the Société des Pétroles d'AEF (SPAEF) found numerous traces of potassium salts. Actually this deposit had been discovered by the mines service in 1940, but the petroleum company's researches provided more precise data that aroused the interest of the Bureau Minier. In 1954 the SPAEF, the Bureau Minier, and the Mines Domaniales des Potasses d'Alsace formed a syndicate to prospect the region and study the means of shipping the output. Transportation seemed to present few difficulties, for the deposits were located near a navigable tributary of the estuary and could be stocked at Owendo port. The first results of the syndicate's operations were disappointing, but the second attempt was more promising. No decision to extract potash has yet been reached.

Miscellaneous ores

Various small deposits of corindon, colombo-tantalite, titanium, tin, and tungsten have been discovered in scattered parts of AEF, often as the result of prospecting for other minerals. Thus far these ores have been found to be present either in insufficient quantity or in inaccessible locations that make their extraction uneconomic. Colombo-tantalite, corindon, tungsten, and tin have all been mined and exported, but irregularly and in very small quantities. Prospecting for additional deposits, however, is being continued by the Bureau Minier and the federal mines service.

CHAPTER 17

Labor

Labor is far weaker in AEF than in French West Africa as to numbers, skills, and organization. This is true not only because the population is smaller and opportunities for gainful work are fewer, but also because the history, traditions, and psychological conditioning of wage earners in the former federation militate against the growth there of a strong labor force.

Before World War II

During the early period of the French occupation, when the trade in rubber and ivory was at its peak, a permanent labor force of about 25,000 men was considered by the concessionary companies to be indispensable. At first it was thought that AEF was an inexhaustible reservoir of manpower, but it soon became obvious that the coastal tribes could not supply any such number and that the hinterland peoples would work only under compulsion. The companies were able to win a virtually free hand from the local administration, and could thus exploit the Africans living in their vast domains (see pp. 12–16). By the turn of the century, French public opinion had become so incensed against the companies that the Minister of Colonies had to find some more indirect means of compelling the French Congolese to work. In 1902 he hit upon the device of imposing a head tax as "the only way we possess of gradually inducing the natives to labor."[1]

Unfortunately for both the government and the Africans, this tax was made payable in kind and was collected by the companies at their own evaluation of the produce, which not surprisingly was far below current market prices. This regime became so patently abusive that in 1906 the government ordered that Africans bringing in their rubber-tax be paid in cash. Because no way was found to enforce this regulation, however, official policy changed again three years later and money was required for all taxes theretofore paid in kind.[2] This measure, too, proved impossible to enforce, and widespread revolts might well have broken out in AEF had it not been for the fact that before World War I only about one-fifth of the total population paid any taxes at all.

Aside from the purely financial consideration of acquiring revenue through taxation, there remained the basic problem of how to promote the economic development of the country through the agency of a population whose attitude toward labor had been conditioned by years of coercion and who had no desire to work even for wages. In fact, the Africans had no interest in growing crops for sale, though they often were willing to carry such produce long distances as gifts for friends and relatives. As early as 1900, the government considered importing West Africans to supplement the local labor supply, but this proved to be too complicated and too expensive. Then in 1907 a plan was officially approved to bring in Asian workers, but Parliament failed to vote the funds necessary to carry it out. Gradually some carpenters and coopers filtered into AEF from nearby British colonies, a few miners came from Portuguese Cabinda, and a handful of plantation foremen immigrated from São Thome, but the total was numerically insignificant and in any case these newcomers performed only fringe occupations. AEF seemed condemned to get along with only its own skeleton labor force.

As more industries developed, particularly those of forestry, the labor shortage became more acute. A circular issued by the government-general on October 10, 1911, frankly told officials that it was their duty to provide French settlers with "the hands necessary for the maintenance of their undertakings."[3] However, coercive measures were increasingly applied to productive enterprises such as lumbering and to the growing of cocoa, coffee, cotton, and food crops rather than to the gathering of uncultivated produce for the sole benefit of the European companies. By the early 1930's, forced labor was restricted to "minor works for communal purposes" and was limited to 12 days out of the year, and in some instances it was made redeemable in cash. Yet by its very nature, the system remained open to grave abuses, and because the Africans subjected to it gained nothing personally thereby, their recalcitrance to such labor grew steadily greater. Little or nothing was done to make work attractive to them or to train them to become skilled in any trade. Though cocoa cultivation took hold spontaneously in Woleu-N'Tem after the growers of this crop began to realize cash profits from it, not all of the AEF Africans had evolved to the point where their desire for imported goods was sufficiently strong to induce them to earn the money needed to purchase them.

Despite the fact that no attempts seemingly were made by the French before World War II to understand why the Africans were so "lazy and inefficient" and so unresponsive to the profit motive, the government gradually became concerned about remedying the demographic causes of the labor shortage. By the end of World War I it had become obvious, at least in Gabon, that a major cause of the dearth of manpower was forced labor, which was held largely responsible for the high mortality rate and for emigration to Spanish Guinea. To make the population more accessible to medical care (as well as to facilitate administrative tasks) was the aim of the first regrouping of Gabonese villages. This failed because the government had counted too much on the villagers' capacity for adaptation and had not tried to win their prior consent. Since this attempt to concentrate the small labor force in easily accessible areas did not succeed, employers were compelled to seek workers ever farther afield, for in AEF most of the forest, agricultural, and mining enterprises were situated in regions where indigenous manpower was conspicuously deficient. Even in the more densely populated north, the inhabitants were very unevenly distributed, and when they were brought south they did not easily adjust themselves to the different food and climatic conditions in the forest zone.

In the early 1920's, both the Metropolitan and the federal governments took the first effective steps to protect AEF labor, though a few regulations regarding minimum wages and the recruitment of workers already were in force. Parliament went so far as to declare in May 1922 that, except for works of general public interest, laborers in AEF were free to work where they pleased. If they voluntarily agreed to work for more than three months in an enterprise, they and their employers would have to sign a two-year contract, which must specify the wages to be paid, the furnishing of free lodging for the laborer and his family, and the food ration, rest periods, and leave to which he was entitled. Labor disputes must be submitted to an arbitration council, composed of an official as chairman and representatives of both employers and workers. It should be noted that neither Europeans nor African day laborers were similarly protected by law because at that period there were very few of either category of such workers in AEF.

Three years after Parliament had made this declaration it was contravened by the governor-general, who announced that the imminent construction of the Congo-Ocean railroad would demand for an indefinite period the services of some 10,000 African workers. To raise such a labor supply, quotas were assigned to each colonial governor, who, in turn, divided this number among the regions and districts under his administration. Those not called up were to raise the crops required to feed the men actively engaged in building the railroad. By its role in eliminating human portage in Moyen-Congo this railroad eventually proved of immense benefit to the local African population, but its construction had the immediate effect of emptying villages in the Niari region and of causing large-scale emigration to adjacent territories. When reports reached France of the terrible mortality rate among the railroad laborers, public opinion there became aroused and strongly censured the AEF government for its negligence in having failed to provide proper working and living conditions for those workers.

From 1927 on, the government did vastly improve the conditions complained of, and during the ensuing decade it established additional legal safeguards for workers of all categories in AEF. In 1930 further restrictions were placed on the use of forced labor, and in 1931 instructions were issued that the "demographic protection of the communities from which workers were drawn" must be taken into account. Two years later it was specified that the maximum number of laborers who might be recruited each year was 33,000 in Moyen-Congo, 9,500 in Tchad, and 8,500 in Oubangui, and where such recruitment was authorized, employers must specify the number of workers they desired and the tasks to which they would be assigned. Written contracts containing the precise terms of an individual worker's employment must thenceforth be signed by both parties in the presence of the administrator of the region where the enterprise was located. The exact amount of the wage had to be specified in the contract, and in no case could it be lower than the minimum annually set by the territorial governor. Wages were to be paid in cash and in full, at least once a month, and to them must be added a minimal food ration similarly established. Workers were also to be supplied without charge by their employer with lodgings, cooking utensils, and one blanket a year. The maximum working day was set at ten hours, interrupted by a two-hour rest period, and one day of rest weekly was made obligatory. Although these provisions were gradually extended to noncontract workers, in all cases too much still depended on the individual employer, for the labor inspectorate created in 1936 was largely a paper organization. Legally, contract workers were now adequately protected, but no effective machinery existed for enforcing the law or for punishing infractions.

World War II and Thereafter

AEF's participation in World War II required that its population make a tremendous effort to produce the materials needed by the Free French forces and their allies. In order to get the maximum work out of AEF's small labor force, Offices du Travail were set up in July 1942 in each of the territories. Their main task was to determine and make available the number of workers to be employed in given enterprises, and secondarily to keep the territorial governors informed on all matters relating to the hiring and utilization of labor. This had to be done on a rough and ready basis and without adequate knowledge of the conditions prevailing in each region, and by the end of the war these Offices had clearly outlived their usefulness. Moreover, the liberal legislation of the 1945–46 period entailed a drastic revision of AEF's entire labor policy.

Allowing for the admitted incompleteness and inaccuracy of the data shown in Table 8, there obviously was a marked growth in the wage-earning class in all the territories except Oubangui during the period 1949–58. It is also clear that Tchad, the most populous territory, still has the smallest number of wage-earners, though that component almost doubled in the course of the period mentioned. This has been largely caused by the expansion of its civil service, which now comprises about one-third of all those gainfully employed there. Moyen-Congo, the territory with the second-smallest population, has the largest working class, but here too functionaries account for a very large proportion because about 40 per cent of all the federation's civil servants work in that territory. For AEF as a whole, however, those employed in the private sector are more than three times as numerous as those working in the public service. As to occupations, the element working for wages in agriculture and allied

TABLE 8.—NUMBER, OCCUPATIONS, AND DISTRIBUTION OF WAGE-EARNERS IN AEF IN
THE YEARS 1949 AND 1958 (IN ROUND NUMBERS)

		1958		
	1949	Private Sector	Public Sector	Total
By territory:				
Gabon	26,000	33,100	8,500	41,600
Moyen-Congo	52,000	46,200	17,200	63,400
Oubangui-Chari	54,000	44,400	5,400	49,800
Tchad	18,000	23,500	11,300	34,800
Total, federation	150,000	147,200	42,400	189,600
By occupations:				
Mining	26,000			13,700
Agriculture and related occupations.	40,000			40,600
Construction and public works.....	15,000			18,800
Industries	13,000			20,700
Transportation	7,000			11,800
Commerce	6,000			21,900*
Domestic service	9,000			18,600
Functionaries and other government workers	34,000			42,400

* Including the liberal professions.
Source: *Afrique Equatoriale Française* (ed., E. Guernier), p. 238; *Marchés Tropicaux*, October 11, 1958.

activities is both remarkably small and static, considering the predominantly rural character of AEF. In the postwar period the curtailed output of the long-existent mining enterprises and their greater mechanization—not to mention the more completely mechanized petroleum companies recently established there—are reflected in the halving of the labor force so employed. There has been a great increase in the number of workers in other industries, however, and in commerce there are now about three and a half times as many employees as in 1949. The rapid growth of the European community can be deduced from the doubling of workers in the domestic-servant category. Finally, the improvement in the federation's infrastructure is to be seen in the increasing numbers of those employed by the transport companies and services.

AEF's over-all shortage of labor and its uneven distribution were more acutely felt in the early postwar years than ever before. This was because more and better-trained workers were needed to carry out the ten-year Plan and because a widespread refusal to work for wages was the initial African reaction to the abolition of forced labor on April 11, 1946. A contributory cause was the dearth of consumer goods on which wages might be spent, and this was an influential factor particularly in Oubangui and Tchad until 1950. Two of the federation's oldest industries, forestry and mining, tried to offset the local labor shortage by importing workers from Nigeria, but the British authorities there not only limited the number of such emigrants but also restricted the area and type of work in which they could be employed. This left all but the forest industry of

Gabon largely dependent, as before the war, on contract workers brought in from the more populous northern territories to supplement the scanty local supply of labor. In regard to such workers, however, there now arose new obstacles—some psychological, others political or material.

Taking advantage of their new freedoms, the northern Africans were less inclined than before to bind themselves by contract, and they preferred —if they emigrated at all—to go to the towns, where they either worked as day laborers or lived off their more prosperous friends and relatives. Furthermore, the Oubangui and, to a lesser extent, the Tchad territorial assembly opposed large-scale recruiting of laborers for work in the south, when they were needed locally to carry out their own development projects. These assemblymen also claimed that the health of men from the millet-consuming savannah region suffered when they were transplanted to the humid forest zone, where, moreover, the basic food was manioc. So the government worked out a somewhat complicated system whereby, in return for Tchadians taken to work in the dry areas of Oubangui, an equivalent number of Oubanguians would be released from that territory's forest zone for labor in Gabon and Moyen-Congo. Opposition to this southward move-ment of labor gradually evaporated when it was realized that many of the emigrants, when they returned to their home territory, had become skilled laborers, and that those who remained in the south to work for higher wages partly relieved the unemployment that began to weigh on the feder-ation beginning in 1952. Generally speaking, the African elite are no longer opposed to intraterritorial labor migrations if such recruitment takes place in urban centers and not in the producing zones.

Southern employers, for their part, made more of an effort than before the war to reduce their labor needs by mechanizing operations, and also to stabilize their labor forces by making working and living conditions more attractive. This was particularly true of the forest and mining com-panies, but they were hampered by the lack of foreign currency with which to buy the machinery they needed in non-franc markets. Then, too, many of the plantations either were situated in areas or grew crops that did not readily lend themselves to large-scale mechanization. Because of the limitations placed by man or nature on mechanization and because of the federation's very limited labor supply and growing number of in-dustries, employers tended to become unscrupulous about the means they used to get workers. Pirating laborers from other enterprises became a not-uncommon practice in isolated regions of the south, but the number of laborers involved was in any case too small to mitigate the over-all shortage. The inducements generally used were wage increments, though some employers also tried to improve their workers' living conditions above what they were required by law to provide. Some assigned their workers a plot of ground on which food crops could be grown, and liberality was shown in granting leave to workers wanting to return to their native villages. For the Nigerian immigrants, employers were more or less compelled to provide sports fields and meeting halls.

Nevertheless, none of these measures succeeded in stabilizing AEF's

rural laborers, who continued to casually quit work to go hunting or fishing. To transform nomadic herdsmen and shifting cultivators into assidu-
ous and conscientious wage earners proved to be a difficult and, in some
cases, an insuperable task. Rural workers labored less hard than did their
urban counterparts, for it was easier for them to lapse into their traditional
milieu, whereas the town dweller had no other resources than his daily
labor unless he could find a friend or relative willing to support him.
The problem was psychological as well as material, and the authorities
grappled with it successively or simultaneously by policies of force, persuasion, training, and legislation.

Blocked both by Metropolitan legislation and by the attitude of the
African elite from forcibly assigning workers to productive enterprises,
the French administration cast about for means of inducing the AEF Africans to work. The obvious method was to pass laws creating better
working and living conditions for wage earners, and in formulating them
the government for the first time called on experts to analyze the African
attitude toward work, particularly in the towns. The studies conducted
by sociologists Pauvert, Balandier, and Soret threw considerable light on
the causes of the Africans' reluctance to work for wages or even to grow
food for sale, aside from the long-standing factors of climate, undernourishment, disease, and resentment against forced labor in the past.

In most of the tribes, the men alternated between periods of intensive
work and leisure, and the women grew such food as was required by their
families. As yet the great majority of rural Africans felt only limited
needs, and once these were satisfied they saw no reason to work more.
Payment of taxes and the bride price were almost the sole incentives to
labor for wages, though in the towns the desire for imported goods, better
housing, and more diversions provided additional stimuli. In the south,
the bride price had reached such astronomical sums that most of the laborers
there were bachelors. In certain regions, too, sizable cash outlays were
required by specific traditions, such as that prevailing among the Batéké
tribes, who shrouded their corpses in hundreds of *pagnes* (loin cloths).
On the other hand, offsetting these incentives to wage-earning and savings
was the widespread custom of harboring impecunious relatives and friends,
who attached themselves to all who held a good job or had acquired
"wealth." The studies made by French sociologists and by groups of psychotechnicians indicated that the Africans' oft-cited inefficiency and lazi-
ness were not inherent but were linked to specific circumstances that could
be altered. Obviously more was required than improving the physique of
Africans and making their work more remunerative. It might be supposed
that to inculcate in them the desire for better living conditions and a pride
in their work should be comparatively easy and might be accomplished
through the force of example, better technical training, and even by legislation. Yet the question was more complicated than that, and the solution
eventually worked out by the French was the *paysannat*. In such communities the group prospered as a unit, and the traditional occupations and

social milieu were gradually transformed by contact with modern techniques and by producing for world markets.

Building up *paysannats* was a long-term task, and in the meantime
the development of AEF's economy required that immediate steps be
taken. When the Africans' first reaction to the abolition of forced labor
in 1946 took the form of strikes or individual refusals to work, it looked
as if AEF might soon return to a subsistence economy. This would have
confirmed the worst fears expressed vehemently at the time by the federation's employers, and would have indefinitely delayed execution of the
Plan. The African elite also became alarmed when their compatriots'
long-pent-up resentment against forced labor expressed itself in the declining production of food crops. At the Pahouin Congress at Mitzic in
1947, a resolution was passed to the effect that "work should be required
for the output of food crops and for operations of public utility, such as
the building of roads, schools, and dispensaries, but that the number recruited for such labor must be related to the utility of the enterprise concerned."

Then and now, African politicians have apparently not been opposed
to forced labor on principle, but only to its use by and for enterprises which
they cannot control and which they feel will benefit solely non-African
interests. Thus, when an African Grand Councilor, early in 1948, proposed
revising the penal code in order to legalize the forcible return to their
villages of the urban unemployed, it was rejected by his colleagues not
only because it would run counter to African traditions of hospitality and
family solidarity but also because it would give too much power to the
administration and the police. This viewpoint underwent a radical change
during the following decade, particularly after 1957, when Africans came
to control the territorial governments. They were then able to do what
it would have been impossible or impolitic for the French to have attempted
—the resettlement projects planned and carried out by Boganda and Youlou
were in fact a form of forced labor.

Labor Legislation

Although after the war the African elite were openly suspicious of any
legislation that might restore the administration's control over the labor
supply, they did agree with the government that new regulations must
supplant the outdated labor laws of the 1930's. Moreover, the Native Labor
Code of June 15, 1945, for Black Africa had been nullified by the grant of
French citizenship to all the inhabitants of Overseas France on May 7,
1946. Clearly, steps had to be taken not only to cope with the existing social
unrest but also to attract and train the workers needed to carry out the ten-
year Plan. So in October 1946 the government-general set up territorial
labor-advisory committees, on which membership was divided equally between officials and representatives of management and labor, for the purpose
of reclassifying the federation's workers and assigning a wage scale to each
category set up. This task occupied the advisory committees throughout

1946–47, and by the end of that period AEF employers had allocated all of their staff to one or another of the new categories, for each of which the committees had established minimum wages based upon what was then deemed to be the workers' "incompressible needs." Furthermore, three or more wage zones were set up in each territory to take into account the differences in living costs of AEF's various regions.

Inevitably opinions among the committee members were often sharply at variance in regard to the *minimum vital* of workers and the delimitation of wage zones. Furthermore, the workers' representatives tended to make excessive wage demands, and the employers' delegates in some cases refused to treat with them on a footing of equality.[4] Sometimes the official chairman of a committee had to intervene and settle the issue arbitrarily. Nevertheless, as time went on the committees functioned more smoothly, and on May 26, 1948, the government-general made them into permanent bodies on both the federal and territorial levels. In addition to their task of establishing wage scales and wage zones, they were given competence to advise on all questions affecting local labor. By that time, too, there was an imperative need for more local action on labor matters, for conservative elements in France had succeeded in shelving the draft labor code of October 17, 1947, for Overseas France by the device of referring its provisions back to the newly created territorial assemblies for their suggestions. It was not until December 15, 1952, that an overseas labor code was finally passed by Parliament, and in the interval AEF had to take piecemeal action to fill in the gaps in its own labor regulations.[5]

The deputies chiefly responsible for the long delay in passing the overseas labor code were AEF's European representatives, Malbrant and Bayrou. They fought its passage step by step in the National Assembly, claiming that the federation could not possibly afford such legislation financially and that it would be preferable for each overseas territory to draft its own labor laws. Despite these and other local Cassandras, however, application of the code to AEF did not provoke strike action as it had in French West Africa, in part because the federal government had anticipated by local regulations many of the code's provisions. In regard to AEF, the code's major innovations were the family allowances for wage-earners' children (though Moyen-Congo already had such a system on a small scale) and the residential qualifications to be required of worker delegates elected to the parity advisory committees. In general, the code simply extended to all the federation's wage earners the legal safeguards already in force for contract workers in regard to medical care, the labor of women and children, working hours, and the like. Governor-General Chauvet repeatedly stressed that the overseas labor code had been the object of grave misconceptions in AEF. It was not, he said, meant to provide automatic wage rises, as some workers seemed to believe, nor was it intended to permit increases in the prices asked for the federation's output, as another segment of the population claimed was justified.[6] Rather, its main aim was to improve relations between employers and wage-earners.

Actually, the only serious debates to which application of the code gave rise in 1953 concerned the authenticity of the spokesmen for labor to be elected to the territorial advisory committees. Here the government was obviously afraid lest outsiders succeed in getting elected as "representatives" of AEF workers, but it eventually accepted a compromise measure whereby such delegates would be required to have lived and been employed in AEF for one year prior to their election.[7] Much longer and more heated were the later assembly debates that preceded the territories' decisions regarding the rate and financing of family allowances, and disagreement on these subjects was responsible in large measure for the fact that the code was not generally applied to AEF until four years after it had become law.

Of all the provisions of the new code, the one instituting family allowances and other bonuses related to the children of wage-earners proved to be the most controversial in AEF. To be sure, since 1950 Moyen-Congo had allocated 100 CFA francs per month per child for such purposes, but the sum was so small that it did not greatly affect that territory's economy. However, when it came to extending much larger family allowances to all the federation's wage-earners, the employer organizations claimed that this would constitute too heavy a burden for them and for so poor a country as AEF. If it had to be imposed at all, they insisted that the system be financed by taxation. To this the African elite and the government were firmly opposed, on the ground that it would be unjust to spread such a burden over the whole population for the benefit of the 6 per cent or so of AEF's total inhabitants who formed the wage-earning class.

Anticipating passage of the overseas labor code, the federal government in 1951 had ordered the labor inspectorate to collect data relevant to applying locally what were likely to be its provisions regarding family allowances. In the first two months of that year the inspectorate undertook a sampling of 3,000 wage earners so as to estimate the number of children likely to be eligible for allowances. Its report indicated that from one-third to one-half of the federation's adult wage-earners were either unmarried or childless.[8] Though this inquiry was admittedly incomplete, the data it brought to light provided ammunition for those who claimed that the payment of family allowances would constitute only a minor burden for AEF employers and, moreover, that it would provide a stimulant badly needed to raise the local Africans' low birthrate.

After the principle of family allowances became consecrated by law, long wrangling took place in all four territorial assemblies about what proportion should be supplied from public funds and what should be the rate for the monthly allowances to be paid for each child, for prenatal assistance to parents, and for bonuses to young married couples. The Grand Council agreed to allocate from the federal budget 50 CFA francs per month per child, but each assembly was left free to determine the rate for its own territory according to its own economic potential. The only uniform measure they agreed upon, as being in the interests of administrative economy, provided for establishing a central *caisse* to handle the separate territorial accounts. When the rate issue finally came to a vote, Moyen-Congo granted the highest allowance of all—400 CFA francs per month per child—Gabon settled for 225 CFA francs, and Oubangui and Tchad for 220 CFA francs. The percentage to be paid by employers also differed from one territory to another: in Moyen-Congo they were to pay 65 per cent of the total, in Gabon 57 per cent, and in Oubangui and Tchad 68 per cent. It took so long to reach agreement on these rates and percentages that the *caisse* did not start functioning until July 1956, three and a half years after the overseas labor code had become law. By March 1958 it was possible to evaluate more accurately than before its incidence in relation to AEF's total population. At that time Moyen-Congo was paying allowances for 15,000 children of wage-earners, Gabon 4,637, Oubangui 10,207, and Tchad about 2,600. In all there were only about 32,000 children on the family-allowance lists—a significant reflection of the ratio of the wage-earner component to the total population, and also of the demographic situation prevailing throughout AEF.

Workmen's compensation was even slower than family allowances in being applied to the federation's wage-earning class as a whole, though for contract laborers some stop-gap legislation in this respect was contained in the regulations of June 28, 1950, and November 30, 1954. Because workmen's compensation had not been included in the 1952 code, it was the object of a special law passed by Parliament on February 24, 1957. Nevertheless, the existence of local legislation in the matter, although temporary and incomplete, had already brought about an increase in the number of work accidents declared to the authorities. These had risen sharply from 58 in 1949 to 1,887 in 1954, but in the view of the federal labor inspector the latter figure probably represented considerably less than the number of accidents that had actually occurred, considering the degree to which AEF enterprises had become mechanized during the postwar years.[9] The law of February 24, 1957, left to the individual territories the task of settling how and by whom its provisions would be financed, and, as in the case of family allowances, this gave rise to acrimonious debates in the assemblies. Finally, by mid-1958, all the territories had voted to entrust this operation to the family-allowance *caisse,* against the strongly expressed preference of the employer groups for its handling by private insurance companies.[10]

On May 29, 1954, the governor-general sent to the territorial labor inspectors a circular urging them to negotiate collective wage agreements as rapidly as possible. For some time the federal government had been anxious to withdraw from its activities in establishing minimum wages, and in this attitude it was supported by the representative assemblies and the trade unions. Because collective agreements were a novelty in AEF, however, and because there was disagreement as to whether they should be made on a federal, territorial, or professional basis, it was not until June 1954 that the first one was signed. Moreover, it affected only 75 per cent of the railroad employees and was confined to the single territory of Moyen-Congo. This agreement was comparatively easy to negotiate because it involved, on the one hand, a limited group of workers organized into two unions and, on the other, the Congo-Ocean railroad, which was under government control.

Far longer and more tortuous were the negotiations that led to the signing of the first truly collective interterritorial agreement on December 5, 1956, by representatives of the industrial workers of Moyen-Congo, Oubangui, and Tchad, and the employer organizations of Syndustrex and the Petites et Moyennes Entreprises. It was completed the following month by a new wage-scale schedule for the various categories of industrial workers in the territories concerned. (Characteristic of Gabon's insistence on its own measures was that territory's abstention from participating in the foregoing agreement, and it was not until 1958 and 1959 that the Mba government negotiated agreements between local transport and forestry workers and the relevant employer groups.) Once the pattern had been set and precedents established by the industrial-workers agreement, others followed at a faster tempo. In 1957 two more collective agreements were signed, which determined the pay rates for commercial and bank employees throughout the federation.

Completion of these collective agreements coincided with the coming to power of African-dominated councils of government in all the territories, and they lost no time in raising the minimum wages for all categories of workers. Less successful were their efforts to reduce the number of wage zones from nine in Moyen-Congo, four in Gabon, six in Oubangui, and three in Tchad. Although they made some headway in this respect, they intend to reduce the number further, for all the new African governments want to close as far as possible the gap between the minimum wages prevailing in the various regions of their republics.

Law Enforcement and the Labor Inspectorate

As has been noted above, a sizable body of labor legislation and a labor inspectorate existed in AEF before passage of the overseas code in 1952, but the effectiveness of the former depended very largely upon the latter's powers of enforcement. A federal inspectorate had been created as early as 1936, but it had little authority and virtually no staff. The law of September 1, 1944, went far to remedy the former situation, but the personnel of the inspectorate then comprised only one official per territory. For some years after the war, administrators in many areas continued to be responsible for the enforcement of labor laws—an anomalous situation, as was frequently pointed out, because the government itself was the single largest employer of labor in the federation. A law in 1950 aimed to make labor inspectors more independent of the local administration by having them appointed by and responsible to the Minister of Overseas France, but the number of inpectors in AEF remained so small that they were unable to utilize their newly acquired authority to any marked degree. In fact, the inspectors were so ineffectual at that time as law-enforcement agents that some African Grand Councilors proposed that their posts be suppressed.[11]

Passage of the overseas labor code added to the duties but not to the staff of the labor inspectorate. For once it was not the lack of funds that was the cause of this shortage, because all of the territorial assemblies had voted the credits required to employ more inspectors. Rather, it was because the terms of service in France's overseas dependencies were less favorable than in France that the government-general had difficulty in finding candidates to fill the posts of inspectors in AEF.[12] A mission of the French Union Assembly which visited AEF in March 1954 to study the labor situation placed most of the blame for the incomplete application of the overseas code in the federation on the scarcity of territorial inspectors.[13] At that time there were only six in all AEF, and of these, three were about to go on leave and only two replacements were being sent from France.

The creating in 1954 of ten labor courts, presided over by magistrates, somewhat lightened the burden placed on AEF's handful of labor inspectors. Nevertheless, they continued to spend a very large part of their time at their desks in the territorial capitals, occupied with the tasks of establishing the *minimum vital* for workers, drafting regulations for the application to AEF of the new labor code, and negotiating the federation's collective agreements. On the rare occasions when they were able to inspect the enterprises, scattered over vast distances, for which they were responsible, they were often called back to the capital to settle a labor dispute that had arisen during their absence. Even after the labor courts had begun to function, the presence and advice of labor inspectors were indispensable to the presiding magistrates.

Aside from their numerical inadequacy and excessive duties, the labor inspectors operated under another grave handicap: they were not welcomed with open arms by many of the federation's employers. As the federal inspector gently informed the Grand Council on May 3, 1956, "My staff does not invariably find understanding and comprehension everywhere in the territories." He found that, on the whole, rural employers of labor showed greater respect for the law than did their urban counterparts.[14] Yet the French Union Assembly mission in 1954 did not give rural employers— especially those in mining enterprises—a clean bill of health. They found that some delayed paying wages to their workers, failed to keep proper accounts, stretched the statutory 40-hour week to 45 hours, practiced no uniform policy in regard to overtime pay, and committed other infractions.[15] Later that same year, after a tour of enterprises in northern Moyen-Congo, the head of the Confédération Française des Travailleurs Chrétiens (CFTC) unions of AEF confirmed those findings (see pp. 524–25).

Thus, while it can be said that AEF's labor legislation is relatively complete—albeit too closely modeled on that of France—many of the laws will remain a dead letter until the machinery for enforcing them is strengthened by a larger staff of inspectors.

Technical Education

For many years, official French policy has favored giving technical education to young AEF Africans, both to enable laborers to obtain better wages and to improve the quality of their work. As long ago as the mid-1920's, the Metropolitan government became concerned about the lack of skilled workers in AEF and sent an expert to study the situation on the spot and to make recommendations. He reported[16] that the small work-shops of that era, which trained a few workers, were worse than useless because employers treated their apprentices as servants and only incidentally —if at all—taught them a trade. Most of the enterprises then functioning in the federation were in any case too small in scale and too scattered to train many workers, although he excepted the forest and river-navigation com-panies from this generalization. He did, however, approve the principle of apprenticeship, provided that Africans were thereby taught the value and dignity of manual labor along with a skill. Among the recommenda-tions he made were that recruits be selected from among the best students in the manual-training sections of village schools, and that they be paid during their apprenticeship a small wage in conformity with a model con-tract he drew up. He also suggested that vocational schools be set up in each territorial capital, and that the most promising pupils from these schools be sent for higher training to a federal institution to be located at Brazzaville.

A few of these suggestions were carried out before World War II, but no complete network of technical schools was created and technical training never became more than an auxiliary activity of the public-school system. A federal professional school was founded at Brazzaville, *maisons de l'artisanat* were built at Bangui, Fort Lamy, and Brazzaville, *écoles des métiers* were constructed at Owendo, Fort Archambault, and Bangui, and manual-training sections were added to some of the primary schools, and in all of these the stress was placed on practical instruction. An apprenticeship tax was imposed on employers so as to provide the funds needed to supple-ment the federal budget's allocations to AEF's various apprenticeship centers. However, one of the recommendations made at the Brazzaville conference of 1944 altered the practical character of the curriculum in AEF's higher technical schools. Thenceforth they were to be aligned on Metro-politan models in a four-year course, theory and general culture were to be stressed, and graduates would receive a certificate (CAP, or *certificat d'apti-tude professionnelle*) the equivalent of that of France. Beginning in 1946, FIDES granted appreciable funds for promoting technical education in AEF. This made it possible to enlarge the staff and improve the equipment of such schools, and in their curricula priority was given to the training of masons, carpenters, mechanics, and electricians. The ten-year Plan en-visaged that each year 40 students would graduate from each of the terri-torial technical schools, a number then considered adequate for the federa-tion's needs in skilled workers for some years to come.

As of January 1, 1946, there were 42 public schools in AEF giving various types of technical training, of which 8 were located in Gabon, 12 in Moyen-Congo, 13 in Oubangui, and 9 in Tchad. Fourteen Europeans and 47 Africans were then instructing 1,974 boys and 178 girls. All of the latter were taking home-economics courses, while by far the largest number of boys were specializing in agriculture.[17] In addition to the sums allocated by FIDES, the federal government was then expending 0.63 per cent of its budget on technical education.[18] Six years later the number of schools providing technical training had risen to 50, and the teaching staff included 51 Europeans and 137 Africans. The federal budget was then allocating only 0.53 per cent to technical education, but this was now supplemented by the territorial budget allocations as well as by FIDES' continuing contributions. The number of pupils attending these schools, however, had shrunk from 2,152 to 1,907, this decline occurring wholly among boys (from 1,974 to 1,166) while girl students were much more numerous (741 against 178), and the number of scholarship holders from AEF studying in French technical colleges had risen to 58. In AEF itself, the diminution in pupil attendance was marked in the higher classes, and only a handful were being graduated each year after completing the whole course. As of 1951, the federation could count only 34 in the fourth-year class, 126 in the third, 302 in the second, and 677 in the first. Most left school to take jobs, but others were dismissed for either ineptitude or indiscipline.[19]

That vastly improved facilities for technical training in AEF were being used by a steadily declining number of pupils was indeed a paradoxical situation for a country so desperately in need of skilled workers as the federation. Aside from those employed in domestic service or by the administration, the number of skilled workers throughout AEF in 1949 was estimated at 15,000. Until 1947 all of the graduates from the federal school and the écoles des métiers had become functionaries, having been absorbed by the education service as teachers for the apprenticeship and manual-training sections in the territorial schools. From 1948 on, the government tried to orient AEF's few CAP holders to private employment, but this effort met with two formidable obstacles. One was that the graduates of AEF's higher technical schools disdained manual work and wanted only desk jobs, and the second was the attitude taken toward them by private employers. Considering the dearth of skilled workers in AEF, the CAP holders seemingly should have been much in demand by the private sector. Yet most AEF employers, as well as the administration's technical services, preferred either to recruit their own African apprentices or to hire skilled European labor, despite the latter's high cost. They were reportedly unwilling to pay the salaries demanded by African graduates of the technical schools and furthermore were alienated by the graduates' supercilious attitude toward manual work.[20] This situation was blamed by the African elite on the administration, on the ground that it had failed to provide training appropriate to AEF's needs and to assure remunerative jobs for the graduates of its schools. The government took the position that a CAP diploma did not automatically entitle its holder to a highly paid job, and blamed the Africans for insisting on white-collar rather than manual employment.[21] A subsidiary grievance of three-fourths of AEF's assemblymen was that their territories had to subsidize on a basis of equality the Brazzaville school, where, despite its supposedly federal character, the majority of the students were from Moyen-Congo.[22]

Despite the government's obstinate defense of the CAP diploma, its spokesmen had to acknowledge that something was very wrong with AEF's technical-school system. Illustrative of its failure to instill into its pupils a proper attitude toward manual labor was the fact that many attended classes and workshops dressed in unsuitable clothing that included even neckties. Perhaps, it was admitted, too much attention had been paid to theory and general culture, but the government refused to comply with the Africans' plea that the higher technical schools' educational qualifications for admission be lowered, their course shortened, and their examinations made easier.[23] In the general reorganization of the technical-school system in 1954, the CAP standards were maintained, but the curricula of the Brazzaville school and manual-training sections were adapted so as to conform more closely with the needs of the country. The *maisons de l'artisanat* were similarly reoriented, and graduates of the one located at Brazzaville were organized into a cooperative and their output marketed with government aid.[24] As of 1957, there existed 46 technical public schools, supplemented by 51 mission establishments, having a total attendance of 3,414 pupils.[25] The number of students at the federal school had risen from 172 in 1950 to 290 (of whom 40 were Europeans) in 1958, and the government had begun to take more responsibility for placing its graduates.[26]

Although the CAP holders remained the elite of AEF's wage-earning class, the federation's continued need of skilled labor posed a problem for which, during the years since 1949, the government had sought a solution in other directions. At first it had been thought that the answer might be found in an extension of the apprenticeship system. On September 1, 1949, a European Grand Councilor proposed to his colleagues that the companies carrying out the Plan in AEF be compelled by the government to train apprentices. But there was nothing in those companies' contracts that required them to train African workers, and the government was afraid, as always, to press the point lest they decide to pull out of the federation altogether. The African councilors, too, opposed this suggestion because the private firms which had trained apprentices in AEF "did little to improve their skills and treated them badly." European foremen, it was said, became impatient with illiterate youths who were confused by being confronted with complicated machinery for the first time in their lives and by receiving incomprehensible orders rather than careful explanations. Moreover, such employers wanted to retain the services of their own trainees but without paying them additional wages. Thus when the federal labor inspector tried to carry out the overseas code's provision for transforming verbal agreements into written apprenticeship contracts, he found both employers and unskilled laborers equally indifferent to that form of training.[27]

It was in another type of instruction that the government placed its hopes, and gradually the African elite came to share the official enthusiasm for it. This was the establishment of rapid-training centers modeled after those successfully operating in French West Africa. The pioneer in this field was Governor Mauberma of Oubangui who, in 1949, brought from France a team of psychotechnicians to study the Oubanguian laborers and recommend a course for their rapid training. After surveying the local labor market and selecting appropriate candidates, these experts proposed a nine-month course to give basic training in skills for which the territory then had great need. Two such courses were opened in 1950, the first of which was at Bangui and the second at Brazzaville, and in late 1958 a third center was founded at Fort Lamy. So successful have these centers been that the African governments of AEF are now proposing to start them in other towns. They are popularly called "schools of the last chance," because they give the only opportunity open to illiterate African workers to get better-paying jobs than if they remained with the floating mass of unskilled urban day laborers.

These centers are run by the labor inspectorate in collaboration with the territorial administration and Chambers of Commerce. Courses are geared to the current needs of the labor market and hence are subject to change. The aim is not to turn out skilled workers but to train quickly men of above-average intelligence so that they can rise above the run-of-the-mill laborers. Originally oriented to the urban building trade, these centers, in recent years, have been concentrating more on training carpenters for rural areas, electricians, plumbers, and mechanics. By December 1958 the Brazzaville center had graduated seven groups, in which 252 of its 308 pupils had received certificates, and the Bangui center had similarly turned out 217 graduates. In neither center had more than 10 per cent of those admitted failed to finish the course. Continuing urban unemployment has led the authorities to encourage these graduates to work in the rural areas, and in order to help launch them as independent workers they have been given some tools and small loans.[28]

Labor Organizations

The overseas labor code revitalized the multitude of small organizations of both employers and workers that had come into existence during the last year of World War II. Until that time, organized work stoppages had been almost unknown in AEF, though something resembling a strike occurred during construction of the Congo-Ocean railroad when joint action for the improvement of working and living conditions was taken by the laborers and Niari valley villagers. But no labor organizations, properly speaking, existed before they were sanctioned by the law of August 17, 1944, and even thereafter the activity of both unions and employer groups was largely negative for some years. The latter insisted that they alone should set the wage scale for their own enterprises, while the unions were inclined to make wage demands unrelated to the financial resources of the industry in which their members worked. The result was a series of work stoppages in 1946 which so threatened public order and the federation's economy that the government felt compelled to step in and establish wage scales and working conditions for the different categories of laborers.

For some years after the war the administration filled a role in labor matters which the unions were too inexperienced and undisciplined to play. The few unions then in existence were those of railroad workers, functionaries, and urban industrial employees. Rural workers were too ignorant to grasp the value of joint action and too dispersed geographically to be effectively organized. Even in the towns, union leaders found it difficult to make workers understand the value of collective organization as a means of defending their interests. Then, too, the admixture of politics with labor organization made some of the unions suspect in the eyes of the workers, the administration, and employers alike.

Soon after the Liberation the three main Metropolitan *centrales,* the Force Ouvrière (FO), the Confédération Générale du Travail (CGT), and the Confédération Française des Travailleurs Chrétiens (CFTC) sent militants to organize labor in AEF. In addition to the branches they set up there, a handful of autonomous unions came into existence, of which some were barely distinguishable from the many indigenous *amicales* and other forms of spontaneous African association. The history of the FO in AEF was at the same time similar to and different from the course it followed in French West Africa. As in the latter federation, the socialists were the first in the field, their appeal was made mainly to the functionary and white-collar class, and the unions they organized were the only ones to combine European with African members. Where the FO in AEF diverged from its West African counterpart was in the control it early established over railroad workers, mainly because most of the officials of that line were members of the Section Française de l'Internationale Ouvrière (SFIO). But the FO was unable to maintain the early lead it had acquired over its rivals. It is now considered to be the weakest of the big three, though in recent years its fortunes have tended to rise with the growth of the civil-servant contingent, particularly in Tchad. In 1955 the FO was estimated to have about 3,000 members—about half the number claimed by the CGT but twice as many as were said to belong to the CFTC.[29]

Since that estimate, the situation has certainly altered, and today both the CFTC and the CGT seem definitely stronger than the FO. In total membership, the CGT appears to have an edge over the CFTC, but the latter's influence is greater than its numbers suggest, for it has the benefit of support and guidance from the Catholic missions as well as superior African leadership. On a territorial basis, the CGT is strongest in Moyen-Congo, important in Oubangui, weak in Gabon, and in Tchad almost wholly confined to the cotton belt. In contrast to its development in French West Africa, the CGT in AEF finds its support largely in rural areas, though it also has a fair following in the transportation and building industries. The CFTC is naturally most powerful where the missions have been longest established. Hence its main strongholds are in the coastal towns of Moyen-Congo and Gabon, it is weak in Oubangui, and only very recently has it begun to make progress in Tchad. Inevitably union strength is directly linked to economic development, so that all the unions are weaker in the northern than in the southern territories. Furthermore, because of the dispersal of AEF's agricultural, forest, and mining enterprises, all of them are poorly organized in the rural districts. Despite these obstacles, the local branches of the three main *centrales* have been making headway, notably at the expense of the smaller autonomous unions. Moyen-Congo remains the territory where unions are best organized, and in the history of AEF labor it plays a role analogous to that of Senegal in French West Africa.

All of the estimates regarding absolute or relative strength of the various AEF unions are, at best, simply informed guesses. None of the *centrales* publishes figures of its membership, and many of the claims its leaders make verbally are patently exaggerated. In 1955 the total number of unionized workers in AEF probably did not exceed 15,000, or only about one-tenth of the whole wage-earning class,[30] which in itself represented only about 6 per cent of the federation's total population. Moreover, the unions varied widely in membership, ranging from the majority which had fewer than 100 members to the handful that could count several thousand members. However, their numerical weakness has not been the only reason for the failure of the unions to influence the course of the federation's economic or political development. Generally speaking, the administration did not always give them constructive support, they were opposed by the employer groups as a whole, and the caliber of their leadership was poor. Only since the overseas labor code assigned an important role to organized labor have unions acquired significance in the eyes of both the authorities and the working class.

Even today the great majority of the federation's wage earners are still unorganized, attendance at union meetings is small, and dues-paying members are few compared with the number of workers either indifferent or at best passively sympathetic to the movement. In the unions' first years, dues were set at unrealistically high rates, but they have been reduced to the point where the average for the FO and CFTC is about 50 CFA francs a month. Dues in the CGT unions are reported to be considerably higher, because of the need to finance that *centrale*'s extracurricular political activities. Yet even 50 CFA francs a month is more than most AEF workers can afford, and none of the unions is in a financial position to support workers during a prolonged strike. When an AEF worker pays his membership dues, it is often in the expectation that the union he has joined will help him redress a personal grievance. An outstanding CFTC leader of Moyen-Congo told the authors that within 24 hours of joining a union, a new recruit almost invariably filed a complaint against his employer, and that if he did not receive immediate satisfaction he was likely to lose interest in union activity with equal rapidity.

Related to this fundamental misconception of the role of labor **unions** was the fact that at the outset AEF workers expected too much too soon from their leaders, and when their hopes were dashed, disillusionment swiftly followed. In some cases, notably in the CGT unions of Oubangui and Tchad, this was due to the utilization of unions by politically radical leaders, and this mixture of left-wing politics with organized labor was mainly responsible for the administration's negative attitude toward unions during the early postwar years. However, the extreme left has never become important in either the political or labor history of the federation, and none of the outstanding African politicians of AEF has risen to fame as a labor organizer. Indeed, the tendency of AEF's current galaxy of ministers is to regard union leaders not as collaborators but as competitors for influence over the masses, despite the fact that the latter have not yet displayed political aspirations. No training in leadership was available except that given by Metropolitan militants, and it is no wonder that the union leaders were almost as benighted and inexperienced as the rank and file of laborers from which some of them came. Tribal loyalties have dominated the labor as well as the political scene, and unions have tended to divide or to be formed according to ethnic rather than occupational lines. To these obstacles to the development of competent leadership was added the requirement laid down in the law of August 17, 1944, that union officials must be literate in French and able to keep proper financial accounts.

Considering the deficiencies in AEF's labor leadership, it is not surprising to read in the federal labor inspector's report for 1949 that on many occasions union leaders neither participated in, nor succeeded in preventing, strikes. Workers, he wrote, struck without formulating any demands, and to discover exactly what their grievances were he had to interrogate each striker separately. This basic weakness of the leadership, plus the lack of financial resources of both unions and individual workers, probably accounts for the scarcity of strikes during the first postwar years, after the 1946 rash of work stoppages. In 1954, though there were more labor disputes than in 1953, the federal labor inspector described their number as "insignificant." They affected a total of 5,297 workers, but only 22 of these disputes culminated in strikes, and these were short ones. Almost all of the disputes had to do with wages or the dismissal of workers. The only sizable strike that has yet occurred in AEF took place at Brazzaville in 1955. It involved 600 workers of the TEFRACO plant, and the aid which the CFTC gave to the strikers, who got satisfaction for most of their demands, reportedly contributed to the growth of that *centrale* in Moyen-Congo. It has been chiefly CFTC leaders who have taken advantage of the chance given organized labor in AEF to attend conferences sponsored by the ILO or UNESCO, and it is that *centrale* which has shown the most initiative in obtaining a reduction of the wage zones and a rise in the scale of wage-earners' family allowances, particularly in Moyen-Congo. Virtually the only AEF labor leader who has stature outside the federation is Gilbert Pongault, head of the CFTC unions.

The success of concerted action by workers in the TEFRACO strike, combined with the long-delayed application to AEF of the overseas labor code, apparently altered the official attitude toward organized labor. The administration had to find valid spokesmen for labor in order to apply certain provisions of the code, and for the first time it began to encourage union leaders to go to Europe for training. In 1957 Governor-General Chauvet, in a speech to the Grand Council on October 21, even proposed setting up a pilot center at Brazzaville to "train workers in their rights and duties," and he was hopeful that it might eventually be transformed into a workers' university. The attitude of the French administration, though recently more favorable to organized labor than before, still varied with the territory and indeed with the individual high officials. Union leaders with whom the authors talked in 1958 as well as in 1956 found the labor inspectors generally "helpful," but felt that the administration as a whole tended to side with the *patronat*.

As to employers in the private sector, their actions show them to be an exceptionally individualistic group and one profoundly hostile to any outside interference in their dealings with their labor force. Many employer organizations have been formed in AEF, the strongest of which have been the Chambers of Commerce and the Chamber of Mines, the Syndicat Forestier du Gabon, and the Syndicat des Commerçants Exportateurs et Importateurs de l'AEF. The need to formulate joint policies and to participate in the new labor advisory committees induced the great majority of these employer groups, a few days after passage of the overseas labor code, to form themselves into a Comité de Liaison du Patronat de l'AEF (COLPAEF).[31] Though COLPAEF operated smoothly and set up a permanent secretariat which coordinated the four territorial branches, it lacked the strength of similar organizations in French West Africa. In fact, AEF's employers to this day remain highly individualistic, and are still covertly opposed to the unionization of their labor force. Some have been singled out for praise by both the labor inspectorate and the union leaders, whereas others have been denounced for their failure to respect the provisions of the code, and for relying on "paternalistic handshakes" with their African personnel instead of promoting their workers' welfare in any fundamental way.

The widespread impulse to create unions independent of the Metropolitan *centrales* that swept over French West Africa in 1956–57 also affected AEF, but it did not lead to any merger between similarly oriented unions in the two federations. During those same years the CFTC and CGT broke with their "mother organizations" in France and set up autonomous counterparts, which, however, were confined to AEF. Close personal relations were reportedly maintained between David Soumah of the West African CFTC and Gilbert Pongault, but the latter formed a separate Confédération Africaine des Travailleurs Croyants de l'AEF (CATC) in January 1957. Three months later the CGT unions set up a Confédération Générale des Travailleurs de l'AEF (CGTA), after having refrained from sending delegates to the congress held at Cotonou in January 1957 at which the UGTAN was born. In their relations to world organizations of similar trends, both the CATC and CGTA have followed the pattern set in West Africa: the CATC voted to become an integral part of the Conseil des Organisations Syndicales de l'Union Française and the CGT to remain allied with the World Federation of Trade Unions.

Both the CGTA and the CATC have jealously asserted their new-found autonomy vis-à-vis the similarly oriented new French West African *centrales,* and the fear of domination by the latter federation appears to be as strongly felt by AEF labor as by its political leaders. In fact there are indications that the new AEF *centrales* would like to become poles of attraction for similar unions in Cameroun and the Belgian Congo. At all their recent congresses, they have invited delegates from those neighboring territories, and Pongault's founding of a Union Panafricaine des Travailleurs Croyants in January 1959 suggests that his aspirations have already moved beyond the boundaries of AEF. Only the FO has followed a somewhat different course. It did not yield to the autonomy trend until 1958, and in February of that year its Moyen-Congo unions sent delegates to attend the FO congress at Abidjan at which it was decided to form a Confédération Africaine des Syndicats Libres Force-Ouvrière. In this new organization each territorial branch was to remain autonomous, but that of AEF would be represented on an equal footing with those of Cameroun and French West Africa on its executive committee. None of the AEF *centrales,* it should be noted, accepted the invitation to attend the International Confederation of Free Trade Unions (ICFTU) congress held at Accra early in 1957.

The over-all shortage of workers, their uneven distribution geographically, and their lack of skills, assiduity, and organization are the basic problems facing the administration, legislative assemblies, and labor unions of AEF. These problems existed before World War II, but because of the then-undeveloped state of the federation's economy, they were acute only at certain times and for a few enterprises. With the application to AEF of the ten-year Plan and the rise of new industries there, the existing handicaps were more sharply felt and demanded remedial action more urgently. The public authorities, first French and then African, have tried to find solutions to these deficiencies through legislation protecting workers, strengthening the machinery for enforcing such laws, raising wages, and improving the skills of workers. This is at best a slow process, and more has been done in the practical than in the psychological domain, though for the first time experts have been called upon to analyze the causes and propose remedies for the AEF Africans' reluctance to engage in sustained labor for wages or even to grow food crops for sale.

Legislation for the protection of workers now seems fairly complete, but the means for enforcing it adequately are still insufficient. Urban laborers are better paid but less well protected by the law than are rural workers, who are in very short supply and prone to lapse without warning into their traditional milieu. The growth of towns, particularly since the war, has made available to urban employers a surplus of unemployed men, who can be hired on a daily basis and easily replaced if they leave or prove unsatisfactory. Wage-earners, though still poorly paid, are no longer badly recompensed, and indeed they are overpaid in relation to the quality of their output. As to European technicians and skilled workers, it has been calculated that they cost their employers about three times as much as in France, not only because of their higher pay but also because of the free transportation, expatriation bonuses, and other inducements offered them. In fact the pay of both African and European labor is a major cause of AEF's very high production costs.

More opportunities for training have been opened to unskilled workers, and they have been better oriented toward the needs of the current labor market. The demographic situation has been improved by the health service, so that the population everywhere, except perhaps in Gabon, is increasing in number and in stamina. However, little has been accomplished in regard to a better distribution of workers, aside from the importation of about a thousand laborers from Nigeria for the forest industry of Gabon. The wage-earning class in AEF is certainly small and seems hopelessly inadequate for the development of a country of such dimensions as those of the federation. This numerical shortage, however, would not be so acutely felt if the available laborers were more evenly distributed, less unstable, and better trained. The tapering off of FIDES work projects, coinciding with the trade depression of 1952, intensified urban unemployment, for despite the dwindling opportunities for gainful employment in the towns, the influx from rural areas continued. The instability and lack of skills characteristic of all AEF's urban laborers is evident in its most extreme form at Poto-Poto, the larger of Brazzaville's two African suburbs. Indeed, Moyen-Congo is the territory that best illustrates the fundamental dilemma of labor in AEF—towns overflowing with unemployed, unskilled, and parasitic youths who have resisted the government's efforts to make them return to their native villages and to contribute to rural production.

AEF workers themselves have shown little initiative about joining forces to improve their lot. In some places they have even resisted efforts to organize them, for they have not realized the power which their scarcity value could give them. Labor unions have had, and are still having, an uphill struggle in AEF, less because of employer resistance to their development than because the federation's laborers, except in a few towns, have not yet realized the value of self-organization and joint disciplined action. Their leadership is weak, and neither the French nor the African governments have done much to help them acquire training or experience. To date, almost all of the measures taken to improve working conditions have been initiated by the Metropolitan and local governments or by the territorial assemblies. This may continue to be the case for some years to come, for the unions have shown neither the inclination nor the ability to become a political force. Much more time will probably elapse before labor is numerically, organizationally, or psychologically able to influence the course of AEF's evolution.

Distribution of *bulletins de vote* to the electorate of Pointe Noire, Moyen-Congo.

Government-built housing for Africans, Pointe Noire.

PLATE 2

~MERCURIALES~		
POISSON FUME	Kg	60
CHICOUANGUE	PAIN	10
MANIOC FRAIS	Kg	5
FOUFOU	Kg	30
GARY	"	30
MAÏS EGRENE		20
ARACHIDE DECORTIQUEE		45
IGNAME		15
TAROT		10
PATATE DOUCE		10
HUILE DE PALME	Litre	50
RIZ LOCAL	Kg	40

...SSON SUR CHOIX	Hors tax
...SSON 1er CAPITAINE BECUNE ET	
...SSON DE PLUS DE 5 Kg	Kg 90
...SSON 2me CATEGORIE BAR PAGRE	
...RANGUE	Kg 80
...SSON 3me CATEGORIE RAIE	
...NGRE THON	Kg 60
...SSON 4me CATEGORIE BARBILLON	
...SSON SCIE FRITURE	Kg 50
...SSON 5me CATEGORIE	
...CHOIRON SELON REQUIN	Kg 40
...KOUALA	Kg 25

Board posting official controlled prices, market place of Pointe Noire.

Palais de Justice, Brazzaville.

Hotel Mayombé at Pointe Noire.

Market in the African quarter of Brazzaville (Poto-Poto).

PLATE 4

Abbé Fulbert Youlou, successively Mayor of Brazzaville
and Premier and President of the Congo Republic.

Nave of Ste. Anne-du-Congo Cathedral, Brazzaville.

PLATE 6

Diesel-engine train of the Congo-Ocean railroad; Brazzaville station.

Schoolroom in Diosso.

Chief of the village of Diosso, Moyen-Congo, wearing his cap of office.

Print shop (built in 1885 and still in use) of the Catholic mission, Loango, Moyen-Congo.

PLATE 8

Léon Mba, Mayor of Libreville and Premier of the Gabon Republic.

The *Fort-Archambault*—a river boat of the CGTA plying the Oubangui and Congo rivers between Bangui and Brazzaville—as seen from one of its attached barges forward.

New hospital under construction at Libreville.

PLATE 10

Approach to a village on the Oubangui river.

Mobile leprosy clinic at a small village north of Bangui, Oubangui-Chari.

Cotton-textile mill of ICOT at Boali, Oubangui-Chari.

Fishermen's huts on the bank of the Chari river at Fort-Lamy, Tchad.

PLATE 12

Ahmed Koulamallah, head of the Socialist party in Tchad.

The market place in Largeau, an oasis town in northern Tchad.

A government-sponsored center for training cattle to draw plows (in Casier A of the Logone project in Tchad).

PLATE 14

Arcade of the market place in Abéché, Tchad.

Village of the Massa tribe in western Tchad.

Typical structures in a village of western Tchad; l. to r., *grenier* used for millet storage, sleeping platform with millet-drying rack above, thatched *case* (hut), and another *grenier*.

PLATE 16

Construction of a *case* (hut), Bongor region, western Tchad.

Musician of the Massa tribe, near Bongor.

CHAPTER 18

Education

Until the mid-1930's, the government of AEF had neither an education policy nor a school system in the true sense, but only a few hundred public primary schools in which a handful of European instructors and poorly trained Africans dispensed some elementary knowledge to about 6,600 children. The main burden of formal education in the federation had been assumed in the early days by Christian missionaries, who opened the first schools in Gabon 14 years after the French occupation of that colony, and until World War II they maintained their lead over the state schools.

Despite its apathetic attitude toward formal instruction in AEF, the Metropolitan government laid down in the late nineteenth century a few fundamental principles to guide the development of schools there. Three of these principles are still valid in the area—namely, that education be given free of charge and exclusively in the French language, and that all classes be open to Europeans and Africans, boys and girls, on the same terms. Of these early principles, however, two others either have been discarded or not enforced as the result of attacks on them by French liberals or African politicians, or both. These were that only an elite potentially useful to the French administration or private commerce should receive instruction above the primary grades and that mass education must have a practical slant determined by the particular milieu from which the students derived. In the years since 1946, the government-general has co-operated with African aspirations to achieve widespread literacy, in so far as its resources in money and manpower have permitted; it has created a network of secondary schools whose equipment and academic standards are the equivalent of those in France; and through the granting of scholarships to higher institutions of learning in French West Africa and in Metropolitan France it has given AEF Africans their first opportunity to acquire state diplomas. In regard to two innovations introduced by official policy—adult education and the instruction of girls—the African elite are either indifferent or lukewarm, and in neither of these fields has the government been able to make much headway except in the southern cities.

At present the African attitude toward formal education is one of ingenuous enthusiasm, particularly in the towns, where the schools are besieged by far more children than can be admitted. The prestige of *l'homme instruit* and of what the French call the "feudality of the diploma" has become almost an obsession with AEF Africans, and their elected representatives, particularly in the southern territories, have voted funds for school-building and teachers' salaries out of all proportion to territorial revenues. Though the number of schools and of pupils attending them have grown phenomenally since World War II—in 1958 there were 197,032 children in primary schools compared with 21,895 in 1939—the pace is not fast enough to satisfy the local elite, especially in the realm of higher education. Here, perhaps inevitably, the Africans' attitude is somewhat contradictory. On the one hand, they want education at all levels to be the equivalent of that given in France, yet at the same time they are so eager to increase the number of African holders of certificates and degrees that they resent any restrictive or disciplinary measures that the government deems necessary in order to maintain high standards or to conform to existing facilities. When the authorities stand firm on such matters, old grievances come to the fore, and the native elite accuse the government of deliberately denying them an education in order to "keep Africans in a state of ignorance."

Before World War II

Until World War II, such accusations had some factual basis. Throughout the late nineteenth and early twentieth centuries the French government passively allowed the missionaries, both Catholic and Protestant, to pioneer and control such schools as they were willing to establish in AEF, and went no further than to aid them with occasional small subsidies and to issue a few general directives. A decree of April 9, 1883, stipulated that instruction must be carried on only in the French language (to which the school children must devote half their study time) and that it should be given a practical orientation. A regulation of December 24, 1901, led to the creation of a center for agricultural apprentices at Libreville and of an experimental botanical garden at Brazzaville, which two years later became the nucleus of the federation's professional school. The Clementel reforms of 1906 (see p. 15) again stressed the "primarily technical and vocational aspect" that was to keynote education in AEF, but vaguely left the choice of subject matter to be determined by the "needs of the natives." Another regulation, that of May 6, 1907, organized a normal school at Libreville to train African teachers, clerks for the administration, and employees for commercial firms, and it added, seemingly as an afterthought, that two of its most promising pupils might be sent for additional training to some appropriate school in southern France. On the eve of World War I, an education inspectorate for AEF was inaugurated, but it did not begin to function in even a limited way until the mid-1920's.

It was not until May 8, 1925, when the governor-general issued a circular, that any serious attempt was made, even on paper, to organize an educational system for AEF, and it did not go beyond that then in force in French West Africa. According to these instructions, the first three elementary classes were to be organized in villages, whereas the urban and regional schools were to offer the complete primary cycle of a six-year course, and African teachers were to be given a legal *statut*. The principles underlying this organization were much the same as those enunciated earlier, but now they were spelled out. The government's goal was to spread a knowledge of spoken French as rapidly as possible and to give primary pupils rudimentary manual training, but they were to be returned to their own milieu before they developed an antipathy to their agricultural and other traditional occupations. Better to train tens of thousands of artisans, ran the slogan of these times, than a dozen bachelors of arts. As for training beyond the elementary level, it was to be reserved for a few talented students and then only in direct relation to the number of jobs available. But the higher primary school opened at Brazzaville in 1927 soon closed its doors and was not reopened until 1935 as the Ecole Edouard Renard, named for the governor-general who had attempted during his brief incumbency to vitalize education in AEF. Antonetti, and even more, Reste—governors-general of the last interwar decade—were the men who accomplished a reorganization of the federation's so-called school system.

A circular penned by Antonetti forthrightly stated that the existing village schools had "shown themselves unable to teach almost anything" because they were in the hands of incompetent monitors; the urban and regional schools were too preoccupied with preparing students for the *certificat d'études primaires* (CEP) to undertake vocational training in the proper way; and the poor caliber of the "educated" Africans then working for the administration or private firms showed clearly the faults of the whole school system. One of these was the failure of the policy of concentrating educational activity in widely dispersed centers, and it was Governor-General Reste who decided that formal instruction must be brought to the rural populations by opening more village schools. Consequently these schools were regrouped and African graduates of the Ecole Edouard Renard were placed in charge of them, and to emphasize their vocational orientation Reste added farms and manual-training sections to them. As for the urban and regional schools, he gave their European directors the onerous task of touring their educational "constituencies" (called *secteurs scolaires*) to supervise and guide the African monitors teaching in the rural areas. Perhaps more revolutionary were moves extracting the state school system from the control of the Directorate of Political Affairs and transferring it to a genuine education inspectorate, and organizing a secondary-school course at Brazzaville in 1938 modeled after Metropolitan prototypes. Reste also arranged for the admission of AEF Africans to French West African secondary schools, but so few of them were sufficiently qualified that this innovation proved to be of little practical importance.[1]

From the standpoint of increasing primary educational facilities and of organizing them more effectively, the above-described measures marked an advance over any previously taken in AEF. Yet the reforms of the mid-1930's were regarded as reactionary by the African elite because they failed to promote secondary education in the federation and because they gave AEF primary schools a curriculum different from that prevailing in Metropolitan France. Even with these more extensive educational facilities, no more than 7,000 AEF children were receiving instruction in state schools on the eve of World War II. That the system was wholly inadequate to meet the local demand for education was shown by the zeal of some villagers in the two southern colonies who took the initiative in building schools and paying for monitors from their own resources. Governor-General Eboué, in a circular of November 8, 1941, scored official apathy in this matter and described the government's "putting to sleep of education" as one of the greatest dangers then facing AEF.[2]

During Eboué's incumbency, the number of state primary schools rose to 127 and pupil attendance in them to 13,225, and he established better cooperation between public and mission schools by granting the latter larger and more regular subsidies.[3] In the realm of education, as in other domains, Eboué's ideas were chiefly responsible for shaping the relevant resolutions adopted by the Brazzaville Conference of 1944. To be sure, among them were to be found such threadbare clichés as that education should penetrate the masses and bring out the elite, that instruction should be given only in the French language because the local vernaculars were too various and primitive to serve as vehicles for instruction, and that the Metropolitan primary-school curriculum should be adapted to local needs. Also retained was the liberal French principle of free education open to all regardless of race, creed, or sex, and added to it were several new ones that were to be revolutionary for AEF. For the first time, the goal officially set for the federation was universal compulsory primary education (a school was to be opened in every village where there were 50 children of school age), wherein the education of girls was to be stressed as much as that of boys. The new official goals also envisaged a network of secondary and technical schools in each territory, which in every respect would be the equal of similar establishments in Metropolitan France, and would provide liberal opportunities for higher study in France by qualified AEF Africans. It was the first and last of these objectives that aroused the enthusiasm of the local elite, whereas until considerably later they remained largely indifferent to those that pertained to women's education and technical training.

To implement the Brazzaville resolutions, FIDES under the first four-year Plan allocated a total of 1,216,600,000 CFA francs to AEF. Of this amount by far the largest share went to secondary education—965 million—while only about 175 million were allotted to primary schools and 89.5 million to technical institutions. These funds were to be used to construct and equip schools but not to pay their running expenses, which were to be borne by the local populations. In 1947, financial responsibility for primary schools was transferred to the territories, whose allocations for this purpose varied widely but were consistently largest in the southern territories and smallest in those of the north.

With the rapid postwar rise in the number of schools and the teaching staff, the amount of public money spent on education increased spectacularly. In 1939 AEF had allocated a mere 1.18 per cent of its funds to education. The government-general's share rose in 1946 to 4.23 per cent (82 million) and in 1952 to 5.4 per cent (1,495 million), and since 1955 it has averaged annually nearly 12 per cent of all the federation's expenditures. While the territories also have greatly increased such contributions, Moyen-Congo is far ahead of the others and Tchad is last. On the score of financing, the only complaints uttered by territorial assemblymen are in connection with the contributions they are asked to vote for the support of federal schools. They claim that such schools are federal in name only and are in reality institutions that draw their students almost wholly from Moyen-Congo, where all of them are situated. One inevitable consequence of the vastly increased allocations for state schools by the federation, as well as by Metropolitan France, was that for the first time in AEF's history, public schools after World War II came to outdistance the mission schools in every respect.

Mission Education

The first schools in French central Africa were founded at Libreville by the priests of St. Esprit and the Sisters of St. Joseph de Cluny in 1863, and for 20 years thereafter mission schools were the only ones that existed there. In 1850 some American Presbyterian missionaries opened a few schools at Libreville, but they were not regarded by the French naval commandants in charge of Gabon with the same favor as were those of the Catholics, and the Americans soon ceded their place to the Paris Société des Missions Evangéliques. In the late nineteenth century, that Protestant organization spread into lower Gabon and Moyen-Congo, where it left among certain tribes an imprint that was at least as strong as that made by the more numerous Catholics. Neither mission group attempted seriously to install itself in the northern territories until well into the twentieth century.

For many years the French authorities gladly left the task of educating AEF Africans to the missionaries, only requiring them to teach in the French language and be legally incorporated as French organizations. A gubernatorial circular of February 1921 somewhat tightened official controls over them by emphasizing that the "administration would enter into relations with no body whose constitution did not offer a guarantee of the absolute preponderance of French influence in a French country."[4] This provision, however, seems not to have been strictly applied, for in practice both the Catholic and Protestant mission schools not only were financially aided by the government but were permitted to give religious instruction in the vernacular languages. A regulation of May 8, 1925, required mission schools to follow the same curriculum as state schools if they wanted to qualify for official recognition and further subsidies. In terms of the number of schools and pupils attending them, the missions were far ahead of state schools, and in 1929 they were giving instruction to 12,605 students in more than 100 primary schools. Relations between the church and state in AEF were never embittered by the promulgation in AEF of the Metropolitan anticlerical laws. Governor-General Eboué, although a freethinker, recognized the missionaries' great usefulness to AEF in the educational field and cooperated with them fully during his incumbency.

After World War II, mission schools continued to grow both in number and in pupil attendance. They were quickly surpassed in both respects, however, by the state schools, whose curricula and organization the missionaries were bound to follow in order to continue receiving official subsidies, and whose teacher-training programs and pay scales they strove to emulate so as to retain their African staff.

In the first postwar years the Catholics opened normal schools in Brazzaville, Bangui, and Lambaréné, and the Protestants founded similar establishments at Ngouedi and also at Lambaréné.[5] Only the Collège Chaminade of the Marist fathers at Brazzaville gave courses that enabled its graduates to attain the rank of instructor, and the great majority of Africans trained in mission normal schools became monitors. Both Catholic and Protestant missions concentrated on primary education and stressed manual training and the instruction of girls. Equal representation was granted to Catholics and Protestants on the federation's educational advisory boards, and both were consulted in regard to official policies in the education field. In 1950, FIDES, after three years of hestitation, decided to pay thenceforth half the cost of building mission schools, Protestant as well as Catholic, provided they did not duplicate state schools and that the missions assumed full responsibility for their operating expenses. The academic standards maintained by the mission institutions were equally high, and if the Protestant schools were not so numerous as those of the Catholics their influence in the south was at least as great. The fact that Catholic schools received larger subsidies from public funds than did the Protestant institutions was due simply to the fact that the latter taught fewer pupils. As of 1949, the Catholic and Protestant mission primary schools had 25,542 students (almost all in Moyen-Congo and Gabon), their secondary schools 144, and their technical-training establishments 132. Of the total student body attending mission schools only 2,692 were in the Protestant schools of Gabon and 3,566 in those of Moyen-Congo.[6]

When the responsibility for operating primary schools was turned over to the territories in 1947, the matter of subsidizing mission institutions became a subject of debate at each budgetary session of the assemblies. Pleas to increase such subsidies were regularly made by missionaries who were members of AEF's elected bodies and by the African assemblymen who had been educated in the mission schools. Occasionally a European or an African assemblyman would speak out against giving subsidies to any of the missions or want equal sums given to Islamic institutions, either because he was anticlerical by conviction or because he feared that the missionaries might attain in AEF the dominant role that they played in the Belgian

Congo.[7] Generally speaking, however, the principle of allocating public funds for the support of mission schools was never seriously questioned in AEF. Debates on this subject usually centered on just how much the federation and territories could afford to allocate to the missions, and whether or not they could specify the use to which such grants would be put by the missionaries. The federation's elected representatives were usually opposed to granting money for mission secondary education[8] and in favor of raising the salaries of African mission teachers. Until passage of the Lamine-Gueye law of June 1950 the salaries of state and mission teachers, though low, had been roughly comparable. Thereafter the pay and privileges of the public-school teachers increased so greatly above those of their mission colleagues that the latter became the object of special solicitude even on the part of African assemblymen who did not look favorably upon the missions. In 1947 the Grand Council urged the territories to do what they could to raise the level of African mission teachers' pay.

On the whole, relations between the French administration and the missions in the education field have been cooperative, and to a greater extent than in French West Africa. However, the degree of cordiality between officials and missionaries, particularly in the rural areas, has been determined by individual personalities and not by ideologies. The Africans have almost invariably welcomed mission schools and wanted no transfer to AEF of the Metropolitan controversy regarding lay and clerical education. The Gabonese Grand Councilor, Evouna, seems to have summed up the attitude of most of his compatriots when he said to his colleagues on May 8, 1949: "At present our major preoccupation is education, and whether it comes from the state or mission schools matters little to us. The essential is that our education be French, essentially and exclusively French, and that it be controlled by the state."

Attendance at mission schools is growing in all four of AEF's former territories,[9] and probably mission influence will increase, particularly in the two southern republics, many of whose present leaders are former students of mission schools. Nevertheless, there are variations in the degree of favor shown the missions in the four territories, which have been reflected in the percentages of public funds allocated to mission schools.[10]

Because Gabon has been longest the scene of mission activity and contains proportionately the largest number of Christian converts, its territorial assembly has consistently and almost unanimously voted the largest percentages of its education budget to mission schools. Despite budgetary stringency in 1952, it spent 3 million CFA francs to close the gap between the salaries paid to mission and to state teachers.[11] When a program for expanding educational facilities in Gabon was drawn up in 1955 by the territorial advisory committee, a larger role was assigned to mission than to state schools. During the next four years it was planned to increase Catholic schools by 25, Protestant schools by 9, and state schools by 26.[12] At the time this policy was adopted, there were 16,000 children attending the 101 Catholic and 31 Protestant primary schools compared with 15,200 in smiliar state institutions, and 200 Africans were being trained in the Catholic Collège Bessieux and in the Protestant secondary school at Lambaréné.

Tchad represented the other end of the scale in missionary penetration and influence. Neither Catholics nor Protestants tried to establish themselves firmly in the northern territories until after World War II, and in Tchad only the Catholics have made any real headway. Here the predominant Muslim population was in general suspicious of any but Koranic schools and in particular feared those run by Christian missionaries. To some extent this distrust has been dispelled, for, as one Muslim assemblyman told his colleagues on September 24, 1957, "Tchadian parents now realize that if their children attend a mission school they will not necessarily be converted to Christianity." The number of children in Tchad's mission primary schools rose from a mere 150 in 1949 to nearly 4,000 by 1957, and each year since 1952 the territorial assembly has voted some 12 million francs for the support of such schools.

In their attitude toward mission education, Oubangui's territorial assemblymen occupy a place about midway between those of Gabon and Tchad, though since the MESAN government came to power in 1957, subsidies to mission schools have been substantially increased. In the first postwar years, the assembly was inclined to support financially only the schools run by the Bangui vicariate and to ignore those of the Catholic mission at Berbérati and the Swedish Protestants because of the "poor quality" of the education they dispensed.[13] Some of Oubangui's assemblymen, such as Condomat, were disinclined to allocate territorial funds to any mission schools,[14] but a subsidy was regularly voted. After the former priest, Boganda, became active in Oubanguian politics, these allocations were greatly increased and, with them, attendance at mission schools. In 1949 only 3,000 children were in mission primary schools compared with 8,000 in state schools, but by 1958 the missions were instructing 22,000 students, or nearly half of the total primary-school attendance in the territory.[15] Though the territorial subsidy in the latter year had risen to 63.5 million CFA francs, the Catholic mission was then in such financial difficulties that it had to offer its African teaching staff the choice of resigning or accepting big salary cuts. This the African teachers refused to do and on October 31 they went on strike, insisting that the government not only restore their previous salaries but put them on its own payroll. The then Minister of Education, who had already been accused of being hostile to missionary schools,[16] held out against giving mission teachers the status of functionaries. Public opinion in Oubangui became so stirred by the controversy, however, that he had to raise the mission subsidy to 85 million CFA francs in the 1959 budget. Currently the Central African Republic is paying 80 per cent of the cost of operating its mission schools.

In Moyen-Congo, the question of subsidies to mission schools has been complicated by the Balali's identification of the Catholic missions with the French administration and by the influence of Protestantism on the

formation of the religio-political sects (see pp. 306 ff.). In their zeal to increase rapidly the literacy rate of the territory, the Congolese politicians
have given substantial and increasing subsidies to mission schools. But
they have allocated five times as much to state as to mission education, and
have insisted that the territorial contributions go toward increasing the pay
of African teachers and not be handed over to the missions as a lump sum
to be used at their discretion.[17] More than in Oubangui, the issue of mission
subsidies became a political one, and pressure was exerted on objecting
assemblymen through a press campaign and organized lobbying on the
part of African mission teachers. (At the 1954 budgetary session, the five
assemblymen who refused to vote an increase in the mission subsidy were
Akouala, Bazinga, Istre, Menga, and Tchitchellé.) Thanks to the conciliatory efforts of Governor Rouys and the territorial advisory assembly
during 1955, the subsidy issue was peaceably resolved and coordination
between the mission and state school programs was assured. But in April
1958 the African mission teachers threatened the Youlou government with
a strike if their demands for increased pay were not met. As the missions
come increasingly under African control, it will be ever harder for the
governments of AEF's new republics to stretch their limited budgetary resources to the point where they can meet the demands that will surely be
more insistently made for complete equality of treatment as between state
and mission schools.

The Education Services

It was not until Governor-General Reste reorganized the school system
in AEF that an education service for the federation, in the proper sense
of the term, was born. World War II intervened before this service could
begin to function effectively, for after 1940 it was impossible to recruit personnel in France. As a stop-gap, Eboué appointed some of the European
instructors then teaching in AEF to act as territorial inspectors of education, and in 1944 he set up education advisory boards at both the federal and
territorial levels. The latter included officials of the education services, administrators, teachers, representatives of the parents of school children and,
after 1946, members of the representative assemblies. Though these com-
mitttees were sometimes criticized as being overweighted with officials, they
survived the war and subsequently rendered important services, especially
in the formulation of official policy and the distribution of scholarships.
    Eboué's other innovation—that of appointing European instructors as
temporary territorial inspectors—proved to be less fortunate, notably in
Oubangui. After the war, difficulties arose there between the acting territorial inspector and the titular head of the service sent out from France
to replace him. Despite the territorial assembly's request for the dismissal
of the acting inspector, he was upheld by the local administration, allegedly
because he had "powerful political friends."[18] The result was the precipitate
departure of three newly arrived professors from France and a rift between

the assembly and Oubangui's education service that has never subsequently been bridged over.[19]

In the light of such misunderstandings and conflicts, Boganda's sharp attack on the territorial education service in December 1956[20] can be better understood. After he had echoed complaints made by the Association of Oubanguian Students in France, Boganda held the local education service responsible for the poor quality of instruction dispensed in Oubangui and asked for a "profound reform" of the territorial inspectorate. Again the result was an exodus of many of the Metropolitan teachers then serving in Oubangui, who asked either to be sent back to France or to be assigned to another overseas territory.[21]

Elsewhere than in Oubangui the limits of authority were gradually better and more harmoniously defined, and the General Inspector of Education for AEF was given a larger and more competent staff. He was made directly responsible for the three federal schools, all located in Moyen-Congo, and for the four territorial services. He also advised the governor-general on all questions affecting state and mission schools, and each year held a conference with the heads of territorial services, in which the adaptation of Metropolitan education regulations to AEF was discussed along with other more strictly local matters. In performing his duties the General Inspector was aided by two inspectors—one for primary and the other for secondary and technical schools. At the territorial level, the heads of the education services were charged with many of the same functions as the General Inspector. Theoretically these officials were *inspecteurs d'académie* but there have never been more than two of such rank at the same time in AEF.

In all of AEF's assemblies, debates have been periodically marred by clashes between their African members and the territorial inspectors. Some of the latter have been charged with "deliberately sabotaging" the Africans' efforts to acquire a formal education, while others have been reproached with their failure to effect a badly needed reorganization of their service. Though the general hierarchy of inspectorates was reorganized in December 1953, the whole system still rested on the *secteurs scolaires* set up by Governor-General Reste in 1937. *Secteurs scolaires* had also been organized in French West Africa and were soon abandoned there. In AEF, however, the lack of qualified staff in its education service prevented that federation from similarly suppressing such a makeshift device, though it had given rise to legitimate criticism long before the territorial assemblies came into being. The fundamental weakness of the *secteurs scolaires* system was that it diverted European instructors from their main task of teaching, and also placed on them the heavy burden of supervising and improving the work of poorly trained African monitors who functioned in village schools dispersed over hundreds of kilometers. More often than not, the head of the *secteur scolaire* lacked adequate means of transportation and so could not visit regularly and frequently the schools for which he was responsible. African assemblymen complained often of this lack of supervision and guidance of village schoolmasters, claiming that monitors left to their own devices were not only incompetent teachers but prone to indulge in irrelevant political activity.[22] In one instance, at least, a European *chef de secteur scolaire* was charged with having abused his authority to the point of slapping an African monitor in front of his class.[23] The government, while admitting the faults of the system, claimed that its retention was a necessary evil until more qualified personnel could be recruited. With the arrival of additional staff from France, the inspectorate became a specialized branch of the education service and European instructors and professors were able to concentrate more and more on their teaching duties.

Teachers

The problems arising from the *secteur scolaire* system underscored the long-recognized need for training more and better African teachers, if there was to be any qualitative as well as quantitative improvement of the education in AEF. Before World War II, there were only some 50 European instructors in the federation, and they were largely preoccupied with administrative duties. Of the 402 Africans teaching in the public primary schools, only 161 held even the rank of monitor. At best the African teacher was the holder of a *certificat d'études primaires* who had received a year's pedagogical training, and at worst he was a totally illiterate agent of the agricultural service.[24] Not only did these teachers lack proper training and supervision, but in some areas they had also to act as interpreters, accountants, and postmasters for the local administration.

The major education goals set by the Brazzaville Conference of 1944 were the replacement of all monitors by instructors and the recruiting of qualified Europeans both to train African teachers and to staff the federation's secondary schools that were to be built for the first time in AEF. During the late 1940's, realization of these objectives was retarded not so much by the lack of funds as by the inability of the federal authorities to induce properly qualified European teachers to come to AEF. From 1946 to 1949, three General Inspectors in succession went to France for the express purpose of recruiting such personnel. Not only were they totally unsuccessful—allegedly because of the "bad reputation" under which AEF labored in Metropolitan France—but also they themselves failed to return to their posts.[25] Of the 73 teaching posts envisaged under the ten-year Plan, only 22 had been filled by 1949, and some of those who had recently arrived in the federation became discouraged by the conditions prevailing there and promptly returned to France.

The Grand Councilors, who regularly bewailed the inadequacies of AEF's education services, proclaimed themselves willing to vote any amount of money within the federation's means to remedy the teacher shortage. So 80 Metropolitan instructors and professors accepted the call, and by the end of 1950 the size of the European staff in AEF's education services had grown to 151. Their number continued to increase during the next three years until they totaled 219 in the federation's public schools (in addition to 179 in the mission schools). The arrival of reinforcements in such quantity enabled the new secondary and technical schools built with FIDES funds to acquire faculties whose academic qualifications closely approximated those in equivalent Metropolitan institutions.

The next and longer task was that of training more African teachers, first for the subaltern posts, which multiplied rapidly with the expansion of the primary-school system, and later to replace the European staff. In respect to numbers, AEF has never experienced the same trouble as has French West Africa in getting enough local Africans to enter and remain in the teaching profession. In fact, so many primary-school monitors were being trained in Gabon and Moyen-Congo that the former territory was threatened with "having more teachers than students,"[26] and the latter was trying to find posts for its trainees in other territories. Only in Tchad was there a numerical shortage of primary-school staff, not simply because of inadequate normal-school facilities but also because the northern tribes were opposed to having their children instructed by southerners, the only ones qualified for teaching posts in that territory.[27] During the first postwar years, Tchad had to rely on the Bambari normal school in Oubangui for training its teachers. Then a normal class was formed at Fort Archambault and in 1955 the *collège* at Bongor was transformed into a normal school, but together these institutions were able to train no more than 30 to 40 monitors a year.[28] As of 1957, Tchad had only 319 Africans teaching in its primary schools (of whom 29 were instructors), while Gabon, with only a fifth of Tchad's population, had more than 300 African public-school teachers (of whom 20 were instructors) and almost the same number in its mission schools.[29]

Aside from Tchad, where an exceptional situation existed, there was no shortage of teacher candidates, for that profession was highly honored among AEF Africans and the issues of rank and salary were early settled in favor of African public-school teachers. Although a few of them left the teaching ranks during the first three postwar years because they did not receive even "a bare living wage,"[30] their status was greatly improved by the establishment of a single cadre for European and African teachers in July 1949.[31] As of October 1, 1950, there were 852 Africans teaching in AEF, but by 1953 their number had risen to 2,238, of whom 1,225 were in state and 1,113 in mission schools.[32] The overwhelming majority of these teachers were ranked as monitors, and the slow rate at which African instructors were being trained (as well as the small number of bachelors of arts) evoked chronic complaint on the part of the African elected representatives.

Aside from the scarcity of candidates educationally qualified to enter the normal schools, there were two lesser obstacles to speeding up the training of Africans above the rank of monitor. One was the reluctance of the assemblymen of the three northern territories to share on an equal basis the financing of the federal teacher-training school at Mouyondzi, the great majority of whose students came from Moyen-Congo. The second obstacle arose from a misunderstanding, widespread among the African elite, as to the diploma granted by the Mouyondzi normal school. They had expected that its graduates would receive the *certificat d'aptitude professionnelle* (CAP) and be entitled to the rank of instructor, but after a four-year course they earned only a *certificat d'aptitude pédagogique élémentaire* (CAPE), which brought with it only the grade of assistant instructor. The dissatisfaction of assemblymen and of students and their parents became so pronounced that in 1955 the Mouyondzi school was transformed into a normal school for girls (at which the same story was repeated), and a new interterritorial normal college for men was founded at Brazzaville. This institution was a replica of Metropolitan normal colleges and awarded the coveted CAP. Candidates for admission were required to have the first part of the baccalaureate degree, and as of 1958 there were 25 Africans studying in this college. By that time there were, in all, 24 teacher-training establishments scattered throughout AEF, about equally divided between state and mission management, and they were attended by a total of 1,623 African students.[33]

Primary Education

Except in Tchad, the growth in teacher personnel has generally kept pace with the rapid increase in the number of primary schools functioning throughout the federation, but this would not be the case if the school attendance of girls were equal to that of boys. Education for girls, pioneered by the missions and pushed by the administration since the war, is only now beginning to interest the African elite in the southern territories. On the other hand, mass literacy for boys has long been the goal of AEF's African assemblymen, and to achieve it they have steadily increased their budgetary allowances. The extent to which educational facilities have been subsidized varies with the territory's resources and their assemblymen's enthusiasm, but everywhere the amount of public money and the proportion granted to schools have grown phenomenally since the war. The assemblies of Gabon and Moyen-Congo have so rapidly increased their budgetary allocations for primary education that within five or six years they can reasonably anticipate 100 per cent literacy for their youthful male populations. Oubangui, too, has regularly increased its education appropriations, but proportionately to its total expenditures these now amount to only half of what Moyen-Congo allocates, and Tchad's percentage is only slightly more than half of Oubangui's. To be sure, the north has bigger and more dispersed populations than the south and it has never received the same attention from mission schools. Moreover, in certain areas of Tchad, the Muslims' attitude toward lay education has handicapped the growth of primary schools, particularly in the case of girls' schooling.

At a conference of overseas teachers held at Paris in 1952, Tchad was declared to have the least-developed primary school system of any of the French Union territories. At that time it could count only 66 primary schools, attended by 8,767 pupils (although the school-age population numbered some 330,000), 95 holders of a primary-education certificate and six

Tchadians studying in Metropolitan secondary schools, and it was spending only 1.3 per cent of its budget on education.[34] Yet even these meager achievements represented a considerable advance over previous years. Because of the long military administration of the colony, the first school in Tchad was not created until 1920 and ten years later the colony still had no more than ten schools, attended by 425 pupils. In 1950, however, 4,000 Tchadian boys and 467 girls were receiving elementary instruction, and primary schools were being built at the rate of 50 a year. Not only had FIDES granted Tchad proportionately less than any other AEF territory for its primary-school building program in a country where construction costs were the highest of any in the federation, but the maintenance of such schools (220,000 francs per year per school) was a heavy burden on Tchad's budget. In southern Tchad, the biggest drawback to the extension of primary education was the shortage of funds and of teachers, but in the north it was the lack of students.

Among the northern and eastern Islamized tribes, Koranic schools taught by faqis (teachers of Arabic and religious learning) were fairly widespread. Ignorant and untrained as were the great majority of these faqis, they gave the only kind of instruction that was generally acceptable there to the parents of school-age children. Even after the advantages of a French education had become more widely recognized, the Muslim populations preferred to have their sons tend herds and their daughters help with household tasks rather than attend lay schools, particularly as the teachers in such schools were the descendants of their erstwhile Negro slaves. In Tchad as a whole, while school attendance was increasing at the rate of about 2,000 a year and congestion in the classrooms of the southern towns was becoming an urgent problem, attendance was stationary or in retrogression in the north and east. In the northern areas, only one child out of a hundred was attending primary schools, and in Ouaddaï, schools that were opened in 1956 at Allacha and Molou, with an attendance of about 20 pupils each, had to be closed within four months as a result of the disappearance of their total student body.[35] Throughout the whole of Tchad fewer than 1,200 girls were in primary schools.

Session after session of the territorial assembly was devoted to discussing ways of remedying Tchad's educational deficiencies. Money was the key to the south's shortage of teachers and school buildings, but elsewhere the problem was more complicated, for it involved the need to "educate" parents as well as children. The program finally drawn up in 1957 by the Lisette government included applying the pressure of example to Muslim parents by persuading the local chiefs to send their children to school, providing free lunches and some boarding facilities in widely dispersed rural schools, organizing separate classes for girls wherever possible,[36] and, above all, training bilingual teachers at Bongor. Experiments in teaching concurrently in French and Arabic, undertaken in Ouaddaï in 1958, were reportedly successful, and will be extended to other Muslim areas when feasible. Actually Tchad, in its present stage of development, is not able to finance or staff primary schools for all of its children. It has been calculated that to attain this aim would cost nearly 1,500 million a year, thus absorbing about three-fourths of the territory's present budget.[37] In the 1958–59 academic year, Tchad spent about 6 per cent of its revenues on education, and 8.4 per cent (32,609) of the territory's school-age children (then numbering 386,427) were in school. Of these, about one-sixth attended mission institutions.[38]

Proportionately to the number of its inhabitants, Oubangui has made greater strides in education than Tchad, partly because it has no large bloc of Muslims recalcitrant to lay schools and because its population is less dispersed. Moreover, mission schools have played a larger and rapidly increasing role in supplementing state education, the territory's normal schools have turned out more African teachers,[39] and it has devoted a bigger percentage of its revenues to enlarging its educational facilities. Oubangui's particular handicap has been a running battle between its African assemblymen and its education service, which has led to the resignation of some of the territory's few European teachers (totaling about 50) and has harmed the *esprit de corps* of those who have remained. This has affected Oubangui's secondary more than its primary schools, but public education in all spheres received a setback that in part explains the upward surge of mission education in the territory within the past few years. Oubangui's expenditures on education rose during the 1950's from 10 to 12 per cent of its resources, and the number of children attending primary schools increased from about 11,000 in 1949 to nearly 39,000 in 1957,[40] of whom almost 4,000 were girls.

Though the school-age population attending schools had risen in that period from 10 to 24.5 per cent, Oubangui's assemblymen were not satisfied by such progress, and to emphasize this they voted a symbolic cut of 1 franc in the education appropriations for 1958. Apparently this impelled the MESAN government to draw up a four-year plan, by which girls' schooling was to be pushed[41] and the school attendance rate for the whole territory was to be raised to 40 per cent by 1962. A problem that has greatly plagued Oubangui's education service has been the absenteeism of school children in the rural areas. They reportedly refuse to attend school during the rainy season (July–August) and during the dry weather leave their classes to hunt or fish or to aid their parents in picking cotton. Some of them simply played hooky, but others left school at the urging of their parents or with their consent.[42]

In one field related to that of primary education, a remote village, 320 kilometers north of Bangui, was chosen as the scene for an experiment in *éducation de base* modeled on the experience gained in French West Africa. In June 1952 a team of African doctors, midwives, and agricultural and education monitors, headed by a European expert, spent four months at Boykota, among an animist tribe that was virtually untouched by contacts with the outside world.[43] Their aim was to raise the tribe's living standards by improving their agriculture, hygiene, and housing, and secondarily to combat illiteracy. Later a similar experiment was undertaken in Tchad, but neither was an outstanding success and apparently such experiments have not been repeated elsewhere. Though these two ventures were not financed by AEF, its African elite have tended to consider them a waste of time and of money which they would prefer to see spent on the regular school system.[44] Though the literacy classes for adults started in a few Oubanguian towns were not much more successful, the territorial assemblymen were more sympathetic to such efforts. In 1948 both lay and mission teachers initiated evening classes in which illiterate adults might acquire some rudimentary knowledge, but attendance fell off so rapidly that they were soon abandoned.[45] Nevertheless, the Oubangui assembly voted funds the next year for such efforts to be pursued at Damara.

In Moyen-Congo, the territory's perseverance in the field of classes for adult illiterates was better rewarded after a start as discouraging as that in Oubangui. Begun in 1948, they had to be closed within 12 months for lack of attendance, though courses for functionaries and clerks eager to improve their professional skills acquired a growing following. Revived a few years later, the adult illiterates' classes became popular in the towns, and by 1956 they were attended by some 3,500 auditors.[46] In this as well as in all but one field of primary education—that of girls—Moyen-Congo has been in the vanguard of AEF territories. The Congolese are very proud of their high literacy rate, and now 75 per cent of the school-age population throughout the territory (86,500 children) attend primary schools compared with 37 per cent (30,717) in 1949.[47] Its assembly raised the allocations for education from 19 per cent of total expenditures in the latter year to 25 per cent by 1954, and now it has plans for achieving a 100 per cent record within five years. Because of the concentration of mission and state normal schools in Moyen-Congo (at Brazzaville, Dolisie, Mouyondzi, and Fort Rousset), there has never been any dearth of African monitors, who, moreover, in recent years have been offered refresher courses and opportunities for promotion. As of 1959, 560 Congolese were engaged in studies that, if successfully completed, would give them the rank of instructor.

Although Moyen-Congo stands at the head of all French Black African territories in regard to primary education, it still has two main weaknesses to overcome. One is the uneven distribution of school attendance and the other is the relatively undeveloped state of girls' education. School attendance is highest in the Pool region, where the Balali early accepted education as a major goal for their children and where the *lettré* enjoys tremendous prestige.[48] In fact, it was to check the Balali's monopoly of the school benches (and consequently of posts in the administration) that the local government introduced a quota system in 1934 so as to open a bigger place to students from other tribes.[49] In the Pointe Noire area, the rate of school attendance is almost as high, but it is weak in the north, especially in the Likouala-Mossaka and Sangha regions. In women's education, Moyen-Congo is far ahead of the northern territories, but as yet only about 28 per cent of the students attending primary schools are girls. It was in large part to remedy this weakness that a territorial plan was drawn up in 1954. The graduation of the first Congolese women instructors from the Mouyondzi normal school in 1959 should soon improve the percentage of girls attending primary schools. Generally speaking, however, Moyen-Congo is not short of teachers or of school buildings. Rather, its chief remaining problem in regard to primary education as a whole is that of finding enough money to maintain and enlarge the existing system.

Gabon's record in the field of primary education approximates that of Moyen-Congo, and in respect to girls' education it is even more advanced,[50] even though it has been spending less (20 per cent) of its revenues on schooling than has Moyen-Congo (25 per cent). Like Moyen-Congo, Gabon had the advantage of being the site of the first mission schools, and its urban population is just as eager for a French education as are the Congolese. In the rural areas, Gabon faces the same problem as do all the territories in regard to absenteeism among children of school age and wide regional variations in school attendance. As of 1955, in the coastal zone of Moyen-Ogooué, Ogooué-Maritime, and the estuary, as well as in Woleu-N'Tem, the percentage of school-age children going to school ranged between 60 and 82 per cent, whereas the lowest rates were found in the N'Gounié and Ogooué-Lolo (23–28 per cent) and there classrooms were also overcrowded (45 to 58 students per class).[51] Mainly with a view to remedying this situation, a territorial plan was drawn up that year, in which the announced goal was compulsory primary education for all children living within a radius of five to six kilometers of a school. In 1959, when the school-attendance rate for the whole of Gabon had reached 75 per cent, education was made obligatory for all Gabonese children between the ages of 6 and 16, and it was expected that by 1965 attendance would be 100 per cent.[52]

In over-all policy, the postwar French governments have cooperated with the Africans' drive toward mass literacy, with certain modifications, restrictions, and compromises. In the realm of concessions to African wishes, the AEF education authorities have aligned the primary-school curriculum on the Metropolitan model more closely than in prewar days and have reduced their stress on manual training. Inevitably more time is given in AEF schools than in France to the study of French and to instruction in hygiene, and local materials and examples are used to illustrate the study of history and geography. Such deviations from the Metropolitan curriculum are acceptable to Africans so long as the certificates awarded primary-school graduates are recognized as equivalent to those for similar studies in France. Where the difficulty has come is in the government's policy, initiated in 1952, of ceasing to construct new primary schools except in Tchad and parts of Oubangui, and of curbing the "anarchic growth of the student body."[53]

This policy was inspired partly by the education service's conviction that the cost of maintaining the multitude of new schools and the difficulty in staffing them had already outrun AEF's resources. In part, it was prompted by the marked falling off in pupil attendance after completion of the first half of the primary cycle, not only because parents withdrew their children to help with family tasks but also because many village schools offered only three years of the full six-year course. Many of the children who had to leave school at that stage became frustrated semi-literates. Moreover, the fact that so few pupils completed the full primary cycle meant that there were relatively few students qualified to enter the higher school grades.

The curtailment of school building, as well as the enlargement of ex-isting schools, seemed reasonable enough to most African assemblymen, but they balked when the governor-general issued a regulation on November 23, 1953, restricting the primary-school population to specified age groups. On the ground that education in AEF's limited school facilities should be reserved to the most promising youthful segment of the population, Chauvet placed the age limit of nine years on candidates seeking admission to primary schools. Such a weeding-out of "over-age children and of those who fruitlessly repeat classes" aroused the indignation of the African elite. They claimed that this policy was both impolitic and short-sighted in a country so desperately in need of educated men, and that it was also unfair because an *état civil* (registry of vital statistics) was almost nonexistent except in the towns. They also warned the government that a "massive rejection of education-hungry children" might well lead to an increase in the federation's juvenile delinquency.[54] Nor were they mollified by the government's compromise proposal to set up more manual- and vocational-training facilities for children who had reached the prescribed age limit. Indeed, they went so far as to urge the government to make primary education compulsory in AEF on the same terms as in France. Because they recognized that this was then impossible for practical reasons, they accepted a stop-gap proposal to the effect that primary education would be made obligatory only in the areas where there were enough schools and teachers to permit the realistic application of such a law.

On the matter of education for girls, the French government was only one jump ahead of African opinion during the first postwar decade. Before 1939, such concern as officialdom had shown in the field of primary education was for the elementary instruction of boys, and it had left that of girls almost wholly to the missionaries. As of 1939, a total of 3,699 girls in all AEF were attending primary schools, and the great majority of these were being taught in mission establishments. Some progress was made during the war, but how little can be deduced from a speech made by Acting Governor-General Soucadaux to the Grand Council on November 24, 1947. In it he stressed that the number of girls attending state primary schools had increased during the preceding year from 2,900 to 3,000. However, the fact that he thought such a meager advance worth citing showed a change of heart on the part of the French authorities. They had come to realize that to promote an elite composed wholly of talented boys was to create a dangerous imbalance in the African family. Not only was an *évolué* compelled to take an illiterate wife, *faute de mieux,* but her ignorance was being ominously reflected in the indiscipline and cultural backwardness of her offspring.

When it came to making amends for past neglect in this field, the French showed themselves less concerned in raising the African girl's general culture than in training her for her future role as wife and mother. The attendance of girls in the public primary schools was encouraged, but as of 1953 only 18,349 all told in AEF were receiving such instruction.[55] For the few who completed the primary cycle there were three courses in professional training open to them—of which two were in the teaching and one in the nursing field.

Under the ten-year Plan, home-economics courses were to be organized by Frenchwomen in each territorial capital, and they were to be opened to young girls qualified to become teachers of similar courses and also to older women interested in acquiring some skill in cooking, sewing, and child care. In such classes as were visited by the authors in 1956 and 1958, the instruction given was of an informal and practical type. Obviously training in home economics is direly needed in AEF, but at present it is on too small a scale to be effective. Here, as in other phases of the problem of girls' education, the key to progress lies in training more African women teachers, of whom there are still only a handful. Almost none of them has a rank higher than that of monitor, and most of them are employed in the schools where their husbands also teach.

After World War II, some classes for training women teachers of primary grades were opened in the federation, but it was not until 1955 that a normal college was created for them at Mouyondzi, in the locale that had served until then as a similar institution for young men. Though 30 pupils attended its first classes, this venture soon proved as ill-fated as its predecessor, and for almost identical reasons (see pp. 288–89). To get the credits required to complete even its first four-year course, the government had to promise the Grand Council that territorial normal colleges would be built as soon as possible, after completion of which Mouyondzi would revert to being a Moyen-Congo institution.[56] In April 1959, Premier Youlou closed the Mouyondzi school and established at Brazzaville a normal institution for girls which would grant its graduates the CAP that entitled them to the rank of instructors.

No satisfactory formula has yet been found for the education of AEF girls. The African elite are gradually evincing more interest in this problem, at least at the primary level. But the average African in the federation shows as yet little interest in the education of his daughters, and if they go to school at all he is likely to withdraw them at an early age so as to obtain their bride price.

Secondary and Higher Education

If the official attempts during the early postwar years to promote the education of girls and of illiterate adults generally failed to arouse African enthusiasm, quite the reverse was true of the new opportunities for higher education opened widely to the populations of the overseas territories after World War II. The AEF Africans saw in the establishing of local secondary schools, and particularly in the scholarships offered qualified students to study in French universities, their first chance to acquire the diplomas and degrees that would make them professionally the equal of Europeans. In this sphere, as in that of primary education, the goals set by the government and the African elite were much the same, but disagreements arose in regard to the methods used and the timing set by the French authorities for their achievement. Because there had been no secondary schools, let alone higher ones, in AEF before World War II (aside from a small secondary class organized at Brazzaville in 1938 mainly for the benefit of Europeans) and because few French professors were willing to come to AEF after the war, it took nearly ten years for the network of colleges and technical institutions envisaged under the Plan to begin functioning. By 1955, however, the federation possessed eight secondary schools giving courses leading to the first or both parts of the baccalaureate. These comprised one *lycée* at Brazzaville and seven modern and classical colleges, of which five were state and three were mission institutions, which had been built and thoroughly equipped by FIDES and staffed with qualified French professors.[57]

One of these colleges deserves special mention, for it was not simply the reproduction of a Metropolitan secondary institution but an educational venture unique in French Black Africa. This was the Collège Franco-Arabe at Abéché, on the eastern frontier of Tchad. In 1945, Governor-General Bayardelle first conceived the idea of establishing a center of higher Islamic learning in Tchad that would serve to offset the attraction exercised upon the Muslim populations of that territory by the universities and religious schools of Egypt and Sudan. His proposal bore no fruit at the time, however, for French officialdom in general was not so aware as he was of the political influence over Islamic AEF that was being acquired by Tchadian students who had been trained at Cairo and Khartoum. Moreover, during the first postwar years neither the funds nor the French professors of Arabic needed for such an institution were available. It was not until December 1951, when Governor-General Chauvet visited Ouaddaï and found some former students of Al Azhar University teaching at Abéché, that the decision was made to found there a *collège* at which both French and Arabic secondary courses would be taught. A French professor of Arabic who had had experience in North Africa was named director of the *collège*, which began functioning in temporary buildings in 1952. Six years later classes were transferred to the building provided for the *collège* by FIDES, to which boarding facilities were later added.

The curriculum consisted of two wholly separate programs, of which one was identical with that of French secondary schools and the other consisted of courses in Arabic similar to those available in Egyptian schools of higher Islamic learning. Most of the Egyptian-trained *faqis* who had already been teaching at Abéché were absorbed into the faculty of the new *collège,* and they were given pedagogical instruction and also lessons in French history and the French language by the director of the *collège.* Opinions as to the merits of this *faqi* faculty vary widely in Tchad, but the feeling is unanimous that they are very poorly paid. A former teacher at the Abéché *collège* told the writers in 1958 that the *faqis* did little more than read aloud a few lines of Arabic a day to their pupils, and the rest of the time either slept or sipped tea. The director of the *collège,* on the other hand, asserted that the *faqis* were exceptionally broad-minded and eager to acquire modern knowledge, and that they even urged Tchadian parents to send their children to schools where French as well as Koranic lore was taught. However, he did add that he tried to de-emphasize religious and political discussions. This may have been the result of an episode that occurred in 1954, when two of the *faqis* teaching at the *collège* were dismissed because they had allegedly led a campaign against the sultan of Ouaddaï. Thereafter the authorization of that potentate became a prerequisite for the admission of any Ouaddaian to the *collège.*[58]

From the outset, the Abéché *collège* was a success in the number of students it attracted, and by 1958, 800 were studying there, somewhat more than half of whom were Ouaddaians. There were said to be 100 Tchadian students at that time in Cairo.[59] But the difficulty encountered by students trained in Egypt and Sudan in finding jobs upon their return to Tchad, because they spoke little French and held no diploma recognized by the AEF authorities, has heightened the popularity of the Abéché *collège.* The great majority of the latter's student body take the French course and at the same time study Arabic, and most of the graduates have entered the local administration. This school is considered a success by the French in that it has kept under supervision in Tchad youths who, had it not existed, would surely have gone to study at Cairo or Khartoum, but whether it will be perpetuated in its present form by Tchad's African government is open to doubt. Relations between its director and students and between him and the Minister of Education have become so strained, both on personal grounds and on those of policy, that a change in the program and management of the *collège* seems inevitable.

AEF's other secondary schools that were built after the war in the territorial capitals were gradually provided with boarding facilities for students coming from outlying districts, and they were fed, clothed, lodged, and given pocket money from public funds.[60] In 1949, six years before this network had been completed, the French government ruled that no more students from Black Africa should be granted scholarships for study in Metropolitan secondary schools. The French authorities maintained that too many of the African students then studying in France had been poorly selected, were badly prepared for their work there, changed courses capriciously, were easily distracted from their studies, and could not adjust to so different a climate and environment.[61] Inasmuch as the Metropolitan *lycées* and *collèges* were already overcrowded and as there were now enough

secondary schools in AEF for the limited number of local students then
qualified to enter them, there was no longer any reason to grant scholarships for study in France below the university or higher technical level.
None of the foregoing reasons, however, seemed valid to the African elite,
and when 41 students[62] were sent back to AEF in 1950–51, the African
assemblymen objected strenuously. They claimed that such a measure was
not only flagrantly discriminatory but also an indication that the government was reverting to its prewar policy of refusing a "first-class education"
to their youthful compatriots.[63] In time, however, they became reconciled
to the new policy as both reasonable and practical, particularly as it did not
affect the number of scholarships granted for higher degrees in France and
as the local network of secondary schools continued to grow. In fact, it
was soon evident that there were not enough AEF students qualified to fill
the new *collèges* that had been constructed in AEF, and the federation
found itself in this quarter as overequipped as it was in port facilities and
electrical energy.

For a country that had had virtually no secondary-education facilities in
1945, it was no mean achievement to have 1,315 Africans studying in such
schools by 1955, but the fact that there were more than twice as many un-
filled places in the new local schools rekindled old grievances and gave rise
to more complaints from the African elite. If there were then only six AEF
African bachelors of arts and hundreds of aspirants had failed to pass the
secondary-school entrance examinations, this was—they claimed—because
of the poor quality of the federation's primary education. It being obvious
that this situation could not be remedied overnight, the African elite insisted that in the meantime the doors of AEF's secondary schools be opened
more widely and the conditions for admission of students be eased. At this
point, the government reminded the African elite that it was they who had
demanded secondary schools identical with those in France, and that any
letting down of the bars would be self-defeating because it would undermine the value of the diplomas locally awarded. Though the education
service remained adamant against lowering the academic standards in
AEF's secondary schools, it did make more elastic the rules governing the
age of students seeking admission to them. In 1955 the age limit for girls
entering the federation's secondary institutions was raised by three years
above that set in France, and for boys by two years.

Much the same conflict arose between the government and the African
assemblymen in regard to the award of scholarships for university study in
France. The government-general, which had the final say in recommending
persons for such grants[64] to the Minister of Overseas France (after consultation with the local advisory committees), laid down rules that were felt by
the Africans to be too rigid, not only in the matter of a candidate's age but
also in the matter of his academic record, his family situation, and the type
of studies he would pursue. Easing of the age limit for admission to local
secondary schools automatically raised that for students applying for university scholarships, but the government did not yield in the matter of

sending married men with children to France nor would it—after 1955—award grants for studies unrelated to the future needs of the federation. Specifically, the French authorities favored students oriented toward higher technical or medical studies, and they were disinclined to award scholarships to those wanting to specialize in literature or law.[65]

This policy, Governor-General Chauvet explained to the Grand Council, was based on the lessons learned over the years since the first scholarship holders were sent to France in 1947 and on the proved aptitudes and attitudes of African students there. After studying personally the dossier of every scholarship applicant, he had found that for every seven of them interested in literature there was only one specializing in the natural sciences.[66] Since the federation was too poor to grant an unlimited number of scholarships, it must choose candidates willing to specialize in the fields most urgently needed for the federation's future development and for which jobs in AEF were assured them. Not all of AEF's scholarship holders, he added, had appreciated the sacrifices made by Metropolitan France and by their compatriots to give them opportunities for higher study, and some had prolonged their stay in France unnecessarily and fruitlessly. AEF would continue to send and France to welcome qualified African students, he assured the Grand Councilors, but they must be more judiciously selected.

In 1955, there were 40 AEF Africans studying in French universities. In extracurricular activities, they were either too few in number or too apolitical in their interests to follow in the footsteps of their fellow Africans from Cameroun or French West Africa. Though they had their own *foyer*, lodgings, and student associations, they did not become similarly involved in radical politics or organizations like the Fédération des Etudiants de l'Afrique Noire Française, nor did they publish firebrand articles in such media as *Présence Africaine, Voix de l'Afrique Noire, L'Etudiant de l'Afrique Noire,* and *Tam-Tam*. When they neglected their studies in France, according to reports from the Metropolitan authorities, personal rather than political complications were responsible. This appeared to be the logical sequence of their behavior in AEF's secondary schools. There have been occasional student strikes in almost all of AEF's secondary institutions, often chronologically following those in Senegal and Dahomey, but they did not have similar motivation. In most cases, AEF students have struck for trivial reasons, such as a dislike for the food served in their dining halls or for certain professors,[67] and in one instance students refused to attend classes because the local administration refused to assure them jobs at a specified salary after graduation. On the whole, however, the zeal to acquire certificates and diplomas among AEF students has been deep-rooted, and as yet they have developed little taste for political agitation.

Because of the backwardness of education in prewar AEF, most of the students there are the offspring of uneducated parents, and far fewer than in French West Africa have come from a milieu of *évolués*. Furthermore, AEF's political evolution has moved so fast that there is a minimum of frustration among students and a multitude of opportunities open to educated men. The most regrettable tendency thus far displayed by students in the federation is their passive assumption that the state will provide them with everything, from a free education to guaranteed and well-paid jobs for life.[68] Though AEF's present leaders are vaguely aware of the dangers inherent in such an attitude, they remain consistently indulgent toward students' demands and lack of discipline, and are still convinced that the key to their country's future progress lies in increasing the number of degree holders.

In 1956, after the *loi-cadre* was passed, responsibility for granting scholarships was turned over to the four territories, which since have increased the number of such awards. As of 1958, 65 AEF Africans were studying in France and 2,494 in the federation's secondary schools (plus 713 Europeans), and more than 27 per cent of the school-age children were attending primary schools.[69] In the near future one may expect to see as many Africans pursuing higher studies as the four republics can afford to send and as the Metropolitan universities are willing to accept. The new African governments of AEF already have at their disposal far more educated men than ever before, but for many years to come the number of qualified men and women will fall far short of meeting the tremendous need for such services.

CHAPTER 19

Religion

The Christian Missions[1]

In 1490 the King of Portugal first sent a few Franciscan and Capuchin missionaries to the Kongo kingdom, where they and their successors were extraordinarily successful for about 250 years. They were centered in Angola, and it was not until 1663 that they founded at Loango the only mission in what later became French territory. Concentrating on the conversion of the king and the upper classes of the Bakongo tribes, these early missionaries did not try to win over the population in general, although the Capuchins made some attempts to establish hinterland posts. They did not trouble to learn the local languages, and for many years they preached and heard confessions through an interpreter. Moreover, they made remarkable concessions to local custom, including the toleration of polygamy and pagan practices among their converts, though occasionally some of the more zealous priests tried to destroy fetishes. The "Christian" rulers of the Kongo, for their part, used the missionaries and the religion they brought as a means of reinforcing kingly authority, and they included the cross among the royal insignia as the symbol of their judicial power. Later the cross, statues of saints, and some of the church ritual were absorbed into animist practices to such a point that, in the Loango region, the cult of the Virgin Mary became almost indistinguishable from that of the local earth goddess.

This process of absorption and adaptation went so far that by the time the second wave of Catholic missionaries reached the coast of central Africa in the late eighteenth century they found it almost impossible to enforce strict Christian practices among their African converts. Frenchmen predominated in this group of missionaries, members of the Order of St. Esprit, and they were accompanied by nuns of St. Joseph de Cluny. In the late nineteenth century one of their number, Father Augouard, worked closely with Brazza in opening up the Congolese hinterland, and he founded two mission stations at Linzolo and Brazzaville that were to become the most important in Moyen-Congo. A network of missions was set up in the heart of the Balali country, owing to the zeal of Augouard and his aides, who besides being priests, were explorers, builders, and managers of farms and workshops. They trained Africans to become carpenters, masons, and blacksmiths, and even tried to raise meat animals so as to wean their con-

verts away from cannibalism.[2] Under Augouard's successors, mission posts
—to which primary schools were added—multiplied in the lower Congo
basin, and others were founded in the Likouala and Haute-Sangha regions.

During the seventeenth century, Italian Capuchin missionaries had
tried intermittently to evangelize the tribes of coastal Gabon, and in 1775
they were joined by two French priests, but none of these early missionaries
left lasting traces in the country. Two French fathers of the St. Esprit
Order, who had been forced to leave the Ivory Coast, went to Gabon in
1843, and were persuaded by the French naval officers stationed there to
remain in the country rather than return to France. One of them, Bessieux,
began work on a dictionary of the local language, and his companion, Le
Berre, wrote the first grammar of any Gabonese language. Both missionaries tried to penetrate the hinterland, but because of the difficulties of
communication and the hostility of the tribes there, they retired to the
coast and made their headquarters at newly founded Libreville. They were
soon joined by other missionaries and nuns. In 1861–62 they constructed
a large mission compound, comprising a chapel and a school, that became
the model for other concentrations of Catholic missionary enterprise in
Gabon. Le Berre, after he succeeded Bessieux as bishop of Libreville, made
a second and more successful effort to evangelize the rural Fang, and in
1878 he founded the missions of N'Gounié and Okané. Even more than
in Moyen-Congo, mission posts in Gabon became economic enterprises, in
which the raising of food crops was as vital to their survival as was the
establishing of schools to attract Africans and make converts.

For many years Catholic missionary activity in AEF remained within
Moyen-Congo and Gabon, and only in the twentieth century did it spread
to the north. By 1909 the evangelization of Oubangui had reached the point
where its capital was made an apostolic see. Mission work in that colony
was confined to the Bangui area until about 1925, when it started pushing
into the M'Baiki and Bambari regions and radiated as far as the Sara
country of southern Tchad. In 1938 the missions at Bangassou, Doba, and
Bozoum (with headquarters at Berbérati) were reorganized as an apostolic
vicariate, distinct from that of Bangui, and entrusted to the Capuchins who
had come to AEF from Ethiopia after the Italian conquest of that country.
In Tchad, except for the Moundou area, mission work spread even more
slowly than in Oubangui. A Jesuit military chaplain began trying to evangelize the tribes living on the banks of Lake Tchad in 1934, but it was not
until 1947—when eastern Tchad was detached from the Khartoum vicariate
—that the Vatican asked the Jesuits to organize a mission in that territory.
At that time, the rank of an apostolic prefecture was conferred on Tchad,
except for the southwestern zone, which remained a part of the Berbérati
vicariate.

The ecclesiastical organization of the Catholic missions in AEF kept
pace with the growth of their activities, and both increased rapidly in the
years that followed World War II. At the end of the nineteenth century
there were only three ecclesiastical circumscriptions—at Loango, Brazza-

ville, and Libreville—to which that of Bangui was added in 1909. Between 1927 and 1947 the arrival of the Capuchins and Jesuits led to the creation of two more, at Berbérati and Fort Lamy. By 1956, however, the federation boasted nine distinct jurisdictions, of which two were archbishoprics (Brazzaville and Bangui), two were apostolic prefectures, and five were major dioceses. Of these nine jurisdictions, six were in the hands of missionaries of the St. Esprit, two were in those of the Capuchins, and one was entrusted to the Jesuits. Ministering to the faithful were 300 European missionaries, 248 being French and the balance divided among six other nationalities, and 38 African priests.[3]

The small proportion of African priests, both absolutely and in relation to the number of European missionaries, is striking, especially in view of the attention that was given to training Africans during the first years of missionary enterprise in AEF. Yet the situation in 1956 represented an improvement over that which had existed six years earlier, when there was a total of only six African priests. The sole African priest in the Fort Lamy apostolic prefecture was not ordained until 1957, and this was considered an event of such importance that it was attended by two archbishops, three bishops, and the head of the Papal Delegation for French Black Africa, who came from Dakar expressly for the ceremony.[4] For some years after the war, the Catholic missionaries of AEF, apparently discouraged by the turn taken by two African priests whom they had regarded as shining examples,[5] had not pushed the training of an African clergy. Because of the lack of secondary-school facilities in AEF until the mid-1950's, politically ambitious young Africans, such as Boganda and Youlou, naturally had been attracted to the priesthood as the only way of acquiring the higher education they needed to rise in the world. This trend became accentuated in 1955 when the Vatican initiated a policy of consecrating as rapidly as possible Negro bishops who could take over from the missionaries the management of churches in French Black Africa. Today, more than thirty Africans are studying at the Grand Séminaire of Brazzaville and 241 in the small territorial seminaries of M'Bamou, Mayumba, Libreville, Berbérati, and Fort Sibut.

The relations between the Catholic missions and the administration were never so marked by distrust as in French West Africa, and they have improved considerably in recent years. Most of the French naval officers who first governed Gabon came from conservative, strongly Catholic families, and they welcomed the missionaries as warmly as did their counterparts in Cochin China. Moreover, the missionaries rendered vital services to the government, by actively helping to open up the hinterland, acting as intermediaries with tribal chiefs, and even quelling revolts (notably that at Lastoursville in 1897), and also by spreading French influence by means of their schools. Passage of the Metropolitan anticlerical laws in the early twentieth century, however, even though they were not promulgated in AEF, led to less cordial relations between the missionaries and civilian officials. The latter tended to believe that the missionaries were trying to create a state-within-a-state and their own zone of influence, and that they were weakening native society by their attacks on polygamy and their support of the emancipation of youths and women from traditional authority. The European lay community in general was inclined to judge harshly the African products of mission schools, holding the instruction they received there responsible for the Africans' aspirations for greater freedom as well as for their lapses from honesty and truthfulness. Basically the antagonism among European officials and merchants alike toward African Christians was based on the latter's insistence on being treated as a privileged group and their resistance to performing tasks they considered menial.[6] Many seemed to forget that for years the missions had provided almost all African interpreters and clerks for the administration and trading firms.

With the growth of the Messianic cults, relations between the Catholic missionaries and French officials became more cooperative in the face of what they both regarded as a common danger. If the missionaries denounced the new cults as a resurgence of fetishism, they saw in them also a revolt against their ecclesiastical as well as against lay authority. In a sense, the missions, cooperating with the government in trying to suppress the new cults in Moyen-Congo and Gabon, virtually declared a war of religion on the aberrant Negro churches.[7] Conversely, the missionaries were surprised and shocked by the hostility displayed by some African parishioners toward them during the fiftieth-anniversary celebrations of the founding of the Linzolo mission. Although even the most fanatical adversaries of the Catholic mission then feared to make an open attack on it, they apparently hoped to isolate and weaken the missionaries fatally by refusing to provision them.

Whereas the administration and Catholic missions were drawn closer together during the interwar period by their common fear of the Messianic sects, quite the reverse was true of the attitude of most French officials toward the Protestant missions. American Presbyterians had been the first Protestants to come to Gabon, as early as 1844, and six years later they founded a post at Libreville. In 1871 a Protestant church was built at Baraka, in 1874 a small post at Balambila on the Ogooué, and in 1882 another at Talagouga. In the mission schools they founded, these Protestants taught Africans in the vernacular, and when the government issued regulations in the 1880's forbidding this, "they were not prepared to teach in French, nor did they show any desire so to prepare themselves."[8] Highly placed French officials, including Brazza himself, pleaded successfully with the Paris Société des Missions Evangéliques to lend French teachers to the Presbyterian missions. But this proved to be only a palliative and relations between the Presbyterians and the government became increasingly strained, with the result that they ceded their work in Gabon to the Paris society in 1892.[9] Protestant activity spread progressively to the rural areas, where they built dispensaries, primary schools, and vocational training institutions, the most outstanding of which were the agricultural station of Samkita (founded in 1909) and the forestry station and sawmill of Ngomo (in 1913).

At about the same time, Swedish Protestants of the Svenska Missionsförbundet came to Moyen-Congo and founded a station at Madoua in the Kinkala area. There they built their first primary school in 1911, which was subsequently cited as a model by the territorial education service. Their work was particularly successful in Boko district, where they soon acquired a following among the Bakongo and thus aroused the hostility of the Balali Catholics, who were in the majority there. The Swedish stations multiplied to the number of 12 in Moyen-Congo, and subsequently another Swedish organization, the Orebre Missionsförening, established three posts in Oubangui. In the latter territory they were joined during the interwar period by some American Protestant groups, notably the Sudan Mission and Mid-Africa Mission, which later extended their work to Tchad.[10]

In both northern territories, the going is hard for all the Christian missionaries because they lack facilities for reaching the tribes scattered over immense areas, and because of the fact that most of the federation's Muslim populations are to be found there.[11] The situation was very different, however, in the south, where the Africans were highly susceptible to Christian proselytizing and the means of communication were comparatively good. This was particularly true in the conventional zone of the Congo where, under the provisions of article 11 of the treaty of St. Germain, "missionaries have the right to enter, circulate, and reside there, with facilities to pursue their religious work." The signing of this treaty in 1919 opened the way not only for the established Protestant denominations to create as many posts as their resources would permit, but also for the advent of two new evangelical organizations, the Salvation Army and Jehovah's Witnesses. In recent years both have taken root in AEF, particularly the former in the Niari region of Moyen-Congo.

During the interwar period, the movement started by the Salvation Army spread rapidly through the region served by the Congo-Ocean railroad, where some villagers even abandoned their homes and fields to participate in the ceremonies organized by its agents. In fact, the Army's officers were disconcerted by the sudden success of their efforts, because of the aberrations to which they gave rise. Their African auxiliaries, fascinated by the uniforms, regalia, and hymns of the Army, increased greatly, and, poorly trained, they enthusiastically spread distorted doctrines. This led to the celebration of mystical rites that were strangely akin to the practices of the traditional secret societies. This did not become a widespread phenomenon, but elsewhere and in other ways the Salvation Army contributed to the development of some of the most extreme aspects of the Messianic cults (see p. 311), and its centers in Moyen-Congo served as places of refuge for a number of their leaders who were sought by the police.

The Watch Tower movement of Jehovah's Witnesses did not gain a foothold in AEF until after World War II. Their influence has extended to Oubangui, but it is mainly felt in the towns of Brazzaville, Dolisie, and

Pointe Noire, where the Watch Tower is called Kinsinga. The extremist doctrines preached by the Witnesses resemble those propagated by the radical fringe of the Messianic cults, but the methods they use have alienated a segment of the African population. In 1956 the authors were told by a high French official that a fight had recently broken out between African Catholics, Protestants, and Witnesses in Oubangui because in some areas the Watch Tower propagandists had taken advantage of the temporary absence of the men from their homes to visit their wives and give them "instruction."¹

Although the policies of the Salvation Army and Jehovah's Witnesses in AEF have been inimical to the French administration, the orthodox Protestant denominations have taken no such stand and have closely collaborated with the government in the field of education. The administration in turn has granted as many favors to Protestant as to Catholic missionaries, even though most of the former are foreigners whereas the latter share the faith of most French officials and in great majority are of French nationality. During World War II, when the Protestant missions were cut off from their parent organizations, they received generous grants from French public funds.[12] After eight of the Protestant missions came together in 1941 in a Fédération des Missions d'AEF, the government called upon its members for advice in formulating policy on social questions.[13] In the postwar years, the Protestant missions have been treated on exactly the same basis as those of the Catholics in respect to official subsidies and representation on educational advisory boards.

Nevertheless, there is little doubt that the administration, for purely secular reasons, has preferred to see African converts enter the Catholic rather than the Protestant fold. Although Catholic missions at times have been considered by French officials to be an overly independent and socially disruptive force, as well as one that aroused the antagonism of some of the African elite, Catholic priests have been far more diligent than have Protestant pastors in supervising and often controlling the activities of most of their converts. Moreover, AEF was one of the very few French-speaking countries in Black Africa where the Vatican's prelates apparently were not instructed in 1955 to come out openly in favor of African self-determination, and where the Holy See has not forced the pace of creating African bishops or of replacing French missionaries by Catholics of other nationalities.[14]

No overtly subversive activities on the part of the Protestant missionaries can be held responsible for having aroused the administration's mistrust of their sincerity or purposes. Nevertheless, the mere fact of the presence of their numerous denominations in AEF—which has broken the united Christian front and caused antagonism between African Christians—has been held mainly responsible for the development of the Messianic sects, with their dangerous doctrinal deviations. Because the basic Protestant creed of individual responsibility fitted in with their yearning for emancipation, the Africans adopted it and interpreted it to mean that they no longer owed obedience to the lay authorities but only to God. Furthermore, the majority of Protestant missionaries were linked neither by nationality nor by religion to the colonial regime, and the Swedes in particular were able to acquire a political influence far greater than might be inferred from the number of their converts. Reportedly the Swedish pastors in Boko district were not disconcerted by the spread of Kimbangism among the Bakongo there but, rather, considered it only the natural conse-quence of their teachings.[15] Though they rarely participated directly in Moyen-Congo's postwar politics, it is interesting to note that a Swedish missionary was among the candidates for election to the Ouesso municipal council in November 1956.

Although the Protestants' success with dissident African elements natu-rally cannot be duplicated by the Catholics, who must perforce be intolerant of any movements that threaten their claim to universality and insistence on unity, both missionary groups have encountered much the same obstacles to their work in AEF and drawn many similar conclusions from their long experience there. Among the common handicaps to their progress are the discouraging results of working with the unstable, cosmopolitan, and easily distracted urban populations; the increasing difficulty of recruit-ing African catechists, because of the attraction of better-paid jobs; and the amount of time and energy devoted by missionaries to economic enter-prises not directly related to their main task of evangelization. On the other hand, positive lessons have been derived from their common experi-ence: both Catholics and Protestants have learned to concentrate their mission activities in a few large complexes rather than in numerous small posts; both have become increasingly convinced that they must train their African auxiliaries better and in larger numbers in anticipation of the prospective transfer of their churches to native management;[16] and both have found schools even more effective than hospitals as a means of attract-ing and influencing the Africans.

Where Protestant and Catholic policy has mainly diverged is in the methods used to win converts. To build their church on as broad a founda-tion as possible, the Catholics have striven for mass conversions, and to this end have sent out catechists to live in the villages and try to win over their inhabitants en bloc. The Protestants, on the other hand, have placed their primary emphasis on the individual, and they have been reluctant to baptize any African who has not given proof of good conduct.[17] Both policies have been successful in vastly increasing the number of their re-spective African converts, and though there are now more than twice as many native Catholics as Protestants (about 484,000 compared with some 218,000),[18] the latter's relative numerical weakness has been offset—at least in Moyen-Congo and Gabon—by the influence in depth exerted by the Protestant missions. Since World War II, the Catholic missions have been trying to regain their hold over the elite by sponsoring the Christian trade-union movement and organizing *Action Catholique* groups, one of whose activities has been to publish the weekly paper *La Semaine de l'AEF*.

After more than a century of effort on the part of some hundreds of Christian missionaries and the expenditure of large sums of money, Catholic and Protestant Africans together constitute no more than a seventh of AEF's total population. The Muslim element in the Federation is twice as numerous and the number of animists more than triple that of the Christians.[19] Despite the still-marked preponderance of animists, their number is being steadily reduced by the expansion of Christianity and Islam at their expense. Islam is moving south from its stronghold in Tchad, where over 1,200,000 of AEF's Muslims are concentrated.[20] In Moyen-Congo and Gabon, Islam offers no hard core of opposition to the spread of Christianity, and the animist cults there are too localized and unorganized to hold their own against the Catholic and Protestant missions, and particularly the attraction exercised by their schools. Yet even there the number of baptized African Christians comes to no more than 25 to 30 per cent of the total population, and it is mainly among them that there have developed the Messianic cults which are in opposition to Christian mission activity.

The Messianic Cults[21]

In AEF, the Messianic movement has been confined almost wholly to the southern territories, which are geographically the most exposed to outside influences and where other conditions also existed that were particularly favorable to their growth.[22] These conditions were especially propitious among the Bakongo tribes of Moyen-Congo and the Fang of Gabon. Both are remarkably enterprising groups, conscious of their cultural heritage. Both have been long worked upon by Christian missionaries and dominated by Europeans, to whom they lost both political and economic power. Their efforts to reconstitute themselves as cohesive units involve related peoples living beyond AEF's political frontiers, and so have naturally been opposed by the colonial administrations of Belgium, France, Portugal, and Spain. Groping for some form in which to express their aspirations that would be acceptable to the authorities and also conform to African traditions and psychology, they gravitated toward religious manifestations, for which the ground was inadvertently prepared by mission activity.

So lax and superficial had been the evangelical work carried on by the Portuguese Catholic missionaries in Angola, beginning in the fifteenth century, that only a few Christian symbols and rites survived among the Bakongo living in what later became Belgian and French colonies. Actually the cross, Catholic ritual, and saints' statues became so much a part of local animist practices that this residue furthered the proliferation of syncretistic cults more than it aided the work of the missionaries who came in the nineteenth and twentieth centuries to convert the Bakongo to more orthodox forms of Christianity. Moreover, the mutual antagonism between Catholics and Protestants, the denominational divisions among the latter, and the eventual entry upon the Congolese scene of the Salvation Army and Jehovah's Witnesses, opened the way for further deviations from, and adaptations of, imported Christian practices. Generally speaking, the Bakongo and Fang took over from the established Christian churches and organizations what appealed most to them emotionally (vestments, uniforms, ceremonies, and hymns) and also what they felt would bring them unity and strength as a group (the ecclesiastical hierarchy, the rejection of sorcery and fetishism, and an ethical code that included most of the Ten Commandments). They excluded, however, tenets that were too onerous or were incompatible with African customs (such as the renunciation of polygamy). From traditional practices they conserved some of the rituals, the cult of ancestors, and taboos—whatever would best serve to perpetuate their specific cultural heritage. Needless to say, this eclectic process was a gradual one and subject to considerable variations. It reached so far afield, in at least one instance, that it borrowed the practice of passive resistance from the Hindu followers of Gandhi in South Africa.

Yet for all its diversity and the ephemeral nature of some of the sects to which it gave rise, the Messianic movement in AEF was most profoundly and consistently influenced by the Christian missionaries, and everywhere it gave evidence of a common motivation and goals, both material and spiritual. It was the Protestants who made the deepest impression, for in their advocacy of the individual's freedom to interpret the Bible according to his own lights the African sects found a "legitimate" means of expressing their hostility to white domination, including that of the missionaries. From the Bible they took such passages as justified revolts against an alien authority and prophesied an imminent end to the existing order. In the history of the early Christians they found the examples of martyrs whose blood had been the seed of the church. It required little effort of the imagination to apply these images to the contemporary scene. Throughout southern AEF, the newly born religious sects took on a political coloring that deepened with each socioeconomic crisis through which the central African tribes passed during the interwar period. Soon the political aspect of the Messianic movement began to transcend (as well as reinforce) its religious motivation, and some of the cults, theretofore confined to ethnic groups, came to regard their members as a chosen people, like the Jews of the Old Testament, destined to lead neighboring tribes. This imperialistic trend has been most pronounced among the Bakongo, but it has also been characteristic of some of the cults of western and northern Moyen-Congo.

The two most durable Messianic cults among the Bakongo—Kimbangism and Kakism—derived from the Belgian Congo, while the Lassyism of the Pointe Noire region and the Ngol and Labi[23] cults of northern Moyen-Congo were almost wholly indigenous in origin.[24]

Because the majority of Bakongo lived south of the Congo and were, on the whole, more prosperous than those on the French side of the river, and because the grip of the Catholic missions was stronger in the Belgian

colony, Messianic leaders first came to the fore there and enjoyed great
prestige among the related tribes in Moyen-Congo. The first of them to
emerge was Simon Kimbangou, a catechist of the British Protestant mission
at Thysville who had failed in the examinations that would have led to
his ordination as a pastor. In March 1921, at the age of 32, Kimbangou
was touched by grace, and so rapidly did he acquire renown as a healer
and worker of miracles that he proclaimed himself to be not only a prophet
but the son of God.[25] His fellow catechists were proud to become his
disciples, and through the religious literature and hymns written by Kimbangou in the Kikongo language they spread his cult widely in Belgian
territory and also among the Bakongo of Moyen-Congo. Kimbangou borrowed from Christian practices the ritual of baptism and the confessional,
and from African tradition the ancestral cult. However, by also stressing
those Biblical passages that incited the "oppressed" to revolt, he soon
alarmed the Belgian authorities, who arrested him in September 1921.
Some years later he died in prison at Elisabethville.

The "martyrdom" of Kimbangou and the persecution of his followers
firmly established the movement he had initiated, and a potent myth was
built up around his person. Kimbangou became the symbol of resistance
to the colonial administration and also to the Catholic missionaries, who
were believed to have cooperated with the government in trying to eradi-
cate the sect he founded. He became the prophet of a golden age that was
soon to dawn in central Africa after white colonialism had been eliminated,
and was venerated as the founder-martyr of a religion that had been directly
revealed to a Negro without any alien intermediation. In the eyes of the
Bakongo, Kimbangou was gradually elevated to a position similar to that
of Moses for the Jews or of Mohammed for the Arabs, and his followers,
like the early Christians, lived in expectation of an imminent second coming of their Messiah. The French Bakongo were less affected by Kimbangism than were their Belgian relatives, and the Brazzaville government
thought it had suppressed the movement by deporting its three most turbulent local leaders to Tchad in 1922. But after it was learned that seditious
Kimbangist hymns had been sung in all the Bakongo temples on both
sides of the Congo on Christmas Day, 1923, the government again applied
strict controls that for a few years arrested the spread of the sect and confined it mainly to the Bakongo living in Boko district.

Although the Balali and Bassoundi elements of the Bakongo remained
under the influence of the Catholic missions at Linzolo and M'Bamou,
they did yield to the spell of the Amicale organization founded by André
Matsoua (see pp. 480–88), which was clearly political in its orientation and
only gradually acquired a religious character. Both Kimbangism and
Matsouanism were movements of protest that had a xenophobic aspect,
and because they drew strength from the same emotional sources they
were able to relay each other when official persecution forced one or the
other of them underground. From October 1926, when some of the Kimbangist leaders returned from their exile in Tchad, until January 1931,

when the administration closed the Kimbangist temples and forbade their members to hold meetings, that cult was in the ascendant. But after the trial of André Matsoua, his followers took up the torch. Both movements profited from the general malaise created by the world economic depression and from the administration's attempt at that period to regroup villages and reorganize the *chefferie*. Throughout the early 1930's, one or another of Moyen-Congo's seven main Kimbangist organizers—who frequently sought refuge from the police with the Salvation Army—managed to give continuous leadership to the movement, and by 1935 its temples were being rebuilt and its spirit revitalized.

In 1939 another Messiah appeared in the Belgian Congo, Simon Mpadi. He combined the role of St. Paul with that of John the Baptist, for he claimed to be both the herald of Kimbangou's return and, in the interval, the organizer of his church. Like Kimbangou, Mpadi had been a professional worker with an organized Christian group—in this case the Salvation Army, in which he held the rank of lieutenant. After Mpadi had received a divine revelation in 1936, he broke with the Army and entered into contact with Kimbangou's former disciples. In September 1939 he established the Mission des Noirs, more popularly called Kakism because of the color of the uniform worn by its adherents. Mpadi organized his church at meetings in Léopoldville and Kinkoni, where he expounded doctrines similar to those of Kimbangou. World War II having just broken out, the Belgian administration was in a state of alert and promptly arrested Mpadi. He managed to escape to French territory, where he was also imprisoned and eventually extradited, but later he was able to return a second time to Moyen-Congo. Despite the brevity of his sojourns among the French Bakongo, Mpadi was able to build his church there on the foundation laid by Kimbangism, and to it he added the uniform, symbols, and military structure that derived clearly from his Salvation Army background. Like Kimbangou before him, Mpadi fought sorcery, fetishism, alcoholism, and adultery, and though he tolerated polygamy he strove to restrict its practice. But more than did Kimbangou, he gave his movement a totalitarian character and xenophobic slant. To his followers he stressed the need for achieving a unity and universality that would transcend tribal boundaries and help them to maintain sustained opposition to the administration. He also insisted on their breaking away from the Christian missions, which he represented as having deliberately misled the Congolese people. Indeed, so effective were the doctrines and the organization with which Mpadi endowed Kakism that it was able, after Matsoua's death, to modify the Amicalist movement, with which it was gradually merged under the aegis of a new trinity of deities—Kimbangou, Matsoua, and Mpadi.

As of 1941, there were altogether 16 organized Kakist churches. Only one of these was in French territory, in Boko district, but it was able to make its influence felt among the non-Bakongo tribes of Mindouli and Madingou by attracting to its fold an increasing number of malcontents, including a large number of mission catechists and functionaries. This spread of Kakism was going on while Nazi Germany was conquering Western Europe, and Mpadi's followers were encouraged thereby to express openly the hope that the Germans would soon take over the Belgian and French colonies in central Africa and install Matsoua and Kimbangou as kings of the north and south banks of the Congo respectively. This scarcely increased the popularity of Kakism with the colonial administrations, and after the German conquest of Africa failed to materialize, little further was heard of the cult's activities during the war. Yet the movement continued underground and reportedly spread north among the M'Bochi tribes. With the birth of elected political bodies in 1946, the position of Moyen-Congo's Messianic sects underwent a marked change. They remained sufficiently powerful that their support was sought by the newly risen African politicians, who, in return, championed the sects' pleas for official recognition and for the grant of land on which to build a "cathedral." No less a personage than Tchicaya, the territory's RDA deputy to the National Assembly, defended the Bakongo sects.

In the western part of Moyen-Congo, Tchitchellé performed similar services for Lassyism, a new Messianic cult that took root among the Vili tribes in the early postwar period. Zépherin Lassy, the son of a Vili Notable and cousin of a militant trade-union leader, had a background even more colorful and cosmopolitan than had his Bakongo colleagues—if the biographical data offered by his followers are to be believed. Though he, too, spent some time in the Belgian Congo, the movement Lassy founded was more indigenous to Moyen-Congo than were any of the other major sects. Born at Pointe Noire about 1908, Lassy attended a local Catholic school, after which he emigrated to Belgian territory and signed up as a cabin boy with the Belgian merchant marine. In this capacity he visited many lands, including the United States, where he reportedly met Father Divine. Returning to Moyen-Congo in 1946, Lassy settled for a time in Dolisie, where one night while reading the Bible he first heard the voice of Jesus. In 1951 he joined the Salvation Army, with which he remained for two years, but never rose above the rank of a soldier. In 1953, with Tchicaya's aid, he got permission to build a church on an abandoned coffee plantation near Hollé. There he held prayer meetings at which he exhorted his audience to give up superstition and destroy fetishes. Soon he became so renowned as a miracle worker that local chiefs began asking his aid, and villagers for miles around called on him to drive out evil spirits, heal the sick, and even revive the dead.

The administration was not aware that the movement had spread to Pointe Noire until one night in September 1953 the police stumbled on a group of some hundred persons in the African quarter praying by candlelight.[26] By that time, the authorities had learned that persecution simply promoted the growth of such sects, and since the Lassyist meetings did not disturb public order, they did not make a frontal attack on the movement. Nevertheless, the police did gather enough evidence of Lassy's profiteering from his followers' credulity to enable the government to bring suit against him in October 1954. Although the state's witnesses refused to confirm in court the testimony they had previously given the examining magistrate and the suit consequently failed, Lassy was sufficiently alarmed to give up his career as healer and to confine his future role to that of prophet and church organizer. Lassy's doctrines differ little from those of the Bakongo sects and he also repudiates any links with the missions, but he recognizes the established order and is neither anti-European nor an advocate of violence. Backsliding among his followers is punishable only by excommunication, and—as the authors know from experience—he welcomes to his church Europeans, among whom he is said to have made a few converts. So long as his movement develops no aggressive political trends, Lassy seems to be safe from official interference.

Quite different from Lassyism is another, even more indigenous, cult that developed after the war in northern Moyen-Congo and from there spread to southern Gabon. It is called Ngol—a name derived from both that of General de Gaulle and the Congolese word *ngolo,* meaning power and strength. Like all the other Messianic sects, Ngol adopted the ecclesiastical hierarchy of the Christian churches and a part of their ethical code, stressed monotheism and the evils of sorcery and fetishism, and conserved tribal traditions in certain ceremonies and taboos. But its character was far more violent than that of Lassyism, for infractions of discipline were punished by death, it attacked other sects, and the chiefs who refused to join its ranks were penalized. Ngol was the organized expression of the spirit of revolt by youth against the traditional authority of the tribal elders, particularly strong in that part of Moyen-Congo. Since this tendency also permeated Fang society, it is not surprising that a similar cult called Malifu developed in the N'Gounié region of Gabon, but it survived for only a short time there.

Much more firmly rooted and widespread among the Fang was another, older cult known as Bwiti.[27] This cult first appeared in the early twentieth century in lower Gabon, where it attracted the laborers and soldiers who had been displaced from their native villages, and it was gradually spread to the center and north of the territory by them and by itinerant traders. During the 1920-30 decade, Bwiti temples multiplied in the Lambaréné and Kango regions, and from there the movement expanded to Libreville, along the Ogooué, into Woleu-N'Tem, and even among the Fang of Cameroun. Its growth alarmed the missions and the administration, for both saw in it a challenge to their authority, and this was the cause of their early hostility to the Bwiti leader, Léon Mba (see p. 350), and of the severe penalties imposed on Bwiti adepts in 1930-31. Inevitably such persecution strengthened the cult and also led to its clandestine development in the inaccessible region between Médouneu and Coco Beach. It was not until after World War II that Bwiti again emerged into the open and its character changed. It became less anti-European and comparatively open to outsiders, on condition that they underwent its initiation rites and followed its rules, and its members even began to participate in the territorial electoral campaigns. Balandier describes this movement as the first attempt at tribal regeneration by the Fang, and their first organized opposition to the religious activities of the missions.[28]

All of AEF's Messianic cults have developed according to a common pattern, and only the degree to which they borrowed from outside sources or conserved local traditions has differentiated them. Despite such variations, they expressed a need deeply felt by the central Africans for a truly Negro church, in whose ceremonies they would find self-expression and in whose organization they could attain unity and the sense of being jointly protected against sorcery and tribal disintegration. They came into being as a spontaneous movement of resistance to alien authority, both temporal and ecclesiastical, and their members drew no clear distinction between the religious and political aspirations that motivated their activities.

With the coming into being of elected representative institutions after the war, Africans gained another outlet for expressing many of the same emotions that had inspired and promoted the growth of the Messianic cults. Throughout the first postwar decade, these cults remained powerful enough to make it advisable for AEF's apprentice politicians to solicit their support, and in exchange they protected the cult's followers and aided them in their relations with the administration. But since the territories have become autonomous republics, the position of the politicians has been greatly strengthened and their need of cult support correspondingly lessened. (This, of course, does not apply to a man like Mba, who is at the same time both a political and a cult leader, and whose status is thereby enhanced.) Indeed, in one instance an outstanding political leader has felt compelled to assert his authority against the politico-religious cult through whose support he climbed to power. This is the case of Fulbert Youlou, who derived his electoral strength at the outset of his political career from the Balali's belief that he was the reincarnation of André Matsoua and who is now clamping down on the die-hard Matsouanists because they have shown themselves to be as opposed to his government as they were to the French administration. In time, other politicians may come to regard the cults as rivals for popularity with their constituents and may take steps to repress them. Thus the future of the Messianic movement in southern AEF is uncertain, and it now appears that the cults most likely to survive are those which concentrate on the purely religious aspect of their activities.

CHAPTER 20

Radiobroadcasting and the Press

In the early 1920's, it had been hoped to create in AEF a broadcasting station that would be the most powerful in central Africa. The project came to nothing, however, and even the pylons that had been constructed at Brazzaville were taken down in 1924.[1] Eleven years later a few enthusiasts among Brazzaville's European community started a Radio Club there, themselves supplying the money needed to buy equipment and hire technicians.[2] It was through this club that clandestine messages began to be broadcast in June 1940, and two months later General de Larminat took over its facilities in the name of the Free French. General de Gaulle, on the occasion of his first visit to Brazzaville, used them to make an address to the peoples of AEF in October 1940.

Attempts to increase the radius of this station failed, and in 1941 the Free French government ordered much more powerful equipment (50 kilowatts) from the Radio Corporation of America. Its delivery and installation took time, and Radio Brazzaville did not begin to function effectively until May 1943. Thereafter it played an outstanding role as a medium for propaganda not only on behalf of Free France but for the whole Allied cause. In 1946 Radio Brazzaville was taken over by Radiodiffusion Française, and thereafter its policy was formulated by the Quai d'Orsay and its operation was financed by the French treasury. Since that time it has steadily enlarged its audience and increased its influence. In 17 daily programs geared to an international audience, Radio Brazzaville broadcasts in French, English, Spanish, and Portuguese, and it has listeners in North and South America, Europe, including the Iron Curtain countries, and the Near, Middle, and Far East.[3] As its secondary function, Radio Brazzaville serves the French subsidiary stations at Dakar, Yaoundé, Douala, Abidjan, and other points, and its broadcasts to the Americas and Europe are timed so that they can be picked up throughout West Africa, just as its Near and Middle Eastern programs are scheduled so that they can also reach listeners in East Africa. In December 1954, a tribute was paid Radio Brazzaville by the Washington periodical *African News,* which observed:

> As a result of its remarkable technical effectiveness, it has continued to build audiences throughout the world. . . . This is so not only because it comes in loud and clear, but largely because since the war it has been building a name for fast, comprehensive, and objective reporting—a rarity in state-controlled radio.

Its director, in an article in *Le Monde* of February 1, 1956, claimed that it was mainly due to Radio Brazzaville that Radiodiffusion Française then held fourth place among the world's short-wave broadcasting services.

Though AEF Africans are proud of the accomplishments of Radio Brazzaville, they have often expressed the wish that it would do more to provide news of events in the country where it is located and that the federation had some say in the making of its policies. To some extent, AEF has profited by the presence of Radio Brazzaville in the federal capital, for its two local stations—Radio AEF and Radio Tchad—were at the outset also placed under the technical control of Radiodiffusion Française. Radio AEF benefited more by this association than did Radio Tchad because the former was situated in Brazzaville, but in neither case was the arrangement considered satisfactory, either financially or technically. In October 1953, Radiodiffusion Française canceled its agreement with the federal government on the ground that the two local stations were causing it to run a large deficit. The Grand Councilors, for their part, felt that the annual subsidy of 17 million CFA francs granted to Radiodiffusion Française not only was more than the federal budget could afford but was over-large in view of the mediocre quality of Radio AEF's six-hour daily broadcasts.[4] They had no qualms about suppressing Radio Tchad, because it had never been more than a poor and highly localized medium for disseminating news and propaganda, but they did want to salvage Radio AEF if its program could be made more effective and less costly. After prolonged negotiations in Paris, Radiodiffusion Française agreed to accept an annual subsidy of 10 million CFA francs for two-hour daily broadcasts over Radio AEF, and to improve its technical facilities and programs so as to reach and hold larger audiences. In 1953, Radio AEF could be heard clearly only in the Brazzaville area, and reception was nil at Pointe Noire, bad in Gabon, and poor in Oubangui.

The projected reforms began to take effect in 1954, with a change in Radio AEF's wave length and in the timing of its broadcasts (6:30–7:00 and 8:00–9:30 P.M.). Gradually programs were given in an increasing number of vernaculars, until by 1956 these included Lingala, Sangho, Monokotouba, Mféné, and Sara. To speed up the reception of news in outlying districts, a network of local correspondents was created throughout the three southern territories, and new features were introduced each week. The three programs that remained staple fixtures were the twice-weekly "L'Afrique Vous Parle" (which gave local news of the federation), a 15-minute daily newscast of world events, and "L'Heure Africaine," which included African music, folk tales, educational talks, and sports events. If the absence of complaints in sessions of the federation's elected assemblies can be taken as significant albeit negative evidence, Radio AEF was giving more satisfaction to its audiences in the late 1950's than at any other time in its history.

In 1955, by the construction of a new station at Fort Lamy, Radio AEF was relieved of the burden of broadcasting to Tchad. The decision to revive Radio Tchad in a more effective form was made under the second four-year Plan, not only because reception of Radio AEF's broadcasts had never been good in that territory but also because a growing number of Tchadians were believed to be listening to Cairo's "Voix des Arabes" program. Some French journalists and politicians were becoming disturbed by the government's apathy in the matter of counteracting the effects of the fiercely anti-Western propaganda broadcast from Cairo.[5] Consequently, Metropolitan France decided to use FIDES funds to build a station that could be heard even beyond Tchad's frontiers and to defray half of its operating expenses, the other half to be paid in equal shares by the federal and Tchad budgets. For Tchad this expenditure would amount annually to about 5 million CFA francs—a large sum for so poor a territory—and some of its assemblymen urged that the French treasury assume all the costs. But in December 1955, the assembly finally voted to pay its share on condition that it be represented on the station's managing committee and thus have some voice in policy decisions and some control over its programs. The latter were of the same type as those of Radio AEF but were broadcast in only three languages—French, Arabic, and Sara. In 1958, the number of weekly broadcasts was raised from 37 to 50, in part to satisfy the assemblymen who wanted additional programs that would appeal to Tchadians living away from their home territory.[6]

How far AEF's two radio stations have served to provide education, entertainment, and information for its population is difficult to tell. In many places reception is still poor, and public-address systems remain confined to the federal and territorial capitals. The number of receiving sets probably does not exceed 25,000[7] and they are concentrated in the hands of Europeans and African évolués. For some years the Grand Councilors urged the government to distribute to Africans without charge several thousand battery-powered sets,[8] but such largesse was clearly beyond the federation's means and only the cercles culturels could be so endowed. Certainly the number of listeners far exceeds that of receiving sets, and audience reaction is surprisingly strong. In 1958 the authors were shown samples of the 400 or more letters received monthly by Radio Tchad. Some were well written, even typed, and they ranged from suggestions for program improvement to the lively expression of approval or disapproval of recent broadcasts. (The station, for example, had just received 20 letters of violent protest against a broadcast in which the speaker had urged ill Tchadians to "use medical drugs instead of the water washed off a slate on which a verse from the Koran had been chalked by a celebrated faqi.")

After AEF was transformed into four republics, each of them wanted its own radio station, though it was agreed by their four premiers in June 1959 to retain Radio AEF under the name of Radio Inter-Equatorial and to coordinate their individual programs. In July Radio Gabon began experimental broadcasts, as did Radio Congo the following month, and in

these ventures they were being aided financially by Metropolitan France
and technically by the French Société de Radiodiffusion de la France
d'Outre-Mer (SORAFOM).

For many years the press in AEF has suffered from so many handicaps
that its very survival is surprising. These handicaps are mainly financial
and are due less to insufficient capital funds than to the lack of readers,
for only a little more than a fourth of the federation's small population are
literate and they are dispersed over a vast area. The local press is concentrated in Brazzaville, where newspapers meet with severe competition from
the more amply financed and better produced Léopoldville dailies, which
are easily and rapidly distributed on the north as well as the south side
of Stanley Pool. Moreover, since air transportation between France and
AEF has become more frequent and rapid, the European population of
the territorial capitals has increasingly subscribed to Metropolitan journals
and decreasingly bought the Brazzaville papers, which cost almost as much
and are slower in reaching them. Furthermore, to gain circulation the
Brazzaville press must try to appeal to both Europeans and Africans—a
difficult task because Europeans are stirred by events in the world and in
France to which the AEF Africans are indifferent. French journalists in
the federation confessed to the authors that even after years of experience
they could not always tell just what foreign news would interest the AEF
African elite. The latter showed some concern about what was happening
in immediately neighboring countries but not much farther afield, and
only in regard to news of these Africans' home localities and of sports
events were the journalists sure of arousing their lively and sustained
interest.

Before World War II, the press in AEF had even harder going than
today, for the European community was much smaller, as was the percentage of literate Africans. Among the ephemeral papers of that period
were *L'Etoile de l'AEF, Paris-Congo,* and *France de Brazzaville.* Some
reflected big business interests (such as G. Boussenot's *Presse Coloniale*)
or the settlers' viewpoint (Raoul Monmarson's *Annales Coloniales*), some
simply voiced the grievances of their owner-editor (Marcel Homet's *Don
Quichotte*), and none of them survived the war. There are still a few
examples of the one-man newspaper in AEF, but the postwar period has
not been propitious for such enterprises. One publication in this category
is *L'AEF,* taken over and run by one of Youlou's European backers, Christian Jayle, after it had served as a Free French vehicle during the war.
Its advertising is said to bring in revenue to its proprietor and its contests
to be a replica of the *Cameroun Illustré* of Douala.[9] However, the highly
personal tone of journalism in AEF has been preserved, albeit in a wider
field, by many of the publications that serve as organs for political parties
and labor unions. By airing personal or group grievances and aspirations,
they may usefully serve their owners in terms of propaganda or simply
in psychological release. By far the great majority of such publications,

however, are so insecure financially that they can appear only irregularly and the circulation of even the most flourishing of them probably does not exceed a few hundred copies.

As to the press that confines itself to printing straight news and information, the attitude taken by the government and the Grand Council has been somewhat ambiguous. Each year during the 1950's, grants-in-aid, amounting annually to about 3,600,000 CFA francs, were allocated in a lump sum and divided among their recipients on the basis of their respective circulation figures. But the amount each received was small and did little more than enable them to keep going. Then, to get some return on these subsidies, the government inaugurated in 1953 a policy of taking a fixed percentage of the total edition of each paper it subsidized, for free distribution to its officials and bureaus, and this reduced the sales that might otherwise have been made. According to Mrs. Kitchen,[10] "a civil servant of rank in AEF would consider himself humiliated if he had to buy his own newspaper."

This practice was naturally decried by the local press, but the resentment of private journalism throughout all French Black Africa was directed chiefly against Agence France Presse (AFP), which was regarded as unfairly competitive there. This agency was heavily subsidized by both the French treasury and the territories in which it produced a mimeographed daily news bulletin and supplied the information that it received by wire from its Metropolitan headquarters to the local radio stations. Not only did the AFP's activities cut into the circulation of the private press but by soliciting advertisements for its bulletin it absorbed some of the revenues that might have gone to the local newspapers. In the mid-1950's, protests from the overseas press were brought before the French parliamentary bodies, and they effected a change in the AFP's operations. From that time on, the AFP daily bulletin ceased to appear wherever there was a privately run newspaper that could perform the same function. In some instances, withdrawal of the daily bulletin proved to be premature, for a number of the newly established newspapers could not afford the same facilities as the AFP, and consequently the printed news available to the public was less than before.

To a certain extent this was the case in two towns of AEF. *L'Eveil de Pointe-Noire* was founded by an active French member of the local Chamber of Commerce, who had come to AEF after being forced to give up a business he had conducted for many years in Indochina. Although he used the AFP wire service for world events, he told the authors in 1956 that he alone gathered local news in such spare time as he had and that he printed only about 250 copies of each issue. In Bangui, the place of the daily bulletin was taken by *La Presse,* owned by such big business interests as SCOA, CFAO, and Unilever. To run it they enlisted the services of the AFP bulletin's editor, who deliberately modeled *La Presse* after a newspaper in a small town in the United States where he had lived for some years as a journalist. He informed the writers that *La Presse* was unique in the annals of AEF journalism, in that—being locally mimeographed at great cost—the more copies it sold the greater the loss it incurred, and that financially its predecessor had been comparatively prosperous. At Libreville, the AFP did not start issuing a daily bulletin until the early months of 1955. A year and a half later, its editor told the authors, its bulletin was serving all of Gabon, where it had 500 subscribers and therefore a circulation and revenues twice that of *L'Éveil de Pointe-Noire*.

The story of Brazzaville's press is perhaps the most edifying of all, for it illustrates most clearly the difficulty of maintaining a daily commercial newspaper even under the most favorable circumstances existing in AEF. That capital has the largest concentration of potential readers and the least obsolete printing presses, as well as the best means of communication with the rest of AEF and the outside world. Except for its vulnerability to invasion by Léopoldville's newspapers, Brazzaville might seem to offer private journalism the best opportunity to be found in any town in the federation. As a matter of fact, the only commercial daily of AEF that appears regularly and is wholly produced locally is published in Brazzaville, but it has gone through several incarnations and survives only because of official subsidies.

For some years after the last war, *L'Equateur Quotidien* and the weekly *France-Afrique* appeared to have more vitality than any of their predecessors or rivals. The former was edited by a French journalist who had long lived in Africa, and the latter by an erstwhile employee of Radio Brazzaville who had obtained financial backing from the small businessmen's organization, PME. Both were eventually forced to close down, however, for lack of money, and in August 1952 they were reborn as a single daily, *France-Equateur*. Although it was not above seeking a subsidy from the federal budget, *France-Equateur,* unlike other such enterprises, was sponsored by a company that included prominent local Europeans among its shareholders, it did not ask for a loan from the Crédit de l'AEF, and it was distributed through regular commercial channels. It failed to take hold in the territorial capitals, however, because it reached them after the news it carried had already been received over the radio or through the daily AFP bulletin, and because air transport added considerably to its price. In July 1955, when its circulation did not exceed 800, *France-Equateur* received an almost fatal blow as the result of the appearance in Brazzaville of a rival daily. This was the Brazzaville edition of the Léopoldville newspaper *L'Avenir,* which had sounder financial backing and a more attractive layout. *France-Equateur* was on the verge of bankruptcy, and the Grand Council was of two minds about saving it.[11] Critics of the paper claimed that it was poorly edited and contained news that was not always reliable and that it could never be made an economically viable publication. But its defenders maintained that as it was the sole French-owned and French-produced daily in AEF and the only paper giving reports of the Grand Council sessions, it should be supported. They finally won the day and *France-Equateur* was voted a small subsidy.

A wholly different sector of the AEF press consists of a few weeklies, fortnightlies, and monthlies directed toward special-interest groups. In this category are the political-party organs, such as the RDA's *L'AEF Nouvelle*, MESAN's *Bangui Lasa*, the BDG's *Union Gabonaise*, the UDDIA's *Le Progrès*, and the UDSG's *Le Pilote*. These publications appear irregularly, flourishing before and during an electoral campaign and then going into eclipse after it is over. Although they contain no news, properly speaking, and only the political opinions and polemics of their party leaders, they are interesting in that they are virtually the only current form of African journalism and are, for the most part, published by and for Africans. More permanent, though also more limited in their appeal, are the vehicles of the labor unions, such as *La Voix des Cadres de l'AEF*, *AEF–Force Ouvrière*, and *Solidarité*, whose circulation in no case probably exceeds a few hundred copies. There are also the equally specialized bulletins of the federation's various Chambers of Commerce, Gabon's Syndicat Forestier, and the PME, which similarly reach only a small public, though inevitably a very different one.

Perhaps more generally informative for the student of AEF affairs are the publications aimed at various religious and cultural groups. By far the most important and influential of these is *La Semaine de l'AEF*, the counterpart for AEF of French West Africa's *Afrique Nouvelle*. This weekly, which is edited by a missionary of the St. Esprit Order, is the organ of Action Catholique. Founded in 1953, within three years it acquired a circulation of some 4,500, mainly but not exclusively among AEF's African Catholics. It caters to the African readers' interest in village news, its social policy is very progressive, and it has many unpaid African correspondents and only one professional journalist. Though it combines news with feature articles, the subsidy of 15,000 CFA francs per issue that it asked of the Grand Council was refused on the ground that it was not a newspaper but a "journal of opinion."[12]

For the federation's Muslim populations, two other socio-religious publications were established. One of these, *Islam–AEF*, was founded at Brazzaville by a French convert to Islam, whose name is variously given as Edouard Eliot or L. Hyet, or in its Arabized form of Mohammed el Amin el Yet. Employed full time by Radio Brazzaville, Eliot showed linguistic abilities and anthropological interests that won him the confidence of the Muslims living in the federal capital. Nominally the organ of the Centre Musulman d'Action Sociale et Culturelle en AEF (see p. 96), *Islam–AEF* is produced by its director, a Senegalese Muslim expatriate of Poto-Poto named Youssouf Bakhoum. The quality of the articles written by Eliot in *Islam–AEF* was winning it an ever-larger place among the literate Muslims of Moyen-Congo when in December 1956—at the point where its circulation had reached some 1,800—Eliot withdrew from its editorship and announced that he would start a less specialized monthly.

An even shorter-lived and quite different attempt to appeal to a Muslim audience was made by another monthly, *L'Etoile du Tchad*, which appeared in both a French and an Arabic edition. This was not initiated by an individual but was an official venture started by the government of Tchad in 1951 at the request of the territorial assembly in order to provide the Islamic populations of that territory with their first local publication in their own language. For lack of a suitable press in Tchad, *L'Etoile* was printed in Algiers and edited by a French official of the North African Muslim Affairs Bureau, to whom a monthly stipend of 25,000 Metro. francs was paid for this service. The annual subsidy required to publish *L'Etoile* amounted to 1,200,000 CFA francs, and at each of the budgetary sessions from 1952 through 1955, the advisability of maintaining this publication was questioned. *L'Etoile* was criticized partly for its poor editing and for arriving so late in Tchad that the news it contained was already stale but even more for being couched in an Arabic unintelligible to the Tchadian Muslims. To reduce its cost, various proposals were made and rejected by the assembly, and finally in December 1955 its complete suppression was voted.

In view of the discouraging history of journalism in AEF, the prospects for establishing a financially sound, independent, and informative press there are not good.[13] This was apparently the conclusion reached by Charles de Breteuil, owner of a successful chain of French West African newspapers, who, after studying the situation in AEF in 1954, decided not to enter that field,[14] and the situation seems to have changed little since then. Under African governments, the four republics may consider it even less worth while than in the past to grant subsidies to the press from public funds. Without such subsidies, and with a probable shrinkage in the resident European community, it is hard to see how more than a handful of the federation's current publications can survive. Journalism is a field into which the AEF Africans have not yet ventured on a truly professional basis. Yet with their fondness and facility for verbal self-expression, they may well take it up in the future, though probably in a form different from that which now prevails in the country.

CHAPTER 21

Population and Social Welfare

The African population of AEF is extremely complex as to ethnic composition and its origins are still to a large degree veiled in mystery. About 90 per cent are Negroes, and the nomadic Touareg, Toubous, and Peulhs, who form the remaining 10 per cent and who call themselves white, are probably of Hamitic or Semitic stock. The Negrillos or pygmies, who live in small units in the forest clearings, are thought to be the oldest inhabitants of AEF. The Negro majority are sometimes roughly classified into 20 main groups.[1] Of these, the five most important, going from south to north, are the Bantu-speaking sedentary farmers, whose related tribes spread over an enormous area in central Africa; the Fang or Pahouin, a seminomadic people inhabiting Gabon and overflowing into south Cameroun; the highly diversified Oubanguian tribes, composed of hunters, fishermen, farmers, and traders, who are concentrated mainly in northern Oubangui; the peoples of the Chari-Ouaddaian linguistic group in Tchad; and, finally, the Nilo-Tchadian sedentary Negroes of the Tibesti.

So various are these Negro groups that it is almost impossible to generalize about them. One authority[2] believes that, if the pygmies and Islamized tribes were excluded, the family—in the widest sense of the term —could be taken as the basic unit of AEF's Negro population. In addition, there are bonds that have been forged not through blood relationship but by sentiment, time, and circumstances. To some extent, the belief that they have a common origin binds together the Bavili, Bassoundi, Bakongo, and Batéké of Moyen-Congo. On a geographic basis, feelings of village unity and even regional solidarity are manifested in the opposition that sets the southern and northern peoples in the same territory against each other. This is the case with the Balali and M'Bochi in the Congolese basin and the Sara and Muslim tribes of Tchad. Trade and the sharing of religious practices have also created ties, as have languages that are spoken over a wide area. Kikongo, a simplified form of the Bakongo language, is the *lingua franca* in what was formerly the kingdom of the Kongo; Lingala, a version of the Boubangui tongue, is understood by all the river peoples along the Federal Artery; Sango is spoken throughout central Oubangui from 5° to 8° N. latitude; and a degenerated form of Arabic is the language used among Tchadian Muslims.[3] Since France took over AEF, a common administration and the French language have become the outstanding unifying forces, and French is virtually the sole means of intercommunication between the African elite from all parts of AEF.

If there is no fundamental unity among the AEF Africans, there has also been none among European observers as to their demographic status. When the Europeans first came to the area, they found its small population concentrated in the two river basins of the Congo and Tchad and along the narrow littoral plain, and the northern desert of Tchad and the great forest of Moyen-Congo and Gabon were virtually uninhabited. Within the relatively populous zones, the tribes were not only scattered but unstable, because of the practice of shifting agriculture or that of nomadic herding. The early explorers quickly grasped the fundamental role played by climate and terrain in determining population concentrations, and in the Congolese basin and Gabon they also noted that slave raiding, trade, and tribal relationships largely determined the distribution of the inhabitants there.[4] After the French occupied AEF, the recruitment of labor for the concessionary companies, public works, and the forest industry increased the population's mobility, as did the later development of a wage-earning class, the administration's regrouping of villages, and the drift to the towns, which began during the world economic depression and became sharply accentuated after World War II.

Before the French occupation, the only large clusters of population in what became AEF were to be found in the Islamized regions of Tchad, but most of them have since lost much of their population and all of their importance. Except for Abéché, all the towns in contemporary AEF are the creation of Europeans,[5] who dominate them and who themselves form an overwhelmingly urban group.

The growth of AEF's European population, slow before World War II, became very rapid in the years immediately thereafter, owing to the enlargement of the civil service and to the greater job opportunities opened up by the Plan. Immigration reached its peak in 1950, when 2,200 Europeans disembarked in AEF and gravitated mainly toward Moyen-Congo's principal towns. That year, 44 per cent of the European population was to be found in Moyen-Congo, 22 per cent in Gabon, 21 per cent in Oubangui, and 13 per cent in Tchad. Particularly striking was the growth of Brazzaville, whose European population—which numbered only 284 in 1900 and 1,104 in 1938—rose to 4,353 by 1950. In 1950 the European element in Pointe Noire totaled 1,996 and that in Libreville 2,085, and those two towns, together with Brazzaville, contained half of AEF's total white population.[6] The trade recession of 1952 stemmed the flow of European immigration, and by 1955 the total European population had fallen to 20,700 from 21,500 five years before. During that span of years, there were important shifts in its concentration: the Europeans living in Moyen-Congo declined numerically from 10,200 to 7,800, but the number resident in Gabon rose to about 4,600, in Oubangui to 5,000, and in Tchad to 3,300. Since that time the European component has remained fairly steady around the 20,000 mark (of whom some 7,900 are women), but it may be expected to diminish in proportion as the new African governments assign their nationals to the posts of command formerly monopolized by the Europeans.

Jean Dresch's oft-quoted phrase, "Les villes, créations des Blancs, se peuplent des Noirs" is even truer today than when it was written soon after the last war.[7] If the number of Europeans coming to live in AEF's towns has grown phenomenally since 1945, that of Africans inhabiting the peripheral suburbs and *quartiers* has risen even faster. In 1938 the African urban population was 85,400 and by 1949 it had increased to 174,500.[8] During those 11 years, the African population of Brazzaville increased by 226 per cent, that of Pointe Noire by 358 per cent, Libreville by 216 per cent, Fort Lamy by 181 per cent, and Port Gentil by 95 per cent. Dolisie, which in 1936 had been only a station on the Congo-Ocean railroad, in 1949 had a population of 18,000 Africans (and 379 Europeans).[9] The mushrooming of AEF's African urban population has continued despite the government's efforts to prevent it and to deflect migrants away from the towns and toward the depopulated rural areas.

Because of the instability of AEF's population, both European and African, its exact number is not known. Then, too, the administration's method of taking censuses, changes in territorial boundaries, and the lack of a registry of vital statistics have caused further uncertainty. In respect to the African segment of the population, confusion has been caused by the custom that prevails in some regions of frequently changing an individual's name and, in the case of the Matsouanists, of refusing on religious grounds to be included in the census. The foregoing reasons account for much of the inaccuracy, inconsistency, and incompleteness of AEF's population statistics. In the late nineteenth century, Brazza stated simply as his impression that the population of Gabon and the French Congo then came to 5 million, and on no more scientific basis rested Challaye's estimate in 1909 of 8 to 10 million, or of Bruel's more conservative figure of about 5 million in 1914. After the head tax was imposed throughout AEF, it was assumed that guesswork as to population figures would be appreciably reduced, but the chiefs who drew up the rolls had an interest in falsifying them (see pp. 74–75) and even the administration had its own *raisons d'état* for stressing or ignoring certain population statistics.[10] On the assumption that the size of AEF's population had declined markedly since the French occupation, opponents of Western imperialism have seized on such figures as would support their viewpoint. Indeed, far more ingenuity has been used to "explain" AEF's population decline than to ascertain the accuracy of the statistics on which such a conclusion was reached.

Since World War II, the government has made a greater effort to take accurate censuses, and in this it has been aided by the development of an *état civil* in the towns. Table 9 not only shows the wide variations in population estimates during the interwar and postwar periods but also indicates the steady growth that has occurred in the number of inhabitants in the two northern territories. According to the figures of January 1, 1957, AEF had a population totaling about 4,848,000, an area of approximately 2,510,000 square kilometers, and thus an average density of fewer than two inhabitants to the square kilometer.[11] Between 1950 and 1957 there had been an over-all increase of about 1 per cent each year, the most rapid

TABLE 9.—POPULATION, POPULATION DENSITY, AND AREA OF AEF,
IN CERTAIN YEARS, 1921–57

Territory	Population (in thousands)					Area (thousands of sq. miles)	Pop. density, 1957, per sq. mile (approx.)
	1921	1936	1946	1950	1957		
Gabon	389	410	382	405	400	103	3.9
Moyen-Congo	582	746	651	675	749	132	5.6
Oubangui-Chari ...	608	834	1,060	1,067	1,128	238	4.7
Tchad	1,272	1,433	1,901	2,238	2,571	496	5.2
Total, AEF.....	2,851	3,413	3,994	4,385	4,848	969	5.0

Note: Apparent declines and increases in population totals reflect to some extent changes in territorial boundaries.

growth being registered in the northern territories, which were already the most densely populated. If one disregarded the immense, virtually uninhabited areas such as the BET, whose 538,000 square kilometers contained only 41,000 persons, the average density would rise to over three per square kilometer—a figure not greatly inferior to that of French West Africa and Cameroun. Nevertheless, even for central Africa, AEF remains a country of exceptionally sparse population. And if uncertainty and controversy surround the question as to whether or where the population of AEF has been increasing or declining over the years, the main causes of its sparsity are well known. As in many tropical African countries, they are the low birth rate and high death rate attributable to alcoholism, the bride-price system, undernourishment, and disease.

Alcoholism

A long-time subject of concern to the government, missionaries, and some European residents has been the ravages caused by alcoholism among the African population of AEF, but the African elite apparently have turned their attention to this social problem only in the past 20 years. As long ago as 1913, a group of French missionaries, merchants, and officials in Gabon, headed by the local director of the Société du Haut-Ogooué, petitioned the Chamber of Deputies to stop the exportation of alcoholic beverages to that colony. This petition failed to win parliamentary support because the government feared that such a measure would have undesirable repercussions on Gabon's budget. The subject was attacked on a far wider basis after France had signed the international Convention of St. Germain, by which she undertook to forbid the exportation of certain types of intoxicating liquor to her African colonies.

During World War II, a local regulation of September 3, 1941, called the Sicé decree, carried such prohibitive legislation much further with respect to AEF. By its provisions, a ban was placed not only upon the sale of all imported alcoholic beverages to AEF Africans, but also on the local manufacture of palm wine and millet beer. African reaction to this measure was strongly adverse, and the elite have never ceased to ask for its abrogation. In all of AEF's elected bodies, the African members have recognized that the wine, beer, and stronger liquors imported in ever-greater amounts are doing serious damage to their compatriots, but their antagonism seems to have been aroused mainly by the discriminatory aspect of the existing legislation. "What is bad for an African," said one Grand Councilor, "is equally bad for a European."[2] He and his colleagues were equally incensed by the law's prohibition against making palm wine, which they described as a healthy, traditional beverage.[13]

Since World War II, various steps have been taken in a futile effort to arrest the spread of alcoholism in AEF, to supplement the provisions of the St. Germain Convention and the ineffective and unpopular Sicé decree. Import duties were raised, a control of the quality of imported wine through laboratory analyses was instituted, and shops authorized to sell alcoholic beverages were restricted to certain areas and their number limited to one per 2,000 inhabitants.[14] From time to time the question of permitting the territorial governors, at their discretion, to impose a quota on imported liquors was discussed in French parliamentary bodies and the local assemblies, but the proposal was finally rejected for various reasons. One was the effect on AEF's precarious revenues of such a limitation, and another was the risk of enhancing the attractiveness of certain liquors by forbidding their sale.[15] Even more important, however, was the effective lobbying done by interested French manufacturers and merchants. So long as French citizens in AEF, including naturalized Africans, were allowed to import liquor freely, clandestine sales to Africans obviously would continue, because they were highly profitable.

Moyen-Congo was the territory in which alcoholism was most acute, for it had the largest number of moneyed Africans, and, moreover, Pointe Noire was the main port of entry for French imports into the federation.[16] Fortunately, the consumption of alcohol in Tchad, the most populous of the territories, was inhibited by the Muslim faith professed by over half of its population. Imported alcoholic beverages accounted for most of the inebriation in the coastal towns, but in the hinterland most of the liquor consumed by Africans was brewed by them. In September 1955, a territorial committee to study the problem in Moyen-Congo was constituted, but its recommendations have been no more successful in checking the increase of alcoholism there than legislation has been. Whether or not the African governments of the four republics will consider alcoholism a sufficiently serious social evil to take effective steps against it remains to be seen.

The Status of Women, and the Birth Rate

European travelers and residents in AEF have often publicly expressed sympathy for the hard lot of African women who are to be seen toiling in the fields or performing onerous household tasks surrounded by a brood of clamoring children. It seemed clear to these onlookers that if African men paid a high bride price for African girls, it was not only because the possession of numerous wives was a sign of wealth and prestige, but also because women were a productive economic asset to them as laborers and bearers of children. With few exceptions, all the efforts made in the course of many years by French missionaries and officials to raise the status of African women either have been ineffectual or have backfired.[17] Not only have they failed to emancipate the African woman but they have aroused the passive resistance or hostility of the male segment of the local population.

Inevitably polygamy was the first target of the missionaries' attack, for they regarded that institution as the main stumbling block in the way of the Africans' conversion to Christianity, and they put considerable pressure on the government to prohibit polygamy by law.[18] The government, though in sympathy with their general objective, found the missionaries' frontal attack on the problem too disruptive to native society, and it particularly frowned on the missions' practice of sheltering young girls who were trying to escape from parental authority. Furthermore, the few African girls educated at mission schools were regarded with disfavor by their elders because of their independent behavior. Yet the Metropolitan government was not more successful in emancipating African women when it attempted a legalistic approach. Neither the Mandel nor the Jacquinot decrees, of 1938 and 1951 respectively, succeeded in their aim of permitting young Africans to marry without being unduly retarded or actually prevented from doing so by the excessive demands made by a prospective bride's family. These laws became dead letters because the Africans regarded as undue outside interference with custom any such attempts to give freedom of marital choice to girls and widows, to allow young people over 21 years of age to marry without the consent of their parents, and to regulate the bride price.

More successful in winning African cooperation was a new policy initiated in AEF by the Free French government during World War II. First General de Gaulle himself contributed a sum of money to enable impoverished and meritorious young men to marry, and later the territorial assemblies voted regular allocations to this "bride-price fund." Then, in another direction, Governor-General Eboué went much further than any of his predecessors in a circular he issued on August 25, 1941. In it he proposed to impose a special tax on polygamists and to make monogamy a prerequisite for any African aspiring to the status of *Notable évolué*. After him, Governors-General Bayardelle and Soucadaux worked out another project whereunder bachelors would be subject to higher taxation than married men, fiscal exemptions would be granted to the monogamous parents of three children, and only monogamists would be admitted to the local functionary cadre. When this project was submitted to the territorial assemblies in 1947, their various reactions reflected their respective demographic and sociological situations.[19] Gabon's assemblymen, worried by that territory's declining birth rate, favored the proposals, as did those of Oubangui and for much the same reasons. Tchad's assemblymen hedged their approval with reservations that reflected the Muslim viewpoint on marriage. Moyen-Congo's rejection of the whole project, except for one favorable vote, showed its representatives' anxiety in regard to the growth of prostitution and divorce among the local urban populations.[20]

The debates concerning this and similar proposals in the Grand Council and territorial assemblies[21] are evidence of the dilemma in which the male elite of AEF find themselves in regard to the status of women. While they wanted to appear progressive and modern and therefore in favor of monogamy, they refused to allow the marital status of an African functionary to play a part in determining his eligibility for family allowances, and they have also displayed an antifeminist attitude. In principle they favor offering greater educational facilities and professional opportunities to African women and are also concerned that the bride price should be kept within reasonable limits, but at the same time they want to make it more difficult for African women to get a divorce, take up prostitution, and escape masculine authority in general. Any implication on the part of Europeans that African women are treated as merchandise or as beasts of burden is hotly resented. By and large, the attitude of the male elite has been that custom in such matters should not be assailed by alien laws but should be modified only at the Africans' own pace and according to their wishes. The contradictions inherent in this viewpoint are reflected in a few of the laws that have been passed by some of the new republics. In Gabon and Tchad the head tax for women has been suppressed, and in all of the republics appropriations for the education of girls have been increased. At the same time, other regulations of a repressive nature have been issued, such as the law passed by the Oubangui legislative assembly shortly after it was constituted forbidding nudity throughout the Central African Republic.[22]

Despite all this mixture of traditionalism, puritanism, and progressiveness, the main concern of the elite is that African family solidarity should not be further undermined, and that the emancipation of women should not adversely affect the local birth rate. Studies carried out by French sociologists in AEF since the war have shown that fewer children are born to polygamous than to monogamous marriages and that great disparity in the ages of a couple also contributes largely to sterility, as does, of course, venereal disease.[23] Although these experts brought to light the wide variations in tribal fecundity, they did not always agree as to whether high infant mortality or a low birth rate was chiefly responsible for the small size of AEF's total population. It appears from such statistics as are available that about one-third of the federation's population is made up of children under the age of 15, which suggests a currently high birth rate, but they show also that approximately one-third of African infants die before they complete their first year.[24] Indisputably, improvement in the health of AEF's population is the main key to its demographic problem, and in this respect AEF suffers from an unusually long roster of serious diseases to which resistance is lowered by the prevailing undernourishment.

Undernourishment and Diet

Before World War II, undernourishment was vaguely recognized by the government and employers of AEF as a prime cause of the local Africans' poor health and inefficiency. Gabon's foresters early realized that to keep their labor force they must provide them with more food, but they usually resorted to the easy solution of increasing the manioc ration. This pleased the laborers who were indigenous to the forest zone and for whom manioc was the basic food, because it gave them the impression that they were eating their fill. Yet it made their diet even more unbalanced than before, and among the immigrant workers who were accustomed to millet, so much manioc was conducive to intestinal maladies.[25]

Before and since the last war, official efforts to cope with the under-nourishment prevalent in AEF have consisted principally of attempts to introduce new food crops and to promote the production of traditional ones, with the exception of manioc, the output of which was spontaneously increasing in certain areas. Since 1952 this policy has been pursued more intensively, but with only mediocre success (see pp. 164–65). To assemble much-needed data on which to base administrative action, the government undertook two scientific surveys, in 1948–49 and in 1956–58. The first related to urban diets and was confined to three of the federation's largest towns, and the second pertained to the food consumed by rural Africans in Moyen-Congo and Tchad.

Among the rural populations studied, only those in certain areas of Tchad were very exceptional in having an ample and well-balanced diet, based on the consumption of millet, milk, meat, and fish. As to the manioc-eating tribes of the forest zone, their most serious lack was animal proteins, for they practiced no animal husbandry and the supply of meat from hunting was sharply limited both by official restrictions on firearms and by the scarcity and small size of game. The meat-starved forest peoples ate every animal they could lay their hands on, including caterpillars, termites, and palm rats. This last-mentioned food element was found to be dangerous to them both because of the bush fires they started in order to force the rats into the open and also because of a widespread malady induced by the consumption of their flesh.[26] To remedy these and other deficiencies in the forest and savannah zones, the government has been encouraging the rearing of tsetse-resistant Ndama cattle, the production of more vegetable fats (palm and peanut oil), and the breeding of tilapia in family ponds, but the supply of food is still far below the demand and the needs of the rural populations.

This was also true in regard to the residents of AEF's fast-growing towns, but there the problem was somewhat different. In the surrounding areas there was plenty of land to supply even the ever-growing number of town dwellers with enough food, but the farmers there were either unwilling to supply food or had themselves drifted to the cities. Soret tells of an attempt to improve the food situation of Brazzaville by cultivating the unused lands north of the town and on M'Bamou island, which failed because of the adamant refusal of the women in adjacent villages to farm them.[27] Scarcity of food supplies, however, was not the sole cause of urban undernourishment in AEF, for cost and eating habits also played a part. The Africans were acquiring a taste for the meat that was being flown into the southern towns from Tchad, and for European imported foods, such as flour, refined sugar, and condensed milk. Despite some official price controls, all of these items were still so expensive that their purchase strained the budgets of urban Africans, even though their incomes were larger than those of their rural compatriots. Thus, after pay day, they ate abundantly, but their meals became poorer and more irregular as the month drew to a close. Moreover, even in the days when the cost of food was not a primary consideration, they had no conception of a well-balanced diet and were also given to spending a considerable share of their income on alcoholic beverages.

To remedy this situation in Brazzaville, the Sociétés Indigènes de Prévoyance (SIP) started communal restaurants in Poto-Poto and Bacongo, for which the initial funds were provided by the administration and the equipment by private groups (such as the Chamber of Commerce and the Importers-Exporters syndicate). Well-balanced, inexpensive meals were served in them—826 each working day in 1952—and the men who ate there regularly, it was noted by their employers, showed marked improvement in physical stamina.[28] At about the same time, professional social-welfare workers in each territorial capital began to organize cooking classes, in which they taught African women how to prepare wholesome meals from locally available ingredients. A third venture, this time with the aid of the United Nations International Children's Emergency Fund (UNICEF), consisted of distributing several tons of powdered milk to school children in Moyen-Congo. In 1955 it was reported that it had taken a year to persuade the children there to drink the milk and their mothers to follow the instructions as to how it should be prepared.[29]

History of the Health Service

A number of military doctors, outstanding among whom was Noël Ballay, accompanied the early French explorers of AEF, and some of them stayed on to organize a health service during the years 1900 to 1908. These first doctors set up some very rudimentary posts, and after difficult beginnings gradually accustomed the populations to Western medical treatment in general and to anti-smallpox vaccinations in particular. Between 1908 and 1912 they managed to establish 23 medical posts, although for this purpose AEF received only a tenth of the funds allocated to French West Africa for its health service.[30]

Also in the opening years of the twentieth century, the first scientific medical mission was sent to the French Congo with funds supplied by the Paris Geographical Society and related organizations. For the study of trypanosomiasis in Brazzaville, Emile Gentil gave land, a laboratory, and a hospital pavilion to this mission, which was the nucleus of what became in 1908 a branch of the Pasteur Institute. Gradually this institute began training Africans for work with trypanosomiasis patients, gave a special course in local conditions to all doctors coming to practice in AEF, and extended its activities to deal with a wide range of diseases. In 1932 it moved into new buildings, and five years later began experimenting with animals, specializing in the study of venomous snakes and cattle diseases. During World War II, it began the manufacture of locally needed serums and vaccines that could no longer be imported from the mother institute in Paris, and in recent years it has been able to supply them also to Cameroun and the Belgian Congo. In 1948 it moved once more, into more modern and better-equipped buildings, and in 1959—after 14 years of indecision—decided to build an annex at Bangui.

On the eve of World War I, an effort was made to improve the equipment of the archaic territorial hospitals that dated back to the first years of the medical service, and a new one, on a smaller scale, was built at Fort Archambault. In 1914 the mobilization of many of AEF's army doctors and nurses reduced the service there to a holding operation, and the only forward step taken during the war years was the training of larger numbers of African auxiliary staff in the federation's hospitals and medical centers. Even before the hostilities ended, it was discovered that sleeping sickness had been spreading to new areas and reappearing in old ones. Specifically to combat this disease, Parliament voted a million francs in December 1917, and every year thereafter it made a similar grant for the same purpose. These funds enabled a trypanosomiasis specialist, Dr. Jamot, to create ten mobile units between 1925 and 1929, which operated out of Nola, the center of Oubangui's most infested region. By the mid-1930's, 60 doctors were giving their full time to combating trypanosomiasis, 1,250,000 persons had been examined for symptoms and a card index of them set up, 40,000 new cases had been treated, and the most afflicted victims segregated in about 50 treatment centers. On the eve of World War II, sleeping sickness was in retreat in Gabon and Moyen-Congo but was still virulent in the regions of Nola and the Logone. Also during the interwar period, AEF's regular medical service had conducted anti-smallpox campaigns, had begun to segregate lepers in special villages, had built more medical posts and dispensaries, and had begun to concentrate on the care of mothers and children. Considering the limited staff and funds at the disposal of AEF's medical organizations, their accomplishments were remarkable. As of 1936, the European staff comprised only 80 doctors and 46 pharmacists, nurses, midwives, and health workers, and the African subordinate personnel numbered some 650 nurses, dressers, and sanitary agents. In addition to the mobile units, AEF as a whole could count 5 hospitals, 46 medical centers, and 52 dispensaries.[31]

Organization of the Service

By a decree of September 2, 1914, which extended to AEF a regulation drawn up three years earlier for New Caledonia, authority over the federation's public health service was centralized in the hands of the governor-general. This worked well enough for some years, but in the late 1930's Governor-General Reste decided on a decentralization of medical activities analogous to that which he was undertaking in the field of education. He gave greater powers to the General Inspector of Public Health but—and this was more important—he stressed the need for preventive medicine and education in hygiene in the rural areas. Just as he favored establishing primary schools in villages rather than concentrating educational facilities in a few centers, so he instructed doctors to care for the sick in their own rural milieu and no longer to count on their seeking medical care in the large settlements. Since the days of Reste, there has been no fundamental change in the organization of AEF's health service, which from the outset has been modeled on that of the army. However, authority has been further decentralized, AEF's hospitals, medical centers, and dispensaries are much more numerous and their equipment has been vastly improved, the range of activities of the mobile units has been increased, and the staff of European and, above all, of African doctors has been enlarged.

The *Journal Officiel* for December 1945 published two regulations re-organizing the public health service so that in respect to the management of hospitals, medical centers, and dispensaries, authority was transferred from the General Inspector to the territorial medical directors.[32] At the same time a new Service Général d'Hygiène et de Prophylaxie, of which the precursor had been Dr. Jamot's anti-trypanosomiasis mobile units, was created, and it was permitted considerable initiative, although it was nomi-nally under the authority of the General Inspector. Besides continuing to campaign against sleeping sickness, this service was assigned the enormous task of tracking down and treating AEF's other major epidemic and endemic maladies, destroying such carriers of disease as tsetse flies, mos-quitoes, and rats, and improving the population's sanitary practices in regard to food and housing. For the operations of this service, the federa-tion was divided into 19 principal and 7 secondary sectors, whose basis was the ethnic group and not the administrative unit. In each sector, one or more teams, each composed of an African doctor or nurse and aides under the supervision of a European medical officer, was to visit regularly every village in its area. There the inhabitants would be assembled by the village authorities to be examined, inoculated, and—if necessary—treated. Shortage of staff and of equipment delayed the creation of teams for all of AEF's sectors, but each year their number was increased by one or two, and by 1957 the roster was complete.

In 1952 the need to adapt the work of the mobile units to the new treatment for leprosy entailed another reorganization, and in each territory they were placed under the control of the local health inspectorate. This proved to be more difficult than anticipated, for the mobile units were accustomed to having considerable autonomy and balked at the new re-strictions aimed at coordinating their operations with those of the fixed medical units. Nevertheless, by 1955 greater regional unity had been attained. Passage of the *loi-cadre* the following year led to a further de-centralization, and all the federal health organizations except one charged with coordinating medical campaigns against the major diseases were suppressed. In October 1959, the health ministers of AEF's four republics met at Bangui to work out joint policies that would guide the operations of that organization.

Hospital and Medical Facilities

In 1949, when the Plan was first being applied to AEF, the federation possessed 5 major and 3 lesser hospitals, 61 medical centers, 92 infirmaries, 30 leper villages, and about 55 centers for the segregation of sleeping-sickness victims. Hospital beds for Europeans numbered 316, and those for Africans 11,968.[33] In addition, there were the medical facilities provided by private organizations such as the Red Cross, the territorial child-welfare centers (*Berceaux*), companies employing large labor forces, and the Christian missions, of which the best known was Dr. Schweitzer's hospital at Lambaréné.

Before World War II, the only health service in the federation that was relatively well provided with funds was the one which combated trypanosomiasis, but after the war, much greater sums were spent on AEF's medical work. Under the ten-year Plan, AEF was allocated 5,131 million francs to be used for the construction and equipment of medical buildings. Even before the Plan became operative in AEF, however, work on the Sicé hospital at Pointe Noire had been begun with money supplied by the federal budget, and in Oubangui and Tchad maternity centers financed from the Cotton Supporting Fund were being built.

When it came to determining which projects were to be undertaken by the Plan, disagreement arose between the FIDES directorate on the one hand and the federal health service and elected assemblies on the other. The latter objected to the predilection shown by the FIDES directorate for improving urban medical facilities (in particular the construction of a huge federal hospital at Brazzaville) and to its neglect of rural health units. All were agreed that Brazzaville's dilapidated and dirty hospital required drastic improvement, but the federal health service and the Grand Council felt that its replacement by a grandiose structure three times the size of Léopoldville's hospital was disproportionate to the federation's needs and that to maintain it would put too great a strain on AEF's resources.[34] After repeatedly and vainly criticizing this project, the Grand Councilors voted a resolution on September 6, 1951, asking that "plans for the Brazzaville hospital be reviewed more realistically" and that the funds saved in consequence be spent on the territorial hospitals and rural units. To be sure, this vote was partly inspired by the northern councilors' habitual resentment that, under guise of building a federal structure, Moyen-Congo was once more being unfairly favored. Nevertheless, the Grand Council also felt that FIDES' desire to construct a hospital that would outdo and impress the Belgians on the south bank of the Congo river was primarily a manifestation of chauvinistic false pride.

As time went on, the fears that had been expressed in AEF seemed justified. The firm that was building the Brazzaville hospital went bankrupt, and that institution did not begin functioning until mid-1957. It

cost the Metropolitan taxpayer over 2 billion CFA francs to construct and
150 million more to equip, and its annual operating deficit was estimated
to come to some 70 million CFA francs.[35] In its favor it could be said
that the Brazzaville hospital was one of the most modern and best equipped
in Africa: it had 731 beds and a staff of 348, of whom 2 were surgeons and
7 were medical specialists. Its completion permitted the immediate transfer
to it of 500 patients from the former obsolete hospital, and it was filled to
overflowing after the Brazzaville riots of January 1959.

Five years before it was completed, Governor-General Chauvet had to
admit that the errors committed by FIDES in respect to planning structures
for AEF's medical units were not confined to the Brazzaville hospital.
On September 30, 1952, he told the Grand Council that delays in getting
the program under way had been due to "insufficient preliminary study
and mistakes made in the initial concept." On a tour of AEF's rural areas
shortly before, the governor-general had been struck by the urgent need
to repair existing facilities, and by the "anarchic dispersal of up-country
units." Progress, he said, had undeniably been made in building more
medical centers and rural dispensaries, but work could not be begun on
the new territorial hospitals until 1953.

Once under way, construction progressed with fair speed, and by 1957
the program envisaged under the Plan had been virtually completed. By
then AEF possessed 6 large, well-equipped hospitals, 120 medical centers
in regional headquarters, and 209 dispensaries, and it was said that no
African need go more than 50 kilometers to reach some unit providing
medical care.[36] In 1956, AEF's medical installations were supplemented
by the establishment at Djoué of a regional branch of the World Health
Organization, on land and in buildings offered it by the federal government "on terms of unequaled generosity."[37] This was the second international health organization that within the year had chosen AEF as an area
for specialized medical activities (see below).

Although these international organizations contributed to AEF's medical facilities and FIDES paid all the initial cost of the structures it built
there, the latter's operating expenses, including those for personnel, were
borne by the federation's budgets. Since the war the proportion of federal
and territorial revenues spent on medical and health work has risen steadily.
In 1958 the territories were devoting between 13 and 20 per cent of their
total expenditures to such activities, most of the outlays going to cover the
medical units' operating expenses.[38]

Prevalent Diseases

Statistics for the year 1949 showed that 33 per cent of the ailments
treated by AEF's health services were of a contagious nature and of either
endemic or epidemic intensity, 45 per cent were sporadic or involved
surgery, 12 per cent were venereal, and 10 per cent were cutaneous.[39]

For many years, yellow fever was considered to be equatorial Africa's
most dangerous malady, but owing to mass inoculations it never became
a major threat in AEF. As a result of systematic and large-scale vaccination,

smallpox, too, which formerly occurred in epidemic form in some parts of the federation, has now almost disappeared except among the nomads of Batha, whose way of life makes them difficult to vaccinate and carriers of this disease.[40]

Malaria is still the principal endemic malady of AEF, and one especially serious for African children between the ages of three and five. It is to be found everywhere throughout the federation, its incidence being especially high in Moyen-Congo and the hinterland of Gabon, and in recent years it has appeared as far afield as the oases of northern Tchad.[41] After World War II, the health service began periodic spraying of African urban homes with DDT and supplied quinine or synthetic substitutes without charge to school children. In 1952, it organized an anti-malaria service on a territorial basis, and by 1957 this service was treating about 130,000 malaria patients a year, of whom 105,000 were children of school age or under.[42]

Yaws ranks after malaria in the number of known cases in AEF, and since 1939 the federation's doctors have been treating annually from 80,000 to 100,000 persons so afflicted. Incidence of yaws is particularly widespread in the forest zone, diminishes in the higher altitudes, and is rarely found north of the Chari river. The control of this disease, which is easy to detect and treat, has brought great prestige to Western medicine in the eyes of the African population.

Less prevalent are such maladies as cerebrospinal meningitis, trachoma, venereal diseases (although nearly 80,000 such cases were treated in 1957, of whom half were syphilitic), and tuberculosis. Beginning in 1956, the mobile teams made a special study of tuberculosis by testing 12,000 individuals, and they were reportedly astonished to learn that it had been spreading rapidly in all the AEF towns except those of Tchad.

Special mention should be made of two diseases in AEF—trypanosomiasis and leprosy—not only because they are among the most serious afflictions borne by the African populations but also because their treatment by the health service has been particularly effective. As long ago as the 1890's, sleeping sickness was recognized by the French to be a major cause of mortality and mental illnesses among the riverine peoples of AEF, and it has been the object of close study since the early years of the twentieth century. Only gradually was it realized that the French occupation had accelerated the spread of trypanosomiasis, which in pre-European days had been confined to certain regions and populations. With the increase of trade, human portage, and the recruitment of laborers, this disease was carried to new areas where it caused terrible ravages among the population. A gubernatorial circular issued in 1925 noted that sleeping sickness, long stationary, had developed so intensively during the preceding decade that special measures must be taken against it (see pp. 332–33). After World War II, the Office de la Recherche Scientifique et Technique d'Outre-Mer (ORSTOM) carried out a systematic search for all the tsetse-fly breeding grounds, and discovered that sleeping sickness existed in an epidemic or marked endemic state throughout an area of about 350,000 square kilometers and in a weak endemic form in an additional 700,000 square kilometers.

To cope with its unexpectedly widespread incidence, the anti-trypanoso-miasis mobile teams were increased and reinforced by specialized personnel. Through their operations, sleeping sickness was brought under control, and at the end of 1957 it could be reported that only 700 new victims had been found that year, whereas in the early 1950's the number of cases discovered each year averaged about 5,000. Since these mobile teams were reorganized, they have treated more than 100,000 trypanoso-miasis cases.

An even more remarkable victory by AEF's health service has been that won over leprosy in recent years. Segregating lepers in agricultural villages was long the classical method of dealing with this disease, and in 1944 the biggest such village established up to that time in AEF was started at Agoudou-Manga, 50 kilometers from Bambari, in Oubangui. As of 1947, nearly 1,000 lepers and their families were living there, in the charge of a Catholic missionary who was himself afflicted with that disease. Subsequently, smaller leper colonies were created in Gabon, of which the outstanding was that of Oyem. These colonies still serve for the segregation of lepers from inaccessible regions, but beginning in 1952 Colonel Dr. Richet initiated a wholly new type of treatment with sulfa drugs administered by mobile units that has revolutionized the whole problem, particularly in the south. In 1951 there were in Moyen-Congo 37,500 known lepers, only 2,200 of whom accepted treatment. By 1953 the number treated rose to 12,000, and the following year nearly 90 per cent of the known cases of leprosy were being regularly treated by members of the mobile units.[43] Estimates of the incidence of leprosy have had to be rapidly revised upward, and it is now estimated that 2.4 per cent of the total population is so afflicted. This high figure is thought not to indicate any spectacular spread of the disease but rather to reflect the greater willingness of lepers to be medically treated in recent years because they no longer fear segregation. As of 1957, the number of known lepers in the southern territories had risen to 140,000, of whom 12,000 had been pronounced cured and 120,000 were being more or less regularly treated, and the health service was planning to extend its work into Oubangui and Tchad. Even two years earlier, the success already won by AEF's health service in its anti-leprosy campaign had been so impressive that it attracted international attention and commendation. To promote this campaign, on which the federal government was spending annually some 45 million CFA francs, UNICEF in 1955 allocated a supplementary $215,000 with which to purchase drugs and vehicles for use by the mobile units.

As can be seen from the success story of AEF's recent anti-leprosy operations, the attitude of the African population is a vital determinant. In the early days of AEF's medical service, sick Africans—still wholly under the influence of sorcerers and fetishers—fled from the French doctors. Only gradually did they gain confidence in the superiority of Western medicine, but the number of those treated by AEF's medical facilities has risen very rapidly since the war. In 1946, about 350,000 patients received such treatment, and ten years later 3,200,000, and during the same decade the number of Africans hospitalized rose from 65,000 to 90,000. All patients, regardless of sex, creed, or color, were treated without charge by the health service, as were those hospitalized if they were certified to be indigent. Because African patients have always been averse to separation from their families, the growth in the number of those hospitalized is particularly significant. To encourage ill Africans to submit to hospitalization, the Grand Council asked the General Medical Inspector to permit those from distant villages to keep a relative with them.[44] He promised leniency in this respect but could not accede to the councilors' other request that sufferers from tuberculosis and venereal diseases be promised tax exemption (as was already the case with victims of trypanosomiasis) if they would accept regular medical treatment. Actually Africans are already sufficiently convinced of the efficacy of Western medicine that they no longer require additional inducements, and only in parts of Tchad is there now any difficulty in getting them to submit to medical examinations. There, it has been reported, the *goumiers* who round up villagers for the doctor's periodic visits exact money from the population, and some of the Muslims refuse on religious grounds to remove their robes for an examination.[45]

Personnel

The results achieved by AEF's health service are the more remarkable in view of the perennial shortage of staff from which it has suffered. Until 1944, it was completely dependent for doctors on the army medical corps, and there are still no doctor-training facilities in AEF beyond the premedical courses given in some secondary schools. The shortage was especially severe during World War II, when the number of doctors stationed in the federation, which had been 87 in 1938, fell to 57 in 1943. Nine military doctors arrived in 1944 to care for the Free French troops, but the civilian population continued to be neglected for some years after the war ended. As of 1947, the European staff working in AEF consisted of 71 doctors, 6 pharmacists, 59 male and female nurses, 9 midwives, and 2 administrative officers. This staff was increased slightly during the next few years, but the penury in French medical personnel was not really eased until 1954, when 94 army doctors who had been serving in Indochina were posted to AEF. During the first postwar years, the government-general had tried to induce French civilian physicians to come to AEF, but it was unsuccessful because the salaries offered them could be no higher than those earned by the military doctors.[46] Eventually this obstacle was overcome, and by 1957, 30 civilian doctors were serving under contract in AEF.[47] In addition, there was a handful of private practitioners in the main towns, whose paying clientele was extremely limited for several reasons. The main one was that all officials were entitled to free treatment from government doctors. The latter, moreover, were allowed after hours to receive private patients for small fees, the scale of which, set by the administration, private practitioners were not permitted to exceed.

Before 1954, the doctor shortage in AEF would have been even more serious than it was had it not been for the advent of an increasing number of African assistant doctors. In 1944 the first six came to the federation from the Dakar school of medicine, and by 1947 the African staff comprised 25 assistant doctors, 1,037 male and female nurses, and 7 midwives.[48] Because the federation had at that time no students of its own qualified to enter the Dakar medical school, it began to offer scholarships at Dakar to West Africans willing to serve for some years in AEF after graduation. By 1950 it was subsidizing 8 student doctors and midwives at the Dakar school, at an annual cost of 6,280,000 CFA francs, but the Grand Councilors were increasingly dissatisfied with the results of this policy. In the first place they were chagrined by the continued inability of AEF students to qualify for admission to the Dakar school, and second, they resented the West Africans' refusal to remain in AEF after their contractual term of duty there had ended. The nurse shortage, however, was not so acute, for in the mid-1950's a federal school of nursing was established at Brazzaville, and nurses were being trained for the local health service at all the territorial hospitals.

Inevitably, the allocation of AEF's limited medical personnel to the four territories gave rise to some dissension. Gabon, as the territory where the demographic situation was most critical, was assigned proportionately the largest number of doctors and midwives. As of 1955 it had one doctor for every 10,800 inhabitants, compared with one per 11,900 in Moyen-Congo, one per 28,200 in Oubangui, and one per 56,000 in Tchad.[49] Within each territory, the criterion used for the distribution of doctors was the number of patients served by the various medical units. Reasonable as this criterion seemed to be, it failed to accomplish the health service's objective of getting the maximum number of sick Africans to undergo regular medical treatment, for only in an emergency would Africans go to medical units that were not staffed by a doctor. The only way to induce those suffering from noncritical illnesses to come regularly for treatment was obviously to allocate doctors to regions in relation to the size of their populations, but there were not yet enough doctors to permit such a solution.

As of 1957, the federation as a whole could count 181 doctors (averaging nearly 4 per 100,000 of the total population), 1,900 midwives and nurses, 300 sanitary agents and laboratory technicians, and 1,600 miscellaneous employees.[50] The number of African assistant doctors serving in AEF had by that time risen to 40, but with the elevation that year of the Dakar school to the status of a Medical Faculty its standards for admission had to be raised and consequently the size of its student body was reduced. Thus, after 1957, any African aspiring to practice medicine in French Black Africa had to earn a state medical diploma, either at Dakar or in France. This meant that fewer—though better-trained— African doctors will be available for service in AEF, unless the governments of the four republics decide to lower this high standard until such time as there will be enough students from their countries educationally qualified for admission to a Medical Faculty.

PART II

The Political and Economical Development
of the Territories

CHAPTER 22

Gabon (République Gabonaise)

Territorial Politics

"Gabon," wrote Philippe Decraene early in 1959,[1] "is not only the most Gallicized of AEF territories but is the best-balanced, politically and economically." He might have added that it is also the smallest and least populous of the new states.

If compared with the Afrique Occidentale Française (AOF) countries, it most closely resembles Senegal culturally and Ivory Coast economically. Traders began coming from France to the Gabon and Senegal coasts in the sixteenth century, and French contacts with those areas have been consistently maintained over a longer period than those with any other parts of the AEF and AOF federations. Economically, and to a certain extent politically, Gabon is more like Ivory Coast in that it wants closer ties with France and looser ones with neighboring countries, which it has had to help out regularly because its great resources have given it a prosperity denied to them. Geographically and demographically, Gabon is unique. Though the dense forests that cover almost the whole territory contain nearly all of its present and future sources of wealth (okoumé wood and minerals), and though its waterways and ports provide the means of internal and external communications to a limited extent, they have also served to discourage the creation of a road network, so that the cost of shipping out ores is almost prohibitive. Furthermore, the terrain has been largely responsible for the dispersal of the Fang, or Pahouin, Gabon's dominant population group, and for the anarchy and degeneration that have characterized its tribal formations.

The political history of Gabon has been mainly that of the Fang peoples, who have been the subject of many European studies,[2] and who have inspired chronic concern on the part of the administration. Beginning in the latter half of the eighteenth century and lasting for about 150 years, the migrations of the Fang were almost incessant. It may well have been the Peulh conquest of northern Cameroun that started their drive southward from the savannah to the forest zone, in the course of which they conquered or drove out many weaker tribes. Warriors and traders, the Fang scorned agriculture and animal husbandry, and with a sure eye they settled in the areas economically best suited to their considerable talents. For historical and geographical reasons, the Fang are most cohesive and dynamic in north and central Gabon (in the Woleu-

343

CAMEROUN

FERNANDO-PO

Kribi

SPANISH
GUINEA

Rio Mouni
MONTS DE CRISTAL

Bitam

Oyem

Cocobeach

Médouneu

Mitzic

Mékambo

Makokou

Sibang
Libreville

Gabon

Ivindo

Kango

L. Azingo

Pt.Gentil

Lambaréné

Lastoursville

Ogooué

Ogooué

Fougamou

Ngounié

Franceville

Mouïla

Ndendé

Sette-Cama

Tchibanga

Nyanga

MOYEN-
CONGO

Mayumba

GABON

KILOMETERS

0   100   200   300   400

PLT

N'Tem and Ogooué-Ivindo regions) and most dispersed in the dense-forest areas. The Ogooué river valley was the southernmost point of their migrations, and there they are to be seen today in their "state of maximum confusion."[3] Some mid-nineteenth-century explorers moving eastward by way of the Ogooué were surprised to encounter Fang migrants swarming toward the coast, and at the time it was thought likely that the Fang might colonize the whole coastal region because it was then the key to trade with the hinterland. The French occupation not only checked further Fang expansion but first turned them from conquest to commerce and, much later, diverted some Fang to cocoa farming and politics.

The Fang of Gabon are widely scattered and, except in the north, do not live in homogeneous and compact groups as do those of Cameroun and Spanish Guinea. Pax Gallica made it unnecessary for them to live together in large fortified villages and encouraged a mobility that was in any case heightened by their attraction to the best trading zones. In fact, so nomadic did the Fang remain for years that the French administration made repeated—and unsuccessful—efforts to regroup them in villages located in accessible regions. The only areas in which this forced resettlement policy has been a success are Ogooué-Ivindo and Woleu-N'Tem (except for Mitzic district) and in the vicinity of Libreville. In the former regions, cocoa cultivation and its resulting income have created a real Fang peasantry, and around Libreville the Fang have found their greatest opportunities for trade, education, and political power. Elsewhere, in the forest zone, these "unemployed conquerors"—to use Balandier's phrase—live in small, scattered villages, clinging to their traditions and resisting the administration's efforts to control them. In 1906 a small-scale revolt broke out in lower Gabon because of French curtailments of Fang trading activities, and a few years later the Fang opposed actively or by emigration an attempt to impose on them the payment of taxes in money. At the time the Federation was set up in 1910, there were still three Fang districts controlled by the military authorities. But generally speaking, the Fang withdrew to isolated villages deeper in the forest instead of offering active resistance, and this tendency accounts in great part for their failure to develop effective organizational and numerical strength.

Of a total of some 550,000 Fang living in central Africa, only 127,000 or so inhabit Gabon, but there they account for more than a quarter of the whole population. (The artificial frontiers created by European colonization have long divided the Fang of Gabon, Cameroun, and Spanish Guinea, and they are only now beginning to overcome their mutual ignorance and isolation.) In northern Gabon the Fang are comparatively stable and robust and are increasing numerically, but in the south their number has been declining over the past century because of emigration and a shrinking birth rate. Here the depopulation, fragmentation, and interclan rivalry result partly from a division of economic occupations and partly from social traditions. Trade drew men to the coast, and the

forest and mining camps attracted others, while the women carried on
subsistence agriculture in their lonely villages. Another more indirect
cause of the declining birth rate was the Fang social organization, in
which there existed no rigid hierarchy or strong chiefs. Pre-eminence was
based on tribal genealogy and age, and wealth was gauged by the number
of wives. Thus the old men in Fang villages were able to control trade
and monopolize the women, creating a demographic situation that was
made worse by the emigration for long periods of the able-bodied youths.

This social anarchy of the forest Fang was paralleled in the early
twentieth century by the economic anarchy resulting from the rule by
concessionary companies. Lacking in organization and in knowledge of
the country's resources, these companies were wasteful of Fang manpower,
particularly after the fall of rubber prices in 1907, which threw many
Fang rubber gatherers out of work. In the days before the company
regime the Fang had lived by the prevalent barter trade, serving as intermediaries in bringing down ivory and rubber to the coast and distributing merchandise and salt to the hinterland. Now they were perforce
dependent on a European economic system over which they had no
control, and their situation was aggravated by the administration's attempts during World War I to attract Fang workers to the regions of
European enterprise.

One constructive result of the government's labor policy was that it
drew attention for the first time to the decline of the Fang population.
An official Commission for the Study of Marriage and the Family, set
up in 1918, made a series of recommendations that were never successfully
carried out. To increase the population and reduce the number of disputes
over women, the commission proposed raising the marriage age for girls,
restricting divorce, and imposing penalties for adultery. Above all it urged
that the bride price be limited and that it be required to be paid in money,
so as to facilitate the marriage of young wage earners and curtail that of
older men who had only merchandise to offer. Perhaps the most disturbing evidence produced by the commission's report was that depletion of
the rural community had led, among other evils, to the formation of an
embryonic proletariat in Libreville and Lambaréné. Both phenomena
caused increasing concern as the forest industry began pulling out of the
post–World War I slump, and for the first time the government considered
importing laborers. It took another 20 years for the timber companies to
begin mechanizing their enterprises, and 30 years for them to bring in
workers from Nigeria, and throughout the interwar period, except in the
depression years, they claimed that they must have a labor force ranging
from 20,000 to 30,000 men between the ages of 20 and 40. This number
corresponded to approximately the total Fang male population in that
age group, with the result that forced labor was the order of the day.
Contracts were made for a two-year period, but by the time they expired
the worker had usually become so indebted to the company that he had
to stay on. As this practice kept young men away from their villages for

years at a time and as the mortality rate among forest laborers was high, the birth rate dropped rapidly. It has been calculated that 75 per cent of the unmarried workers never returned to their home villages and, detribalized, wandered from one forest camp to another.[4]

The world-wide depression of the 1930's compelled the local administration to try a new tack. Inspired by the success of cocoa planting in Cameroun, the government created in 1930 the first *paysannat* based on cocoa cultivation, in the Woleu-N'Tem region. Despite the difficulties involved in forcibly transforming the Fang into a peasant and the attraction exercised by Cameroun and Spanish Guinea, whose proximity made escape across those frontiers easy, this program was surprisingly successful. Within five years the flow of Fang emigrants had been arrested, villages had been stabilized, housing and clothing in Woleu-N'Tem became strikingly Europeanized, the towns of Bitam and Oyem expanded rapidly, and new ties were formed with fellow Fang in Cameroun through trade. Once the Fang comprehended the benefits of growing cocoa, they began cultivating it with enthusiasm, and they even worked out spontaneously a new division of labor whereby the men farmed and the women marketed the crop. Cocoa brought a prosperity, stability, and vigor to the northern Fang not shared by their relatives in the dense forest, and this differentiation widened the gap between them and after World War II was reflected in their political divisions.

World War II intensified rubber collecting, and this further depleted the Fang population in lower Gabon, causing some villages to be clandestinely displaced into the depths of the forest. Again the administration became alarmed, but this time their concern began to be shared by Fang leaders. The postwar political reforms now gave the Fang their first chance not only to express such anxiety but to try to reorganize their social order through a regrouping of clans and tribes.[5] But by this time, the differences that had developed between northern and southern Fang were paralleled by a cleavage between the generations, particularly in lower Gabon. The older Fang, living mainly in rural areas, clung to animism and the traditional privileges granted them by seniority. Many of the younger generation were urban wage earners, converted to Christianity, who had long nursed grievances against their elders, particularly on the matter of marriage.

A Commission on Population created by the administration in June 1946 undertook a study not only of the practical consequences of the population decline but also of the whole structure of Fang society. This commission, like its predecessor, had little practical effect and simply served once again to point up the problems and their interrelationship. More significant was the Congrès Pahouin called by the governor of Gabon at Mitzic in February 1947. It was attended by some 50 delegates, including canton chiefs, the Fang representatives in the territorial assembly, and a group of Libreville *évolués* led by Léon Mba. To the administration's surprise and consternation, Mba seized the leadership of this conference. The discussions ranged over a wide array of subjects, but economic problems, those of the *chefferie,* and the question of suppressing the Bwiti cult (see below) aroused the liveliest debates. The economic resolutions passed by the congress were quite orthodox, perhaps because no representatives of organized labor were present. Delegates asked for the encouragement of industrial crops and animal husbandry, the mechanization of agriculture and forestry enterprises, a plan for Gabon's industrialization, more means of communication, a reorganization of trade, better protection of laborers, and the like.

An instructive debate on the status of chiefs disclosed remarkable unanimity on the part of the nonofficial delegates. Both the *évolués* and the traditionalists denounced the administration-appointed canton chiefs as being prone to abuse their powers in regard to tax collection and the regulation of family disputes, and as serving only their interests and those of their official superiors. The real chiefs, it was said, were unknown to the administration, and they must be sought out and restored to their rightful authority so that the Fang could regain their tribal solidarity. For its part, the administration maintained that it had never tampered with chiefs at the village level but had had to create such units as the canton and *terre* because strong chieftaincies were lacking in Fang society. In this debate, Léon Mba maneuvered with such skill that he not only got the problem of the *chefferies* placed on the congress agenda but persuaded the canton chiefs present to vote in favor of electing a paramount Fang chief. To be sure, the Woleu-N'Tem delegates were unfavorable to this proposal, feeling less need of a symbolic leader than did the forest and town Fang because their social structure had not crumbled away as had that of the latter, and the canton chiefs refused to accept Fang political unity as the framework for creating new chieftaincies.

The administration's failure to take action on this resolution was largely responsible for a growth of the movement initiated by the Fang themselves to regroup their clans. If the Fang delegates at Mitzic did not see wholly eye to eye, the Pahouin congress at least showed their common desire for unity and an improvement in their demographic status. It also served to alert the administration to the role that the *évolués* now proposed to play by taking over leadership from the discredited appointed chiefs—a role, if need be, in opposition to the government. It indicated the rise of a new elite in the south, composed of urban *lettrés,* war veterans, artisans, and traders, led by a wholly indigenous tribal leader. In 1948 the proliferation of new organizations, notably the Union Démocratique et Sociale Gabonaise (UDSG) and the Comité Mixte Gabonais (later the Bloc Démocratique Gabonais), foreshadowed a crystallization of the two main Fang groups of Woleu-N'Tem and Libreville around the personalities of Jean Aubame and Léon Mba, respectively.

Varying circumstances, as well as the rivalry between those two leaders, caused the Fang revival to take different forms in the north and in the south, though both factions were inspired by a common concern to remedy the corrosion of Fang society. In the south the Fang lived interspersed with other tribes; there the dominant element was made up of *évolués* and wage earners, though the numerical majority consisted of rural conservatives. In the countryside, the Fang reaction to colonialism in general and the proselytizing of the missions in particular took a religious and traditionalist form—adherence to the Bwiti cult. This was a truly indigenous religion, though its membership included some non-Fang and its organization borrowed freely from the Catholic church. No great sacrifices or formalities were demanded of members, who, moreover, acquired a new self-confidence through mystical revelations and a sense of ethnic solidarity induced by practice of the cult. Primarily it served as an organizational framework for the rebuilding of Fang tribal unity, and Léon Mba was outstanding in his ability to utilize this cult in establishing his political ascendancy in lower Gabon.

In Woleu-N'Tem the unity movement took another, less religious form. There it was directly inspired by the organizational activity of the Fang from adjoining Cameroun, where it had developed in 1944–45 at about the same time that the local *chefferies* had been reformed. Its aim there was to strengthen clan ties and the tribal hierarchy, and simultaneously to modernize Fang society. This objective appealed strongly to the Woleu-N'Tem Fang, among whom the movement spread rapidly from 1947 on. To bring some order into their confused relationships, the northern Gabonese drew up a "book of the clan" and a "code of the tribe," and to reinforce their sense of kinship they held tribal meetings that combined some of the characteristics of a village celebration and a New England town meeting. From 1947 to 1949, under the leadership of Aubame, villages were regrouped according to clan affinities, and clan groups were formed to work together on projects of common interest, such as the building of roads, schools, and houses. Stress was placed on education, hygiene, and other modern concepts, and the newly devised tribal hierarchy was modeled after that of the administration at the canton, district, and village levels. The new tribal leaders improved plantations, settled disputes, and acted as intermediaries between the administration and the people. Yet the government was worried by the very fact that these elected leaders showed that they possessed genuine authority and obviously aimed at supplanting the chiefs appointed by the administration. Although the new organization was careful to operate within the existing administrative structure, and its leaders repeatedly gave assurances of their loyalty, the government veered from its initial attitude of encouragement to one of guidance and control. Faced for the first time with a Fang-initiated movement toward unity and regeneration, some French officials came to oppose it as a potentially nationalistic, even possibly communist-dominated movement. The Bwiti cult in the south, being a widely diffused religion, was hard to combat, but the northern movement, more localized and concrete, was vulnerable to the obstructionist tactics resorted to by officials and missionaries alike.

Such opposition was in part responsible for the decline of the Fang unity movement from 1950 on, but there were other contributary causes. The north's attempt to extend its movement to the south reawakened latent antagonisms, and the competition for rank within the new hierarchies aroused personal jealousies. Many clans in Gabon were by now too fragmented and dispersed to achieve more than artificial unity, and funds were lacking to carry out the ambitious modernization program. Both in the north and in the south the movement tried to straddle the old and the new, to combine the revolutionary with the reactionary, the *évolués* with the traditionalists. Had qualified leaders been more numerous, unity might have been attained, for their basic aims were much the same. But the rivalry between Aubame and Mba was transferred to the territorial assembly, and in the political void created by the abdication of the *chefferie* both men tried to advance their political fortunes by utilizing the postwar parties and representative institutions.

Organized political activity in Gabon began during the post–World War I depression, and though not a strictly Fang movement it did include Fang at the village level in the Libreville region. This was the Gabonese Section of the League of the Rights of Man. Although this organization was acceptable to the administration because it aimed to increase the well-being of the African population, it symptomatized—in another sphere—the yearning of Gabonese *évolués* to acquire a greater share in the management of public affairs. The latter objective clearly motivated the founding of the colony's first real political party, Jeune Gabonais, and of a political journal, *Echo Gabonais*. Jeune Gabonais was made up of the youthful elite, particularly in Libreville and Port Gentil, who could find no outlet for their political aspirations and therefore occupied themselves with obstructing the government's policy. But Jeune Gabonais gradually weakened because of the administration's opposition, personality conflicts, antagonism between the component ethnic groups, and especially an improvement in the economic situation. By 1926 it apparently had ceased to exist as an organized party.

Early in the 1930's, the depression gave new impetus to political agitation, which facilitated the rise of Léon Mba, one of the two outstanding Gabonese leaders of the postwar period (see above). As an educated young man specializing in the study of Fang customary law, Mba had attracted the favorable attention of the administration, and he was appointed canton chief in one of the most backward Fang regions of lower Gabon. Seeing in the Bwiti cult a chance to regenerate Fang society, Mba became one of its most influential adherents, but in contributing to its spread he came into conflict with his superiors. Although his dismissal as canton chief turned him to trade, his chief preoccupation thenceforth was to build himself up as the Fang leader of southern Gabon. It was not until the Pahouin congress of 1947, however, that the extent of his influence in that region became widely apparent.

Also in the early 1930's an Amicale des Métis was founded at Libreville, where mulattoes make up 10 to 15 per cent of the population. This organizational activity on the part of both mulattoes and Fang not unnaturally led other ethnic groups to follow suit. In 1937 a Comité Mpongwé was formed, in response to which another Fang group—the Comité de Défense des Interêts Pahouins—was forthwith established. Balandier points out[6] that the first truly political reactions of the Fang were directed less against the colonial administration than against the rise of other tribal groups. Official reports on the eve of World War II indicated that the Fang minority of Libreville was especially concerned by and resentful of the greater political maturity of the mulattoes and Mpongwé. Naturally the administration could not but benefit by the proliferation of ethnic parties, yet considered as a whole they reflected a disquieting restlessness on the part of the evolved minority in each racial group.

With the coming of representative institutions to Gabon after World War II, the Fang, as the single largest ethnic group in the territory, were able to dominate the territorial assembly elected in 1946. While the first electoral college, which had to share its deputy with Moyen-Congo, regularly returned the same European, Bayrou, to the National Assembly, the second college, which could elect a deputy solely to represent Gabon, with equal regularity returned a Catholic Fang from Woleu-N'Tem, Jean Aubame. It was not until the Pahouin congress of 1947 that Léon Mba became prominent at the territorial level and founded his own party, the Comité Mixte Gabonais. Probably inspired by the RDA's policy in French West Africa at that period, Mba began to intervene in local labor disputes and in the functioning of the customary courts, and organized a mutual aid society. His leanings toward the then radical RDA, plus Aubame's desire to play a lone hand, probably contributed to the breakdown of the Fang unity movement described above. In any case, by 1950 the Fang in the territorial assembly were divided into two groups, the UDSG led by Aubame and the Bloc Démocratique Gabonais (formerly the Comité Mixte Gabonais) under Mba.

The newcomer to Libreville or Port Gentil is at once struck by the fact that the coastal Gabonese are far more Europeanized than are Africans living in any other part of AEF. Almost all the urban Africans in those towns wear European clothes and have attended French schools. Owing largely to the Christian missions, French is not only widely spoken there but is often the language used by Africans among themselves. And the existence of a large mulatto component testifies to the long-established affinities between the white and black populations.

French subjects since 1839, the Gabonese are proud of the fact that they have been French longer than the residents of Nice or Savoie.[7] To be sure, Gabon barely escaped being exchanged for Gambia in 1870, and in 1885 it was excluded from the Congo Basin Convention. Until 1910, the territory had the same type of administration as Senegal's. Then Dahomey, after its conquest by the French, was annexed for a time to Gabon and governed from Libreville, which was then the administrative center and main port of the whole colony.

With the creation of the AEF Federation in 1910 the special position of which the Gabonese were so proud began to be undermined. Then the building of the Congo-Ocean railroad and the development of the "Federal Artery" (the *voie fédérale*) from Pointe Noire to Bangui dealt a blow to Gabon's shipping primacy, just as the founding of Brazzaville had entailed the displacement of Libreville as the administrative center. Resentment was aroused, too, by the fact that Gabon's revenues were regularly diverted toward construction of the towns and means of communication that were to increase the relative importance of Moyen-Congo. Mainly because of its wood exports, Gabon was the only AEF colony that showed a consistently favorable trade balance, but its surpluses were used to rescue neighboring territories from their financial deficits and not for local improvements. Although Libreville's old-fashioned charm survived, it soon languished as a backwater; Gabon had no roads outside the two main towns and much of it was covered by impenetrable forest; and its small, scattered population was shrinking at an alarming rate. Inevitably the Gabonese resented the burdens imposed on them by the federation without commensurate returns, and they developed a special hostility toward that spoiled upstart, Moyen-Congo.

Wartime changes in AEF's economic orientation led to still closer integration of Gabon into the AEF ensemble, but this time the territory benefited. Since Gabon was cut off, because of the war, from France—with which it had been assimilated as regards tariff regime—the Free French government took steps on September 21, 1940, to include this territory in the customs system of the Congo Basin Convention. Gabon was thus freed from paying both fiscal and customs surtax on imports of foreign origin. When the question of restoring the tariff structure *quo ante bellum* came up in 1950, a proposal made by Aubame and the socialist and Mouvement Républicain Populaire (MRP) deputies for a reconsideration of Gabon's position and its detachment from the AEF Federation was debated in the French Union Assembly.[8] The arguments then advanced in support of giving Gabon administrative, economic, and financial autonomy were much the same as those used in 1910, with the added claim that since the war little had been done by Metropolitan France to equip that territory, compared with other parts of AEF. At the time, the traffic handled by Libreville and Port Gentil was larger than that passing through Pointe Noire, even though the latter port had been equipped on a much more lavish scale. Since almost all of Gabon's exports, except for a few thousand tons of cocoa shipped through Cameroun, moved out of Gabonese ports, the validity of maintaining Gabon in the AEF customs zone seemed debatable. Furthermore, Gabon's economy, based on big forest and mining enterprises and their derivative industries, differentiated it sharply from the other AEF areas.

Opponents of this proposal argued that it was to Gabon's advantage to remain linked with AEF, which provided it with federal technical services and a labor supply readily accessible from adjacent territories, and that to concede autonomy to Gabon might set a risky precedent for other countries of the French Union. Gabon's special problems, the French Union Assembly felt at that time, could be solved by a genuine decentralization of the AEF government-general that would benefit the other territories as well. A few decentralizing measures were indeed adopted, but these did not appease the Gabonese, whose bitterness grew with the years and took an acute turn in consequence of the discovery in their territory of sizable deposits of manganese, iron, and petroleum. Not a session of its territorial assembly passed without complaints being voiced against the role of milch cow being forced upon Gabon by its "greedy and impoverished" neighbors. And the project to export Gabon's manganese ores by way of the Congo-Ocean railroad to Pointe Noire added fresh fuel to the flame of such protests.

In demanding greater autonomy vis-à-vis the federation and closer ties with France, the Africans and Europeans of Gabon displayed a harmony of viewpoint that has almost always been evident in their relationship. This has been due in part to their long past in common and in part to the identity of the problems they must face together. Both elements must combat too much water, too dense forests, too small a population, and too strong a tendency to dwell on the so-called glories of the past. To be sure, apathy also plays a certain role there. As one French resident told the authors: "Gabon will probably be the last territory to leave the French Union, if for no other reason than that the local population hasn't the energy to throw us out." But above all it is probably Gabon's isolation that has been responsible for the easy social relations between blacks and whites both in the towns and in the forest and mining camps, where an authoritarian and semifeudal paternalism seems to reign to the general satisfaction of employers and employees. As Balandier puts it:[9]

> Gabon remains filled with social groups belonging to another age—pioneers with their clientele—though not numerous enough to create another Brazil. . . . Gabon rapidly exhausts the men trying to serve her. One must have an exceptionally strong personality or vital material interests to hold out against a natural and human environment that shows an astonishing capacity for annihilation.

Although both Europeans and Africans, beset by almost overwhelming odds, realize that they must maintain a united front, there are inevitably some rifts between them and inside each group. With the recent and considerable influx of outsiders, from other African countries as well as from France, attracted by the development of Gabon's new sources of wealth, more seeds of discord have been sown and the division of interests has deepened. As to inter-African disputes, the importation of Nigerian workers has given rise to few conflicts, but the presence of Togolese and Dahomeans has caused friction. One of the rare outbreaks that have occurred in postwar Gabon was directed mainly against the latter elements working in Port Gentil, but the significance of the incidents of June 1953 should not be exaggerated. Some of the violence then shown derived from secondary ethnic antagonisms, the penalties imposed—ranging from one day to three years in prison—were mild, and time showed that the conflict was a minor and localized one.

In the European community a certain amount of competition has developed between the foresters and oilmen in regard to the labor supply. The foresters, claiming most of the credit for developing the territory, complain about the petroleum company's high-wage policy, while the company's officials accuse the foresters of fanning political agitation by their old-fashioned attitude toward their workers. Much the same type of jealousy pervades the sentiments of the inhabitants of Libreville, the century-old cultural and administrative center, toward those of Port Gentil, the booming commercial capital of the plywood and petroleum industries. But this inter-European rivalry, somewhat similar to though less personal than that which divides the Fang political groups, is based on a division of interests that is purely local and largely superficial. Normally all such feeling is put aside when the larger interests of Gabon as a whole are considered to be at stake. Unity of this sort may appear artificial or superficial, but its maintenance is sedulously cultivated by all the politically conscious Gabonese, and for that very reason it may prove to be more enduring than in other countries with a greater natural and demographic homogeneity.

Gabon's political tranquillity can, of course, be attributed largely to a prosperity that has been sustained except for the 1952 crisis in the wood industry. Full employment has been the rule despite the influx of French West Africans to the towns and of Nigerian laborers to the interior. Housing and sometimes food are scarce in fast-growing Port Gentil, but the Africans working there have learned skills and earn exceptionally high wages. It is noteworthy, in this respect, that the emissaries of the French Communist party who toured AEF towns in 1948 failed to visit only those of Gabon.

Until very recently, elections aroused little emotion among the Gabonese, although about half the registered voters regularly cast their ballots. For years the same deputies (Aubame and Bayrou[10]) and senators (Gondjout and Durand-Reville) were re-elected. As a rule, too, Europeans were presidents of the territorial assembly and chairmen of its key committees. Especially appreciated was the work of the popular forester Pierre Flandre, who as president not only of the territorial assembly but also of the Grand Council of AEF labored hard to defend Gabon's interests vis-à vis the federation. Aubame, to be sure, was not a prominent member of the National Assembly, but he occasionally spoke up in debates to stress the good Franco-African relations prevailing in Gabon and to urge replacement of the dual by the single electoral college.[11] Relations between the administration and the territorial assembly were far more cooperative and debates in the latter much less acrimonious than in other AEF territories. While Aubame belonged to the Indépendants d'Outre-Mer (IOM) and Mba was affiliated with the Rassemblement Démocratique Africain (RDA), those ties were loose and did not give rise to local discord as did similar ones in some French West African territories.[12]

A cloud appeared on the horizon of this idyllic political scene with the election of Mba as mayor of Libreville in November 1956 and as vice-president of the government council in May 1957. To the politically alert this suggested that the star of Mba, tribal spokesman for the south, was rising as that of the northern Fang Catholic leader, Aubame—absent much of the time in Paris—was waning. Mba had come a long way in the 23 years since he had tangled with the French government, and the latter had also learned to be less rigid in its dealings with African politicians. Mba was increasingly attracting to his Bloc Démocratique Gabonais (BDG) some Mpongwés and other non-Fang tribes, and on his list of candidates for election to the Libreville municipal council in 1956 he tactfully included a number of Europeans, including one Frenchwoman. Aubame, on the other hand, carried on his campaign with less skill and had only African candidates on the list that he sponsored. In a talk which the writers had with Mba on the eve of the municipal elections, he expressed his feeling that Gabon was the territory best suited to serve as an example of Franco-African unity, and though his policy might in some respects, he said, resemble those of Boganda and Youlou, he had no direct association with those two African leaders. Fluent, poised, and affable, Mba left us with the impression of being a thoroughly regional product, typical of that Franco-African blend that makes Gabon unique in AEF.

Elections in the spring of 1957 to the territorial assembly gave almost equal representation to Aubame's UDSG and Mba's BDG, so maneuvering began at once to win over the six Independents who held the balance of power. Mba managed to acquire a two-vote majority in an assembly whose membership had risen from 30 to 40, and to become in due course prime minister of a government that included three members of the opposition. With so slender a margin of support in the assembly, the Mba government was highly unstable, and one political crisis followed another throughout 1957 and 1958. The three UDSG ministers resigned in the autumn of 1957, only to be taken back into the cabinet as "Independents" in February 1958. In the following May, Gondjout, leader of the BDG at Port Gentil, was re-elected president of the territorial assembly, but the month after, he failed to be re-elected to the French Senate, being, surprisingly, defeated by a European. Indirectly this caused Flandre, who was held responsible for his downfall, to resign later as Minister of Finance. In April 1958 the Libreville College was closed down because of a "political strike" that had aligned a UDSG student majority against a BDG-oriented faculty. The failure of a no-confidence motion in the Mba government, introduced in December 1957, had caused the UDSG immediately to announce that it would enter into a "vigilant and firm opposition until the cabinet has been modified in accordance with the wishes of the elec-torate."[13] But on June 18, 1958, the day after Mba had unexpectedly in-creased his majority by one vote, Aubame expressed his willingness to have UDSG members reoccupy ministerial posts. Elections in Gabon's four new communes on April 13 reflected the party line-up in the terri-torial assembly and confirmed—if the urban vote could be regarded as a barometer—that the territory was still about equally divided between UDSG and BDG supporters.

Local dissensions were still the main cause of UDSG-BDG rivalry, but for a short time it seemed that the growing tension between the big West African political groups might spread to Gabon and still further aggravate interparty discord. When the IOM under L. S. Senghor's leader-ship was transformed into the Convention Africaine and later became the Parti du Regroupement Africain (PRA), Aubame and the UDSG followed suit. Mba, on the other hand, remained loyal to the RDA and Houphouët-Boigny. For years these attachments had been largely nominal or, in the case of Aubame, had operated only at the parliamentary level. But after the *loi-cadre* decrees were applied throughout French Black Africa and the issue of the primary federation came to the fore, the West African leaders began courting their counterparts in AEF for additional support. Mba was the only African member of the Gabon RDA to attend the party congress in September 1957 at Bamako, where he expressed shocked sur-prise at the views aired by the radical faction.[14] Thereafter he assiduously supported Houphouët's views and was regularly present at the meetings of the RDA directing committee. By July 1958, Aubame and his lieutenant, Jean-Marc Ekoh, attended the first PRA congress at Cotonou, which opted for independence and a federal executive. After it was over, Aubame po-litely voiced his pleasure at the success of the congress, but failed to endorse any of the extremist views put forward there. Given Gabon's strongly pro-French and pro-autonomy sentiments, Aubame could no more conform to the PRA party line with respect to independence and the federal execu-tive than Mba could adhere to the views of Sekou Touré.

Both issues came to a head for all French Black Africa in the summer of 1958 with de Gaulle's proposal for a referendum on the Fifth Republic's constitution. For Gabon they became even more cogent in view of the rapidity with which plans were then shaping up for exploitation of its manganese and iron deposits, and the Gabonese were unanimous in their determination that they and not the federation should be the beneficiaries. Three times the territorial assembly, without a single dissenting vote, went on record as "categorically opposed to the creation of a federal executive," and it even refused to send a representative to discuss with the other AEF territories a common *statut* for civil servants. There is little doubt that Mba was expressing a widely prevalent feeling when he said publicly on July 25, 1958:[15]

> We reject the principle of a federal executive on the African level, and Gabon asks to be linked directly to Metropolitan France. We are not betraying our African neighbors, but we have had enough of working for others. We can

no longer consent to our money being used to help Brazzaville mushroom while we have neither roads nor infrastructure. Nor will we any longer agree to letting certain federal administration organizations hamper our economic development when their role should be to promote it. We have noticed some obscure maneuverings designed to deprive Gabon of the enjoyment of its patrimony. Some of them even aim to take Mékambo away from us. If this strategy persists, we shall take precautions, and our reactions may not take place in complete calm. Gabon will renounce its membership in AEF and ask to be linked forthwith to the Metropole, for we are deeply attached to France.

Aubame and the UDSG agreed in general with these sentiments of Mba, but because of their membership in the PRA they apparently felt they should temporize. "Independence," said Aubame over Radio Brazzaville in late August 1958, "does not mean secession (from France). We have been fighting for a federation since 1953, so we cannot logically refuse to be federated with France . . ." And he went so far as to propose a meeting at Brazzaville later that month with other AEF leaders to "study the possibility of creating a state of Equatorial Africa," but one unlike that proposed by Abbé Fulbert Youlou of Moyen-Congo.

When it came to a showdown, as it did in the referendum of September 28, 1958, Aubame and Mba stood shoulder to shoulder and Gabon turned in a 97.7 per cent affirmative vote. Both men rejected the status for Gabon of an overseas department or territory and opted for that of member state in the new Franco-African Community. Only about 10,000 of Gabon's 261,682 voters failed to follow their lead. The dissenters were mostly members of a new party, the PUNGA (Parti d'Union Nationale Gabonaise), composed almost wholly of non-Fang groups from south-central Gabon, and malcontents other than members of the UDSG, such as the Conseil de la Jeunesse, students, labor leaders, and a miscellany of those who were simply against the Mba government. The PUNGA, having been formed so recently, is difficult to appraise correctly: one of its leaders is Prince Berre, who asks strict application of treaties made with his ancestors by France in 1839, and it seems to appeal mainly to those who are resentful of the Fang control of Gabonese politics. PUNGA's president is Sousatte, a former French Union Assemblyman, who went so far in September 1959 as to demand immediate independence for Gabon. Sousatte's declaration was apparently motivated by his anger over the Mba government's refusal to sanction new elections to the Gabon legislative assembly, for which he held the French largely responsible.

Gabon's overwhelmingly affirmative vote in the 1958 referendum has been followed by a marked tendency toward compromise, both internally and with its neighbors. Early in October 1958, Mba accepted a UDSG proposal to reshuffle his government, reducing the number of ministers from 11 to 10. In that month also he sent a representative to confer with the premiers of the other AEF states, after which Lisette reportedly said that it was now not impossible that Gabon might agree to some form of coordinated activity with its neighbors.[16] A few weeks later, in Paris, Mba said that "Gabon is not hostile to a secondary community of AEF states," and on January 17, 1959, he agreed to enter a tariff and transport union with them.

No vital issues at present divide the Gabonese population, and personal rivalries such as that between Aubame and Mba have been exaggerated by some of their followers for reasons of self-interest. Both leaders are deeply tribal and local in their orientation, and both have to meet much the same problems inside as well as outside their respective parties. Gabonese of all political stripes fear being smothered by the more numerous peoples around them and want to preserve their territorial patrimony for their own use, and they realize that they must remain united if they are to succeed in this objective. Gabon's good economic and financial position is likely to improve still further in the near future, and this provides an additional reason for fostering the already exceptionally cordial Afro-European relations that have long been maintained in the territory.

The Territorial Economy

The Plan

Application of the ten-year Plan to Gabon has done little to alter its fundamental economic pattern. In fact, it has accentuated the territory's dependence on wood exports, drawn more of the population to the urban centers, and failed to improve appreciably Gabon's means of communication. In its first operations FIDES concentrated on road building so as to bring Gabon into closer touch with other parts of the federation and to make accessible the isolated areas of the hinterland not served by navigable waterways. Though a few roads were laboriously built, this program as a whole bogged down and had to be classed as a costly failure. Not much more successful were FIDES' attempts to enlarge Gabon's ports and to modernize living conditions in Libreville and Port Gentil.[17] The latter town had to wait many years before being provided with a proper lighting and water system, and the continued inability of the Gabonese to grow more food crops has made the provisioning of its fast-growing urban population a grave problem. FIDES, however, certainly has contributed to Gabon's equipment in the social domain, in the form of a modern *lycée* and hospital at Libreville, as well as schools and dispensaries throughout the territory.[18]

By and large, the funds that FIDES has placed at Gabon's disposal have been too small to show conspicuous results in a territory where both labor and materials are very scarce and expensive, the cost of living in Libreville the highest anywhere in AEF, and the terrain exceptionally difficult. Gabon's existing industries probably have been the main beneficiaries, for FIDES has helped to modernize the equipment used in its forest and mining camps and to build the largest plywood factory in the world at Port Gentil. Gabon's *paysannats* have been financed in large part by the Plan, as have experiments in the cultivation of export crops. But the greatest changes that have been wrought recently in Gabon's economy must be credited not to FIDES but to two enterprises financed more directly by Metropolitan France—the Bureau Minier and the Société des Pétroles d'AEF (SPAEF), which have been responsible for its mineral and petroleum prospecting. Exploitation of these new resources should certainly lessen Gabon's dependence on okoumé exports, bring new life to neglected and underpopulated regions, and lead to unprecedented prosperity for the whole territory. Gabon already has attracted (and welcomed) the largest foreign-capital investments in the federation and is likely to receive a great deal more. There is poetic justice in the prospect that this smallest and apparently least favored territory may become the wealthiest in all AEF.

Finances

The fact that Gabon has a small and probably declining population scattered throughout a vast, trackless, and unhealthful tropical forest might seem to doom that territory economically to stagnation if not total eclipse. Its great forest, however, contains a unique and precious wood, the okoumé, the export of which has regularly supplied the federation with the largest part of its revenues. Beneath the forest surface, also, are huge deposits of manganese and iron ore, some gold, uranium, and potash, not to mention valuable petroleum deposits along the coast. Though Gabon has seen lean financial years, it consistently has had larger surpluses than any other AEF territory and its future promises to be even brighter. Gabon's prosperity and bright prospects have made its elected representatives adamantly opposed to any union with its sister republics that would require it, as in the past, to help finance the deficits that they incur. Conversely, the strength of the sentimental ties which Gabon has developed over the years with France has not been impaired by certain of France's postwar economic policies that the Gabonese feel have been particularly harmful to their territory.[19] These include two currency devaluations, the termination of their special tariff status and an enforced customs union with the rest of AEF, and application of the principle of federal financial solidarity.

In 1947 Gabon's Grand Councilors and territorial assemblymen made the first of many appeals for the grant of financial autonomy to their territory. Little heed was paid to their pleas during the first five postwar years, for this was the period described later—in the light of the federation's far greater financial stringency—as "euphoric." In those days, Gabon's financial structure and problems were much the same as those of the other territories. Its budgets were smaller in volume and the increase in its expenditures proportionately less, but its area and population were also less sizable. Until 1951 the territory was able to balance its budget and even finance an equipment program from rebates on its earnings and from its own resources. That year a 30 per cent increase in its expenditures, caused by application of the Lamine-Gueye law, elicited an exceptional grant of 10 million CFA francs by the Grand Council, and this enabled Gabon to balance its budget. But the blow fell in 1952, when Gabon's territorial councilors were shocked to learn that their accumulated indebtedness amounted to 220 million francs, their reserve fund was empty, and they could expect no more than 50 million as rebate from the federal budget.[20]

Retrenchment was the order of the day, for it was felt that Gabon's population could not stand increased taxation. All new works projects were canceled, Libreville and Port Gentil taking over some of the housing and road-construction programs for their respective areas. For three successive years Gabon was unable to finance any development program, and this intensified its assembly's resentment of the Plan's penury and hostility toward the federal government. Said the president of the assembly:[21]

> Our budget simply pays past debts and functionaries. We are subjected to a federation that stifles us, returning to us only a small part of what we earn. Our poverty is due to this situation and we are the poorest territory in AEF in investments and public works.

For many years, but particularly at that period, the keynotes of Gabon's assembly debates were its persecution and neglect by the government-general. Its members harped on the theme that Gabon had not been enabled to diversify its economy and had become too dependent upon wood exports, but they rarely mentioned that the territory's timber industry had been saved by "federal solidarity" during the crisis of 1952. They did, however, accept a rise in the head tax, and Gabon was the first territory in AEF to agree, under certain conditions, to impose a *taxe vicinale* ranging from 75 to 300 francs according to the region.[22]

With the revival of the wood industry in 1953 and 1954, the financial situation improved rapidly, despite successive cuts in the federal subsidy and only a slight reduction in the territory's indebtedness (amounting to 200 million francs by the latter year). Of the budget for 1954, which totaled 1,034 million francs, personnel expenditures accounted for 54 per cent of the total and those on social works for 39 per cent. As a reward for the austerity that had characterized Gabon's recent budgets and the large contributions made by that territory to the federation's revenues, the Grand Council granted it in 1954 a subsidy sufficient to wipe out almost all of its past debts. Nevertheless, the volume of Gabon's budgets continued to grow steadily, rising from 1,114 million francs in 1955 to 1,321 million in 1956, and with them increased the territory's deficit in its annual operations. As elsewhere in the federation, Gabon's revenues grew only slowly but its expenditures mounted wildly. However, the return to the rebate system in 1957 and the strengthening of the territories' budgetary autonomy throughout AEF that year brought greater financial ease to Gabon. Though the volume of its budget for 1958 rose steeply to 1,869 million francs, the newly installed Mba government felt that it could afford to suppress the head tax for women and to raise the minimum wage and the rate of family allowances. Eventually the revenues to be anticipated from the exploitation of Gabon's mineral wealth should make it the richest of the new republics of AEF.

Transportation

Roads. In the 1920's a beginning was made in giving Gabon's capital and its most economically productive areas a few short roads. First Libreville was linked to nearby loading stations on the coast (Sibang, Owendo, and Kogou), then some navigable points on the N'Gounié river were connected, and finally Woleu-N'Tem was able to communicate by road with both Cameroun and the Gabon coast by way of N'Djolé. Altogether, 600 kilometers of such roads had been built by 1936, when the need was felt to establish overland contact with Moyen-Congo at Dolisie. Though this road was very hastily and poorly constructed by local administrators, it did give access to south Gabon over· a distance of about 300 kilometers. The greatest wartime road-building effort made in Gabon involved the improvement of communications between Cameroun and the Congo-Ocean railroad, and to span the Niari river, which crossed this route, the longest bridge built in AEF was constructed. Elsewhere forest camps were given access tracks, as were some of the regions earmarked for mineral prospecting. All of these means of overland communication were exceptionally poor, even for AEF, and almost impassable during the rains. Their condition was such that very few motor vehicles circulated in the territory, and truckers were able to demand very high prices for their transport services.

To rescue Gabon from its isolation, both external and internal, the ten-year Plan laid down a big port- and road-building program. The latter's main feature was the transformation of the Dolisie-Cameroun route into a real highway, 1,200 kilometers long, with branches to Mayumba, Libreville, and Woleu-N'Tem. Though much of Gabon would still remain roadless, it was thought that this highway would drain the output of its most productive regions to the ports. The territory's road construction was entrusted to a Metropolitan firm, the Compagnie Générale des Colonies, which proved a most unfortunate choice. Extravagant and incompetent as this company soon showed itself to be, the cancellation of its contract would have been very costly to Gabon. Moreover, its territorial assemblymen had little faith that the slow-moving Public Works Service would do any better.[23] Emissaries sent to Gabon by the Grand Council in 1949 and 1951 reported that such roads as the territory possessed were in a deplorable state.[24] Funds for road building then were not lacking—they had simply been badly utilized. Most of the blame they placed on the company, though it was also admitted that Gabon's climate and topography were exceptionally unfavorable to road building.

From 1950 on, the situation became progressively worse. Not only did a large segment of the original plan have to be abandoned, but certain sectors of the existing network deteriorated so far that Gabon's various districts became isolated from each other.[25] Woleu-N'Tem, which till then had been precariously linked to the Ogooué-Ivindo region, now had as its sole outlet the Camerounian ports of Kribi and Douala. The N'Gounié-Nyanga area of southern Gabon could be reached only from Dolisie. The

Ogooué basin became "autonomous economically," and Libreville found itself blocked off from its hinterland. Gabon's small road network (2,800 kilometers) was broken up into bits and pieces, and it was the only territory in AEF in which some administrative posts could not be reached by motor vehicles.[26] In certain places the cost of building a kilometer of new road came to 20 million CFA francs, instead of the 3 million originally estimated. Then, too, it began to appear that construction of the Cameroun-Dolisie highway might be an economic mistake as well as technically difficult. Circumstances born of the war had led to the concentration at Dolisie of supplies for distribution to the north, and under normal conditions the value of building an inland road paralleling the coast was open to question. For all these reasons, Gabon was forced to revise its road program several years before the other territories reconsidered theirs.

The pervasive feeling of hopelessness among the territorial assemblymen about Gabon's roads was pointed up by the failure of an enterprising agent of the Agricultural Service to build a motorable road connecting the great natural palm grove of Moabi with the nearest regional market.[27] For its construction he had been able to recruit laborers by paying them in meat he obtained by hunting. But when they realized that the money returns from the sale of palm products amounted to very little, they would not maintain the road, which soon reverted to jungle. Gabon's population, at all events, was too sparse and scattered to count on for sustained effort in road building or upkeep, and it became apparent that such infrastructure as the territory acquired would have to be a gift, pure and simple, from France. Unfortunately this realization came at the same time as a drastic reduction in FIDES funds and a reorientation of the Plan toward *rentabilité*. Gabon perforce had to devise a new road program that would be more in keeping both with its terrain and with its reduced income.

Applying the hard lessons learned over the past years, the authorities decided to concentrate on short roads of local utility. A modest beginning was to be made on the 103-kilometer stretch between Libreville and Kango, which was to be prolonged by stages to Lambaréné. Then in north Gabon, the Mitzic-N'Djolé road was to be tackled and the Crystal Mountain region given access to the N'Komor basin. In southeastern Gabon, Lastoursville was to be linked with Franceville. By 1955 most of these local roads had been built and a small-scale experiment in mechanized road upkeep had been successfully undertaken. But the Gabonese did not feel that the corner had been turned until their capital was connected by road with Lambaréné in 1958, for this enabled Libreville to maintain contact with the principal hinterland settlements.

Gabon still has the poorest and shortest road network of any AEF territory, and the circulation of motor vehicles is still largely confined to Libreville and Port Gentil. Nevertheless, the Gabonese have reason to be optimistic about the future. The imminent exploitation of Franceville's manganese and uranium and the possible mining of Mékambo's iron deposits should open up two regions that have remained among the most isolated in the territory. In May 1959 the legislative assembly accepted a proposal made by the foresters' syndicate to finance jointly with it the building of two roads in okoumé-rich regions. One of these—from Kougouleu to Médouneu—would also permit the output of Woleu-N'Tem to be exported from a Gabonese port, while the second, from N'Djolé to Lastoursville, would give access to a theretofore undeveloped region.

Waterways. Of all the AEF territories, Gabon is the best-provided with waterways, whose total length is over 1,000 kilometers. Though they are navigable only in segments and at certain times of the year, they have to some extent offset the territory's lack of a road network, and have been the *sine qua non* of the expansion of Gabon's timber industry.

The region of the estuary is served by two small ports, that of Libreville on its northern bank, and Owendo, nearby, on the southern shore. For many years Libreville's port was the most active in the federation, but by the late 1930's, Port Gentil was catching up with it, and it has now definitely been relegated to the position of AEF's third port, following Pointe Noire and Port Gentil. Libreville has a well-sheltered port but one that is difficult of access and, above all, lacks deep water. In 1950 its traffic amounted to 130,000 tons, and this volume, taken in conjunction with Libreville's importance as the territorial capital and center of a prosperous region, induced the authors of the 1952–56 Plan to go ahead with the project drafted in 1946 to build a steamship dock there. The ten-year Plan for the wood-loading port of Owendo, on the other hand, was eliminated,[28] and it has remained in an undeveloped condition. The estuary, on which Owendo is well located, is considered only a mediocre outlet, for it receives the water of no sizable river and serves as no link with the hinterland.

Port Gentil, though situated on an island, is admirably protected by Cap Lopez and is potentially an important deep-water port. It is the outlet for the great Ogooué river, which, with its tributary the N'Gounié, drains Gabon's richest forest regions and is the territory's main lifeline. As far as Lambaréné the Ogooué is navigable throughout the year, to N'Djolé from October to May, and up to Alembé under certain conditions. On its upper reaches, shallow-draft boats can reach Lastoursville from Booué between mid-November and mid-June. The N'Gounié, which flows into the Ogooué at Lambaréné, is navigable as far as Sindara and, after being cut by rapids, from Fougamou to Mouila during the months from October to June. Another of the Ogooué's tributaries, the Ivindo, is accessible to small boats for the same period of time from the Cameroun frontier to Makokou. For a time, in 1956, it was hoped that the Ogooué could be used for the shipping of manganese ores from Franceville to Port Gentil. But the estimated cost of making it navigable for only six months of the year was higher (7 billion CFA francs) than that of constructing a railroad that would be usable the year round.[29]

Even without the manganese of Franceville, the Ogooué network has played a large part in making Port Gentil the federation's second-ranking port. Its future hung in the balance for a number of years.[30] Although a slow starter, Port Gentil forged ahead of Libreville during World War II and, after a pause, has been growing rapidly since 1956. The ten-year Plan to transform it into a well-equipped deep-water port has never been carried out, partly because of its island location and concentration on wood exports, and partly because of a costly blunder in executing the initial project in 1947.[31] Some improvements have been made, however, and the amount of tonnage it handles has been growing rapidly. Port Gentil's recent rise has been due not only to a growth in its wood exports of all types, but to new shipments of petroleum, which is extracted from deposits nearby.

Agriculture

Because of the territory's topographic and demographic situation and the structure of its economy, Gabon's agriculture is the least developed in AEF. Much of the land is covered by dense forest, which produces the valuable okoumé tree and some wild rubber but automatically limits agricultural production. Moreover, it creates difficulties of communication that prevent the export of perishable crops outside the producing area. Then, too, the territory's active male population prefers urban trading or wage earning in the forest or mining camps, from which larger monetary returns are forthcoming than from agricultural pursuits. Food-crop cultivation is left to the village women, who usually grow enough to take care of their families' needs. Agricultural output for sale or export is confined almost wholly to four regions—the Woleu-N'Tem and Ogooué-Ivindo for cocoa and coffee, the Ogooué area for oil-palm products, and the Tchibanga district for rice.

The indifference of the Gabonese to growing food crops has long disquieted the administration. To compel them to increase such output, the government after World War I regrouped some villages along the territory's few means of communication and ordered their populations to cultivate nearby more manioc—their basic food—and vegetables. This policy failed to win the cooperation of the Gabonese, and they started only token plantations. In the hope that the local administrator would not leave his car for a closer inspection, the villagers planted a few crops along the roads nearest to official headquarters, and let it go at that.[32] Apparently discouraged by such failures, most of the government's efforts in the agricultural domain turned toward the increase of export crops—cocoa, coffee, oil-palm produce, and hevea. The only two agricultural stations set up in Gabon, at Oyem and Kango, and the experimental plantation of the Compagnie Générale des Oléagineux Tropicaux (CGOT) near Lambaréné have concentrated on hevea, cocoa, and oil palms, and only in recent years have the Sociétés Indigènes de Prévoyance (SIP) and *paysannats* begun actively to promote food crops.

The food situation, poor as it long had been, did not become serious until the urban population began to grow rapidly during World War II. Not until the abolition of forced labor in April 1946 led to a sudden fall in the production of local food crops, even of manioc, could it be called

critical. This caused concern not only to the administration but to Gabon's
elected representatives, who saw in the prevailing undernourishment a
main cause of the population's decline in numbers and health.[33] They
tried to popularize food-crop cultivation among their compatriots, but
found the Gabonese singularly unresponsive to this propaganda because
of the low price paid for such produce.[34] Next the government introduced
or encouraged the cultivation of beans, potatoes, onions, and peppers, but
only in its promotion of mountain rice in the Tchibanga district did it
meet with even partial success. During the postwar years the production
of cocoa, coffee, and palm kernels and oil rose steadily, but with the
exception of paddy, production of food crops did not keep pace.

One reason for the last-mentioned phenomenon was the almost universal unpopularity of the SIP, which was virtually the only agency used
by the government until 1950 to promote food production. Year after year
the African assemblymen protested against the SIP as an "abusive and
useless" organization. It was claimed that it rendered no services to Gabonese farmers in return for their 25 CFA francs' annual dues, and that its
commercial operations not only were superfluous but interfered with the
local merchants' legitimate trade.[35] To be sure, Gabon also had five cooperative societies functioning, but only one of them was concerned with
agricultural production and its crop was oil palms.[36] Obviously some other
formula had to be found, and in 1950 the government began preparing
to set up *paysannats* in Gabon's three main producing regions—the Woleu-
N'Tem, Ogooué-Ivindo, and the N'Gounié-Nyanga—each of a different
character.

In the Woleu-N'Tem little remained to be done except build schools,
markets, and dispensaries, for in that region there had been a spontaneous
regrouping of villages as far back as the 1930's and the population was
already settled on the land because of the remunerative cultivation of cocoa.
Parts of the Ogooué-Ivindo were similarly well advanced, but a great deal
had to be done for the *paysannats* set up at Batouala and Djidji in the way
of technical and material aid. It was in the N'Gounié-Nyanga area, however, where the population was very dispersed, that a whole network of
roads and tracks had to be built before the *paysannats* could be created at
Imeno M'Bila, N'Zensélé, and Moabi. Because such construction opened
up large areas and affected well over 15,000 persons theretofore stagnating
in a closed economic circuit, and because food production was combined
with a cash crop, the *paysannats* are the most promising agricultural development in Gabon today, though they have by no means solved the
problem of provisioning fast-growing towns such as Port Gentil. In 1955
a small-scale experiment with the mechanical cultivation of crops was
undertaken at Kango, but even should it be successful, it is doubtful that
its lessons can be applied to any sizable segment of the territory. The
largest single achievement to date is the extension of paddy cultivation
in the Tchibanga district, and this is one of the rare successes that must
be chalked up to the credit of the SIP.

Tchibanga is the only region in Gabon where rice is grown, and its production climbed steadily from about 400 tons in 1947 to nearly 900 tons in 1955. This increase has posed marketing problems for the government despite the fact that Gabon is a rice-importing territory. The main stumbling blocks are high transportation costs, the mediocre quality of Tchibanga's output, and the marked preference of the Gabonese for manioc as a basic food.

Lack of roads in the Tchibanga area has necessitated shipping rice by plane to the consuming centers, which are limited to some of the coastal towns and the forest and mining camps. Because of this air transportation, the price for locally grown rice is higher there than that of rice imported from the Far East or Madagascar, and the latter is, moreover, of superior quality. Husking the paddy also is a stumbling block, for the only mills operating in Gabon are small ones belonging to the SIP and a private one at N'Dendé, none of which turns out a satisfactory product. To popularize the eating of rice, the government has carried on a campaign among buyers, and has introduced it as a basic food in the rations served in state schools, hospitals, and prisons. But the forest and mining laborers who are used to the imported article object to eating Tchibanga rice, and their employers hesitate to force the issue, so some hundreds of tons of rice continue to be brought into the territory each year.[37]

As the marketing difficulties increased with rising local production, the government was forced to reverse its policy of encouraging paddy cultivation and to reduce the area planted to rice in 1955. As this measure did not wholly remedy the situation, however, it proposed and the territorial assemblymen reluctantly accepted the imposition of a higher duty on imported rice (6 per cent, formerly 2 per cent). They also agreed to buy Moyen-Congo's rice surplus on condition that its price and quality approximated those of Far Eastern rice. In recent years a better balance has been reached between local production and Gabon's consumption needs, which amount to some 750 tons a year. But the handicaps of high internal transportation costs and of the unpopularity of rice as a food among the Gabonese have not been overcome. Even the Tchibanga paddy farmers, it is said, prefer to eat manioc and to sell the rice they grow.

North Gabon is the only area in the whole territory where agricultural products—cocoa and, to a lesser degree, coffee—have been instrumental in creating a stable and relatively prosperous peasantry. Indigenous coffee has long been grown in small amounts in lower Gabon, as well as in other parts of AEF, but it was not until 1925 that this crop was officially encouraged, and then chiefly in Woleu-N'Tem. Unlike Oubangui, where Europeans pioneered its commercial cultivation, coffee has been grown in Gabon exclusively by Africans and on a much smaller scale. Under the ten-year Plan, new areas in both northern and southern Gabon were to be brought under coffee cultivation and the territory's output increased to 1,700 tons by 1956. It was not until 1952, however, that the local government began actively working to increase the yield and improve the quality of the product. Since that year the area planted to coffee in Gabon has been greatly extended, chiefly in the N'Gounié, Nyanga, and Haut-Ogooué regions. By 1956 it covered 5,500 hectares, production had risen from about 200 to nearly 600 tons, and exports to some 550 tons. Although the uncertain and generally low returns to its growers resulted in clandestine exports to Spanish Guinea and have tended to inhibit the further expansion of coffee culture, production increased still further in 1958, reaching nearly 1,000 tons.

Much more successful have been the government's efforts to promote cocoa cultivation. Seeds brought to Libreville's Botanical Garden in 1889 from the Portuguese island of São Thome led to the creation of European plantations in the estuary. Some Africans followed their example, and cocoa soon became the basic crop of the littoral and from there spread to lower Gabon. By 1906 the territory had a total of some 500,000 cocoa bushes on 40 plantations, and it exported 91 tons of good-quality cocoa under the trade name of *fermenté du Gabon*.[38] Production continued to increase until about 1914, when the development of the okoumé industry began to absorb all the labor and capital available and led to the almost complete abandonment of cocoa cultivation in lower Gabon. After World War I, a French army captain, using coercive methods, introduced the crop into Woleu-N'Tem, and by 1928 African plantations in that region were producing 200 tons a year of marketable cocoa. Natural conditions there were very propitious for this crop, and its cash returns were attractive in relation to the effort involved in its cultivation. The creation in 1931 of a cocoa *paysannat* in Woleu-N'Tem had a salutary influence on the evolution of a local peasantry and the development of its farming methods. By 1936 compulsion was no longer necessary, for the Africans of that region were voluntarily increasing their production under the technical guidance of the Agricultural Service. By the eve of World War II they were growing about 1,000 tons of cocoa for export, which was bringing in an annual income averaging several thousand francs to each producer.

Even the war did not arrest this development. By 1950 production was more than double the prewar figure, and cocoa cultivation had spread to Mitzic and Medouneu and into neighboring Ogooué-Ivindo, covering a total of some 2,000 hectares. However, yields were poor, for the African farmers were prone to neglect their plantations and ignore the advice of technicians.[39] The conditions under which this crop was marketed not only were chaotic but were detrimental to the grower, for the local merchants who bought the crop (dominated by the powerful Société du Haut-Ogooué) profited by the farmers' inability to stock so perishable a product and their ignorance of market prices.[40] Consequently the administration stepped in to improve the quality of Gabon's cocoa exports and to assure a minimum price to the grower.

By the importing of selected plants, the encouragement of better methods of farming and of drying beans, the restriction of sales to controlled markets, and the standardizing of exports, the reputation for quality already enjoyed by Gabon's cocoa was enhanced. (In 1957, after a brief return to the free sale of cocoa, the controlled markets were reinstituted in order to check a rapid decline in the quality of exports.) A territorial Supporting Fund, set up in 1948 and financed by about half the income derived from the 22 per cent tax on cocoa exports, helped to cover the expenses of the Agricultural Service's operations and also to cushion local farmers against the sudden price falls to which their output was subject. That this latter objective was not wholly attained was shown by the continuation of clandestine cocoa exports to Spanish Guinea, where the price paid was higher than in AEF and the quality factor was ignored.[41] Bad climatic conditions and a sharp drop in the world price for cocoa beginning in 1954 determined the government-general to reorganize the Supporting Fund on a federal basis, even though Gabon's output accounted for 96 per cent of the federation's entire cocoa exports.[42]

The government's policy seems to have been justified by the improvement of the quantity and quality of Gabon's cocoa production and the growing prosperity of its farmers. By 1958 the yield in Woleu-N'Tem had reached 2,700 tons, of which more than 73 per cent was of superior quality, and its decline to 2,200 tons the following year was attributable to drought. When the newer plantations in neighboring areas come into bearing, the output of Gabon's cocoa—all of which is shipped to Douala for processing and export—is expected to rise to 4,000 tons.[43]

In the realm of oleaginous crops, Gabon is a potential rather than an actual producer. Small amounts of peanuts are grown nearly everywhere, but only in the more northerly and southerly regions are they produced in relatively large quantities. No attempt was made to increase the territory's peanut output, which amounted to only 20 to 25 tons a year, until 1953, when a peanut more marketable than the indigenous variety was introduced from the Loudima agricultural station into the Mitzic district of Ogooué-Invindo.[44] Two years later an experiment was undertaken in semimechanized peanut cultivation in the mediocre soils of lower Gabon near Tchibanga. In 1954 Gabon exported 123 tons of nuts and since then production has been increasing in the N'Gounié and Nyanga regions. In 1959 a record crop of 1,300 tons was harvested.

A more hopeful future seems in store for oil-palm products, which come from three main producing centers. One is the great natural grove of Moabi, which is exceptional in its extent (over 10,000 hectares), the density of its producing palms (80 to 100 to the hectare), and the number of Africans living nearby (10,000). Improvement of 3,000 hectares of this grove has been financed by FIDES and carried out by the territorial agricultural service. Access roads into the grove have been built, a 500-ton-capacity oil mill has been built there, and a cooperative called COOPAL has been organized for the gathering, processing, and sale of nuts. In consequence the output of kernels has increased from 300 tons annually to 500. Kernels and oil are sold either locally or in Libreville, and provide much-needed fats for the populations of those areas. A major handicap to this grove's further development is the isolation of the Moabi region, which creates transportation difficulties. A much smaller natural grove at Kango, covering 1,000 hectares, has been developed by the CCAEF.

Soon after the war the CGOT acquired a plantation in the neighborhood of Lambaréné, and the success of its experiments in palm cultivation was such that the decision was made in 1955 to enlarge it to 700 hectares. (By 1959, 500 hectares had been planted with palms, of which area 200 hectares were in full yield.) Since this necessitated the displacement of numerous African villages, the CGOT became unpopular among the African territorial assemblymen. Consequently, when the CGOT proposed granting a concession of 1,500 hectares nearby to a subsidiary of Unilever, the Société des Palmiers et Hevéas du Gabon, the assembly demurred.[45] Then Unilever itself was beset by doubts, finding labor scarcer and wages higher in AEF than in neighboring countries. Eventually, however, an agreement was reached between it and the assembly, and if its plantation proves successful, "Gabon may become in the foreseeable future a non-negligible producer of palm oil."[46]

Forests and forest products

For about half a century Gabon's economy has been almost completely dependent upon its wood industry, in particular on its okoumé exports. Agriculture never has played more than a small part in the territory's productivity, and only in very recent years have petroleum and mineral deposits promised an appreciable diversification in its output. Even today it is the sales of okoumé in foreign markets that determine almost wholly the tempo at which the whole territory can be developed, the volume of its imports, and the living standards of much of its population. Fortunately for Gabon, the demand for okoumé in the world market has been both large and consistent since the end of World War I, except during the great trade slumps of the interwar period and World War II, and briefly in 1952 and 1956.

Gabon is a timber territory *par excellence,* for most of its surface is covered by the dense tropical forest, which is dotted with lakes and traversed by a network of rivers that flow from the heart of the country to the Atlantic coast. Along with Spanish Guinea and Moyen-Congo, Gabon has a monopoly of the okoumé tree, which is not only ideal for the manufacture of plywood but so light that it can be floated to the seaports as soon as it is cut down. European lumber companies have operated in the territory since the turn of the century, but since 1946 their operations have undergone a drastic change in regard to both locale and the methods used.

Until World War II, the European firms both cut wood themselves and bought timber from Africans, who either felled trees on the companies' concessions or logged independently. During this period, African concessionnaires were fairly numerous, and a few of them made a fortune in the lumber business, but the great majority of African foresters worked for the big European companies, mostly as wage laborers. Some 20,000 Africans were thus employed, and labor was the single most important factor in the timber business. The work of felling trees and rolling logs to the nearest watercourse was a hard and back-breaking task—sometimes it took 30 men an entire afternoon to move a log 100 meters—and in the case of trees whose branches intertwined with those of their neighbors the ground had to be cleared for a considerable radius around before they could be cut down.[47] Gabon's population was small and dispersed, and besides the difficulty of recruiting workers there was the problem of housing and feeding them. The tsetse fly had eliminated the chance of procuring much meat by hunting, and not infrequently the nearest village growing food crops was 50 kilometers from the camp and had little surplus for sale. Furthermore, manioc and bananas were too perishable to stand long-distance transportation. Some of the companies complied with the government regulations requiring them to grow their own manioc, but for the most part the forest laborers had to subsist on tinned goods, especially sardines, and imported rice, local fruit, and vegetables.

A forest company's troubles were not over when it had recruited and fed its laborers, for it had to depend upon the local chiefs to round up enough skilled rowers to propel the lumber rafts to the loading port. Many logs were lost en route when the rafts became marooned on sandbanks or were being loaded onto freighters anchored in the open roadstead, and the rowers were not above selling some of the logs to the river villagers, who deftly substituted old logs for those freshly cut. Time was of the essence from the beginning to the end of these operations. Logs must be got to the river bank during the only period when the waters were high enough to float them downstream, and to the loading points when the freighters—whose port charges were heavy—were available to transport them to Europe, where the wood market was seasonal and demanding. The cost of maritime shipping was so high that only high-quality logs were worth transporting, and those that had lain in the forest for a year before shipping were so damaged by insects as to be virtually unsalable. Rowers were given a bonus for conveying a timber raft rapidly to the coast, and they were also spurred on by the fact that they could find little food, and that at very high prices, en route or in the port towns. Often, however, they could not resist the temptation of stopping off for a few days to celebrate a festival in one of the river villages or of squandering what they had earned on tobacco and alcohol at Libreville or Port Gentil.

The sharp decline in Gabon's lumber exports during World War II led to a reduction by about half in the wood industry's labor force, many of whose members became workers for the mining companies. In 1937 production amounted to 675,000 cubic meters, but by 1942 it had fallen to 30,000 cubic meters. A revival of exports began in 1947, owing to the high price then being paid for okoumé, but it was not until 1951 that they returned to prewar levels. Various causes were responsible for this slow recovery of Gabon's wood industry: the disappearance of valuable tree species from the accessible coastal area, the depletion of its matériel, the rise in taxation[48] and freight rates, and the increased difficulties of recruiting, provisioning, and paying its laborers. The postwar freedoms had made the Gabonese more reluctant than ever to work in the forest camps, and laborers at high wages had to be brought in from Nigeria. All this added up to very high production costs, and to reduce them the big companies decided to mechanize their operations to the maximum.[49] Here the French treasury aided them by allocating to them 10 per cent of the hard currency earned by Gabon's wood sales in foreign markets, on condition that it be used for the purchase of mechanical equipment. It took some years for such orders to be filled, but when tractors arrived in large numbers they revolutionized the production of Gabon's timber in two ways— by vastly reducing its dependence on manual labor and by gradually eliminating the small foresters, both African and European, from the field.

Tractors—of which there are now over 100 in the Libreville region alone—are used for handling logs and for building access tracks. The rowers of rafts have been replaced by motorized lumber barges, and trucks sometimes transport logs to the ship-loading points. Mechanized equipment has made possible the development of Gabon's so-called second forest zone, which penetrates deep into the tropical forest, but it can be worked only by heavily capitalized companies. Forest enterprises in Gabon at present number about 150, and of these only 20 small ones are owned by Africans.[50] The machine is not the only cause for the progressive Europeanization of this industry—another has been the dizzily rising prices at which cutting permits have been auctioned, and still another, in the accessible first zone, is the extension of forest reserves, where felling is no longer permitted.[51] Then, too, many African foresters have failed through poor management of their enterprises and through the parasitism of their relatives and hangers-on. If, as Léon Mba told the territorial assembly on January 25, 1956, there were no longer any African lumber magnates whereas there had been a number of such millionaires in the interwar period, the reasons are multiple, and one of them is deeply rooted in indigenous society.[52]

Inevitably the European foresters who have been able to survive and even prosper in so tough, hazardous, and competitive a business as Gabon's lumber industry are a hardy and individualistic lot of men. Russell Howe, a British journalist who is not tender toward many aspects of French colonialism, describes[53] the foresters of Gabon as—

> the most realistic of pioneers. . . . [They are] for the most part of the more constructive breed on which empires should be built, if empires are built at all. Rough and ready, cut off from the Metropolis by everything except a certain liberal way of thinking . . . they are of the old-trader sort that Conrad respected and that history teaches us to admire. Their allegiance is to Brazzaville, not Paris (despite their deep attachment to France itself) and to Brazza himself and what he stood for, rather than to the Minister [in France] . . .

It is easy to see how men of such a stamp are, by their temperaments and lives, recalcitrant to any official controls over their activities. Until World War II, the many regulations governing Gabon's forest industry were never effectively enforced, with the result that the zones nearest the watercourses were wastefully denuded of valuable trees and little effort was made to reconstitute the growths or to check soil erosion. The forest companies operated as laws unto themselves, as did the countless middlemen who sold their output in European markets.

With the aim of putting an end to the devastation of AEF's forest resources and to the anarchic marketing conditions, the Office des Bois d'AEF was created during the war. However, it was not until this Office was granted a monopoly of okoumé purchases and sales in foreign markets, on October 12, 1945, and the government's representative was given a decisive vote in its decisions that Gabon's foresters began to voice strenuous objections through their own organization, the Syndicat Forestier du Gabon. Largely as a result of the pressure brought by Gabon's producers, the Office was progressively modified in its powers and directorate. They did not, however, succeed in getting rid of the Office and reviving free trading in wood, and gradually they became reconciled to such controls as it continued to exercise, particularly after the trade recession of 1952 had shown how useful such an organization could be to them. The attitude of the Gabonese elite, on the other hand, has always been favorable to the Office, which they regard as the defender of the small foresters vis-à-vis the big companies. So when the Mba government was constituted in 1957, it began to insist that the Office be "territorialized" and that it be given control of the directorate—a policy to which the producers' organizations were firmly opposed.

If the Gabonese elite looked with favor on the Office des Bois from the outset, the same could not be said of their attitude toward the Forestry Service, and only in recent years have they come to recognize its usefulness. At almost every session of the territorial assembly, its African members complained that the Service was extending forest reserves at the expense of African villages and was imposing unduly severe penalties upon those inhabitants who continued to farm and to cut wood in such areas. Every year the surface classified as forest reserves has been growing, and it now covers about one million hectares. At the same time the area over which okoumé-cutting permits have been granted has also been increasing, at the annual rate of 30,000 to 60,000 hectares, and it now comprises nearly 1.5 million hectares. Concurrently the Forestry Service has reforested over 6,000 hectares in okoumé trees, made an aerial prospection of the Ogooué basin, and taken an inventory of the valuable species growing on more than 75,000 hectares. It also established a scientific experimental station in 1954, which is managed by the Service's research section. Although these are long-term operations, the African elite are beginning to see their value in preserving and enriching Gabon's forest resources, particularly as some of the older reserves are being opened up for controlled felling. In

1956 the territorial assembly accepted the Forestry Service's proposal that Gabon's forests be divided into two separate zones, the first and more accessible one to be reserved for concessions and cutting permits over 500 to 2,500 hectares, and the second for those of 10,000 to 25,000 hectares. In this way small and medium-sized enterprises are assured of a minimal area which is suited to the means of development at their disposal, while the general reform effected by the law of May 1955 has guaranteed to all the Africans their traditional rights over the use and ownership of land (see pp. 159–60). In mid-1959 the legislative assembly was told that an increasing number of okoumé-cutting permits were being granted to Africans.

The importance of Gabon's forests to the territory's economy has been enhanced since 1946 by the development of its wood-processing plants. Before World War II, almost all of Gabon's wood exports were in the form of undressed timber; there were two small wood-peeling plants at Port Gentil which exported their output to Metropolitan plywood factories, and only a few sawmills, the most important of which, at Macok, manufactured ties for the French railroads. During the war this sawmill was able to turn out 2,500 cubic meters of sawn wood for the local market, but its labor requirements were so large that it proved to be not a paying proposition. After the Liberation, the Office des Bois built a wholly mechanized sawmill at Port Gentil, and four other companies in the estuary and along the Ogooué followed its example. All of these enterprises processed logs that were unsuitable for export as undressed timber. Now there are 22 sawmills in Gabon, with an annual capacity of about 35,000 cubic meters of sawn wood. The domestic market for their output is small—only a few thousand cubic meters a year—and because of its high price, sawn wood occupies a very minor place among Gabon's timber exports. In 1952 the mill of the Ateliers Mécaniques had to close down, and none of the territory's sawmills operates to capacity. In 1958 Gabon produced 25,600 cubic meters of sawn wood.

Far more important for the territory's economy is the plywood, peeled-wood, and veneer-wood industry, though the plants concerned also operate well below capacity and have a hard time finding markets for their products. The early postwar demand for plywood far exceeded the supply available, and an ambitious project was conceived of constructing the world's largest plywood and veneer-wood factory at Port Gentil. For this purpose the Compagnie Française du Gabon (CFG) was formed, with the aid of the local government and of the U.S. Plywood Co., but the opposition of the Metropolitan plywood manufacturers had not been reckoned with, and they succeeded in barring the European market to the Gabon company's exports. Inevitably the CFG was unable to operate at anywhere near its annual capacity of 50,000 cubic meters of plywood and veneer wood, and it ran into financial difficulties that necessitated its reorganization in 1952. Since that year, when it came to an uneasy modus vivendi with its Metropolitan competitors, it has been able to increase its output to about 75 per cent of capacity—some 39,400 cubic meters in 1958 compared with about

18,000 in 1953. The CFG has also compressed its operating expenses by reducing its European staff from 125 to 70 and by increasing the number of its African employees from 700 to 1,300. Not only has this change of policy brought out more skilled Gabonese workers but the latter's wages total annually some 100 million CFA francs and the territory's revenues benefit by about 30 million CFA francs in the taxes and duties paid each year by the CFG.[54]

In one form or another the products of Gabon's forests are still of major importance to that territory, where they regularly account for 96 per cent of the tonnage and 87 per cent of the value of its exports. Wood exports, which are virtually tantamount to production in Gabon, have hovered around the 400,000-ton figure in recent years, and that appears to be about the maximum compatible with the healthy management of its forest resources and the capacity of the world market to absorb. It now seems likely that in the near future Gabon's dangerous dependence upon a single industry whose prosperity is determined by fluctuating world prices will be mitigated by the development of more diversified resources.

Animal husbandry

Natural and human conditions in Gabon conspire to make that territory singularly unsuitable for animal husbandry, and none of the official attempts to introduce it there has thus far been very successful. The presence of the tsetse fly throughout the great forest zone has been a grave obstacle to the rearing of indigenous cattle, and the few thousand scrawny chickens, pigs, sheep, and goats to be seen in Gabonese villages receive little or no care or food from their owners. The town dwellers are irregularly and inadequately provisioned in beef from Cameroun, which exports to the seaports some 500 cattle a year, and in mutton to the extent of a few hundred tons received during the year by plane from Tchad, but the rural populations have to depend on the even more limited and insufficient supply of meat acquired through hunting. As the amount of game in Gabon is in any case small and as the government has strictly limited the number of firearms owned by the local population to about 3,000 guns, the dearth of meat in the Gabonese diet is considered to be a prime cause of decimation of the territory's inhabitants.

To offset this shortage, an experimental farm for the rearing of pigs, poultry, and (later) cattle was created at Owendo, and four assistant veterinaries were sent on inspection tours of Gabonese villages to advise their inhabitants regarding the care and feeding of livestock. Both of these efforts failed lamentably, for the choice of Owendo as a site for such experiments proved to be unfortunate and the itinerant African veterinaries were too few and too untrained to instill in the Gabonese villagers any interest in proper methods of animal husbandry.[55] Even the selected breeding animals shipped to Owendo from the Brazzaville station at Kilometer 17 failed to do well there, and the African assemblymen repeatedly asked the government to suppress that "useless and expensive farm" and increase the number of firearms and hunting permits allocated to Gabonese farmers.

The government, however, heartened by its success in introducing cattle husbandry into Moyen-Congo, persisted in its attempt to popularize the rearing of meat animals in Gabon according to a new formula developed under the second Plan. The Owendo farm was retained, but only as a point for relaying imported N'dama breeding stock to villages in the savannah regions of Nyanga and N'Gounié. Under a sort of sharecropper contract made with the administration, each of the village chiefs or Notables who received a few animals for breeding purposes was required after four years to return the number he had been given but was allowed to keep the offspring produced during the interval. In the forest zone, where cattle husbandry could succeed only in the hands of experts, selected sheep and poultry were to be distributed to villagers, but only in the places where the territorial veterinaries could supervise and instruct owners in their care. A beginning was made, also, in scientific pig rearing in the Tchibanga district, where by-products of the rice harvest assured an adequate supply of feed.[56]

Though the foregoing experiments are too recent to appraise, animal husbandry has been introduced with at least partial success in zones of south Gabon where it never before existed, and a few Gabonese are serving their apprenticeship as herders. But aside from the time required to train the rural population in an occupation alien to its traditions, there remain the lack of natural fodder, the adverse nature of Gabon's climate and terrain, and the omnipresent tsetse fly. Undoubtedly Gabon can and will appreciably increase its own animal resources, but if there is to be real improvement in the local diet, it will still have to import the greater part of its meat supplies for many years to come.

Fisheries

Deep-sea fishing is carried on by villagers the length of the Gabon coast, but on a full-time basis by only one tribe, located at Fernan Vaz. The resources offshore from Cap Lopez and Pointe Denis have attracted Dahomean fishermen from the Popos, who have set up seasonal villages there from which to operate, and those of the estuary have induced a European to establish a plant at Ozouri, near Port Gentil, for the purpose of smoking and salting the catch of that region. The largest-scale fishing enterprise off the Gabonese coast has been conducted by European whaling companies, whose activities have fluctuated widely depending upon local and international regulations and the number of whales frequenting Gabon's territorial waters.

Before World War I, no regulations existed limiting the destruction of whales, and in the late 1930's eight Norwegian, French, and British companies operated in the Atlantic off Cap Lopez. The war caused the cessation of their activities, and in 1920 two Franco-Norwegian companies acquired the three licenses then issued by the Gabon government for whale fishing in the vicinity. As a result of competition from other companies and the whales' abandonment of the Gabon coast, the Franco-Norwegian companies suspended operations from 1926 to 1934 and again from 1937 until the outbreak of World War II. In 1949 a single Franco-Norwegian company was formed, the Société des Pêcheries Coloniales à la Baleine (SOPECOBA), which built a processing plant at Cap Lopez, hired a staff of over 200 technicians, and obtained from the territorial government a ten-year monopoly of whale fishing in Gabonese waters. Almost overnight this company became an important element in Gabon's economy, paying into the local treasury in 1949–50 taxes and duties amounting to 22 million CFA francs. In its first three seasons SOPECOBA killed nearly 3,800 whales and processed 27,500 tons of oil at Cap Lopez, but in 1952 it caught very few whales and the following year decided to suspend operations.[57] In March 1959 the territorial assembly renewed SOPECOBA's permit for a year in exchange for 1,000 tons of oil to be processed from an authorized catch of 600 whales.

As to fresh-water fishing, the lakes of Gabon form one of the federation's three main sources of production, and their output is estimated at 8,000 to 10,000 tons of fresh fish a year.[58] Probably because of the abundance of such local resources, the federal government did not start the construction of family ponds for tilapia breeding in Gabon until the end of 1955, and then only in N'Gounié and Woleu-N'Tem. The next year these were extended to Ogooué-Ivindo, but as of 1957 Gabon had only some 110 such ponds. In Libreville the authors were told in late 1956 that the local population, as apathetic as it is amiable, had expressed its willingness to go along with the government's tilapia-stocking project, and thus increase their supply of protein, provided that the officials agreed to catch the fish.

Trade

Though data on Gabon's trade go back as far as 1862, they are incomplete, and until 1891 they were never the subject of annual reports. In the former year, the colony's external commerce amounted to over 3 million francs; two years later it fell to about half that sum, and from 1869 to 1891 the data on it are either fragmentary or nonexistent. Even in the post–World War II period, official statistics naturally cast no light on the extent of Gabon's clandestine exchanges with Spanish Guinea, which are said to represent a value of some 40 million CFA francs a year.[59] In 1958 the volume of Gabon's known trade came to 1,207,102 tons, valued at 15,851 million CFA francs.

During the first half of the twentieth century, uncultivated produce supplied the great bulk of Gabon's exports. As occurred in some other regions of the African forest zone, ivory, wild rubber, gold, and diamonds declined in importance, and two cultivated crops—cocoa and coffee—began to appear in the customs statistics during the interwar decades. For a time, both before and after World War II, whale oil was listed among Gabon's export commodities, but for years on end it disappeared wholly from their midst. Wood, and particularly okoumé logs, has been the most constant and valuable of the territory's exports, dwarfing every other of Gabon's products until 1958. In 1951 timber accounted for 96 per cent of the tonnage and 77 per cent of the value of its total exports. After the sharp price fall in 1952, wood made a swift comeback, and by 1957 it supplied three-fourths of the territory's entire shipments. Agricultural produce for export has amounted to only a few thousand tons annually and has brought in, on the average, less than 300 million CFA francs a year. Gold and diamond exports, which long held third place, slumped after 1956 because of the exhaustion of deposits.

In 1957 the structure of Gabon's economy was suddenly modified by its first shipments of crude oil, and the next year petroleum rose to second rank in both tonnage and value. Oil was still far outdistanced, however, by timber exports, which climbed spectacularly from 1954 on. In 1955 Gabon shipped out 540,000 tons of wood worth 5 billion CFA francs, and two years later its exports had increased by 50 per cent in tonnage and also in value. The imminent development of its manganese, uranium, and iron deposits is expected not only to diversify Gabon's exports and increase its revenues, but also to strengthen its position as the leading exporter among the four republics of the former federation. For many years Gabon supplied from two-thirds to three-fourths of AEF's export tonnages. In terms of value, they accounted for about one-third of all the federation's shipments until 1957, when their proportion rose to 41 per cent, and in 1958 they represented 43 per cent.

Gabon's consistently favorable trade balance, except for a few years, has resulted in part from its comparatively small imports. Not only is it the least populous of the AEF territories, but its location and lack of means of communication have made it difficult to provision. During the first postwar decade, Gabon took about 10 per cent of the federation's total imports, but since 1955 its share has risen to about one-fourth in terms of value, though tonnages have not risen so markedly. Between 1956 and 1957, imports almost doubled, largely because of the influx of equipment goods ordered by the petroleum company, and in the latter year Gabon's imports accounted for 29 per cent of the federation's total. Among them foodstuffs have also increased sharply in recent years, and in 1958 Gabon bought 22 per cent of the flour, 20 per cent of the rice and fish, 41 per cent of the alcoholic beverages, and 24 per cent of the fuel brought into the federation, although it possessed only 8 per cent of AEF's African and 16 per cent of its European population.

The swift rise in Gabon's imports reflects the territory's rapid industrialization, its deficiencies in food production, and the prosperity traceable to growing wood and petroleum exports. Though the timber industry is still mostly in the hands of Europeans, Gabonese Africans have profited as wage earners from its record export tonnages. Moreover, despite the small volume and fluctuations of Gabon's cocoa and coffee exports, their continued increase has played a part in enhancing the purchasing power of the hinterland tribes. With the current and future extension of industry in the territory, food and other imports may be expected to increase. For some years the difficulty in provisioning the coastal towns (as well as the forest and mining camps) has been a major and worsening problem, and it accounts to a large degree for the high prices charged for their goods by the numerous merchants of Libreville and Port Gentil.

Perennially, the franc zone has been Gabon's main external market and provisioner, no matter under what tariff regime the territory has been placed (see p. 212). In 1958 the French Union swelled its percentage of the value of Gabon's exports to 63 per cent from 56 per cent the previous year, owing to its absorption of the totality of Gabon's petroleum shipments, while Germany both before and since the war has been the territory's principal client outside the franc zone. Also in 1958, the franc zone supplied 72 per cent of Gabon's imports by value. Other provisioners were the dollar and sterling-zone countries, followed by West Germany, Italy, and Holland. That year, exports of wood accounted for 6,023 million CFA francs, those of crude oil for 1,556 millions, those of cocoa for 408 millions, and those of gold for 121 millions.

Industry

Until the discovery of Gabon's petroleum deposits in 1956, virtually the only industrial enterprise in the territory of any importance was that of wood. Processing of Gabon's timber is almost wholly a postwar phenomenon, but because of labor shortages and marketing difficulties, the sawmills and plants for producing sawn wood, veneer and peeled wood, and plywood erected since 1946 do not yet work to capacity. Oil from whales caught off the Gabonese coast has been intermittently processed locally, and a few hundred tons of rice are milled in the Tchibanga district. Mining is the sole industry that can be said to rival that of wood, and in recent years not only has its character changed but its importance has been vastly enhanced.

In the early 1950's gold and to a lesser extent diamonds were the only valuable products of this industry. Gabon was the last territory of the federation in which gold was discovered, but it soon proved to have the richest alluvion deposits of any. From 1950 through 1953 it produced half of the gold mined in AEF, amounting to over a ton a year, and its output came almost wholly from the mines in the N'Gounié region operated by the Compagnie des Mines d'Or du Gabon. Progressive exhaustion of these rich deposits, however, caused a sharp decline in production beginning in 1956, and current prospecting has made no new and valuable discoveries. Diamond mining, also localized in the N'Gounié area, has followed the same downward course as that of gold, and it was also carried on almost exclusively by a single company, the SOREDIA. In any case, however, Gabon's diamond output was never very considerable, having accounted at its peak in 1952 for no more than 10 per cent of AEF's total ouput, and in December 1957 SOREDIA suspended its mining operations.

Fortunately for Gabon, petroleum was found in its coastal region in

1956, after many years of fruitless and expensive research. It has given an enormous impetus to the industrialization of Port Gentil, jobs to several thousand Africans there, and hundreds of millions of CFA francs to the territory's revenues in the form of taxes and royalties. The manganese and uranium deposits of Franceville and the iron of Mékambo are already providing jobs for several thousand more Africans, and when these minerals enter the export stage they should enrich the republic's coffers by large additional sums. Lake Azingo's potash should also add to Gabon's revenues, but on a much smaller scale.

Gabon's mineral wealth has not yet been completely surveyed, and each year new and valuable deposits are discovered. The location of most of them, not to speak of Gabon's difficult terrain and climate, makes prospecting a long and costly process and also foreshadows colossal transportation difficulties. Each new find is hailed by the Gabonese with mixed emotions. On the one hand, naturally, they are delighted by the prospect of a profitable industrialization of their isolated and underpopulated territory, and they have welcomed the private capital needed to bring this about by passing laws and granting long-term fiscal concessions designed to attract it. On the other hand, they fear that their country's wealth will be not only a wasting asset but one that will benefit others more than themselves. In particular they resent the export of manganese ores to Pointe Noire for processing by means of the cheap electrical current that is to be provided by the Kouilou dam, for Gabon has its own hydroelectric potential that is now wholly unutilized. Furthermore, they had hoped that shipment of the ores from Franceville would entail the construction of a railroad that would end the isolation and contribute to the development of the Haut-Ogooué region. In this respect the compromise reached—an aerial cableway connecting with a short railroad line—has not satisfied them, and perforce they must accept the industrial primacy given to Pointe Noire by the Kouilou project. However, they have succeeded in requiring the mining companies operating in Gabon to establish their headquarters there and to admit the territory's representatives to sit with their board of directors and the local government to share in their capitalization.

To the leaders of the Gabon republic, the working of the Mékambo iron mines, and even that of the small potash deposits of Lake Azingo, is of more interest than the operations of either SPAEF or COMILOG. To ship out Mékambo's ore, a 500-kilometer railroad will have to be built that should greatly benefit the economy of the region through which it passes, and if a decision is made to mine Gabon's potash, it will be sent to Owendo for export. These will be wholly Gabonese enterprises in the geographical sense of the term, and the country can profit by them over and above the revenues brought in by taxation and the employment given to a few hundred manual laborers.

Before World War II, Libreville was one of three towns in AEF and the only one in Gabon to have a public distribution of electrical current, and its plant was operated by a small private firm, the Compagnie Générale de Distribution d'Energie Electrique (CGDEE). Port Gentil had to wait until after the war, when the Compagnie Française du Gabon built a generating plant for its plywood factory that supplied current also to a portion of the town. Elsewhere a few individuals and industries had their own diesel generating plants, as did administrators in the main hinterland settlements.

The ten-year Plan envisaged the progressive electrification of Port Gentil, Lambaréné, Mouila, Oyem, and Bitam by the CGDEE, and also a peripheral project for eventually utilizing the waterfalls of Fougamou and Kinguéla. Before and since World War II, technicians have studied such projects, and since 1946 Gabon's territorial assembly has discussed the means for carrying them out. However, the sparseness of Gabon's population and its dispersion have deterred even the most enthusiastic assemblymen, for it was estimated in 1954 that if electric-power distribution were to be undertaken in the hinterland towns, it would be so expensive that a rate of 100 to 150 CFA francs per kilowatt-hour would have to be charged.[60] By 1956 they decided that such a scheme would be worth executing only in Lambaréné, and the assembly then voted to earmark for that town all of the 3 million CFA francs the territory had been allocated by FIDES for the electrification of secondary centers.[61] It was hoped that the other settlements on the 1946 list would be able to raise loans for such a purpose after they were raised to the rank of mixed communes.

Time has justified the cautious approach to the issue, based on Gabon's lack of potential consumers and the high cost of its current. Even in Libreville the use of electrical current has increased slowly, largely because it costs about 30 CFA francs per kilowatt-hour. Its 1,170-horsepower diesel plant generated only 1,435,000 kilowatt-hours in 1953 and 1,658,000 in 1954. The greatest progress in the territory has been made at Port Gentil, where the wood, fishing, and petroleum industries have created a fast-rising demand for current. There the EEAEF helped in 1950 to finance a new company of "mixed economy," the Société d'Energie de Port-Gentil. It bought the 5,850-horsepower diesel plant from the Compagnie Française du Gabon, and by 1954 was selling to consumers 1,327,000 kilowatt-hours a year, compared with 989,000 in 1953. Five years later, natural gas produced from nearby petroleum deposits was substituted for imported fuel in its operations—reportedly the first achievement of this kind in Black Africa.[62]

Some of the bitterness felt by the Gabonese toward Moyen-Congo was due to the choice of Pointe Noire instead of a point on Gabon's coast to become the federation's deep-water port, and now this sentiment has been aggravated by the selection of Kouilou in preference to some of the Ogooué waterfalls for construction of AEF's major hydroelectric-power plant. This will mean that Gabon's manganese ore must be exported to Pointe Noire for processing, and the Gabonese feel that the wealth of their country is slipping through their fingers to the benefit of their traditional southern rival.

Labor

Paradoxically, Gabon has both the smallest population and, in proportion to it, the largest number of wage earners in AEF, and it is also the territory in which labor is the least strongly organized. In a population of less than half a million, there were in 1958 some 41,600 wage earners, of whom 33,000 were employed in the private sector (mainly in forestry and mining) and 8,500 in the public one. This represented a rise of more than 15,000 wage earners since 1952, and reflected the rapid industrialization of Gabon.

The large size of the wage-earning class has been due in part to the demographic and social structure of Gabon (see pp. 343–47) and in part to the early development there of the forest industry, which, in the interwar period, employed 20,000 to 25,000 laborers a year. The virtual stoppage of wood exports during World War II, and later the mechanization of that industry, as well as the importation of Nigerian workers, have markedly reduced the demands made by the forest companies on local manpower. As of 1952, only 10,000 of the 26,000 estimated wage earners in Gabon were employed in the forest industry, or only 2,000 more than were then engaged in mining.[63] In the late 1920's, the government intervened to stop the recruitment of Gabonese workers for labor outside the territory, and in 1953 it again stepped in to prevent in some cases their employment outside their home districts. In the first instance official policy was inspired by the determination not to depopulate further a colony whose inhabitants were retrogressing in numbers and in health, and also to safeguard the forest labor supply. By 1953 the demographic factor had become paramount, particularly in the trypanosomiasis-ridden districts. During the war, many of the laborers dismissed from the forest camps turned to mining, for in that period stress was placed on increasing the output of minerals. Since the Liberation, Gabon has seen the development of other industries, which compete for the services of its meager manpower, and the imminent development of the Franceville and Mékambo mines, despite their high degree of mechanization, may be expected to intensify the local labor shortage.

Until the postwar development of the wood-processing and petroleum industries, little attempt had been made to train Gabonese laborers. By 1947, Gabon's public-school system possessed one Ecole des Métiers at Owendo, one *section artisanale,* and six *sections d'apprentissage,*[64] and only 13 per cent of the territory's wage earners could be classed as skilled workers.[65] This failure to train workers was due chiefly to the nature of the labor required by the early forest industry, but it also derived from the seasonal and fitful character of the territory's labor supply. The forest provided hinterland Gabonese with their basic food needs, and so they worked only enough to pay taxes and the bride price, and to buy a few meters of cloth, a little tobacco, and alcoholic beverages. Dr. Schweitzer, in reminiscing about his first years at Lambaréné,[66] describes how European planters would see their laborers desert when crops were ready to harvest and foresters could find no one to cut down trees just at the time they received urgent orders from their customers, simply because the workers felt a compelling desire to hunt or fish. The Catholic missionaries managed to train a few carpenters and blacksmiths in their own workshops, but had no success in teaching their converts gardening, masonry, shoemaking, or how to care for animals.[67] The latter occupations the Gabonese regarded as fit only for slaves or women and, if they had to work at all, they wanted to become either clerks or retail merchants. This disdain for certain types of work which were considered to be lacking in prestige, along with a dislike for occupations requiring hard and continuous labor, accentuated the existing shortage of laborers in the territory.

The government has attacked the problem from various angles but as yet has made little headway in turning the Gabonese into skilled workers. Though it increased the number of technical schools to 11 and spent 1.82 per cent of its budget on that type of education, the pupil attendance in such establishments had fallen to 261 by 1952.[68] Some of this decline could be blamed on the difficulties encountered by graduates of the Owendo Ecole des Métiers in finding remunerative jobs, and this naturally discouraged others from applying for admission to its three-year course in iron- and wood-working. Gabon is the only AEF territory that has not yet been provided with a rapid-training center for manual workers. For some years after the authorities had failed to regroup Gabonese villages (see p. 345) official policy concerning manual laborers remained largely negative and mainly took the form of forbidding labor recruiters to hire Gabonese for work on the Congo-Ocean railroad. Aside from efforts to improve the general health of the population, the government's most positive contribution was that of bringing into Gabon workers from other parts of the federation, Algeria, and Nigeria. But immigrants from the north had a hard time adjusting themselves to the climate and food of Gabon, and the only successful venture in this domain has been the importation of Nigerian workers from a zone geographically similar to that of Gabon.

In 1947 the federal government began negotiations with the British in Nigeria for the emigration of 10,000 laborers to Gabon. It took over a year to persuade the Gabon territorial assembly to accept such a measure, and two years to reach an agreement with the British authorities. This was finally signed in May 1949 on terms that differed considerably from those initially proposed by the French. The number of migrants was much reduced, they must not be used in mining enterprises or outside the districts of Libreville, Kango, and Port Gentil, and the conditions posed in regard to their recruitment, transportation, pay, and various emoluments pointed to outlays far larger than the forest industry had expected or had been paying to local laborers. In Nigeria, recruitment was entrusted to an Anglo-Spanish employment agency, volunteers signing a two-year contract underwent medical examination before they left home and after their arrival in Gabon, and responsibility for their welfare in the forest camps was shared by a British official stationed at Libreville and the territorial labor inspectorate.

Despite the precautions with which this migration was organized, relations between the Nigerians and their employers, as well as their Gabonese co-workers, were strained at the outset.[69] In part this was because of language barriers but in part also because of the inaptitude of the Nigerians for the work assigned them and of their demands for certain amenities not given to Gabonese laborers. Through the consistently good working relations between the French and British governments, most of these difficulties were ironed out by 1952, and every year since then a few hundred Nigerian laborers have come to work in Gabon. Each of the thousand or so Nigerians at present laboring in the territory costs his employer about 4,650 CFA francs a month for his recruitment, wages, and travel expenses, and in addition the forest companies have built sports fields and meeting halls for them. A locally recruited Gabonese laborer costs considerably less (3,540 CFA francs a month), and he is said to be no more inefficient and ill-adapted than his Nigerian counterpart.[70] In fact, it took the arrival of the Nigerians to make European foresters in Gabon appreciate the qualities of local labor, which, except for its numerical deficiency, was in every way more satisfactory to employers than were the immigrants.

Given the scarcity of indigenous labor in Gabon and the high proportion of wage earners to the total adult population, one would expect to see develop there strong unions able to exact high wages and good working conditions from employers. Yet unions are conspicuously weak in Gabon, apparently because of the dispersal, lack of skills, and illiteracy of the forest workers, who account for about one-quarter of all the territory's wage earners. As of mid-1957, only about 1,000 of the nearly 13,000 men employed by the forest companies in the isolated camps scattered throughout the hinterland were organized. Naturally the strongest unions were those in Libreville and Port Gentil, where they were concentrated in the wood-processing, petroleum, and fishing industries, but even there their influence has been both politically slight and, on the whole, ineffectual in obtaining better pay and working conditions.[71] The least weak of the Gabon unions is the Confédération Française des Travailleurs Chrétiens (CFTC) and the one with the smallest following is the Confédération Générale du Travail (CGT), in both cases because of the dominant role played by the Catholic missions in coastal Gabon. Such improvements as have been made in the position of Gabonese labor can be ascribed almost wholly to the initiative of the government and, to a lesser degree, that of the territorial assembly. The latter's African members have been concerned in seeing not only that labor should get a fair deal and that the territory's productivity should be increased, but that a higher birth rate should be encouraged through raising the laborers' living standards.

Owing to the cooperation between the administration and the assembly, the Overseas Labor Code was applied to Gabon without encountering major obstacles. On March 15, 1953, a territorial labor-advisory committee was set up under the auspices of the local labor inspectorate. The following year, labor courts were established at Libreville and Port Gentil, and in 1957 the assembly voted unanimously to establish in the capital an Office de la Main-d'Oeuvre for all Gabon. The greatest interest shown by the African assemblymen in any labor question has been in regard to family allowances, and despite the opposition of employer organizations they raised the rate to the same high level as that of Moyen-Congo at the session of November 5, 1957. Thanks to this move, each of the 27,000 or more children of Gabon's wage earners was to receive 400 CFA francs a month, the prenatal allowance was set at 500 CFA francs, and the premium for births at 2,500 CFA francs. Between June 1, 1958, and June 1, 1959, 86 million CFA francs were paid out to 8,350 wage earners for the support of their children.

After the Mba government came to power in 1957 it began negotiations which in March 1958 resulted in the first collective agreement reached in Gabon—that between the maritime and river-transport companies and the local CGTA branch of workers. Much more important, with regard to the number of laborers affected, was the second collective agreement, signed in mid-July 1959, between the CATC and CGTA forest workers and the powerful Syndicat Forestier. In November 1959, Premier Mba announced that 13 collective agreements had been drawn up, with the aid of Gabon's *comité paritaire*,[12] which covered almost all the republic's occupational categories; that the minimum wage had not been raised as of the preceding January; and that all workers were now insured against accidents.

CHAPTER 23

Oubangui-Chari
(République Centrafricaine)

It would be hard to find a greater contrast to Gabon than the territory of Oubangui-Chari, often called simply Oubangui for the sake of brevity. Oubangui has more than twice the area and nearly three times the population of Gabon, and there is no dominant tribal group such as the Fang. It has an excellent system of internal communications, both roads and rivers; comparatively small forests and great stretches of savannah; and only one real town, which is both an administrative and a trading center. While Oubangui has no great resources comparable to those of Gabon, its economy is fairly well balanced: it is mainly agricultural, with a few small mining industries.

Again in contrast to Gabon, Oubangui is land-locked—it has 4,000 kilometers of artificial frontiers with non-AEF countries, and for centuries it has been a crossroads for central Africa. French explorers did not reach this area until the last decade of the nineteenth century. Though it was occupied pacifically, it soon felt the full brunt of the concessionary-company regime, and became the scene of the worst revolts in the history of AEF. To this day, relations between Africans and Europeans seem to be more tense in Oubangui than anywhere else in French central Africa. The political struggle here has been almost wholly between Africans and the administration, and not between African factions as in Gabon.

Geography has played an exceptionally influential role in determining the history of Oubangui. Its 1,200 kilometers of river frontier with the Belgian Congo, repeatedly altered by a series of agreements in the late nineteenth century, gave rise to some friction between the French and Belgians exploring its northern reaches and setting up trading posts along its banks. High-level diplomacy smoothed this over, as it did subsequent Belgian anxiety lest unrest in Oubangui contaminate the populations on the other bank of the river.[1] More recently, the amount of clandestine trade between the Belgian and French African riverine peoples has aroused mutual official concern. More than 600 kilometers of frontier in the east is shared with the Sudan but, except for the flight of a few refugees into Oubangui in 1955, this proximity has led to few incidents. The 400 kilometers

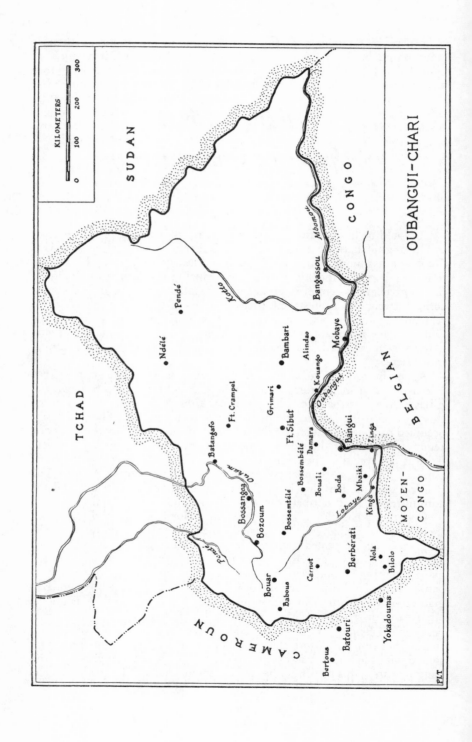

KILOMETERS
0   100   200   300

SUDAN

TCHAD

Pendé

Ndélé

Ft. Crampal

Batangafo

Grimari

Ft. Sibut

Bambari

Alindao

Kousngo

Mobaye

Bangassou

CONGO

OUBANGUI–CHARI

Bossangoa

Bozoum

Bossemtélé

Bossembéle

Damara

Bouali

Bangui

Boda

Mbaiki

Zinga

Kinga

Berbérati

Nola

Bilolo

BELGIAN

MOYEN–CONGO

Bouar

Babous

Carnot

Batouri

Bertoua

Yokadouma

CAMEROUN

PLT

of border with German Kamerun were involved in two important changes prior to 1914, but since France was given the mandate over Cameroun after World War I there have been no further modifications. Oubangui's boundary with Tchad has been the most unstable of all. In 1906 the two territories were united to form the colony of Oubangui-Chari-Tchad. But by 1911, proliferation of the administrative posts in the regions of M'Bomou and Haute-Kotto led to the reconstitution of Oubangui as a separate unit comprising six military and five civil circumscriptions, with the territorial capital located at Bangui, now given the status of a commune.

The absence of strong natural barriers has inevitably made of Oubangui a major crossroads and trading center, and the multiplicity of its ethnic groups testifies to the number of migrants who have settled there over the centuries. Eboué in his study of the local populations in 1923 divided them into four main groups and 20 subgroups, of which the Baya branch of the Mandjia tribes in the southwest is perhaps the most important historically. Owing to Oubangui's terrain and the enterprise of Governor Lamblin, the territory today has the best road system in AEF, motorable throughout the year, and many of the main north-south and east-west highways that connect the territory with other parts of central Africa pass through Bangui. Moreover, Oubangui is blessed with a dense network of rivers, although the courses of many of them are partly obstructed by rapids. Bangui is the terminus of the navigable stretch of the southern Oubangui river, and thus communicates directly with Brazzaville and thence indirectly with Pointe Noire by means of the Congo-Ocean railroad. Yet the fact that Bangui is situated 1,400 kilometers from the sea means that its communications with the outside world are slow and costly. Airplanes now link Bangui with France and with other parts of Africa, but Oubangui's imported goods remain small in volume and high-priced, and its exports have to bear heavy freight charges.

Oubangui's geographical position and above all its river system made it a natural springboard for penetration of the areas to the north, east, and west. The early explorations were peaceful in nature and contrasted sharply with the period of ruthless exploitation that followed. It was the great misfortune of Oubangui (and of northern Moyen-Congo to a lesser degree) that the concessionary regime survived there longer and probably more brutally than anywhere else in AEF. It was particularly in the Lobaye and Haute-Sangha regions[2] that the worst abuses seem to have taken place, or perhaps it may have been that such practices were more actively resented by the Baya people than by other tribal groups. It will be recalled that in 1925 it was at Boda in the Lobaye that Gide was shocked by the brutalities committed by agents of the concessionary company with the connivance of the local administrator (see pp. 17–18), and three years later a revolt broke out among the Baya that lasted until 1930.

Marcel Homet, in 1932, wrote a vivid account of this revolt, which he did not himself see, but whose details he gathered from eye-witnesses.[3] Having harbored a long-standing resentment against the concessionary company and against the taxes imposed by the government, the Baya finally rose up against both when men were forcibly recruited from among them to work on the Congo-Ocean railroad. White hens were sacrificed by the old men of the tribe as the ritual signal for a revolt, and the next time that militiamen came to collect laborers they were not only promptly killed but eaten by the Baya, according to Homet's story. The concessionary company not unnaturally was alarmed and called on the administration for help. At first the Oubangui government did not, it seems, take the revolt seriously, and after some delay sent out only a small column of 20 militiamen commanded by a civil official. It was quickly routed by the Baya, and the official with the other survivors hastily retired to the post of Boda, where they were besieged. This repulse of the whites was a heady stimulant to the uprising, which then spread swiftly throughout the whole region from Tchad to Cameroun.

So indifferent did the government-general at Brazzaville remain to this development that the company agents appealed to Paris for action, going so far as to claim that France risked losing all of Oubangui if the rebels went unpunished. Prodded by Paris, the Bangui administration sent out more militiamen, this time commanded by a lieutenant, whose mission was to relieve the Boda post. When he in turn was defeated, Brazzaville began to worry, as did the Belgians in the Congo, who reportedly convinced the French government that white civilization in the whole area was endangered. Further reinforcements eventually rescued beleaguered Boda and the war was carried deep into the Baya country. Tribes antagonistic to the Baya were called upon to help crush the revolt, and allegedly were told that they could pillage the country as their reward. The nightmare campaign that followed was said to have been marked by gruesome cannibal feasts and the enslavement of women and children to the point of decimating the Baya tribes for years thereafter. Although the revolt may have been exaggerated in Homet's secondhand account—little news of it appeared in the Metropolitan press—it was sufficiently prolonged and its repression was severe enough to have left its mark on the whole region to this day.

Territorial Politics

A background knowledge of the Baya uprising, which was succeeded by minor outbreaks in the mid-1930's and 1944, is essential to an understanding of the postwar history of Oubangui, especially of the Berbérati affair of 1954 (see pp. 392–93), and of the career of Barthélemy Boganda, a native of the Lobaye region.

On the local scene, Boganda did not become prominent immediately after the war, although he was elected with the backing of the Mouvement Républicain Populaire (MRP) to the National Assembly in 1946 and regularly re-elected thereafter. Oubangui's perennial deputy was born in 1910 at Bobangui, and was graduated from the Catholic seminary at Yaoundé, which has sometimes been called the William Ponty School of French central Africa because it trained so many of the present leaders of that region. In 1935 he was ordained a priest, but 11 years later he forsook his parish for politics, a career then opened to Africans for the first time. For the next few years he lived in Paris, where he married his French secretary and was therefore defrocked. Though he was no longer recognized by his church as a priest, Boganda retained among the Oubanguian Africans considerable prestige as a religious leader, not only because of his clerical background but also because of a paternal connection with certain animist practices. He made a point of informing whites—and told the authors—that his father had been a sorcerer and a cannibal. At any rate, there is no doubt that in the eyes of his African followers, Boganda possessed occult powers, and this was certainly largely accountable for the hold he came to exercise not only over the electorate but over men of the stamp of Antoine Darlan.

The Darlan brothers, Georges and Antoine—albeit mulattoes—were the outstanding Africans in Oubangui's first territorial assembly. Georges became its president in 1949 by defeating a European candidate, and also a Grand Councilor for AEF. Antoine, in his early phase, was moderate enough in his views to have proposed in 1947 that AEF change its name to that of Equatorial France. But after he joined the RDA he became the stormy petrel of the assembly and the administration's *bête noire*. He founded the local RDA branch, called the Union Oubanguienne, and wholeheartedly adopted the RDA line during that party's most radical period. Antoine Darlan was then widely believed to be a communist, and it was even rumored that he had been trained as a revolutionary agent while on a visit to Moscow. From 1947 to 1952, Darlan used every opportunity in the assembly to attack the local administration and members of the first college, and in this he was actively aided at the outset by two other African assemblymen, Yetina and Condomat.

In their early years, all the territorial assemblies of French Africa suffered from the 1946 law's failure to define clearly the powers to be exercised by them and by the executive. But in Oubangui this imprecision gave rise to acute friction not only between the assembly and administration but between the first and second colleges. The life span of the first territorial assembly synchronized with the struggle that the French government was carrying on throughout Black Africa against the RDA, and in Oubangui not only was officialdom conspicuously conservative but most of the first-college assemblymen were members of the local branch of the RPF, Union pour la Défense des Interêts Oubanguiens.

Responsible in various degrees for the markedly acrimonious character of Oubangui's political life were the background of bad Franco-African relations, the local tradition of administrative authoritarianism, and the unusually rapid rotation of territorial governors.[4] Two incidents in 1948 contributed further to resentment between Africans and Europeans. Raymond Barbé, French Communist party spokesman in the French Union Assembly, reportedly told 200 African listeners, during his visit to Bangui that year, that "those who follow the colonialists and the RPF are enemies of the Negroes, and when we are masters of the country we shall have their throats cut."[5] And the same year, Oubangui's deputy Boganda, when on a parliamentary mission to the territory, was refused admission to one of Bangui's hotels on the ground that he was an African.

It was thus in an atmosphere of growing tension that Antoine Darlan and his supporters began attacking the administration for using every means to curtail the powers of the assembly, for ignoring the resolutions passed by that body, for rigging elections, and for neglecting African welfare generally. They charged that the administration cut short assembly discussions on the excuse that members were infringing the powers of the executive and that they were giving every subject debated a political coloration. Specifically the accusations ranged all the way from the administration's stinginess in allotting vehicles for the transport of second-college members to its refusal to let the assembly appoint missions to investigate conditions in the interior. Such missions were a bone of contention from 1948 until 1950, and the second-college members accused those in the first college of abetting the administration's efforts to have them suppressed. Defending the administration's attitude, its spokesman asserted that he had been lenient about such missions until he learned that Darlan had been using them in 1947 to organize branches of the Union Oubanguienne in his constituency, and that Yetina had profited by a similar mission to publicize the bad conditions prevailing in up-country jails.[6] In 1950, however, the second college won a victory when the Minister of Overseas France confirmed the assembly's right to send out investigatory missions provided they did not deviate from clearly defined objectives.

Settlement of the missions issue, however, did not bring about a truce. In the matter of land concessions the administration was said to have expropriated African villagers wantonly, especially in the Bangui area, where they had been resettled in an unhealthful place far from the center of the town, where many of them worked. Any matter relating to African land or hunting rights, the distribution of rationed imports, and the like was always good for fiery verbal duels, as was any expenditure made by the government without specific authorization from the assembly.[7] Squabbling over such trivia took up a great deal of time, and the administration tried to bypass the plenary sessions by working through the assembly's permanent committee, which had only five members. In turn, this made the second-college members refuse to delegate powers to the permanent committee during intersession periods, particularly in regard to forest and mining concessions.[8]

As the years went on, the big guns of the second-college members were trained on two main issues—the arrogant behavior of French civil servants toward Africans in general and their assemblymen in particular, and the former's interference in territorial elections. The most restrained expression of the Africans' feeling of frustration at the up-hill battle they were waging against official obstructionism was made by Georges Darlan in his presidential address to the assembly on September 20, 1951. In it he spoke of "the spirit of conservatism displayed by some administrators who have been used to a certain system and who until now have alone enjoyed certain prerogatives. This is but natural, because it is a question of habit. For this reason our (assembly) discussions and decisions have not been widely appreciated." Much more outspoken was Georges' brother, Antoine, when he said, "You, gentlemen of the administration, use the basest methods to delay the evolution of Oubangui-Chari. You employ intimidation and corruption to induce people to leave one party and join another."[9] Yetina cited Berbérati as a region that suffered acutely from bad administration, and after reading a petition from the inhabitants of Bozoum asking to be relieved of an unpopular official, he added: "These administrators get funds for road maintenance but they don't pay their laborers, perhaps giving them some cloth, textiles, salt, or even a medal. Some officials imprison villagers for two weeks for having failed to salute them; others they arrest on the pretext that they are vagabonds."[10]

Another source of grievance imputed by Antoine Darlan and his friends to the French civil servants was that the latter favored only those Africans who shared their political affiliations.[11] Unfortunately, political divisions in Oubangui between the RPF and the RDA followed racial lines rather closely, and Darlan's charges that the regional administrators tried to block expansion of the Union Oubanguienne were probably not unfounded. That party was founded in September 1947, but some months elapsed before it could get under way. A year later its founder reported that it could count 18 regional branches, more than 20,000 members, and funds amounting to one million francs. Stressing the party's social aims as paramount, he asked the assembly for a modest subsidy of 50,000 francs from the territorial budget to aid its program of building schools, dispensaries, canteens for workers, and two brick factories. That the sentiments of the majority of his colleagues were at that time overwhelmingly favorable to the Union Oubanguienne was shown by the prompt vote of the assembly to raise this sum to 300,000 francs.

By late 1949, however, the atmosphere in the assembly had changed, as indicated by its response to two demands made by Antoine Darlan. When he asked for a subsidy to be given the Cercle Africain, Yetina and Condomat went so far as to back up the administration's refusal, on the ground that Darlan was using a cultural organization as the headquarters for his party operations.[12] By 1950 they were even less inclined to go along with Darlan, whose speeches against the administration had become increasingly vituperative and whose use of his position as assemblyman to carry on RDA propaganda had grown more and more obvious. In August 1950, Darlan was given an unmistakable rebuff when he asked the assembly to send him on a mission to Haute-Sangha and Ouham-Pendé. He refused to divulge the purpose of this mission, on the ground that he should be given *carte blanche* as a matter of principle. Significantly, both his African and European colleagues opposed granting Darlan's request unless he first defined his mission's objectives, and several even voiced the suspicion that Darlan was simply going on a propaganda tour for the RDA.[13]

From that time on, Antoine Darlan's stock went down sharply. Though he remained a member of the RDA after joining a purely local party, he became increasingly absorbed by his duties as a member of the French Union Assembly (to which he was re-elected in October 1953) and faded out of Oubanguian politics. Primarily responsible for his local eclipse was the *volte-face* of the RDA high command in 1950, but perhaps an even more important cause was the appearance of Boganda on the Oubangui political scene.

It was in 1952 that Boganda founded his own party, the Mouvement d'Evolution Sociale en Afrique Noire (MESAN), was elected to the territorial assembly in March,[14] and to the Grand Council of AEF a month later. A thoroughly African leader with a magnetic personality and oratorical ability, Boganda enjoyed wide popular support. He was able to steal much of Darlan's thunder without the appearance of being tied to a radical all-African party like the RDA, and without so deeply antagonizing the local administration. To be sure, the administration had learned a lesson from its failure to bring about Boganda's defeat in the elections of June 17, 1951, to the National Assembly, in which it had tried to whip up support for the RPF candidate, Marcel Bella.[15] A friendship even developed between Governor Sanmarco and Boganda, despite the latter's chiding of the administration for its policy of forced cotton cultivation, its poor education services, and its stuffy officials.

The political line-up of the territorial assembly elected in March 1952 showed little change in the first college: all 14 of its members were affiliates of the RPF, and their candidate, Robert Aube, was later elected to the French Senate. The second college was composed of 9 Independents, led by Songomali, and 17 members of MESAN, led by Boganda, with A. Darlan in a very secondary position. Since 1952 the political history of Oubangui has been almost wholly that of MESAN, and MESAN meant Boganda. Doubling of the electorate between 1951 and 1956 brought forth no serious opponents to challenge his rule. Boganda was easily re-elected to the National Assembly on January 2, 1956, by 155,952 votes against 20,230 for Songomali, his nearest rival. But he spent little time in Paris, devoting his main energies to building MESAN into a mass party from headquarters on his coffee plantation near Bangui. By that time the RDA in Oubangui was but a shadow of its former self, though Antoine Darlan continued to attend its major meetings. Boganda had the local situation well in hand, and the prevailing calm had not been fundamentally disturbed by what came to be called the Berbérati affair.

On April 30, 1954, the bodies of two Africans were discovered on the property of a European incongruously named Bontemps, who was the employer of one of the deceased. The Baya of nearby Berbérati, suspecting that Bontemps was responsible for the deaths, demanded that he be either arrested or turned over to them. When the local administrator refused, on the ground that there was insufficient evidence of Bontemps' guilt, he and two French assistants were attacked by the crowd and wounded. Shortly thereafter, another European, who tried to come to their rescue, was stoned by the Baya and killed. Troops were rushed in, the governor appeared, and so did Boganda, who appealed to the Baya to refrain from further violence and trust to the justice of the courts. Soon Bontemps was duly charged with murder, but being able to prove an alibi, was released on July 12. Such was not the case for the 102 Baya who had reportedly sung war songs and shouted anti-white slogans. They were charged with armed rebellion and tried at Berbérati the following September. Though they were defended by four French lawyers, 10 of them were sentenced to terms ranging from five to ten years' forced labor; 67 to imprisonment for from six months to three years; and only 25 were acquitted. This incident is hard even now to evaluate. Politically it appears to have been significant only in so far as it showed how easily memories of earlier Baya revolts could be reawakened, and it did serve to draw the authorities' attention to the "defective status of a backward peasantry."[16] It is noteworthy that the court's verdict was received without a murmur, and that it was followed by no serious violence in the Baya country.

Whether the appeal for calm by Boganda or the presence of troops was the more effective in restoring order it is impossible to tell. At all events, Boganda's prestige was enhanced by this incident, and he was now more clearly established than ever as the single most powerful political figure in the territory. Such eminence, naturally, aroused antagonisms and jealousy. When the authors visited Bangui in 1956, they found the European community inclined to distrust Boganda as a demagogue. On the other hand, local church dignitaries were tolerant to the point of then seeking a reconciliation with their black sheep. Boganda was an animated, nonstop talker, who alternated anecdotes with perorations on the need for Franco-African amity and the evils of international communism. The number of African followers waiting outside his office was impressive, yet it was said at the time that a minority of the elite resented his failure to do more for their advancement as a group. Apparently Boganda found little leadership material in the territory, for he never hesitated to call on outside talent for advice and support. His closest counselors were reportedly Europeans (Guérillot and Naud), and he brought in as his candidate for election to the Senate from Oubangui a Guiana lawyer, Hector Rivierrez.[17] Later in his career, Boganda surrounded himself with more Oubanguian associates, but his one-man, one-party rule inevitably bred malcontents, and in time they moved over to the local ranks of the MSA and RDA opposition.

Being firmly in the Oubanguian saddle, Boganda could now turn his energies to a wider field. The fact that he had called his party a Mouvement d'Evolution Sociale en Afrique Noire indicated that as early as 1952 he had hopes for its spread beyond his territorial confines. When his MESAN candidates were all elected in March 1957 to the territorial assembly, Boganda was assured of heading without opposition the government council to be set up under the *loi-cadre*. It was at that time that he first started negotiations with Gabriel Lisette, then political leader of Tchad, with a view to founding a branch of MESAN in Tchad territory. In June 1957, Boganda was elected president of the Grand Council of AEF by 19 votes against one abstention.

Boganda's overwhelming success in this election was probably traceable to the inability of the RDA and MSA members of the Grand Council to agree upon sponsoring one of their number, so that they swung their votes to a neutral candidate. Boganda, however, apparently interpreted such unanimous support as a mandate to lead all AEF, and he lost no time in springing into action. In a series of violent speeches, starting with a peppery reply to Governor-General Chauvet's address inaugurating the October session of the Grand Council, Boganda attacked the French administrators of AEF at both the federal and the Oubanguian levels. "Il faut décoloniser" became his favorite slogan, but at the same time he was careful to proclaim his unwavering loyalty to France. The *loi-cadre,* he insisted, must be modified and supplemented, lest conflicts arise because of a two-headed administration.[18] He denounced the survival of a colonialist spirit among the present administrators, and if there were no Africans qualified to take their place, he said, this was clearly the fault of the education services. He proposed suppressing the administrative units known as regions, "which have become screens erected between ourselves and the French Republic and between the territorial governments and our toiling African populations." A federal executive, he thought, "might be useful, but is certainly not indispensable at the present moment." Political autonomy was the goal, with Metropolitan France contributing only financial and technical aid. "What we need," he wound up his diatribe, "is fewer functionaries and more technicians, so that we can bring to the great French family and the Common Market the fruit of our work and our efforts."

Reaction to these outbursts was not slow in coming from the organized French functionaries, and the vigor of their protests in turn evoked more oratory in the Grand Council. Its members, on November 16, 1957, unanimously voted their "full confidence in President Boganda," and they also asked the governor-general to penalize any civil servants who failed to act in conformity with the spirit of the *loi-cadre*. This resolution represented an undeniable personal success for Boganda and marked the high point of his popularity in the federation. The RDA, which at that time was gathering strength and closing its ranks throughout AEF, was no longer content to have so popular an outsider as Boganda head the Grand Council. And in April 1958, Boganda was barely re-elected president of that body, receiving only ten votes to nine for the RDA candidate.

Two months later, the coming to power of General de Gaulle in France foreshadowed an early and profound change in French Black Africa's orientation, and Boganda was quick to seize the opportunities thus offered for the materialization of his vision of hegemony. He did not, however, want to burn his bridges with France, and lost no occasion for stressing his francophile sentiments.[19] When de Gaulle visited Brazzaville, Boganda thanked him effusively for "being faithful to his promises and speaking without equivocation."[20] Yet it was Boganda who presented the general with a petition in which the French government was asked to insert in the forthcoming constitution France's recognition of her overseas territories' right to independence, "a right whose benefits they could reap when they so wished." As to the referendum of September 28, Boganda early took an affirmative stand, and Oubangui turned in a 98.1 per cent vote in favor of the Franco-African Community.

Boganda did not wait for the outcome of this vote before trying, by means of an extensive correspondence and the sending of personal envoys, to enlist support outside of Oubangui for his plan to create a central African state. Almost at once he ran into competition from Fulbert Youlou, the mayor of Brazzaville, and to lesser degree from Aubame of Gabon, while Lisette remained noncommital for Tchad. Actually the only encouragement Boganda received came from Opangault and Tchicaya of Moyen-Congo, and this automatically caused the RDA leaders to oppose his project. By early November it had become apparent that Boganda's appeal had fallen not only on deaf but on hostile ears. Nevertheless he persisted in hoping that he might at least induce Moyen-Congo to fall in with his plan, not fully realizing the extent and force there of Youlou's opposition. In a press statement, he said:[21]

> In proposing the central African state, our aim is to reconstitute the Congo and to form a Great Congo which would be open to all and whose capital would be at Brazzaville. We would like to preserve AEF in a form more efficacious and less costly than the old one. . . . Faced with reservations on the part of the governments of Tchad and Gabon, this single state will for the time being be confined to Oubangui-Chari and Moyen-Congo.

Eventually Oubangui had to go it alone, and was the sole territory forming the Central African Republic unanimously proclaimed by its territorial assembly on December 1, 1958, to be a member state of the Community. Yet Boganda did not renounce his ambitious plan to make it the core of an ensemble to be called the United States of Latin Africa, that would be expanded in three stages to include first the French-speaking lands of AEF, Cameroun, and the Belgian Congo, then Portuguese Angola, and finally Spanish Guinea.[22] Needless to say, this grandiose scheme caused a flurry not only in Moyen-Congo, whose leader had similar aims, but in neighboring territories as well. Boganda did succeed in persuading all the AEF states to hold a round-table conference at Paris on December 15, but its results fell far short of what he wanted. Instead of deciding to form a genuine federation that he himself might head, the delegates opted merely for coordinated activity on the economic and technical levels.

On December 6 the first government of the Central African Republic was invested by the Legislative Constituent Assembly, with Boganda as premier and his two principal Oubanguian aides, David Dacko (a cousin) and Abel Goumba, as Ministers of Interior and Finance, respectively. As an all-MESAN body, the assembly did not hesitate to give the new government almost unlimited powers until the constitution was promulgated, and it also voted two puritanical laws, proposed by Boganda, forbidding nudity and vagabondage. For some time it had been evident that Boganda intended to take Oubangui's economy firmly in hand, when he set up a "Comité de Salut Economique" in January 1958, and now it looked as if he would try to force the "unemployed parasites of Bangui" back to cultivation of the land. In early 1959 the draft constitution prepared by a committee presided over by Naud, president of the Bangui Chamber of Commerce, was profoundly modified by the government before being submitted to the assembly on February 9. Not surprisingly, all the changes thus made tended to concentrate power in the hands of the premier, and Oubangui alone of all the new AEF republics acquired a presidential cabinet.

In several speeches made later in February, Boganda said that he still intended to work for creation of the United States of Latin Africa,[23] but for the next two months he was preoccupied with preparing the ground for elections to the new 50-member legislative assembly in April. That he intended it to be a rubber-stamp body was shown by the government's arbitrary elimination in three out of the four electoral districts of the lists of candidates drawn up by the RDA and the MSA. Then overnight the picture changed drastically, for at the height of this electoral campaign, Boganda was killed in a plane accident on March 28. With the sudden disappearance of the man who for the past seven years had completely dominated Oubangui politics, panic spread through the ranks of MESAN and there was much speculation as to how the voting would go, since Boganda's death seemed to leave the field wide open to dark horses. As it turned out, the elections passed off quietly. Voter participation was 58 per cent—a little higher than in previous elections—except in Bangui circumscription, where it was only 36 per cent. MESAN candidates swept the boards, winning 48 of the 50 seats. The new assembly unanimously expressed its confidence in David Dacko as premier; with the exception of Maleombho, elected president of the assembly, all of Boganda's ministers were retained in the Dacko cabinet and three new ones were added; and Senator N'Gounio was chosen to succeed Boganda as president of MESAN. All signs pointed to the likelihood that the party would survive in fine shape the disappearance of its founder.

Dacko's inaugural speech to the assembly closely followed the Boganda line. After stressing the need to abolish all traces of tribalism and racialism so as to build a strong central African state, he expressed the hope that the other three republics of AEF would eventually consent to form a federation with the Central African Republic. Dacko soon discovered, however, that this assembly was not going to be so docile to him as its predecessor had been to Boganda, and even his MESAN party refused him its full support. During his one and a half months of untrammeled power, the

Dacko government had created a Central African jurisdiction and rural collectivities, replaced the administrative regions by four provinces, accepted a new plan for the republic's economic development, and established a special tax on hunting guns. This last-mentioned measure aroused popular protests, but it was to the "multiplicity of administrative organs and the abuses committed by some officials" that the MESAN high command objected. And at its closing meeting in mid-June 1959, the assembly unanimously rejected a draft law that would have renewed the full powers which had been readily granted to the Boganda government.

During the next few months, this struggle for power between the government and the assembly was utilized by two outstanding members of MESAN to wrest the party leadership from Dacko. These men were N'Gounio, elected in June senator from Oubangui and mayor of Bangui, and Maleombho, president of the legislative assembly. They succeeded in persuading 18 deputies to sign a manifesto censuring the Dacko administration and calling for its resignation on the ground that Dacko was abusing his authority and intended to dissolve the assembly. However, at the end of a long closed session on October 6, the assembly unanimously voted its confidence in Dacko, who five days later formed a new government in which he took over the Interior portfolio and dropped two of his ministers, Abel Gouma and Sato. To all outward appearances the rift in MESAN was thus bridged over, and the ease with which that party had won the municipal elections of the preceding June suggests that its rule is not threatened, for the time being, by rival political groups. Dacko has been trying to enhance his popularity as Boganda's "spiritual heir" by stressing the absence of Europeans from his government and the rapidity with which he is Africanizing the administrative cadres. Whether or not he can retain the party leadership in the face of formidable rivals remains to be seen, and it should be noted that there is still before the assembly a project for modifying the constitution in such a way as to augment the powers of the legislature at the expense of those of the executive branch.

The Territorial Economy

The Plan

In many respects nature has favored Oubangui-Chari, particularly in its geographical attributes and vegetation, and this has been conducive to a balanced relationship between export and subsistence crops. Its northern districts, 500 kilometers in breadth, form part of the sahel zone, whereas its southwestern region belongs to the humid equatorial forest. Between the series of plateaus that lie along its eastern and western boundaries is the central valley of the Kémo and the Gribingui rivers, where the territory's cotton is grown. Coffee, sisal, and tobacco are cultivated on the plateaus, on the extremities of which are to be found Oubangui's diamond deposits. Though deprived of maritime facilities because of being land-locked and distant from the sea, Oubangui has the best road network of any AEF territory, and its capital city, Bangui, is the northern terminus of the Federal Artery.

There are, however, certain unfavorable aspects in this otherwise harmonious economic picture. Rainfall is inadequate throughout much of the territory, and the eastern and northeastern regions are particularly arid. Erosion has attacked some of the areas where the forest has been cut down to make way for plantations. Oubangui's foreign commerce suffers from a transportation system that is both slow and expensive. This weighs heavily on its exports, which, with the exception of diamonds, are bulky and of low value, as well as on its imports, which are vital for the equipment of this underdeveloped country. Labor is scarce and unskilled, and particularly resistant to mining and to growing cotton for export. To a great extent these handicaps are man-made, and can be traced to the abuses of the concessionary-company regime and the authoritarianism of the territorial administration. This heavy legacy of the past not only has hamstrung Oubangui's capacities for production but has made for obstructively acrimonious relations both between the administration and its elected representatives and between the two colleges of its assemblymen.

From the outset, Oubangui's territorial assemblymen were determined to wrest from the administration the right to discuss and control the Plan's operations. They wanted priority to be given to improvement of transportation facilities and to the acquisition of labor-saving equipment.[24] Years of human portage had depleted Oubangui's manpower resources, the forced cultivation of cotton had turned its farmers against growing crops for export, and the long-standing monopolies granted to certain European transport and business firms had aroused African resentment against such servitudes. To the African assemblymen the hopes aroused by the Plan centered on the mechanization of agriculture and mining, and on the farmers' receiving a greater share of the proceeds from their toil. In the matter of improved transportation and equipment, their aspirations were not incompatible with those of their European colleagues and the administration, but the latter were primarily concerned that the Plan should increase the territory's salable output. So there was general accord as to the need to speed up freight services on the Federal Artery, build a railroad from Bangui to Tchad, and apply more scientific knowledge to the territory's agricultural output. But there was a parting of the ways when it came to who was to control the purchase and distribution of the supplies imported under the Plan, which projects would be first carried out, and what group of men would supervise their execution. The administration insisted that the assembly had no legal right to intervene and was consulted about the Plan by courtesy only—in other words, that the drawing up of FIDES programs and the decisions regarding priorities rested with Paris and Brazzaville alone.[25]

This struggle was more emotionally acute in Oubangui than in any other territory, and it had also a more unrealistic character there. Because Oubangui lacked any economic base on which FIDES could operate, the credits allocated to it could not be used until sufficient equipment materials and construction companies had been brought in and an adequate local labor supply had been assembled. This took three years from the time AEF's first Plan was drawn up, and in the meantime FIDES' allocations to Oubangui fell unproductively into its reserve fund. During this period of enforced inaction, the territorial assemblymen had a chance to examine the Plan for Oubangui more closely and to modify some of their earlier views. Federal funds had indeed bettered the territory's communications with the outside world and eased its postwar shortage of imported materials. But there was a growing feeling that the Plan for Oubangui itself had perhaps laid too great stress on the infrastructure in general and on the improvement of Bangui in particular. The territorial capital was to be provided with a better lighting and water system, a new hospital and college, improved port, air, and road facilities, and an abattoir, while comparatively little was to be done for the rural areas.[26]

For some time the territorial assemblymen had been worried about the decline in Oubangui's food and cotton production and by the unhealthy growth of Bangui to the detriment of the countryside. The ending of forced labor in 1946 had been followed by a reduction in Oubangui's millet and manioc output, and to ensure there being enough left to feed the rural population the government two years later had to limit the amount of food being brought into urban markets.[27] At first the African assemblymen came out strongly against such controls because they wanted the farmers to profit by scarcity high prices, but gradually they came to realize the dangers of declining rural production.[28] When the territory's revenues began shrinking as the result of smaller cotton exports, they became eager that the Plan should lay more stress on agricultural output—an insistence that grew with the territory's financial responsibility for the Plan's operating expenditures.

Fortunately this change in viewpoint coincided and harmonized with the orientation given by Paris to the second four-year Plan. For the 1952–56 period, Oubangui's share of FIDES funds came to 3,500 million CFA francs, of which 805 million were to go to economic development and 516 million to social equipment. Infrastructure still got the largest slice, but this was because a large proportion of Oubangui's high production costs was due to heavy transportation charges. By diversifying the range of its products Oubangui had probably escaped the dangers of monoculture, but it still produced in too small quantities. To bring new areas under cultivation, the government was urged to "make an inventory of the soil" but the Agricultural Service claimed it lacked the staff to do so. In any case, the main cause of Oubangui's mediocre production was not believed to be its lack of arable land or the small size of its population, for in both respects it ranks second among all the AEF territories. Rather, it was probably due to the Oubanguians' disaffection for certain agricultural occupations and ignorance of scientific farming methods. A proposal to regroup some scattered villages and to create experimentally a few *paysannats* in the cotton country, following the patterns established in Gabon and the Belgian Congo respectively, seemed to offer a possible solution and one acceptable to both the administration and the assembly.[29]

When the MESAN took over Oubangui's government in 1957, it lost no time in launching a territory-wide campaign as a reinforcement of the Plan to increase agricultural production. Its leader, Boganda, toured the country urging a "return to the land," preaching "work as a social duty," and soliciting the support of private capital to finance the new program.[30] To guide and supervise his own 15-year agricultural plan, Boganda created a Franco-African 16-man Comité de Salut Economique in January 1958. According to its directives, more *paysannats* were to be set up, farmers were to be scientifically trained at a special center, coffee cultivation was slated for a big expansion, and more peanuts were to be planted. While conditions of village life were to be made more attractive and production in all spheres encouraged, a main goal of the committee was to reorient Oubangui away from overdependence on cotton, for whose cultivation local farmers had been showing a "disquieting disinclination" during the preceding three years.[31]

In Oubangui's Plan for 1958–62, totaling 5,408,501,000 CFA francs, over 1,745 million were to be devoted to increasing production, mainly agricultural, approximately the same sum was earmarked for social equipment, and the balance was to be used to continue improving the infrastructure.[32] From the beginning, Oubangui's new leaders have realized that the task they set themselves would take many years to accomplish, but in December 1958 (less than a year after the committee had been formed) Premier Goumba was able to report to the assembly that its work was already showing results and that there had even been a 30 per cent increase in cotton production.

Finances

In 1948, as in 1947, Oubangui not only had a simple operating budget without any territorial-equipment program but it also ran a deficit that, by the end of the year, amounted to 100 million CFA francs. At first the assembly blamed this state of affairs not on the local administration, "which has compressed its expenditures to the maximum," but on the government-general "which absorbs most of our revenues and only returns to us what it pleases."[33] As Oubangui's expenditures continued to mount and the Grand Council (which now controlled the federal budget) declined to increase its rebates to the territory, the assembly in August 1948 refused to vote the draft budget for 1949 and forced the local government to revise its estimates. The head tax, complained one African member, had been raised for his compatriots while the income tax, which fell almost wholly on Europeans, remained unchanged, and the rapidly rising cost of living was more than offsetting the small increase now granted in the guaranteed price for cotton paid to the producer.[34] European members were equally disgruntled, but mainly because of the continuing shortage of imported goods and the delays in getting the Plan under way. The French president of the assembly, speaking of the second draft budget presented to the assembly a month later, declared:[35]

> I find this proposal as miserable as its predecessor, and I am not even sure that this budget will be balanced. I believe that our taxpayers will find little improvement in their status or in the country's welfare. It seems to me that the government-general has done nothing to meet our desires or to change its practice of taking over our resources.

Despite his urging that this draft budget, too, be rejected, the assembly finally accepted it by a vote of 14 to 9, and along with it another increase in taxation. By that time Oubangui had accumulated 41 million francs from unutilized FIDES funds in its reserves but had a current budgetary deficit amounting to 127 million.

Territorial expenditures shot up tremendously, and by mid-1949 they had risen by more than 60 per cent compared with those of the preceding year. According to Governor Delteil, 80 per cent of this increase was caused by the new salary scale voted by Parliament and 20 per cent by the cost of new official recruits.[36] Revenues were not up to the estimates made a few months before, though Oubangui was said to have the heaviest taxation of any territory of the federation. However, the territory now had nearly 380 million francs in its reserve fund, a sum almost identical with that by which the 1950 draft budget exceeded the one for 1949 (848 million compared with 468). Since a 174-million deficit was anticipated for 1950 and only a slightly larger subsidy from the federal government could be expected, it looked as if the reserve fund would be virtually emptied if the budget was to be balanced.

Yet by the time the assemblymen got around to discussing the 1951 budget, it appeared to them that the territory's financial position a year before had been one of "comparative ease."[37] Expenditures for personnel would absorb 51 per cent of the total, compared with 45 per cent in 1949; Oubangui could afford no equipment program of its own; it had only 19 million francs left in the reserve fund; and it had received no accounting of its wartime and early postwar indebtedness. Governor Colombani claimed that the Notables-in-council were agreed that the head tax could easily be increased, inasmuch as in most circumscriptions it was lower than in 1938. Its average rate, he said, was only 150 francs, or three-fourths of the price of a chicken in the Bangui market, and cotton farmers as well as laborers had a larger income than ever before. The first-college assemblymen concurred that "Africans pay ridiculously low taxes" whereas Europeans had to surrender 20 per cent of their annual income.[38]

Not unnaturally the African councilors disagreed vehemently with this viewpoint, and asserted that the Notables' consent was not valid because they were not truly representative of the indigenous taxpayer. They were against permitting the chiefs to continue as tax-collecting agents, but admitted that the administration had neither the funds nor the agents required to alter the existing system. (In any case it was hard to collect taxes because many Oubanguians were mobile, and especially difficult to get them from Bangui's large floating population.) After considerable debate the assembly finally agreed to a 113 per cent rise in the rate of the head tax and to lesser increases in those for the *chiffre d'affaires,* licenses, and patents. As matters worked out, the sacrifices demanded of Oubangui's taxpayers proved to have been greater than they needed to be. The changes made that year in the federal budget's rebate system and in the export duty on cotton brought to Oubangui's coffers larger revenues than had been anticipated. Yet so strong remained the territorial assemblymen's suspicions of the government-general that many of them regarded these moves as a trap designed to force Oubangui to shoulder a larger share of federal personnel costs.[39]

The budget for 1952 was examined under unexpectedly difficult conditions, for the cotton harvest was smaller in size and fetched a lower price than had been expected. Moreover, expenditures had once again soared, and the volume of the budget now reached 1,593 million francs. For Oubangui, 1952 turned out to be a very bad year financially, as it did for the whole federation, and the territory ended it with a current deficit of 80 million francs. The assembly refused a plea from the federal government to raise the rate of its head tax, and even worse conditions prevailed throughout 1953. Oubangui was forced to turn to the Grand Council for special aid and, in the end, to increase its head tax, since this was the condition imposed by that body for an exceptional grant of 25 million francs. A similar supplementary sum was allocated to Oubangui in 1954, which saw a general improvement in the territory's trade. Consequently, by the end of that year Oubangui had wiped out its past debts and was even able to place 295 million francs in its reserve fund.[40] But in 1955 its financial position once more deteriorated, for the assembly voted that year to liquidate its wartime stocks at heavy cost and took on new burdens in the form of family allowances. Once again the Grand Council came to Oubangui's rescue, and the budget for 1956 was balanced at a lower total (1,566 million francs) than for the preceding three years. But the course of Oubangui's finances did not run smooth in the latter months of 1956. Annoyed by a reduction in the federal subsidy to the benefit of Tchad, Oubangui's assemblymen refused to vote the tax increase requested of them by the Grand Council, and the year ended with a budgetary deficit of about 30 million francs.[41]

The cost of setting up the first council of government in 1957 and 1958 involved Oubangui in a rash of new and large expenditures. Notwithstanding the fact that Metropolitan France, to help defray such expenses, made special grants to all of the territories, Oubangui's financial status became even more precarious than before. The new African ministers earned great local popularity and brought about economies by accelerating the Africanization of the civil service. At the same time, they had the courage to refuse to grant the special salary rises demanded by the African functionaries' union on the ground that this could be done only at the expense of the already heavily overburdened rural taxpayer.[42]

The budget for 1958 resembled all of its predecessors in being strictly an operating one, but its volume was slightly larger (1,792 million francs) and it did include larger allocations (totaling 82 million francs) to the services of education, health, and agriculture. Territorial revenues were almost stationary, and Oubangui had no prospect of great future increments, as did the southern territories from mining and the Kouilou project. Its only hope seemed to lie in persuading the population to produce more and cheaper export crops. The assembly did accept a tax on fuel consumption (for a new Road Fund) but rejected proposed taxes on textiles and other imported goods to finance a Tobacco Supporting Fund, as well as a tripling in the rate of family allowances.[43] This setback came late in the budget debate, and to get a quick affirmative vote on its general budgetary proposals the MESAN government decided to postpone presenting the much more drastic fiscal reforms that it had up its sleeve and that required the prior approval of the other new AEF republics.

Early in 1958 the government began dropping hints as to the fiscal changes it would sponsor, which had the local companies and Chamber of Commerce worried. Boganda was outspokenly determined to have done with Oubangui's "budgets of misery" and to extricate the territory from its chronically parlous economic and financial situation.[44] His budget for 1959 would still be mainly an operating one but it was to be inspired by his concern to "divide the fiscal burden as equitably as possible." This meant no rise in the head tax or *impôt cédulaire,* but a 25 per cent increase in other forms of direct taxation. Specifically he proposed, and the assembly accepted on December 30, 1958, the creation of a tax on nondistributed profits, a 10 per cent ad valorem sales tax on imported textiles, and a rise in the duties on alcoholic beverages imports and the circulation of motor vehicles. The main increases in expenditures were for the upkeep of roads (99 million), for education (72 million), and for health (42 million). This brought the volume of the 1959 budget to over 2,696 million francs, or an increase of more than 700 million compared with that of 1958.

Transportation

Roads and road transport. With the object of prolonging the Federal Artery northward from its river terminus (just south of Bangui), French army engineers built Oubangui's first road from the territorial capital to Damara during World War I. The Fort Sibut–Fort Crampel stretch was the next to be constructed, and gradually Bangui attained communication by road with Fort Archambault in Tchad. This work was facilitated by Oubangui's lateritic soil, relatively dry climate, and abundant labor supply. But it was Governor Lamblin and other technically unqualified administrators who gave to Oubangui during the interwar period the best, longest, and most cheaply constructed road network in all AEF. Because of their enterprise, Bangui was linked by road to Bambari and Bangassou in the east, and to M'Baiki, Carnot, Berbérati, and the Cameroun network in the west. And in 1938 a second overland connection with Cameroun was established via Bossembélé and Bouar.

During World War II, Oubangui's strategically important road to Tchad was the one that profited most by improvements, but throughout much of the network an effort was also made to build bridges and eliminate ferry crossings. Both these enterprises were continued after the Liberation, and more *pistes* were built in the cotton and mining zones. When members of the Grand Council mission visited Oubangui in 1949, they were struck with admiration for its road system, and the only suggestions they made were to urge the construction of more bridges and that road laborers be paid in cash rather than in kind (usually salt).[45] Oubangui's territorial assemblymen heartily concurred, but they had an additional grievance— the slowness with which the Public Works Service was carrying out its road work. They wanted a private firm to take over the construction envisaged under the Plan, in which improvements to the road systems of Oubangui and Tchad were given top priority and treated as an ensemble.[46] This wish was gratified, and the contract for the Oubangui road work was awarded—albeit without consulting the territorial assembly—by FIDES to the big Parisian Société des Batignolles.

The assembly's satisfaction was short-lived, and in nearly every session throughout 1950 and 1951 this company was assailed for its extravagant organization and high-handed attitude toward both the public and the territorial authorities. It was criticized for having too many European employees, failing to train Africans to replace them, and repatriating its profits instead of reinvesting them in the territory. By tearing up old roads and interfering with motor-vehicle circulation it showed itself indifferent to the comfort and needs of the public, and by dealing only with Brazzaville it flouted the authority of the local government and assembly.[47] Nevertheless, this company had built the best single road in the federation, from Bangui to Damara, and was modernizing the Bossembélé-Bouar route so as to assure Oubangui of an all-weather connection with Cameroun, and in mid-1951 a mission sent out by the Grand Council singled it out for special praise.[48]

In the matter of roads, in fact, Oubangui was in such a favored position that it felt the curtailment in the 1952–56 Plan less than did the other territories. During that period Oubangui concentrated on improving its links with Tchad, especially in the cotton zone. By 1955 it was reported to have a network of 17,570 kilometers—nearly one-third of which was usable throughout the year—and a fourth of all the motor vehicles in the federation.[49] Transport remained a controversial question in the territorial assembly, not in regard to the road system but in so far as truckers were concerned.

This truckers controversy, which was one of the many subjects that divided the two colleges of the assembly, was touched off by the creation in July 1950 of an African cooperative (TRANSCOOP) by Condomat, an indigenous assemblyman. He lost no time in asking the assembly to bring pressure on the government to give the TRANSCOOP some of its official business, and on the European companies to share with it a part of the lucrative transport of cotton, which they monopolized. The European companies involved were the Société des Transports Oubangui-Cameroun (STOC), the Compagnie des Transports Routiers de l'Oubangui (CTRO), and Uniroute, a firm that operated mainly in Tchad; of these firms, the first was the most important. All of these companies had been in Oubangui for about 20 years, and from very modest beginnings had built up fleets of trucks, of which by 1958 STOC had 170, CTRO 150, and Uniroute 53.[50] By virtue of short-term contracts with the territorial government, these companies held a monopoly of the territory's transport business. The government announced its willingness to make similar contracts with any transport company able to provide as efficient and cheap service as the European ones, but TRANSCOOP with its rudimentary and small-scale equipment knew that it could never compete unless wholeheartedly supported by the assembly. This support its members were unwilling to give, not only because TRANSCOOP inspired little confidence as to its probable performance but also because they were offended by Condomat's attempt to use his post as assemblyman for his personal benefit.

Although, as of 1958, the big three continued to monopolize Oubangui's transport to the detriment of medium and small truckers, their position has never aroused such opposition as has that of the big truckers in Tchad.

Waterways. It is fortunate for Oubangui that its good road system and its capital's position as the northern terminus of the Federal Artery have made it largely independent of its own river network as a means of communication. A number of the Oubangui river's important tributaries, such as the Lobaye and Sangha, are shared between it and Moyen-Congo, but their usefulness to the more northern territory is distinctly limited. Like all of AEF's rivers, they are only partly and seasonally navigable, and many of them flow through little-inhabited regions untouched by external trade. The most used of these waterways is the upper Oubangui, which can be negotiated for a distance of 600 kilometers by boats up to 100 tons, between Ouango and Ouadda, from mid-June to November. The usefulness of this stretch is greatly diminished by its being cut off north of Bangui by 50 kilometers of rocks and rapids. The traffic using the upper Oubangui is estimated to total between 7,000 and 8,000 tons annually.

As to Bangui itself, its river port was neglected both before and after World War II. Before 1939, its equipment, poor as it was, sufficed to handle the limited tonnages brought there. Even under the ten-year Plan, its enlargement was postponed until that of Brazzaville port was completed. It was not until 1950 that improvements on Bangui's river port were undertaken, and then it was in conjunction with the town's urbanization plan. A major reason for this long delay was that during the low-water period on the Oubangui, the cargo brought up from Brazzaville had to be unloaded 100 kilometers downstream from Bangui, put aboard a narrow-gauge railroad seven kilometers in length, and then reloaded on small boats for the remainder of the journey. But with the improvements effected under the Plan in the navigability of the Oubangui and with the growth in the traffic carried on that river, Bangui's port took on much greater activity. In 1950 it handled about 80,000 tons, but by 1957 the volume had increased to 107,000 tons, of which 75,000 represented imports and 35,000 exports (including 23,000 tons of cotton).[51]

Agriculture

Oubangui enjoys far better facilities for agricultural production than does Gabon. Its population is larger, its output is more varied and balanced as between subsistence (manioc, rice, sesame seed, and peanuts) and export crops (cotton, coffee, sisal, palm oil, and tobacco), and it imports very few foodstuffs. Yet Oubangui's agricultural potential is far from being realized. This phenomenon is due in part to tribal traditions and in part to the government's past policy.

In many parts of Oubangui the population can get enough food to survive with a minimum of effort, particularly in the forest zones where uncultivated produce can be had for the gathering. Tribal traditions in the savannah country assign to men the tasks of fighting, hunting, and fishing, and "it is considered dishonorable for a male from the age of 15 upward to till the soil."[52] Agricultural cultivation is the work of the village women, who plant a little manioc and a few banana trees around their huts, and only among the populations of Ouham and the northeast are genuine farmers to be found. Forced labor, first on the big companies' concessions and then on the administration-sponsored cotton fields, completed the Oubanguians' alienation from an occupation that was traditionally antipathetic and currently hard and unremunerative. So in 1946, as soon as they were free to do as they pleased, many of them left the fields and drifted to the towns. Others followed in their wake, for the continued forced cultivation of cotton in many parts of the territory and its low purchase price caused the burden of taxation to be felt more heavily by the rural population than by the town dwellers.

Cotton was not the only crop to suffer from this rural exodus. Manioc and rice production also declined, and by 1949 the provisioning of Bangui in food had become difficult.[53] Exhaustion of the soil in the immediate environs, as well as the proximity of urban attractions, had led to a desertion of the countryside around Oubangui's main towns. For this situation the African assemblymen blamed the government in general for having over-stressed cotton production, and the agricultural service in particular for having done nothing to promote indigenous food crops. They pointed out that three of the territory's five agricultural stations were devoted to cotton (Bambari, Bossango, and Gambo), one (at Boukoko) worked on coffee mainly for the benefit of European planters, and only the Grimari station gave any time to developing African food crops. The administration was urged to mechanize and otherwise modernize African farming techniques, to make an inventory of the territory's soils and resettle some of the rural population on the unused arable land, and to pay higher prices to the producers of export crops.[54]

In the early postwar years, three of Oubangui's leading African politicians added emphatic denunciations of the SIP to the foregoing criticisms. Each of these men was the founder of a fledgling cooperative—Antoine Darlan of COTONCOOP, Condomat of TRANSCOOP, and Boganda of the Société Coopérative de la Lobaye-Lessé—for which they were trying to obtain subsidies from the territorial budget.[55] In so doing they sounded a popular note by claiming that the operations of the SIP, which they aimed to replace, were "scandalous" and that the administrators in charge of them were "enriching themselves at the expense of the population."[56] Since all of the assemblymen were at this time in favor of suppressing the SIP, the new cooperatives had little trouble in getting sizable sums of public money, but as time went on the enthusiasm of the African representatives cooled. In part the cooperatives' difficulties arose from their inexperienced management, which was in no way equipped to compete with the entrenched and well-organized European cotton, transport, and trading companies. To some extent, however, they could also be ascribed to the dishonesty of some of their officers as well as the political orientation given them by a few of their leaders. By 1954 they had all gone bankrupt or been voluntarily liquidated, but even four years earlier the territorial assembly had become chary about subsidizing them further and had voted against suppressing the SIP.[57] By playing a waiting game and letting the cooperatives slowly destroy themselves, the territorial government had been able to save the SIP, but it did not find it so easy to sidestep the other criticisms of its agricultural policy voiced by the African elite.

The local administration, though it admitted that it had pushed cotton cultivation to the detriment of food crops, claimed that it had neither the money nor the staff to undertake a soil survey or to experiment with mechanized farming. Its spokesman also reminded its critics that the government no longer had the legal means to resettle the population, and it was they themselves who opposed any revival of the forcible prewar regrouping of villages and constituting of grain reserves. Nevertheless, beginning in 1950, a greater official effort was made to enlarge the personnel of the Agricultural Service, encourage Africans to plant coffee, peanuts, tobacco, and rice, and discourage them from making their manioc flour into "whisky." Furthermore, after an abortive attempt to start a cotton *paysannat* at Kohiri (see p. 172), the government began to set up others in four regions of the territory, in which food production was associated with more remunerative crops. Of the nine *paysannats* created between 1952 and 1956, six (Bilolo, Baya, Kouzindoro, Mbi, Gaigné and Zandé), specialized in coffee cultivation and one (Kembé) in oil palms; two of them (Kouzindoro and Niakari) aimed to stabilize the populations that tended to migrate to Bangui and Bangassou respectively; and two others (Bilolo and Baya) were oriented toward the development of individual farming among the M'Bimou and Baya tribes.

As in the other territories of AEF, each *paysannat* has been treated as an individual problem in the light of its demographic and geographic situation and the farming aptitudes of the populations concerned, and some are still in the experimental stage. The fact that cotton growing has not figured heavily in the *paysannat* program and that all of the more than 32,000 farmers involved in it are volunteers has greatly contributed to its success. While the area planted to cotton in Oubangui has become progressively smaller in recent years despite the improvement in the price paid to the growers, that devoted to coffee and peanut cultivation has been expanding. A vast increase in the output of those two crops (as well as of cotton) is the main goal of the official Comité de Salut Economique. Though its "return to the land" appeal has met with no territory-wide response, agricultural production has certainly increased, and for this success the *paysannat* program launched in 1950 is at least partly responsible.

Along with that of other food crops, production of paddy declined during the first postwar years in the regions of Lobaye, Bambari, and Bossembélé, where local husking mills formerly turned out sizable quantities of rice. In 1948, when only 804 tons were harvested, the administration tried to revive interest in this crop by bringing in seed from the Belgian Congo, but instead of planting it the farmers either ate or sold it.[58] Undiscouraged, the authorities made another effort in 1950 to increase production: experiments with irrigated cultivation were undertaken in the Bangui region and the four existing husking mills were modernized. Some success attended this venture, and in 1953 about 1,000 tons were harvested, of which 300 tons came from the Lobaye region. The government then learned, however, that it was hard to market such a crop, for the Oubanguians were confirmed manioc eaters and simply did not care for rice.[59] Since that time the official policy has been to stabilize production at about 700 tons, which represents the limit of the present consumer demand.

Oubangui was the first territory in which cotton cultivation was officially sponsored, beginning under the indefatigable Governor Lamblin in 1924. During the next few years, monopolies in clearly defined zones were accorded all four of AEF's cotton companies, of which the most important locally was COTONAF (see pp. 175–76). Planting was extended year by year until it covered a very large part of the whole territory, even after considerable portions of the land had been proved unsuitable for this crop. So varied are Oubangui's climates and soils that a series of experimental stations had to be set up at Grimari, Ouham, and Alindao to develop the varieties best suited to the surrounding area and the means of combating local pests and plant diseases—notably the wilt disease which spread into the eastern region from the neighboring Belgian Congo. Until the end of World War II, Oubangui continued to plant an improved form of

Triumph, but after the IRCT set up research stations at Bambari and Bossanga, which developed other strains, the Banda variety began to replace it in the area between Fort Sibut and Fort Crampel and in the region of M'Bomou, and Triumph is cultivated only in the western districts. By 1956, selected plants of the new varieties covered two-thirds of Oubangui's total cotton area.

Under the Plan for Oubangui, its cotton output was slated to rise by two-thirds between the years 1947 and 1956, and until 1954 marked progress was made toward that goal. The area planted to cotton grew from about 120,000 hectares just after the war to 159,000 in 1954, and production rose in that period from some 39,000 to 43,252 tons. But beginning in 1955, every year witnessed a shrinkage in the area planted to cotton and in the number of farmers cultivating that crop. However, production—with some seasonal fluctuations—was maintained at about the same level owing to improved yields from planting (from about 230 to 285 kilograms to the hectare) and from ginning (from 18 to 25 per cent of fiber). In 1958–59 a record harvest of 43,561 tons was produced, even though the area planted to cotton had shrunk by 26,000 hectares and the number of cotton farmers had declined by 56,000 compared with the 1954 peak.[60] This shrinkage was not experienced everywhere, for in some areas cotton had spread to new districts and had disappeared from other zones where it had formerly been planted. The bumper crop of 1958–59 resulted from the intensified efforts of Oubangui's faithful cotton planters and not to any revival of interest in this crop on the part of the 50,000 or so farmers who had abandoned it.[61]

This disaffection of African farmers for cotton was far stronger in Oubangui than in Tchad, where the Negro population was more agriculturally minded and where there was no possible competition in the cotton zone from better-paying crops. The Oubanguians certainly preferred hunting to farming. When they cultivated the soil they grew peanuts and coffee wherever it was possible to do so, in preference to cotton, which required more labor and brought in smaller cash returns. Oubangui's political leaders maintained, however, that there were still other reasons for the abandonment of cotton cultivation—the coercive methods used by the administration, the brutality of the boys-coton, the abusive profiteering of local chiefs, the crushing weight of taxes, and the like. It was they who in the territorial assembly and Grand Council voiced the loudest and most bitter complaints, denouncing the government's cotton policy as a form of forced labor and the companies for making 30 to 40 per cent profits out of their monopolies. Boganda told the assembly on June 25, 1956, that he had been arrested and his family persecuted when he had tried to warn the authorities that "cotton is the cause of our present malaise and also of AEF's decline in population from 8 to 4 million in 40 years." Antoine Darlan drew a sad picture of the Oubanguian peasant who had to leave his hut before dawn, walk five kilometers to the cotton fields, meeting panthers and snakes on the way, and was able to nourish himself at noon only with a little manioc under the eye of an armed militiaman.[62] The lot of his wives, fellow-toilers in the field, apparently was even worse:[63]

> At the end of April or early in May when the rains begin, the countryside comes alive. Agents of the administration called *boys-coton* are sent out to allocate the work to be done by each village, family, and individual. For the following month they zealously watch their charges. They spare no one and are accompanied by guards who mete out physical punishments and even prison sentences. During the war Oubangui gave the impression of a vast forced-labor camp. Women had to work in the fields with babies tied to their backs. It was they who harvested the crop and took it to market, and in consequence many of them and their children died . . .

Pitiable as the lot of the Oubanguian cotton farmer certainly was, it served some of the local politicians as a handy issue on which to make a popular appeal to the electorate. Every move during the postwar years to improve the situation was greeted with open suspicion and provided them with the opportunity to recall past conditions. When it became known that under the 1949 agreements the cotton companies would build a textile factory near Bangui, this reminded territorial assemblyman Yetina that "during the war we had to get textiles from the Belgian Congo to clothe our soldiers and even our population. Even today only 200,000 of Oubangui's total population of 1,200,000 are decently clothed."[64] And when the purchase price for cotton was raised sharply in 1951 to 25 francs per kilogram, Antoine Darlan insisted in the French Union Assembly that this would bring no improvement in the cotton growers' purchasing power because the cost of imported merchandise had risen to even greater heights:[65]

> The cotton production of a family averages 80 kilograms a year, from which the peasant gets 1,200 francs. Of this the *fisc* takes 450 francs as head tax for himself and another 450 francs for his wife. The SIP, that unpopular institution of legalized theft, takes 50 to 60 more francs from him, and he has barely 200 francs left with which to buy a meter of cloth for his wife. . . . The other six months of the year not devoted to cotton growing are taken up by various services to the administration, notably the upkeep of some 15,000 kilometers of roads and *pistes,* which serve only the vehicles belonging to a small minority of the population. . . . The Oubanguian peasant has no time in which to grow food crops, repair his hut, or care for his impaired health. . . .
>
> If we want cotton growing to become really profitable for the farmers we must rethink the whole problem, give up the present system, mechanize cultivation, eliminate the crowd of middlemen, and put an end to the monopoly of the cotton companies which enables them to make scandalous profits. The unanimous wish of the growers is that a mixed organization be set up which would take over from the companies the purchase and processing of cotton. . . .

Darlan had indeed founded such an organization in February 1948, the COTONCOOP of Bangui, an enterprise that was unique in AEF. The following month the territorial assembly voted 32 million CFA francs to help it through its formative years. But when in July 1950 Darlan claimed that over 24,000 members were already enrolled in his cooperative, the assembly was somewhat disconcerted to learn that he had been collecting dues from them "in the name of the government and without its fore-knowledge."[66]

If there is little doubt that the subject of Oubangui's cotton gave rise to demagoguery, it is also certain that cotton was an increasingly unpopular crop in that territory, even after its purchase price was raised, better farming methods were taught, and the element of coercion was removed. The Comité de Salut Economique, set up by the MESAN government in 1958, conducted a territory-wide propaganda campaign urging that a doubled crop goal of 80,000 tons be set for that season. Allowing for the adverse climatic conditions during that year and the fact that the committee's campaign began too late and was subject to frequent changes, the output nevertheless came to only 37,468 tons. The companies' 21 gins worked far under capacity, for they were capable of ginning 60,000 tons. However, the outlook for the future is brighter, for soon the territory's new oil mills will be producing 600 to 700 tons of cottonseed oil a year, and the textile factory of Boali is increasing its capacity. The government has not given up its aim of coaxing back into cotton production the thousands of marginal planters who have abandoned the crop during the past five years. As Oubangui's premier Goumba said forthrightly:[67] "In some quarters it is mistakenly said that MESAN intends to reduce cotton cultivation. I say without equivocation that any persons who think this are totally mistaken." Cotton remains Oubangui's principal crop and accounts for about 64 per cent of its total exports in tonnage, though only about one-fourth in value.

Sisal was first planted in 1930 at Fadama, and during the ensuing decade its production grew very slowly, reaching only 27 tons by 1940. Almost all of this was taken by local craftsmen to make string, cord, and rugs for the domestic market.[68] After the war, output picked up rapidly, rising to 235 tons in 1947, 331 in 1948, and 614 in 1949. In the last-mentioned year, 583 tons, valued at over 26 million CFA francs, were exported, the balance being sold locally.

Pierre Gilliaux, an experienced colonist, was the pioneer of sisal in Oubangui, and his Société de Gérence Industrielle et Agricole (SGIA) produced almost all of the territory's output on its six plantations covering 3,000 hectares in the eastern region. This company received technical aid from the agricultural station at Bambari, where IRCT experts experimented with sisal cultivation. During the early postwar period of high sisal prices, the SGIA planned a big increase of its activities, with the aim of producing 15,000 tons of fiber a year by 1955. It started a new plantation at Pembolé (Ouanga district) in 1952, and proposed to plant sisal there at the rate of 1,000 additional hectares annually for the next five years. The SGIA also began construction in 1952 of a spinning mill in the heart of the producing area at Kouango, which was also the center for the ten artisanal-type decorticating enterprises of the region. The Kouango mill was completed in 1953 and had a capacity of 2,000 tons of finished products a year. It was also planned then to build at Pembolé six modern plants to turn out string, cord, and rugs on an industrial scale.

The high prices prevailing for sisal, the enterprise of the SGIA, and the exceptionally favorable natural conditions under which sisal could be grown in Oubangui persuaded other companies to begin new plantations. In the forest zone, sisal matured at the end of five instead of the usual eight years, and gave yields of two tons to the hectare.[69] The territorial agricultural service began experimenting with small plantations under the guidance of the IRCT in central and western Oubangui, and two other private companies, the SOCANA (Société des Plantations du Café Nana) and the Société Sanghamine started planting sisal in the Berbérati and Carnot regions. To varying degrees all of these companies had to contend with transport and labor difficulties, although those situated in the Sangha region were more favored in both respects. The SGIA expected to mechanize eventually almost all of its operations, but in the meantime it had to bring in a contingent of 1,000 Sara laborers from Tchad in 1952. No trouble was anticipated in finding a market for Oubangui's sisal, as France took 45,000 tons of that fiber annually.

In the early 1950's the outlook for the territory's sisal looked very promising, and Governor Raynier hailed it as "a crop with a future."[70] But this future very rapidly became a dark one. A fall in price that began in 1952 became catastrophic by 1954: the SGIA had to stock most of its output for lack of a paying market and ran into such heavy financial seas that control of this enterprise passed into the hands of the Degrain interests. The government vainly tried to help this company by lowering export duties and transport costs for sisal in 1954.

Little further has been heard of the activities of any of the sisal-growing companies, and exports fell steadily to the low point of 500 tons in 1957. Though they revived in the following year and Oubangui shipped out 1,500 tons, worth 52 million CFA francs, sisal production is generally regarded as a failure in the territory, where the MESAN government has not even mentioned that crop in the program for agricultural expansion laid down by its Comité de Salut Economique. Exceptionally enterprising and technically well prepared as it was, the SGIA sadly illustrates the fate of various AEF companies which have fallen victim to price fluctuations in the world market for tropical raw materials.

Oil palms occupy a very small place in Oubangui's economy both because of the smallness of their yield and because of their concentration in the southern tip of the territory. So great has been Oubangui's preoccupation with cotton, and to a much lesser extent with coffee and peanuts, that its 3,000 or so hectares of natural palm growths in the Lobaye, Kembé, and Ouango have largely been ignored. The local populations gather some of the kernels and extract an oil of mediocre quality, most of which they consume or sell to soap factories in Bangui, and the balance—about 1,000 tons a year—is exported. The territorial agricultural service and SIP have somewhat improved the Kotto grove and set up an oil mill nearby, but the tribes around Kembé have not cooperated in this development for they were afraid that they would lose ownership of the palms.[71] In 1953 the CGOT selected three possible sites for plantation development—two along the Oubangui river, near Bangassou in the east and below Bangui in the south, and the third on the banks of the Sangha river south of Berbérati. Thus far only one of these, in the Zinga-Mongoumba area, has been planted with selected palms, and they have not yet come into full bearing.[72]

In the savannah lands of Oubangui, peanuts have long been grown for family consumption. Only since the war, however, have its African farmers grown, in rotation with cotton, a small surplus for sale locally or for export.

Just how many peanuts are grown in the territory is unknown, but the area planted to this crop is probably close to 25,000 hectares. The amount of peanuts produced in Oubangui has certainly increased in recent years and is perhaps three times as much as the quantity sold in the local markets, which recently has averaged between 3,000 and 4,000 tons a year. More than half of this output comes from the northwestern regions of Ouham-Pendé and Ouham. The growth of Bangui's soap industry and the construction in 1955 of two modern oil mills at Bohina and Alindao, with a crushing capacity of 1,500 and 1,200 tons of nuts a year respectively, have certainly stimulated peanut production. In 1955 the sale of Oubangui's peanuts brought in about 60 million CFA francs to their growers.[73]

The leaders of the newborn Central African Republic are encouraging the culture of peanuts as a crop more remunerative and less onerous than cotton, and they have created controlled markets for its sale. But they are encountering the same difficulties as did the French administration before them. The terrain on which peanuts can be grown is limited and corresponds roughly to the 175,000 hectares given to cotton cultivation. Moreover, transport costs weigh heavily on such a "poor crop" as peanuts. Still another drawback is the fact that Metropolitan France is willing to purchase only limited tonnages at a price higher than that prevailing in the world market, and it has been found almost impossible to sell the surplus over that amount profitably elsewhere. No oil at all is exported from Oubangui, and the shipments of shelled nuts—though increasing—have not yet reached 1,000 tons a year. Even local sales fell to around 2,000 tons in 1957 and 1958 because the peanut farmers found the price level set by the government too low. To bring stocks out into the open in the latter year the authorities had to lift the embargo on selling outside the controlled markets.[74] In 1957 the peanut growers had shown their dissatisfaction with the official price by either consuming more nuts and oil themselves or bartering them clandestinely in the Belgian Congo against imported merchandise.

To offset some of these difficulties, the MESAN government is trying to persuade France to increase Oubangui's peanut quota and to guarantee for the next three years a price higher than the world level for the tonnages it accepts. And to increase the income of local peanut farmers, it has announced its willingness to contribute toward an interterritorial Price Supporting Fund for Peanuts.[75]

Although coffee holds second rank after cotton in this territory's agricultural exports, Oubangui is by far the biggest producer of coffee in AEF. An indigenous variety grows along the Oubangui river and in the Haute-Sangha region. To offset the decline in rubber production in those areas, Governor Lamblin in 1922 gave orders that Africans wherever possible should plant coffee around their villages. But it was not until seven years later that plantation development began, when Europeans at first timidly and then on a large scale began planting areas to the *excelsa* variety. In 1935, when the European-planted surfaces aggregated about 20,000 hectares, it was anticipated that coffee would become Oubangui's outstanding crop and soon cover nearly half of the territory. A blight, however, which appeared the next year, quickly wiped out more than 10,000 hectares of *excelsa* bushes and caused Africans to abandon this variety almost completely. The European planters saved what *excelsa* areas they could, but elsewhere they began planting *robusta,* a more disease-resistant variety but one that gave smaller yields. As of 1949 the coffee-growing areas still totaled 14,000 hectares, of which 7,500 hectares were planted to *excelsa,* 5,500 to *robusta,* and 1,200 to *nana.*[76]

Oubangui's coffee production has gone through vicissitudes but on the whole it has been marked by a steady rise in tonnages. Output rose from 788 tons in 1936 to 2,900 on the eve of World War II. In 1942 and 1943 the *excelsa* bushes were struck by a new blight and production slumped, but the following year the *robusta* planted in the late 1930's came into bearing, and the quantity grown throughout the territory increased to 4,759 tons in 1944. The harvest fell again in 1945 because of the waning productivity of old bushes and in 1947 because of labor shortages. Yields ranged widely between 230 and 750 kilograms per hectare, but from 1949 on, Oubangui's production became stabilized around 4,000 tons annually, an amount that provided about 4 per cent of the coffee then consumed each year in France. Virtually all of Oubangui's coffee was shipped to France, and to standardize and maintain its high quality a control service for exports was set up by the territorial government during the war. Another wartime innovation aimed at improving Oubangui's coffee production was the Boukoko station established in the forest zone in 1942 to experiment with insecticides and the development of disease-resistant and high-yielding coffee bushes. In the latter domain success did not crown that station's efforts until 1954, but in the interval its staff aided European planters with technical advice and with an insecticide-spraying service by plane.

The abolition of forced labor in 1946 posed an acute problem for European planters, and to offset the shortage of laborers, felt especially at harvest time, they experimented with bringing in Sara workers from Tchad. But the latter belonged to millet-eating tribes and could not adjust themselves to manioc, which was the basic food of Oubangui's coffee-growing regions. For some years, therefore, it looked as if the ceiling of the territory's coffee production had been reached, but in 1950 a marked rise in the world price for coffee began to alter the local picture. Africans started once more to plant coffee on about 1,000 hectares in the Lobaye region and around Berbérati. The yields and quality of their output were poor, for they planted coffee on scattered holdings without concern for the suitability of the soil or for the upkeep of the bushes. Although the administration at that time did not favor such an extension of the coffee-growing areas, it realized the need to give guidance to African planters and in 1950 created a special coffee section in the territorial agricultural service.

At first this service was extremely unpopular with both the African coffee farmers and the territorial assemblymen.[77] Its members were accused of trying to turn Africans from coffee to cotton planting and of favoring European coffee planters to the exclusion of their African colleagues. Specifically the Africans resented the agricultural service's revival of regulations dating back to the mid-1930's, which provided penalties for coffee growers who failed to keep up their plantations or root out diseased or over-age bushes. Later this feeling of antagonism gave way to appreciation when the government, in 1954, began to encourage African planting with the new bushes developed at the Boukoko station. Even the sharp drop in the world price for coffee from 1954 on did not arrest the extension of Oubangui's coffee plantations, for coffee grown in the French Union now benefited by some protection in the Metropolitan market and it was a crop that could be profitably stocked against a future price rise. As of June 30, 1957, the total area planted to coffee in that territory came to 16,881 hectares. Although European plantations still accounted for the great majority, the African share in the coffee-growing surfaces had risen to 2,609 hectares, of which 1,430 belonged to individual farmers and 1,179 to *paysannats*.[78]

Under the encouragement of the Comité de Salut Economique, the Africans of Oubangui have been fired with enthusiasm for this crop, and the tempo of African planting and processing has been rapidly accelerated. Until 1957 the territory produced more coffee than it had the facilities to process, but in that year the SIP organized cooperatives for processing at Berbérati, Mbaiki, and Nola, and in 1958 they turned out the first 200 tons of good-quality beans. In 1958, too, African farmers planted 2,600 new hectares to coffee compared with the 1,800 so planted in the preceding year. By the end of 1958, coffee bushes covered 23,500 hectares in Oubangui, of which 7,000 hectares were in African hands and the proceeds from the territory's exports of this crop brought in to its growers 877 million CFA francs, or about half as much as the sum realized from the sale of cotton. In 1959 the Boukoko station was able to distribute large amounts of improved *excelsa* seed, and it is confidently expected that by 1965 Oubangui will be able to export some 15,000 tons of coffee.

The MESAN government is anxious to maintain Oubangui's reputation for high-quality exports and to concentrate on increasing yields rather than extending the area under coffee cultivation. It is also determined to maintain a remunerative price for the planters, but is not happy that the recently created Price Supporting Fund for Coffee was set up on a federal basis and that Oubangui was not given a larger representation on its executive committee. But these are minor difficulties compared with those involved in marketing Oubangui's rapidly growing output. The French market for overseas coffee, except for *arabica,* is saturated, and Oubangui's soil and climatic conditions are not suited to the development of that variety. Moreover, high production and transportation costs strictly limit the sale of Oubangui's coffee in nonprotected markets.

The cultivation of imported varieties of tobacco was slower in starting in Oubangui than in Moyen-Congo and has never developed as rapidly, because of less favorable natural conditions and of the inferior farming abilities of its inhabitants.

Three years after it initiated Maryland-tobacco cultivation in Moyen-Congo, the Service d'Exploitation Industrielle des Tabacs et Allumettes (SEITA) mission was invited in 1949 by the Oubangui administration to prospect favorable zones in its territory. It was also offered the collaboration of the territorial agricultural service for cultivation of the crop and a monopoly of sales for export as well as of the local manufacture of cigarettes.[79] SEITA agreed to start experiments in the Bossembélé sector and embarked on a more successful operation in the environs of Berbérati, where it also constructed a processing plant. By 1957 Berbérati was furnishing 200 of the 237 tons of tobacco produced yearly in Oubangui, the balance coming from the M'Bomou region. A ceiling of 750 tons has been placed on Oubangui's tobacco production by SEITA, but there seems little prospect that this will be reached in the near future.

Forests and forest products

Although a steadily increasing amount of timber is being produced both for the local market and for export, the wood industry will probably never occupy more than a minor place in Oubangui's economy. Only a small proportion of the territory is covered by forests, comparatively few of the trees grown therein are commercially valuable, and the cost and difficulties of transporting its wood to foreign markets automatically limit exports to periods during which the world price for lumber is high.

Oubangui's dense forest is concentrated in the Lobaye and Haute-Sangha regions, which border on Moyen-Congo. Elsewhere there are only wooded areas, which have been fast disappearing with the extension of plantation agriculture and with the spread of urban populations. As recently as 1957 the territorial assembly was warned by one of its African members that Oubangui would become a desert in 50 years if trees continued to be cut down at the current rate.[80] Yet here as elsewhere in AEF, the African elite have blamed European planters and the fuel needs of industries such as the Union Electrique Coloniale (UNELCO) for this devastation, rather than the local population's practice of shifting agriculture and of setting bush fires. And they continue to reproach the Forestry Service for classifying an ever-larger area as reserved forests (which now total about 70,000 hectares) and for reforesting only a very small surface (less than 200 hectares).

As of early 1959, 18 permits for cutting trees, in an area totaling 91,500 hectares, had been issued, and during the preceding year some 73,000 cubic meters of timber were produced in Oubangui. This represented an impressive increase over 1952, when wood-cutting permits covered only 58,000 hectares and production amounted to some 50,000 cubic meters. From 1946 to 1949 there had been little increase in output—in fact, the wood shortage in Bangui was acute—but from 1950 on, newly mechanized sawmills began increasing their output both for local consumption and for export to neighboring territories. Until 1957 all of the timber cut in Oubangui was sold to the territory's ten sawmills, which exported to Tchad, the Belgian Congo, and Cameroun several thousand tons of sawn wood every year besides marketing locally about 30,000 tons. But the currency-devaluation moves of August 1957 and December 1958 opened up export markets for Oubangui's best-quality output of limba in western Europe and South Africa, and this new development was aided by a lowering of transport rates for wood on the CGTA's barges and on the Congo-Ocean railroad. Since Oubangui's lumber trade has never been subject to official controls as in Gabon, the course of its future exports will probably depend simply on the market demand and price.

Animal husbandry

In Oubangui, animal husbandry, though an important occupation, is a secondary one. This is the case partly because large areas are infested by the tsetse fly, particularly in the south, and partly because the Oubanguians are by inclination not herders but hunters. Only the nomadic Bororo Peulhs are professional cattlemen, and even they get Negroes to guard their animals during the rainy season; they practice no selection in breeding, and willingly sell their young bulls to the fetishist tribes for religious sacrifices.

On the eve of World War II the government succeeded in introducing cattle husbandry into the Bambari region of eastern Oubangui. Until then, only the Ouham-Pendé area of western Oubangui possessed sizable herds, whose number was difficult to estimate because they grazed for part of the year in Cameroun. After study had shown that the Bambari area had tsetse-free pastures, cattle were brought there from Ouham-Pendé and flourished in the care of Bororo herders. An early postwar census of Oubangui's animal resources indicated that at that time some 200,000 head of cattle existed in western and 81,000 in eastern Oubangui.[81] No exact figures were available as to other kinds of animals, but it was thought that in the territory as a whole there were perhaps 75,000 sheep, 300,000 goats, and 10,000 pigs.

Despite such considerable animal resources, the Oubanguian people suffered then as now from a shortage of meat. Because of the Peulh tradition of keeping cattle unproductively as capital or for payment of the bride price, only about one-fifth of the local herds was used for meat, and each year some 20,000 head were driven south to the Bangui market from Tchad. Then, too, not all of these were slaughtered for local consumption, for several thousand each year were shipped farther south to Brazzaville. The only meat consumed by rural Oubanguians was that of the sheep, goats, and pigs that they reared negligently in their villages. Hunting was sharply restricted by an administration anxious to check the wasteful destruction of wildlife and to turn enthusiastic hunters into settled cultivators of cotton. Because they were thus deprived of a congenial and ancient pastime and forced to grow a crop they disliked, the Oubanguians deeply resented this policy. Their spokesmen in the territorial assembly held the government responsible for the rural exodus, in large part because it had created a shortage of meat in the countryside.[82]

Besides their chronic opposition to any and every official policy, the African assemblymen of Oubangui had special grievances against the animal-husbandry service. They claimed that this service helped only the Bororo herders and their cattle and had totally neglected the sedentary farmers and their small-scale rearing of sheep, goats, poultry, and pigs.[83] On such grounds they were opposed to any increase in the veterinary staff, though the government pointed out that no improvements could be expected so long as there were only three or four veterinaries for a territory larger than France, one of whom was wholly occupied in ascertaining the condition of animals reaching the Bangui market. Despite such handicaps, this service in 1949 succeeded in creating a third cattle-husbandry zone in the M'Bomou region and was continuing to build up a herd there. Finally the assembly agreed to vote the sum needed to increase the veterinary staff, and the government promised to use some of the additional personnel to undertake a survey of suitable pastureland currently unutilized for animal husbandry.

Under the second four-year Plan the administration was able to meet the assembly's demands for the development of small-scale husbandry. Already in 1949–50 it had begun building a station for poultry rearing at Bangui and pig-husbandry stations at Bambari and Bouar. These were provided with breeding stock from France and from Brazzaville's experimental farm at Kilometer 17, and in due course their progeny were distributed to Oubanguian farmers. At the same time cattle husbandry was promoted through extensive inoculations against epidemic diseases and through the teaching of farmers and herders to feed and shelter their animals. The export of hides and skins was encouraged and a new abattoir was built at Bangui, as well as cold-storage space. Thus Bangui's meat supply was slowly improved, though the rural situation in this respect remained almost stationary.

Gradually the African assemblymen ceased to berate the animal-husbandry service, in view of its success in increasing the number of animals reared in the territory. Nevertheless they continued to complain about the hunting restrictions and the depredations of the Bororo cattle on the crops of sedentary farmers. In recent years the service has concentrated on finding new pastures and improving existing ones, for Oubangui's cattle continue their ceaseless migrations, which are bad for the health of the herds and for the relations between farmers and Bororos. Because of the continuing failure to utilize to capacity its existing animal resources, Oubangui still has to import half of the 10,000-odd tons of meat its urban populations consume annually. To increase the supply of meat in the rural areas, N'dama cattle were experimentally introduced in 1956 into regions new to animal husbandry in the south.

Fisheries

Fishing is widely engaged in by the tribes living along the Oubangui, but a considerable portion of their catch is sold or bartered on the Belgian Congo bank of the river, and Oubangui has consumed less fish per capita than any other territory in AEF.

To remedy this situation the federal government created a secondary research station at Landjia near Bangui, and in 1955 began a special effort to popularize tilapia-breeding throughout the territory. Three official pisci-culture stations were established, at Bangui, Bambari, and Berbérati, in addition to those operated by the SIP and Catholic mission at Alindao. Tilapia-breeding first took hold in the western part of the territory, and by 1956 some 1,500 ponds had been built there, compared with 180 and 120 in the eastern and central areas respectively.[84] Total production of tilapia that year amounted to only ten tons of fish, but the enthusiasm with which the Oubanguians of the hinterland have taken up pond installation gives the authorities hope that rapidly increasing production will supply an element much needed in the local population's diet and will also enable them to earn a supplementary cash income.

Trade

Despite the declining production of export commodities in recent years, Oubangui still holds third rank among AEF's territorial exporters, though its percentage has fallen from a fourth to a fifth of the federation's total exports. Oubangui's products are more diversified than are those of Gabon and Tchad but they are also less valuable: compared with those of Moyen-Congo, their range is smaller but they bring in bigger revenues. Cotton is by far the most important export of Oubangui, and it is followed by coffee and diamonds. Trailing those three commodities at some distance come oleaginous produce, sisal, wood, and hides. In 1958 Oubangui's cotton brought in 1,741 million CFA francs, coffee 877 million, diamonds 351 million, oleaginous produce 148 million, sisal 52 million, wood 48 million, and hides 22 million. Since 1953, the value of the territory's total exports has ranged between 2,400 and 3,400 million CFA francs. When the MESAN party took over control of the government in 1957–58, its leaders at once started a drive to increase the production of both export and food crops, which has been successful to some extent in arresting the downward trend of output.

The growth of imports in recent years, which has been out of proportion to Oubangui's exports, succeeded a period of stagnation. For five years after the Liberation, the African members of the territorial assembly were chronically indignant not only over the shortage of imported goods but also over what they considered to be their unfair distribution. Their complaints were directed mainly against the big European trading firms which dominated the Bangui Chamber of Commerce, but also were aimed against the itinerant Haoussa merchants, to whom the big importers ceded some of their wares. The Haoussas, it was claimed, were impoverishing Oubangui and making proportionately even larger profits than did the Europeans.[85] Although admittedly they were performing a useful service by provisioning the countryside, it was said to be at the expense of the consumer and of the territorial budget, for they managed most of the time to escape being taxed. The reaction to both these "monopolistic" groups was the setting up of a number of indigenous consumer-cooperative societies, but the latter were short-lived (see pp. 169–70). The Haoussas continued to thrive as small-scale traders and diamond smugglers, and one of the first moves made by the MESAN government was an attempt to curtail and regulate their activities.[86]

In the early 1950's the shortage of imported goods had become much less acute in Oubangui, and as a result of the better prices received by cotton and coffee growers, the local Africans' cash income had increased. Apparently Oubangui's imports grew markedly from 1955 on, though in the customs statistics it is hard to disentangle the territorial destinations of the goods brought in by way of Pointe Noire. Food imports mounted, though proportionately less than in the other territories because of Oubangui's greater local production of the major items in the local diet. In order of importance as named, the territory's principal imports were motor vehicles, cotton cloth, gasoline, household wares, wines, tires, corrugated iron, sugar, cement, flour, and beer. The franc zone was Oubangui's main provisioner as well as its biggest external market.

In 1950, the territorial assembly's overriding desire in relation to trade was that the administration should eliminate its controls over purchases in the internal market.[87] Its African members were especially resentful of the government's placing of limitations on the amount of food brought into the urban markets and on the prices of the merchandise sold there. Yet the rise in living costs after the currency devaluations of 1957 and 1958 induced the African government of Oubangui to devise even stricter price controls and also to forbid trading in raw materials outside the officially established markets.[88]

Industry

By reason of their variety, the proximity of an important segment of the Federal Artery, and the existence of a source of hydroelectric power, Oubangui's industries present a picture that resembles closely that of Moyen-Congo. The Boali falls supply power to a sizable textile mill, and also to the large Mocaf brewery located at Bangui. At Ouham-Pendé is situated one of AEF's three tanneries, which supplies leather to a small shoe factory nearby. Oubangui also has the most flourishing soap industry in the federation, which utilizes locally milled palm oil. Its sawmills are turning out increasing quantities of sawn wood, and its cotton gins are beginning to produce cottonseed oil for the local market. None of these industries has any difficulty in marketing its wares, and the industrial outlook could be viewed optimistically were it not for the decline in the production of raw materials, as a result of which the already small scale of output has been still further reduced.

As for gold mining, the exhaustion of Oubangui's alluvion deposits has been mainly responsible for reducing production to virtually nothing. Even the output of the diamond industry has been curtailed for the same reasons, though the territory is still the chief diamond producer of AEF.

No public system for the distribution of electricity existed in Oubangui until World War II, when a small plant was built at Bangui with such materials as were then available. In 1942, consumption there amounted to 72,000 kilowatt-hours, and three years later the concession to distribute electricity in the capital was granted to UNELCO on a long-term contract with the local administration. After the war the demand for current rose very rapidly, and UNELCO was unable to meet it, particularly in the years 1948–49. Oubangui's assemblymen attributed this failure to UNELCO's deliberate refusal to expand its facilities, particularly in regard to lighting Bangui's African suburbs, and the proposal made by a French assemblyman that UNELCO should be expelled from the territory was greeted by enthusiastic applause from his colleagues.[89] Their irritation reached the explosion point when UNELCO demanded a loan from the local budget as the condition for increasing its supply of electrical current.

What preserved UNELCO from the wrath of Oubangui's representatives was the decision made at long last in 1951 to construct the Boali hydroelectric dam and power plant, the second project recommended by the EDF mission in 1947. This project was delayed by the equivocation of AEF's cotton companies, whose participation was vital both for financing the plant's construction and for consuming the current it would generate. Opposition to the scheme came also from Jacobson, head of the Plan Committee for the French Union Assembly, who claimed that the Boali plant would never be profitable and that it would be better to enlarge UNELCO's facilities. This twofold opposition was finally overcome, but meanwhile the cost of constructing the dam and generating plant at Boali, as well as the power line that was to connect it with Bangui 80 kilometers away, had risen to over 1 billion CFA francs. Advocates of the project pointed to the tenfold increase in Bangui's electrical consumption between the years 1943 and 1950, and to their expectation of industrial development in the Ouban-guian capital.

In May 1955 the Boali plant began functioning, with a capacity for producing annually 3,200,000 kilowatt-hours, or about twice as much as Bangui was then consuming. The Boali textile factory is its biggest cus-tomer, but the anticipated industrialization of Bangui has not yet mate-rialized and the plant is not working to capacity. Furthermore, UNELCO, far from being dispossessed, is now responsible for distributing Boali's cur-rent and is considering plans for handling also the lighting of such sec-ondary territorial centers as Bambari, Berbérati, and Bouar.

Labor

In two respects the labor situation of Oubangui differs from that of any other AEF territory: the number of its wage earners has declined since the war, and the territory is both an importer and exporter of labor. As for urban unemployment, the slow growth of unions, and the decline in the number of boys attending technical schools, Oubangui resembles the rest of the federation.

As of 1949 there were an estimated 54,000 wage earners in Oubangui, about 14,000 of whom were employed in mining and 13,000 on agricultural plantations.[90] By 1958 the total had sunk to 49,800, of whom 44,400 were said to be in the private sector and 5,400 in the public sector.[91] In so far as technical schools were concerned, these consisted on January 1, 1946, of one Ecole des Métiers at Bangui, two sections artisanales, and eight sections d'apprentissage, which were giving instruction to 42 girls (in home eco-nomics) and 517 boys (398 in agriculture, 72 in local crafts, 28 in woodwork, and 19 in mechanics). By 1952, though there had been no diminution in the number of technical schools, only 279 boys were attending them and the territory was spending no more than 0.91 per cent of its budget on this kind of education. It should be noted, however, that the number of girls taking home-economics courses had risen during the interval to 500.

That the number of wage earners was declining while the size of the population as a whole was increasing was attributed by local African politi-cians to the legacy of the concessionary-company regime and to the con-tinuing forced cultivation of cotton. They also blamed the government for permitting workers to be recruited in the savannah zone for labor in Gabon and Moyen-Congo.[92] Whatever the main causes of the difficulty may have been, employers in Oubangui—particularly the mining companies—had such trouble in assembling and retaining their labor force that they brought in workers under contract from Tchad and from Cameroun. In 1948 the government, to remedy this curious situation, forbade the hiring among those already locally employed of laborers for work outside the territory, and also banned such recruitment completely in the regions of Haute-Sangha, Lobaye, Bri, and Haut-M'Bomou. Despite the official pledge to confine recruiting thenceforth to the unemployed of Bangui, where only 8,000 of some 45,000 residents then had jobs, the assembly adopted unanimously on November 16, 1948, a resolution to the effect that no more Oubanguians should be hired for work outside the territory, particularly for construction of the port of Pointe Noire. This vote was inspired by fear lest not enough local laborers should be available in Oubangui to carry out the territorial-development Plan and that workers who had once been employed at Pointe Noire might refuse to return home and take jobs at lower wages. On September 20, 1949, Governor Delteil told the assembly that the governor-general had assured him that no further call would be made by the southern territories on laborers from Oubangui. However, he insisted that this pledge in no way affected the government's right to replace with freshly recruited Oubanguians those whose work contracts at Pointe Noire were on the point of terminating. The governor did add the promise that such replacements would be recruited only in the forest zone, where conditions were analogous to those in Moyen-Congo, and that the same number would be brought in from Tchad to work in Oubangui's savannah regions, where they easily adapted themselves to the climate and food.

From 1950 on, the question of labor recruitment in Oubangui for work in other AEF territories ceased to be a major concern for local politicians, particularly after unemployment in Bangui became acute. The African leaders, first Antoine Darlan and then Boganda, found that the local labor situation offered convenient ammunition to use against the territory's big companies and also the French administration. They and their followers claimed that unjust dismissals, bad working conditions, and starvation wages accounted for the instability and inefficiency of Oubanguian laborers.[93] They asked that the companies be compelled to respect such labor laws as were in force and also to provide dispensaries and schools for their staff. They also wanted the existing labor unions to be consulted in the formulation of regulations for settling labor disputes and improving working conditions, pending passage of the Overseas Labor Code still before Parliament. To these demands the territorial labor inspector replied that he, more than anyone else, regretted the absence of complete labor legislation and of collective agreements in Oubangui, and also of the staff needed to enforce existing labor laws. As to the unions, he claimed that they were too unrepresentative and their membership too small to be regarded as valid spokesmen for the wage-earning class.

Though there was little agreement as to the exact size of that class, it was widely conceded that the total number of organized workers did not exceed 2,000[94] and that the distribution of laborers varied markedly from one area to another. Although the wage-earning group might comprise one-fifth of the adult male population—which numbered somewhat over 300,000 throughout all of Oubangui—there were, for example, in Lobaye only 10 per cent gainfully employed. Moreover, few classified as wage earners worked throughout the year, either because of the seasonal nature of their occupations or because they would suddenly leave their jobs when the urge to hunt or fish became too strong to resist. Under such circumstances it was difficult to form unions among workers in the rural areas. Indeed, as recently as 1955 the 200 to 300 African workers on an experimental farm refused to listen to a militant unionist who had come expressly from Bangui to organize them.[95]

Union strength in Oubangui, such as it is, remains restricted largely to the towns. Probably the Confédération Générale du Travail (CGT) is numerically the strongest of the three *centrales,* particularly in the south, but it has suffered from the political eclipse of the RDA and of its spokesman, Antoine Darlan, who sponsored its early growth. As elsewhere in AEF, the Force Ouvrière (FO) attracts chiefly the white-collar class, combines African with European members, and is the weakest of the big three. Under the missions' guidance, the territorial Confédération Française des Travailleurs Chrétiens (CFTC) has steered clear of political involvements and has concentrated on trying to promote its members' professional interests. In Oubangui, despite the politically tense atmosphere in that territory, strikes have been very few, and none was successful in meeting most of the workers' demands.[96]

In 1956, application of the Overseas Labor Code and passage of the *loi-cadre* brought some improvements in the workers' position. In April of that year the CFTC, CGT, and FO unions agreed to form an "interunion cartel so as to pool their resources and assure the defense of the territory's wage earners."[97] Despite this organizational reinforcement, the demands formulated by the union spokesmen in July 1956 for a 25 per cent rise in the minimum wage and a reduction of the three wage zones to two were not granted. The year after, Oubangui's first two collective agreements were signed,[98] and these won appreciable wage rises for the workers involved, but there is little evidence that the unions played a major role in negotiating their terms. Working conditions in the territory have been improved gradually, first through the initiative of the French administration and more recently by the MESAN government.

Governor Mauberma was the first official to experiment in AEF with rapid labor-training centers. On the basis of studies made by two missions of French experts to Oubangui, such a center was created at Bangui in November 1949. Until 1954 this center was oriented toward the building trades, but with completion of most of the infrastructure projects financed by FIDES it began to train carpenters and masons to improve rural African housing. By December 1958 it had graduated 217 skilled workers (for whom the Labor Inspectorate easily found jobs), and they have been earning wages markedly higher than those of their unskilled compatriots. The more stringent educational requirements for the Ecole des Métiers, also

located at Bangui, and the limited demand for the output of the leather-
workers, wood- and ivory-carvers, and bookbinders it trains, has restricted
the number of pupils admitted to that school to about nine a year.

The MESAN government is far more sympathetic to the rapid-training
center than to the Ecole des Métiers, but its efforts to better working conditions have taken a very different direction from that of increasing the
number of locally skilled workers. Its advent to power coincided with an
aggravation of the unemployment problem, particularly in Bangui, where
the head of the Office de la Main-d'Oeuvre stated at the end of 1957 that
there were no more than 6,000 individuals then holding jobs.[99] At the
same time, in the rural areas more and more cotton farmers were abandoning cultivation of the soil (see pp. 409–11). Boganda energetically tackled
the problem from two angles. By means of editorials signed "Boganda,
peasant of the Lobaye" in the party organ *Bangui-Losa,* he told his compatriots that tilling the soil and increasing rural productivity were Oubangui's only salvation, and in the spring of 1958 he sent out members of his
government and of the newly created Comité de Salut Economique to
preach the gospel of the "dignity and grandeur of manual labor" throughout the land. At about the same time he increased the minimum wage
by 15 per cent in the first zone and by 13 per cent in the second and third
zones, and in July 1958 he announced that the monthly allowance of 220
CFA francs then being paid to 18,036 children of wage earners in the
territory would be augmented.

Unfortunately for those leaders who had long maintained that "the
prevailing miserable and inhuman working conditions" were responsible
for the Oubanguians' reluctance to take jobs, these benevolent measures
did not succeed in appreciably increasing the number of those gainfully
employed. Soon after Oubangui became the Central African Republic, its
assembly voted Boganda's proposal to penalize by three to six months'
imprisonment "all idlers and vagabonds without regularly assured incomes,
18 years of age or over, who are mentally and physically sound and who
have refused to work."[100] Then in January 1959, the MESAN government
followed the example set by Youlou in Moyen-Congo. It more or less
forcibly dispatched to a 2,000-hectare area adjoining the road between
Bangui and M'Baiki an initial contingent of 100 unemployed youths recruited in the capital city. For the first three years this land was to be
jointly cultivated by its settlers and at government expense, after which
it was to be divided into individual lots and become the property of its
farmers in exchange for a percentage of their harvests.[101]

CHAPTER 24

Tchad (République du Tchad)

All the handicaps confronting other AEF territories, aside from those of labor supply, are to be found in Tchad on a larger scale and in aggravated form. The largest country of the former federation—its area is twice that of France—it is also the least prosperous, and its population, which accounts for more than half that of the whole federation, is more fragmented and more ridden by tribal and other antagonisms. In particular, the problem of the chiefs is more acute here than in any other AEF state.

Like Oubangui, Tchad is landlocked and easily accessible to neighboring foreign countries, but Tchad is even more vulnerable to outside influences and is farther from the sea. Moreover, the length of its common frontiers with Sudan, Libya, Cameroun, and French West Africa exceeds that of Oubangui's boundaries Nor has Tchad any compensatory system of good internal communications, for few roads exist in the territory and it has only one river system, that of the Logone and the Chari. Tchad's produce is poor and undiversified, its economy being based almost wholly on animal husbandry in the north and east and on cotton in the southwest. Traders and truckers abound in the towns, but there are only two industries, livestock and cotton ginning. Desert covers the northern half of the country, sahel[1] the eastern part, and only a meager agricultural zone is to be found in the southwest.

In the southwestern towns the populations are the most evolved. Politically, Tchad was slower in developing than were the more dynamic countries to the south, and in recent years it has become unstable more rapidly than they. But Tchad possesses two advantages in this field: politics have not divided Africans from Europeans, for all the major parties have members from both groups; and moreover, all Tchadians have an awareness of their territory's weaknesses that has made them exceptionally cooperative with both Metropolitan France and adjacent territories.

Because of their geographical location and lack of natural frontiers, the indigenous Negro populations of Tchad were overwhelmed time and again by waves of white or mixed-blood Muslim invaders coming from the north and east, and this undoubtedly accounts for the multiplicity of ethnic groups found there today. These invaders forcibly Islamized a majority of the local peoples and organized them into strong sultanates. One of these, that of

Kanem, after waging a 200-year struggle with the pagan Sao communities, succumbed at the end of the sixteenth century to the Bornou sultanate. Other powerful states, particularly those of Baguirmi and Ouaddaï, also rose and fell during the course of the centuries, weakening themselves by constant warfare and internal strife, and decimating their Negro neighbors by successive slave raids. The legacy of this slavery can still be seen in the bitter hostility felt by Negro Tchadians toward their former Arab masters. It is also evident in the contempt tinged with jealousy shown by the Arabs toward their former slaves, who have now become more prosperous and better educated than they and who today form the elite in the towns and farmlands of the south.

No reliable basis has yet been found for classifying the Tchadian populations. Often they are designated simply as Muslims, pagans, or Christians, but these religious affiliations are not permanent, especially as to the pagan element, for steady inroads are being made on it by the other two more aggressive creeds. Another looser and even less satisfactory practice has been that of classifying the Tchadians as Negroes or whites, but this does not take into account the considerable cross-breeding that has blurred the lines between them. The largest authentically Negro group is that of the Sara fetishists, who have long formed the backbone of France's combat troops in AEF. Living near them in southwestern Tchad are other Negro tribes, including the Massa of the Logone and the Baguirmi in the Fort Lamy region. One such tribe, the Kotoko, deserves special mention. They are the Islamized descendants of the Sao (a tribe more numerous in Cameroun). In Tchad they form a distinct bloc and live by farming and fishing along the banks of the Chari. The so-called "white" Tchadians—Arabs, Peulhs, and Toubou—despite profound differences between them have more in common than have the Negro tribes. They are almost all nomadic herders, aggressive Muslims, strongly hierarchized, and they speak a debased form of Arabic that is mutually comprehensible. The Negroes, on the other hand, have no common religion or occupation or native language.

When the French reached Tchad almost 60 years ago, they found a heterogeneous population whose primitive economy was conditioned by the generally poor terrain, hot and dry climate, and lack of intercommunication. In the desert and sahel regions of the north and east, animal husbandry was the only economic activity carried on by the nomadic Arabs, Peulhs and Toubou, though wheat, dates, gum, and salt were produced in small amounts by their Negro slaves. In the savannah lands of the south and west, sedentary Negroes eked out a precarious livelihood by growing millet and by fishing. Trade was confined to barter, ivory and cattle taking the place of money, and it was greatly limited by the lack of internal means of communication in a country of immense distances. The nearest seaport was nearly 2,500 kilometers away, and the only permanent and utilizable rivers—the Chari (1,200 kilometers long) and the Logone (970 kilometers) —underwent sharp seasonal fluctuations. Water flowed in the eastern

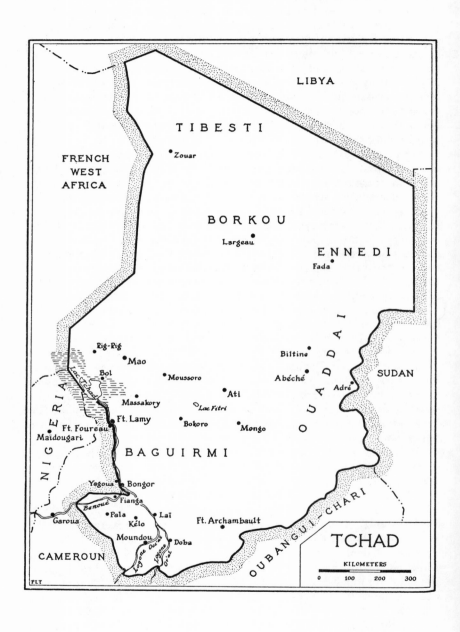

LIBYA

T I B E S T I

• Zouar

FRENCH
WEST
AFRICA

B O R K O U

• Largeau

E N N E D I

Fada •

Rig-Rig •

• Mao

Bol •

Biltine •

Abéché •

O U A D D A I

SUDAN

Adré •

• Moussoro

• Ati

Massakory •

○ Lac Fitri

N I G E R I A

Lac Tchad

Ft. Lamy

Bokoro •

• Mongo

Ft. Foureau •

Maidougari •

B A G U I R M I

Yagoua • Bongor

Fianga

Benoué

• Pala

• Laï

Garoua •

Kélo •

Moundou •

• Doba

Logone Occidental

Logone Oriental

Ft. Archambault •

O U B A N G U I - C H A R I

CAMEROUN

TCHAD

KILOMETERS

0   100   200   300

FLT

oueds[2] for only a few weeks of the year, and to the north lay the great Sahara. Lake Tchad, on which the frontiers of Nigeria, Cameroun, French West Africa, and Tchad territory converged, lay in a vast, shallow depression, and its indistinct papyrus-covered shores had a circumference that varied between 100 and 250 kilometers.

The first task facing the French was that of establishing order in a generally insecure country whose innumerable chiefs had found no way of asserting their authority other than by force or of prospering except by raiding the manpower and possessions of their weaker neighbors. To pacify Tchad took 15 years, and another five were required to set up an administrative network. Between 1900 and 1920, France never worked out any coherent policy in her dealings with the local chiefs. Nevertheless, the trend was unmistakably toward cutting down their power whenever and wherever conditions of security permitted.

An instructive case history is that of Baguirmi, described by Gentil as the pivotal region of all Tchad. In 1897 its sultan had called on the French to help repel an invasion by Rabah (see pp. 10, 99). After the latter's defeat, four successive treaties were made with the sultan of Baguirmi by the military officers then commanding in Tchad. The Baguirmi people continued to be ruled by their sultan under a protectorate agreement, but the pagan areas which the sultan had previously annexed were directly administered by French officers. In return for the sultan's pledge to give up slave-raiding and his claims to the left bank of the Chari, he was paid an indemnity of 10,000 francs.[3] As the years went by, this subsidy was reduced, on the ground that the sultan was not living up to his treaty obligations, and so were the various taxes and tithes that he was allowed to collect from his subjects, the French claiming that his exactions were imposing an undue burden on the people. By 1915, Baguirmi was considered sufficiently pacified to be turned over to a civilian government, which rapidly moved toward direct rule, collected the taxes itself, and encroached more and more on the local chiefs' jurisdictional authority. Despite the opposition of the sultan and his successors to this altered policy, its application was not seriously hampered, and much the same procedure characterized France's handling of the other paramount chiefs. Yet, circumscribed as their power now was by more direct French rule, the chiefs continued to wield great influence over their subjects, especially in the peripheral regions of Ouaddaï, Kanem, and Mayo-Kebbi. During this period, the far north remained untouched and largely unexplored, and even today the Borkou-Ennedi-Tibesti region—frequently called the BET— is still under military control.

It was not until two years after the end of World War I that Tchad became a distinct territorial entity, but even more time was needed to give it a real administrative organization. As of 1925, it took four to five months to reach Tchad from France, either by the southern water route or overland by caravan. Fort Lamy, the territorial capital, had only one European merchant, and the total number of Frenchmen then living there did not exceed 50.[4] From 1920 until World War II, the government-general at Brazzaville, which was then deeply committed to and preoccupied by the building of the Congo-Ocean railroad, left Tchad to fend for itself. Considering the territory's isolation and its meager revenues—in 1926 the budget came to only 6.5 million francs—the local officials performed marvels. To strengthen its one existing source of wealth, the administration made great efforts to increase the northern herds, and to supplement an animal husbandry confined largely to the north and east, the government in 1929 forcibly introduced cotton cultivation in the southwest. In time, cotton became the second largest revenue-earner for the federation and the only source of cash income for many Negroes in southern Tchad.

Félix Eboué was governor of Tchad when World War II broke out, and his rallying to the cause of Free France in 1940 profoundly affected the fate not only of that territory but of all AEF as well. Tchad became the operational base for Colonel Leclerc's trans-Saharan drive to Bir Hakeim, and this greatly promoted the territory's economic and psychological evolution. Aside from the concrete benefits to Tchad in the form of equipment and money for the payment of troops and their provisions, it put the territory on the map so far as the French and Allied peoples were concerned. Tchadians, both black and white, became ardent Gaullists, and they have never ceased to regard their country proudly as the "cradle of the Resistance." This sentiment accounts for the impressive following built up in Tchad by the Rassemblement du Peuple Français (RPF) when representative institutions were created there in 1946, and to this day the *mystique* of Gaullism is a living force even though the RPF as a political factor has declined sharply.

Territorial Politics

Strangely enough, the inhabitants of this poor, vast, underdeveloped, and artificially constructed territory have become intensely political-minded over the brief span of 14 years.[5] At first, the European members of the Union Démocratique Tchadienne (of the RPF), supported by an administration of the same political complexion, had things pretty much their own way. But beginning in 1953, the Negro element belonging to the opposition parties came increasingly to the fore. This did not necessarily mean that all the other individuals or groups went into eclipse: Europeans have continued to play an important, though now subsidiary, role. The chiefs have gradually come to realize that the decisions reached by the territorial assembly affect their prestige and revenues. They now regard membership in that body as more than a pretext to visit Fort Lamy periodically and be well paid for it. Since 1955 the political tempo has speeded up, tensions have increased, parties have organized branches even in the northern oases, and politics have now permeated every stratum of Tchadian society.

In October 1945 the first elections took place in Tchad for deputies to be sent to the National Assembly. The first-college candidate (shared with Oubangui's European electorate) was René Malbrant, an ultraconservative

French member of the RPF widely respected for his role in the local resistance movement. He was duly elected, and continued to sit in the National Assembly until the dual college was abolished late in 1956, although his record of persistent obstructionism to such liberal measures as the Overseas Labor Code, the Municipal Reform Bill, and the single-college proposal ran increasingly counter to the temper of the times.

The RPF's local branch, the Union Démocratique Tchadienne (UDT) succeeded in getting another of its members, Colonel de Boissoudy, elected as deputy in 1945, by the second college, but he failed to win a renewal of his mandate in the November 1946 election. By that time, the number of voters in Tchad had more than doubled, rising from 7,907 to 17,598. More important, a local branch of the RDA had been organized at Moundou in the interval, as the Parti Progressiste Tchadien (PPT), and it had rapidly gained popularity. The man responsible for its growth was an Antilles Negro, Gabriel Lisette, who had studied in Paris and married a Frenchwoman. After graduating from the Ecole Coloniale, he served as an administrator successively in Morocco, Moyen-Congo, and Tchad, and, like all the other local candidates, he had been prominent in the Free French movement. Comparatively unknown at the time of his election to the National Assembly,[6] Lisette sprang into prominence just at the time when the RDA was in its most radical phase. Inevitably this drew down on him the hostility of the local RPF and the administration at the same time that it won him the votes of the Negro elite of southwestern Tchad, especially the Sara évolués.

Although Lisette followed Houphouët's change-over to a more moderate line in 1950 and eventually advocated collaboration with the administration, French high officialdom exerted all the pressure at its command to bring about his defeat when he ran for re-election as deputy on June 17, 1951. At that time, Béchir Sow and Sou Quatre, both African members of the UDT, were elected and Lisette, though he continued to be an active member in the territorial assembly, did not reappear on the Paris political scene until he was again elected a deputy in 1956.

In Tchad the years 1947 to 1953 were lean ones for all the local politicians who were not members of the UDT, and the administration's hand weighed heavily on any functionary who actively showed PPT proclivities. In 1947 and again in 1948, the RDA deputies in the National Assembly vainly queried the Minister of Overseas France as to why some regions in Tchad were being "reorganized for political reasons" and why officials belonging to the PPT had been either dismissed or transferred to obscure posts.[7] The government of course denied that any such changes had been politically motivated. In any case, penalized African functionaries had no effective means of redress and found little support in the territorial assembly, which was then a thoroughly docile body. In fact, on the ground that Tchad was politically inexperienced, a majority of its members voted in 1947 for maintaining the double electoral college—a stand diametrically opposed to that of all other similar bodies in French Black Africa at the time. Of Tchad's 30-member assembly, 10 were Europeans, and 27 of the total membership belonged to the UDT. Most of the African members were chiefs, sultans, or Notables, and not unnaturally they offered no opposition to the government's program. This was not true of the PPT members, but in the first assembly their group numbered only three.

Elections held in March 1952 for renewal of the assembly netted the PPT a gain of one seat, but the total membership in this body had meanwhile been raised to 45. The UDT, whose name had been changed to Action Sociale Tchadienne (AST), now held 33 seats, and the remaining 8 members were either independents or belonged to the UDSR (linked to Pleven's group in the National Assembly), or to the small Parti Socialiste Indépendant du Tchad, led by a Muslim merchant, Ahmed Koulamallah. Until 1948, Koulamallah had worked with the PPT, but Lisette's radicalism at that time caused the former to break away and form his own group, which he soon affiliated with the Metropolitan SFIO. The outstanding Independent in the new assembly was a long-time European resident of Tchad, André Kieffer, who was a passionate defender of the Tchadian cotton grower, and a thorn in the flesh of the AST, the local administration, and Lisette. A rugged individualist and easily the most aggressive and controversial figure of the 1952 assembly, Kieffer later joined the Union Démocratique Indépendante du Tchad (UDIT). At first, however, he functioned as a one-man opposition party, attacking the AST's monopoly of the presidency of the assembly and the chairmanships of its key commissions. Though by 1952 the AST majority had been cut down, the party still enjoyed the administration's full support, which it continued to receive during the five-year incumbency of Governor Colombani.

Shortly after the March 1952 elections for membership in the second territorial assembly, violence broke out in the Logone region. The government held that this was provoked by the PPT in revenge for its defeat in a region which it had theretofore regarded as its stronghold. But the PPT and its left-wing supporters in French parliamentary bodies[8] insisted that the local population had simply shown its indignation at the electoral frauds perpetrated by the administration. One incident involved the arrest or dismissal of local Notables or functionaries who had dared to vote against the UDT. A graver incident, also in April 1952, was what the radicals came to call the "massacre of Bébalem." A series of confused events in this village led to the firing of shots at a seated and unarmed crowd that had gathered in front of the local administrator's office to protest the arrest of one of their number who had reportedly opposed an exaction of the local canton chief. Neither at the time nor during the trial in the following December of 22 Bébalem villagers accused of armed revolt was there much publicity in the press. Later, contradictory statements were issued as to the number of killed and wounded, and even in regard to the sentences passed on those found guilty by the criminal court of Fort Lamy. Basically the incident was probably personal rather than political, but the disorder attending it could certainly be laid to the atmosphere of tension stirred up by the recent elections. At all events, the tragic happenings at Bébalem were utilized by a wide variety of malcontents to attack—variously—the administration, rival political leaders, and even the Protestant missions.[9]

Taken by themselves, neither the foregoing incidents nor Kieffer's persistent attacks on the AST majority and the administration would probably have altered the political situation in Tchad, but they were somewhat responsible for the marked change that occurred late in 1953. What then brought matters to a head and fundamentally revised political alignments was the election in October 1953 to the French Union Assembly of a former governor of Tchad, Rogué. During his nearly five years' tenure of office just after the war, Rogué made an indelible impression on the territory as a fantastically energetic administrator who ruled Europeans and Africans alike with a firm hand. His strong personality had made probably more enemies than supporters in both camps, for he alienated conservative and left-wing elements alike. The AST strongly opposed his candidacy, as did the Colombani administration. The PPT, perhaps influenced by one of its leaders, François Tombalbaye, who had reportedly been dismissed from his post during Rogué's governorship, even chose to support the latter's AST rival. Since this meant voting for Laurin, an arch-conservative Frenchman, Koulamallah for the second time broke with Lisette and re-formed his own socialist party. (In 1952, Koulamallah and Lisette —after Lisette's defeat in the National Assembly elections—had got together again in their mutual opposition to the administration.) This election also marked the decline of the Union de la Défense des Interêts Tchadiens, a splinter group of the RPF which Béchir Sow had formed shortly before, and with it the fading from the Tchad political scene of Béchir Sow and another RPF African parliamentarian, Ibrahim Babikir. It also brought into being the Union Démocratique Indépendante du Tchad (UDIT), with an able mulatto merchant, Jean Baptiste, as its leader and Rogué[10] as its adviser, and to this new group gravitated Kieffer and some former members of the UDSR. A short-lived communist party composed of PPT radicals who refused to go along with Lisette's more moderate policies also came into existence at about this time. But soon one of its leaders, Jean Charlot, rejoined the PPT and the other, Malah Pleven, entered the ranks of Koulamallah's socialists.

All in all, these confusing and amoeba-like developments served to strengthen the opposition forces in the assembly. Africans took an increasing part in the debates, which grew more personal and acrimonious as the months passed. Kieffer's attacks on William Tardrew as a "dictatorial" president of the assembly and on the administration as "perpetrator of electoral frauds" grew in virulence. In the midst of two such diatribes, Secretary-General Bergerol left the assembly hall, and, in March 1955, Governor Colombani also quit the hall pointedly, before Kieffer could make a reply to the gubernatorial address opening the assembly session. Even Béchir Sow rose to support Kieffer's denunciation of the political pressure that the administration continued to exert upon up-country officials as well as on assemblymen, and also Kieffer's charge that AST members were involved in a current financial scandal.[11] The changed temper of the assembly was shown by its strong vote in favor of instituting the single college for elections under the municipal-reform bill[12] that finally became law in December 1955. Considering the amount of time devoted to sheer obstructionism, it is no wonder that at the expiration of their mandate in March 1957, the members of this assembly could not look back upon any remarkable accomplishments. They had indeed managed to clear up a bad financial situation, gain more control over the civil services, and promote primary and technical education. But little constructive work had been done, and many of their resolutions had been ignored by the administration, particularly those favoring a less cumbersome governmental machinery.

The campaign preceding the National Assembly elections of January 2, 1956, was an unusually brief and hectic one. Shortly before it opened, Koulamallah changed the name of his party to Mouvement Socialiste Africain (MSA) and at the same time stressed its direct ties with the Metropolitan SFIO.[13] But a fraction of his erstwhile followers continued to call themselves the Parti Socialiste Indépendant du Tchad and later moved into the PPT-UDSR orbit. For the electoral campaign, Lisette's forces organized the Sara regions so thoroughly that the PPT won a decisive victory in the south, particularly in the Mayo-Kebbi, Logone, and Moyen-Chari regions, where voter participation reached 79 per cent compared with 59 per cent in the other parts of Tchad. Two of the outstanding members of the 1952 assembly were defeated. One was Kieffer, who toured his constituency in a jeep and used loudspeakers to broadcast military music and his own speeches translated into the local dialects.[14] The other was Béchir Sow, who—like Kieffer—subsequently retired from political life. The AST, however, did succeed in bringing off the election of two of its members, Arabi el-Goni and the perennial René Malbrant.

The impressive comeback of Lisette after five years in the political wilderness was the outstanding feature of the 1956 campaign and foreshadowed the end of the AST's reign in the territorial assembly. The AST leaders had failed to organize their party in depth throughout the territory. Apparently they had counted overmuch on the support of the administration and of the chiefs, whose influence, they seemingly did not realize, had been gravely weakened by the recent modifications of their status (see pp. 74–78). Lisette's victory in the January 1956 elections was followed 11 months later by his election as mayor of Fort Lamy, with control over 18 of the 33 seats on its municipal council.

The territorial-assembly elections of March 31, 1957, simply confirmed the ascendancy of the PPT and the decline of the AST. Of the AST's former members, 23 were not re-elected, and the party won only 9 of a total of 65 seats. By that time, the abolition of the double college had cut down the influence of the European conservatives. And the tripling of the electorate (which had risen from 308,000 in 1952 to 1,196,000) had now given the younger generation of Tchadians their first chance to express their aspirations. For this campaign the PPT teamed up with the UDIT and some UDSR members to form an Entente Républicaine. Everywhere except in Batha and Ouaddaï, where the chiefs' authority was still strong, the PPT and its allies campaigned against the AST as the "party of the white men and of the chiefs." The new Entente did not include the MSA, whose leader Koulamallah was defeated by a slim margin in his traditional fief, the Chari-Baguirmi. The victors won a comfortable majority in the new assembly, and an African, Senator Sahoulba Gontchomé, was for the first time elected its president. This did not, however, denote the elimination of either the chiefs or Europeans as influential members of the assembly, though the latter no longer dominated its key committees. All the major parties continued to have among their members both chiefs and Europeans.[15] Furthermore, a new and more liberal governor, René Troadec, had replaced Colombani in late 1956, and the administration's more neutral stand in the 1957 elections may well have accounted for the exceptional calm in which they took place.

The Entente Républicaine, which had served its purpose well during the electoral campaign, did not long survive the establishment of Tchad's first government council. Lisette, as leader of the Entente's dominant party, became premier, and in his ten-man cabinet he gave portfolios to four non-PPT members. Jean Baptiste, leader of the UDIT, was named Minister of the Plan; two European members of the UDSR, André Vazel and Fernand Sallet, were made Ministers of the Interior and Public Works respectively; and an African leader of the AST, Djibrine Kherallah, became Minister of Finance. From the outset the new assembly ran into difficulties, both procedural and political. So many of its members were newcomers and inexperienced in parliamentary procedure that debates became confused and were endlessly prolonged. Though the administration was reproached, as in the past, for having failed to document the assembly properly and for its extravagant and top-heavy structure, it was no longer the assemblymen's main target. The struggle now became an inter-African and highly partisan one, in which grievances against a less powerful administration were relegated to the background and those against the PPT-dominated government came to the fore.

The first issue on which horns were locked was that of forming political groups inside the assembly. Advocates of their formation argued that party discipline would operate to put an end to the anarchic and interminable debates. Opponents retorted that young assemblymen should be given the chance to speak at will and thus serve their political apprenticeship. A more telling argument used by those opposed to party grouping in the assembly was that it would deepen the discord between the southwestern and northeastern members, which was already becoming apparent. Four months passed before an affirmative decision was reached by the assembly, and events of the last months of 1957 soon justified the fears of those opposed to party organization.

In November, after the PPT and the UDSR had formed one intergroup and the UDIT had similarly joined forces with the AST, friction arose over the allotment of seats in the Finance Committee. No sooner was this smoothed over than fresh trouble developed in January 1958, concerning Tchad's representation in the Organisation Commune des Régions Sahariennes (OCRS) (see p. 466). The difficulty did not relate to Tchad's placing 45,000 square kilometers of the BET region within the OCRS's operational zone—the assembly was only too pleased by the prospect of getting outside aid for developing that area—but as to which party's members should be selected to represent the territory. Sharp words were exchanged between Jean Baptiste and Lisette because the latter insisted on passing over the UDIT assemblyman who represented the BET region. Eventually, two PPT members were chosen by the assembly majority, one of them (Ahmed Mangué) a Sara from Moundou and the other (Moussa Yayami) a Kanadja from Largeau. Their only apparent qualification was that they had been loyal PPT wheelhorses.[16] Throughout 1958 similar dissension arose in regard to other government appointments, especially those regarded as political plums. The most flagrant and amusing case was the government's sending to Paris, as Tchad's representatives at the Congrès Mondial des Mères, a local spinster and an unmarried mother who had organized the local women's branches of the PPT.[17] Such practices were so strongly denounced by the UDIT-AST opposition that Jean Baptiste was relieved of his post as Minister of the Plan.

More unsettling to the Lisette government than the UDIT's defection was the growing opposition by Koulamallah and the MSA to the PPT spoils system and its politicization of the civil service. Though Koulamallah was not a member of the 1957 assembly and had taken little part in the debates of the 1952 body, both the administration and the PPT considered him a dangerous man. As local head of the Muslim Tidjaniya sect, a descendant of the Arab chieftains of Baguirmi, and a merchant with many business and family ties in Sudan, he not only was regarded as a personal enemy of Lisette but also was rumored to be anti-French and a supporter of the Arab League. Twice he had broken with Lisette after brief periods of cooperation with him. Antagonism became acute between the two men after Koulamallah's narrow defeat in the March 1957 elections through what he asserted had been unfair PPT electioneering practices in Chari-Baguirmi. The Council of State eventually confirmed Koulamallah's charges and ordered the holding of fresh elections in that region on June 1, 1958. This step deeply perturbed Lisette, for an MSA victory in Chari-Baguirmi would deprive his government of seven seats that he needed for its support.

Two apparently unrelated events contributed to raise the temperature of the April–May 1958 electoral campaign in Chari-Baguirmi. In August 1957 a savage fight took place in one of its cantons, Massakory, between its sedentary Arabs and the Peulh nomads who were passing through that area with their herds on the way to pastures in the north. In a two-day battle, 31 were killed and 41 wounded, and even more blood might have been shed had it not been for the intervention of the district chief and of Koulamallah, who settled the dispute in conformity with customary law. Next, in April 1958, at the village of Am Tanabo, about 100 kilometers east of Fort Lamy, another pitched battle between the same elements left 19 dead on the field. Koulamallah, as spokesman for the Baguirmi Arabs, blamed the PPT government for not maintaining order, to which Lisette retorted that the socialists were trying to give these incidents a false political coloration. There is little doubt that both the PPT and the MSA used every means at their disposal to win over the Baguirmi electorate, and violence continued to prevail in their relationship there for some time after Koulamallah won the election.

In consequence of the MSA's victory in Chari-Baguirmi, another inter-group emerged in the assembly—the Union Socialiste Tchadienne (UST), which now controlled 26 seats against the 39 held by the PPT and the UDSR together. The UST was composed of the MSA, the AST, and the UDIT, the adherence of the last-mentioned party being due, it was said, to the influence of its European adviser, Rogué, long a friend of tradition-alist Islam. When Koulamallah triumphantly resumed his seat in the assembly, his entry was greeted by tumultuous applause from the gallery. In fact, so vociferous and rowdy did the public spectators become when-ever Koulamallah rose to speak that the sessions had to be suspended several times. Such "participation" by party followers in the meetings of the assembly was unprecedented, and it foreshadowed the organized mob action that became a crucial factor in the political crises of November 1958 and January 1959 (see below).

The changed balance of party forces in the assembly incited the UST in June 1958 to demand the resignation of the Minister of the Interior, André Vazel, who had headed the defeated PPT candidates in Chari-Baguirmi. Lisette refused to comply, but he did offer the UST wider representation on the assembly committees and a portfolio or two. These sops were promptly rejected by the UST as inadequate, and it announced, on June 30, that it would withdraw all its members from assembly com-mittees and enter into formal opposition to the government's program. The immediate effectiveness of this move, however, was vitiated by the intrusion of external events on Tchad's political horizon during the ensuing four months.

How Tchad would vote in the September 28 referendum and what its future relations would be with the other AEF territories became such burning questions of the hour that for a time they even submerged partisan politics. De Gaulle's brief stopover at Fort Lamy on the first leg of his African tour in August 1958 rekindled Tchad's Gaullist fervor but did nothing to revive the AST as a political force. The summer of 1958 proved to be a busy and trying time for Lisette, for he had to operate simultaneously on two different levels. In the National Assembly, he had always been more absorbed by his duties as a spokesman for the RDA than by those of a territorial deputy, and now as one of Houphouët's right-hand men he became involved in his chief's struggle with Sekou Touré. At the same time, as premier of the Tchad government, he had to cope with an aggressive and powerful minority in the assembly. To strengthen his shaky majority there, he came increasingly to depend on the support of a newly formed political group, the Groupement des Indépendants et Ruraux du Tchad (GIRT), which controlled nine seats in the assembly. The leader of GIRT was none other than Senator Sahoulba, and its members were mainly traditional chiefs whose loyalty to Lisette was far from certain. Later on, in January 1959, it was the defection of GIRT that caused Lisette's government to be overthrown.

In the meantime, the warring parties declared a political truce during the weeks immediately preceding the referendum. Actually, September 28 came and went without causing a ripple of discord: all the territory's political leaders were agreed that Tchad should enter the Community, and the electorate turned in a 98.7 per cent affirmative vote. Disagreement did arise, however, as to the role that the territory should choose in the Community. Lisette wanted Tchad to become a member state, whereas Koulamallah (and Sahoulba) inclined toward maintaining its existing status as an overseas territory. On August 23, Koulamallah had declared in the name of the MSA that "our vocation is independence, but it would be of no benefit for us to obtain it right now. Independence would mean a multiplication of the burdens that the people of Tchad would have to bear. The MSA favors maintaining the status quo until independence is achieved."[18] But Koulamallah's stand was not adamant, and on a trip to Paris soon afterward he was apparently persuaded by his SFIO friends to change it and came out in favor of a member-state status. Thus there was no opposition on November 28 when the assembly proclaimed the Republic of Tchad to be a member of the Community and ready to cooperate in some new grouping with the other AEF territories. In fact, the assembly showed little interest in the various proposals made by Boganda, Youlou, and Aubame as to the form that such future cooperation should take. And Lisette, faithful to Houphouët's stand against a strong federal executive, was left pretty much of a free hand to deal with this matter. The prime concern of all the local political parties was that Tchad should continue to receive French financial and technical aid. Secondarily, they wanted to ensure harmony with their AEF neighbors, on whose good-will the economy of Tchad perforce depended. On January 17, 1959, the republic agreed to join a customs and transport union with the other former AEF territories.

If such weighty questions as Tchad's future relations with France and the other AEF territories were settled without a hitch, not so the purely local problem as to which party should control the government. While Lisette was preoccupied with high-level negotiations, the UST opposition was busily engaged in creating a situation intended to force the dissolution of the assembly and the holding of new elections. Twice in November, troops had to be used to disperse crowds bent on forcibly preventing meetings of the assembly. Although Lisette was consequently persuaded to promise fresh elections early in 1959 and to take some opposition members into his government, the UST determined to oust him as soon as possible. The decision of GIRT to join the UST brought into being still another political formation, the Mouvement Populaire Tchadien (MPT), which then controlled 34 of the 65 seats in the assembly. Taking advantage of Lisette's absence in Paris, where he was attending the first executive meeting of the Community, the nine MPT ministers resigned from the government, which was duly overthrown on February 10, 1959, by 30 votes to 17.

Sahoulba then formed a government composed solely of former opposition members. But a month later he was compelled to resign after the announcement of a working agreement between the MSA and the PPT. Then Koulamallah, on March 13, tried his hand at forming a union government in which all parties were represented, but it survived only 11 days. On March 25, the fourth provisional government of the four-month-old Republic of Tchad was installed, with François Tombalbaye as premier. Tombalbaye—a trade-union leader, stalwart member of the PPT since its beginnings, and Grand Councilor for Tchad—had long represented Moyen-Chari in the assembly. Although he did not persuade the MSA to join his cabinet, Tombalbaye at least obtained a pledge from Koulamallah that he would not "systematically oppose" the new government. On the heels of the assembly's vote of confidence, Tombalbaye made an emphatic appeal for unity, saying:

> For the past two months, we have lost valuable time in playing politics. Our energies and the country's vitality have been dissipated, work has slowed down, disorder has entered the administration. The prestige that we won outside of Tchad by 18 months of constructive work has evaporated. We have become the living example of irresponsibility and instability. It is time for us to unite.[19]

After delivering this well-merited scolding, Tombalbaye proceeded to submit to the assembly a constitution for the Republic of Tchad. One of its chief aims was to make future governments more stable and the next assembly more responsible.[20] Tombalbaye next took steps to control the movements of ministers during an electoral campaign so as to avoid any repetition of those "past incidents that have undermined the public's confidence in the government."

That these precautions were effective seems evidenced by the unusual calm in which the elections of May 31 took place. The first legislative assembly was to have a total of 85 seats, which meant one deputy for every 30,000 inhabitants. All the familiar parties put up candidates, but this campaign brought together strange political bedfellows. In Guera, local alliances were formed between the AST and the PPT and between the UDIT and the MSA; and in Batha, the GIRT and the PPT made common cause. Surprisingly enough, the PPT gained an early lead, coming out ahead even in the Mayo-Kebbi, the GIRT's stronghold, where Sahoulba was defeated, and in Kanem, where the MSA had a big following. In all, the PPT won

57 of the 85 seats in the new legislature and 68 per cent of the votes cast, hence it was assured of a working majority. Lisette's comeback this time was even more remarkable than his victory in 1956.

For more than a year, observers had been commenting on the decline of Lisette's popularity. Because he was a thoroughly Gallicized Antilles Negro, it was said that his days were numbered as a political leader of Africans, who had come to regard him as an outsider. The fact that he was a Catholic and that his main support came from the Sara Christians and pagans was thought to have made him *persona non grata* with the northeastern Muslims in general and the chiefs in particular. The MSA victory in Chari-Baguirmi in June 1958 was taken to be the beginning of Lisette's downfall, and the defection of supporters from both the more conservative elements (GIRT) and the radical fringe (Jeunesses Progressistes) later that year was expected to give him the *coup de grâce*.

A report written in April 1958 by a visiting French official[21] described Lisette's party as that of the "little people" and Koulamallah's as the party of the chiefs and the Arab League. Both leaders sharply objected to this description of their organizations.[22] In a verbal exchange with Lisette in the territorial assembly, Koulamallah said:

> A few of us here guide the Arab elite in Tchad. It is said that we are an FLN and that we are representatives of Nasser. Time will show the truth. . . . The French are here to build up the country. As for me, I work for my country and I am above all a Tchadian and an African. . . . I speak in the name of the MSA . . . a movement affiliated with the Metropolitan Socialist party, and it collaborates with other parties here.

And on July 1 he told the assembly that the press had labeled him a communist because on two occasions he had worked with Lisette, but that he had never replied to this accusation.

> This failure to answer such charges was not due to inability. If I speak French badly, I know that I possess another culture which enables me to reply to all who criticize me. . . . It has been said in a report that I am a member of the Arab League and that my party is that of the chiefs. . . . I am going to Paris to complain against the author of this report and those who gave him such information. . . . I am French and I will continue to say so. And it is not out of fear that I say I am French.

To the authors, who talked with Koulamallah in his modest dwelling in Fort Lamy in October 1958, he repeated many of the foregoing assertions, and their tone was sincere. Although Koulamallah's French is defective, it is understandable, and he appeared genuinely to admire France and especially General de Gaulle. Above all, he seemed to be a thoroughly indigenous product, representative of the Muslim Arab aristocracy. Yet Koulamallah told us that he had alienated a number of the chiefs, including his own relatives, by his socialistic views, and his generosity to the many Africans who haunt his doorstep is proverbial in Tchad. Koulamallah's record, unlike that of some other Tchadian politicians, is not marred by nepotism and self-seeking, and his reputation for disinterestedness and frankness is one of his strongest political assets.

The Tchad political picture is extraordinarily complex not only because of the number and instability of its political parties but also because none of them embodies any single dominant trend. Actually Koulamallah no more represents only the chiefs than does Lisette the "little people": both of their parties include chiefs and members of the urban elite. Nor is there any very distinct geographical division as to their following, though among Lisette's supporters are to be found many Sara pagans or Christians while Koulamallah's partisans come mainly from the Muslim elements, especially the Arabs of Baguirmi. The basic economic, social, and ethnic cleavage that exists between the Negro farmers of the south and the "white" herders of the north is not truly reflected in Tchad's present party alignments. A basic difficulty is that Tchad's economic evolution has not kept pace with its political development.

Despite certain conspicuous differences between them, Lisette and Koulamallah do not stand very far apart politically. Both want greater local autonomy and also the continuance of close ties with France until Tchad can build up the cadres it sorely lacks and the Tchadians can forget their former slave-master relationship and live peacefully together without requiring European arbitration. Lisette is indeed suave, lucid, and intelligent, and he possesses a cosmopolitan background and contacts which Koulamallah lacks. Though Koulamallah is more truly "indigenous" than Lisette, his short tenure as premier suggests that he does not have Lisette's diplomatic or organizing ability.

Lisette may well have learned the lesson of his defeat in January 1959 and have become less obviously partisan in his appointments and policies.[28] Whether the forces who oppose him have learned how to pursue a long-term united policy is debatable. At Tchad's present stage of development, Lisette appears to be indispensable. And when the time comes for a truly local leader to replace him, in all likelihood Lisette will be useful to the RDA in another capacity. At the RDA congress at Bamako in September 1957, Lisette was elected a vice-president of that movement, and in AEF he remains the outstanding advocate of Houphouët's policies for French Black Africa. His present over-all objective appears to be that of finding a compromise between those leaders who want some form of federation among the new countries of the former AEF and their opponents who desire closer, individual ties with France. Lisette is credited in some quarters with having initiated the four-premier meetings which have preserved certain aspects of the federation's unity.

On the local Tchadian scene, it is imperative that he come to some modus vivendi with his political opponents. Efforts by the PPT during the summer of 1959 to bring about unity among Tchad's political factions not only came to naught, but were accompanied by outbreaks of fighting between partisans of the GIRT and the PPT at Bongor (in June) and between members of the MSA and the PPT at Fort Lamy (in July). And in

September Koulamallah announced that the MSA would remain an opposition party. If any real unity is to be attained in this sprawling country, and among its heterogeneous peoples, Lisette and Koulamallah will have to work together to that end.

The Territorial Economy

The Plan

It is sometimes said that Tchad's real assets consist more of its large and industrious population than of its cotton and livestock, and that this territory's main liabilities are its great distance from the sea (2,500 kilometers from Pointe Noire, 1,500 from Douala), lack of internal communications, and vast unproductive area in the north. Its resources and handicaps are much the same as those of Oubangui, but on a bigger scale. Tchad is the largest of the territories and contains half of the federation's population—double the number to be found in Oubangui and four times greater than that of Gabon or Moyen-Congo—but its contributions to AEF's economy have not been proportionate.

Semihumid in the south, it grows progressively drier as one goes north until it becomes total desert in the BET region. The eastern part of Tchad lies in the sahel zone, whereas in the west the valleys of the Logone and the Chari are inundated for nearly half the year. The development of Tchad's Mesopotamia, as this last-mentioned region is often called, is the only large-scale project now being carried out in the territory, and its purpose is to increase rice and cotton production. The climate and soil of Tchad preclude any possibility of growing rich export crops there, such as cocoa, coffee, bananas, or oil palms, and no great mineral wealth has been discovered as yet, though surveys recently being made in Tibesti may disclose exploitable uranium deposits. Because of the immensity of this country and its location off the main routes of continental Africa, its industrial potential is limited, capital investment is discouraged, almost insuperable transportation problems exist, and production and living costs are multiplied.

Tchad's present economy is founded exclusively on agriculture and animal husbandry, and all the plans drawn up for the territory have been placed within their relatively narrow frame of reference. Almost the totality of the subsidies granted Tchad by France and the federal budget have gone to increase the territory's two main exports—cotton and meat—and little has been done to raise local living standards by expanding the internal market. Such revenues as its population enjoys—and the Tchadians' purchasing power has been slowly growing—derive from the expansion of its foreign trade, and this has been made possible solely by the investment there of French public funds. The concern to improve Tchad's means of transport, externally and internally, and to create new sources of water has motivated the planners for this territory's development. Because it was wholeheartedly conceded that the problem of transport dominated all others, one finds none of the same disagreements as in the other AEF territories as to the stress laid by the first Plan on improvement of the infra-structure. From the outset the main difficulties encountered by FIDES' operations in Tchad have been practical ones.

Two plans for Tchad were drawn up at about the same time, one by the territorial government and the other by the government-general, but as a result of the difficulties of communication between Fort Lamy and Brazzaville, they were not coordinated. Because the territorial program was delayed in reaching the federal capital, the Grand Council, in September 1948, approved that drawn up by the government-general, and Tchad was the gainer thereby. Curiously enough, the latter had allocated more funds to Tchad than the territory had asked for.[24] The authors of both programs were in substantial agreement that one-third of FIDES' credits should go to social equipment and to improving the means for shipping out the territory's exports, but they disagreed as to the sums to be spent respectively on road-building and on animal husbandry. It took time for the FIDES directorate to iron out this difference of opinion, but Tchad's total lack of the essential basic equipment and labor force would in any case have delayed execution of its Plan.

In 1950, when at long last the technical conditions required for the Plan's operations had been fulfilled, new practical obstacles reared their heads. Vital documents had somehow gone astray between Fort Lamy, Paris, and Brazzaville, and when they were found it was discovered that some of the construction already started had not been authorized.[25] Worse still, the initial appropriations[26] had later been cut, and at the same time the cost of equipment materials had greatly risen. In the interval, moreover, misgivings as to the wisdom of undertaking certain projects (such as the big Fort Lamy hospital) had prompted another revision of the Plan, the work and money that had gone into making many preliminary studies was wasted, and confusion reigned. At the end of the year the French Union Assembly was told by a Tchad representative[27] that no headway had yet been made on the pastoral-hydraulics program and that not one kilometer of road had thus far been built in the territory. A year later Deputy Malbrant, just returned from a trip to Tchad, reported to the National Assembly that execution of the Plan there had been stopped before getting well started, and he blamed this on the lack of preparatory studies, poor administration, and the cut in FIDES credits. Because the money had run out, matériel destined for Tchad had been diverted to Pointe Noire, planeloads of technicians had been sent back to France, and a thousand African laborers had been dismissed at Fort Lamy.[28]

Actually, Tchad's disillusioned and disgruntled parliamentarians had painted an over-black picture. Under Tchad's first Plan (which was extended into 1954 because of the delays in carrying it out), the territory was allocated 3,705 million CFA francs. Of this sum, 672 million was spent on improving the rural economy (agriculture and forestry), 425 million for animal husbandry, and 2,510 million for building roads and airfields.[29] With these funds work was continued or begun on a host of operations,

including the Logone valley project, experimental cotton farms, a reforestation program, construction of a laboratory and abattoir at Farcha, and
the like. With the 543 million assigned to social-development works, hospitals were built or enlarged in Tchad's main towns, colleges were constructed at Abéché and at the territorial capital, and work was done on
Fort Lamy's water and lighting systems. This Plan's worst failure was its
road-building program, on which huge sums had been spent with very
meager results. Its accomplishments were real and constructive, but they
were only a drop in the bucket of Tchad's almost limitless needs.

In view of Tchad's underdevelopment and handicaps, the division of
funds between AEF's territories under the second four-year Plan seemed
to its assemblymen shockingly unfair. Up to the end of 1951, when this
Plan was prepared, Tchad and Oubangui together had received no more
than one-fourth of the credits allotted them by the Grand Council. Their
assemblymen had been given to understand that under the first Plan, priority must be given to the coastal areas so as to facilitate the importation
of equipment goods, and that the northern territories would receive their
due later on.[30] But under the 1952–56 Plan, Tchad and Oubangui were
accorded no more favorable treatment, with the result that Tchad's two
most neglected areas, the BET and Ouaddaï, remained without the prospect
of development for another four years. To be sure, there already had been
some improvement in the BET's social equipment, but its population of
fewer than 50,000 was reported to be "discouraged" because FIDES had
no project to build more water wells there or to increase the agricultural
output of their oases.[31] As to Ouaddaï, its 460,000 inhabitants were said
to be even worse off: they could not live by locally produced meat and
millet alone, and needed help to develop exports of livestock, peanuts,
and gum arabic. Worst of all, in the eyes of the Tchadian elite, was the
lack of progress toward solving the territory's external transport problem.
In 1948 it had been decided at Brazzaville to give priority to the Benoué
route, but little had been done to make this a reality. No decision at all
had been reached on the long-mooted question as to whether Tchad's
future railroad should be built to Douala or to Bangui.

The first year of the second Plan, 1952, also brought the trade recession
that was felt throughout AEF, but it affected Tchad less adversely than
any of the other territories. Tchad's economy was too rudimentary to
feel as great a shock, and Metropolitan and federal subsidies maintained
the price paid to the territory's cotton farmers. The local situation worsened in 1953 owing to a fall in the world price for cotton, but Tchad's
financial position improved in 1954 and again in 1955. By 1955 its economy
had become more diversified, exports and imports had revived, its pastoral-
hydraulics program was beginning to show results, and its system of communications had been improved. Under the next Plan, 27.5 per cent of
all the funds granted by FIDES to AEF were allocated to Tchad, and at
the same time its assembly acquired more control over their distribution.[32]

The changes wrought in Tchad's governmental structure did not imme-

diately alter the territory's economic policies. Despite their political instability, the new African governments have simply carried forward earlier
plans to intensify and diversify the production of Tchad's established exports, and the only new items on the agenda are a proposal to increase output
for domestic consumption[33] and one to develop the BET region with funds
placed at Tchad's disposal by the OCRS.

Finances

Until 1952 Tchad had the most flourishing budget of any of the AEF
territories, and even a small self-financed equipment program. To be sure,
this comparatively favorable financial situation was in part due to subsidies,
for Tchad along with Moyen-Congo received the largest share (28 per cent)
of the federal rebates. It also resulted to some extent, however, from the
relatively large number of persons paying direct taxes and, above all, from
the expansion of its production of cotton—one of the federation's two main
exports. In 1952, nevertheless, Tchad, like the federation, found itself in
a precarious position. It had been living beyond its means without taking
into budgetary account the accumulation of past debts which, by the end
of that year, totaled 310 million CFA francs. Moreover, its revenues had
sharply declined with the fall in the price of cotton, personnel now absorbed
53 per cent of ordinary expenditures (compared with 36 per cent in 1948),
and Tchad had to begin paying interest to FIDES on an equipment program that had barely got under way in the territory.

Tchad was now forced to impose on itself what one of its assemblymen
described as "the regime of the great repentance." Its assembly reluctantly
voted to double the head tax, which already provided a larger proportion
of Tchad's revenues than was the case in any other territory. With the
aim of getting rid of the many parasitic unemployed who had swarmed into
the capital during the first postwar years, the rate of this tax in Fort Lamy
was set at 700 francs, double that prevailing in the rest of the territory,
except in the BET and Ouaddaï, where it was much lower. This exceptional treatment was due to the fact that the BET was almost devoid of
population and taxable produce, while Ouaddaï not only was impoverished
but was losing thousands of young men each year to adjacent Sudan. Elsewhere, theoretically, the tax rise was to affect equally the southern cotton
farmers and the northern herders. But in reality it fell harder on the former
than on the latter group. The sedentary population of the south could
not escape taxation as easily as did the nomads of the north, who dissimu-
lated the size of their herds and acquired untaxed income from the clandestine export of their livestock to Nigeria.[34]

By the end of 1953 the situation had distinctly improved, for the public
debt had been reduced to 200 million and there was even a surplus of 240
million in current revenues over expenditures.[35] The administration had
made economies and its tax collection had become more efficient. Because
the territorial assembly had "shown its willingness to make a greater fiscal
effort," Metropolitan France granted exceptional aid to Tchad's cotton

farmers and the federation allocated a larger subsidy to the territory. But when the administration called on the assemblymen in 1954 to wipe out the whole of Tchad's back debts, they responded with a chorus of reproaches. The administration was charged not only with extravagance in the past but with currently poor accountancy methods, delay in taking an accurate census of the human and animal population, and failure to restrain the chiefs' abusive collection of taxes.[36] The government spokesman in reply stressed the cost and time required to revise all of the tax rolls and assured the assembly that its financial accounts were now accurate and up to date. "We have at last finished with the nightmare of past debts," he said; "our reserve fund stands at over 66 million francs, and the only black spot that remains is the warehouse stocks that in large part are unsalable."[37]

The budget for 1955, which came to over 1,545 million CFA francs, was duly voted by the assemblymen, though it marked an increase of 41 million over that of the preceding year and included no equipment program. The members balked, however, at voting a new tax (taxe vicinale) proposed by the government. Not that the assembly was against the principle of this tax, whose proceeds were to be used wholly for development of the region in which they were collected, but it wanted an elected assembly to handle such funds and, above all, opposed any increase in the population's fiscal burdens. In its session of December 8, 1954, Ahmed Kotoko graphically described the already dire plight of the tax-ridden cotton farmers whom he represented:

> In the region from which I come, the peasant pays a head tax of 400 francs, plus 30 francs to the SIP, a total of 430 francs. Each taxpayer must either himself work on the upkeep of roads or, if he cannot leave his fields, pay for a substitute at a cost of 1,500 francs. Then each year men are recruited for the army, each canton supplying a fixed number of men, and if the peasant wants to hire a volunteer to replace him that means another 1,500 francs that he must pay. Next he must furnish bullocks to the Veterinary Service: for a young animal he is paid 500–700 francs when he could get 2,000–2,500 francs for it in the open market. He is also asked to supply the authorities with millet, at the rate of 100 kilograms per taxpayer. He is paid for this millet at the rate of 9 to 10 francs a kilogram when it sells normally for 15–17 francs, and this means an additional loss of 1,500 francs. All of the foregoing burdens cost him 5,000 francs. And, in addition, the canton chief steals from him God knows how much . . . Our peasants are exploited, and for all of these reasons we members of the Socialist party refuse to vote any tax increases. Rather, we ask that they be decreased, especially for the town of Fort Lamy.

Kotoko's plea proved effective, and in 1955, for the first time in Tchad's history, its taxes were reduced, by 50 francs in the cotton districts and 25 francs in the herding areas. This reduction, however, mainly applied to Fort Lamy, where the exceptionally high head tax had failed to eliminate the idle and unproductive elements of the population and where the sum-

mary methods used by the police in collecting taxes had often been denounced.[38] Indeed, expenditures for the security forces—who seemed
unable to check the growth of crime in Fort Lamy—were increasingly
criticized in the assembly because they were disproportionately large as
compared with those for more constructive services.[39] Despite the growth
in expenditures and reduction in taxes, the year ended with a small surplus
(6 million); the reserve fund had attained its statutory minimum of 80
million francs; Tchad made a 5-million-franc contribution to the newly
created FERDES; and the territory's own equipment program was revived,
with a backing of 40 million francs.

In 1956 Tchad's financial position continued to improve but the volume
of its budget also grew, rising from 1,492 million francs in 1955 to over
1,824 million. Personnel now accounted for 60 per cent of its expenditures
and operating costs for 22 per cent, the remaining 18 per cent going to
payments on the debt, maintenance, and the equipment program. Charges
for the Plan were also increasing while the shrinking investments made
by FIDES were mainly concentrated in the unremunerative field of social
works. Not only were revenues virtually stationary but they derived far
more from persons (76.5 per cent) than from the productive activity of
the territory (14 per cent). Moreover, it was becoming apparent that the
tax reductions recently voted were bringing little real relief to the population. Insufficient publicity had been given the new rates, and the chiefs
reportedly continued to collect the same sums as before and to pocket the
difference. Nevertheless, the assembly accepted a new tax on imported
alcoholic beverages and the principle of family allowances to wage earners.
Federal and Metropolitan subsidies came to the rescue and the year ended
with a 66-million-franc surplus.

The budget for 1957 showed the same characteristics as its predecessors.
Its volume increased by nearly 243 million francs, but expenditures continued to grow more rapidly than revenues and had to be devoted almost
wholly to operating costs. On the credit side of the ledger was a more
substantial subsidy voted by the Grand Council, the assumption by Metropolitan France of a larger share of personnel expenditures, and a better
yield from the taxes on animals, of which a more accurate census had
been taken. In 1958 the budget (2,520 million) took another and more
sensational leap upward, mostly because of the expenditures involved in
setting up the new government. During the debate on this budget the
assembly voted no changes in the fiscal picture beyond suppressing the
head tax for women and increasing that for men by 50 per cent. But as
the year wore on, additional income had to be sought from taxes (on sugar,
salt, textiles, cotton, tobacco, income, and the *chiffre d'affaires*) and the
territory had to negotiate two loans totaling about 350 million francs.[40]
At the same time, Tchad received larger grants than before from both the
federation and Metropolitan France, and also a windfall of 100 million
francs from the OCRS for a pastoral-hydraulics program in the BET region.

The draft budget for 1959 provided for larger allocations for the health and education services but also for a severe compression of general operating expenditures. It came to the unprecedented total of 2,938 million francs and was adopted only after two days of heated debate, in which confusion reigned because of the number of unknown factors in the current situation. Without waiting to learn how much France and the federation would grant that year to Tchad, the new Minister of Finance announced fiscal reforms in January 1959. The better to equalize the tax burden among the various elements of the population, he proposed lightening the duties on imports of prime necessity (salt, sugar, and flour) and increasing the export duty on cotton from 10 to 12 per cent.[41] On October 15, 1959, the name of the head tax was changed to that of "civic tax," apparently in the hope that the patriotic aura of the new name would make the collection of this tax easier and more rapid.

Transportation

Roads and road transport. Before World War II, no roads at all, properly speaking, existed in Tchad—only *pistes,* laid out by the military authorities. The most important of these connected Fort Lamy with Fort Archambault, and was usable in the dry season over a length of 580 kilometers. In the mid-1930's the *pistes* connecting Fort Lamy and Fort Archambault with Abéché and Adré were improved for the benefit of herders in the Ouaddaï region. On the eve of World War II a great many minor *pistes* were opened in western Tchad around Bongor and in the Fianga-Lai-Pala area in order to encourage cotton cultivation there. Since Cameroun was the natural zone of attraction for that whole region, the Tchad network was extended to Garoua on the Benoué river. Doba and Moundou, on the other hand, were oriented toward Bangui and the Federal Artery.

Road building and maintenance in southern and eastern Tchad were comparatively easy, for the soil and climatic conditions resembled those of Oubangui, but they were very difficult in the richest region of the whole territory—that of the Chari and Logone rivers. Because of their extensive seasonal inundations, motor traffic ceased there entirely between June and November, road-blocks being erected in order to prevent the rutting of *pistes* by heavy trucks. Another handicap to motorized transport in western Tchad has been the lack of permanent bridges. Rudimentary ferries must be used on all the main routes out of Fort Lamy, Fort Archambault, Bongor, Lai, and Moundou, and this means frequent transshipments because of the limit placed on the weight of trucks.

During World War II almost all the road work done in Tchad was concentrated on the Lamy-Archambault route, used by Leclerc's army for his desert campaign. This was transformed into an all-season road, and progress was also made on extending it to Moussoro and Faya-Largeau. Under the ten-year Plan, 3,180 million CFA francs were allocated for the improvement of 1,300 kilometers of Tchad's *pistes,* in conjunction with the Oubangui network. Those two territories received the lion's share of FIDES grants for road building in AEF, but even expenditures on such a scale did little to meet Tchad's basic needs, for road transport was more important there than in any other part of AEF. Furthermore, neither on the federal nor on the territorial level could agreement be reached as to which main projects would benefit by the funds available.

Aside from plane transport, this vast landlocked territory had four outlets through which it received and shipped out the merchandise on which its economy depended. The least important was the Abéché-Adré link to Sudan, which served only the impoverished Ouaddaï. Goods taking this route had to be carried in trucks across 1,150 kilometers of desert *pistes* to El Obeid, and from there 1,506 kilometers by rail to Port Sudan. For the three remaining outlets, the advantages were balanced by the disadvantages. First there was the Federal Artery, and the roads connecting Fort Lamy and Fort Archambault with Bangui were the best in the territory. But by this route, more than 3,000 kilometers separated Tchad's main towns from the seaport of Pointe Noire, the road and river portions of the Artery were not fully usable throughout the year, and successive transshipments added to transport cost and delays. Improvements since the war in the navigability of the Oubangui and in the equipment of the river boats and railroad have gradually speeded up the service on this itinerary, but transport is still slower and more expensive than on Tchad's alternative outlets to Cameroun and Nigeria. Partisans of the Federal Artery stress that it lies wholly inside French territory and that its use contributes to federal solidarity. They believe that its attraction could be greatly enhanced by building a railroad from Bangui to some point on the Chari or Logone, whence goods could be carried by water to Fort Lamy if the navigability of those rivers were somewhat improved.

There remained the Camerounian and Nigerian routes, the least costly of all Tchad's outlets, but they also involved road, river, or rail transport, or all three. Trucks could take either the road to Garoua or one of the two *pistes* that led to Maiduguri. At Garoua, merchandise could either be floated down the Benoué and the Niger to the sea, or be carried by truck 1,200 kilometers to Yaoundé and thence 300 kilometers by rail to Douala. The all-Cameroun route was more expensive but usually faster—the time factor being conditioned, however, by the degree of congestion on the Yaoundé railroad and at Douala port. Transport on the Benoué, which was both slower and cheaper, had two special handicaps—this river could be used only during the period of high water, the same three months that Tchad's roads were closed to traffic, and the capacity of Garoua port and the Benoué flotilla were limited to handling 30,000 tons a year. Another possibility was truck transport via Maiduguri and Kuru (Nguru), the terminus of the Nigerian railroad, and it was along this route that most of Tchad's imports and some of its cotton exports traveled. It was the cheapest of all, but shared with the Benoué route the drawback of being dependent on the capacity and willingness of British companies to carry Tchad's trade and of necessitating outlays of foreign currency estimated at the equivalent of about one billion CFA francs a year.

Inasmuch as no one of these itineraries was clearly superior to the others, the federal government decided to use its road-building funds to make improvements in all of them—with a slight preference accorded in 1948 to the Benoué route. In this the federal authorities received cooperation from the Cameroun administration in enlarging the ports of Garoua and Douala, and from the Nigerian government in increasing the capacity of the Benoué flotilla and in improving the roads around Maiduguri. Inside Tchad itself, the chief objective was to build bridges at former ferry points on the roads leading south and west from the main towns, and minor improvements were made on the *pistes* between those towns and Abéché. Between 1952 and 1956 FIDES granted the territory 1,198 million CFA francs for road work, and to this a small sum was added from Tchad's own resources.

Soon after the third Plan got under way in 1956, two new elements appeared on the scene that further confused the situation and forced another postponement of the decision as to which—if any—of Tchad's outlets were to be given a railroad. Until this time the only projects under consideration were those put forward by rival business interests in Douala and Bangui, both intent on capturing Tchad's foreign trade. Now the British decision, reached at long last, to prolong the Nigerian railroad to Maiduguri and its proposed construction of a trans-Sudan railroad from the Red Sea to Nigeria's network have given new aspects to an old problem that must be tackled by the African government of the Republic of Tchad. Though these recent developments have widened the range of Tchad's choice, they have also added political imponderables to a situation that proved too difficult to deal with even when it involved only economic considerations.

As for the human side of Tchad's transport problem—that of its truckers —it likewise began by being a purely economic matter and has recently taken on sociopolitical overtones.

The local custom of granting transport monopolies by long-term contract dates back to 1931, when the government granted to the Compagnie Française de l'Ouham-Nana a ten-year monopoly of its official business between Fort Lamy and Fort Archambault. The fact that this Dutch-owned firm was guaranteed the transport of a minimal annual tonnage at rates double those paid to local truckers angered many French colonists.[42] But criticism of the monopoly system did not prevent the grant of a similar contract at about the same period by COTONFRAN, Tchad's sole cotton company, to a French firm known as Uniroute. The main condition laid down was that this trucking concern should be "ready at all times and in all places with the number of vehicles required to collect and ship the totality of the cotton crop."

Uniroute, like its European colleagues in Oubangui, had built up from modest beginnings in the interwar period a large and efficient business able to cope with the extension of cotton cultivation after the war. During the six months open to motorized traffic in Tchad, Uniroute had to collect from the most isolated parts of the producing zone about 60,000 tons of cotton in the boll, and also carry some 17,000 tons of cotton fiber from the hinterland to seaports 1,200 kilometers away. The remainder of the year was spent in repairing its fleet of trucks and preparing for the coming season.[43]

After 1945, war-surplus trucks, left in Tchad from Leclerc's campaign, became available, and local Africans were thus enabled to enter the transport field. Improvements in the territory's road system opened up remote areas where slow-moving oxcarts could be replaced by trucks and buses, and for some years after the war there was enough business to occupy all the transporters. Until 1948, transport costs were lower in Tchad than in Oubangui; from 1948 to 1950 they were about the same; but in 1950 those in Tchad suddenly became higher. The government intervened and rates were stabilized until 1952, when once again they soared, ostensibly because of the higher cost of fuel and of imported trucks. This development coincided with a fall in the price of cotton and a diminution in the size of that crop, an expansion of local air-freight services, and the general trade recession throughout AEF. When a study then made of the cotton industry showed that transport accounted for two-fifths of its production costs, Tchad's Grand Councilors were moved to ask the government-general (which controlled transport activities in the federation) to end Uniroute's monopoly. They argued that African truckers should be given a share in the handling of cotton because it was the only really remunerative sector of that business in Tchad.

The government, for its part, did persuade Uniroute to reduce its rates by 13 percent, and in 1954 imposed a further cut of 10 per cent on all transporters without asking their prior consent. But in general the administration took the stand that it had no right to intervene in regard to the private contract made between COTONFRAN and Uniroute, and stressed the fact that any transport firm was free to bid for the former's monopoly contract. To this the African Councilors replied that obviously the indigenous firms, with their few and decrepit trucks, could not hope to compete on equal terms with Uniroute, and in view of the current shrinkage in the transport business the many small-scale African truckers could not survive without government support.[44]

In fact, Uniroute's monopoly left freely open to the African truckers only the transport business between Tchad and Nigeria, but from 1953 on, their control of this run was increasingly jeopardized. More and more, Tchad's importers began to patronize the Nigerian truckers, whose rates were about half those of their Tchadian competitors. The latter still carried most of Tchad's exports that took the Nigerian route, but often they were compelled to stay for weeks, even months, in Maiduguri awaiting a return load. Since Tchad's imports by way of Nigeria were far larger (45,000 tons a year) than its exports, the situation of the local truckers became desperate and they appealed to the territorial assembly for help. Its African members then renewed their pressure on the administration, not only to end Uniroute's monopoly but to negotiate with the Nigerian government and with local importers a more equitable arrangement whereby a share of the import trade would be reserved to Tchadian truckers. The territorial authorities agreed to open negotiations with Nigeria but claimed that they could do nothing about Uniroute or with local importers unless Tchad's innumerable small truckers formed themselves into a responsible organization. Talks with the Nigerian government dragged on fruitlessly for years, and in the meantime no progress was made in organizing Tchad's illiterate and increasingly indebted truckers. The only alternative to monopoly, as Governor Colombani told the territorial assembly on November 26, 1954, seemed to be anarchy.

Finally, in August 1955, the impasse was broken by the organization of a Coopérative des Transporteurs Tchadiens, the combined capacity of whose trucks came to only 1,000 tons. Yet within a year this cooperative had raised the total to 2,600 tons and gained 166 members.[45] At long last, the African truckers were in a position to negotiate with the local importers, and owing to the combined efforts of the administration, the assembly, and the Chamber of Commerce an agreement between them was reached in December 1956. On condition that the African truckers' cooperative employ a European supervisor, build a warehouse at Maiduguri, and insure its members' trucks, they would be given all the importers' transport business except shipments of fuel and heavy machinery.[46]

In its first operating year, the cooperative handled a volume of business amounting to 42.5 million CFA francs, and this emboldened it to ask for a 45-million-franc loan from the CCOM and to attack Uniroute's cotton-transport monopoly. It succeeded easily in its first objective, but not until all the truckers other than Uniroute had become members of the cooperative was it able to wrest from that company the right to transport all the cotton produced in one zone and 5,000 tons that had been grown elsewhere.[47] But this success did not end Tchad's transport troubles, both internal and external. To put order into a still-chaotic situation, a study committee was formed in mid-1957 to collect data on the ownership and condition of the territory's 3,000 or so trucks, and to lay down rules governing the truck-driving occupation. At about the same time the new territorial government had to begin negotiations anew with the Nigerians, who were naturally displeased by the agreement reached between Tchad's importers and the transport cooperative, and with the Oubangui authorities, who had recently placed heavy taxes on the Tchadian truckers operating in their territory. Transport remains a vital problem for Tchad, and one for which a satisfactory solution has yet to be found.

Waterways. Tchad's usable waterways are concentrated in the southwestern part of the territory, and are comprised in the Chari-Logone network. A few stretches on these rivers are navigable throughout the year by small craft, but their meanderings, sandbanks, and seasonal variations in water level greatly diminish their usefulness and make them inferior (and at best supplementary) to roads as a means of communication.

Of the two navigable sectors of the Chari, that between Fort Lamy and Fort Archambault (800 kilometers) is the more important. Used chiefly when the road connecting those two towns is cut, it serves for the transport of merchandise unloaded at Bangui and destined for northern Tchad. During the high-water season, July to February, the barges of its two navigation companies (COMOUNA and UNIFAC) can carry about 5,000 tons of merchandise.[48] The navigable stretch between Fort Lamy and Lake Tchad, which is difficult but possible for shallow-draft boats throughout the year, is used for the transport of natron, quarry stone, and dried fish.

The Logone is navigable for about the same period between Fort Lamy and Kéré, but the shifts of its sandbanks and the variations in water level are even more marked. Its two tributaries, the Pendé and Bahr-Sara, present even graver difficulties for navigation and are little used. There is no doubt that the Chari-Logone network could be made more serviceable than it is today, but in the present stage of Tchad's economic development the expense of such improvements is considered to be unjustified. When, in late 1957, the question arose as to the territory's participation in the newly founded Interterritorial Service of Navigable Waterways, many of its assemblymen opposed Tchad's joining this organization on the ground that its usefulness would not justify even the small expense (2.2 million CFA francs) involved.[49] Tchad's existing riverine facilities, it was claimed, met current needs, and only the building of the proposed railroad north from Bangui to Bousso would warrant spending great sums on improving the navigability of the Chari.

Agriculture

Tchad's agricultural situation is both better and more complicated than that of any other territory of the federation. Here lives a numerous and robust population of born herders and farmers who are able to feed themselves and even export surplus products, despite periodic locust invasions and droughts. Cotton is the main cash crop, and its cultivation is spreading, as is that of peanuts, which in most of the appropriate regions are grown in rotation with it. In addition, the territory produces a wide variety of cereals, the most important of which are millet, rice, wheat, and corn. Most of the complications in Tchad's agricultural situation are of comparatively recent origin, having arisen from the change in relations between the chiefs and the peasantry, between nomads and sedentaries, and the consequent conflicts over the use of land and watering points and the ownership of harvests, particularly those of dates.

Millet is the basic food of most Tchadians, consumed in the form of flour or beer, and its sale provides the only income for certain regions of the territory. It is cultivated in both the savannah and inundated zones, and also in the sahel up to a line running about 100 kilometers north of Rig-Rig, Mao, and Arada. Four main varieties are grown and harvested at different times of the year; yields vary widely from 350 to 1,000 kilograms to the hectare; and a total of some 700,000 tons annually is produced throughout the territory.[50] The administration has been buying about 4,000 tons of millet a year for its own services, public institutions, and the army. Each year until 1958 the prices paid by the government for its purchases were fixed in accordance with whether or not millet was the sole cash crop of a region and required extensive transport to bring it from the producing area. If the crop was poor in a region in which millet was the sole cereal grown, the government also forbade its export from that area, and through the SIP it also constituted stocks for Fort Lamy. Though Tchad's assemblymen recognized that these measures were designed to protect consumers, they resented what they considered to be excessive official authoritarianism, claiming that the government's purchases had the character of requisitions and were made at prices below the local market level.[51] Pressure from the assembly succeeded in raising the official price paid for millet in Batha, Ouaddaï, and Salamat, and in November 1958 the sale of millet was completely freed from restrictions.

Although paddy cultivation was introduced into Tchad only on the eve of World War II, this territory is now by far the biggest rice producer in AEF. In a comparatively short time paddy has become an important crop in the Logone valley, where the districts of Bongor, Lai, and Kélo account for all of the territory's present output. A marsh type of rice is grown there, and its productivity depends largely on the extent of the river's annual inundations. Because of the variability of this factor and because of the primitive methods used by the Logone farming families, yields are generally poor (750 kilograms to the hectare), though in some places they have amounted to more than 1 ton per hectare. Production has risen from 3,000 tons of paddy in 1947 to over 20,000 tons each year since 1954, and rice farming is carried on by 20,000 to 30,000 individuals in the Logone area. They consume almost all of the output, but some 2,000 tons are sold annually through official organizations either as paddy or as rice after being husked at three mills situated in Lai.

In this family production of paddy the government has intervened only to a very limited degree, for the territory's output approximates current consumption, no competition from imported rice exists, and for the time being there is no prospect of large-scale exports. Selected seed has been developed and distributed by the Boumo agricultural station and better cultivation methods have been taught by agents of the territorial agricultural service, but these efforts have been small in scale. This picture may change radically in the future, however, when and if Casier A of the Logone Project (see pp. 458–93) turns from cotton to rice production. Technically such a transformation seems to present few difficulties. On the other hand, it involves the delicate task of persuading the Massa tribes of that area to grow and eat more rice, besides posing the question of disposing of huge tonnages of paddy whose profitable export depends on the solving of Tchad's basic transport problem.

Corn is cultivated widely throughout Tchad, chiefly on the periphery of villages. In most regions it serves only as a food to tide the population over between millet harvests, but in the Lake Tchad area it is the main cereal, and production in Bol district is estimated at 3,000 tons a year. There and throughout the polders of Kanem it is grown alternately with wheat. In recent years the area planted to corn and wheat has fluctuated widely as a result of the lake's breaking through the African-built dykes in 1950 and 1955, but it has rarely exceeded 1,000 hectares. The administration has been trying to increase wheat production by introducing tender varieties developed at the Bailli station, building a strong dam at Bol, and creating an embryonic *paysannat* in the region. With the completion of the Bol dam, 4,000 hectares of arable land should become available, and consequently there should be a great increase in the wheat harvest. This is expected to augment the food supplies for the Arabized populations of northern Tchad, help provision Fort Lamy, and possibly lead to the construction of a flour mill by the Grands Moulins de Paris.[52]

Date palms also grow in the *oueds* bordering on Lake Tchad, and in the past few years have acquired an importance far out of proportion to the size or quality of their output. Their dates are in fact reputed to be among the poorest produced in Africa, but they are vital to the overpopulated Kanem region as a food and for bartering against millet. Since 1957 a dispute has gone on between the chiefs of Mao district and the cultivators of date palms in the *oueds* regarding division of the harvest. Through circumstances peculiar to that area, ownership rights, deriving from both Islamic and customary law, are extremely complex, and they gave rise to such a feeling of tension that the government sent a French expert of ORSTOM, J. P. Trystran, to make a special study of them in 1958.[53] Though the situation in the date-palm groves of Mao was exceptionally acute, it was also symptomatic of a revolt, widespread in northern and eastern Tchad, on the part of the peasantry against the exactions of their customary chiefs (see pp. 76–78). Not only were the new political freedoms arousing the farmers everywhere to demand a greater share in the produce of their labor, but the growth of the population in such regions as Kanem, where the arable land was very limited, necessitated constructive action on the part of the authorities. Trystran urged that a study be made of all the Kanem *oueds* so as to see which were suited to agriculture—some were so permeated with natron as to be better adapted to herding—and then to enlarge the arable zone. But above all he recommended that ownership rights in Kanem be clearly and officially defined, even though this would involve a drastic revision of the whole land-tenure system.

That this is urgently required has been shown by another conflict peculiar to Tchad, which has led to violence in recent years—that between nomad herders and sedentary farmers. After the French occupation had brought peace to a territory long afflicted by tribal warfare, more and more of the population became sedentary farmers and began to encroach on the areas traditionally used by nomadic herders as trekking grounds for their animals. Watering points in arid Tchad were inevitably the places where most disputes arose, and these became more violent as the human and animal population grew in numbers. Even the well-digging program, pursued intensively by the government since 1955, has done nothing to assuage these difficulties. One African assemblyman declared that "an incredible number of persons are killed every year in fights over water and pasture rights."⁵⁴ Conflicts regarding property ownership are not confined to any one region of Tchad, and they are now beginning to appear even in the BET areas. Thus far the government has not felt able to undertake the radical reform required and has simply tried to cope with each outbreak as it occurs.

In other, related domains, however, the government has been more constructive and active. Since cotton growing has been the province of COTONFRAN and of various Metropolitan and federal agencies, the territorial administration has been able to concentrate on crops of direct concern to the Tchadian consumer. To increase food production it runs an agricultural station at Bailli, and it utilizes the SIP as its main agency for distributing selected seed and purchasing harvests. For the same reasons as elsewhere in AEF, the SIP is an organization unpopular with the African elite, but it has been better tolerated there than in any other territory except possibly Moyen-Congo. This has been due in part to the SIP's effectiveness in provisioning Tchad's main towns in foodstuffs, and in part to the early demise of the territory's three cooperative societies.⁵⁵ The territorial assembly got its fingers badly burned by guaranteeing loans to the cooperatives, and so decided to retain the SIP, as least until a better-managed cooperative movement could be developed. In December 1957 the Lisette government apologized to the assembly for not having had time as yet to reorganize the SIP, but it is now regarded as certain that they will be gradually transformed into Sociétés Mutuelles de Production Rurale (SMPR) as a step preparatory to their ultimate conversion into cooperatives.

Paysannats have been set up in Tchad, as in other parts of the federation, but they were slower in starting and have developed differently there than elsewhere. To break up over-large settlements that clustered around watering points and were exhausting the land nearby, the government wanted to create *paysannats* that would develop the as-yet-uncultivated arable areas. Though these *paysannats* simply aimed to increase the production of Tchad's traditional crops of cotton and food, their members were to be trained in the use of draft animals and fertilizers and also to combine farming with herding. Since new sources of water were the prerequisite for such enterprises, *paysannats* could not be founded until more wells were dug or irrigation provided by controlling inundations from the Logone and Chari rivers. A modest beginning was made in 1955 when the SIP created a market-gardening *paysannat* in the Chari-Baguirmi to provision Fort Lamy. The next year saw the start of four *paysannats*—two in Mayo-Kebbi (at Youhé and Torok) and two in the Logone (at Doulougou and Dade)—and in 1957 ten others were created. None of these *paysannats* as yet groups more than about 1,000 persons, and they are all small-scale operations compared with the great enterprise that the French government has been carrying out in "Tchad's Mesopotamia."

On May 17, 1947, the French government set up a Scientific Commission of Logone-Tchad under ORSTOM to settle a 40-year-old controversy as to whether or not the Benoué river was capturing the waters of the Logone. As the latter river supplied about one-third of the water in Lake Tchad, it was feared that that lake might be in process of drying up. The commission consisted of 21 members, headed by General Tilho, who had been the first explorer of the Tchad basin at the turn of the century, and its initial tasks were to make hydrological and soil surveys. Two years after it was created, the commission was asked by the Minister of Overseas France to include in its work studies of the possibility of improving the navigability of the Benoué and aiding agriculture through irrigation of the great plains bordering on the middle Logone. There for six months of every year the Massa population of farmers and herders took refuge with their animals on hillocks, while the surrounding flat lands were inundated by the overflow of the Logone river. During the dry season they cultivated millet on the plains, where they also led their animals to graze, but it was becoming increasingly difficult for the Massa to produce enough food for their rapidly growing numbers. In its first report the commission concluded that Lake Tchad was in no imminent danger of disappearance and that controlling the flow of the Logone for the improvement of agriculture on the adjacent plains would be of immediate economic benefit to the local populations.

Although this proposal drastically altered the original project and vastly enlarged its scope, it was decided to add agronomic and social studies to those already undertaken, and to extend the hydrological survey to include the middle portion of the Logone. In 1952 FIDES financed the participation of technicians from the Bureau Central d'Etudes pour les Equipements d'Outre-Mer, and later that of two sociologists to appraise the probable effect upon the local Massas of the radical change that execution of the new project would bring to their physical environment.[56] This reorientation of the Logone project required a great deal more time and money than had been originally envisaged, for the area to be examined was vast and heterogeneous and the Massas exceptionally reluctant to accept innovations.[57] Metropolitan France paid for all the research and half of the works undertaken, the federal government set up a Comité d'Aménagement du Logone-Chari and contributed the services of its rural engineers, and the territory was asked to pay for half of the expenses involved in building dykes and a drainage system.

The new committee soon decided to cut down the ambitious initial scheme of dyking all of the Tchad bank of the Logone between Lai and Katoa, because of the danger of flooding the Cameroun side of the river, where a rice-growing project was under way. In 1953 it began by reinforcing a much shorter dyke running north of Bongor, which had been built by Africans under the direction of local administrators. Though this dyke was subsequently broken twice by the force of the waters, to the discouragement of the technicians and of the Massas who had begun cultivating supposedly protected land, and the drainage system had to be revised several times, the technical difficulties of dam construction and irrigation are now thought to be resolved. This cannot yet be said of the agronomic and human problems involved, though progress has been made in both those domains.

Casier A is the name given to the area of some 57,000 hectares now protected from the river's overflow, and it consists of two very different zones.[58] The northern one is underpopulated, and in 1956 it was conceded to a private company called Syndicat Agricole du Logone-Tchad (SALT) for experimentation with cotton cultivation, on condition that the company respect the rights of the few African inhabitants and cooperate with an agricultural station set up in 1954 at Biliam-Oursi in the heart of the Casier. The southern zone is more populous, and the villagers living there on hillocks are only slowly and with difficulty being won over to a new type of economy. They have claimed that the project has interfered with their fishing and also has forced them to drive their herds too far afield to find pastures. But gradually the increase in the land on which they can grow millet not only has reconciled them but has led to a small but growing stream of Massa immigrants. The 18,000 or so Massa now living in Casier· A even seem willing to add a cash crop to their millet production, though their wants are minimal in regard to imported goods. They are also increasingly inclined to use their cattle as draft animals, whereas these animals heretofore either have been slaughtered for religious festivals or have served as payment of the bride price.

What is only now in the process of being determined is what cash crop to grow in Casier A. When the writers visited the project late in 1958 it appeared that the experts of the Biliam-Oursi farm and of SALT had come to the conclusion that the soils and climate of Casier A were not propitious for cotton cultivation and that rice would be planted progressively over most of the reclaimed land. Not only did paddy grow better there than did cotton, but its cultivation did not interfere with the fishing and herding activities of the Massas and its output would find a market in Fort Lamy. The trend in favor of paddy seemed confirmed in 1959 by the territorial assembly's decision to build a rice mill in Casier A.

The Logone committee aims eventually to double the zone now under cultivation, extend the area planted to paddy at the rate of 1,000 hectares a year, and persuade the Massas to grow millet on the dry plains and cotton on the hillocks. But the Massas show no inclination to substitute rice for millet as their basic food and they will accept only very small increases each year in the area of land to be cultivated. Because of the costliness of the investment—well over one billion CFA francs—and the lack of any prospect of immediate returns, the French taxpayer has reportedly been disillusioned as to the Logone project. Government officials both French and African, however, stress that even if the project never becomes even self-supporting it is socially and economically vital for the Mayo-Kebbi region.

Though it will cost large sums every year for upkeep of the dyke and drainage canals, Casier A must continue to be developed, for in the increased cultivation of the great Logone plains lies the only hope of feeding the growing Massa population and of raising its living standards. That the pace of this development cannot be forced beyond the Massas' willingness to cooperate has been one important lesson learned from the experience of the past few years.

Development of cotton as a major crop was slower in Tchad than in Oubangui, but it has come to cover a larger area (about 230,000 hectares) and to provide a steady occupation for more farmers (at least 400,000). Its area is also more concentrated than is the case in Oubangui, though in very recent years cotton has been spreading eastward from its traditional stronghold in the Logone-Chari-Baguirmi region. Moreover, its production is monopolized by a single company, COTONFRAN, with the result that its output is more uniform and the percentage of yellow cotton smaller. Cotton is both absolutely and relatively more important to Tchad's economy than it is to that of Oubangui, accounting for about 80 per cent of the territory's exports in value and approximately one-third of its budgetary resources. On the other hand, transport is a bigger factor in Tchad's production costs, as its cotton is mainly carried in trucks to the Benoué and from there by boat (or truck) and rail to the sea, whereas Oubangui's has a shorter land trip to make before reaching the Federal Artery.

COTONFRAN began operating first in Moyen-Chari in 1928 and the next year spread to Moyen-Logone and Mayo-Kebbi, whence it gradually extended its operations throughout southern Tchad. With only a few setbacks, the production of cotton from that territory has risen steadily and swiftly from 17 tons in 1929 to 80,467 tons in 1957–58. The main producing areas are the Logone (35,700 tons from 106,000 hectares), Mayo-Kebbi (26,500 tons from 64,000 hectares), Moyen-Chari (16,000 tons from 52,000 hectares), and the fifth zone of the Salamat region (2,000 tons from 18,000 hectares).[59] Between 1953 and 1954 production almost doubled, largely owing to the almost total replacement of the ordinary Allen variety by the improved or N'Kerala species developed by the eight research stations belonging to the IRCT and COTONFRAN. Yields are higher per hectare (about 350 kilograms) than in Oubangui, as are those from ginning (36 per cent of fiber). In 1958 Tchad's farmers received an aggregate income from cotton sales of 2,165 million CFA francs.

Tchad's elected representatives, both European and African, have been at the same time more constructive in their campaign to get better prices for local cotton farmers and less virulent in their criticisms of the government's cotton policy than have been those of Oubangui. A. Kieffer, almost single-handed, fought the good fight for Tchad's cotton growers in the Grand Council, and though he was not devoid of political ambitions, he was obviously sincere in his championing of the local underdog. From the Tchadian Africans one hears the same sort of complaints as from their colleagues in Oubangui, but they are only pale echoes of the barbed criticisms voiced by Messrs. Darlan and Boganda. Tchad's indigenous assemblymen have asked that the company create more purchasing centers and the government exercise more control over them in order to better protect the farmers against false weights and parasitic middlemen and chiefs.[60] The same spokesmen also wanted more trained agents to replace the *boys-coton* and to teach Tchad's farmers better cultivation methods. They bewailed the presence in Fort Lamy of laborers from the cotton regions, claiming that the latter would return to the land if cotton were made a more remunerative crop. On August 23, 1951, Ahmed Kotoko, who came from Tchad's cotton belt, told the French Union Assembly:

> . . . a farmer who takes to market the 250 kilograms of cotton that is the result of 90 days' labor receives for it 3,750 CFA francs. Of this sum the village chief appropriates 150 to 250 francs for the head tax. As farmers usually have several wives, he thus pays to the chief about half of what he earns. Merchants at the market charge steep prices for their goods and he must spend 300 francs for a shirt. In the end he returns home with 200 francs or nothing. . . . It is true that cotton cultivation has slightly raised our farmers' living standards, but it has above all gone to increasing the companies' revenues and the budget's resources. Throughout the whole cotton region there is not a single indigenous African who owns a store or a truck except a few chiefs who have got their money through premiums on cotton production and who are therefore prone to apply force.

Even after the average planter's income had risen to 7,300 CFA francs in 1951, he had to pay out some 4,000 francs in various types of taxes and had left over only 3,300 francs wherewith to pay the bride price, customary dues, and miscellaneous essential expenditures.[61]

Tchad's African assemblymen regarded as of almost equal importance to the goal of increasing the income of cotton farmers the need to drive down the transport costs for Tchad's cotton and to break the monopoly held in this domain by Uniroute (see pp. 450–52). This has been gradually accomplished, but a more radical change may be expected as a result of the new cotton-company contracts due to be negotiated in 1959–60.

Cotton is so overwhelmingly important to Tchad that there is no question but that whatever government controls the new republic will strive to promote it. In September 1957 Premier Lisette set up a Special Committee for Cotton Affairs, and in a report made to the territorial assembly on December 7 of that year he stated that "cotton remains the key to our economy." When production fell by 15 per cent in 1958, the Tchad government drew up a special program to revive the output of that crop.

In very recent years peanuts have been hailed as Tchad's "crop with a future." This enthusiasm has been prompted more by the rapidity with which their production has spread in that territory since the war than by any firm assurance as to how this crop will develop in the years to come. There is no doubt that Tchad, in conformity with the government's policy, can produce many thousand more tons of peanuts than at present, but the problems relevant to their transport and sale have not yet been solved.

Over an immense area the natural conditions are propitious for the growing and stocking of peanuts, and Tchad has the population density required for increasing the cultivation of this crop. Even without using selected seed, a conscientious Tchad farmer can get yields of 1,500 to 1,700 kilograms to the hectare, and the nuts grown in the territory have a high percentage of oil and a low degree of acidity. During the past decade, peanut planting has been increasing in Tchad more rapidly than in any other territory of AEF, but, as in Oubangui, the total of peanuts sold locally and exported gives no accurate clue to the quantity of nuts grown. Estimates of the area planted to peanuts vary widely between 80,000 and 170,000 hectares, and estimates of their output range between 45,000 and 144,000 tons. Apparently about one-tenth of the nuts grown are used for seed, and only a very small part of the total harvest is sold. Recently, from 5,000 to 6,000 tons a year have been marketed locally, less than 400 tons of shelled nuts have been exported, and about 200 tons of oil have been pressed in the territory's few mills.

In 1955, for the first time, selected seed was distributed to Tchad's farmers, and this resulted in a rapid enlargement of the planted area. Until then peanut cultivation had been confined almost wholly to the cotton belt. More than one-third of the territory's peanuts came from Chari-Baguirmi, especially Bokoro district, and the other main producing areas were Batha and Mayo-Kebbi. These are still the principal regions, but beginning in 1956 peanut cultivation spread rapidly eastward along the 13th parallel as far as Ouaddaï. Tchad's farmers having realized 110 million CFA francs from peanut sales that year, the government encouraged this expansion in the hope that peanuts would provide a remunerative occupation for the impoverished inhabitants of eastern Tchad and arrest emigration to the Sudan.

The Lisette government, which came to power in 1957, began zealously to promote peanut cultivation. It set up an experimental farm at Dilbini, near Bokoro, to develop and distribute selected seed, and the staff of this station was instructed to preach the virtues of peanut growing among the farmers for whom this crop was a novelty. In November 1957 the sale of peanuts was restricted to controlled markets, and a few months later an inspectorate was set up to standardize the quality of the nuts sold therein. Only in Ouaddaï, where no commercial network existed, was the SIP given a monopoly of peanut purchases with the proviso that it would reserve seed sufficient to increase the planted area the following season.

This monopoly was unpopular with Tchad's assemblymen, who were perennially opposed to the SIP, but it was the price at which the SIP purchased the peanut crop that aroused the ire of Ouaddaï farmers.[62] To their complaints the government replied that the immensity of the area over which this crop was grown caused wide variations in transport costs, and that the latter were necessarily reflected in the official prices established for peanuts in the different producing zones. That it was desirable to pay pea-

nut farmers a higher price for their output the government freely acknowledged, and since the territorial budget was in no position to provide the
necessary funds, it was decided in September 1958 to set up a Peanut Price
Supporting Fund. This fund did not begin functioning until May 1959,
and in the meantime a bad drought in Ouaddaï had so blighted the peanut
crop there that seed for planting the following season had to be obtained
from neighboring areas.

The question of price, though very important, is not the only one that
makes the future of Tchad's peanuts uncertain. In view of Senegal's huge
production of oil and nuts it is improbable that France will enlarge its quota
of peanut imports from Tchad. Then, too, unless the territory's external
transport problem is adequately solved, no marked improvement can be
expected in the present small tonnages of nuts carried by truck to Nigeria.
Transport is also a costly element in developing local sales, and as yet the
domestic demand for peanut oil is not large enough to justify the construction of modern oil mills. Ideally Tchad's immense peanut potential should
be utilized for the production of oil not only for export but for consumption
by a population that is short of vegetable fats, and of cake to serve as fodder
for the territory's vast animal herds. Such a development, however, would
require capital investment on so big a scale that it is unlikely to be forthcoming soon. In 1959 Tchad's production of peanuts for sale amounted to
2,200 tons of shelled nuts, of which 1,300 tons were exported to France
via the Federal Artery.

Fisheries

Along the Chari and Logone and their tributaries and around Lake
Tchad live the largest number of professional fishermen in AEF, and the
output of the whole Tchad basin is now estimated at 60,000 to 80,000 tons of
fresh fish a year. Perhaps one-sixth of this catch is smuggled across the
Camerounian and Nigerian frontiers, and the rest is consumed by the producers or sold dried or smoked in nearby markets—chiefly Fort Lamy,
which buys over 600 tons a year. A European company, the Société de
Pêcheries Taransaud, was established in the region of the Chari after the
war, but its output is very small compared with the African catch. Varied
and ingenious equipment is used by the region's professional fishermen,
outstanding among whom are the Boudouma and Kouri who live on the
islands of Lake Tchad, and the Kotoko who fish along the lower reaches of
the Logone and the Chari. Since 1952 seasonal fishermen have been coming from distant areas of Mayo-Kebbi and the Logone to a place reputed to
be one of the most productive fresh-water fishing zones in central Africa—
the juncture of the Chari and Logone rivers. Here the barrages they have
built, with the object of forcing the salanga species returning from their
spawning grounds in the lake to take the Chari route, have operated to the
advantage of north Cameroun's fishermen and to the disadvantage of
Tchadians fishing on the lower Logone.[63]

In part it was to study this situation that the Water and Forestry Service created the Centre d'Etudes de la Pêche in November 1953, placed it under the direction of two ORSTOM specialists, and gave it a staff of 19 African agents and monitors, a laboratory at Fort Lamy, and a motorized barge.[64] This center's main tasks, however, were to bring up to date the inventory of Tchad's fresh-water fish made by Théodore Monod in 1926, determine which of its 125 species were of economic interest, what regions—if any— were overfished, and compile reliable data as to the number, location, catch, and markets of the Tchad-basin fishermen. A first report was completed in time to be presented to the inter-African conference on fresh-water fishing held at Brazzaville in July 1956, and further studies have been made since that time. It appears from the center's reports that the sales made by Tchad-basin fishermen bring them in nearly 1 billion CFA francs a year and that their production is far below the region's potential. Because of the increase in the population and in marketing facilities, there are probably today three times as many fishermen in the territory as in 1926, and they are moving from greater distances to new fishing centers.

Fishing appears to be the local activity which now gives the best returns for the effort involved, but the fishermen's cash income could be greatly increased by the use of stronger equipment and above all by better processing, packing, and transport. Working in close cooperation with the Camerounian fish station at Fort Foureau, the Tchadian center is trying to improve local fishing and marketing techniques, and it has already made headway in the type of dugouts and nets utilized, has guided African fishermen to new fishing zones, and has raised the price at which their catch is sold.

Forests and forest products

In comparison with other territories of AEF, Tchad has no real forests, only wooded areas, and virtually their only salable product is gum arabic. Barely 500 cubic meters of wood are sawn annually in the territory, and Tchad gets most of such supplies from Oubangui. The local Water and Forestry Service has prospected the wooded zones, classified 235,000 hectares as protected forests, and reforested some 150 hectares. This work has been done almost wholly in the southern part of the territory to arrest soil erosion there and to protect the wood supplies of the urban populations.

For some years the Forestry Service attempted to interest the populations of Massakory, Rig-Rig, Mao, and Ouaddaï in the production of gum arabic, which, in the 1930's, had amounted to between 300 and 400 tons annually. But in more recent years the market price was too low to induce them to make the necessary effort, and the quality of the gum produced was too uneven and transport costs too high to attract local merchants. In 1957, however, after the price for gum arabic rose appreciably in Metropolitan France, the situation changed rather abruptly. Officials of the Forestry Service selected the most favorable producing zones, the SIP purchased, prepared, and standardized the output, and that year more than 200 tons were sold for export (compared with 150 produced in 1956) and they brought in some millions of francs to a few of Tchad's most impoverished regions. It is believed that the territory could easily produce 2,000 to 3,000 tons of gum arabic annually, but this depends on maintaining a high purchase price for that product.[65]

Animal husbandry

Livestock, after cotton, is Tchad's greatest resource, but it is one that is still far from being fully utilized. In recent years the government's intensive efforts to promote this aim have taken two forms. One has been to increase the size and improve the quality of existing herds, and the other, to alter radically the nature and direction of the export trade. Both policies have been on the whole successful, but the novel elements introduced in the course of their execution have given rise to unexpected problems, some of which have not yet been solved.

In regard to the quantitative and qualitative improvement of Tchad's herds, the territorial veterinary service has used the classical methods of protecting animals against epidemic diseases by mass inoculations and of cross-breeding with imported stock. Under the Plan, a big laboratory for research and the manufacture of serums was built at Farcha, on the outskirts of Fort Lamy, and since 1954 its products have been used in Cameroun as well as throughout AEF. Despite their joint financing of this laboratory, its upkeep proved to be so expensive that in 1957 it was taken over on a 25-year lease by the Metropolitan Institut d'Elévage et de Médicine Vétérinaire des Pays Tropicaux. The serums produced at Farcha have enabled the Tchad veterinaries to wage a successful fight on rinderpest, which formerly decimated the territory's cattle, and the laboratory is now turning out, in addition, serums aimed at eliminating other animal diseases, particularly trypanosomiasis, which has been spreading since 1956.[66] So effective has been the use of such serums that it has altered the suspicious attitude of Tchad's herders toward the veterinary service. For some years now they have insistently demanded an increase in the number of veterinaries and have even driven their herds for hundreds of kilometers in order to have them inoculated whenever an epidemic threatens.[67] This demand has been particularly strong in recent years among the cotton farmers of southern Tchad, who were long neglected in favor of the more numerous professional Arab cattle herders of the north.

To expand its activities in the south, the animal-husbandry service began in 1951 to import N'dama cattle to its station located at Fianga. Owing to the enlargement of this station in 1957, it has been possible to increase the number of trypanosomiasis-resistant cattle distributed throughout the cotton belt. Small-scale experiments in the cross-breeding of local mares with imported stallions have been carried on at the N'Gouri station in Kanem, with a corresponding growth in the size of the territory's horse population. A costly and resounding failure, on the other hand, has been the government's attempt to cross astrakhan with local sheep. An initial experiment on the eve of World War II seemed so promising that an elaborate station was built with Plan funds at Abougoudam, near Abéché, which later had to be abandoned and is now an impressive ruin. Still another experiment, which is both more recent and still hopeful, is that of cattle ranching, conducted by two private companies with official French and American technical aid. In 1953 the Compagnie Pastorale, which had long and successfully been ranching in Cameroun, asked for a 5,000-hectare concession in the Massakory district on which to create a pilot ranch with 1,000 animals. If after a few years the outlook proved to be promising, the Pastorale proposed to ask for a 50,000-hectare concession so as to be able to graze a herd of 15,000 cattle. In return, it pledged to improve its pastures and dig wells, to respect the trek routes of the region's nomadic herders, and to lend its thoroughbred bulls for cross-breeding with local zebu cows. A mission composed of officials and assemblymen visited the site of the future ranch, found it contained excellent pasture and no inhabitants, and therefore recommended that it be ceded to the Pastorale on condition that the whole area be fenced.[68] This development prompted the STEC company, a meat-packing firm already established at Fort Lamy, to ask for a concession in 1955. This also was granted but with more reservations by the assembly, for it concerned a relatively populous area. From the outset the STEC enterprise encountered difficulties, but that of the more experienced Pastorale is reportedly successful and its herd now exceeds 3,000 head. The chief expenditure involved in ranching in Tchad is that of fencing and well-digging, and the cost of installing a herd of 5,000 head there in 1957 was calculated to be 115 million CFA francs.[69]

The second postwar novelty introduced for the purpose of improving the number and quality of Tchad's herds has been the program of well-digging in both the sedentary and nomadic zones. Vast grassy pasturelands that exist in the territory are unutilized because of their lack of surface water. Every year northern Tchad's herds move south for four to five months in search of water and pasture, and the loss in animals is estimated at 25 per cent of the total as a consequence of their continual migrations.[70] Obviously the stabilization of herds would automatically increase their number and size, and would also, it was expected, eliminate many of the conflicts between the nomads and sedentaries. The southern farmers naturally resented the destruction of their crops, which the famished animals from the north either ate or trampled down. Accordingly, the first wells dug under the Plan were in the Baguirmi region, and later the program was extended to the great trek routes. In both those quarters, unexpected complications resulted.

In the south, it may be said that the well-digging accomplished was oversuccessful in attracting the nomad herders to settle with their animals around the new watering points. By 1957 the whole Chari-Baguirmi region had been provided with wells, and more were being dug in the Logone and Bas-Chari. But far from lessening the antagonism between the nomads and sedentaries, the settling of the northern herds in the south caused more and bloodier conflicts. In part this was due to the current political situation in Chari-Baguirmi (see pp. 436–37), but more fundamentally it derived from the "profound change effected in the social organization of a population that has been formed by the seasonal need to seek pastures and water elsewhere."[71] The "impressive list of dead left by these conflicts over the past year" led the assembly to consider ways and means of "passing from the regime of the open range to that of fenced pastures without causing undue harm to the basic rights of both elements."

The well-digging program that got under way in the sahel trek zone in 1952 gave rise to another type of problem. The first pilot wells were dug in the Bokoro–Lake Fitri region, then in Ouaddaï, Salamat, and Batha, where water was struck at depths of 40 to 60 meters. Of the expenditures involved, 55 per cent was borne by FIDES, but the territory was responsible for the remaining 45 per cent and for the cost of upkeep. Then the question arose as to what organization would manage the wells' operations and who would pay for their maintenance and the cost of fuel to pump up the water. As always, the territorial assembly was opposed to enlarging the attributes of the SIP but could think of no alternative way of running the wells, and there was a division of opinion as to whether or not the herders should be required to pay for the water they used.[72] As time went on, it became obvious that some of the nomads preferred to pursue their traditional treks rather than pay for water from the new wells, and in June 1958, after some of the wells had ceased functioning for lack of funds, the Lisette government proposed temporarily stopping the well-digging program until the problem of financing the upkeep of wells had been resolved.[73] By then it was realized that the whole pastoral-hydraulics program needed to be revised, for its execution required a fundamental and time-consuming re-education of both herders and sedentaries. Yet when the OCRS in September 1958 asked the Tchad assembly how it could help develop the BET region, the latter body voted to build a chain of wells along the track leading from Largeau to Sallal or to Ouaddaï, the natural market for the BET's livestock. In that semidesert area, water is the prime essential of animal husbandry and there is little likelihood of discord developing between the herders and as yet nonexistent sedentaries.[74]

All of the foregoing measures have undoubtedly increased the size of Tchad's herds, though to exactly what extent is not known. An estimate made in 1949 by the head of Tchad's animal-husbandry service placed the number of cattle at 3,500,000, sheep and goats at 6 million, horses at 125,000, donkeys at 175,000, camels at 250,000, and poultry at 4 million.[75] ·Because of the herders' reluctance to declare the extent of their herds and flocks, these figures are in all cases two, three, or four times larger than those shown in the official animal census, which, moreover, in Tchad takes into account only adult animals that are liable to taxation. In any case Tchad's animal resources, particularly in cattle, are greatly in excess of the population's needs, and for many years there has been a brisk export trade in cattle, horses, camels, donkeys, hides and skins, and butter with neighboring countries. In 1957 such exports were sold for 700 million CFA francs compared with 560 million the previous year.

Tchad as a whole consumes little beef—less in the north than in the south, where small animals do not flourish—but considerable amounts of mutton and goat meat are eaten, and four-fifths of the hides and skins produced are locally used, as is most of the milk and butter. The several hundred thousand animals slaughtered each year in the territory's 20-odd official abattoirs probably do not represent more than one-tenth of the meat consumed each year in Tchad, yet there remains a considerable surplus for export. Here again it is freely admitted that the official figures do not reflect the much larger reality, for the most considerable export of livestock is that of cattle (well over 200,000) to Nigeria and to a lesser extent Sudan, both of which are the object of a clandestine trade. Many persons in Tchad and neighboring countries are involved in this illicit traffic, which includes undercover currency dealings and the barter of animals for consumer goods. For years the government has tried vainly to stop this trade, because it has meant a serious loss of hard currency and tax revenues to Tchad, but perforce it is now tolerated within certain limits. Official policy, however, now has turned toward a reorientation of the territory's cattle exports to the south and a change in their form to that of frozen meat.

The severe shortage of meat in the diet of all the AEF populations except those of Tchad has long been of concern to the government, but it was not until a few tons of fresh meat were flown by the animal-husbandry service from Fort Lamy to Brazzaville in 1947 that a program of large-scale meat shipments by air was conceived. Soon afterwards two private companies, the STEC and SICAT, began to ship meat by plane from Fort Lamy and Abéché respectively to the southern towns of AEF and also to Léopoldville, Douala, and Yaoundé. The government aided by building or improving airfields at the loading points and started the construction of modern abattoirs at Fort Archambault and Fort Lamy. The quantities of meat transported by plane grew rapidly, from 471 tons in 1950 to 3,154 tons five years later. Already during this period of expansion, however, it was becoming apparent that it would be hard to make such operations pay. By the end of 1952, the SICAT had to cease its activities because the population of Ouaddaï could not afford to buy the imported goods that alone would have supplied a remunerative return freight. Its successor, the Société Africaine de Boucherie d'Abéché soon went bankrupt, and it was taken over by TREC (Transports Régionaux de l'Est et du Centre) only after the territorial assembly had guaranteed financial support.[76] Then the STEC began to lose its Belgian Congo markets to lower-priced competitors from Kenya and South Africa, though it was able to increase its shipments to the southern towns of AEF and Cameroun. The rising costs of plane transport and the difficulty of finding a return load were already making the position of this meat-shipment trade precarious when the completion of the refrigerated abattoir at Farcha in mid-1958 unexpectedly worsened the situation.

After a mission sent to Tchad in 1953—to investigate the commercial potentialities of a meat-export trade from Fort Lamy—had submitted a favorable report, FIDES decided to build at Farcha a refrigerated abattoir with an annual capacity of 6,000 tons of meat. At that time, Tchad was exporting only 2,800 tons of meat a year, hence the Farcha abattoir required at least 1,500 more tons if it were not to operate at a loss. Moreover, several private companies—of which the most important was TREC—had their own abattoirs, in which the cost of slaughtering was lower than at that of Farcha, and there was no way of compelling them to utilize the more costly new abattoir. In fact the private companies were openly hostile to the Farcha enterprise, for it opened the way for anyone to enter the meat industry and threatened the established firms with extinction. Over the preceding eight years these companies had built up a regular clientele and trained personnel, and on a yearly operating basis were able to offset the wide seasonal fluctuations in the prices they paid for the animals they slaughtered. The opening of the Farcha abattoir meant that an individual or company could, without previous experience or fixed overhead expenses, buy animals for the meat industry when their prices were low and hold off when they rose high. The prospects for a solution of this situation have not been improved by its admixture with politics, and the sessions of the assembly given over to debating the Farcha abattoir question have been stormy and fruitless. There is no doubt that the Farcha abattoir is too big for the current meat industry and too expensive for the territory to operate,[77] yet if it does not function, Tchad risks alienating FIDES, which had sunk 300 million CFA francs in its construction. The basic error behind its conception was the supposition that if over 200,000 live animals were exported to Nigeria each year, it was simply because adequate slaughtering and refrigerating facilities were lacking in Tchad. Meat shipments by air, despite their increase, have not made a dent on Tchad's livestock exports, and local traders have even found it cheaper to drive animals to Maroua for slaughtering than to have it done at nearby Farcha.[78] The local market is too slight to count toward bringing down the cost of Farcha's operations, and in any case the African consumer vastly prefers fresh to frozen meat.

The one bright spot in the current picture is that two new markets have been opened up for Tchad's meat, in the Saharan oases and in South Africa, but they are expected to take only about 500 tons a year.[79] All the responsible authorities in Tchad are agreed that for some years to come the Farcha abattoir will operate at a loss but that some solution must eventually be found to make it pay.[80] The territory's already vast animal resources and the demand for meat in the southern coastal cities is likewise large and steadily increasing. Already the towns of French Black Africa within a 2,000-kilometer radius of Fort Lamy depend to a great extent upon Tchad's meat shipments, and many Tchadians are also dependent upon the meat-export industry for their livelihood. The sole and still unsolved problem of this industry is that of bringing down its high cost, for which the rates of plane transport and taxation are almost wholly responsible. Only when the Farcha abattoir can work profitably to capacity can the Tchad government hope to check the uneconomic export of livestock, which represents a heavy monetary loss to the territory and a waste of its animal resources.

Trade

Tchad's trade has been characterized by chronic deficits, high prices for both its imports and exports, monopolies held by foreign firms, flourishing contraband exchanges with Nigeria and to a lesser degree with Sudan, and its dependence on cotton exports.

Cotton has played an even more important role in Tchad's commerce than has okoumé in that of Gabon, because it is an African crop and because Tchad has no secondary major export that can aspire to a place such as petroleum has come to occupy since 1957 in Gabon's foreign trade. Livestock is Tchad's longest-established export, and even if the extensive clandestine export of animals is taken into account, this trade trails far behind cotton in both volume and value. In the postwar years, Tchad has developed two new exports, meat and peanuts, and its fish and hides shipments bring in increasing revenues, but none of these has more than minor importance. It is because of cotton—a crop that has been grown in Tchad only since the interwar period—that the territory ranked second among AEF's territorial exporters for the past five years, accounting fairly regularly for about one-quarter of the federation's total exports in value. In 1958 Tchad's exports were sold for about 4,875 million CFA francs, of which ginned cotton—despite a comparatively poor crop—accounted for 4,181 million, livestock for 342 million, meat for 178 million, hides for 133 million, and fish for 41 million.

Tchad's main imports are petroleum products, motor vehicles, sugar, cloth, machinery, building materials, hardware, drugs, chemicals, alcoholic beverages, and flour, in that order of importance. With the higher prices being paid to cotton growers, the output of cotton has been growing steadily in recent years, and imports consequently have been increasing. Tchad's trade deficit, which stood at 1,400 million CFA francs in 1956, rose abruptly to 2,300 million in 1957. In the latter year, Tchad paid 5,800 million CFA francs for its imports and received only 3,500 million for its exports. From November 1957 on, the cost of living—always high in Tchad—rose more rapidly than before, despite the government's freezing of the prices for imported goods after the currency devaluation of the preceding August 10. In 1958 the relatively poor cotton harvest reduced the Tchadians' purchasing power and with it the trade deficit, and it also encouraged smuggling of goods into the territory from Nigeria.[81]

The high prices charged for legally imported goods are not the sole reason for inflation in Tchad. Others are the large and continuing military expenditures there, not only for the construction of an army air base but also for veterans' pensions, which aggregate a larger sum in Tchad than in any of the other territories. Then, too, the rises in wages and family allowances voted by all the territorial assemblies were supplemented in Tchad by a consumers' tax placed on imported sugar, textiles, and alcoholic beverages to compensate for the loss of revenue entailed by suppression of the head tax on women in December 1957. These developments have created difficulties in the internal market, already plagued by transport problems arising from Tchad's distance from seaports and by the rains that close the territory's roads and bridges to traffic for almost half of every year. Except for the very costly air-freight services, the transport of all of the territory's import and export goods must be concentrated in about six months.

Another undesirable feature has been the quasi-monopoly of trading held by seven large firms long established in Tchad. Of these, three—the Kouilou-Niari, SCOA, and France-Congo—have for years controlled about 70 per cent of the merchandise imported into the territory; one company, COTONFRAN, monopolizes its cotton exports and has also ceded a monopoly of its transport to a single trucking firm, Uniroute. The debates of Tchad's assembly have been filled with protests against the grip of these firms on the territory's trade, and some African members have blamed them for the lack of a local indigenous bourgeoisie. Gabon and Oubangui, it was said,[82] had a nascent native middle class, but Tchad did not have a single African millionaire merchant. The situation had not been improved when the big companies, at the administration's behest, began to provision the rural areas in 1954. Rather, it was worsened, for the superior organization, experience, and capital of these companies enabled them to undersell the local African retailers in the districts and thereby to strengthen their hold on the whole commercial circuit.[83] Although this was obviously to the advantage of the consumers—temporarily, at least—the African government of the Tchad republic has tried with some success to bolster the position of the small African retailer and trucker. There has been allotted to them a percentage of the transfrontier transport and commerce, particularly with Nigeria, as well as a portion of the territory's hard-currency reserves, and at the same time the cost of trading licenses required of the big firms has been raised. It was soon apparent, however, that such props were not enough and that African merchants and transporters would have to learn the need for keeping proper financial accounts and organizing themselves into efficient and responsible groups.

Industry

In sharp contrast to Moyen-Congo, Tchad is rich in manpower and natural resources, except minerals, but because of its lack of power and its inaccessibility it is industrially the least-developed country in AEF. A little rice is milled at Lai, but the output is far below local demand, a small milk-and-butter industry exists at Massakory but has difficulty in marketing its few tons of products, and less than 500 tons of dried and smoked fish are turned out by two artisanal-type plants on the Logone and Chari rivers. Only the cotton and meat industries of Tchad can be considered important. COTONFRAN's gins are now working almost to capacity, and that company has recently added to Tchad's industries by turning out cottonseed oil. The meat industry is a postwar venture of increasing importance for which the territory has ample resources and ready markets, but it has not yet solved its slaughtering, storage, and transport problems.

Tchad's lack of coal and hydroelectrical sources of power, as well as the cost of imported fuel, are formidable handicaps to its industrial expansion, though they may be partially overcome if the decision is made to construct an atomic pile at Fort Lamy. There is also the possibility that current prospecting will bring to light substantial mineral deposits in Tibesti, but the difficulties of processing and transporting the output—if any—would be almost insuperable.

In conformity with its industrial underdevelopment, but not with the size of its population, Tchad has the smallest electrical installations of any AEF territory. After World War II, Fort Lamy was provided with a 390-horsepower diesel plant, run by a municipal *régie,* which produced 902,000 kilowatt-hours in 1953 and 952,000 in 1954. Its small capacity reflected the inadequacy of its equipment and of its clientele, and subsidies from the local budget were required to keep the cost of current within the price range of its few consumers. No other town in Tchad had a public distribution of electrical energy.

In 1950 the municipal *régie* at Fort Lamy was replaced by the Energie Electrique d'AEF (EEAEF), to which was entrusted two years later the task of constructing a new and bigger diesel plant and distributing its current. Though the demand for current in the Tchadian capital was growing, especially in the African quarters, the expense of building branch lines and the difficulties of wiring *poto-poto* (mud-brick) structures were generally prohibitive obstacles to its satisfaction. FIDES allocated less for the development of electrical energy in Tchad than for any other territory, and the plan to enlarge Fort Lamy's plant was also held up by indecision in regard to its site. It was not until 1954 that construction was actually begun, and it started functioning late in the following year. The demand for current increased immediately to the point where its price could be reduced by 10 per cent in 1956, but even then it cost 37 CFA francs per kilowatt-hour.[84] Early in 1957 it was decided that the plant must be further enlarged, and the assembly was asked to guarantee a loan of 25 million CFA francs required for the work.

Before this project could be carried out, a new element entered the picture and made the plan obsolete. This was a proposal by the EDF, which worked closely with the Atomic Energy Commissariat, to build a small atomic pile at Fort Lamy. Admittedly the idea of utilizing this form of power was related to the discovery of uranium and thorium deposits in Ennedi,[85] and the scheme had the additional attraction of eliminating the importation of fuel, which was largely responsible for the high cost of electrical current in Fort Lamy. In 1958 the cost of such a pile was estimated at one billion CFA francs, and neither the indispensable funds for its construction nor purchasers of the current so generated were immediately in sight. Under present circumstances only the meat industry and the army at Fort Lamy are likely to be large-scale consumers, hence for the time being the construction of an atomic pile there remains in the category of enterprises that have been accepted only "in principle."

Labor

Tchad has the largest population and the fewest industries of any AEF territory, and it appears to have virtually no labor problems. From time to time, evidence of the survival of forced labor in various disguised forms and of unemployment in Fort Lamy has come to light, but it is soon dismissed by the authorities as either fictitious or as merely a passing and localized phenomenon. Only recently has labor been organized in the territory and, except among some cotton-company laborers, unions are confined almost wholly to the towns. Tchad's territorial assemblymen have shown very little interest in labor questions, and only one of them, Jean Charlot, has been a militant labor organizer.

Of a population numbering over 2 million, only about 34,800 are classed as wage earners (23,000 in the private and 11,300 in the public sector), and almost all of these are unskilled and are employed in the building and cotton industries. Compared with the situation in 1949, this represents a big numerical increase, almost doubling the number then estimated to be wage earners, but there have been few opportunities for these laborers to acquire skills. As of January 1, 1946, the Tchad public-school system had two *sections artisanales,* six *sections d'apprentissage,* and one Ecole des Métiers at Fort Archambault. These schools were giving technical instruction to 18 girls (in home economics) and 375 boys (303 in agriculture, 32 in local crafts, 23 in woodwork, and 17 in mechanics). By 1952 the number had dropped to 109 boys and one girl, and at that time Tchad was spending only 0.43 per cent of its budget on technical education.[86]

For some years the several thousand youths who could not find work in the impoverished eastern regions went to pick cotton or gather gum arabic in Sudan, but because of worsening economic conditions after that country became independent this seasonal emigration has now fallen off. Steadier but numerically less important outlets for Tchadian laborers exist in Oubangui and Gabon. In the cotton belt of Oubangui they find a way of life comparable to that at home, but the 500 or so Tchadians who go to work each year for the petroleum and plywood companies at Port Gentil have a more difficult time adjusting themselves to different climatic and food conditions. However, they are compensated by higher wages than those prevailing in Tchad and by a training in Gabon that makes them into skilled workers. The great majority of these migrants are seasonal, and ultimately almost all of them return to settle in their home areas. Tchad's politicians recognize the value of these extraterritorial labor markets for their compatriots, and are concerned only that the labor inspectorate and assemblymen from the districts where they are chiefly recruited (Logone and Moyen-Chari) should carefully control the terms of the laborers' contracts and the conditions under which they live and work in Gabon.[87]

It was not until 1954 that an "employment problem" was spoken of in Tchad, and then only in regard to its capital city. For some years before that, the assembly had voted to raise taxes in Fort Lamy far above those prevailing in the nearby countryside in order to force the growing number of idlers there to return to farming. As of late 1954 it was said in the assembly[88] that only one out of every six residents of Fort Lamy then had a job, but that for the first time since the war not all of the unemployed were simply parasites preying on their wage-earning relatives and that those who genuinely wanted to work were unable to find employment. This was, of course, a situation common to all of AEF's towns, but it arose in Fort Lamy later than elsewhere because the construction financed by FIDES had been slower in getting under way (and hence in terminating) in Tchad than in any other territory. Fortunately for Tchad, the slack was soon taken up by a revival of building at Fort Lamy for the new military installations of the army there and for enlargement of the civilian airfield.

The survival of forced labor in three disguised forms has caused recurrent, though fitful, concern in the government and assembly. One of these, that of a slave trade said to flourish in Tibesti, aroused little interest in Tchad but was given a great deal of publicity in France. In 1954, Dr. M. G. Schenk, a Dutch writer, published a book at Amsterdam in which he claimed that prosperous pilgrims taking the overland route from west Africa to Mecca brought with them retainers whom they sold or exchanged for arms and ammunition in Tibesti. This aroused some Parisian journalists either to make their own on-the-spot investigations or to query the geologists, *méharistes,* and officials of the antilocust service who frequented that inaccessible region.[89] All were agreed that such reports were more sensational than true because the nature of the country and the limited number of wells along the main *pistes* would make it impossible for any clandestine caravans carrying slaves to assemble in Tibesti without the knowledge of the administration.

Of more local concern was the exaction of forced labor by autocratic chiefs, particularly in the big sultanates, and this problem could be approached only indirectly, in relation to the whole question of the status of the Tchadian chieftaincy (see pp. 76–78). Much easier to deal with was the more or less forced labor demanded by regional and district administrators for the upkeep of roads. Here the burden fell mainly on the canton chiefs, who were not provided with sufficient funds to pay such labor adequately, and who were therefore faced with the choice of displeasing the administration if they failed to maintain the roads or the local peasantry if they used compulsion to do so. Primarily this was a financial matter that fell within the tax-regulating powers of the assembly, but it also involved the continued utilization of rural administrators and chiefs for tasks that properly lay within the competence of the labor inspectorate. The assemblymen were not opposed in principle to the use of compulsion in road maintenance, but they insisted that laborers so taken be regularly and sufficiently paid in cash and that their term of duty be limited definitely to either two weeks or a month.[90]

Application of the Overseas Labor Code to Tchad met with few difficulties except perhaps in relation to the cotton company. Tchad was assigned only two inspectors and one *controleur,* who natually centered their activities in the towns where the largest concentrations of wage earners existed. Similarly the territory's two labor courts were set up in 1954 at Fort Lamy and Fort Archambault, and in 1957 Tchad's sole Office de la Main-d'Oeuvre was established in the capital city. In the rural areas administrators were generally empowered, as they had been before the war, to see that the labor code was enforced. It was in respect to this that the assembly complained that district and regional officers were either too busy or indifferent to take steps to see that the cotton company carried out the new law's provisions in regard to its employees. Workers were said to be dismissed without justification in order to avoid giving them paid leave, seniority, and other benefits now legally due them. Among employer groups, COTONFRAN was singled out as the worst offender in this respect, and was also upbraided for its refusal to recognize the newly organized trade unions.[91]

As is not surprising, labor was slower to organize in Tchad than elsewhere in AEF. Though the first union was formed there in 1939 by a French member of the Confédération Française des Travailleurs Chrétiens (CFTC), it was confined to a handful of European functionaries. The CFTC is still the outstanding union in Tchad, and though it is now under an indigenous leader, Victor Malot, who has received some training in Europe, its membership is small (33 unions with about 1,300 members) and remains confined to the urban white-collar class. In October 1958 Malot told the writers that he maintained close relations with other branches of the CFTC in AEF, and also with those of French West Africa. Dues are 50 CFA francs a month, and its membership has increased at the expense of the small autonomous unions in proportion as the CFTC has been effective in getting salary rises for its members. The Force Ouvrière (FO) was similarly organized in Tchad by a Metropolitan militant, shortly after the war, but its appeal, aimed also at the functionary white-collar class, has brought to its fold far fewer members than the CFTC has gained.

The last of the big Metropolitan *centrales* to organize branches in Tchad was the Confédération Générale du Travail (CGT), and it now occupies a position midway between that of the CFTC and FO. It was set up in 1947 but made little progress until the return to Fort Lamy four years later of its present leader, Jean Charlot. After serving in Europe with the Free French forces, this Franco-Tchadian mulatto pursued his formal education in France and at the same time worked with the *cheminots* in the Paris region. There he became interested in organized labor, joined the CGT and, although not a communist, went as a member of that union on two trips to Moscow. This was enough to damn him in the eyes of the French administration of Tchad, which, he told the writers in 1958, tried to frustrate his attempts to revitalize the CGT unions there. In contrast to the situation prevailing elsewhere in Black Africa, the CGT in Tchad is strongest in the rural areas and claims a large membership among the cotton laborers and building trades despite the high monthly dues (75–150 CFA francs). Since he feels that education is the outstanding need of the territory's laborers,

Charlot teaches classes of workingmen once a week, trade by trade. He is on good terms, he said, with the CFTC, which he conceded is the strongest union in the territory, and stated that he had seceded from the Metropolitan CGT and maintained only nominal ties with the UGTAN of French West Africa. All of the labor leaders with whom the writers talked disavowed any political aspirations or even links with local political parties. Though it is impossible to get exact figures as to union membership for any of the *centrales* in Tchad, the total number of organized workers probably does not amount to even one-fourth of all the territory's wage earners. Whether the unions are even growing numerically is open to doubt, but it appears reasonably certain that in very recent years the three main *centrales* have been gaining members at the expense of the multitude of small autonomous unions which formerly dominated the Tchad labor scene.

Such improvements as have been made in the workers' status are traceable mainly to the government's initiative and very secondarily to the support of the territorial assembly and the unions. In December 1958 the administration opened the territory's first rapid labor-training center, thus supplementing the small professional school (Ecole des Métiers) that has existed at Fort Archambault since 1946. Employers in Tchad pay an apprenticeship tax, which provides funds for the Archambault school and for the territory's various apprenticeship centers, and some of them also train their own laborers. The minimum wage for most categories of workers has been raised several times in recent years to keep pace with the steadily rising cost of living, and it appears now to have reached about the limit which the few industries of Tchad are able to pay. When in June 1958 the Lisette government decided to increase the monthly family allowance by 50 per cent (from 200 to 300 CFA francs per child of wage earners), it was said that Tchad's rate in relation to minimum wages was the highest of any territory in the federation.

CHAPTER 25

Moyen-Congo (République du Congo)

Of all the AEF territories, Moyen-Congo is the least favored by nature and the best equipped by man. The northern half of the territory is covered by a dense forest in which the struggle for mere survival absorbs almost all the energies of its sparse population. Moreover, this forest contains few of the okoumé trees that have made the fortune of Gabon, and it covers no known mineral resources such as those possessed by Gabon in the iron of Mékambo or the manganese of Franceville.

The southern part of Moyen-Congo is better suited to human habitation and the formation of urban centers, but it has only one truly fertile region, the Niari valley, which has been developed solely through the enterprise of a few white settlers. The Niari colony is unique in AEF, and similar attempts to cultivate crops on the Batéké plateau to the northeast have proved failures. A few industries have been set up in the south, but more have failed than flourished. Brazzaville itself, which contains a seventh of the territory's total population, is a "great window opening onto nothing," for it lacks a supporting hinterland. When the Kouilou dam is constructed, a strong industrial complex may develop in the Pointe Noire region. But thus far Moyen-Congo has lived almost wholly by its transit trade, of which Brazzaville is the pivot for the rail line leading to the ocean and for the cargo boats plying between it and Bangui.

Moyen-Congo has two assets that have won for it exceptional treatment on the part of the French government. The first is its location, bordering on the Congo river and the Atlantic Ocean; the second is the presence in the Congo basin of the Bakongo, one of the most evolved and enterprising tribes in central Africa. Brazzaville grew to be the largest town and became the capital of the federation not only because it was located at the southern extremity of the Congo's longest navigable stretch but also because it was the habitat of a tribe capable of adapting itself to a European-type economy without losing its own traditions, vitality, and social structure. To fulfill its role in the transit trade, Brazzaville—like Léopoldville on the opposite bank of the Congo river—had to be linked with the coast by a railroad that turned out to be very difficult and costly to build. And at the western terminus of this rail line, an artificial port was built at Pointe Noire on such a scale that it has not yet been used to capacity.

That this poorest of all AEF territories in natural resources has today the only railroad in the federation, the largest towns, the biggest port, and the finest administrative buildings can be ascribed in large measure to the contributions in manpower and money made by the other territories, which are perforce dependent on its transit facilities. Moreover, the prospective transport of Gabon's mineral ores and the electric power to be produced by the Kouilou dam foreshadow an increase in their dependence and Moyen-Congo's economic importance.

Territorial Politics

Moyen-Congo ranks as the second-smallest territory of AEF in area and population. About one-third of its 700,000 inhabitants live in small villages scattered throughout the northern forest, and for the most part they belong to the M'Bochi tribe. Another, smaller population concentration is that of the Vili tribes who inhabit the region around Pointe Noire. The third and most important tribal group is the Bakongo, who straddle the Congo river and whose most progressive branch in Moyen-Congo is that of the Balali or Lari. Although other tribes live interspersed with or near the Bakongo, the latter are relatively homogenous and compact in the Brazzaville region. They number nearly 100,000 there and have given their name to one of the two main African villages that make up the non-European suburbs of the federal capital. The Bakongo in general and the Balali in particular are proud of their historical past (see pp. 4–5), are eager for self-improvement, and have been refractory to control by the French administration. They also are desirous of maintaining close ties with their relatives in non-French territory and of asserting their leadership over the other tribes living in Moyen-Congo.[1]

The French occupation caught and checked the Bakongo, as it did the Fang of Gabon, in a period of expansion. The Bakongo had already moved across the Congo and, after pushing the Batéké onto the plateau north of Brazzaville, had settled along the river's northern bank. Farmers and traders like the Fang, the Bakongo were better able than they to adapt themselves to the new economy brought in by the Europeans without suffering a similar population decline or breakdown of their hierarchized social structure. In this connection, it should be noted that no European-style plantations, forest camps, or mining industries were set up in the Bakongo area such as those that have acted as a solvent for Fang society. Although 22 per cent of the Bakongo are now town dwellers, they have not become detribalized, and have retained close ties with the land and with their rural relatives. Generally speaking, the crops raised by the Bakongo farmers— manioc, fruit, tobacco, and the like—are not especially remunerative, but the Bakongo do gain some cash income from palm-oil products and the contraband and legitimate trade they carry on with the Belgian Congo. Bakongo clothing and housing reflect higher living standards than those of neighboring tribes.

Unfortunately for the Bakongo, their ambition to raise themselves to

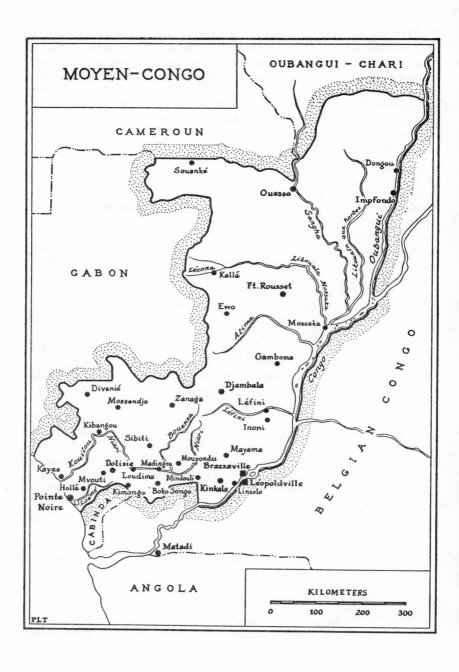

MOYEN-CONGO

OUBANGUI - CHARI

CAMEROUN

GABON

Souanké

Dongou

Ouesso

Impfondo

Sangha

Lécona

Kellé

Ft. Rousset

Ewo

Likouala

Mossaka

Litouala aux herbes

Oubangui

BELGIAN CONGO

Alima

Mossaka

Congo

Gamboma

Divenié

Djambala

Mossendjo

Zanaga

Léfini

Léfini

Kibangou

Inoni

Sibiti

Bouenza

Mayama

Niari

Mouyondzi

Kayes

Koulou

Dolisie

Madingou

Brazzaville

Mvouti

Loudima

Mindouli

Léopoldville

Hollé

Niari

Kimongo

Boko Songo

Kinkala

Linzolo

Pointe
Noire

Loémé

CABINDA

Matadi

ANGOLA

KILOMETERS

0   100   200   300

PLT

the level of Europeans has exceeded the opportunities locally available.[2] During periods of economic depression when the Bakongo's earnings have sunk below their already low level, tension has developed between them and the European community, which they hold responsible for their losses. Willing, even anxious, to adopt any European novelties that would bring them profit, the Bakongo have not yet fully grasped how the system into which they have been drawn operates, and their response to the exercise of arbitrary administrative authority has been recalcitrance. Thus for some 16 years, beginning in 1914, the Bakongo resisted all the government's moves to regroup their villages, in the belief that this was only the prelude to tighter administrative controls. But after the Congo-Ocean railroad was built, they spontaneously settled along this new means of communication, for they realized that it would offer them greater opportunities for trading.

Much the same attitude of both suspicious and enlightened self-interest characterized their early relations with the Christian missions. They availed themselves of the educational facilities provided by the mission schools but fought shy of submitting to any such control as was exerted by Catholic missionaries in the Belgian Congo. Later, when the Swedish evangelists and the Salvation Army came to Moyen-Congo, the Bakongo were at once attracted to their missions. Protestantism appealed to them more than did Catholicism, because of the greater freedom inherent in its more individualistic doctrines and because the Protestant missionaries were not of the same nationality as the colonial administrators. Just as the Bakongo took over those aspects of the European economic system in which they could see an immediate material advantage, so they adopted and adapted those facets of Christianity that lent themselves to their acquiring greater spiritual autonomy. The fact that Christian missionaries had been laboring in the Bakongo country since the end of the fifteenth century meant the early development of a larger literate group than was to be found among other Moyen-Congo tribes. This naturally gave the Bakongo, especially the Balali, a marked head start in entering the administrative services, the priesthood, and later the professional classes. Their early success in those fields enabled the Bakongo to emulate the white community and confirmed their belief that they had the "mission" to lead all the other tribes of Moyen-Congo.

To reach their goals, the Bakongo realized that they must develop a strong internal unity, but in their efforts to attain this they often encountered opposition on the part of the colonial administration. The failure or checkmate of their first political organizations led the Bakongo to abandon, as a rule, frontal attacks on the citadels of authority in favor of more indirect methods. Throughout the interwar period the Bakongo's technique consisted of absorbing from the Europeans only what seemed useful to them and of offering passive resistance to any official measures that they felt ran counter to that end. Furthermore, they were able to disguise their striving for greater freedom behind an outwardly Christian façade. Thanks to the syncretistic Messianic sects that burgeoned in the Brazzaville region, the Bakongo were able to carry on an underground resistance to the administration, for the latter found it much harder to clamp down on what were apparently religious organizations than on the earlier, more frankly political formations.

By far the most important of the Bakongo political organizations was that founded by André Matsoua at Paris in 1926. A Bakongo Christian and a minor official in the customs service of AEF, Matsoua had fought in both World War I and the Rif campaign of 1924–25. In 1925 he returned to Paris, where he got a job as an accountant, became a French citizen, and entered into contact with other Negroes in Metropolitan France, especially with those involved in the pan-Africa movement of that period. Although by his experience with these groups he acquired a political education in colonial problems, Matsoua did not succumb to the invitation to join a communist organization, the Union des Travailleurs Nègres. He concluded that the main task facing his fellow Negroes was that of raising their living standards to approximate those of the white world, and to accomplish this he felt that some form of organization and the acquisition of French citizenship were indispensable. So, with some official support and the aid of four other Congolese, he founded a mutual-aid society called the Société Amicale des Originaires de l'AEF. As this name suggests, its founder hoped to appeal to the French central Africans living in France, but it was actually in AEF that the movement took root, at first in Bangui and Libreville. However, it was among the Bakongo that the two emissaries sent by Matsoua found the readiest response when they went to Moyen-Congo on a propaganda and dues-collecting tour in 1928–29. At that time, Matsoua remained in Paris and began writing letters to the French government protesting against the *indigénat* in French Black Africa, the practices of some Brazzaville commercial firms, and the general stagnation of AEF's economy compared with that of the Belgian Congo. This activity, plus the resistance campaign adopted by Matsoua's followers in AEF—estimated officially in 1929 to number some 13,000—led to his arrest and then to his trial at Brazzaville the following year. The administration's case against Matsoua was strengthened by the evidence that was brought to light of some financial skulduggery on the part of the movement's leaders, and he was exiled, along with three Balali disciples, to Tchad, from which he managed to escape five years later.

Matsoua's trial took place in an atmosphere of great tension, and the verdict led to outbreaks against the administration by the Bakongo, among whom the Amicale movement now spread with heightened rapidity. The majority of its adherents were clerical employees and members of the *chefferie,* the elements most closely linked with the administration, and they combined traditionalist with modernist tendencies in about equal proportions. It was at that point that the Matsouanist movement acquired a rudimentary organization which generally followed the administrative divisions, and at all levels efforts were made to attract to it other tribes besides the Bakongo. Thus early in its growth Matsouanism aimed at creating unity among all the Congolese, and it became most dynamic in the region closest to the Belgian Congo. There it found affinities with a somewhat similar movement that had spread to Moyen-Congo in the early 1920's from the Belgian side of the river. This was Kimbangism, propagated by a former catechist, Simon Kimbangou, who used religion as a screen from behind which he attacked white rule (see pp. 309–10).

This mixture of religion with politics soon came to characterize increasingly the Matsouanist movement, and its founder, in the eyes of his followers, began to seem a Christian martyr. The popular idealization of Matsoua was greatly facilitated by his practice of leaving the organizational and fund-raising work to his followers and appearing in AEF only during the periods when he was on trial. From the time of his trial in 1930, Matsoua became "the symbol of all protests against colonial society," and neither the exposing of his shady financial deals nor his constant demands for money from his followers detracted from his popularity and pseudo-divinity. Later, when the administration tried to return the money it had seized from the Amicale treasury, the Matsouanists refused to accept it. Apparently they believed that the administration, by taking these funds, had obligated itself to accede to their demands for greater rights. An attitude of passive resistance characterized the Matsouanist movement throughout the 1930–40 decade. Its members and sympathizers refused to grow the new crops proposed by the administration, including peanuts—even though peanut seed was offered without charge—and to pay the 3-franc dues to the Sociétés Indigènes de Prévoyance (SIP) when they were set up in Moyen-Congo. They even opposed with some effectiveness the taking of a population and animal census and the recruitment of laborers for the Congo-Ocean railroad. As one leader summed up their attitude at the time, "We are tired of obeying."

Because the economic depression was spreading at the time of the incidents provoked by Matsoua's trial in 1930, the administration was misled into believing that they were solely manifestations of economic discontent. But the efforts, beginning in 1931, to improve local agricultural methods, water supply, and medical facilities did not touch the heart of Bakongo grievances, which were even more psychological than material. And they were in fact aggravated by the administration's move in 1934 to curtail the educational opportunities open to the Bakongo, in order to strengthen the *elite* of other tribes. Passive resistance at all levels of Bakongo society continued through the whole prewar decade.

After a brief period of improved Bakongo-French relations during the opening months of World War II—during which many Balali volunteered to serve in the army—a new crisis arose in April 1940. This was caused by the rearrest of Matsoua, this time accused of disseminating pro-German propaganda. Two years later he died a natural death in prison, but the authorities made the great mistake of burying him secretly. His followers refused to believe that he had died, and thereafter as a myth and a divinity he became a more powerful force than when he was alive. Though Matsoua's arrest had been followed by new outbreaks, during which the chiefs and the Native Guard had been attacked as collaborators of the administration, the movement began to take on a more distinctively religious coloration. "Jesus Matsoua" was said to be de Gaulle's divine helper and responsible not only for Free France's military successes but also for the reforms initiated at the Brazzaville conference in 1944. De Gaulle was not the only mortal to benefit by Matsoua's supernatural guidance. In 1941 a sect called Kakism was launched by Simon Mpadi, who claimed to be both the reincarnation of Kimbangou and Matsoua's local deputy. This blend of politics with religion, of the living with the dead, and of tradition with modern reforms was a phenomenon that shaped the Bakongo political evolution in the years that followed.

Until 1956 the Bakongo remained quiescent in the local political game, for they were addicted to their own forms of "protest" and looked with suspicion upon political parties and labor unions as alien formulas foisted upon them by the administration.[3] Yet for all its seeming passivity, Matsouanism had lost none of its vitality, as was indicated by the number of new chapels built soon after the war and by the growing cult of the Congo river as the symbol of Bakongo unity. Although in 1949 there were probably not more than 4,000 active Matsouanists, Balandier then estimated that nine-tenths of the Bakongo population were sympathetic to the movement.[4] At election times, the Bakongo voted—if at all—for André Matsoua, writing his name on their ballots in the place of candidates put up by the regularly constituted political parties. By their persistence in voting for a dead man, the Bakongo left the political field wide open to the Rassemblement du Peuple Français (RPF) and to the two other main tribal groups of Moyen-Congo, the Vili and M'Bochi.

The RPF never became as prominent in Moyen-Congo politics as it did in Tchad, but *Gaullisme* continued to exert an emotional appeal in the territory where Free France had been born overseas, and this sentiment was almost as strong among Africans as among Europeans. When Raymond Barbé, the Communist Party spokesman in the French Union Assembly, visited Moyen-Congo in 1948, he made ill-advised attacks on both de Gaulle and the territory's RPF deputy, Bayrou. The African war veterans present at the meetings he addressed in the Brazzaville suburb of Bacongo and in Pointe Noire took strong exception to his jibes, for Bayrou had commanded many of them on the celebrated trans-Sahara march to Bir Hakeim. At Brazzaville the meeting broke up in disorder, and at Pointe Noire Barbé had to leave the hall under a police escort.[5] In the first postwar territorial elections to the National Assembly, the only real contest was that between two European RPF candidates, Bayrou and Seignon, and the administration—in the form of Governor Sadoul—was accused of favoring the latter unduly.[6] When Bayrou's election was subsequently validated, however, the excitement died down, and there was little talk for some years thereafter about electoral pressure being exercised by French officialdom.

Such reticence is noteworthy, for it illustrates the difference between the ways in which the Rassemblement Démocratique Africain (RDA) developed in French Equatorial and French West Africa. It is true that the French government's hostility to the RDA's aggressive radicalism in 1949 was probably responsible for the resignation from that movement of several territorial assemblymen and of two Moyen-Congo parliamentarians, Senator Malonga and French Union Assemblyman Dadet. But though the RPF candidate Bayrou was regularly returned to the National Assembly by the European electorate of Moyen-Congo (and Gabon), so was the Vili leader, Jean-Félix Tchicaya, as consistently re-elected by the African second college. This occurred despite the fact that Tchicaya had been a member of the RDA from its earliest days. To be sure, Tchicaya was no Lisette and never was actively associated with the RDA high command, and his contributions to National Assembly debates were confined mostly to protests against the double electoral college.[7] Never, it appears, seriously opposed by the local administration—especially after Cornut-Gentille became governor-general—and supported as he was by many traditional chiefs and a few of the big Moyen-Congo trading firms, Tchicaya built up an effective local branch of the RDA, called the Parti Progressiste Congolais (PPC).

Many other political parties were born in Moyen-Congo, but most of them withered away after elections were over, and the only one that offered any real competition to the PPC was the local branch of the Section Française de l'Internationale Ouvrière (SFIO), led by a minor African official in the judicial service, Jacques Opangault. Actually both the PPC and the SFIO, though directly linked with their respective parent organizations, were tribal groupings. The PPC was composed very largely of Vili tribesmen from the Pointe Noire and Niari regions, while the great majority of SFIO members were from the M'Bochi tribe that peopled northern Moyen-Congo and formed the principal element in the Brazzaville suburb of Poto-Poto.

The territorial assembly elected in 1952 had in its second college 17 PPC members to 7 for the SFIO. There was little to distinguish this body from similar assemblies in other parts of AEF. The assemblymen, Europeans and Africans alike, chided the administration for submitting incomplete projects to it at the last minute, for ignoring 90 per cent of the resolutions it passed, and for trying to by-pass plenary sessions by submitting controversial matters to the smaller and more malleable permanent committee. All these were the classical reactions of all such assemblies, and only in a few instances did that of Moyen-Congo show a more original trend. Perhaps more than in other territories were Moyen-Congo's parliamentarians rebuked for their failure to attend assembly sessions and for not exerting themselves enough to further the territory's interests in Paris.[8] It may be, too, that the territorial assembly was more stubborn than its counterparts in refusing or drastically cutting down the administration's proposals for heavier taxation, secure in the conviction that Moyen-Congo's deficits would always be made up by the Metropolitan or the federal government. From time to time, the Matsouanists opposed—though not by force—such measures as that of census-taking, claiming that they owed allegiance only to God through André Matsoua.[9] By and large, however, neither Moyen-Congo's electorate nor its territorial assembly set off any political fireworks until the legislative elections of January 2, 1956.

This deceptive background of seeming political calm made the January 1956 outbreaks at Brazzaville stand out in startling relief. Unfortunately they were but the forerunner of other riots of increasing violence, which are no longer confined to the Brazzaville area and of which the end is not yet in sight. To outward appearances, the 1956 outbreaks were caused by the spectacular rise of a new political leader, the Abbé Fulbert Youlou. More fundamentally, they were the recrudescence of old tribal hostilities and at the same time afforded opportunities for paying off personal scores.

Fulbert Youlou, a Balali born at Brazzaville in 1917 and educated at the Yaoundé (Cameroun) Seminary, had for some time been well known to his compatriots through a school that he founded and by some of his writings. Behind the mild, even unctuous, demeanor of a simple parish priest, Youlou cherished political ambitions that displeased his ecclesiastical superiors. When he decided to be a candidate for election to the National Assembly in January 1956 and thus make the contest a triangular one between Tchicaya, Opangault, and himself, a letter from his bishop was read aloud in Brazzaville churches forbidding the faithful to vote for him. As it turned out, the Catholic missionaries made a strategic error in pitting their authority against the popularity of Youlou, but the church prudently stopped short of defrocking him as it had done Boganda. To this day, Youlou wears the cassock and is thus able to add the prestige of the priesthood to that of an authentic tribal leader.

For some days before the election, it was apparent that the campaign was taking on a definitely tribal character and that Youlou had the incredible good fortune of being accepted by a majority of the Balali as André Matsoua's heir. Not all the Matsouanists of Brazzaville, however, were willing to vote for him,[10] and, in addition, there were many Batéké residents of the capital who were partisans of Tchicaya and the RDA. Thus the stage was set for the election-day riots of January 2, 1956, in which the zealous followers of both Youlou and Opangault attacked the supporters of Tchicaya and the die-hard Matsouanists. These riots caused the death of at least one person, wounded 46 others, and wrought property damage estimated at over 25 million CFA francs. They also resulted in the arrest of 474 persons, all but 26 of whom were immediately released. When those who had been detained were tried at Brazzaville the following September, they were acquitted for lack of evidence.

This was a strictly inter-African outbreak in which only one European was molested. For the most part, the pro-Youlou Balali and the M'Bochi adherents of Opangault joined forces against their common foe, Tchicaya and the PPC. When the election results were announced, the votes were so evenly distributed among the three candidates that the Balali and M'Bochi again united in asking the government to annul the election. They complained jointly to Paris about the "defective organization of the polling, frauds practiced in counting the ballots, and the moral pressure exerted by Tchicaya upon the electorate."[11] Youlou was able to raise several hundred thousand francs from his devoted followers to finance a trip to Paris for the purpose of protesting the election of Tchicaya in person, and the crowd that saw him off at the airport was reportedly even larger than the one that greeted General de Gaulle during the war.

Though Youlou's protests to the Paris government were unavailing, and therefore the pledges that he had made to his supporters could not be fulfilled, this failure seemed not at all to diminish his popular appeal. As had been the case with Matsoua before him, dubious financial practices that would have discredited a politician of Western Europe were regarded indulgently by the abbé's followers. They happily provided him with an automobile, a chauffeur, and a monthly stipend so that he could pursue his political career without concern for his material needs. The next goal that Youlou set for himself was that of winning the municipal elections at Brazzaville the following November 18, and in that Balali stronghold he won the mayoralty by a landslide. Even at Pointe Noire, the candidates whom he sponsored jointly with the socialists won a clear-cut victory over the PPC. By that time it was obvious that Tchicaya's debatable success in January had been in reality his swan song, and that the next real trial of strength would lie between Opangault and Youlou. Enactment of the *loi-cadre* in June 1956 had given an unprecedented importance to the March 1957 elections for the next territorial assembly, since on their outcome would depend which of the two men would control Moyen-Congo's prospective government council.

After promising the French authorities that their campaign would be peaceably conducted, the two rivals got under way in earnest. With the advice and material aid of some Europeans, Youlou organized his own party, the Union Démocratique pour la Défense des Interêts Africains (UDDIA), and he toured the territory preaching the need for social reform and—ironically enough—for unity. The decision that had been reached by the socialists of Brazzaville in January 1957 to group all the local branches of the SFIO into a single territorial party, the Mouvement Socialiste Africain (MSA), resulted in an increase in its over-all membership, but they had a hard time closing ranks and getting trade-union support. Their mainstay continued to be the northern M'Bochi and their southern stronghold, the Poto-Poto suburb at Brazzaville. The PPC, whose zone of influence had formerly extended as far as Dolisie, was having trouble in maintaining its strength even in the Pointe Noire region, and to all intents and purposes it could no longer be considered a serious contender. Politics were becoming increasingly tribal and personal, and party labels and platforms meant less to the voters than did their symbols. A Balali voted inevitably for Youlou, whose symbol was a crocodile, and a M'Bochi just as automatically for Opangault, whose emblem was a cock. According to those lively reporters, Pierre and Renée Gosset,[12] the Balali took delight in sacrificing cocks ritually in public, while the M'Bochi retaliated by throwing pepper

486   DEVELOPMENT OF THE TERRITORIES

in the eyes of the baby crocodiles brandished aloft by the Balali. And each party took pains to enlist the support of one or another of the many politico-religious sects that flourished in Moyen-Congo.

In all, 102 candidates presented themselves for election to the 45 seats in the 1957 territorial assembly. Of these, 17 were Europeans, and for the first time former RPF members were sponsored by the socialists, while none of them was to be found on the UDDIA list.[18] Youlou owed a great deal to his own European supporters, especially Joseph Vial and Christian Jayle, who were his financial and legal advisers respectively, and he later rewarded them with cabinet posts. The inconclusive outcome of this election was at the root of Moyen-Congo's later political difficulties, for the UDDIA and the MSA each won 21 seats, the 3 remaining places going to Independents. Inevitably it led to a coalition government and to a tug of war between the UDDIA and the MSA to win over the Independents. As two of the Independents had socialist sympathies, Moyen-Congo's first government was headed by Opangault. But the personality of the third Independent, Stéphane Tchitchellé, was the strongest of all, and on his future alignment the fate of the government seemed at that time to depend. Tchitchellé was a station-master by occupation and mayor of Pointe Noire by election. As a Vili he had been a PPC member of the assembly as recently as 1952. In the 1957 elections, however, he was labeled a member of both the MSA and the UDDIA, and to many Europeans in Pointe Noire he appeared to be covertly anti-French. Whatever may have been his real sentiments, he soon went over to the UDDIA, in which he became an invaluable aide to Youlou and was his outstanding Vili collaborator.

Tchitchellé may have been prompted to take this step by the successful outcome of long-drawn-out negotiations between Youlou and the RDA emissaries sent to him by Houphouet shortly after the 1957 elections. Although in May the UDDIA announced that it would not merge with the RDA but would only make an alliance with it, Tchicaya was thus effectively isolated from the party of which he had been a founding member and his local political potential was still further reduced. Another consequence of this RDA move to increase its influence in Moyen-Congo was the strengthening of the socialists' organization. In September 1957 the local branch of the MSA held its first territorial congress at Brazzaville, to which even socialists from the Belgian Congo came as observers. Of the 86 delegates, 8 were Europeans. But on the principle that the Moyen-Congo party should be under wholly African leadership, the European members declined to run for office, and the pre-eminence of Opangault and his lieutenant Kikounga Ngot was unanimously confirmed.

The shaky coalition government headed by Opangault survived until November 1957, when the resignation of four UDDIA Ministers—including Tchitchellé—brought to a climax the political tension that had been building up over the preceding six months. What precipitated their resignation was a "libelous and insulting" article entitled "The Gravediggers of the Franco-African Community" that appeared in Opangault's newspaper, *Climats d'Afrique et d'AEF,* and this was followed by an anonymous letter (presumably from the same source), circulated among members of the territorial assembly, in which the four ministers in question were more specifically denounced. Official oil was poured on the troubled waters by Governor-General Chauvet and Governor Soupault, and Opangault and his socialist colleagues were persuaded to express publicly their regret at having made "outrageous and discourteous comments" and to appeal anew for union. On December 24, Opangault and Youlou issued a joint declaration of their intention to work together thenceforth for the public good in peace and harmony. Few in Moyen-Congo were inclined, however, to believe that this entente would long endure.

A rumor circulated to the effect that the truce was prompted primarily by the desire of both leaders to extricate themselves from the overzealous tutelage of their respective European backers. More likely it was traceable to the overwhelming preoccupation of all the Moyen-Congo elite with the decision then pending in Paris to build the Kouilou dam. For no sooner had the French government committed itself to that project than on January 11, 1958, trouble broke out anew, this time at Dolisie, between the MSA and the UDDIA. The fact that this town, which till then had been a political no-man's-land between the zones of Vili and Bakongo influence, was chosen as the site for a UDDIA meeting was interpreted by the MSA as a provocative attempt by the UDDIA to extend its influence there. As soon as the MSA militants showed signs of belligerence, the police forbade the UDDIA members to hold further meetings, which were then transferred to Brazzaville. Disorders continued, however, after their departure: huts were burned, one person was killed, and eleven others were wounded.

Youlou forthwith announced that he was going to Pointe Noire to meet with Opangault so that together they might take the steps necessary to restore calm. But Opangault refused to receive him and in a communiqué stigmatized the behavior of the UDDIA at Dolisie as an "incitement to disorder."[14] Naturally the UDDIA responded to this by charging the MSA with responsibility for the Dolisie outbreaks, and for the next ten days Moyen-Congo's government functions almost came to a standstill.[15] During this interval the French administration tried to effect a reconciliation between the two groups. But when the MSA insisted on the resignation of the UDDIA Minister of Finance, Joseph Vial, Youlou pronounced this condition to be unacceptable and the situation reached a deadlock. To understand the bitterness of MSA feeling, it must be remembered that Youlou's sudden and spectacular success on the Moyen-Congo political scene had upset the socialists' applecart. Opangault, a conscientious minor functionary somewhat older than his rival, had waited patiently for ten years on the sidelines without once changing his political allegiance, which made him a rarity among African politicians. Then, just when the SFIO came to head the government in France and Tchicaya's star was definitely on the wane in Moyen-Congo, Opangault saw the power that was almost within his grasp fall into the hands of a newcomer.

In the spring of 1958, two events transpired that caused a further deterioration in the already bad political situation. On March 28 the PPC held its first congress in 12 years, officially severed its connections with the RDA, and voted to join the MSA opposition to the UDDIA. This was almost the only positive move left open to the PPC and, coming almost a year after the announced alliance between the UDDIA and the RDA, the step must have been taken by Tchicaya with the greatest reluctance, for he knew that it would cost his party a loss in membership. The second event was the death in mid-April of the MSA territorial assemblyman from Kouilou in an automobile accident, which led to short-lived disorders in that region as the result of a rumor that he had been poisoned.

In May the election of Christian Jayle as president of the territorial assembly, in place of another European (A. Garnier) who had been chosen for that post the preceding year through the socialists' support, indicated that the political impasse was about to be surmounted in favor of the UDDIA. This trend was confirmed two months later when the by-election held in the Kouilou region sent a member of the UDDIA to the assembly. The consequent increase, modest as it was, in the UDDIA majority induced Youlou to ask for Opangault's resignation as premier. But the socialist leader would not step down, and the French administration—after an appeal from both parties to arbitrate—refused to intervene, on the ground that it had no legal power to do so.

In part because this new deadlock occurred at the time when all were preoccupied by preparations for the September 28 referendum, still another potential crisis was averted. Although the UDDIA was now in the RDA camp and the PPC-MSA aligned with the PRA, all the parties favored joining the Franco-African Community. The result was a 99.1 per cent affirmative vote, the highest percentage registered in any territory of the federation. Such virtual unanimity in a territory so ridden by politics as Moyen-Congo was certainly traceable to the widespread eagerness to assure French aid in building the Kouilou dam. And the almost equally overwhelming acceptance of some type of close cooperation in the future with neighboring AEF territories grew out of a general comprehension that Moyen-Congo was not economically capable of going it alone locally. Where differences arose, however—and here they followed party lines—they had to do with the form that such cooperation should take. For some time, Opangault and Tchicaya had been openly receptive to Boganda's overtures, and the fact that Youlou was himself hatching a similar project had some bearing on their reaction. Actually there was little to choose between the two schemes except in the vital matter of leadership. Here Youlou certainly had the advantage over Boganda, for he was an authentic Bakongo and was said to be in close touch with fellow tribesmen in Belgian and Portuguese territories who cherished the same dream of restoring the ancient Bakongo kingdom. However, these competitive projects had not matured to the point of bringing about a head-on colllision between the UDDIA and the MSA-PPC before there took place a development in the territorial assembly that was to tip the scales definitely in favor of the UDDIA.

This event occurred during the session of November 28, 1958, at which the assembly proclaimed Moyen-Congo to be the République du Congo and an autonomous member-state of the Community. An assemblyman named Georges Yambot, who had for many years vacillated between the two rival parties, suddenly announced that he was shifting his allegiance to the UDDIA. Youlou thereupon claimed the right to form a new government and to transfer the capital from Pointe Noire to Brazzaville. When the socialist militants of Pointe Noire learned of Yambot's defection, they invaded the assembly hall to wreak vengeance on him. With considerable difficulty the police and gendarmes restored order, but the socialist assemblymen refused to discuss the draft constitution submitted by the UDDIA and then left the hall. So the UDDIA assemblymen, forming neatly the required quorum of 23, were able without opposition to invest Youlou as premier and to vote the capital's transfer to Brazzaville. The serio-comic scene that ensued when the socialists invaded the hall was aptly described by Philippe Decraene as a scenario worthy of a Western movie:[16]

> Premier Opangault seized the microphone, with which he struck the president of the assembly (Jayle). Then Fulbert slipped out of his cassock and in the middle of the meeting armed himself with a gun, while his friends covered the retreat of Yambot—more dead than alive—with a variety of projectiles. The day ended with another picturesque scene. Having succeeded by legal means in overthrowing the Opangault government, Youlou's followers had only one idea—to get safely out of Pointe Noire, fief of their adversaries, and regain the security of Brazzaville. The RDA councilors feverishly surrounded Fulbert at the Pointe Noire station, some of them obviously armed. Up to the last minute they hesitated to board the *micheline* that had been especially chartered, for fear of their opponents' vengeance. Would they be safe? But a motorized hand-car, manned by well-armed militiamen, cleared the way for the *autorail* on the track.

The departure of the panicky UDDIA assemblymen with all their families did not bring calm to Pointe Noire, where rioting throughout the day led to the death of four persons, the wounding of 16 others, and considerable property damage. Such incidents continued until the departure of Youlou for Brazzaville on December 1, accompanied by Tchitchellé, the mayor of Point Noire and his outstanding Vili ally.[17] Once back in his home town, Youlou tried to reassure those distressed by the undemocratic character of the first laws passed by the assembly. In a press conference he stated that there would be a place in the government for representatives of the minority after order had been restored.[18]

Yet in the government that Youlou set up with no little difficulty on December 8, no portfolios were assigned to the opposition,[19] and none of the MSA or PPC members would attend sessions of the assembly until a date was officially set for holding new elections to that body. The UDDIA assemblymen decided that for the time being the territorial capital should not be transferred from Pointe Noire (pending a possible decision on the federation level to reinstate Brazzaville as a federal headquarters) but that

Brazzaville should serve as the temporary seat of government and meeting place for the assembly. This decision was badly timed, as the rioting that took place across the river in Léopoldville on January 4–5, 1959, inevitably had repercussions in Brazzaville, where the situation was already tense. In fact, tension was widespread in Moyen-Congo, particularly as the Youlou government after it came to power had, for political reasons, transferred many MSA civil servants to different posts and sent Bakongo to occupy positions in M'Bochi country. Feeling in that area ran so high that in mid-January the M'Bochi population of Fort Rousset refused to permit a UDDIA official arriving from the south to take up the post he had been assigned there.

The M'Bochi of Poto-Poto in general, and Opangault in particular, have been generally charged with being mainly responsible for starting the riots that broke out in Brazzaville on February 17. These were the bloodiest that that town had ever known: after five days of intermittent rioting the official toll stood at 98 persons killed, 170 wounded, and 350 arrested. Four French surgeons worked day and night in the new Brazzaville hospital, where they performed 160 operations in 72 hours. Thousands of African refugees poured across the Congo to the Belgian side or sought shelter with Europeans or in the camps provided to receive them. No Europeans were killed nor was their property damaged, as had been the case during the Léopoldville riots five weeks earlier. This was a wholly African, intertribal conflict, and pointless savagery marked the fighting. Many African women and children were among the victims hacked to death or badly injured by knife wounds. The donning of their traditional headgear by both the M'Bochi and the Balali facilitated the massacre, for it made them easily distinguishable from one another. The mere fact of belonging to the rival tribe was apparently sufficient provocation for an attack to kill. To quell the riots, 1,300 troops were brought into Brazzaville, and within 48 hours of their arrival the slaughter ceased. This was accomplished without their firing a shot: the troops simply patrolled the streets and conducted a house-to-house search for arms. Not even the arrest of Opangault and Ngot incited their followers to fresh violence.

Such a shocking outburst of tribal hatred, not to mention such a proof of political immaturity, was scarcely reassuring to the French government that had just granted autonomy to Moyen-Congo and had promised to help build the Kouilou dam. Youlou, now that his main opponent was safely in jail, promised to hold elections for a new assembly as soon as order was completely restored. But in March he gave the whole question an unexpected twist: he proposed that a referendum be held in northern Moyen-Congo, by means of which the M'Bochi there would indicate whether they wanted to remain in the Congo Republic or preferred to form a separate and independent state of their own. Youlou's proposal was thought to be motivated by his evident desire to slough off an economic and political liability that was both a drain on the territory's resources and a threat to the UDDIA's political supremacy.[20] Secession by the north would serve to advance the fulfillment of Youlou's ambition to form a homogeneous Bakongo state with his fellow tribesmen south of the Congo river. On the local political scene, moreover, it would give him a clear working majority. Inasmuch as the existing party affiliations in Moyen-Congo were based on tribalism, there was little hope otherwise of ending the permanent stalemate that had resulted from the almost equal numerical proportions of the UDDIA and the MSA.

As was inevitable, Youlou's proposal met with opposition from various quarters. The French administration was displeased by the prospect of a further balkanization of tropical Africa. As for the northern M'Bochi themselves, they were faced with Hobson's choice. If they voted to remain in the Congo Republic, this might be interpreted as a vote of confidence in Youlou, and if they broke away, their brethren in the south would be left a small socialist minority at the mercy of the UDDIA. Because the north was too poor to be viable as a separate state, it would perforce have to join Oubangui-Chari, and there was no evidence that Boganda would be willing thus to add to his own burdens. Youlou must have realized almost immediately that his referendum proposal promised no real solution of the problem, or he may never have intended that it be taken seriously—in any case, he has let the matter drop. It remains to be seen whether the Bakongo leader can find some more constructive way to apply the lessons to be learned from the Brazzaville massacres.

Even before his referendum died stillborn, Youlou was busying himself with more immediately urgent matters. On February 21 his UDDIA assemblymen duly and unanimously approved the constitution he had drafted for the Congo Republic and also the agreement reached the month before at Paris for an interterritorial customs union. The next item on Youlou's agenda was to ensure a UDDIA victory in the elections for the legislative assembly, to be held June 14. To this end he created new electoral circumscriptions and increased the number of assembly seats to 61. Since the MSA had been formally blamed for the February riots and was leaderless, it had been reduced to impotency and semiclandestinity. Moreover, Youlou could count on at least the benevolent neutrality of local French officialdom, for France's chief concern in the Congo was that the Republic should have a stable government. Even with so many cards stacked in his favor, however, Youlou must have been astonished by the extent of his victory on June 14. Calm had marked the campaigning as well as the election, and the electorate, as expected, simply voted on tribal lines and not for party platforms, which in any case presented few differences. The UDDIA won 64 per cent of the popular vote and 51 of the 61 seats in the assembly.

Hard on the heels of the UDDIA's triumph, however, rioting broke out again in the Brazzaville area on June 18, which seemed to show that Youlou had the situation less well under control than the elections would indicate. First reports spoke of a spontaneous uprising by the Matsouanists, who were refusing to submit to census-taking and the payment of taxes to the Youlou government, just as they had done previously with the French administration. Later evidence indicated that these riots were very different from those of the preceding February in regard to their scope, motivation, and participants, being strictly between Bakongo groups and not between two different tribes. Order was restored quickly and without the large-scale intervention of troops. It appeared, too, that the rioting was no spontaneous expression of resentment by the UDDIA militants against a group that had refused to vote for their leader or help to finance his government. Rather, according to one astute observer,[21] the government had deliberately utilized mob violence to liquidate the Matsouanists as a politico-social force. Yet the government had reportedly given orders "to punish but not to kill," and this won it the approval of some European observers. The latter noted that Youlou had been compelled to deal with a problem inherited from the French administration, which had failed to solve it after more than 25 years of effort. The attack on the Matsouanists not only gave gratifying practical results but was followed by wisely conceived measures on the part of Premier Youlou. Within 48 hours after the riots ended, taxes and requests for identity cards flowed in from the Matsouanists as never before. Then on June 30 the new assembly voted unanimously in favor of an amnesty that liberated almost all local political prisoners, including Opangault and other MSA leaders. And in the new government he formed early in July, Youlou included as ministers two members of the opposition (Bazinga and Okambo), although the MSA controlled only ten seats in the new legislature.

Satisfaction over these developments, however, was short-lived, for a new and more violent clash between UDDIA militants and Matsouanists occurred in late July and early August. The government, apparently convinced that the MSA no longer represented a threat to its power, adopted a tougher line toward the Matsouanists and forcibly deported about 500 of the most turbulent of them to the Fort Rousset region. This time the Matsouanists struck back, and at least 35 persons were killed and 17 wounded in the ensuing melee. Subsequently the assembly voted exceptional powers to the government, which was authorized to impose a curfew, forbid meetings of more than five persons, and set up a special court that could inflict without appeal the death penalty on all "fomenters of trouble," including those who advocated the nonpayment of taxes. From this point on, the government exercised increasingly dictatorial powers in various ways. Beginning in September, Youlou altered the designation of "regions" and "districts" to "prefectures" and "subprefectures," organized a seminar in political training for about 30 influential members of UDDIA so as to "intensify their antisubversion action,"[22] and took steps to force the unemployed youths of the Congolese towns to work. Then, as the crowning touch, he permitted himself in November to be elected president as well as premier of the Congo Republic, after the assembly had amended the constitution for the specific purpose of creating this post for him.

The Territorial Economy

The Plan

Moyen-Congo owes what little prosperity it has known almost wholly to its geographical location, for it possesses virtually no natural resources— with the possible exception of petroleum—that are large revenue earners. To be sure, the Mayombé forests contain valuable wood and the Niari valley comprises one of the few comparatively large areas of fertile soil in the federation, but they would never have achieved their present stage of development had it not been for their proximity to the Congo-Ocean railroad. And AEF's only railroad would never have been built across the mountainous Mayombé forest had Moyen-Congo not possessed in the west an outlet on the Atlantic Ocean capable of being made into a great port, and in the east the southern terminus of the Congo's longest navigable stretch. It is also true that three of AEF's main towns—Brazzaville, Dolisie, and Pointe Noire—lie within the boundaries of this territory, but none of them has a supporting hinterland whose products it can drain, and all owe their rise to their location along the federation's major trade routes. Brazzaville, which has been the federal capital since 1910, has already been described as a dying city, kept alive only by its administrative and political functions, and as a result of the disappearance of the government-general it may revert to being simply a point of transit or a trading post.

For many years the "parasitic role" played by Moyen-Congo in the federation's economy was a source of irritation to its neighbors, particularly to Gabon. Men and money coming from the countries to the north were poured into Moyen-Congo to build its railroad, administrative buildings, and ports. And to the detriment of their native villages and farms, many of these emigrants stayed on in Moyen-Congo to swell the unproductive element of its urban populations. A large proportion of this territory is covered by a forest so dense and so inhospitable that its few and scattered inhabitants can barely eke out a livelihood. And once they have experienced life in the southern towns they prefer to remain there even under miserable living conditions. This over-rapid expansion of Moyen-Congo's urban centers in general, and of their commercial structure in particular, began before World War II but has been greatly aggravated since 1945.

Of the 1,545 million CFA francs allotted to Moyen-Congo under the first Plan, about 60 per cent was devoted to its infrastructure, almost all of which benefited its towns with the exception of the portion assigned to road building and the railroad. Even the 28 per cent of FIDES credits allocated to works of a social character were concentrated for the most part in the towns.[23] Only 12.3 per cent went toward direct aid for the peasantry through the creation of *paysannats,* equipping the SIP, constituting animal herds, and reforestation. An attempt to develop agriculture scientifically on the Batéké plateaus ended in failure, for their terrain was unsuitable and their populations proved uncooperative. Elsewhere, marketing turned out to be the major difficulty, as Governor-General Reste had discovered when he tried to encourage coffee and peanut cultivation in the 1930's. Even today the selling of its products is a problem in the Niari valley, the one bright spot in Moyen-Congo's production picture, where a unique experiment in modern farming has been conducted since the war by a colony of white settlers.

With the progressive shrinkage in FIDES funds and especially during AEF's trade recession in 1952–53, the situation of Moyen-Congo became even more critical than did that of the other territories. For its small output and even for the transit trade, Moyen-Congo proved to be overequipped. The newly installed railroad and port equipment was far from being fully utilized, and there were purchasers for only about one-sixth of the electrical current that the recently built Djoué dam was capable of supplying to the Brazzaville region. Obviously production must be increased; hence the second Plan was oriented far more than the first toward improving the rural economy. To exactly what extent this was done is hard to discover, because here as in the budgetary domain funds for federal projects of the nonproductive type (such as Brazzaville's general hospital) are difficult to disentangle from those for Moyen-Congo proper. Of the strictly territorial credits it appears that 32.4 per cent was allotted to the rural economy, 52.1 per cent to infrastructure, and 15.5 per cent to social equipment, and they were mainly distributed over multiple operations rather than concentrated on a few major projects in the urban centers.

Before the effects of this reorientation of the Plan could be felt, Moyen-Congo's economic situation further deteriorated. The number of unemployed men in the towns increased alarmingly, and the government's attempt to induce them either to return to their villages or to work in the Niari valley was largely unsuccessful. The tempo of investments slowed to a grinding halt; many trading firms, especially the smaller ones, went to the wall, as did some recently installed industries. When the authorities tried to rescue the survivors by lightening their tax burdens, this increased the already large deficit of the territorial budget.[24] By 1955, however, a revival of the federation's foreign commerce had begun to swell Moyen-Congo's revenues from the transit trade, and concurrently its own economic situation improved. At long last the investments made under the Plan were being felt in terms of the increased output of crops, fish, and livestock products, and the like. At this time, too, the whole structure of FIDES was decentralized, so that the territory gained more control over its operations. In the spring of 1956 its territorial assembly was able to carry out an often-expressed desire to constitute its own Committee of the Plan,[25] and the following year Moyen-Congo's newly constituted African government acquired the power to allocate a larger portion of its credits.

The political orientation of Moyen-Congo's present government makes it unlikely that the funds for production will be sharply increased. Even before 1956 its territorial assemblymen were often reproached for having voted sums to carry out social works disproportionate to the percentages allocated to those economic enterprises that could provide the wherewithal required for their maintenance. Gabon had its okoumé, Oubangui its cotton and coffee, and Tchad its cotton and livestock, but Moyen-Congo never developed any such stable exports and continued to rely overmuch on the revenues derived from its transit trade and on subsidies from the federal and Metropolitan budgets. It is noteworthy that it was a group of private interests, not the new territorial government, that in 1957 sponsored creation of a Committee for the Economic Development of the Pool Region.[26]

Hopes appear now to be centered on the Kouilou project, but the glamorous vista which this has opened to Moyen-Congo will affect only the western and central parts of the territory. Already some industries have been transferred from Brazzaville to Pointe Noire in anticipation of the expansion of that port and the establishment of an industrial combine nearby. This suggests a further economic eclipse of the Brazzaville region, which may ultimately be reduced to handling the river and rail transit trade to and from the countries to the north.

Finances

So top-heavy and poorly balanced is Moyen-Congo's economy that its budgets regularly have had, proportionately, the largest operating deficits in the federation. Every year the other territories as well as Metropolitan France have been called upon to sacrifice some of their revenues to pay for Moyen-Congo's running expenses. Not only has the spirit of federal solidarity worn thin under this practice but it has further contributed to Moyen-Congo's parasitism. In the first postwar years Moyen-Congo's real budgetary position was somewhat disguised by the fact that its expenditures were not always kept distinct from those of the federal government. But as time went on, complaints from the other territories grew louder that "Moyen-Congo gets everything and contributes nothing."

Resentment against Moyen-Congo reached a new pitch in 1952 when its territorial assembly refused to raise the rate of its head tax in order to meet its current deficit and back debts (which then totaled 180 million francs).[27] The following year, however, it was forced to do so in order to qualify for a special federal subsidy of 45 million. Now expenditures had not increased as much in Moyen-Congo as in some other territories, and its finances were exceptionally well administered. Nor could it be said that its back debts and the subsidies it received were the largest in the federation. Yet the feeling persisted elsewhere in AEF that Moyen-Congo was not making the fiscal effort of which it was capable. It had never had any self-financed development program and, as of 1954, it had failed to collect back taxes amounting to 110 million francs.[28] Its assemblymen admitted that Moyen-Congo had no heavier financial burdens to bear than did the other territories, but insisted that it was too poor to shoulder them.

In 1954 Moyen-Congo had to raise a loan of 170 million to help liquidate its debts and to meet the running expenses of a budget described as one of "prudence and pause." The austerity preached by Governor Rouys was undermined by the federation-wide rise in officials' salaries, for personnel now accounted for 57.4 per cent of Moyen-Congo's total expenditures. Yet at the end of that year the assembly budgeted increased allocations to the social services (40.2 per cent compared with the previous 38.4 per cent), despite the territorial governor's criticism that such a rise was disproportionate to Moyen-Congo's resources and productivity.[29] If this course were pursued, he added, Moyen-Congo would be unable to lighten taxation for the purpose of attracting investments, just at the time when the Kouilou project seemed on the point of materializing. In 1956 and 1957 Moyen-Congo's budgets continued to rise (to 1,517 and 1,591 million CFA francs respectively), but personnel charges had been slightly reduced (to 56.8 per cent) and the public debt brought down to 63 million. In presenting the budget for 1956 Governor Rouys was even able to look back over the preceding three years with some satisfaction at the "marked progress" made.[30] Taxes had been only slightly increased and their burden was more equitably distributed; half of the territory's back debts had been paid; and there was in prospect even a small development program costing about 6.5 million francs.

Although the years 1956 and 1957 proved to be better financially for the territory than had been anticipated, their budgets were still unbalanced and Moyen-Congo had to raise another loan to meet current deficits and what remained of its past indebtedness. Mainly because of the expenditures involved in setting up the new territorial government, the budget for 1958 soared to a new high of 2,362 million francs. So greatly was Moyen-Congo counting on the revenues expected from execution of the Kouilou project to help defray its anticipated expenditures that the finance committee of its territorial assembly proposed that the budget not be voted until France had formally pledged construction of that dam.

Moyen-Congo continues to be dependent upon French generosity to balance its budget. Its current deficit in 1959 amounted to 800 million CFA francs, in addition to which it owes France 68 million, which in 1957 was loaned it for five years, interest-free, to establish its new political institutions.

Transportation

Roads. Before 1925 no roads at all existed in Moyen-Congo, and travelers going overland from the coast to Brazzaville had to take the Belgian railroad from Matadi to Léopoldville. Between Brazzaville and Loango there was a difficult mountain trail over the Mayombé, used only by African porters. Northward from the federal capital there were virtually no *pistes* until 1929, because of the unproductive nature of the Batéké plateaus and because the Congo-Oubangui rivers provided easy if slow access to the northern colonies. Building of the Congo-Ocean railroad (see pp. 140–42) necessitated the construction of a parallel service road, but its progress was even slower than that of the rails and it did not reach Pointe Noire till 1938. In the early 1930's, small roads branching off from the rail line were built from Loudima north to Sibiti and Mossendjo and south to M'Boko-Songo. A few years later Governor-General Reste took action to further the construction of intercolonial routes, notably that between Dolisie and Cameroun. He was also responsible for the construction of a second *piste* north from

Brazzaville, which it was planned to extend eventually to Carnot in Oubangui-Chari. This route passed by way of Mayama and Djambala and at Fort Rousset joined the *piste* from Brazzaville to Ouesso which had been begun in 1929. At the western extremity of the colony, *pistes* linked Pointe Noire to Loango and to Portuguese Cabinda.

During World War II, almost no new construction was undertaken except for the replacement of wooden bridges by permanent ones over the Niari and Nyanga rivers in conjunction with improving the Dolisie-Gabonese route. As of 1945, Moyen-Congo had a road network whose total length was variously claimed to be 4,000 and 7,500 kilometers. In any case the best of its roads were little more than poor *pistes,* very few of which permitted motor circulation even during the dry season. Moyen-Congo's road program, as laid down in the ten-year Plan, was less ambitious than that of any other AEF territory, for it possessed the only railroad in the federation and good river communication with the north. The Plan for Moyen-Congo's roads consisted almost wholly of improving existing ones in the Niari region and the territory's links with Cabinda and Gabon. Because they lacked economic interest, the two roads north from Brazzaville were neglected and are still in very bad condition.

By 1955, Moyen-Congo had a network totaling nearly 9,000 kilometers, but of these only 269 kilometers could be described as improved dirt roads,[31] and though it had far more macadamized roads (108 kilometers) than any other territory in AEF they were all to be found within the limits of its three main cities. This last-mentioned phenomenon accounts for the fact that the number of motor vehicles of all types in Moyen-Congo greatly exceeds that of any other territory. As of January 1, 1958, it had well over 10,000 of them—almost three times as many as Oubangui, its nearest competitor in this respect—and more than one-third were concentrated in Brazzaville.[32]

Even though Moyen-Congo's road network was relatively unimportant to its economy as a whole, there were regions in which it was vital. When FIDES funds were cut in 1955, work on the much-used Pointe Noire–Cabinda road and on the link between the Niari region and Brazzaville had not been completed, and there was also need to build many more permanent bridges. Moyen-Congo's budgetary situation was so precarious that no money for roads could be expected from that quarter. Its territorial assembly tried in vain to have part of its network reclassified as federal roads and to persuade FIDES to assume some of the maintenance charges.[33] Consequently the local government in November 1955 proposed following the example of French West Africa in setting up a Roads Fund that would be financed by a tax on imported fuel. As one man, the Brazzaville Chamber of Commerce, the territory's many small truckers, and the forest and agricultural companies rose up in arms. Their view was that it was the government's business to build and maintain the territory's roads without adding to their already heavy fiscal burdens.[34] It took more than a year of maneuvering on the part of the administration to persuade the assembly to accept even the principle of creating such a fund. Only by stressing that the proposed fund would reduce unemployment but not the subsidies from FIDES or the federal budget, and by pledging that it had no intention of asphalt-surfacing the Brazzaville–Pointe Noire road (calculated to cost 6 to 7 billion CFA francs) was the administration able to get a favorable vote from the assembly in December 1956. It was not until its March 1958 session that the assembly could bring itself to decide exactly how much the supporting fuel tax would be (3 CFA francs per liter of gasoline).

Waterways. Although the Oubangui and Congo rivers flow along Moyen-Congo's eastern and southern frontiers and the latter is not navigable downstream from Brazzaville, the sector between the federal capital and Bangui is the territory's most important waterway. A few of the many tributaries that pour into the great artery have long navigable stretches. The Likouala is accessible to small steamers throughout the year as far as Etoumbi (350 kilometers), and its tributary, the Kouyou, to Fort Rousset (125 kilometers). The Alima can be used by similar small craft and also throughout the year as far as Délé (300 kilometers), and its tributary, the Mpama, to Ossélé (75 kilometers). Of all the rivers flowing into the Oubangui-Congo artery, the Sangha is the most important and the most used. Boats drawing 1.20 meters can navigate it at all times along the 1,180-kilometer stretch between Mossaka and Salo, and smaller craft as far as Ouesso. The freight transported by the Compagnie Générale des Transports en Afrique (CGTA) on the Sangha has steadily increased, rising from 3,000 tons in 1952 to 7,000 in 1954, and an agreement made in 1954 between that company and the Compagnie Française du Haut et Bas Congo (CFHBC), which granted the CGTA a monopoly of its traffic, further added to the cargoes carried on this waterway.[35] But even the Sangha, and to a lesser extent the other tributaries of the Oubangui and Congo rivers, are not fully used to their present capacities. Though they give access to isolated settlements, they traverse generally unproductive regions. The craft plying those waters are mainly dugouts, which provision the villages along their banks and bring out articles of an artisanal nature. If northeastern Moyen-Congo should acquire more economic interest, further study of the potentialities of these tributaries for navigation might become worth while.

Despite successive plans to rebuild Brazzaville's inadequate river port, dating back to 1911, no lasting improvements were made in it until FIDES came to the rescue after World War II. In 1931 a few of its quays were enlarged, but their foundations proved defective, and little was done to repair the damage, build warehouses in which to store merchandise in transit, or prevent the river there from sanding up. In 1949 the work of rebuilding the port was undertaken, and was coordinated with the improvements being made at the same time in the Congo-Ocean railroad which it served. In consequence of this and of the growth in traffic along the Federal Artery, the tonnage handled by Brazzaville port rose steadily from 84,000 tons in 1948 to over 200,000 tons in 1957. By 1955 not only was the port's budget balanced (both Oubangui and Moyen-Congo contribute to its operating expenses) but it was able to begin payments into a renewal fund. Of the traffic handled by this port in 1957, 121,000 tons represented imports and 81,000 tons exports, including over 20,000 tons of copper ore from the Belgian Congo.

Agriculture

The great equatorial forest blankets much of Moyen-Congo, and about one-third of the territory's total surface is covered by poor, sandy soil that can give only mediocre harvests. Yet Moyen-Congo grows so many crops—manioc, rice, bananas, citrus fruits, tobacco, sugar cane, fiber plants, coffee, cocoa, peanuts, oil palms, and others—that there is risk of receiving a false impression of the importance of its agricultural output. Not even oleaginous products, which are its principal agricultural export, are grown on a large scale, and some of its crops—such as bananas, citrus fruits, cocoa, and rubber—could be best described as promising rather than actually significant.

Considering its area, Moyen-Congo has a very small rural population and a disproportionate number of sizable towns, for whose residents it now imports foodstuffs. If rice and corn were cultivated intensively, enough could be grown to fill the territory's needs, but the government has had little success in persuading the Congolese to substitute those foods for manioc, and not even manioc is grown in sufficient quantity. Farming villages are few and far between, and they no longer hold much attraction for young men who can find work in the towns or live there parasitically on their relatives' earnings. One must have visited the isolated river settlements of Moyen-Congo, overwhelmed by the surrounding tropical verdure, to realize how miserable and monotonous are the lives of their inhabitants. The decline in the number of the territory's farmers has increased the difficulties of provisioning the growing urban populations, and the inducements offered by the government to the towns' unemployed youths either to return to their villages or to work on the big agricultural plantations have met with little response.

The authors of the ten-year Plan attacked Moyen-Congo's agricultural problems with especial vigor, not only because they were becoming crucial but also because that territory seemed to be a promising field for experimentation. Three regions were selected for development—the Sangha, the Batéké plateaus, and the Niari valley—and later, a fourth, the Mayombé, was added. To some extent the cultivation of cocoa, tobacco, and oil palms has become established in the Sangha area, but because of that region's relative inaccessibility it has by no means yet reached its potential development. The vast project to transform the arid Batéké plateaus by the introduction of mixed farming was started without sufficient preparatory study of either the soils or the local populations' agricultural aptitudes. The Inoni station, installed there in the first flush of postwar enthusiasm, proved to be an expensive failure and was closed down in 1955. A much more recent attempt to promote banana cultivation in conjunction with a limba reforestation program in the Mayombé cannot yet be appraised. The one success chalked up by the planners of 1946 is the Niari valley project, and this has been appreciably modified since its inception. Conditions there were exceptionally favorable for experiments with mechanized cultivation and even small-scale animal husbandry. Three-fourths of the valley's nearly 400,000 hectares were covered by a comparatively thick layer of humus, and what is more, it lay adjacent to the federation's only railroad. Few problems were posed by the displacement of African villages, for the valley was almost uninhabited. Moreover, the Metropolitan scientific organizations and companies that spearheaded the Niari's agricultural experiments had the good fortune to find already installed there a remarkably enterprising group of French pioneer farmers, who gladly cooperated in applying the lessons learned from the newcomers' research.

In 1946, 20 families belonging to the Resistance *maquisards* of Aubeville in France decided to maintain their wartime unity by accompanying their leader to AEF, where they would farm as a group in the Niari valley. Some brought with them a little capital realized from the sale of all their possessions in France, whereas others had nothing to offer but their labor. Upon disembarking at Pointe Noire, they were held up by the imposition of 2 million francs of duty on the equipment they were bringing.[36] An appeal was made to Governor-General Luizet, who not only smoothed out that difficulty but granted them a concession of 5,500 hectares near Madingou. Their first five years in the Niari were very difficult ones, for they encountered insect pests, plant diseases, drought, and even hailstorms. The men built their own houses and workshops and even hired out their services to nearby African farmers, and the women reared poultry and did handiwork for sale. Some gave up, but the majority survived through sheer grit, hard work, and the spirit of *camaraderie*. As a group they jointly financed indispensable trips back to France by some of their members, and even marriage expenses for bachelors.[37] Besides market gardening they tried out new crops such as paddy, peanuts, and tobacco, and some of them associated animal husbandry with farming. Aside from what they actually produced, the Aubeville cooperative offered a salutary example to its African neighbors, for this was the first time that the latter had ever seen white men working with their hands.

Alongside these settlers the Metropolitan research organizations and five companies set up research stations and plantations. Oil-palm cultivation was engaged in by the Institut de Recherches pour les Huiles et les Oléagineux (IRHO) at Sibiti, and palm oil was manufactured at a mill built by the Société Industrielle et Commerciale Africaine du Pool (SICAP), as well as by the local SIP; mechanized peanut culture was done by the Compagnie Générale des Oléagineux Tropicaux (CGOT) at its Loudima station, and by the Société des Fibres Coloniales (SOFICO) and the Société Industrielle et Agricole du Niari (SIAN); urena was planted by the Institut de Recherches du Coton et des Textiles Exotiques (IRCT) in conjunction with SOFICO at Madingou; paddy was mechanically cultivated by SOFICO at Malolo; sugar cane was planted by SIAN, which also built a refinery at Jacob; and citrus fruits, bananas, and pineapples were grown by the Institut des Fruits et Agrumes Coloniaux (IFAC) on 50 hectares of the Loudima station. The Institut d'Etudes Centrafricaines (IEC) and agricultural service sent experts to study the Niari soils; the forestry service started nurseries of limba; the Bureau Minier prospected for mineral deposits; and a private company, the Société Africaine d'Elévage, cooperated with the animal-husbandry service in constituting a herd of about 2,000 head of N'dama cattle. The Niari valley was a microcosm of the Plan for all of AEF, and it became a vast laboratory in which nearly everything tried out in the federation was represented. In large part this was due to the impetus given by the planners of 1946, but the Niari's recent evolution has resulted from the orientation given to the federation's agricultural policy since 1952.

From the outset of his incumbency as governor-general, Chauvet had been impressed both by the confusion prevailing in the Niari and by that valley's great potential. Represented there were all stages of agricultural evolution, from vast plantations mechanically cultivated by European technicians, companies, and settlers, to the small, scattered villages of Africans, who continued to farm by their primitive traditional methods or worked as laborers on large-scale enterprises. Some 35,000 persons in all were cultivating only 50,000 of the Niari's nearly 400,000 arable hectares, and the area covered by European concessions was about twice as large as that farmed by Africans. If Moyen-Congo's agricultural output was to be increased and the valley's great resources utilized, some new means must be devised to expand cultivation rapidly. And experimentation with new methods and crops had now reached the stage where their results could be applied.

Chauvet's first move was to give the Niari valley, which formed a geographic whole, an administrative unity that it had until then lacked. In place of the former division of its area between the Regions of the Pool and Dolisie, he set up under his own chairmanship an advisory Comité de la Vallée du Niari. Its competence extended far beyond the area then under cultivation and its membership included representatives of the relevant technical services, research organizations, the territorial assembly, the private sector (both producers and traders), and African farmers and Notables. After further basic studies had been made, a development program for the Niari was drawn up, on which the committee was to submit annual progress reports. Its main function, however, was to guide the rational development of the Niari as a whole, through a close correlation of European and African enterprise.[38] As there was little prospect of any further large-scale white immigration or the advent of more European companies, the main instruments to be used were the African *paysannat* and, to a lesser extent, the SIP. Thus the African farmer was now assigned the star role in developing the Niari, and was no longer relegated to a position peripheral to the European mechanized enterprises which had been in the forefront of the original Plan.

The first orthodox *paysannat* was set up in November 1952 at Divenié in the forest region of the Niari, but experiments with embryonic *paysannats* in the more accessible part of the great valley had already been carried out at Loudima and Madingou by the CGOT and SIAN with their African employees. The two companies used their tractors to prepare the ground for planting, and the families of their wage earners sowed, cultivated, and harvested the crop. This they sold in part to the CGOT and SIAN, which processed and marketed it, taking 4 per cent of the proceeds in payment of their services, and the African producers retained what they needed for their own food. At Komono and Mankassou, *paysannats* of the Divenié type were formed, in which food crops were combined with oil palms, coffee, peanuts, and urena. As to the rest of the territory, the *paysannat* of Souanké specialized in cocoa, while that of Moulenda was of a more experimental type, whose major objective was the reforestation with fruit trees of an eroded region. A totally different type of *paysannat* (and one that has not been conspicuously successful) was created at Madingou in 1956 for the purpose of winning back to agricultural production some of the unemployed laborers of Brazzaville.

On the whole, these *paysannats* have been successful in increasing agricultural production, stabilizing Africans on the land, and improving their cultivation techniques. Some of the European companies have been in financial straits and none of them has been able to declare a dividend, but the African members of the *paysannats* have seen their incomes increase fivefold.[39] Only occasionally has friction developed between their members and the European settlers, when their respective herds have grazed at times beyond the boundaries of their owners' land.[40] The fact that it is now African and not European colonization of the Niari that is being encouraged makes the project more acceptable to the new territorial government. In fact, Premier Youlou in April 1959 announced his intention of forming a company of "mixed economy" for the Niari in which the Congo Republic, African *paysannats,* and European companies and settlers would all be shareholders.[41]

All of the rice grown in Moyen-Congo is of the dry variety, and it is both a European and an African crop. European production is concentrated in the Niari valley, where mechanical cultivation is carried on by the CGOT, SOFICO, SAPN, and the Aubeville colonists according to techniques developed at the Loudima, Botouali, and Inoni agricultural stations and in conjunction with other crops. European-grown rice is of luxury quality and amounts to only about 500 tons a year, compared with the 2,000 or more tons produced by African farmers. Among the African producers, Mossendjo subdivision is the largest, followed by three districts of the Pool region, the Ewo area of Likouala-Mossaka, and a few places in Alima-Léfini and the Sangha.

Under official encouragement, paddy cultivation generally expanded during the first postwar decade, though with wide annual variations. From 1947 to 1952, about 1,000 tons a year were harvested, then production fluctuated from 3,000 tons in 1955 to 1,000 tons in 1956 and to over 3,500 tons in 1957. This instability can be traced not only to varying climatic conditions but also to experimentation in the Niari valley with imported varieties of rice, some of which have given yields of as much as 25 tons to the hectare whereas others have failed completely.[42] Variations in output are also caused by husking and marketing difficulties, for rice is making only very slow headway as a basic element in the local African diet. There is a growing market for this cereal in Moyen-Congo's three main towns, but even there it has to compete with the rising consumption of bread and with the urban population's preference for the cheaper and tastier imported rice. Laborers in rural areas will accept rice as a "gift" supplementary to their other rations but not as a basic food.[43] A modern rice mill built by the SAPN in 1952 had to cease operations two years later because of the irregularity of paddy supplies, and the husking now done in small SIP mills is regarded as unsatisfactory. More than anything else, however, it has been the variable and usually very high prices at which local rice is marketed that have made it unpopular with the African consumer.

In recent years the government has decided that it must put a stop to the extension of paddy cultivation and stabilize output at between 3,500 and 4,000 tons a year, which is the amount currently consumed in Moyen-Congo. At the same time an effort is being made to prevent further deforestation such as has resulted from the spread of paddy cultivation in the Pool region, to improve husking and marketing facilities, and to bring down production costs so that locally grown rice can be sold at a more uniform and generally lower price to consumers throughout the year.

There are many indigenous varieties of bananas in AEF, and that fruit is a basic food for many of the inhabitants of the forest region, especially in the Chaillu mountains and the Mayombé, where some tribes cultivate the plants extensively around their villages. About 1932, the territorial agricultural service distributed some plants of the *gros michel* variety to African farmers in the Mayombé, who used their output for food. The difficulties of organizing a purchasing system in that inaccessible region and of shipping the fruit by way of Pointe Noire handicapped the development of banana production for export, and it was not until 1955 that the first European banana plantation was started there.

This was undertaken on an experimental basis and at the instigation of the local government, which had been inspired by the success of the Belgians in developing banana plantations in their section of the Mayombé by means of what were called banana-timber contracts. Under this formula, the entrepreneur was pledged to clear the forest over an area of at least 20 hectares, plant bananas there, and care for the limba trees that the Forestry Service would set among his banana plants. For the expenditures incident to cutting down the forest, the entrepreneur was to be recompensed at the rate of 10,000 CFA francs for each hectare he cleared, and during a ten-year period he was to receive the total income derived from the sale of the

trees cut down in that process and also of the bananas grown on his plantation. The territory stood to benefit by a reforestation of the Mayombé in
limba trees and also by acquiring full ownership of the plantation upon
termination of the contract.[44]

Although this is too recent an experiment to appraise its success, by 1957
there were already in existence two European plantations in the Mayombé,
covering a total of 270 hectares, and another concession near Pointe Noire
of nearly 300 hectares. In 1956 AEF exported its first 214 tons of good-
quality bananas, and in 1957 shipments reached nearly 550 tons. Most of
these exports came from European planters working under the contract
system, but some were produced by the 248 hectares of African plantations,
and as of mid-1958 their situation seemed so promising that it was predicted Moyen-Congo would soon be exporting 15,000 tons of bananas annually.[45] Mainly responsible for this satisfactory development has been
the advice given planters by IFAC experts at the Loudima agricultural
station, where they are also guiding the cultivation of 63 hectares of bananas
in the Niari valley and encouraging the planting there and in the Pool region of citrus-fruit trees.

In many parts of AEF, African farmers grow citrus fruits, including
pomelos, and many years ago their cultivation on a limited scale was begun
in the Brazzaville botanical gardens. IFAC has been promoting the cultivation of citrus fruits in the Pool region, where the soil is not suited to the
growing of industrial crops and where about 150,000 fruit trees and innumerable pineapple plants are now in bearing. In 1957 a Union Fruitière
du Pool was organized to improve the quality of output, find markets for
it outside AEF, and experiment with the manufacture of orange essence.
That year, sample shipments of fruit from the Pool were sent to the Belgian
Congo, Cameroun, and France. They were said to have been well received
in France, especially Moyen-Congo's pineapples, which had the good fortune of arriving on the market at a season when there was no competition
with pineapples from other French Union countries.[46] The Union Fruitière and the agricultural service are trying to train Pool Africans to care for
their fruit trees and to pick the fruit rather than to simply shake it off the
branches and thus injure it by its fall to the ground.

Since 1938 the commercialized production of fiber plants in Moyen-
Congo, and the export of their fiber, have been in the hands of the Société
des Fibres Coloniales (SOFICO). This company was created by the
Groupement des Industriels Français du Jute to develop jute substitutes in
Overseas France. World War II interrupted its activities, but they were
resumed in 1947 with greatly increased financial and technical backing. The
objectives assigned to SOFICO were the encouragement and improvement
of African production of punga, a plant indigenous to parts of Moyen-
Congo and Gabon, and the cultivation and processing by mechanical means
of another jute substitute called urena, or paka, in the Niari valley. It was
also expected to grow selected urena seed for distribution to African farm-

ers, supervise their cultivation methods, buy their output, and ship it to France after sorting and classifying the fiber. Every year at the beginning of the planting season SOFICO was to set the price for both punga and urena, based on that for Indian jute, at which it would purchase the entire African output of both crops. In all of these activities SOFICO had the cooperation of the government-general and was also aided technically by the IRCT and financially by FIDES.

Despite wide price fluctuations that have adversely affected output, SOFICO's punga program has been a success among the forest populations of Moyen-Congo, where production of punga has easily entered into the traditional economy. No cultivation of punga is required, and the African women simply gather and ret the fibers of plants which grow spontaneously around their villages. Agents of SOFICO purchase their output, and stock, sort, and pack it at a central point 5 kilometers east of Dolisie. With some annual variations, punga production has risen from 67.5 tons in 1949 to about 740 tons in 1957, despite a minimum of encouragement on the part of the authorities. Punga is considered an inferior jute substitute by French industry, hence SOFICO's efforts have been concentrated chiefly on the production of urena.

Within the context of the Niari valley project, SOFICO was granted a 5,000-hectare concession for urena cultivation at Malolo, and it was aided by French public and private capital in building a stocking and sorting plant near Dolisie and a pilot decorticating factory at Louvakou. Experiments with mechanical cultivation and with selected seed were begun on 600 hectares at Malolo under the technical guidance of the IRCT, and urena was rotated there with paddy and peanuts. By the end of 1951, when SOFICO was ready to enter the industrial phase of its operations, it had invested a total of 450 million CFA francs in the cultivation of urena, both on its own concession and on African farms in the Niari and Pool regions, and had harvested 532 tons of that fiber.[47] Beginning in September 1952 it undertook experiments in industrial decortication at Louvakou, with a fresh grant of funds by FIDES and the Fonds d'Encouragement à la Production Textile.

From this time on, SOFICO ran into increasing trouble on a number of fronts. In the realm of cultivation, an unknown plant disease suddenly damaged the urena crops and the IRCT did not succeed in getting it under control. Then the decortication project, in which a wholly new process was being tried out, encountered seemingly insuperable technical difficulties. Finally, the price for both urena and punga, which had begun falling in 1951, dropped even lower in the following years, and the local Africans lost what interest they had had in cultivating urena, and even in harvesting the urena grown on the Malolo concession. Production fell from about 800 tons in 1951 to 150 by 1953, despite redoubled efforts by SOFICO to distribute seed to African farmers. Given time, the technical difficulties might have been ironed out, for the IRCT was working hard on developing a disease-resistant urena variety and was also experimenting with another promising indigenous fiber plant called kenaf or dah. But SOFICO's Metropolitan backers became discouraged by the disparity between the results obtained and the investment they had made. In 1956, when the area planted to urena had reached 500 hectares, the Malolo concession and the Louvakou factory were abandoned and SOFICO went bankrupt.

Nevertheless, the local government refused to write off urena cultivation completely. So as not to discourage African growers with this crop, the SIP and agricultural services purchased the output in 1957–58, SOFICO was transformed into a sorting and packing company, and a price-supporting fund for jute-type fibers was set up with a subsidy of 4.5 million CFA francs from Metropolitan France.[48] During the past few years urena production has hovered between 300 and 400 tons, and any considerable increase in the output depends largely upon the government's future ability to pay a bigger price to its producers.

Palm oil and kernels occupy the first place among the agricultural exports of Moyen-Congo, and both before and since World War II almost the totality of AEF's shipments of those products have come from that territory. Export tonnages, however, have not returned to the record level of 1938, when Moyen-Congo shipped out 6,000 tons of oil and 14,000 tons of kernels. In a few years, however, the territory's production should top those figures, and already the quality of its oil has vastly improved, owing to the combined efforts of the Metropolitan, federal, and territorial governments and of private enterprise.

Moyen-Congo has both the most extensive natural growths and the largest plantation of oil palms of any territory in AEF. For many years the exploitation of its natural growths was considered economically precarious, for yields were irregular, small, and of poor quality. Most of these growths were located far from markets and on inaccessible mountain slopes or marshy ground, and the few tribes inhabiting the vicinity were too nomadic or lacking in incentive to collect and crush even a small portion of the nuts available. Production fell sharply during the war, and the shortage of fats became so acute that the government-general determined to create the first federal oil-palm experimental station, covering 350 hectares, at Sibiti in the south-central part of the territory. In January 1946, IRHO took over this station, and a little later it was given the management of the 24,000-hectare Boudouhou plantation near Sibiti, on which FIDES was to finance experiments in the mechanical cultivation of oil palms. Since that time, IRHO has developed selected palms on the site of the original Sibiti station and has taught nearby African oil-palm planters how to improve their output by the use of scientific methods and the organization of a cooperative. However, after the federal government decided in 1955 that it could no longer bear the heavy expenses incident to IRHO's experiments in mechanized cultivation, the Boudouhou plantation was divided up among the *paysannats* recently created in the region, where the basic crop was oil palms.[49]

Valuable as IRHO's experiments have been, they have done little directly to revive Moyen-Congo's exports of palm products, and the greatest contribution to this end has been made by private companies, notably the Compagnie Française du Haut et Bas Congo (CFHBC). This old-established firm has vast holdings in the Congolese basin, and around 1920 it started planting palms at Etoumbi and Lebango in the Likouala-Mossaka region, where its plantations now cover more than 2,000 hectares. Since 1948 it has built oil mills (producing about 3,000 tons of oil annually) and has experimented with mechanized cultivation near Ouesso and Mokouango in the Sangha area, where by 1958 it had planted nearly 900 hectares with palms developed by IRHO. It planned to continue planting progressively at the rate of 300 hectares a year, with the aim of reaching by 1965 the goal of 3,000 hectares giving yields of 2,000 tons of oil to the hectare.[50] Already the CFHBC is turning out each year over 2,300 tons of high-quality oil (3 per cent acidity) from its mills at Etoumbi and Lebango. It expected not only to modernize and enlarge its activities in the Likouala-Mossaka region but also to build a mill at Ouesso capable of producing nearly 6,000 tons of oil a year. When completed, the whole Ouesso enterprise will probably cost nearly 1 billion CFA francs—an investment which few other companies in AEF could afford. Nevertheless, the example of the CFHBC has inspired smaller-scale efforts by other private companies, notably the CAFRA in the Kouilou area and more recently the SICAP in the Likouala region. (Its methods have also been followed by the territorial agricultural service on its farm near Mouyondzi and by the SIP in the Regions of the Pool and Niari.) Naturally these private companies, in undertaking such enterprises, are motivated by purely economic considerations. They thus differ sharply in their orientation from such government efforts to extend and improve palm-oil production within the context of African society as those at the *paysannats* of Komono and Divenié (see pp. 171–72).

In 1957 Moyen-Congo exported 6,500 tons of palm kernels and 3,800 tons of oil (in addition to 950 tons of oil supplied to the five local soap factories and the domestic market), valued altogether at 311 million CFA francs. Almost all of this oil was produced by the territory's 31 mechanized mills, of which 22 belonged to private companies and 9 to the SIP. It is expected that Moyen-Congo's palm-oil production will soon reach 8,000 tons a year, and it should greatly exceed that amount when the big Ouesso plantation comes into bearing.

Although an increasing number of Africans in the territory are taking up peanut cultivation, this crop remains essentially a European one, being produced and crushed by mechanical means primarily for export. It was in two underpopulated areas of Moyen-Congo that the ten-year Plan proposed to undertake the production of peanuts with the participation of only a minimal amount of African labor. On 200,000 selected hectares near Loudima in the Niari valley, CGOT undertook experiments in mechanical cultivation which, it was hoped, would encourage the Europeans of that region to follow in its wake and eventually take over the responsibility for this crop. In an agreement made with the AEF government in 1950, CGOT was pledged to form a subsidiary local company to carry on its work after it had ironed out the technical difficulties and developed seed suitable for propagation in the area. At the same time similar experiments were to be carried out at Inoni, on the arid Batéké plateaus north of Brazzaville, by experts of IRHO and ORSTOM, who were given charge of an experimental station installed there. It was expected that the output of both areas could be easily shipped on the railroad to the well-equipped port of Pointe Noire for export. By 1955 the Inoni experiments had unquestionably failed, but those of the Loudima station and the Niari valley have been technically if not financially successful. Though climatic conditions still largely determine the output of this area, CGOT has been able to produce two crops a year, with yields of well over 2 tons to the hectare.

In the Niari valley, CGOT was fortunate in having as co-pioneer in this field a financially prosperous French company, SIAN, and also the co-operation of the European colonists of Aubeville (see p. 500). When SIAN first came to Moyen-Congo in 1938 it was devoted to the cultivation of manioc, but after it was taken over in 1949 by an industrial group headed by the Grands Moulins de Paris it turned toward the production of peanuts and peanut oil. More recently it has developed a major interest in sugar production, but in the early 1950's its experiments in mechanized peanut cultivation on a plantation situated between Loudima and Madingou supplemented those of CGOT, and in addition it built there a motorized oil mill capable of crushing 6,000 tons of peanuts a year. This mill has not yet worked to capacity, but it has produced high-quality oil for both export and the domestic market, including local soap factories. Smaller mills, with a daily crushing capacity of 20 tons of nuts, are operated by the SIP and some *paysannats*; they handle the increasing quantities of peanuts grown by African farmers in other parts of the Niari and in the Pool Region.

Since World War II, the production of peanuts has made more progress than has that of any other crop in Moyen-Congo. In 1947 only 700 tons of shelled nuts were sold in the whole territory. Ten years later, 4,400 tons of shelled nuts and 5,800 tons of nuts in the shell were marketed locally, and 3,400 tons of shelled nuts, 3,800 tons of nuts in the shell, and 500 tons of peanut oil were exported from this territory, with a total value of 275 million CFA francs.[51] Of this total, African production accounted for one-third of the output of nuts in the shell.

The future of this crop in Moyen-Congo appears uncertain, less because of its quantitative variations than because of its cost and the difficulties of selling the surplus abroad. European planters who practice mechanized cultivation have high fixed charges, and to make any profit they must associate peanuts with other crops and, if possible, with animal herding. The trend now appears to be in the direction of a closer association between the European and African types of production, with machinery preparing the soil and shelling the nuts, and African farmers growing and harvesting the crop. If European production can be maintained and African output continues to increase, it should be possible for Moyen-Congo to reach by 1965 the goal of 22,000 tons of nuts set by the first Plan.

In 1949, sugar cane was one of a number of crops with whose cultivation SIAN began experimenting in the Niari valley. In view of the success of the Belgians in growing sugar under analogous conditions in a nearby region of the Congo, SIAN planted 50 hectares to sugar cane in the environs of Jacob, a station on the Congo-Ocean railroad. By 1952, the Jacob plantation had grown to 325 hectares and was giving big yields, and SIAN proposed to build a refinery there with a capacity for manufacturing 10,000 tons of sugar a year. Despite a loud outcry from Antilles sugar planters and the Metropolitan beet-sugar industry, the French government gave its blessing to the SIAN project on condition that it would produce exclusively for the AEF market.

Economically this project seemed sound, for AEF imported 11,000 tons of sugar a year from France (of which four-fifths was consumed in Tchad) and, in addition, absorbed 5,000 tons smuggled into the country from Nigeria and Sudan.[52] Obviously the African population was avid for sugar and was only deterred from consuming more by its very high price and scarcity.[53] Technically, too, SIAN'S scheme for a local mill was pronounced feasible by visiting Dutch experts who were experienced in sugar cultivation and processing in Java. Financial backing was provided in 1954 by a loan from the Caisse Centrale de la France d'Outre-Mer (CCOM) and by private capital from French and Dutch industrialists and bankers. The recruiting of labor proved more difficult, for to run its sugar plantation (which now covered 1,200 hectares) and its refinery SIAN required the permanent services of 50 Europeans and 1,500 Africans in addition to 500 African laborers for planting and cutting the crop. Seasonal workers were the hardest of all to find, for all those locally available were already employed on other plantations and the unemployed youths of Brazzaville and Pointe Noire showed no inclination to take up agricultural work. (In 1956, 400 laborers whom SIAN had recruited in Pointe Noire for its plantation took the train to return there—for no known reason—the day after they had arrived at Jacob.) Not only were workers hard to come by, but their wages and the salaries of its European employees were a very heavy burden on SIAN'S budget.

Despite all these difficulties and the unsuitability of some equipment brought in from Europe, the refinery was built in record time and in October 1956 turned out its first lumps of sugar. But the plantation's yield that year was very low and in 1957 it was even worse—barely 5 tons of sugar to the hectare, when double that amount had been anticipated. Three successive dry years had so reduced the yield that only 7,000 tons of sugar were produced, even though the area planted to cane had been enlarged by 50 per cent.[54] A new appeal for capital had to be made and eventually SIAN was taken over by the Vilgrain interests, which control the Grands Moulins de Paris.

The last word has not yet been said on SIAN's expensive experiment, and a few good harvests may radically alter the present rather dismal picture. Because of a protective duty, SIAN's output is priced slightly lower than imported sugar, and there is no difficulty in selling it in AEF. It should also optimistically be noted that the price of sugar in the federation has risen since 1956 by only 8 per cent compared with an average rise of 30 per cent in the price of other foodstuffs.

With the exception of a few very small plantations started in the Likouala region at the turn of the century, Moyen-Congo's interest in cocoa cultivation dates back only to 1947, when this crop was planted in the Souanké district. In recent years it has spread to Likouala-Mossaka and along the Oubangui river, and also to the Kayes and M'Vouti districts of the Kouilou.

Although there are two small European plantations in the Sangha, covering a total of somewhat over 200 hectares, cocoa in Moyen-Congo is an African crop and one carefully nurtured by the local agricultural service. Under the guidance of that service, 25,000 bushes were planted around Souanké in 1950, exports have been controlled so that 90 per cent of them are graded as of superior quality, access tracks have been built in the producing region, and the local SIP has aided in transporting and marketing the crop. With the encouragement of the SIP and that of a territorial cocoa committee, cocoa cultivation in the Sangha has grown much faster than was anticipated. Production there came to 100 tons in 1956, doubled that amount in 1957, rose to 365 tons in 1958, and is expected soon to reach 1,000 tons. New planting is being carried on at the rate of 250 hectares a year and is spreading eastward as far as Ouesso. Shipping out cocoa from the Souanké area presents such difficulties that no trading firm is willing to undertake its transport over 280 kilometers of particularly bad roads to a loading point on the Sangha river south of Ouesso, and this task has devolved wholly on the local SIP. The shipment of the output from the Kayes and M'Vouti plantations, which are expected to come into bearing in 1960, presents far fewer difficulties.

Probably for some years to come, cocoa production in Moyen-Congo will remain on a very small scale. At present it represents only 4 per cent of the federation's exports of that commodity.

The well-organized production, processing, and export of commercial tobacco in Moyen-Congo is the result of close collaboration between the French *régie,* the local administration (through the SIP and the agricultural service), and a private company at Brazzaville. In 1946, the Metropolitan tobacco monopoly (Service d'Exploitation Industrielle des Tabacs et Allumettes, or SEITA) sent a mission to AEF to study the possibilities of growing tobacco there suitable for use by the French cigarette industry. Indigenous varieties were soon found to be too heterogeneous, but various areas in the territory were thought to be propitious for the growing of imported types of tobacco. Consequently seeds of Maryland and Kentucky tobacco were distributed through the SIP to African farmers in the Niari valley, the Batéké plateaus, and the Djambala district of Alima-Léfini. The territorial agricultural service supervised the family cultivation of these crops, the SIP purchased the harvest, and agents of the SEITA built warehouses in the Brazzaville region for stocking and sorting the output and organized exports to north Africa and France. In 1948 the well-known French tobacco company, Job, built a factory at Brazzaville to manufacture cigarettes for the local market through a subsidiary called Société Industrielle et Agricole du Tabac (SIAT).

A few years had to pass before this network was operating smoothly. Farmers in the Niari valley and on the Batéké plateaus found the cultivation of imported tobacco too onerous and wasted the seeds given them, but those of the Djambala area in time proved to be more adept and amenable. Then, too, delays and technical difficulties beset the SIAT because at the outset it used only indigenous tobacco, and it was able to survive only through government aid.[55] By 1950, however, harvests of the imported varieties were assuming marketable proportions, and the SIAT worked out a satisfactory formula in which it combined them with smaller amounts of indigenous tobacco and was thus able to produce a cigarette that has become increasingly popular with the local African clientele. In contrast to its small output in 1950, when it processed 67 tons of locally grown tobacco, the SIAT factory is now handling over 350 tons a year and is turning out about 1.5 million packages of its "Brazza" brand. Much larger tonnages are shipped to France for cigarette manufacture by the French *régie*.

The territory's production of Maryland tobacco, which has been steadily displacing native varieties, amounted to about 200 tons annually between 1947 and 1950. Since 1950 it has increased irregularly—the harvest depending upon climatic conditions—but has not yet exceeded the 724 tons produced in 1955. Its cultivation has been abandoned in the extreme north of the territory and in the forest zone of the Niari, and has come to be concentrated in the Regions of Alima-Léfini (65 to 70 per cent), the Pool (20 to 25 per cent), Likouala-Mossaka (5 to 6 per cent), and Niari-Bouenza and Loudima (4 to 5 per cent).[56] The quality of exports is rigorously controlled, and growers are paid premiums for superior grades. In the Alima-Léfini Region the popularity of tobacco cultivation is due to the regularity of the revenues it brings to producers and to the absence of such competitive cash crops as peanuts. For some years the SEITA has placed a ceiling of 850 tons a year on Moyen-Congo's output, but the prospect of opening up non-French markets in Europe has led to a reconsideration of this limit, which may soon be raised to 1,000 tons.

Fisheries

The fishing grounds off the Moyen-Congo coast are more productive than those of Gabon, and Pointe Noire is the site of the IEC's oceanographic service and of the two largest European fishing companies in the federation

—the LIPA and SAPAC. The oceanographic station, established in 1951, has made an inventory of the fish frequenting the territory's coast and lagoons and has been studying their reproduction and migration habits. It has also cooperated with the two fishing companies in experimenting with the breeding and conservation of sardines, oysters, and tuna. The SAPAC and LIPA between them have trained Africans in modern fishing and processing techniques and possess a fleet of six motorized trawlers, a processing plant at Pointe Noire, and refrigerated freight cars in which to ship fish by rail to Brazzaville and Dolisie. They have been steadily enlarging their markets along the Gabonese coast, in the Pool region, and in the mining and forest camps of the hinterland, and their annual catch is said to exceed 1,500 tons. Although this figure reflects a big advance over preceding years, it is far below Moyen-Congo's potential, but the development of deep-sea fishing on an industrial scale in this territory hinges on the use of more equipment and the anticipated construction of a large ice-manufacturing plant at Pointe Noire.

In regard to fresh-water fishing, the Mossaka region is the most productive in the territory, but the catch there probably does not total more than 4,000 tons a year. Moyen-Congo has been the site not only of AEF's main inland research and experiment station—at Djoumouna, 23 kilometers outside of Brazzaville—but also of the Water and Forestry Service's most intensive efforts to popularize the construction of tilapia-breeding family ponds. Four propaganda teams have been working in the districts of Niari, Boko, and Mindouli-Mayama, and by 1956—three years after they had been sent out by the Djoumouna station—5,500 tilapia ponds had been built in the territory, of which the yield adds up to more than 30 tons a year.[57] The fishing industry in Moyen-Congo, both maritime and hinterland, seems to have such a promising future that in 1958 the territorial assembly asked FIDES for more funds to devote to research, the development of a tinned-fish, fish-cake, and fish-oil industry at Pointe Noire, and the installation of more tilapia ponds.

Animal husbandry

Until World War II, Moyen-Congo received all its meat in the form of livestock from the northern territories or from Douala and Angola. All attempts to acclimatize cattle, horses, and donkeys brought in from Tchad had been uniformly unsuccessful, for those animals, worn out by the 2,000-kilometer southward journey, did not long survive so radical a change in climate and fodder. Such small herds as Moyen-Congo had been able to constitute were decimated during the war, and the rapid growth in its urban population made imperative an increase in its meat supplies. The project of developing cattle breeding in the territory was inspired by the prosperity of the Van Lancker ranch in the Belgian Congo, and both during and after the war, N'dama breeding animals were brought from there and from their native Guinea to form herds for the government station at Mindouli. Just before the election of Moyen-Congo's first territorial assembly, two private companies financed in France obtained large concessions for cattle ranching on the eastern slopes of the Mayombé and in the Mouyondzi area. Of these companies, the Société Africaine d'Elévage (SAFEL) was by far the more important, but it did not get actively under way until 1953.

In the meantime the government made two abortive attempts to create meat reserves for Brazzaville by constituting herds of Tchad, Oubangui, and Cameroun cattle on the Batéké plateaus and on M'Bamou island in Stanley Pool. The only cattle that flourished in the territory were the trypanosomiasis-resistant N'dama, and it was with this breed that the administrative stations and the SAFEL ranch were successful. By 1949, 500 N'dama were living and multiplying rapidly under the care of European experts and settlers, whereas African farmers kept only some 4,000 sheep and about 6,000 pigs. Under the ten-year Plan, experimental stations in poultry- and pig-rearing had been set up at Kilometer 17 near Brazzaville, for eventual distribution of the progeny throughout the federation, while that of Dolisie performed the same function for Madingou district and the Niari region.[58] It was hoped that eventually the Mindouli station would provide breeding animals for southern Gabon, and in the meantime it aimed to encourage cattle husbandry among the Africans of the Pool and the northern regions.

Obviously it took time to develop enough breeding animals for distribution throughout the southern territories, and even longer to make herders out of Africans who neglected even the small livestock that roamed in the neighborhood of their villages and who were frightened by large animals.[59] In the interval the territory's three main cities urgently required meat, for which the African demand was steadily growing, consumption having risen from 1,000 tons in 1946 to 1,800 tons annually a decade later. This demand could be met in part because of the enterprise of Pierre Receveur, head of Tchad's animal-husbandry service, who initiated the plane transport of beef from Abéché and Fort Lamy to the southern cities of AEF and the Belgian Congo. By sending three tons of fresh meat in 1947, by air, as a Christmas gift to the governor-general at Brazzaville, Receveur pioneered an industry that was later developed by the SIP and two private companies in Tchad. With the construction of modern abattoirs in Tchad and cold-storage space at Brazzaville's Maya-Maya airport, meat shipments by air to the federal capital (some of which are relayed by rail to Dolisie) are increasing rapidly, and Pointe Noire is now provisioned in meat more from Tchad than from Cameroun. Though the current average consumption of 20 kilograms of fresh meat a year by Moyen-Congo's urban populations seems small, it is nevertheless larger than ever before.[60]

By 1954 the herds reared in the territory's stations had become numerous enough to permit distribution of animals to some of the African farmers living in Kimongo district, where pastures were fairly abundant and where the SIP could supervise their care. Four years later, when the recipients were required to return to the breeding station the same number of animals they had originally received, there were nearly 1,500 cattle in African hands. By then, herding had become an accepted—because remunerative—African occupation in southern Moyen-Congo, though there were some disputes about the ownership of grazing land. Being primarily farmers, the local Africans continued to prefer rearing poultry because cattle and pigs tended to destroy cultivated fields in their search for food.[61] Under the tutelage of the SIP and agricultural agents supervising the *paysannats,* the rural Africans of Moyen-Congo have made progress in caring for their animals, but it is unlikely that they will ever become enthusiastic herders.

As a European occupation in the Niari region, cattle husbandry has been an outstanding success, and the Mindouli station, which has built up a homogeneous herd of over 2,000 N'dama cattle, is now able to meet the settlers' demand for some 100 breeding animals a year. But it is the SAFEL enterprise on its 5,000-hectare concession in the Mouyondzi region that is credited with the most remarkable achievements. Not only did it constitute a herd of over 4,000 cattle in the space of four years, but it pioneered the ranching form of cattle husbandry in AEF. Its concession is located in a particularly favorable area of vast pastureland, permanent running water, and few forests and swamps. Moreover, this zone, which has only a small African population and is unsuited to agriculture, is situated near the railroad and the territory's main markets for meat. To reach its goal of 10,000 N'dama cattle, the SAFEL in 1956 asked for an enlargement of its concession, which the territorial assembly reluctantly granted but only on condition that the SAFEL would fence the whole of its grazing area.[62] This has greatly added to the expense of an enterprise that required a large initial investment and a wait of ten years before receiving any returns on it.[63]

Although the importance of increasing the territory's meat supply has to some extent been grasped by its African politicians, they are much less keen on promoting ranching than the French administration has been. They have always viewed with suspicion large-scale enterprises that can be undertaken only by Europeans and that require big concessions of land. As elsewhere in the federation they cling to the belief that the meat scarcity would be remedied if only the government were more indulgent in the matter of hunting permits and firearms.[64] While the territorial animal-husbandry service points with justifiable pride to the creation of a cattle population of more than 15,000 healthy animals in a territory where only a few hundred head of undernourished cattle existed before the war, the Africans tend to think almost wholly in terms of farming and to regard animal-rearing as a very subsidiary and unrelated occupation, and one that requires no training.

Forests and forest products

Moyen-Congo's wood industry resembles—though on a smaller scale—that of Gabon, in that it occupies a place of primary importance in the territorial economy. Like Gabon's, too, it is oriented toward the export trade, has increasingly turned to processing in local plants, has given rise to opposition between the interests of big European and small African foresters, and is subject to official controls that are generally opposed by its producer organizations. It differs from that of Gabon in that its current importance dates only from the postwar period, that its two producing areas are widely separated, and that it has a larger local market for its output.

In 1938 Moyen-Congo exported only about 28,000 cubic meters of logs, of which well over half were of okoumé and the rest were of limba, and very little of its production was taken by the domestic market. Almost all of this wood came from the Mayombé region, and it was not until the postwar years that the mahogany and other valuable trees of the Sangha basin began to be cut for export to the Belgian Congo and for provisioning two sawmills in Brazzaville. Execution of the Plan called for substantial local lumber supplies, and beginning in 1946, more and more sawmills and one wood-peeling plant were set up in the western part of the territory. Until 1950 a large part of their output was taken by the local market, but in that year exports returned to their prewar level and began thereafter to climb rapidly. Now, however, it was limba that accounted for the majority of the wood exported, and okoumé was relegated to second place.

This expansion was the natural consequence of the increase in conceded and reforested areas and in the number of local processing plants, but a marked improvement in the quality produced and in the seasoning and storage of soft woods also played a part. By 1957, cutting permits covered 737,600 hectares, of which only 187,600 hectares were for okoumé; the territory's 24 processing plants were turning out each year a total of 215,300 cubic meters of peeled timber, 14,800 of sawn wood, and 5,000 of veneer woods; and exports comprised 143,400 cubic meters of limba, 42,900 of okoumé, and 29,000 of miscellaneous woods.[65] West Germany was by far Moyen-Congo's best customer, buying nearly 1 billion CFA francs' worth of the territory's woods, chiefly limba. In the same year, the territory's forest products—including a few hundred tons of gum copal—accounted for 85 per cent of the volume and 54 per cent of the value of Moyen-Congo's total exports.

Although the sustained market for okoumé greatly facilitated this rapid development of the territory's wood industry, it owed even more to Moyen-Congo's position as the premier exporter of limba, a wood that has many uses for which okoumé is not suitable, and one that is readily sold in western Europe, the United States, and South Africa. The only rival producers are the Belgian Congo, whose limba stands are becoming exhausted and which is even importing wood from the Sangha region, and Portuguese Cabinda, whose reserves have also been declining and which lacks a good loading port.[66] Limba reforestation was started on a very small scale in 1937 in the forest reserve of Boku N'Situ, and after the war, with the help of

FIDES, it was so intensified that by 1957 it extended over 3,859 hectares, al-most all of which are located in the Mayombé, including the 850 hectares so planted under the banana/timber contracts (see pp. 503–04). When the access roads for the Kouilou dam are built, it is expected that they will open up vast new reserves of limba which will strengthen Moyen-Congo's hold on the world market for that wood.

Attractive as this prospect is to both European and African foresters, it has also revived the chronic dispute between the large and small producers in the territory. While the reforested limba areas are easily accessible and can be developed with minimal equipment by African foresters, it is feared that the more distant and difficult limba zones of the Niari forest will be conceded in large blocks to the big companies which alone have the capital and machinery required to work them.[67] For many years the administra-tion has had to defend itself against charges in the territorial assembly that it has helped the big companies—particularly the SCKN—get a monopoly of forest lands, has favored them in the matter of granting loans, and has permitted them to trespass on African plantations. In reply, the govern-ment spokesman said that loans have been granted African foresters with a minimum of guarantees and at a low interest rate by the Crédit de l'AEF, that it had reserved for them a special category of cutting permits as well as a zone in the newly opened-up regions, and that it had trimmed the re-quest by a new company for a concession in the Niari from 70,000 to 25,000 hectares.[68] On two points at least the European and African foresters saw eye to eye—they wanted a simplification of the complicated regulations gov-erning development of the territory's forest domain, and the exclusion of foreign companies "which will try to install themselves in Moyen-Congo for the purpose of controlling the production and price of its timber."[69]

African assemblymen have been the main defenders of the small for-esters, for the latter have done nothing to organize themselves into a group that could take effective action in their mutual interest. The big foresters and sawmillers, on the other hand, are for the most part Europeans, united in an organization called UNIBOIS (Union Professionnelle des Exploitants Forestiers et Usiniers du Moyen-Congo). Almost all of the territory's saw-mills and wood-peeling plants belong to the Compagnie Forestière et In-dustrielle du Congo, the Ateliers et Chantiers de Pointe-Noire, the Société Industrielle des Bois, the Société Forestière du Mayombé, and the South Africa Plywood Company, which in 1957 took over the Plexafric plant. Though there was a rift in UNIBOIS when 17 of its members resigned in 1948, it still represents the great majority of Moyen-Congo's big producers and has been the mouthpiece for that element of the industry which is op-posed to the Office des Bois and any and every official control over lumber production and sales.[70]

It should be noted, however, that the operations of the Forestry Service have not aroused as much resentment in Moyen-Congo as in some other parts of French Black Africa. This is in part because half of its expendi-tures have been financed by FIDES and in part because of the success of its reforestation program and of its inventory of 12,000 hectares of the May-ombé forest. The area it has classified as reserved forests includes only some 70,000 hectares—a comparatively small proportion of the total surface and one that impinges little on the land cultivated by the African population. Moreover, the Forestry Service brings to the territory's revenues some 100 million CFA francs a year. In 1958, the new government of the Congo Republic indicated its interest in the further development of the forest industry by contracting with the Metropolitan Centre Forestier Tropical for a vast survey of the state's forest resources.[71]

Trade

In both the volume and the value of its trade, Moyen-Congo is the least prosperous territory in AEF. Yet in the mid-1950's its exports, in terms of value, bettered their relative position among the federation's total shipments more than did those of any other territory, rising from 11.1 per cent in 1954 to 14.5 per cent in 1956. In two other respects, also, the foreign trade of Moyen-Congo has been noteworthy—its range of export goods is more diversified and it has the largest commercial network of any AEF territory. As to imports, the goods brought into Moyen-Congo are of a sort that reflects the concentration there of AEF's European community and westernized Africans, and the territory has received proportionately more equipment goods (including motor vehicles) than any other in AEF.

Until 1955, agricultural produce, particularly oleaginous materials, constituted Moyen-Congo's most valuable export, for France offered such shipments a guaranteed market and prices higher than those prevailing elsewhere. Among the territory's exports, wood has long supplied the largest tonnages, but in 1955 it rose to first place also in terms of value. Timber exports have since maintained that lead, not only because of favorable conditions in the world wood market but also because an increasing share of the local oleaginous output is being absorbed by the territory's soap factories. From 1953 on, the value of almost all of Moyen-Congo's exports increased, rising from a total of 1,166 million CFA francs in that year to 2,900 million in 1958. In the latter year, wood accounted for 1,709 million CFA francs, oleaginous produce for 489 million, lead for 117 million, and various lesser exports for the balance.

Between 1953 and 1956, Moyen-Congo's imports declined both in tonnage and value. This shrinkage was caused by termination of many of the Plan's infrastructure projects, of which Moyen-Congo had been the main beneficiary, and also by the development of some local industries that lessened the need to import textiles, beer, cigarettes, and, later, sugar. Despite these favorable features, the status of the internal market was a cause of constant concern to the federal as well as the territorial government. Smuggling between Brazzaville and Léopoldville proved almost impossible to curtail, and the excessive number of merchants in the three main towns was reflected in frequent bankruptcies but did not serve to check the tendency of prices to rise faster there than elsewhere in the federation. For these reasons, controls over trade were retained in Brazzaville longer than in other AEF cities. Set prices were imposed by edict on a wider range of merchandise, and hard-currency allocations were made with more of a view to helping out small merchants, for whom the contraband trade and over-much competition were creating special difficulties.

Industry

The roster of Moyen-Congo's industries is impressive, but the meagerness of their output is evident at a glance. The territory boasts two tanneries and a shoe factory, a brewery, sawmills and a plywood factory, a sugar mill, a small plant turning out manioc flour, a few rice mills, and a cigarette factory. It also has a textile and clothing enterprise, two fishing companies, and oil mills and soap factories. Moyen-Congo's handicraft output is also varied: pottery is made in Niari valley, marionettes and statuary in the form of carved wood figures in the Fort Rousset area, bricks and tiles by local artisans in the towns, and the like. Most of these industries produce for the local market, which is very limited, and some are profitable enterprises and capable of expansion, such as those manufacturing cigarettes, beer, and soap. Only the oleaginous and wood industries, which produce mainly for export, could be described as large-scale, and that term can be used only relatively.

In the domain of minerals, too, Moyen-Congo has greater variety than volume. It possesses the only known deposits of lead, zinc, and copper in the federation, but copper mining ceased some years ago, zinc is produced only when market conditions are favorable, and the lead mines are the only ones that are fairly profitably and regularly worked for export. Diamonds have been found in small numbers in the Divenié region, but they are of inferior quality and their future is considered to be "doubtful." Small amounts of gold have been mined near the Gabon frontier, but in the past few years output has fallen to about 290 kilograms from the maximum of 435 kilograms produced in 1950. Sizable deposits of low-grade phosphate have been noted in the Pointe Noire region, and petroleum has been found 20 kilometers from that town along the coast. The extent of these two resources is not yet known.

The whole future of industry in Moyen-Congo hinges largely on the realization of the Kouilou project. If electrical power can be derived from the Kouilou in abundance and at the low price anticipated, a vast industrial combine is planned for the Pointe Noire region. Already two organizations have been formed to study what industries might be developed there, in what markets their output could be sold, and by what means the raw materials involved could be brought to the federal port. Once more, in the industrial domain, Moyen-Congo's geographical position and means of communication have given it a marked advantage over neighboring territories that are more richly endowed with natural resources.

Electrical energy is more widely distributed in Moyen-Congo than in any other AEF territory, though its hydroelectric-power resources are smaller than those of Gabon. Because of the more extensive development of its towns and means of communication, priority has always been given to the expansion of electrical-energy facilities there. Before World War II, both Brazzaville and Pointe Noire had public distribution systems which were entrusted by the government to the Union Electrique Coloniale (UNELCO) under a long-term contract highly advantageous to that private company. In those two towns, small generating plants were built in the mid-1930's, and during the war, consumption amounted to only 531,000 kilowatt-hours yearly in Brazzaville and 448,000 in Pointe Noire. The demand for power rose rapidly in the early postwar years, and to meet it a call had to be made on the resources of a Léopoldville company. Curiously, this situation was briefly reversed, beginning in 1953, when some of the current generated at the newly constructed Djoué dam was sold in Léopoldville pending completion of a new generating plant in the Belgian Congo.

The Djoué hydroelectric dam was the first such project realized in AEF by FIDES, and it was given priority over the two other schemes recommended by the Electricité de France mission in 1947 because of its proximity to Brazzaville. Justifiable doubts as to the industrial future of the federal capital delayed the decision to proceed with the Djoué project until April 1949, and in the two-year interval its cost had risen from the original estimate of 1.5 billion to over 4 billion CFA francs. Built by the Energie Electrique d'AEF (EEAEF), the Djoué dam had an annual capacity of 50 million kilowatt-hours, which was 15 times Brazzaville's yearly consumption at that period. Both the federal and Moyen-Congo governments optimistically believed that Brazzaville's industries would soon grow sufficiently to create the needed demand, but the Grand Councilors from the three other territories were skeptical and agreed only reluctantly to have the federal budget guarantee Djoué's operating expenses for a 50-year period.[72] A five-year contract signed in 1954 with the Belgian Congo government enabled the Djoué plant for a short time to sell more current annually to Léopoldville (12,751,000 kilowatt-hours) than to Brazzaville (10,913,000), but completion of the Zongo dam sharply reduced Belgian purchases of Djoué's current after September 1955. In Brazzaville itself, the textile factory of the Compagnie Française des Textiles (TEFRACO) was the largest consumer, accounting for 10 per cent of that town's total consumption, but the failure of other, larger industrial enterprises to materialize in the federal capital has meant that the Djoué plant has been working to only about one-third of its capacity.

This situation, which bore out the fears expressed by opponents of the Djoué dam, was aggravated by UNELCO's price policy. This private company, which has been the sole distributing agent for Brazzaville and Pointe Noire since 1937 and 1936 respectively, was regularly reproached by Moyen-Congo assemblymen with persisting in charging between 28 and 30 CFA francs per kilowatt-hour rather than lowering its rates so that current would be available to more consumers. After long negotiations, the government succeeded in getting UNELCO to reduce its charges slightly, beginning in 1956, but the contract by which it was bound to that company until 1985 (with the possibility of buying back the concession in 1962) enabled UNELCO not only to retain its distribution monopoly in Brazzaville and Pointe Noire but to add that of Dolisie, where a new plant was built in 1955.

The third of the hydroelectrical schemes recommended by the EDF mission in 1947 involved the harnessing of the falls of Loémé to provide current for Pointe Noire, 75 kilometers away. Power consumption in the federal seaport had risen from 488,000 kilowatt-hours in 1941 to 3,360,000 in 1953, but the Loémé project was never undertaken. By building the Djoué dam first, the EEAEF had time to reconsider Pointe Noire's power situation and to study the possibility of a much more grandiose scheme. This was to construct a dam across the Sounda gorge of the Kouilou river, which would supply enough power not only to process the newly prospected manganese deposits of Franceville but also to create a large industrial complex at Pointe Noire.

In June 1954 a mission of the EEAEF began to study the lower course of the Niari river, which was known by the name of Kouilou, and its work lasted three years. It was soon apparent that Kouilou had enormous advantages over the Loémé project. The Sounda gorge was situated 75 kilometers from Pointe Noire in a direct line, and 90 kilometers from the mouth of the Kouilou river; construction would be technically easy and entail the displacement of only about 3,000 persons and the submerging of one main road and a small amount of arable land. Behind the dam would form an artificial lake of some 2,000 square kilometers that would give access to a forest region rich in okoumé, and probably permit Gabon to increase its exports of that wood by about 150,000 tons a year. The cost of current in the Pointe Noire region, it was estimated, would amount to less than one franc per kilowatt-hour—appreciably less than that anticipated from the Konkouré dam in Guinea. As the site for a vast industrial complex, Pointe Noire with its flat terrain and well-equipped deep-water port seemed admirably suited. Naturally the Kouilou project aroused the greatest enthusiasm in Moyen-Congo and some was felt even in Gabon. Its sponsors cited the billions of francs in revenues that its materialization would add to southern AEF's hard-pressed budgets, and the thousands of jobs it would offer to the inhabitants of Moyen-Congo, who were suffering from chronic unemployment. In a territory where the average peasant income did not exceed 10,000 CFA francs a year, where the electrical supply in towns was precarious, and where the kerosene lamp supplied the only lighting up-country, the vistas opened by the Kouilou project seemed almost utopian. Investments totaling 220 billion francs were anticipated, and an output of hundreds of thousands of tons of ferro-manganese, aluminum, and phosphates, through the processing of imported as well as locally mined ores, was prophesied.[73] To examine the area's industrial potential and markets, as well as to plan for their development, two organizations were formed by the public authorities and private capitalists—the Organisation Régionale Industrielle du Kouilou (ORIK) and the Société pour le Développement du Congo Français.

There were nevertheless doubting Thomases who expressed misgivings about financing the project and about finding enough customers for Kouilou's current. Opposition on principle came from the Metropolitan French known as *cartieristes*[74] who felt that building the Kouilou dam would be simply throwing good money after bad in a country bound to become independent within a few years. They pointed out that the Metropolitan treasury was in no position to finance the project and that in consequence it would be necessary to call on foreign private capital to the extent of some 160 billion francs. To counter such objections, the advocates of the Kouilou scheme insisted that realization of the project would weld AEF to France, consolidate the position of those local politicians who favored membership in the Franco-African Community, and offer France's Common Market partners a chance to manifest their solidarity in tropical Africa.

Opponents of the Kouilou scheme found more solid grounds for their objections when there emerged two other projects potentially competitive with the Kouilou enterprise. Chronologically the first of these was that of a dam across the Konkouré river in Guinea, debated in Metropolitan France at the same time as the Kouilou scheme and bracketed with it for study by the same committee formed in 1955. Studies of Kouilou took longer than those for Konkouré because of Kouilou's greater inaccessibility and the short duration of the season in which they could be made. Moyen-Congo's assemblymen became increasingly worried lest Konkouré nose out Kouilou in the race for the commitment of French public funds, for Konkouré possessed the substantial advantage of being near vast bauxite reserves and the Conakry-Niger railroad, which could easily connect a processing plant with a deep-water port less distant from European markets. Though Kouilou's current would be much cheaper than that to be generated at Konkouré, AEF would have to import bauxite whose processing was expected to account for most of the consumption of Kouilou's power.[75] Moyen-Congo's delegates to the RDA Congress at Bamako in September 1957 succeeded in obtaining adoption of a resolution asking for a rapid decision by France to build the Kouilou dam. A year later, Guinea's sudden acquisition of independence made it unlikely that any of that country's bauxite ores would be available for processing at Pointe Noire.

An even more ominous threat to Kouilou was posed by the second scheme mentioned—the Belgian government in October 1957 announced its decision to build a hydroelectric-power dam at Inga, about 40 kilometers from Matadi port. Only 300 kilometers by direct line from Kouilou, the Inga plant was expected to become eventually the biggest power system in the world, generating 160 billion kilowatt-hours a year, and even after completion of its first stage it would produce more and cheaper current than Kouilou would offer. Moyen-Congo, however, was comforted to note that the cost of building the Inga dam (estimated at 20 billion Belgian francs) would be far greater than that of Kouilou, that studies for its construction were far less advanced than were Kouilou's, and that eight years would be required to build even the first portion of the project. Nevertheless, it was obvious that there would never be either enough customers in the region to consume all the current from both dams or enough capital for the construction of both. The French government was naturally as anxious as the Belgian to avoid sterile competition, and negotiations began late in 1957 between their officials and technicians to work out some modus vivendi. These dragged on inconclusively through 1958, and the Moyen-Congolese became increasingly impatient for some affirmative conclusion to be reached in favor of Kouilou. In fact, in December 1957 the territorial assembly refused to vote the local budget, asked that management of the Kouilou project be transferred to the newly constituted African government, and even threatened to secede from the Community if France refused to build the Kouilou dam.

Finally, in February 1958, the French government decided "in principle" to construct the dam, but it had found no solution to the problem of financing it. The turn taken by political events in Guinea, at Brazzaville, and in the Belgian Congo inevitably made international capitalists more wary than before about investing their money in such a scheme, but at the same time it made the Kouilou project become in the eyes of AEF Africans the touchstone for France's benevolent intentions toward the future development of their countries. In early 1958 the cost of equipping Kouilou was estimated at about 80 billion francs, and that of creating the Pointe Noire industrial complex at 225 billion.[76] The French Minister of Finance was disposed to help finance construction of the dam, and the World Bank, the Common Market countries, and private capitalists were to be asked to participate in this project as well as in launching the industrial complex of Pointe Noire. Currently an access road to the dam site is being built with funds supplied by FIDES.

Labor

The labor situation in Moyen-Congo is particularly instructive, not only because it is a microcosm for all AEF but because its documentation is more complete than for any other territory.[77] Except for the ratio of wage earners to the total population, which is highest in Gabon, most of the phenomena characteristic of labor in the federation as a whole are to be found in Moyen-Congo in their most developed form. Moyen-Congo has the most acute urban-unemployment problem and the greatest dearth of rural laborers, the highest percentage of functionaries among the wage-earning class, the best vocational training facilities available in AEF (which are teaching a declining number of students), and the strongest labor-union movement, despite its abstinence from local politics and the opposition of a large segment of Brazzaville's African population.

As of 1949 there were an estimated 52,000 wage earners in Moyen-Congo, almost half of whom were employed on agricultural plantations and in mining and forest enterprises and the other half in various other occupations.[78] By 1958 the total had risen to about 63,400, of whom 46,200 were in the private and 17,200 in the public sector. Brazzaville being the federal capital,

40 per cent of all AEF's functionaries lived in Moyen-Congo (17,200 of approximately 42,400). As of January 1, 1946, the Federal Professional School, a Maison des Artisans, four *sections artisanales,* and six *sections d'apprentissage* were situated in Moyen-Congo. In these establishments technical instruction was given to 110 girls (in home economics) and to 561 boys (287 in agriculture, 178 in local crafts, 46 in woodworking, 36 in mechanics, and 14 in ironworking). By 1952 the number of such schools and of girl pupils had grown to 23 and 240 respectively, but there were only 517 boys attending them, and the territory was spending not more than 1.15 per cent of its budget on technical education.[79]

As is characteristic of all AEF, whose urban centers are overswollen and whose countryside is depopulated, about one-seventh of Moyen-Congo's population has become concentrated in its three main cities. Brazzaville, as the federal capital—and for a time also the territorial capital—and as the juncture of the railroad and main river route of AEF, naturally received the largest grants of any urban center for execution of the works undertaken by FIDES. Inevitably the opportunities for gainful employment thus created attracted many rural youths, chiefly from the forest regions, where economic conditions were particularly unfavorable. Similarly, though on a smaller scale, work on the federal seaport and on developing the Niari valley contributed to the growth of Pointe Noire and Dolisie respectively. Young men from all the tribes of AEF swarmed to those towns, making their population exceptionally cosmopolitan, mobile, and unbalanced as to the sex ratio. Only the Brazzaville suburb of Bacongo and perhaps Dolisie developed relatively stable and homogeneous populations, whose sex ratio was more nearly normal and whose occupations were more evenly divided between production, trade, and daily labor. Brazzaville's larger African suburb, Poto-Poto, on the other hand, became the most populous, heterogeneous, occupationally unbalanced, and politically conscious town of any of the AEF cities.

Census figures indicate that in the early 1950's from 14 to 22 per cent of Moyen-Congo's town dwellers were day laborers, and of these not more than 25 per cent could be called skilled. Moreover, most of them were inclined to shift frequently from one job to another, which meant that only a handful of workers became skilled in any one occupation. This lack of specialization, along with their instability and their large number, explained to a large extent the very low wages they received. In 1950–52, Soret found that 43 per cent of the workers in Poto-Poto and 31 per cent at Bacongo wanted to change their current occupations for ones considered to be more "honorable."[80] At the top of the preferred list came the occupations of trader and office employee, and in the manual field those of chauffeur and mechanic. This restless urge for prestige employments was thwarted not only by the workers' lack of patience to develop skills but by the parasitism that beset the individual able to get and hold a relatively remunerative job. Soret's investigations showed that whereas only 10 to 14 per cent of the population of Brazzaville's two suburbs earned less than the officially set minimum wage, from 88 to 90 per cent subsisted on less than the minimum wage because African custom required that they support relatives and friends who were not gainfully employed. The usual reply made to Soret's query as to why an individual had chosen such and such an occupation was, "No longer able to find anyone to support me, I had to seek a job."[81] Not only did the wage earner have to extend limitless hospitality but he also had to make periodic gifts to his own and especially to his wife's family. Aside from such expenditures, which perhaps took as much as 10 per cent of his income, 53 per cent of the average budget of an urban wage earner was spent on food, 21 per cent on clothing, 7 per cent on alcoholic beverages, 5 per cent for rent and taxes, and 4 per cent on savings. Under such circumstances, not to mention the distractions of urban life, it is not surprising that fewer and fewer town dwellers were inclined or able to put aside any savings.

Beginning with the economic depression of 1952 and the tapering off of Plan funds during the following years, all of the worst features of Moyen-Congo's town life were accentuated. Despite the fast-shrinking labor market, up-country youths continued to pour into the towns, particularly Poto-Poto, thus aggravating the problems of parasitism and unemployment. To stem this tide and also to increase the territory's productivity, the government offered inducements to these urban idlers and vagabonds to return to their native villages—free transport, exemption from taxes for a limited period, and the loan of seeds and agricultural equipment. But, as Governor Rouys told the territorial assembly on March 27, 1954, "this policy did not receive the welcome it merited," for the number of chronically unemployed in Brazzaville alone by that time totaled several thousand. The deleterious effects of this state of things on the economic situation of Moyen-Congo were obvious enough, but the election riots of January 1956 drew the authorities' attention to their equally harmful political consequences. Although the strikes of 1946 had political overtones[82] and in 1955 Governor-General Chauvet referred to "certain agitators who use the trade unions as a screen behind which they denigrate the intentions of the government,"[83] it was not until his speech of May 23, 1956, that he attributed to Brazzaville's parasitic idlers much of the electoral agitation that had occurred five months previously. He also held a few African politicians to be partially responsible for the failure of his return-to-the-land campaign because they wanted to retain a hold on their urban supporters.

Such egocentric demagogues, however, could not be wholly blamed for the refusal of all but about 250 persons to accept free transportation back to their native villages or the offer of work on Moyen-Congo's plantations and mines. The labor unions, especially the Confédération Française des Travailleurs Chrétiens (CFTC), had long since drawn attention to the excessive gap between wages in the towns and up-country, amounting to as much as 70 per cent as between Brazzaville and the M'Bochi area. Gilbert Pongault, head of the CFTC, made a tour of the territory's rural areas in 1954. In the report he submitted later to the authorities he gave data showing which enterprises were flouting the labor laws in working hours, medical care, and the regular payment of wages.[84] Though he had kind words to say for the labor policy of the Compagnie Minière du Congo Français, he denounced the great majority of employers because they paid starvation wages to their workers and practiced an "arrogant paternalism" instead of improving their laborers' lot. His energy in organizing the up-country workers, as well as the publicity given to his report, was undoubtedly instrumental in reducing the number of wage zones in Moyen-Congo, getting a special fund of 25 million CFA francs from France to provide temporary work for the capital's unemployed, and starting a *paysannat* for unemployed urban youths in the Niari valley.

To be sure, the government and the territorial assembly had already taken steps to improve working conditions. Already in 1950 Moyen-Congo, alone of all the AEF territories, had instituted an allowance of 100 CFA francs per month per wage earner's child, thus anticipating by two years the family-allowance system created under the Overseas Labor Code. To reduce the very high percentage of unskilled workers among the territory's 42,000 or so laborers, the government had established at Brazzaville in September 1950 a rapid-training center geared to current economic needs (building, electrical industries, and auto mechanics). A regulation of March 26, 1954, had set a limit of 20 per cent on the proportion of foreigners who could be employed in any private building or commercial enterprise in the territory. The first collective agreement in all AEF was signed in 1955 at Pointe Noire in the presence of Governor Rouys. By January 1954 almost all of the organizations envisaged under the Overseas Labor Code—advisory committees, an inspectorate, and labor courts—had been installed in Moyen-Congo. But so much disagreement arose between the employer organizations, the territorial assembly, and the workers' groups about the rate and method of financing family allowances that it was not until April 28, 1956, that the final decision was made, and the territorial assembly voted that day in favor of the highest monthly allocation to wage earners' children—400 CFA francs—of any territory in the federation. In helping to attain this goal the CFTC showed itself to be the most influential union in the territory, though numerically it was weaker than the CGT and it did not combine African and European members, particularly the railroad employees, as did the FO. Though none of the Moyen-Congo's unions can be described as strong, they are the best-organized in all AEF, have the most enlightened leadership, and have proved the most effective in improving working conditions. The only strike in AEF that could be considered large-scale was that of 600 workers at the Brazzaville TEFRACO plant in 1955, and owing largely to union support, most of the strikers' demands were met.

These union successes are the more remarkable in that labor organizers have met with a chilly reception from the sizable Bakongo population of Brazzaville (see p. 44) and have generally held themselves aloof from local party politics. The CFTC in particular has indicated that it sometimes feels African politicians to be as much its adversaries as the employer groups, largely because the former are "jealous" of the unions' hold on the masses, and because both elements can apparently see no alternative between crushing and controlling the unions.[85] The UDDIA government, like that of the MESAN in Oubangui, seems determined to take the lead away from the unions in regard to bettering working conditions. Since it came to power the minimum wage has been raised several times in all four of the territory's wage zones. It has also taken a strong stand in regard to the urban unemployed, particularly since the riots of February and July 1959 have shown that calling out the mobs in Brazzaville can be as dangerous for an African government as for the French administration. And the agricultural and youth camps being set up for the "vagabonds and idlers" fall not far short of a policy of forced labor. It is hoped, of course, that the Pointe Noire industrial combine and the various mining projects will, at least for the next five years, absorb many of those currently unemployed.

Conclusion

Many commentators on French Negro Africa have simply assumed that AEF, on a smaller scale, is a replica of French West Africa, only more inaccessible, poorer, and even less populous. Certainly AEF has faced many of the same problems as has its sister federation, and is more backward politically and economically. Although France gave AEF an identical form of administration and applied to it many of the same policies, its history and hence its evolution have differed from those of French West Africa in significant respects. The African political priest, as he has come to the fore in AEF in the persons of Youlou and Boganda, has no counterpart in the western federation. AEF not only has acquired a distinct character of its own but within its confines offers striking contrasts. In the realm of education, for example, AEF has both the highest and lowest literacy rates to be found in any of the French overseas territories. Moreover, constant comparison with French West Africa has created a defensive attitude on the part of AEF Africans. They both envy the greater prosperity and opportunities of their western compatriots and suspect the latter of trying to take over and control AEF's political parties and labor unions.

Because of its geographical location, AEF has been more exposed to inter-African currents than has French West Africa, and this permeability to non-French influences was increased long ago by the inclusion of much of the southern territories in the Congo Conventional Basin. France, by various stratagems and without developing the country herself, was able to keep other nations from trading with and investing in AEF on any appreciable scale, but she could not maintain a monopoly in the educational and religious fields. In both economic and cultural directions the results of this policy were unfortunate for France and for AEF. Economically, it resulted in the scandals associated with the concessionary-company regime, in a precarious demographic situation, in commercial stagnation, and in chronic financial deficits that made AEF highly unpopular in Metropolitan France. Culturally, it led to a covert opposition to alien rule that expressed itself in the birth and growth of politico-religious sects that have developed extremist and sometimes lawless tendencies.

World War II and the years that followed it witnessed a veritable revolution in French policy and in the evolution of AEF. Suddenly and unexpectedly, in 1940, AEF became the African center of Free France and relatively prosperous, and the federation gained the favorable attention and aid of the Western world. After the war, AEF was for the first time provided with an adequate number of qualified administrators and technicians, investment funds on a large scale, and elective political institutions. To be sure, this same constructive policy was applied to other parts of the French Union, but it had an exceptionally great impact on AEF because of that federation's comparatively underdeveloped status.

Considering the long neglect of AEF by the mother country, the loyalty expressed by the great majority of AEF Africans to France during World War II and in the referendum of September 1958 is worthy of note. Neither the introduction there in 1946 of the dual electoral college nor—after the *loi-cadre* was passed 10 years later—the issues of federalism and independence ever aroused such discord or tensions as they did in French West Africa. For some years before AEF was transformed into four autonomous republics, almost all of the Europeans who had been in the political forefront during the first postwar years gradually and inconspicuously withdrew from party activities and left a clear field politically to the Africans. Except in Oubangui, Franco-African relations have been generally more cooperative in AEF than in French West Africa, despite the greater favors shown the latter federation by France, and all of the new republics of AEF are eager to maintain close relations with France. To a large extent this can be explained by AEF's continuing and great need of French financial and technical aid, particularly in the light of the discovery of Gabon's mineral wealth and France's plans to create an industrial complex at Pointe Noire. But it is also due to the fact that since the war the evolution of AEF's political institutions has moved faster than has that of its economy and has also outdistanced the present capacity of the indigenous population to take advantage of all its new opportunities.

In analyzing the current relationship between France and the four republics, the history and psychological climate of AEF must also be taken into consideration. It should be recalled that AEF was occupied by France with virtually no bloodshed, that revolts against French rule have been few and short-lived, and that such long-term and profound resistance as has been offered to the government has taken an indirect and somewhat disguised form. Responsible for this phenomenon was, first, the diversity and dispersion of AEF's tribes, and second, their poverty, illiteracy, and lack of means for intercommunication. Even today, with AEF's vastly improved infrastructure and educational facilities, such political—and to a lesser extent, labor—organizations as exist are largely the manifestations of regionalism and tribalism masquerading under party (or union) labels. Politicians who have acquired a truly popular following are in effect great tribal chiefs, who both by tradition and because of current circumstances almost inevitably gravitate toward one-man, one-party rule, although they retain the forms of democratic representative government. Some of these so-called political parties have shown imperialistic tendencies, but as yet none has been able to assert its complete domination over rival groups, and occasionally ancient tribal antagonisms have broken out of the alien party framework in which they find themselves and have erupted in the form of riot and massacre.

Many AEF Africans are very conscious of their present weaknesses and realize that they need more of almost everything they have except living space. Above all they require additional capital investment, technicians, infrastructure, and population, especially the last, and they are making progress in all of these domains. As to their future, the principal open question is in regard to the shape, if any, that their former unity will take, should it survive. The earlier federation possessed no fundamental geographic, cultural, or ethnic unity, and its only bonds were a common administration, certain institutions, and a few means of communication. All the present leaders of the four republics have refused to re-create a strong federal executive, but they have agreed to maintain a loose form of economic and technical cooperation and some of the established cultural and judicial institutions. It remains to be seen whether this trend to cooperation will be strong enough to counteract the older, centrifugal forces that are tending to reassert themselves. The outcome of this contest will depend not wholly upon the course of events in the four AEF republics, but also upon that which is unfolding among related tribes in neighboring countries.

Abbreviations

AEF	Afrique Equatoriale Française
AFP	Agence France Presse
AOF	Afrique Occidentale Française
AST	Action Sociale Tchadienne
BAO	Banque de l'Afrique Occidentale Française
BCA	Banque Commerciale Africaine
BDG	Bloc Démocratique Gabonais
BET	Borkou-Ennedi-Tibesti region
BIC	Bénéfices Industriels et Commerciaux
BNCI	Banque Nationale pour le Commerce et l'Industrie
BRP	Bureau de Recherches des Pétroles
CAFRA	Compagnie de l'Afrique Française Equatoriale
CAP	*certificat d'aptitude professionnelle*
CAPE	*certificat d'aptitude pédagogique élémentaire*
CATC	Confédération Africaine des Travailleurs Croyants de l'AEF
CCAEF	Compagnie Commerciale de l'AEF
CCOM	Caisse Centrale de la France d'Outre-Mer
CEP	*certificat d'études primaires*
CFA	Colonies Françaises d'Afrique
CFAO	Compagnie Française de l'Afrique Occidentale
CFG	Compagnie Française du Gabon
CFHBC	Compagnie Française du Haut et Bas Congo
CFP	Compagnie Française des Pétroles
CFTC	Confédération Française des Travailleurs Chrétiens
CGDEE	Compagnie Générale de Distribution d'Energie Electrique
CGOT	Compagnie Générale des Oléagineux Tropicaux
CGT	Confédération Générale du Travail
CGTA	Compagnie Générale des Transports en Afrique
CGTA	Confédération Générale des Travailleurs de l'AEF
CMCF	Compagnie Minière du Congo Français
CMOO	Compagnie Minière de l'Oubangui Oriental
COFIREP	Compagnie de Financement de Recherche Pétrolière

COLPAEF	Comité de Liaison du Patronat de l'AEF
COMILOG	Compagnie Minière de l'Ogooué
COMOUNA	Compagnie Commerciale de l'Ouham-Nana
COOPAL	Coopérative des Palmiers
COTONAF	Société Française des Cotons Africains
COTONCOOP	Coopérative du Coton
COTONFRAN	Compagnie Cotonnière Equatoriale Française
COTOUBANGUI	Société Cotonnière du Haut-Oubangui
CTRO	Compagnie des Transports Routiers de l'Oubangui
ECA	European Cooperation Administration
EDC	European Defense Community
EDF	Electricité de France
EEAEF	Energie Electrique d'AEF
EMAC	Société d'Exploitation Minière au Congo
FAC	Fonds d'Aide et de Coopération
FAO	Food and Agriculture Administration
FERDES	Fonds d'Equipement Rural et de Développement Economique et Social
FIDES	Fonds d'Investissement pour le Développement Economique et Social
FINAREP	Société Financière pour la Recherche et l'Exploitation du Pétrole
FLN	Front de Libération Nationale
FO	Force Ouvrière
GIRC	Groupement d'Importation et de Répartition du Coton
GIRT	Groupement des Indépendants et Ruraux du Tchad
GNACA	Groupement National d'Achat des Cafés
ICFTU	International Confederation of Free Trade Unions
ICOT	Société d'Industrie Cotonnière de l'Oubangui et du Tchad
IEC	Institut d'Etudes Centrafricaines
IFAC	Institut des Fruits et Agrumes Coloniaux
ILO	International Labor Organization
IOM	Indépendants d'Outre-Mer
IRCT	Institut de Recherches du Coton et des Textiles Exotiques
IRHO	Institut de Recherches pour les Huiles et les Oléagineux
LIPA	L'Industrie de Pêche en Afrique
MESAN	Mouvement d'Evolution Sociale en Afrique Noire
MPT	Mouvement Populaire Tchadien
MRP	Mouvement Républicain Populaire
MSA	Mouvement Socialiste Africain

OBAEF	Office des Bois d'AEF
OCRS	Organisation Commune des Régions Sahariennes
ORGABON	Compagnie des Mines d'Or du Gabon
ORIK	Organisation Régionale Industrielle du Kouilou
ORSTOM	Office de la Recherche Scientifique et Technique d'Outre-Mer
PFA	Parti de la Fédération Africaine
PME	Petites et Moyennes Entreprises
PPC	Parti Progressiste Congolais
PPT	Parti Progressiste Tchadien
PRA	Parti du Regroupement Africain
PTT	Services des Postes-Télégraphes-Téléphones
PUNGA	Parti d'Union Nationale Gabonaise
RDA	Rassemblement Démocratique Africain
RPF	Rassemblement du Peuple Français
SAFA	Société Agricole et Forestière Africaine
SAFEL	Société Africaine d'Elevage
SALT	Syndicat Agricole du Logone-Tchad
SAPAC	Société Anonyme de Pêche, d'Armement et de Conservation
SAPN	Société Agricole et Pastorale du Niari
SCKN	Société Commerciale du Kouilou-Niari
SCOA	Société Commerciale de l'Ouest Africain
SEITA	Service d'Exploitation Industrielle des Tabacs et Allumettes en A.E.F.
SERP	Syndicat d'Etudes et de Recherches Pétrolières en AEF
SFIO	Section Française de l'Internationale Ouvrière
SGIA	Société de Gérence Industrielle et Agricole
SHO	Société du Haut-Ogooué
SIAN	Société Industrielle et Agricole du Niari
SIANG	Société Industrielle et Agricole de la N'Gounié
SIAT	Société Industrielle et Agricole du Tabac
SICAP	Société Industrielle et Commerciale Africaine du Pool
SICAT	Société Immobilière et Commerciale de l'Afrique Tropicale
SIFA	Société Industrielle Forestière et Agricole
SIP	Sociétés Indigènes de Prévoyance
SMI	Société Minière Intercoloniale
SMPR	Secteurs Modernes de Production Rurale
SMPR	Sociétés Mutuelles de Production Rurale
SOCANA	Société des Plantations du Café Nana
SOFICO	Société des Fibres Coloniales
SOMINA	Société Minière du Niari

SOPECOBA	Société des Pêcheries Coloniales à la Baleine
SORAFOM	Société de Radiodiffusion de la France d'Outre-Mer
SOREDIA	Société de Recherches et d'Exploitation Diamantifère
SPAEF	Société des Pétroles d'AEF
STEC	Société du Tchad et des Entreprises Chemin
STOC	Société des Transports Oubangui-Cameroun
TEFRACO	Compagnie Française des Textiles
TRANSCOOP	Coopérative du Transport
TREC	Transports Régionaux de l'Est et du Centre
UAT	Union Aéromaritime de Transports
UDDIA	Union Démocratique pour la Défense des Intérêts Africains
UDIT	Union Démocratique Indépendante du Tchad
UDSG	Union Démocratique et Sociale Gabonaise
UDSR	Union Démocratique et Sociale de la Résistance
UDT	Union Démocratique Tchadienne
UGTAN	Union Générale des Travailleurs de l'Afrique Noire
UNELCO	Union Electrique Coloniale
UNESCO	United Nations Educational, Scientific, and Cultural Organization
UNIBOIS	Union Professionnelle des Exploitants Forestiers et Usiniers du Moyen-Congo
UNICEF	United Nations International Children's Emergency Fund
UNIFAC	Union Fluviale de l'Afrique Centrale
UNIROUTE	Union Routière Centre-Africaine
UST	Union Socialiste Tchadienne
WHO	World Health Organization

Notes

Chapter 1

1. Very little has been published on the early history of this part of central Africa. For the information contained in this section, reliance has been placed mainly on the works of G. Hardy, G. Balandier, G. Bruel, and H. Zieglé. The best accounts in English are to be found in the studies by R. L. Buell and S. H. Roberts. See Bibliography.

2. Georges Hardy, "Origines et Formation de l'Afrique Equatoriale Française," *Afrique Equatoriale Française,* p. 47.

3. Henri Zieglé, *Afrique Equatoriale Française,* p. 89.

4. See J. P. Lebeuf and A. Masson-Detourbet, *La Civilisation du Tchad.*

5. R. L. Buell, *The Native Problem in Africa,* I, 338.

6. An agreement concluded on September 8, 1919, divided between England and France some small Tchadian states that had not been included in the treaty of 1899.

7. *History of French Colonial Policy,* I, 350.

8. See E. D. Morel, *The British Case in French Congo.*

9. At the time, Vivier de Streel, *chef de cabinet* for Minister André Lebon, was director of six companies holding concessions in the Congo.

10. See French Union Assembly debates, December 21, 1951.

11. See Augouard's correspondence in *Les Deux Congo,* by Baron Jehan de Witte.

12. *Le Congo Français.*

13. Zieglé, *Afrique Equatoriale Française,* p. 99.

14. S. H. Roberts, *History of French Colonial Policy,* I, 350.

15. See René Trautmann, *Au Pays de "Batouala."*

16. P. 25.

17. Paris, July 5 and 7, 1927.

18. See correspondence published in Gide's *Retour du Tchad,* p. 218.

19. *Terre d'Ebène,* p. 6.

20. *La Mort Mystérieuse du Gouverneur-Général Renard.*

21. *Sous le Feu de l'Equateur: Les Secrets de l'Afrique Noire.*

22. *Behind God's Back.*

23. A. Sicé, *L'AEF et le Cameroun au Service de la France.*

24. See Albert Maurice, *Félix Eboué, sa Vie et son Oeuvre;* Eboué's own works; E. Trézenem and B. Lembezat, *La France Equatoriale;* and Albert Q. Maisel, *Africa: Facts and Forecasts.*

Chapter 2

1. For details, see Georges Bruel, *La France Equatoriale Africaine,* pp. 433 ff.

2. Merlin, Angoulvant, Augagneur, Antonetti, Renard, Reste, and Boisson.

3. In French Black Africa, Chambers of Commerce have had a semiofficial status and have been financed in part by public funds.

4. H. Zieglé, *Afrique Equatoriale Française*, p. 170.

5. Previously there had been 49 circumscriptions and 164 subdivisions.

6. W. M. Hailey, *An African Survey* (1938), p. 190.

7. H. Labouret, "L'A.E.F., 1937," *L'Afrique Française*, March 1937.

8. Zieglé, *Afrique Equatoriale Française*, p. 174.

9. Grand Council debates, November 24, 1947.

10. His grandfather, however, had at one time been a naval commandant of the French posts in Gabon.

11. At the September 9, 1949, session of the Grand Council, even so harsh a critic of French officialdom as Stéphane Tchitchellé praised Cornut-Gentille.

12. Grand Council debates, April 20, 1948.

13. See Oubangui-Chari territorial assembly debates, March 15, 1951.

14. Grand Council debates, April 30 and May 9, 1949.

15. AFP dispatches from Brazzaville, August 28 and September 3, 1956.

16. *La Vie Française*, June 28, 1957.

Chapter 3

1. Although the double-college system was established in AEF, French West Africa was accorded different treatment. An account of the reasons for this, as well as further details regarding the decrees referred to, is given in the authors' *French West Africa* (Stanford, Calif., 1958), p. 44 ff.

2. Article 82 of the 1946 constitution provided that citizens who did not hold French civil status might keep their personal status until they renounced it.

3. See National Assembly debates, October 4 and 5, 1946.

4. See National Assembly debates, May 11, 1951.

5. These were the "incidents" of Bébalem in Tchad and Jean Keté in Oubangui. In 1953 there was an outbreak at Port Gentil, and in 1954 a more serious one at Berbérati.

6. French Union Assembly debates, November 8, 1955.

7. The task assigned to AEF's 190 *chefs de région* of drawing up the new electoral rolls proved to be a difficult one, especially as only 1,195,000 had been registered in the previous elections. In the course of this operation, it was discovered that about half of the population of AEF were over 21 years of age and more than half were illiterate, and that they spoke some 50 dialects.

Chapter 4

1. Thomas Hodgkin cites the existence in 1950 of 12 *amicales* at Poto-Poto organized on a tribal basis, each with a membership of around 100. These were composed chiefly of clerks and were concerned with preserving tribal ties in a cosmopolitan and fragmented city. See *Nationalism in Colonial Africa*, p. 86.

2. Grand Council debates, September 6, 1951.

3. This Senator survived longer politically than his European colleagues because the history of the Resistance and of Franco-African relations in Gabon differed from

4. See Pierre and Renée Gosset, *L'Afrique, Les Africains*, vol. I, *France-Afrique, le Mythe qui prend Corps*, p. 116.

5. See *Marchés Coloniaux*, April 6, 1946.

6. See National Assembly debates, February 16, 1950.

7. It is interesting to recall that Gabriel d'Arboussier, who subsequently became one of the most controversial of the West African RDA leaders, held an administrative post in Moyen-Congo and was its delegate to the Constituent Assembly at Paris in 1945. It was not until two years later that he joined the RDA and was elected French Union Assemblyman for the Ivory Coast.

8. This was accomplished through creation of a committee, composed of members of the MESAN and the PPT in equal number, to study how to achieve the "unity of views indispensable to all social, economic, and political questions common to the two territories.' See *Afrique Nouvelle*, May 14, 1957.

9. See *Afrique Nouvelle*, May 7, June 25, 1957.

10. Tchad sent eight delegates and two observers, Moyen-Congo five delegates and one observer, and Gabon three delegates, of whom Mba was the only African. Only Oubangui sent neither a delegate nor an observer. See A. Blanchet, *L'Itinéraire des Partis Africains depuis Bamako*, p. 25. At this conference Lisette was elected a vice-president of the RDA.

11. By Philippe Decraene in *Afrique Nouvelle*, November 28, 1958.

Chapter 5

1. See *Afrique Equatoriale Française* (ed., E. Guernier), p. 196.

2. See F. Eboué, *Circulaire Générale sur la Politique Indigène en Afrique Equatoriale Française.*

3. Perhaps the advantage most appreciated was the exemption of *Notables évolués* from the regime of the *indigénat.*

4. Grand Council debates, June 27, 1952; French Union Assembly debates, July 19, 1949.

5. See French Union Assembly debates, March 17, 1948.

6. The situation improved after Luciani, a former Labor Inspector, became mayor, but he was still urged to change the membership of his council, "which coils around him like a venomous serpent." See Oubangui-Chari territorial assembly debates, August 20, 1948.

7. *Communes de moyen exercice* differed from the full communes of Senegal, whose mayor was elected, in having at their head an official appointed by the territorial governor; but they resembled the full communes in that their councils were elected by all the adult townspeople voting in a single college.

8. Grand Council minutes, June 27, 1952.

9. Loans to AEF municipalities between 1948 and 1951 aggregated 1,040 million CFA francs, which were divided as follows: Brazzaville, 360 million, of which 200 million were for housing and 100 million for roads; and, for housing construction, 250 million to Fort Lamy, 300 million to Libreville, 30 million to Pointe Noire, and 100 million to Port Gentil. Bangui was accorded no loans because it received a larger subsidy from the territorial budget than did any other commune.

10. See National Assembly debates, July 29, 1954. Brazzaville's sole subsidy, that of 1952, amounted to only 22.1 million CFA francs; Fort Lamy's five subsidies came to 0.1 million; and Bangui's—the largest sum of all—totaled 104.6 million.

11. In 1953, municipal budgets of the principal towns were as follows (in millions of CFA francs): Bangui, 267; Brazzaville, 252; Dolisie, 13; Fort Lamy, 102; Libreville, 41; Pointe Noire, 135; and Port Gentil, 68.

12. An interesting development occurred at Port Gentil, where the Council of

State annulled the election as mayor of a local functionary, Etienne Makaga, on the ground of irregularities in the balloting. His successor was a resident French merchant, Madame Piraube, the first woman and the first European to be elected mayor of an important French overseas town.

13. *Marchés Tropicaux,* August 9, 1958. This situation worsened after Boganda's death, and in August 1959 the Dacko government felt compelled to threaten with severe penalties the Bangui residents who failed to pay their back taxes. *Ibid.,* August 29, 1959.

14. Speech to the Grand Council, September 30, 1952.

15. Gabon territorial assembly debates, April 24, 1956.

16. Governor Rouys' speech to the territorial assembly, November 22, 1955.

17. Tchad territorial assembly debates, April 24, 1953.

18. See French Union Assembly debates, July 21, 1955.

19. National Assembly debates, January 14, 1958.

Chapter 6

1. Hailey, *An African Survey* (1938), p. 190.

2. The technical services were also depleted. The Services des Postes-Télégraphes-Téléphones (PTT) had 61 of its 78 posts filled, and the public works department 140 out of 158, but the agricultural service only 7 out of 15 and the education service 16 out of 29.

3. Bruel, *La France Equatoriale Africaine,* p. 439.

4. Oubangui-Chari territorial assembly debates, August 20, 1948.

5. Tchad territorial assembly debates, May 6, 1954, November 23, 1955; National Assembly debates, April 3, 1956.

6. French Union Assembly debates, November 9, 1951; *Encyclopédie Mensuelle d'Outre-Mer,* October 1951.

7. See Moyen-Congo territorial assembly debates, May 17, 1955.

8. Oubangui-Chari territorial assembly debates, October 6, 1949.

9. Gabon territorial assembly debates, March 19, 1948.

10. French Union Assembly debates, January 31, 1952.

11. Tchad territorial assembly debates, December 23, 1954.

12. French Union Assembly debates, November 3, 1949.

13. National Assembly debates, April 4, 1951.

14. Grand Council debates, December 17, 1947.

15. Oubangui-Chari territorial assembly debates, September 17, 1947.

16. Grand Council debates, September 5, 1949.

17. Speech to the Grand Council, November 24, 1947.

18. Permanent civil servants in French Black Africa were placed in one of three cadres—the general, the "upper,' or the "lower." To enter the general cadre, a university degree was required; members of this cadre could serve in different territories. Members of the "upper" cadre were recruited at a lower educational level; they had to pass a competitive examination and could be shifted about within a group of territories. Those in the lower, wholly territorial cadres were required only to hold a certificate of primary studies. Another group, working under contract, were more or less temporary functionaries. The largest category of government employees consisted of auxiliaries, who were usually unskilled laborers.

19. See Aubame's speech to the National Assembly, February 21, 1950.

20. See Grand Council debates, August 23 and September 8, 1951.

21. Grand Council debates, October 15, 1952.

22. See Grand Council debates, November 15, 1950. In 1953, 5,986 African functionaries in AEF—57 per cent of all the Africans on the federation's payroll that year —received family allowances. Of those receiving such allowances, 1,429 were polygamous. Sums paid out to African functionaries in family allowances in 1953 totaled 310,246,538 CFA francs. This represented an increase of 6 per cent in the cost of operating AEFs public services compared with the period in which no family allowances had been paid. See French Union Assembly debates, January 20, 1955.

23. This service had in its employ that year 202 Europeans belonging to various cadres, whose salaries aggregated 178 million CFA francs.

24. The writers were informed in 1956 that some functionaries even took their refrigerators home with them when they went on leave.

25. Tchad territorial assembly debates, November 21, 1952.

26. Oubangui-Chari territorial assembly debates, October 31, 1952.

27. Gabon territorial assembly debates, November 21, 1952.

28. *Afrique Nouvelle,* November 19, 1957.

29. As of 1950, there were 11,000 Africans in government service compared with 1,700 Europeans.

30. National Assembly debates, December 16, 1954.

31. This school also admitted a few other pupils who wanted to continue their education beyond the primary grades.

32. In 1949, 18 of its 20 graduates chose to become clerks in the law courts.

33. See speeches by Tchitchellé and Gondjout in the Grand Council, September 6, 1951.

34. Speech of Governor-General Chauvet to the Grand Council, October 24, 1955.

35. This report was summarized in *Encyclopédie Mensuelle d'Outre-Mer,* May 1956.

36. In January 1953, there were no African secretaries of the administration or any African *greffiers,* but by January 1956 the former accounted for 75 per cent and the latter for 34 per cent of all employees in those categories; in the same period, the proportion of African deputy secretaries rose from 78 per cent to 83 per cent of the total. In the technical services, the percentage of Africans was far lower: in the agricultural service, for example, which had no African *conducteurs* in January 1953, they represented only 3 per cent of the January 1956 total, although the proportion of African deputy *controleurs* increased from 2 per cent to 27 per cent during that three-year period. In the treasury department, the accountants were still Europeans but all their aides were now Africans. In the police, there were no African commissioners or inspectors, but by January 1956 the ranks of deputy inspectors, of whom none had been African three years earlier, were 47 per cent African.

37. In the 1958 budgets, AEF's total contribution—federal and territorial—toward payment of state officials came to 1,126,254,000 francs, of which Gabon gave 64,418,000; Moyen-Congo, 77,962,000; Oubangui-Chari, 94,793,000; and Tchad, 78,400,000. See French Union Assembly debates, January 30, 1958.

38. Only the services of Finance, the Plan, Economic Affairs, Justice, and Mines were to be retained at the Group level.

39. Tchad territorial assembly debates, December 10 and 30, 1957; January 3, 1958.

40. *Marchés Tropicaux,* February 8, 1958.

41. Tchad territorial assembly debates, September 16, 1957.

Chapter 7

1. P. Paraf, *L'Ascension des Peuples Noirs*, p. 83.

2. The mass can be reached only through the [chief] to whom respect is owed because of his birth. . . . I know what some people will reply to this. They will say that the king of such and such a country, clad in ridiculous clothes, his power based on the poisonous abuse of palm wine and women who have worn him out prematurely—they will say that the ill-will of such a man is obvious and his lack of understanding of our orders is total. I know all that; I wasn't an administrator in Oubangui for 25 years without learning such things. Yet I repeat that we owe respect to the chief; if he doesn't deserve it as an individual, then his rank does. . . . Respecting the chiefs, mind you, doesn't mean approving of everything that they do. We must train them. And we know perfectly well that education must be accompanied by the rod, but we must know how to use that rod and we must avoid the easy recourse to brutality. . . . Another mistake we should avoid is to regard the chief as a functionary: he is not a functionary but an aristocrat and should be treated as such. Our main effort should be to educate the chiefs, and in this way the abuses they practice will disappear. (F. Eboué, *Circulaire Générale sur la Politique Indigène en Afrique Equatoriale Noire,* Brazzaville, 1941.)

3. See National Assembly debates, August 9, 1947.

4. Gabon territorial assembly debates, November 29, 1952.

5. Oubangui-Chari territorial assembly debates, September 11, 1948.

6. This time differential was eased for chiefs in northern Tchad in 1953.

7. Gabon territorial assembly debates, November 29, 1952.

8. See Oubangui-Chari territorial assembly debates, October 15, 1949. As recently as May 1959 the government of the Tchad Republic created an honorary category for meritorious customary chiefs, who were to receive special decorations and additional monthly stipends.

9. Oubangui-Chari territorial assembly debates, May 28, 1950.

10. In 1955 the official emoluments of canton chiefs in Gabon totaled 4 million CFA francs, and village chiefs in that territory received 7¼ million as rebate on taxes.

11. In Bangui, for example, there were in 1948 some 15 group chiefs and 90 *chefs de quartier*, some of whom administered fewer than 50 individuals.

12. Chauvet proposed to reduce the number of chiefs, where they were excessive, and to classify them into two hierarchies whose members would be given suitable salaries. He also suggested setting up special courses for selected chiefs so that they should be better informed both as to the extent of their duties and also as to the limitations on their rights. In 1955 such training courses were begun in all of Moyen-Congo's districts.

13. Gabon territorial assembly debates, March 23, 1948.

14. Tchad territorial assembly debates, December 20, 1956.

15. *Goumiers* were usually fed and clothed by their overlords but were paid only a few thousand francs a year.

Chapter 8

1. This chamber was composed of magistrates belonging to the court of appeals plus two officials proposed each year by the attorney-general, head of the federal judicial service, and appointed by the governor-general. Its function was to confirm all verdicts involving more than two years' imprisonment that had been imposed by the second-degree courts.

2. A native-status legal "code" that enabled administrators to impose arbitrarily certain penalties on African noncitizens for offenses other than statutory ones.

3. However, if African litigants so desired, they could carry any cases before the tribunals applying French law, or even before French courts applying customary law.

4. See Governor Soucadaux' speech to the Grand Council, November 24, 1947.

5. See A. Schweitzer, *A l'Orée de la Forêt Vierge*, p. 100.

6. Buell, *The Native Problem in Africa*, II, 221.

7. *Chroniques d'Outre-Mer*, January 1952.

8. National Assembly debates, August 19, 1947; July 1, 1949.

9. Grand Council debates, August 26, 1949.

10. National Assembly debates, November 13, 1951.

11. Grand Council debates, June 27 and September 30, 1952.

12. *Ibid.*, October 21, 1953.

13. *Ibid.*

14. French Union Assembly debates, February 7, 1950.

15. Paraf, *L'Ascension des Peuples Noirs*, p. 117.

16. Grand Council debates, November 16, 1955.

17. Tchad territorial assembly debates, December 23–24, 1954.

18. Grand Council debates, May 6, 1950.

19. See Homet, *Congo, Terre de Souffrances*, p. 109.

20. Moyen-Congo territorial assembly debates, December 14, 1955; Oubangui-Chari territorial assembly debates, September 11, 1948.

21. *Chroniques d'Outre-Mer*, April 1954. In 1955 the daily wage for prison labor was raised to a maximum of 90 CFA francs for inmates of the Brazzaville jail, and this was paid as a lump sum to prisoners on the eve of their liberation.

22. One African Grand Councilor said on August 26, 1949, "To the great majority of Africans, justice is a palaver held under a tree, where everyone talks and gesticulates as he pleases."

23. National Assembly debates, June 25, 1952.

24. Grand Council debates, November 19, 1954.

25. French Union Assembly debates, January 15, 1953.

26. See P. E. Joset, *Les Sociétés Secrètes des Hommes-Léopards en Afrique Noire*, p. 118.

27. Balandier, *Sociologie Actuelle de l'Afrique Noire*, p. 377.

28. See Governor-General Chauvet's speech to the Grand Council, October 30, 1954.

29. Grand Council debates, November 17, 1954.

30. Moyen-Congo territorial assembly debates, December 4, 1954.

31. P. Hugot, "Tchad et Soudan," *L'Afrique et l'Asie*, No. 37, 1957.

32. Moyen-Congo territorial assembly debates, December 4, 1954; Tchad territorial assembly debates, December 20, 1956.

Chapter 9

1. Bruel, *La France Equatoriale Africaine*, p. 473.

2. French Union Assembly debates, November 20, 1956. The reinforcements planned for AEF included three companies to be stationed at Zouar, Largeau, and Fada; three mobile desert groups with headquarters respectively at Zouar, Fada, and Moussoro; and three motorized units, of which two were to be centered at Largeau and one at Abéché.

3. A. Q. Maisel, *Africa: Facts and Forecasts*, p. 250.

4. N. Farson, *Behind God's Back*, p. 507.

5. French Union Assembly debates, July 24, 1956.

6. See F. Aerts, "Les Tchadiens et le Service Militaire," *Tropiques*, May 1954.

7. French Union Assembly debates, February 16, 1954.

8. *Ibid.*, June 23, 1949.

9. Grand Council debates, November 24, 1947.

10. Of these, 8,000 were in Tchad, 4,000 in Oubangui, 1,500 in Moyen-Congo, and 1,000 in Gabon.

11. See Aerts, "Les Tchadiens et le Service Militaire."

Chapter 10

1. A reference to the Asian-African conference at Bandung, Indonesia, in May 1955.

2. Grand Council debates, November 9, 1954.

3. Hugot, "Tchad et Soudan."

4. L. A. Fabunmi, "Egypt and Africa," *West Africa*, December 21, 1957; January 4, 1958.

5. P. Nord, *L'Eurafrique, Notre Dernière Chance*, p. 98. At the Muslim Center of Poto-Poto, the authors were shown some Arab League English-language tracts sent by an organization in Brooklyn, New York. Needless to say, none of the Center's members could understand a word of them.

6. Hugot, "Tchad et Soudan."

7. *Neue Zurcher Zeitung*, December 1, 1951.

8. *West Africa*, May 12, 1956.

9. *Le Monde*, May 18, 1956.

10. J. Lartéguy, *Les Clefs de l'Afrique*, p. 247.

11. *Afrique Française*, August–October 1956.

12. Hugot, "Tchad et Soudan."

13. *Le Monde*, May 11, 1956.

14. For details, see *Afrique Française*, March–April 1958.

15. The Senoussi is a powerful religio-political order founded in north Africa in 1843. By the end of the nineteenth century the Senoussi had conquered a region extending to the western Sudan, which had been nominally under the control of the Ottoman Empire since 1835.

16. P. Diolé, *Dans le Fezzan Inconnu* (Paris 1957), p. 70.

17. *Afrique Nouvelle*, March 25, 1957.

18. *The Economist*, September 10, 1949.

19. See the series of articles by E. Sablier in *Le Monde*, beginning December 24, 1954.

20. *West Africa*, September 21, 1957.

21. *The New York Times*, July 20, 1958.

22. See French Union Assembly debates, May 26, 1955.

23. In the National Assembly 411 to 120, and in the Senate 196 to 92.

24. *Le Figaro*, November 22, 1957.

25. French Union Assembly debates, December 10, 1957.

26. *Le Monde*, December 24, 1957.

27. C.-H. Favrod, *Le Poids de l'Afrique*, p. 239.

28. *West Africa*, October 12, 1957.

29. French Union Assembly debates, March 26, 1956.

30. Imports from the Congo into AEF rose from 416 million CFA francs in 1954 to 637 million in 1955, whereas AEF exports to the Congo were respectively 209 and 256 million (*Marchés Coloniaux*, March 31, 1956).

31. *Le Monde*, January 16, 1959.

32. Belgian Congo Monthly Bulletin, No. 1, January 1959.

Chapter 11

1. "Afrique Equatoriale Française, 1953," *Encyclopédie Mensuelle d'Outre-Mer*, August 1953.

2. Grand Council debates, November 24, 1947.

3. *Ibid.*, May 9, 1949.

4. *Ibid.*, May 10 and 13, 1950.

5. *Ibid.*, October 30, 1950.

6. P. Paraf, *L'Ascension des Peuples Noirs*, p. 28.

7. AEF produced only 0.4 per cent of the world's cotton and its coffee supplied only 2.4 per cent of that bought by French consumers. See Zieglé, *Afrique Equatoriale Française*, p. 117.

8. Grand Council debates, June 19, 1952.

9. *Ibid.*, June 21, 1952.

10. Under this reorganization, a *section commune* was set up at the federal level and separate sections were instituted for each of the four territories. Funds invested in the *section commune*, which was to be prepared by the governor-general and voted upon by the Grand Council and the FIDES directorate, were to go to enterprises involving the whole federation or two or more territories. Through this medium France would finance all such interterritorial projects as health, higher education, housing and town planning, industrial and rural production schemes, and up to 75 per cent of all expenditures on the federation's infrastructure. Projects for the territorial sections, drawn up by the governors and approved or amended by the territorial assemblies and the FIDES directorate, were to concern works of strictly territorial interest.

11. Grand Council debates, May 23, 1956.

12. French Union Assembly debates, January 16, 1958.

13. J. Dresch, "Les Investissements en Afrique Noire," *Présence Africaine*, April 1952.

14. *Congo, Terre de Souffrances*, p. 154.

15. R. Susset, *La Vérité sur le Cameroun et l'Afrique Equatoriale Française*, p. 212.

16. *Marchés Coloniaux*, July 14, 1951.

17. *Ibid.*, August 6, 1955.

18. *Afrique Nouvelle*, April 5, 1955.

19. *Marchés Tropicaux*, August 3, 1957.

20. *Ibid.*, February 14, 1959.

21. French Union Assembly debates, October 25, 1955, and Grand Council debates, April 28, 1950.

22. See *La Vie Française*, October 18, 1957.

23. See Grand Council debates, October 2, 1948.

24. Félix-Tchicaya, speaking in the National Assembly on February 10, 1948.

25. René Malbrant, speaking in the National Assembly on February 10, 1948.

26. René Malbrant, speaking in the National Assembly on January 28, 1948.

27. National Assembly debates, August 3, 1948.

28. *Marchés Coloniaux*, January 13, 1951.

29. *The New York Times,* March 12, 1959.

30. L. Mougin, "La Monnaie et le Crédit," *Afrique Equatoriale Française,* p. 419.

31. *La Situation Economique de l'Afrique Equatoriale Française,* August 30, 1955. Financing the cotton crop alone then required loans aggregating 3 billion CFA francs a year.

32. In January 1955 the latter privilege was taken away from the CCOM and entrusted to a newly created Institut d'Emission pour l'AEF et le Cameroun, for which AEF and Cameroun named three directors apiece. At the time, this was considered the most radical innovation made by Minister Buron in the financial field. See *Marchés Coloniaux,* January 29, 1955. The name of this organization was changed on April 5, 1959, to that of Banque Centrale des Etats d'Afrique Equatoriale et du Cameroun, in which each state of the former federation was represented by an official.

33. *Chroniques d'Outre-Mer,* June 1954.

34. *La Situation Economique de l'Afrique Equatoriale Française,* August 30, 1955.

35. See report to the French Union Assembly, March 22, 1956.

36. Grand Council debates, April 23, 1949.

37. *Ibid.,* May 13, 1950.

38. *Marchés Coloniaux,* January 13, 1951.

39. Grand Council debates, June 21, 1952.

40. *Marchés Tropicaux,* November 16, 1957.

41. *Ibid.,* November 15, 1958.

42. See M. Carcassonne, G. Servat, and P. Jacquot, "Organisation Financière," *Afrique Equatoriale Française,* p. 185 ff.

43. G. Bruel, *La France Equatoriale Africaine,* p. 456.

44. Of this, 21 million francs in 1909 was to reimburse about three-fourths of a 2-million-franc loan contracted in 1900, to pay for public works costing 15 million, and to finance studies required by a development program; 171 million francs in 1914 was to improve certain means of communications; 300 million francs in 1924 was for work on the Congo-Ocean railroad and on the ports of Brazzaville and Pointe Noire; and 1,120 million francs in 1931 was to complete rail and port works, to carry on a medical campaign, and to set up a Supporting Fund for African Production.

45. *An African Survey* (1938), p. 1451.

46. A. Gide, *Retour du Tchad,* p. 216.

47. Buell, *The Native Problem in Africa,* II, 223.

48. These were taxes on gold and transporters, an *impôt cédulaire* on wages and salaries, and a tax on industrial and commercial profits (BIC)—none of which was repealed after the Liberation.

49. *Encyclopédie Mensuelle d'Outre-Mer,* August 1953.

50. Inasmuch as there was no uniform system of budgeting used by all of the territories, it is difficult to compare the volume of their respective revenues and expenditures.

51. Grand Council debates, November 2, 1955.

52. National Assembly debates, June 21, 1949.

53. Grand Council debates, April 27, 1949.

54. Grand Council debates, May 29, 1954.

55. Grand Council debates, October 30, 1954.

56. *Chroniques d'Outre-Mer,* March 1955.

57. French Union Assembly debates, November 18, 1954.

58. Grand Council debates, May 27, 1955.

59. Under the system proposed at that time by the government-general and finally

accepted, with modifications, by the Grand Council, the basic principle laid down was that all funds not needed for the federation's operating expenses should go to the territories. First the minimal needs of all the territories taken together would be determined, and these normally would be supplied by one-third of the revenues from import duties and internal taxes and two-thirds of the export duties collected by the federation. Then, any surplus federal revenues remaining, after the territories' minimal needs and the government-general's operating expenses were provided for, would be divided among the territories in the following percentages: Moyen-Congo 21.3 per cent, Gabon 23.7 per cent, Oubangui 26.5 per cent, and Tchad 28.5 per cent.

60. Grand Council debates, May 23, 1956.
61. *France-Equatoriale,* November 7, 1956.
62. *Marchés Tropicaux,* November 24, 1956.
63. *La Vie Française,* June 28, 1957.

Chapter 12

1. Grand Council debates, April 20, 1949.
2. Tchad territorial assembly debates, December 8, 1954.
3. G. G. Beslier, *L'Apôtre du Congo, Mgr. Augouard,* p. 176.
4. In 1919 the French government had to pay 1.5 million francs to a steamship company because of delays in unloading ships at Matadi. See Buell, *The Native Problem in Africa,* II, 258.
5. *Marchés Coloniaux,* October 9, 1954.
6. *Ibid.*
7. A. Londres, *Terre d'Ebène,* p. 234.
8. *Marchés Coloniaux,* October 9, 1954.
9. Hailey, *An African Survey* (1938), p. 1590; *Marchés Coloniaux,* May 14, 1949.
10. Zieglé, *Afrique Equatoriale Française,* p. 125.
11. Susset, *La Vérité sur le Cameroun et l'Afrique Equatoriale Française,* p. 134.
12. Trézenem and Lembezat, *La France Equatoriale,* p. 118; *Chroniques d'Outre-Mer,* October 1953.
13. *Marchés Coloniaux,* October 11, 1947.
14. Grand Council debates, September 10, 1949.
15. *Ibid.,* October 20, 1952, and June 12, 1953.
16. *Ibid.,* December 18, 1947.
17. *Ibid.,* October 28, 1953, and October 30, 1954.
18. Trézenem, *La France Equatoriale,* p. 118.
19. *Chroniques d'Outre-Mer,* October 1953.
20. Grand Council debates, October 22, 1953.
21. *Ibid.,* October 30, 1954.
22. *Ibid.,* November 12, 1955.
23. Report to the Moyen-Congo territorial assembly, 1956, p. 48.
24. *Marchés Tropicaux,* April 11, 1959.
25. *Ibid.,* April 12, 1958.
26. Hailey, *An African Survey* (1938), p. 1562.
27. Zieglé, *Afrique Equatoriale Française,* p. 129.
28. For details of this Plan, see *Afrique Equatoriale Française* (ed., E. Guernier), p. 437.
29. Gabon, 1,320; Moyen-Congo, 1,650; Tchad, 1,610; and Oubangui, 1,320 kilometers.

30. The Société des Batignolles for Oubangui, SETRAP and Graeff for Tchad, the Société Desplats-Lefèvre for Moyen-Congo, and the Compagnie Générale des Colonies for Gabon.

31. *Marchés Coloniaux,* February 23, 1952.

32. According to Zieglé, *Afrique Equatoriale Française,* p. 129, it was assumed that a road would automatically create prosperity in the regions through which it passed. In 1948 a road was built in an area where there was an annual traffic of less than 100 tons, which had only one inhabitant to the square kilometer, and which was already well provided with water transport.

33. National Assembly debates, November 6, 1952.

34. Grand Council debates, May 27 and June 10, 1955.

35. *Marchés Tropicaux,* February 21, 1959.

36. See Homet, *Congo, Terre de Souffrances,* pp. 161, 227.

37. As of 1950, one ton cost 15 francs per kilometer to transport by road, nearly 5 by the railroad, and 3 by the river route. See Zieglé, *Afrique Equatoriale Française,* p. 132.

38. The writers were informed in 1956 by the captain of one of the CGTA's river boats that the method of pushing instead of towing barges had been copied from the American practice followed on the Mississippi river.

39. *Marchés Coloniaux,* January 24, 1948.

40. In 1949 a kilogram of coffee bought for 140 francs from the grower had to bear 89 francs in freight charges for delivery in France.

41. Governor Rouys' report to the Moyen-Congo territorial assembly, 1956, p. 53.

42. *Marchés Tropicaux,* December 14, 1957, and August 23, 1958.

43. *Encyclopédie Mensuelle d'Outre-Mer,* January 1954.

44. As of 1959, Gabon was said to have more private airfields than any other country in the world. See *Le Monde,* February 24, 1959.

45. *Afrique Equatoriale Française* (ed., E. Guernier), p. 499.

46. Libreville and Port Gentil in Gabon; Dolisie, Ouesso, and Djambala in Moyen-Congo; Berbérati, Bambari, and Bangassou in Oubangui; and Moundou, Fort Archambault, Pala, and Abéché in Tchad.

47. *L'Afrique Française,* January–February 1958.

48. Grand Council debates, August 26, 1949.

49. *Ibid.,* September 8, 1951.

50. *La Situation Economique de l'Afrique Equatoriale Française.*

51. *West Africa,* October 10, 1959.

Chapter 13

1. See Hailey, *An African Survey* (1938), p. 786 ff.; Buell, *The Native Problem in Africa,* II, 233.

2. In Moyen-Congo, 561 titles for 31,068 hectares, and in Tchad, 47 titles for 126 hectares. See *Afrique Equatoriale Française* (ed., E. Guernier), p. 233 ff.

3. National Assembly debates, August 4, 1947.

4. For details, see French Union Assembly debates, October 7, 1952.

5. Oubangui territorial assembly debates, May 6, 1949.

6. French Union Assembly debates, January 31, 1952.

7. Moyen-Congo territorial assembly debates, April 4 and December 18, 1954.

Chapter 14

1. Homet, *Congo, Terre de Souffrances,* p. 127.

2. According to the missionary Briault (*Sur les Pistes de l'AEF,* p. 96), the Africans to whom he showed pictures of some Chinese tilling the soil at once concluded that all Orientals must be slaves.

3. *Afrique Equatoriale Française* (ed., E. Guernier), p. 426 ff.

4. Grand Council debates, November 17, 1950; October 30, 1954.

5. Grand Council debates, September 6, 1951.

6. Gabon territorial assembly debates, November 29, 1952.

7. *Marchés Coloniaux,* April 17, 1954.

8. Between 1946 and 1959 the agricultural services of AEF received from FIDES 8,463 million CFA francs. Of this sum, Gabon was allocated 5,686 million, Moyen-Congo 1,284.6, Oubangui 1,977.6, and Tchad 3,182.6. These figures do not include the investments made in the federation by IRCT, IRHO, IFAC, and the cotton companies. Altogether AEF's agricultural production received funds aggregating about 64,400 million CFA francs. See *Marchés Tropicaux,* July 25, 1959.

9. J. Cabot and R. Diziain, *Population du Moyen-Logone,* Paris, 1955.

10. This has also been true in regard to AEF's contribution of 5 million CFA francs a year to the locust-control service. See Grand Council debates, November 15, 1950.

11. *Ibid.,* June 19, 1953.

12. "Doctrines et Bilans de la Modernisation Rurale en AEF."

13. The name of these organizations was later changed to Sociétés Africaines de Prévoyance, or SAP.

14. Grand Council debates, December 11, 1947.

15. French Union Assembly debates, February 12, 1952.

16. See J. Romieu, *Les Mouvements Coopératifs en Afrique Noire.*

17. Grand Council debates, October 30, 1954.

18. *Doctrines et Bilans de la Modernisation Rurale en AEF,* p. 7.

19. Homet, *Congo, Terre de Souffrances,* p. 112.

20. Zieglé, *Afrique Equatoriale Française,* p. 145.

21. *Marchés Coloniaux,* July 2, 1955.

22. French Union Assembly debates, May 27, 1948; Zieglé, *Afrique Equatoriale Française,* p. 149.

23. Oubangui territorial assembly debates, June 5, 1956.

24. French Union Assembly debates, March 22, 1951.

25. Grand Council debates, May 13, 1950; French Union Assembly debates, May 27, 1948.

26. *Afrique Equatoriale Française,* Paris, 1950, p. 209.

27. Oubangui territorial assembly debates, September 7, 1950.

28. Grand Council debates, May 13, 1950; French Union Assembly debates, March 22, 1951.

29. *Afrique Equatoriale Française* (ed., E. Guernier), p. 384.

30. Grand Council debates, November 23, 1950.

31. See P. Moussa, *Les Chances Economiques de la Communauté Franco-Africaine,* p. 43.

32. Moyen-Congo territorial assembly debates, April 30, 1956.

33. *Marchés Coloniaux,* July 2, 1955.

34. *Ibid.,* April 24, 1954.

35. Between 1947 and the end of 1952 the Supporting Fund had spent 2,579 million CFA francs. Of these, 295 million went to the IRCT, 855 million to technicians' salaries, 533 million for planting bonuses, and 896 million for miscellaneous projects in the cotton zone and elsewhere. See Grand Council debates, October 8, 1953.

36. Quoted in *Marchés Coloniaux*, July 2, 1955.

37. An average of one kilogram of fiber is ginned from three kilograms of cotton in the boll.

38. See Grand Council debates, June 3 and September 30, 1953. This fund was created in 1943 to help subsidize production throughout the French Empire of raw materials used by the Metropolitan textile industry, and it was financed by a tax paid by the French consumer. It aided AEF's cotton to the extent of 239 million CFA francs between 1954 and November 1956, when it was replaced by a Fonds de Soutien des Textiles des TOM.

39. The IRCT now has five stations or farms in Oubangui and six in Tchad. Almost all the *boys-coton* have disappeared and have been replaced by 60 *conducteurs* and over 1,000 African monitors under the supervision of 18 agronomists.

40. Zieglé, *Afrique Equatoriale Française*, p. 150.

41. *Encyclopédie Mensuelle d'Outre-Mer*, July 1953.

42. Grand Council debates, October 29 and 30, 1954.

43. *Marchés Coloniaux*, October 9, 1954.

44. It had determined that the optimum area for a medium-size enterprise was from 250 to 400 hectares, but even so comparatively modest an enterprise required the investment of 8 to 10 million CFA francs.

45. *Marchés Tropicaux*, April 11, 1959.

46. *Afrique Equatoriale Française* (ed., E. Guernier), p. 319.

47. Zieglé, *Afrique Equatoriale Française*, p. 151.

48. National Assembly debates, February 27, 1953.

49. *Encyclopédie Mensuelle d'Outre-Mer*, August 1953.

50. *Marchés Tropicaux*, March 15, 1958.

51. See Balandier, *Sociologie Actuelle de l'Afrique Noire*, p. 174.

52. *La Situation Economique de l'Afrique Equatoriale Française*.

53. Grand Council debates, October 31, 1956.

54. *Ibid.*, November 2, 1955.

55. Gabon territorial assembly debates, January 26, 1956.

56. Schweitzer, *A l'Orée de la Forêt Vierge*, p. 75.

57. Trézenem, *La France Equatoriale*, p. 90.

58. Zieglé, *Afrique Equatoriale Française*, p. 109.

59. *Afrique Equatoriale Française* (ed., E. Guernier), p. 317.

60. *Marchés Tropicaux*, April 20, 1957.

61. Grand Council debates, September 9, 1949; Oubangui territorial assembly debates, September 19, 1950.

62. See Grand Council debates, September 6, 1951.

63. Meat consumption in all AEF has been estimated recently at about 22,000 tons a year, chiefly mutton and goat; it is considered adequate only in Tchad and most deficient in Gabon and rural Moyen-Congo.

64. *Marchés Coloniaux*, October 18, 1947.

65. *Ibid.*, June 22, 1946.

66. Zieglé, *Afrique Equatoriale Française*, p. 141.

67. National Assembly debates, July 4, 1947.

68. *Marchés Coloniaux*, February 5, 1955.

69. *La Vie Française*, May 17, 1957.
70. *Chroniques d'Outre-Mer*, June 1958.
71. Governor Rouys' report to the Moyen-Congo territorial assembly, 1956, pp. 26–31.
72. Zieglé, *Afrique Equatoriale Française*, p. 108.
73. *Marchés Tropicaux*, April 18, 1959.
74. See Grand Council debates, April 26, 1948.
75. *Marchés Tropicaux*, February 22, 1958.
76. *Chroniques d'Outre-Mer*, November 1958.

Chapter 15

1. For more detailed studies see Hailey, *An African Survey* (1958), p. 1347; *Afrique Equatoriale Française* (ed., E. Guernier), p. 409 ff.; Trézenem, *La France Equatoriale*, p. 108; and Zieglé, *Afrique Equatoriale Française*, p. 161.
2. Trézenem, *La France Equatoriale*, p. 110.
3. Since 1951, exports had doubled in tonnage, rising from 387,000 to 772,000 tons in round figures, and in the course of the preceding year they had increased by 2.1 per cent in tonnage and by 3.2 per cent in value.
4. On February 12, 1948, Deputy Tchicaya told the National Assembly that the minimal needs of each inhabitant of AEF were six meters of cloth a year.
5. Speech to the Grand Council, April 29, 1949.
6. Paulin, *Afrique Equatoriale Française*, p. 82.
7. Governor-General Chauvet's speech to the Grand Council, May 27, 1955.
8. Grand Council debates, May 23, 1956.
9. Zieglé, *Afrique Equatoriale Française*, p. 116.
10. *Voyage au Congo*, p. 57.
11. Quoted by Zieglé, *Afrique Equatoriale Française*, p. 162.
12. Their creation and the size of their membership were determined by the governor-general, and their operations were in part financed by public funds. In addition to the activities normally associated with such bodies in the United States, they ran ferry services, managed warehouses, offered courses in stenography, etc. On commercial matters they were competent to advise the administration, which, in some cases, was legally required to consult them but not to follow their advice. The government's negligence in this respect was a source of common complaint by their members. See *Afrique Equatoriale Française* (ed., E. Guernier), p. 415.
13. Grand Council debates, May 9, 1949.
14. Paulin, *Afrique Equatoriale Française*, p. 137.
15. *L'Afrique Française*, November–December 1957.
16. An American journalist's dispatch in the *New York Times* of March 12, 1959, stated that the average income of an AEF family came to $90 a year, and that such a sum could easily be spent within 48 hours in one of the federation's better hotels.
17. *Vente et Publicité*, July–August 1954.

Chapter 16

1. Moussa, *Les Chances Economiques de la Communauté Franco-Africaine*, p. 106.
2. See Moyen-Congo territorial assembly debates, May 14, 1955.
3. Moussa, *Les Chances Economiques*, p. 121.

4. *Afrique Equatoriale Française*, p. 49.
5. *Marchés Coloniaux,* October 14, 1950; *La Situation Economique de l'Afrique Equatoriale Française.*
6. French Union Assembly debates, June 19, 1952.
7. National Assembly debates, March 17, 1953.
8. Moyen-Congo territorial assembly debates, April 4, 1954.
9. Grand Council debates, September 5, 1949.
10. *Ibid.,* May 6, 1950.
11. Zieglé, *Afrique Equatoriale Française,* p. 139.
12. Fontaine, *La Mort Mystérieuse du Gouverneur-Général Renard,* p. 158 ff.
13. These were the Société Minière du Niari (SOMINA) and the Société d'Exploitation Minière au Congo (EMAC), both of which received loans from the U.S. government.
14. *Chroniques d'Outre-Mer,* October–November 1955.
15. About 15 companies mine gold in AEF, and of these by far the most important are the Société des Mines d'Or du Gabon and its subsidiary, the Société Minière de Micounzou, both of which operate in the N'Gounié region. Next in order of importance are the Société Minière Oubangui-Lobaye, which mines in the Kellé region of Moyen-Congo and around Berbérati in Oubangui, and the Société de N'Djolé and the Société Gabon-Congo, both active in Gabon.
16. Grand Council debates, October 30, 1950.
17. National Assembly debates, April 11, 1951; Council of the Republic debates, November 29, 1950.
18. *La Vie Française,* May 17, 1957.
19. *Le Monde,* May 7, 1957.
20. *Chroniques d'Outre-Mer,* July 1952.
21. National Assembly debates, December 17, 1952.
22. This 15-year loan was negotiated in June 1959 at an interest rate of 6 per cent.
23. *Encyclopédie Mensuelle d'Outre-Mer,* March 1957.
24. *Nice-Matin,* October 27, 1959.
25. Moyen-Congo territorial assembly debates, November 26, 1955.

Chapter 17

1. Roberts, *History of French Colonial Policy,* I, 366.
2. Buell, *The Native Problem in Africa,* II, 232.
3. Hailey, *An African Survey* (1938), p. 642.
4. French Union Assembly debates, February 9, 1948.
5. New safeguards for the health of AEF workers were laid down on September 18, 1947; a regulation of July 21, 1949, required that all wage disputes be submitted to arbitration councils composed of representatives of the government, management, and labor on a parity basis; on May 3, 1950, the Grand Council accepted the government's proposal to set up a limited form of workmen's compensation; and on September 8, 1951, it agreed to limit the type of occupations in which women and children could be employed.
6. Speech to the Grand Council, October 30, 1954.
7. Grand Council debates, March 9, 1953.
8. In Tchad, 55 per cent of the laborers investigated were unmarried and 76 per cent had no children; in Gabon, the corresponding figures were 28 per cent and 71

per cent; and in Oubangui, 46 per cent and 81 per cent. See French Union Assembly debates, January 27, 1955.

9. Annual report of the AEF Labor Inspectorate for 1954, p. 21.

10. *Marchés Tropicaux,* May 31, 1958.

11. Grand Council debates, August 23, 1951.

12. National Assembly debates, December 16, 1954.

13. French Union Assembly debates, May 10, 1955.

14. Writing of conditions in 1949, the federal labor inspector said that most urban employers complied with the eight-hour working day and six-day week but that in other respects "the law is observed in towns only up to the point where employers risk penalties for infraction of the sanitary code." *Afrique Equatoriale Française* (ed., E. Guernier), p. 238.

15. French Union Assembly debates, May 10, 1955. The mission's report commented, "Generally speaking, enterprises located in rural areas, and indeed everywhere outside the territorial capitals, have only a slight relation to the new legislation. Because of the distances and lack of uniformity in the territorial regulations, and because of the scarcity of inspectors, working conditions there escape effective controls." See pp. 524–25.

16. E. Picard, *L'Enseignement Technique en Afrique Equatoriale Française,* p. 54.

17. Totaling 1,276, compared with 296 in local crafts, 122 in woodwork, 88 in mechanics, and 14 in ironwork.

18. See *L'Evolution de l'Enseignement Technique Public dans les Territoires Françaises d'Outre-Mer.*

19. In 1951 a number of students at the federal school were expelled for taking part in a "street demonstration."

20. See Gabon territorial assembly debates, December 5, 1952.

21. Grand Council debates, September 1, 1949; October 21, 1953.

22. In 1953, the Brazzaville school had 122 students from Moyen-Congo compared with 15 from Gabon and 4 each from Oubangui and Tchad.

23. Grand Council debates, October 21, 1953; October 30, 1954.

24. *Ibid.,* October 24, 1955.

25. *Afrique Nouvelle,* January 1, 1957.

26. *Marchés Tropicaux,* May 31, 1958.

27. Report of the Federal Labor Inspectorate for 1954, p. 10.

28. *Chroniques d'Outre-Mer,* December 1958.

29. *Encyclopédie Mensuelle d'Outre-Mer,* December 1955.

30. *Ibid.*

31. In 1956 COLPAEF was reorganized and took the name of Union Interprofessionelle de l'AEF.

Chapter 18

1. Scholarships to French West African schools have never been popular with AEF Africans because they do not have in the latter's eyes the same prestige as Metropolitan institutions and the grants for study there are smaller.

2. Zieglé, *Afrique Equatoriale Française,* p. 183.

3. Payments from public funds toward the salaries of mission teachers were first made in 1937.

4. Hailey, *An African Survey* (1938), p. 1267.

5. To avoid duplication of effort, the Catholics transferred their normal school to Mouila from Lambaréné in 1955.

6. *Afrique Equatoriale Française* (ed., E. Guernier), p. 589.

7. Grand Council debates, May 13, 1950.

8. On June 7, 1955, a request by a Protestant mission for modest financial aid in establishing a secondary school was turned down by the Grand Council. Said the *rapporteur* of its finance committee: "We have no objection to any religious body opening such schools in AEF, but they should be supported from its own and not from public funds. There already exist in the federation secondary schools that have cost us dear and which are not fully attended, though they are open to pupils of all religious faiths."

9. According to Dr. Aujoulat, 46 per cent of the students who were receiving primary education in AEF in 1958 were in mission schools (*Aujourd'hui, l'Afrique,* p. 342).

10. For example, in the 1954 budgets, Moyen-Congo allocated 25 per cent of its total expenditures to education, but only 5 per cent went to mission schools. The corresponding figures for Gabon were 15.2 per cent and 4.3 per cent, for Oubangui 10.4 per cent and 2.4 per cent, for Tchad 6 per cent and 0.2 per cent, and for the federal budget 1.3 per cent and 0.06 per cent.

11. As a result of the Lamine-Gueye law, the beginning pay of state school teachers was 7,000 CFA francs a month compared with 4,000 for mission teachers. See Gabon territorial assembly debates, May 9, 1952.

12. *Ibid.,* March 26, 1955.

13. Oubangui territorial assembly debates, September 1, 1948.

14. *Ibid.,* March 3, 1949.

15. *Marchés Tropicaux,* November 15, 1958.

16. *Ibid.,* June 7, 1958.

17. Moyen-Congo territorial assembly debates, December 18, 1954; May 10, 1955.

18. Antoine Darlan speaking in the French Union Assembly, July 29, 1949.

19. On March 12, 1949, Georges Darlan, then president of the assembly, said to his colleagues: "Oubangui has twice the population of Moyen-Congo and three times that of Gabon, and its children are not even half as well educated as the children of those territories. Under such conditions, it would be hypocritical of me to offer my congratulations to our education service, which obviously needs a complete reorganization."

20. Oubangui territorial assembly debates, December 22, 1956.

21. *Marchés Tropicaux,* May 4, 1957.

22. Grand Council debates, December 13 and 15, 1947.

23. Gabon territorial assembly debates, January 26, 1956.

24. Zieglé, *Afrique Equatoriale Française,* p. 183.

25. Grand Council debates, September 9, 1949.

26. Gabon territorial assembly debates, November 30, 1953.

27. Tchad territorial assembly debates, December 27, 1954; March 30, 1955; December 9, 1955.

28. *Ibid.,* November 16, 1957.

29. Tchad territorial assembly debates, September 24, 1957; Gabon territorial assembly debates, January 26, 1956.

30. Grand Council debates, December 15, 1947.

31. The delay in establishing this single cadre, which had been approved in 1947 by both the governor-general and the Grand Council, was attributed by African mem-

bers of the latter body to the ill-will of the then General Inspector of Education. He was accused in the session of August 29, 1949, of having ignored the expressed wishes of the government and Grand Councilors and of having tried to perpetuate the two-cadre system. This prompted a demand by the African elite for his dismissal and for the placing of AEF's education services directly under the French Minister of Public Instruction.

32. *Encyclopédie Mensuelle d'Outre-Mer*, August 1953.

33. *Chroniques d'Outre-Mer*, December 1958.

34. National Assembly debates, July 8, 1952; Grand Council debates, June 9, 1953.

35. Tchad territorial assembly debates, September 24 and 25, 1957.

36. As of 1956 there were five girls studying to be teachers in the normal schools of Bongor and Mouyondzi. Tchad territorial assembly debates, December 7, 1957.

37. *Ibid.*, September 24, 1957.

38. *Chroniques d'Outre-Mer*, December 1958.

39. In 1951 the Bambari normal school graduated its first group of six African instructors.

40. In round figures, the number of children taught in mission primary schools in 1949 was 3,000; in 1957, 22,000. See *Afrique Nouvelle*, January 1, 1957.

41. At this time, eight girls from Oubangui were studying at the Mouyondzi normal school and 12 were undergoing training in home economics at Bangui.

42. Oubangui territorial assembly debates, September 12, 1950.

43. See Paraf, *L'Ascension des Peuples Noirs*, p. 68; *Encyclopédie Mensuelle d'Outre-Mer*, August 1953.

44. Tchad territorial assembly debates, April 28, 1953.

45. Oubangui territorial assembly debates, September 1, 1948.

46. Governor Rouys' report to the Moyen-Congo territorial assembly, 1956, p. 72.

47. In the main towns, over 93 per cent of the boys go to school. *Afrique Nouvelle*, June 5, 1959.

48. See Balandier, *Sociologie Actuelle de l'Afrique Noire*, p. 408.

49. *Ibid.*, p. 359.

50. In 1955, when well over a quarter of the children attending primary schools were girls, the territorial assembly wanted to build its own normal school for training women teachers. This was opposed by the government-general as a needless expense, and Gabon was urged to send its candidates to the federal school at Mouyondzi. The Gabonese, however, preferred to utilize teacher-training facilities in France, and, as of 1956, Gabon was the only territory which sent no pupils to the Mouyondzi school. See Gabon territorial assembly debates, April 25, 1956.

51. *Ibid.*, April 14, 1955.

52. *Marchés Tropicaux*, June 20, 1959.

53. Governor-General Chauvet's speech to the Grand Council, October 30, 1954.

54. Moyen-Congo territorial assembly debates, April 23, 1954; Grand Council debates, November 15, 1955.

55. *Chroniques d'Outre-Mer*, April 1953.

56. Grand Council debates, May 30, 1956.

57. In addition there were five vocational institutions, four of which were run by the state, with an attendance of about 550.

58. Tchad territorial assembly debates, December 27, 1954.

59. Hugot, "Tchad et Soudan."

60. As of 1953, 3,154 Africans were studying on scholarship grants in the federation's secondary schools. See *Encyclopédie Mensuelle d'Outre-Mer*, August 1953.

61. In all the territorial assemblies, the local governors read aloud letters from Metropolitan teachers and African students in France illustrating these points.

62. Eighteen from Moyen-Congo, 11 from Gabon, 8 from Tchad, and 4 from Oubangui.

63. Grand Council debates, September 4, 1951.

64. The territories awarded scholarships for technical studies in France.

65. Grand Council debates, October 24 and November 16, 1955.

66. The authors were told by European teachers in AEF that their African students were especially talented in mathematics and in all studies involving memorizing and verbal facility, but that they were weak in fields that required the objective observation of natural phenomena.

67. Probably an exception to this generalization was the student strike of 1958 in Gabon. There the college had to be closed twice and students sent home because of a dispute with political overtones that occurred not only between the authorities and the students but among members of the faculty. See p. 355.

68. In 1956 the authors were told by an *inspecteur d'académie* of a student at Libreville who had written to the governor-general, as his "father and mother," asking that he send him a watch so that he could get to his classes on time.

69. *Chroniques d'Outre-Mer,* December 1958.

Chapter 19

1. For the early history of the missions, the authors are mainly indebted to the chapters by Bouchaud, Le Comte, Leenhardt, and Oschwald in *Afrique Equatoriale Française* (ed., E. Guernier), and to Balandier's *Sociologie Actuelle de l'Afrique Noire,* p. 45 ff.

2. Concerning Augouard, who came to be known as the Bishop of the Cannibals, an amusing anecdote is told by his biographer, Baron de Witte. During an audience with Pope Leo XIII, Augouard was asked if his parishioners really ate human flesh. "Yes, Holy Father, every day," replied the bishop. "It is curious," commented the Pope, "that among the martyred saints none has been eaten by cannibals." "Well, Holy Father," responded the obliging Augouard, "I shall try to be the first." "Heaven forbid," exclaimed the Pope, "for if you were eaten, we would have no relics." See Baron Jehan de Witte, *Les Deux Congo, p.* 107.

3. *Afrique Nouvelle,* March 20, 1956.

4. F. Méjan, *Le Vatican contre la France d'Outre-Mer?,* p. 229.

5. See p. 388 and p. 484. Relations between Boganda and the church were tensest in 1949–50, but four years later he wrote an article in *L'Observateur* on May 20, 1954, attacking the priests of the Berbérati mission for having conducted different ceremonies at the funerals of the French and African victims of the "Berbérati incident." (See pp. 392–93.) To this, one of the missionaries concerned replied in *Afrique Nouvelle,* on June 30, 1954, that he could not have done otherwise, inasmuch as neither of the murdered Africans had been a baptized Christian, but that he had prayed at their tomb. Subsequently Senator Rivierrez used his good offices between Boganda and the church to such good effect that a reconciliation took place in 1956. To mark the event, the Archbishop of Bangui told the authors, he attended a banquet given him by Boganda the day after Ascension.

That same year, the Abbé Fulbert Youlou made conciliatory overtures to the Catholic mission in Moyen-Congo. Upon his election as mayor of Brazzaville on

November 18, he made a public speech in which he said: "I have not renounced my faith. . . . I want with all my heart to re-establish normal relations soon with the hierarchy of my church." (Quoted in *Marchés Tropicaux,* December 8, 1956.)

6. Dr. Schweitzer recounts in his reminiscences the story of his cook, a convert, who kept an open book beside him while he worked, not because he was able to read but because he wanted to show that he was above the task he was performing. Eventually he became so presumptuous that the doctor dismissed him. (*A l'Orée de la Fôret Vierge,* p. 190).

7. Balandier, *Sociologie Actuelle de l'Afrique Noire,* pp. 218, 224.

8. Norman A. Horner, "The Development of an Indigenous Presbyterian Church in the French Cameroun during the Decade 1938-48," p. 4.

9. It was not until 1935 that another group of American missionaries, the Christian and Missionary Alliance, attempted to evangelize Gabon.

10. All non-French-speaking missionaries working in AEF are sent first to Paris for language lessons given under the auspices of the Comité de Liaison des Missions Evangéliques.

11. Only about 5 per cent of Oubangui's population and 0.1 per cent of Tchad's are Christians.

12. Another evidence of religious tolerance during the war was in the building of Brazzaville's sensationally handsome cathedral of Ste. Anne du Congo. Its construction was sponsored by a free-thinking Negro governor-general, and its architect was a Protestant who refused to accept pay for his work. From the town's residents, African as well as European, came gifts of all sorts, such as cement, bricks, and tiles. It became the custom for anyone starting a business there to make some contribution to the edifice, and even owners of bars and night clubs took advantage of this opportunity to win celestial indulgence. (See Paraf, *L'Ascension des Peuples Noirs,* p. 14.)

13. F. Grébert, *Au Gabon,* p. 214.

14. Méjan, *Le Vatican contre la France d'Outre-Mer?,* p. 165.

15. G. Balandier, "Messianisme des Ba-Kongo," *Encyclopédie Mensuelle d'Outre-Mer,* August 1951. See also pp. 479-82.

16. In 1948, a school of theology was opened by the Protestant missions at Ndounghé, Cameroun, to train future African pastors from AEF as well as from that trust territory.

17. For a comparison of Protestant and Catholic policy in this respect, see Schweitzer, *A l'Orée de la Fôret Vierge,* p. 190.

18. G. Bruel calculated that in 1935 there were only 67,985 Catholics and 12,429 Protestants. *La France Equatoriale Africaine,* p. 453.

19. According to the round figures cited in *Afrique Nouvelle,* on March 20, 1956, AEF's Muslims numbered 1,256,000 and its animists 2,164,000.

20. In 1956 the Archbishop of Bangui told the writers that within the past year he had noted an increase in the number of Muslim missionaries, mostly Haoussas from Tchad, working in Oubangui. Though until then they had made few inroads, he admitted that Islam had a strong attraction for the Africans because it adapted itself more than Christianity to their customs, and he expressed the fear that the day would soon come when it would make a concerted drive for converts in the territory.

21. For most of the material in this section, the writers have drawn upon the publications of G. Balandier, and also upon several typescripts loaned them from the archives of the Moyen-Congo government.

22. In Oubangui, a similar fervor animated the followers of Boganda, to whom they attributed magical and even divine powers, but it remained within the framework of a political party.

23. In regard to Ngol, see p. 313. Labi was the name given to a religious association led by the "prophet" Karineu, a chief of the Haute-Sangha, who in 1928 announced the imminent expulsion of the white man and a subsequent regime of inexhaustible abundance. This movement was shot through with xenophobia and violence, including the massacre of Africans who were hostile to it. After Karineu was killed in combat, it subsided quickly. (See Balandier, *Sociologie Actuelle de l'Afrique Noire*, p. 59.)

24. Lesser and more localized sects in Moyen-Congo are those of "Mademoiselle" in the Ewo region, the Dieudonnistes in the Ganboma area, and the Tchaka-Tchaka in the north.

25. He was given the name of Gounza, symbol of the trinity, and in some places the sect that he founded became known as Gounzism.

26. The role played by candles in this cult led to its being sometimes called Bougisme.

27. Bwiti is the name given to a superior divinity revealed only to the initiated. The name is also given to the sculptured doorpost that supports the entrance to its temples.

28. Balandier, *Sociologie Actuelle de l'Afrique Noire*, p. 228.

Chapter 20

1. Homet, *Congo, Terre de Souffrances*, p. 164.

2. *Afrique Equatoriale Française* (ed., E. Guernier), p. 497.

3. In 1956, it added the programs of Radio France-Asie after that station had been closed by the government of South Vietnam.

4. Grand Council debates, October 22, 1953.

5. In 1958, however, the director of Radio Tchad told the writers that he thought most Tchadians could not understand the Arabic spoken by the Egyptians and that they listened to Cairo broadcasts mainly for the music.

6. Tchad territorial assembly debates, June 17, 1958.

7. *Le Monde,* March 6, 1958.

8. Grand Council debates, May 16 and September 6, 1951.

9. H. Kitchen, *The Press in Africa*, pp. 62, 65.

10. *Ibid.*, p. 63.

11. Sessions of November 16, 1955, and June 6, 1956.

12. Grand Council debates, June 5, 1956.

13. In 1957 it was estimated that throughout that immense territory, probably not more than 7,000 copies of all its various publications were printed each year, aside from the scientific journals of the Institut d'Etudes Centrafricaines and the output of government offices. See French Union Assembly debates, May 14, 1957.

14. Kitchen, *The Press in Africa*, p. 62.

Chapter 21

1. For details, see Zieglé, *Afrique Equatoriale Française*, p. 60 ff.; Trézenem, *La France Equatoriale*, p. 66; Buell, *The Native Problem in Africa*, II, 213; and Hailey, *An African Survey* (1938), p. 105.

2. Zieglé, *Afrique Equatoriale Française*, p. 74.

3. Balandier attributes to the Protestant missions' translation of the Bible into Kikongo a considerable influence on the development of quasi-nationalist sentiments among members of the Bakongo Messianic sects. (See "Messianisme des Ba-Kongo,"

Encyclopédie Mensuelle d'Outre-Mer, August 1951.) Utilization by the Catholic mission of Lingala rather than of the M'Bochi vernacular is thought to be chiefly responsible for Opangault's adoption of anticlerical views and for his joining the Section Française de l'Internationale Ouvrière (SFIO).

4. Balandier, *Sociologie Actuelle de l'Afrique Noire*, p. 50.

5. As used in AEF, the term "Europeans" denotes all who do not have an African civil status, and it includes Syrians and naturalized French Africans and mulattoes. The Portuguese colony is largest in Pointe Noire, Bangui, and Fort Archambault; both Greeks and Syrians are numerically strongest in Tchad. See *Marchés Tropicaux*, September 29, 1956.

6. In 1955, out of 12,013 urban Europeans, Bangui had 1,695, Fort Lamy had 1,259, and Port Gentil had 663. See *Marchés Coloniaux*, July 29, 1955.

7. "Villes Congolaises," *Revue de Géographie Humaine et d'Ethnologie*, No. 3, 1948.

8. *Marchés Coloniaux*, July 29, 1950.

9. In 1949, Brazzaville had 78,000 African residents compared with 4,353 Europeans. The respective figures for Pointe Noire were 21,000 and 1,809; for Bangui, 39,000 and 1,695; and for Fort Lamy, 18,000 and 928. See *Afrique Equatoriale Française* (ed., E. Guernier), p. 96.

10. See Zieglé, *Afrique Equatoriale Française*, p. x.

11. See *Chroniques de la Communauté*, October 1959.

12. Grand Council debates, September 10, 1949.

13. In this stand they have been supported by such an outstanding European as Dr. Albert Schweitzer, who wrote (*A l'Orée de la Fôret Vierge*, p. 156) that "the only important alcoholic beverage that is made in AEF is palm wine, and it represents no serious danger. Palm wine cannot be kept for long periods, and it permits the villagers to get drunk, but only a few times a year. . . . The law forbids the tapping of palm trees, but this constitutes nothing like so great a danger as does the importation of alcohol."

14. Decree of May 20, 1955. Two years later a further restriction limited them to one per 4,000 inhabitants.

15. French Union Assembly debates, November 22, 1949; Grand Council debates, November 9, 1954.

16. In 1947–48, 310 penalties were imposed for infractions of the Sicé decree in Moyen-Congo compared with 220 in Gabon, 260 in Oubangui, and 140 in Tchad. See French Union Assembly debates, January 23, 1951.

17. Some measures have had the unexpected effect of encouraging marital instability and even polygamy. A case in point is the Lamine-Gueye law of June 1950, which made the children of African functionaries eligible for family allowances, for functionaries used these allowances mainly to buy more wives and beget more children and thus obtain additional funds. Then, too, the French law courts in AEF have generally upheld the right of a husband to reimbursement of the bride price of the wife he has repudiated and returned to her family. Gide (*Retour du Tchad*, p. 65) found during his journey in 1925 that the Muslim herders in the north were buying more wives than cows, because wives could not be seized and sold if they failed to pay their animal tax.

18. Briault, *Dans la Fôret du Gabon*, p. 141; Schweitzer, *A l'Orée de la Fôret Vierge*, p. 158.

19. Grand Council debates, May 3, 1948.

20. M. Soret, *Démographie et Problèmes Urbains en A.E.F.: Poto-Poto, Bacongo, Dolisie*, pp. 75, 83, 95; Balandier, *Sociologie Actuelle de l'Afrique Noire*, p. 410.

21. Grand Council debates, May 30, 1956; Gabon territorial assembly debates, March 23, 1948, April 25, 1952, December 11, 1957; Tchad territorial assembly debates, December 16, 1954, December 7, 1957; and Oubangui territorial assembly debates, August 27, 1947, September 1, 1948.

22. That this viewpoint was not confined to Oubangui was shown as recently as December 1958 at Fort Archambault, where a Tchadian girl whose clothing was considered too European and immodest was ill-treated by a mob. *Afrique Nouvelle,* May 15, 1959.

23. Soret (*Démographie et Problèmes Urbains en A.E.F.,* p. 95) found that nearly half the marriages in cosmopolitan Poto-Poto and Dolisie were childless, whereas in Bacongo, where tribal custom had remained stronger and encouraged large families, the percentage was only about a fourth as large.

24. National Assembly debates, December 17, 1954; French Union Assembly report, March 22, 1956.

25. *Marchés Coloniaux,* November 20, 1954.

26. This disease has been studied by Colonel Le Gac of the Oubangui medical service. See *Marchés Coloniaux,* February 24, 1951.

27. *Démographie et Problèmes Urbains en A.E.F.,* p. 125.

28. *Ibid.*

29. French Union Assembly debates, November 17, 1955.

30. See *Afrique Equatoriale Française* (ed., E. Guernier), p. 209.

31. Hailey, *An African Survey* (1939), p. 1177.

32. *Afrique Equatoriale Française* (ed., E. Guernier), p. 213.

33. *Marchés Coloniaux,* July 8, 1950.

34. Grand Council debates, December 18, 1947.

35. French Union Assembly debates, July 16, 1957.

36. *Chroniques d'Outre-Mer,* March 1955; French Union Assembly debates, July 16, 1957.

37. Inaugural speech by Dr. Sutter, deputy director of the World Health Organization (WHO) for Africa south of the Sahara, quoted in *Marchés Coloniaux,* September 8, 1956.

38. *Chroniques d'Outre-Mer,* June 1958.

39. *Afrique Equatoriale Française* (ed., E. Guernier), p. 209.

40. Tchad territorial assembly debates, October 31, 1952.

41. Paraf, *L'Ascension des Peuples Noirs,* p. 57.

42. *Chroniques d'Outre-Mer,* June 1958.

43. Speech of Governor-General Chauvet to the Grand Council, October 24, 1955.

44. Grand Council debates, November 17, 1954.

45. Tchad territorial assembly debates, June 26, 1958.

46. *Ibid.,* December 13, 1947.

47. French Union Assembly debates, July 16, 1957.

48. Speech of Acting Governor-General Soucadaux to the Grand Council, November 24, 1947.

49. Grand Council debates, June 10, 1955.

50. *Chroniques d'Outre-Mer,* June 1958.

Chapter 22

1. *Le Monde,* Paris, January 24, 1959.

2. See P. Alexandre and J. Binet, *Le Groupe dit Pahouin*; M. Briault, *Dans la Forêt du Gabon*; and Georges Balandier, *Sociologie Actuelle de l'Afrique Noire*; to

the last-named work the writers are indebted for much of the data included in this section.

3. Balandier, *Sociologie Actuelle de l'Afrique Noire*, p. 73.

4. *Ibid.*, p. 163.

5. According to Balandier, the line is not always clearly drawn between Fang clans and tribes. Some groups known as tribes in northern Gabon are considered clans in the coastal districts.

6. *Sociologie Actuelle de l'Afrique Noire*, p. 232.

7. *Le Monde*, January 24, 1959.

8. *Journal Officiel*, November 14, 1950.

9. *Afrique Ambiguë*, p. 159.

10. Even the African electorate was gratified to have Bayrou named Secretary of State for Overseas France in 1955, despite his very conservative political viewpoint.

11. National Assembly debates, January 25, 1952.

12. It should be noted, however, that Mba protested the re-election of Aubame to the National Assembly on January 2, 1956, on the ground that "improper pressure" had been exercised by some officials on behalf of Aubame.

13. *Afrique Nouvelle*, December 24, 1957.

14. *Marchés Tropicaux*, October 19, 1957.

15. *Ibid.*, July 26, 1958. In August 1959, a BDG spokesman said it was "unthinkable that Gabon might break away brutally from France," with which it had had close ties for 120 years.

16. *Afrique Nouvelle*, October 10, 1958.

17. See Grand Council debates, September 5, 1949.

18. See Gabon territorial assembly debates, April 14, 1956.

19. *Ibid.*, March 17, 1948.

20. *Ibid.*, October 31, 1952.

21. *Ibid.*

22. *Ibid.*, November 28, 1952.

23. *Ibid.*, March 7, 1948.

24. Grand Council debates, September 9, 1949; September 11, 1951.

25. Speech of Governor Digo to the territorial assembly, November 28, 1955.

26. Trézenem, *La France Equatoriale*, p. 121.

27. G. Balandier, *Afrique Ambiguë*, p. 169.

28. At the same time the plan to improve south Gabon's port of Mayumba was also given up, and its traffic diverted to Pointe Noire.

29. *Chroniques d'Outre-Mer*, December 1957.

30. Zieglé (*Afrique Equatoriale Française*, p. 123) quotes a recent governor of Gabon as saying: "Both the gods and man, especially administrators, were mistrustful of Port Gentil, but the Ogooué gave it its confidence and that was enough."

31. See National Assembly debates, March 24, 1953.

32. M. Briault, *Sur les Pistes de l'AEF*, p. 106.

33. See National Assembly debates, August 6, 1948.

34. Gabon territorial assembly debates, March 17, 1948.

35. *Ibid.*, March 23, September 15, 1948; December 2, 1952.

36. *Ibid.*, May 13, 1952.

37. Grand Council debates, June 1, 1955.

38. *Afrique Equatoriale Française* (ed., E. Guernier), p. 322.

39. *Encyclopédie Mensuelle d'Outre-Mer*, August 1953.

40. Balandier, *Sociologie Actuelle de l'Afrique Noire*, p. 174.

41. Gabon territorial assembly debates, November 28, 1955.

42. *Ibid.*, January 26, 1956.

43. *Marchés Tropicaux*, January 4, 1958; March 14, 1959.

44. *Marchés Coloniaux*, October 9, 1954.

45. Gabon territorial assembly debates, January 24, 1956.

46. Governor-General Chauvet's speech to the Grand Council, October 24, 1955.

47. Schweitzer, *A l'Orée de la Forêt Vierge*, p. 124.

48. As of 1949 the taxes on profits realized from the sale of 300,000 CFA francs' worth of okoumé amounted to 17 per cent; those on profits over a million came to 66.7 per cent.

49. Even for a mechanized enterprise, production costs are high. As of 1954 it was calculated that the average cost of producing one ton of peeled okoumé came to between 3,000 and 4,000 CFA francs and that the profit realized on its sale averaged only 800 CFA francs. Moreover, for such an enterprise to produce one ton of okoumé, 40 African laborers and 1 European were required, the latter's salary alone being at least 100,000 CFA francs a month. Each tractor used by the company cost between 5 and 6 million CFA francs. See *France-Outre-Mer*, August 1956.

50. *Chroniques d'Outre-Mer*, February 1957.

51. Gabon territorial assembly debates, March 23, 1948; January 25, 1956.

52. Pierre and Renée Gosset (*L'Afrique, les Africans: France-Afrique, le Mythe qui Prend Corps*, p. 159) write of a Gabonese named Walter Divine, whose fortune, made in the lumber business, attracted such a swarm of parasites around him that he not only lost all of his money but also served as an example to discourage other Africans from entering the wood industry.

53. In *Theirs the Darkness*, p. 162.

54. *Marchés Tropicaux*, December 28, 1957.

55. Gabon territorial assembly debates, November 4, 1950; November 25, 1953.

56. *Ibid.*, April 24, 1956.

57. *Encyclopédie Mensuelle d'Outre-Mer*, September 1951; *La Vie Française*, May 3, 1957.

58. *La Situation Economique de l'Afrique Equatoriale Française*.

59. *Chroniques d'Outre-Mer*, August–September 1957.

60. Gabon territorial assembly debates, March 26, 1954.

61. *Ibid.*, April 24, 1956.

62. *Le Monde*, December 13, 1958.

63. J. Cl. Pauvert, "La Notion de Travail en Afrique Noire," *Le Travail en Afrique Noire*.

64. In these eight schools 8 girls were then studying (all taking home-economics courses) and 343 boys (288 specializing in agriculture, 25 in woodwork, 6 in mechanics, and 14 in local crafts).

65. Balandier, *Sociologie Actuelle de l'Afrique Noire*, p. 53.

66. *A l'Orée de la Forêt Vierge*, p. 94.

67. Briault, *Sur les Pistes de l'AEF*, p. 96.

68. *L'Evolution de l'Enseignement Technique Public dans les Territoires Françaises d'Outre-Mer de 1946 à 1953*.

69. *Marchés Coloniaux*, October 6, 1951.

70. *Marchés Tropicaux*, April 20, 1957.

71. Sousatte, founder of the PUNGA party, is the only Gabonese politician who has also been a spokesman for organized labor.

Chapter 23

1. Marcel Homet, *Congo, Terre de Souffrances,* p. 35.
2. Headquarters of these regions are respectively M'Baiki and Berbérati.
3. Homet, *Congo, Terre de Souffrances,* pp. 29–35; "Congo Français: Les Troubles de la Sangha," *Revue Française de l'Etranger et des Colonies et Exploration,* vol. 27, Paris, 1876.
4. The gubernatorial succession in this period was as follows: Chalvet, 1947; Mauberma, 1948; Delteil, 1949; Even and Colombani, both in 1950; and Raynier, 1951.
5. French Union Assembly debates, February 16, 1950.
6. Oubangui-Chari territorial assembly debates, March 4, 15, 1949; March 11, 1950.
7. In July 1950, the governor was criticized for having paid from the territorial budget, without consulting the assembly, the traveling expenses of the family of an unpopular European official, of having hired a Frenchwoman in preference to an African, and of having bought for his official use an airplane at a price far above its market value.
8. Oubangui-Chari territorial assembly debates, March 11, 1950.
9. *Ibid.,* October 14, 1949.
10. *Ibid.,* October 6, 1949.
11. At one session, Darlan took the bold step of asking that the governor come in person to defend before the assembly his "politicization of the administrative services." See Oubangui-Chari territorial assembly debates, March 28, 1951.
12. *Ibid.,* October 14, 1949.
13. *Ibid.,* August 26, 1950.
14. His party captured 17 of the 26 seats reserved for the second college.
15. Barbé, French Communist party spokesman, told the French Union Assembly on July 5, 1951, that "In Boucanraga district the administrator threatened the village and canton chiefs with imprisonment if they failed to vote for him [Bella]; at Berbérati, the regional chief campaigned for the RPF; and at Bangui, Capt. Teulière, head of the governor's military establishment, distributed uniforms to African veterans, saying that they had ʾen sent by General de Gaulle, who asked them to vote for M. Bella."
16. Pierre Nord, *L'Eurafrique, Notre Dernière Chance,* p. 84.
17. The list supported by MESAN in the territorial assembly elections of 1957 included one Dahomean, seven Europeans, and two Antilles candidates.
18. *Afrique Nouvelle,* October 29, 1957.
19. In a farewell speech to Chauvet, Boganda said, in a burst of apparent emotion: "We are perhaps *français de la dernière heure,* but we are nevertheless Frenchmen." Quoted by André Blanchet in *L'Itinéraire des Partis Africains depuis Bamako,* p. 118.
20. *Le Monde,* September 10, 1958.
21. *Afrique Nouvelle,* November 7, 1958.
22. *Le Monde,* December 3, 1958.
23. *Marchés Tropicaux,* February 28, 1959.
24. Oubangui-Chari territorial assembly debates, September 23, 1948.
25. *Ibid.,* September 25, 1948; September 20, 1949.
26. *Ibid.,* April 2, 1951.
27. *Ibid.,* September 25, 1948.
28. *Ibid.,* August 24, 1950.
29. *Ibid.,* December 6, 1950; March 17, April 2, 1951.
30. *Marchés Tropicaux,* November 2, 1957.
31. *Ibid.,* January 18, 1958.

32. *Ibid.*, February 8, 1958.
33. Oubangui-Chari territorial assembly debates, August 28, 1947.
34. *Ibid.*, August 20, 1948.
35. *Ibid.*, September 17, 1948.
36. *Ibid.*, September 20, 1949.
37. *Ibid.*, August 24, 1950.
38. *Ibid.*, September 6, 1950.
39. *Ibid.*, March 28, 1951.
40. Grand Council debates, November 17, 1954.
41. *Afrique Nouvelle*, December 18, 1956.
42. *Marchés Tropicaux*, December 14, 1957.
43. *Ibid.*, December 21, 1957.
44. *Ibid.*, January 11, 1958.
45. Grand Council debates, September 21, 1950.
46. Oubangui-Chari territorial assembly debates, September 9, 1949.
47. *Ibid.*, March 15, September 23, 1951.
48. Grand Council debates, September 11, 1951.
49. *Encyclopédie Mensuelle d'Outre-Mer*, March 1957; *Marchés Tropicaux*, February 1, 1958.
50. *Marchés Tropicaux*, February 21, 1959.
51. French Union Assembly debates, March 22, 1956; *Marchés Tropicaux*, August 23, 1958.
52. *Marchés Coloniaux*, April 17, 1954.
53. About 150,000 tons of manioc are grown annually in Oubangui.
54. Oubangui-Chari territorial assembly debates, July 17, September 6 and 19, 1950, and September 20, 1951.
55. There were a host of lesser cooperatives organized at about the same time, such as the Espoir Oubanguien, Coopérative Oubanguienne d'Exportation et d'Importation, and Société Coopérative des Producteurs du Coton de l'Oubangui, whose membership claims ran from under 100 to many thousands.
56. Oubangui-Chari territorial assembly debates, March 14, 1947.
57. *Ibid.*, September 23, 1950.
58. Oubangui-Chari territorial assembly debates, September 19, 1950.
59. *Marchés Coloniaux*, October 24, 1953.
60. The main cotton-growing areas in 1957–58 were Ouakka, with 27,800 hectares producing 3,700 tons; Ouham-Pendé, 27,200 hectares and 7,900 tons; Ouham, 23,000 hectares and 7,200 tons; Basse-Kotto, 15,600 hectares and 3,700 tons; and Kémo-Gribingui, 14,600 hectares and 5,600 tons. Output by companies was topped by COTONAF with some 27,000 tons; COTOUBANGUI and COMOUNA together produced about 10,000 tons; but COTONFRAN's production in Oubangui came to only 1,500 tons. See *Marchés Tropicaux*, August 2, 1958.
61. *Marchés Tropicaux*, November 22, 1958.
62. French Union Assembly debates, August 23, 1951.
63. *Ibid.*, May 27, 1948.
64. Oubangui-Chari territorial assembly debates, September 28, 1949.
65. French Union Assembly debates, August 23, 1951.
66. Oubangui-Chari territorial assembly debates, July 13, 1950.
67. *Ibid.*, October 11, 1957.
68. *Marchés Coloniaux*, August 26, 1950.
69. *Encyclopédie Mensuelle d'Outre-Mer*, May 1953.

70. Speech to the Oubangui-Chari territorial assembly, September 20, 1951.
71. Oubangui-Chari territorial assembly debates, March 12, 1951.
72. A. Teulières, *L'Oubangui Face à l'Avenir*, p. 68.
73. Oubangui-Chari territorial assembly debates, June 5, 1956.
74. *Marchés Tropicaux,* December 27, 1958.
75. *Ibid.,* November 1, 1958.
76. The *nana* bushes were localized around Carnot and Berbérati, the *excelsa* in the savannah country of Kémo-Gribingui and Basse-Kotto, and the *robusta* in the forest zone of Lobaye and M'Bomou.
77. Oubangui-Chari territorial assembly debates, September 6 and 19, 1950.
78. *Marchés Tropicaux,* March 15, 1958.
79. *Marchés Coloniaux,* October 24, 1953.
80. *Marchés Tropicaux,* June 15, 1957.
81. *Afrique Equatoriale Française* (ed., E. Guernier), p. 335.
82. See R. Monmarson, *L'Afrique Franco-Africaine,* p. 183.
83. Oubangui-Chari territorial assembly debates, July 15 and September 19, 1950.
84. *Encyclopédie Mensuelle d'Outre-Mer,* July–August 1956.
85. Oubangui-Chari territorial assembly debates, August 20 and September 25, 1948.
86. *Marchés Tropicaux,* April 18, 1959.
87. Oubangui-Chari territorial assembly debates, December 6, 1950.
88. *Marchés Tropicaux,* September 27, 1958.
89. Oubangui-Chari territorial assembly debates, September 28, 1949.
90. J. C. Pauvert, "La Notion de Travail en Afrique Noire," *Le Travail en Afrique Noire.*
91. *L'Evolution de l'Enseignement Technique Public dans les Territoires Français d'Outre-Mer de 1946 à 1953.*
92. Oubangui-Chari territorial assembly debates, May 9, 1949; March 28, 1950.
93. *Ibid.,* September 29, 1949; July 15, 1950.
94. *Ibid.,* August 24 and September 12, 1950.
95. French Union Assembly debates, May 10, 1955.
96. In 1950, 40 laborers of the STOC walked out, without formulating demands, because they would not accept the management's change in working hours, and in 1958 there were strikes by workers of the SAFA and by the territory's African functionaries.
97. *Afrique Nouvelle,* April 10, 1956. Two other mergers occurred in Bangui at about the same time—that of the Union Territoriale des Cadres de l'Oubangui-Chari and the Syndicat des Travailleurs Metropolitains Expatriés.
98. One with COTONAF and the other with Sycompex and the Petites et Moyennes Entreprises.
99. *Afrique Nouvelle,* December 17, 1957.
100. *Ibid.,* December 19, 1958.
101. *Marchés Tropicaux,* January 24, 1959.

Chapter 24

1. Subdesert regions of sparse vegetation and rainfall.
2. Watercourses of rare and spasmodic flow.
3. Buell, *The Native Problem in Africa,* II, 217.
4. *Marchés Coloniaux,* January 13, 1951.
5. As of the date this book is being written, Tchad's political parties have included

the following (the parties are listed in the order in which they were founded):

Union Démocratique Tchadienne (UDT): A branch of the Metropolitan RPF founded at Fort Lamy in 1945. Its leaders at that time were Tardrew, Malbrant, Laurin, Béchir Sow, Sou Quatre, and Arabi el-Goni. It later became *Action Sociale Tchadienne*.

Parti Progressiste Tchadien (PPT): Founded at Moundou in October 1946 by Gabriel Lisette. In 1952 this party was called briefly the *Front pour l'Action Civique*.

Parti Socialiste Indépendant du Tchad: Founded in 1948 by Ahmed Koulamallah. In September 1955 a majority of its members formed a branch in Tchad of the SFIO, called the *Mouvement Socialiste Africaine* but without ties to the MSA of French West Africa.

Union Démocratique et Sociale de la Résistance (UDSR): Founded in 1950 and affiliated with the party of the same name in the National Assembly. The Tchad branch usually has been allied with the PPT.

Action Sociale Tchadienne (AST): The name taken by the UDT in 1952. In 1958 it formed an "intergroup" with the UDIT in the territorial assembly.

Union de la Défense des Intérêts Tchadiens: In 1953, Béchir Sow broke away from the UDT to form this splinter group. It is not to be confused with the *Union Démocratique Indépendante du Tchad* (UDIT) listed below.

Union Démocratique Indépendante du Tchad (UDIT): Created in 1953 by Jean Baptiste. Its chief adviser is former governor Rogué.

Mouvement Socialiste Africaine (MSA): Formed in September 1955 by a majority of the members of the *Parti Socialiste Indépendant du Tchad*.

Union Socialiste Tchadienne (UST): Founded in April 1958 by the MSA, UDIT, and AST.

Groupement des Indépendants et Ruraux du Tchad (GIRT): Formed in September 1958 by Senator Sahoulba Gontchomé. Most of its members are chiefs.

Mouvement Populaire Tchadien (MPT): Born of an alliance between GIRT and the UST in January 1959.

Parti National Tchadien: A Muslim party founded in February 1960 by Koulamallah. Soon thereafter joined by Jean Baptiste and Djibrine Kherallah.

6. The validity of this election was contested on the ground that Lisette had too recently been an administrator in the Logone and at Fort Lamy to run for elective office. Despite considerable opposition from conservatives in the National Assembly, his election was confirmed, mainly because of the support given him by Lamine-Gueye and the SFIO. See National Assembly debates, May 20, 1947.

7. See National Assembly debates, August 1, 1947, and June 9, 1948.

8. See *ibid.*, February 26, 1953; French Union Assembly debates, March 12, 1953.

9. See Tchad territorial assembly debates, April 21, 1955. To what extent, if at all, the Protestant missions were involved in this incident is not clear. At about this time, however, the Sudan Inland Mission made a ruling that no church member should belong to any political party. In this connection, see *West Africa*, June 23, 1956.

10. *Le Monde* of January 21, 1959, reported: "Installed in a poto-poto hut in the African quarter [of Fort Lamy], he receives innumerable calls all day long from both Africans and Europeans. . . . He has a marked taste for intrigue and likes to have a guiding hand in local politics."

11. See Tchad territorial assembly debates, March 30, 1955.

12. See *ibid.*, April 7, 1955.

13. *West Africa*, September 3, 1955.

14. *Le Monde*, December 22, 1955.

15. Sahoulba himself is a traditional chief of the Moudang tribe in the Mayo-Kebbi region. Of the ten AST members elected to the 1957 assembly, two were Euro-

peans; of the 32 PPT members, only one was a European; and of the UDSR's ten members, five were Europeans.

16. The naming of Moussa Yayami was particularly resented by the UDIT, for he seemingly was being rewarded for organizing a PPT branch in the northern oases, a region theretofore relatively free from political ferment. See Tchad territorial assembly debates, January 4 and June 17, 1958.

17. See *ibid.,* June 17, 1958.

18. *Marchés Tropicaux,* August 28, 1958.

19. *Ibid.,* April 4, 1959.

20. To form a government, the prospective premier must receive two-thirds of the assembly's votes, but if these were not forthcoming within 20 days, the assembly would be dissolved. Furthermore, if the assembly should overthrow two governments during a period of 24 consecutive months, it would be dissolved and its president named temporary premier.

21. J. P. Trystran, "Rapport sur le Régime Foncier des Ouaddis du Kanem."

22. See Tchad territorial assembly debates, June 17, 1958.

23. Twice in 1959 he accepted a secondary place in the PPT-dominated governments, leaving the post of premier to Tombalbaye.

24. French Union Assembly debates, January 26, 1949.

25. *Ibid.,* June 20, 1950.

26. Tchad had been allocated 13 billion CFA francs under the original ten-year Plan.

27. Ahmed Kotoko, at the session of November 9, 1950.

28. National Assembly debates, December 26, 1951.

29. Tchad territorial assembly debates, March 5, 1954.

30. National Assembly debates, December 26, 1951.

31. Tchad territorial assembly debates, November 28, 1952.

32. *Ibid.,* December 4, 1956.

33. *Ibid.,* December 7, 1957; May 2, 1958.

34. Tchad territorial assembly debates, November 21, 1952.

35. *Ibid.,* November 6, 1953.

36. *Ibid.,* March 9, 1954.

37. *Ibid.,* November 26, 1954. These stocks were inspected by the assembly's finance committee, one of whose European members described them to the assembly on December 16, 1954, as follows: "We were really upset by the heterogeneous materials found in the Fort Lamy warehouses, not to mention what must be lying about in the various Regions. What on earth could the officials who ordered this stuff have been thinking of? Our big firms have been understandably forced to invest in certain works the scandalous profits that they made by reselling these materials to an incompetent administration. We can estimate at 3 billion francs the waste in terms of money to the budgets of the territory and of the Plan—without any real benefits being derived therefrom by the local population."

38. Tchad territorial assembly debates, December 28, 1954.

39. In the 1955 budget, 226 million was allocated to the security forces compared with 179 million for agriculture and industry and 117 million for education.

40. *Marchés Tropicaux,* April 12, 1958; Tchad territorial assembly debates, June 24, 1958.

41. *Marchés Tropicaux,* January 10, 1959.

42. Susset, *La Vérité sur le Cameroun et l'Afrique Equatoriale Française,* p. 120.

43. Tchad territorial assembly debates, December 8, 1954.

44. Grand Council debates, October 22, 1952; Tchad territorial assembly debates, April 11, 1953. As of 1957, 2,829 of the 4,090 motor vehicles in Tchad were trucks.

45. Of these, 94 owned only one vehicle and 19 had five trucks or more, and the great majority were residents of the Fort Lamy region.
46. Tchad territorial assembly debates, December 20, 1956.
47. *Marchés Tropicaux,* January 24, 1959.
48. *Le Tchad 1958* (Chambre de Commerce de Fort-Lamy, Casablanca, 1958), p. 138.
49. Tchad territorial assembly debates, September 24, 1957.
50. *Afrique Equatoriale Française* (ed., E. Guernier), p. 304.
51. Tchad territorial assembly debates, June 6 and September 19, 1957.
52. Grand Council debates, October 31, 1956; *Marchés Tropicaux,* May 25, 1957.
53. See Trystran, "Rapport sur le Régime Foncier des Ouaddis du Kanem."
54. Tchad territorial assembly debates, September 21, 1957.
55. *Ibid.,* November 28, 1952.
56. See J. Cabot and R. Diziain, *Population du Moyen-Logone.*
57. *Encyclopédie Mensuelle d'Outre-Mer,* June 1956.
58. See M. Gaide, "Situation Rizicole dans le Casier A, Nord-Bongor."
59. *Marchés Tropicaux,* August 2, 1958.
60. French Union Assembly debates, August 23, 1951; Tchad territorial assembly debates, May 31, 1957.
61. Grand Council debates, November 19, 1954.
62. Tchad territorial assembly debates, December 7 and 14, 1957.
63. *Ibid.,* April 21, 1955.
64. See J. Lemasson, "Les Travaux sur la Pêche dans le Bassin du Logone–Chari–Lac Tchad."
65. Tchad territorial assembly debates, December 7 and 14, 1957; *Marchés Tropicaux,* January 24, 1959.
66. Tchad territorial assembly debates, December 7, 1957.
67. *Ibid.,* October 31, 1952; November 26, 1954.
68. *Ibid.,* December 4, 1953; March 15, 1954.
69. *Chroniques d'Outre-Mer,* December 1957.
70. French Union Assembly debates, January 26, 1949.
71. Tchad territorial assembly debates, May 2, 1958.
72. *Ibid.,* November 21, 1952.
73. *Ibid.,* June 10, 1958.
74. *Marchés Tropicaux,* October 4, 1958.
75. *Afrique Equatoriale Française* (ed., E. Guernier), p. 335.
76. Tchad territorial assembly debates, February 14 and April 21, 1956.
77. Its costs are estimated at 36,500,000 CFA francs a year.
78. Tchad territorial assembly debates, May 9, 1958.
79. *Marchés Tropicaux,* February 27, 1959.
80. That they are still optimistic about the future of Tchad's meat industry is indicated by the government's decision in October 1959 to take over management of Fort Archambault's new refrigerated abattoir, for whose initial operations they have authorized a loan of 7 million CFA francs from public funds.
81. In 1954 considerable indignation was generated in Tchad's assembly by the disclosure of the extent of a clandestine traffic in currency that had been going on between Nigerian and local merchants since the war. The finance department discovered frauds, amounting that year to over 2 billion CFA francs, perpetrated by Fort Lamy traders of Libyan, Iranian, and French nationality. Six persons were arrested and the case was carried before a Paris court but the government was able to retrieve only 30 million CFA francs.
82. In the session of June 10, 1958.

83. *Ibid.*, December 6, 1954.

84. Tchad territorial assembly debates, April 18, 1956.

85. Interview with Lisette, printed in *La Presse du Cameroun*, August 17–18, 1958.

86. *L'Evolution de l'Enseignement Technique Public dans les Territoires Français d'Outre-Mer.*

87. Tchad territorial assembly debates, June 6, 1957.

88. *Ibid.*, December 28, 1954.

89. *Afrique Nouvelle*, August 18, 1954; January 12, 1955.

90. Tchad territorial assembly debates, December 4, 1956; June 24, 1958.

91. *Ibid.*, October 3, 1957.

Chapter 25

1. For almost all of the data on the Bakongo contained in this chapter, the authors are indebted to the book of G. Balandier, *Sociologie Actuelle de l'Afrique Noire.*

2. Balandier has calculated that the average income of a Bakongo villager in the Kinkala district amounted in 1949 to less than 2,000 CFA francs.

3. In 1938 an attempt by the French government to create an organization intended to displace Matsouanism proved a dismal failure.

4. *Sociologie Actuelle de l'Afrique Noire*, p. 403.

5. See *Marchés Coloniaux*, November 20, 1948; French Union Assembly debates, February 10, 1950.

6. National Assembly debates, February 25, 1947.

7. *Ibid.*, October 4, 1946.

8. Moyen-Congo Territorial Assembly debates, April 23, 1954; May 14, 1955.

9. *Afrique Nouvelle*, March 29, 1955.

10. In the 1956 elections, about one-third of the votes still went to Matsoua, but in the 1957 elections for the territorial assembly, only 535 votes were cast for the dead leader.

11. *Le Monde*, January 6, 1956.

12. *L'Afrique, les Africains: France-Afrique, le Mythe qui Prend Corps.*

13. *Afrique Nouvelle*, March 19, 1957.

14. *Ibid.*, January 17, 1958.

15. *La Presse du Cameroun* (Douala), January 22, 1958.

16. *Le Monde*, January 23, 1959.

17. *Time* magazine, in its December 15 issue, described in its inimitable style the delirious welcome accorded Youlou by "5,000 cheering blacks in headgear ranging from French army képis to straw boaters and Davy Crockett caps who were at the airport to welcome him. Even his wizened old mother, after performing a little weaving dance in his honor, fell on her knees before him."

18. *Le Monde*, December 2, 1958.

19. Two Europeans, Kerherve and Vial, were named respectively Ministers of Industrial Production and of Finance, and Tchitchellé was given the key post of Minister of the Interior.

20. *New York Times*, March 11, 1959; *Marchés Tropicaux*, February 28, 1959.

21. P. Decraene; see *Le Monde*, June 21, 1959.

22. *Le Monde*, October 17, 1959.

23. Governor Rouys' report to the Moyen-Congo territorial assembly, 1956, p. 42.

24. Moyen-Congo territorial assembly debates, May 17, 1955.

25. *Ibid.*, April 26, 1956.

26. *Afrique Nouvelle*, August 13, 1957.
27. Grand Council debates, September 30, 1953.
28. Moyen-Congo territorial assembly debates, May 24, 1954.
29. *Ibid.*, November 24, 1954.
30. *Ibid.*, November 22, 1955.
31. *La Situation Economique de l'Afrique Equatoriale Française.*
32. *Marchés Tropicaux*, February 1, 1958; February 21, 1959.
33. Moyen-Congo territorial assembly debates, May 14, 1955.
34. *Ibid.*, November 22 and December 14, 1955.
35. *Marchés Coloniaux*, August 6, 1955.
36. *Ibid.*, August 16, 1952.
37. Paraf, *L'Ascension des Peuples Noirs*, p. 36.
38. Moyen-Congo territorial assembly debates, April 22, 1954.
39. *Marchés Tropicaux*, September 29, 1956.
40. Moyen-Congo territorial assembly debates, December 18, 1954.
41. *Marchés Tropicaux*, April 19, 1959.
42. *Encyclopédie Mensuelle d'Outre-Mer*, May 1953.
43. *Marchés Tropicaux*, November 22, 1958.
44. *Marchés Coloniaux*, June 4, 1955.
45. *Marchés Tropicaux*, July 12, 1958.
46. *Ibid.*, August 30, 1958.
47. *Marchés Coloniaux*, January 12, 1952.
48. *Marchés Tropicaux*, August 16 and November 29, 1958.
49. Grand Council debates, October 24, 1955.
50. *Marchés Tropicaux*, September 20, 1958.
51. *Ibid.*, November 8, 1958.
52. *Chroniques d'Outre-Mer*, December 1954–January 1955.
53. Sugar sold for 80 CFA francs per kilogram in the towns, and for 2 CFA francs per lump in the rural areas when it was obtainable there.
54. *Marchés Tropicaux*, September 27, 1958.
55. *Encyclopédie Mensuelle d'Outre-Mer*, June 1951.
56. *Marchés Tropicaux*, December 6, 1958.
57. Grand Council debates, October 31, 1956; *Marchés Tropicaux*, March 16, 1957.
58. In 1955 the Dolisie station distributed 1,500 chickens and about 100 pigs to applicants in the surrounding region.
59. *Marchés Coloniaux*, June 30, 1951.
60. *Chroniques d'Outre-Mer*, February 1957.
61. See Governor Rouys' report to the Moyen-Congo territorial assembly, Brazzaville, 1956, p. 27.
62. *Ibid.*, p. 29; Moyen-Congo territorial assembly debates, April 12, 1956.
63. It has been calculated that an investment of 300 million CFA francs will be required at Mouyondzi to assemble a herd of 10,000 cattle. In addition to iron fences, dipping tanks and firebreaks must be built. As to staff, one veterinary is needed for the whole herd, one European supervisor for every 3,000 animals, and one cowherd per hundred head in pasture—a larger number than in the American West because horses cannot be used in Moyen-Congo. Each N'dama imported from Guinea costs about 28,000 francs and needs four hectares of grazing land. See *Chroniques d'Outre-Mer*, December 1957.
64. See Moyen-Congo territorial assembly debates, May 17, 1955.
65. *Marchés Tropicaux*, September 20, 1958.

66. Moyen-Congo territorial assembly debates, April 23, 1954.

67. *Ibid.*, May 17, 1955.

68. *Ibid.*, November 26, 1955.

69. *Ibid.*, December 14, 1955; April 20, 1956.

70. *La Situation Economique de l'Afrique Equatoriale Française.*

71. *Marchés Tropicaux*, September 20, 1958.

72. Grand Council debates, June 26, 1952.

73. *Industries et Travaux d'Outre-Mer*, No. 58, September 1958.

74. A term derived from the name of the writer, Raymond Cartier; see his articles in *Paris-Match*, August 11 and 18, 1956.

75. The processing of one ton of bauxite would require 22,000 kilowatt-hours.

76. *La Vie Française*, January 24, 1958.

77. See the excellent studies by Balandier, Soret, and Pauvert. Though the field work of these French sociologists was done in the late 1940's and early 1950's, their conclusions for the most part are still valid for Moyen-Congo's urban centers.

78. The mining and forestry enterprises each employed some 6,000 men, and agricultural plantations 16,000. See *Le Travail en Afrique Noire.*

79. See *L'Evolution de l'Enseignement Technique Public dans les Territoires Français d'Outre-Mer.*

80. M. Soret, *Démographie et Problèmes Urbains en A.E.F.: Poto-Poto, Bacongo, Dolisie*, p. 83.

81. *Ibid.*, p. 88.

82. Zieglé, *Afrique Equatoriale Française*, p. 170.

83. Speech to the Grand Council, October 24, 1955.

84. *Afrique Nouvelle*, December 15, 1954.

85. See *Le Monde*, January 20, 1959.

Bibliography

"A la Gloire des Troupes Noires," *Tropiques*, May 1954.

ABENSOUR, L., and THÉVENIN, R., *La France Noire*, Paris, 1931.

ABOU DIGU'EN, *Notre Empire Africain Noir*, Paris, 1928.

AEF 53 (*Encyclopédie Mensuelle d'Outre-Mer*, August 1953), Paris, 1953.

AEF 56 (*France Outre-Mer*, August 1956), Paris, 1956.

"L'AEF, Banc d'Essai de l'Union Française," *Le Figaro*, Nos, 2798–2802, September 1953.

AERTS, F., "Les Tchadiens et le Service Militaire," *Tropiques*, May 1954.

AFRICANUS, *L'Afrique Noire devant l'Indépendance*, Paris, 1958.

L'Afrique et l'Asie, Paris. (Periodical.)

"Afrique Equatoriale d'Aujourd'hui," *France Outre-Mer*, July 1953.

Afrique Equatoriale Française (editor, Eugène Guernier), Paris, 1950.

Afrique Equatoriale Française: Le Chemin de Fer Congo-Ocean (album), Paris, 1934.

"L'Afrique Equatoriale Française 'Energétique,'" *Marchés Coloniaux*, Jan. 31, Apr. 3, May 15, 1948.

AFRIQUE EQUATORIALE FRANÇAISE, DIRECTION GÉNÉRALE DES SERVICES ECONOMIQUES, *L'Economie de l'AEF en 1955*, Brazzaville, 1956.

———— GOUVERNEMENT-GÉNÉRAL:

Annuaire de la Fédération des Territoires de l'Afrique Equatoriale Française, Paris.

L'Exploitation Forestière au Gabon, Paris, 1931.

Journal Officiel de l'Afrique Equatoriale Française, Brazzaville.

———— GRAND CONSEIL, *Débats*, 1947–58.

———— HAUT-COMMISSARIAT, *Etudes sur le Bien-Etre Rural*, Brazzaville, 1957.

———— INSPECTION GÉNÉRALE DU TRAVAIL ET DES LOIS SOCIALES, *Rapports Annuels*.

———— SERVICE DE STATISTIQUE, *Bibliographie Ethnographique de l'Afrique Equatoriale Française, 1914–1948*, Paris, 1949.

"L'Afrique Equatoriale Française," *La Vie Technique et Industrielle* (supplement to issue of September 1927), Paris, 1927.

L'Afrique Française: Bulletin du Comité de l'Afrique Française et du Comité du Maroc, Paris. (Monthly and bimonthly.)

Afrique Nouvelle, Dakar. (Weekly, 1946 to date.)

ALCANDRE, SYLVÈRE, *L'Emancipation des Peuples Colonisés*, 3 vols., Paris, 1949–54.

ALEXANDRE, P.:

   Le Groupe dit Pahouin (with J. BINET), Paris, 1958.

   "L'Islam en Afrique Noire," *Marchés Tropicaux*, Oct. 19, 1957.

Almanach, 1957 (also *1958, 1959*). (Pub. by *Afrique Nouvelle*, Dakar.)

AMBASSADE DE FRANCE, SERVICE DE PRESSE ET D'INFORMATION, New York, African Affairs Series.

"L'Aménagement et la Mise en Valeur du Casier Nord de Bongor," *Marchés Coloniaux*, Apr. 21, 1956.

ANCEL, JACQUES, "La Formation de la Colonie du Congo Français, 1843–1882," *Renseignements Coloniaux*, June 1902.

ANDRÉ, L.-M., "Le Problème de l'Alimentation des Populations de l'AEF," *Marchés Coloniaux*, Nov. 20, 1954.

Annales Africaines, Dakar. (Periodical.)

Annuaire Noria, Guide Economique A.O.F., Togo, Cameroun, A.E.F., Oran, Algeria. (Yearly.)

L'Annuaire du Tchad, 1950–51, Paris, 1951.

ANTONETTI, M., "L'Afrique Equatoriale Française," *La Vie Technique et Industrielle*, September 1927.

L'Art Nègre (Présence Africaine, No. 10–11), Paris, 1951.

AUGAGNEUR, V., *Erreurs et Brutalités Coloniales*, Paris, 1927.

AUGOUARD, PROSPER PHILIPPE:

   "Lettres de Mgr. Augouard, Evêque du Haut-Congo Français," *Dépêche Coloniale*, March 1902.

   28 Années au Congo, 2 vols., Poitiers, 1906.

   44 Années au Congo, Evreux, 1935.

AUJOULAT, DR. L., *Aujourd'hui, l'Afrique*, Paris, 1958.

BABIKAR, ARBAB DJAMA, *L'Empire de Rabeh*, Paris, 1950.

BALANDIER, GEORGES:

   Afrique Ambiguë, Paris, 1957.

   "Aspects de l'Evolution Sociale chez les Fang du Gabon," *Cahiers Internationaux de Sociologie*, 1950.

   "Les Conditions Sociologiques de l'Art Noir," *Présence Africaine*, No. 10–11, Paris, 1951.

   "Le Développement Industriel et la Prolétarisation en Afrique Noire," *L'Afrique et l'Asie*, No. 4, 1952.

   "La Littérature Noire de Langue Française," *Présence Africaine*, March 1950.

   "Messianisme des Ba-Kongo," *Encyclopédie Mensuelle d'Outre-Mer*, August 1951.

   "Problèmes Economiques et Problèmes Politiques au Niveau du Village Fang," Institut d'Etudes Centrafricaines, *Bulletin*, nouvelle série, No. 1, 1950.

   Rapport de Mission en Pays Fang, Brazzaville, 1949.

   Sociologie Actuelle de l'Afrique Noire, Paris, 1955.

   Sociologie des Brazzavilles Noires, Paris, 1956.

   "Le Travailleur Africain dans les 'Brazzavilles Noires,'" *Présence Africaine*, No. 13, Paris, 1952.

BALANDIER, GEORGES (*contd.*):
"Les Villages Gabonais," (with J. CL. PAUVERT), Institut d'Etudes Centrafricaines, *Mémoire No. 5*, 1952.

BARATIER, A. E. A., *Au Congo: Souvenirs de la Mission Marchand de Loango à Brazzaville*, Paris, 1914.

BERGERY, GASTON, *Air-Afrique, Voie Impériale*, Paris, 1937.

BESLIER, G. G., *L'Apôtre du Congo, Mgr. Augouard*, Paris, 1926.

BINET, J. (with P. ALEXANDRE), *Le Groupe dit Pahouin*, Paris, 1958.

BLACHE, JOSEPH, *Vrais Noirs et Vrais Blancs d'Afrique, au XXe Siècle*, Orléans, 1922.

BLANCHET, ANDRÉ, *L'Itinéraire des Partis Africains depuis Bamako*, Paris, 1958.

BOBICHON, H., *Le Vieux Congo Français et l'AEF*, Paris, 1938.

BORDARIER, P.:
"Développement de l'Enseignement," *Encyclopédie Coloniale et Maritime*, October 1950.
"Tableau de la Littérature," *Afrique Equatoriale Française*, Paris, 1950.
Le Bottin de l'Afrique Noire. (Pub. in Paris by *Afrique Nouvelle*, Dakar.)

BOURDARIE, PAUL, "Les Problèmes de la Politique Indigène et Economique au Congo Français," Société Normande de Géographie, *Bulletin*, Année 28, 1906.

BOUSSENOT, G., "Des Huileries pour y Traiter les Graines de Coton vont y être Créés," *Marchés Coloniaux*, Sept. 27, 1952.

BRIAULT, MAURICE:
Dans la Forêt du Gabon, Paris, 1930.
Sous le Zéro Equatorial, Paris, 1928.
Sur les Pistes de l'AEF, Paris, 1948.

BRITISH GOVERNMENT, FOREIGN OFFICE: HISTORICAL SECTION, *French Equatorial Africa*, London, 1920.

——— NAVAL STAFF: NAVAL INTELLIGENCE DIVISION, *French Equatorial Africa*, London, 1919.

——— *Notes Exchanged between the United Kingdom and France Agreeing to the Ratification of the Protocol Defining the Boundary between French Equatorial Africa and the Anglo-Egyptian Sudan*, London, 1924.

BROUSSEAU, GEORGES, *Souvenirs de la Mission Savorgnan de Brazza*, Paris, 1925.

BRUEL, GEORGES:
Bibliographie de l'Afrique Equatoriale Française, Paris, 1914.
La France Equatoriale Africaine, Paris, 1935.
L'Oubangui, Voie de Pénétration dans l'Afrique Centrale Française, Paris, 1899.
"La Population du Cameroun et de l'Afrique Equatoriale Française," *Renseignements Coloniaux*, September 1927.

BRUMACHE, PAUL, *Le Centre de l'Afrique: Autour du Tchad*, Paris, 1894.

BUELL, RAYMOND LESLIE, *The Native Problem in Africa*, 2 vols., New York, 1928.

BURMAN, B. L., *Miracle on the Congo*, New York, 1942.

CABOT, J., and R. DIZIAIN, *Population du Moyen-Logone*, Paris, 1955.

Cahiers d'Outre-Mer, Bordeaux. (Quarterly.)

CARCASSONNE, M., G. SERVAT, and P. JACQUOT, "Organisation Financière," *Afrique Equatoriale Française*, Paris, 1950.

CASTELLANI, C. J.:
    Les Femmes au Congo, Paris, 1898.
    Vers le Nil Français avec la Mission Marchand, Paris, 1898.

CECCALDI, Médecin-Colonel JEAN, "L'Institut Pasteur," *Afrique Equatoriale Française*, Paris, 1950.

CENTRE CULTUREL ET UNIVERSITAIRE D'OUTRE-MER, *Bulletin No. 8*, Paris, May 1956.

CHALLAYE, FÉLICIEN, *Le Congo Français*, Paris, 1909.

CHAMBRE DE COMMERCE DU TCHAD, *Le Tchad 1958*, Casablanca, 1958.

CHAMBRUN, J. A. DE P., *Brazza*, Paris, 1930.

CHAMPION, J., "Fruits en AEF," *Encyclopédie Coloniale et Maritime*, January 1951.

CHAPPELLE, JEAN, *Nomades Noirs du Sahara*, Paris, 1958.

CHARBONNIER, FRANÇOIS, *Gabon, Terre d'Avenir*, Paris, 1957.

CHAULEUR, PIERRE, *Le Régime du Travail dans les Territoires d'Outre-Mer*, 2 vols., Paris, 1956.

CHAVANNES, CHARLES DE:
    Avec Brazza; Souvenirs de la Mission de l'Ouest-Africain (Mars 1883–Janvier 1886), Paris, 1935.
    Le Congo Français, Paris, 1937.

CHERY, CHRISTIAN:
    La Grande Fauve, Paris, 1955.
    Les Couteaux sont de la Fête, Paris, 1954.

CHEVALIER, AUGUSTE:
    L'Afrique Centrale Française, Paris, 1907.
    Rapport sur une Mission Scientifique et Economique au Chari–Lac-Tchad, Paris, 1905.

Chroniques d'Outre-Mer, Paris. (Monthly. Before January 1951, entitled *Bulletin de la France d'Outre-Mer*; beginning Apr. 1, 1959, entitled *Chroniques de la Communauté*.)

Code du Travail des Territoires d'Outre Mer, Guide de l'Usager, Paris, 1953.

COLONNA D'ISTRIA, CHARLES, "Les Problèmes du Travail," *Afrique Equatoriale Française*, Paris, 1950.

COLRAT DE MONTROZIER, RAYMOND, *Deux Ans chez les Anthropophages et les Sultans du Centre Africain*, Paris, 1902.

COMBES, R., "La Recherche Scientifique en A.E.F.," *Résonnances*, 1954.

COMPIÈGNE, V. L. A., Marquis de, *L'Afrique Equatoriale*, Paris, 1876.

La Conférence Africaine Française, Brazzaville (30 Janvier, 1944–8 Février, 1944), Algiers, 1944.

"Congo Français: Les Troubles de la Sangha," *Revue Française de l'Etranger et des Colonies et Exploration*, vol. 27, Paris, 1902.

CORNET, C. J. A., *Au Tchad: Trois Ans chez les Senoussistes, les Ouaddaiens et les Kirdis*, Paris, 1910.

"Le Coton en Afrique Equatoriale Française," *Encyclopédie Mensuelle d'Outre-Mer*, May 1953.

COUDERT, A.-P., and E. TRÉZENEM, "L'Afrique Equatoriale Française dans la Guerre," *Afrique Equatoriale Française*, Paris, 1950.

COUPIGNY, Dr. J.:

"Au Moyen-Congo, l'Aménagement de la Vallée du Niari," *France Outre-Mer*, July 1954.

"Vallée du Niari, Terre d'Avenir," *Marchés Coloniaux*, Aug. 16, 1952.

COWAN, L. GRAY, "French Equatorial Africa," *Journal of International Affairs*, 1953.

CURAULT, Capt., "Monographie du Secteur de N'Djolé au Gabon," *Revue des Troupes Coloniales*, No. 68, 1908.

CUREAU, A. L., *Les Sociétés Primitives de l'Afrique Equatoriale*, Paris, 1912.

CUVILLIER-FLEURY, HENRI, *La Mise en Valeur du Congo Français*, Paris, 1904.

DAIGRE, PÈRE, *Oubangui-Chari: Témoignage sur son Evolution, 1900–1940*, Issoudun, 1947.

DARNAULT, P., *Régime de Quelques Cours d'Eau d'Afrique Equatoriale et Etude de leur Utilisation Industrielle*, Paris, 1947.

DAVESNE, ANDRÉ, *Croquis de Brousse*, Paris, 1946.

DECORSE, J., *Du Congo au Lac Tchad*, Paris, 1906.

DELAVIGNETTE, ROBERT:

Afrique Equatoriale Française, Paris, 1957.

"Jeunesses d'Afrique Noire," *Pensée Française*, Jan. 15, 1957.

DESCHAMPS, HUBERT, *Les Religions de l'Afrique Noire* (Collection Que Sais-je?), Paris, 1954.

Des Prêtres Noirs s'Interrogent (*Recontres*, No. 47), Paris, 1956.

DIDIER, HENRY, "Aperçu sur le Syndicalisme en Afrique Française," *Encyclopédie Mensuelle d'Outre-Mer*, December 1955.

DIOLÉ, P., *Le Fezzan Inconnu*, Paris, 1957.

"Doctrines et Bilans de la Modernisation Rurale en A.E.F." (mimeographed), Brazzaville, 1956.

DOLISIE, ALBERT, "Albert Dolisie, sa Correspondance," *Afrique Française*, Année 42, Paris, 1932.

DORGELÈS, ROLAND, *Sous le Casque Blanc*, Paris, 1941.

DRESCH, JEAN:

"Les Investissements en Afrique Noire," *Présence Africaine*, April 1952.

"Villes Congolaises," *Revue de Géographie Humaine et d'Ethnographie*, No. 3, 1948.

DROGUÉ, AIMÉ:

"Le Développement Agricole de l'A.E.F. dans le Cadre du Plan Décennal," *Afrique Equatoriale Française*, Paris, 1950.

"L'Evolution des Exportations et de l'Industrialisation Agricoles en AEF," *Marchés Coloniaux*, Sept. 1, 1951.

"Les Industries Agricoles en AEF," *Marchés Coloniaux*, Sept. 15, 1951.

"Les Nouvelles Cultures en AEF," *Marchés Coloniaux*, Sept. 8, 1951.

DU CHAILLU, PAUL, *Explorations and Adventures in Equatorial Africa*, New York, 1861.

DUJARRIC, G., *La Vie du Sultan Rabah*, Paris, 1902.

DUPUIS, M., "L'Office des Bois de l'A.E.F.," *Marchés Coloniaux*, Oct. 18, 1947.

DURAND, HUGUETTE, *Essai sur la Conjoncture de l'Afrique Noire*, Paris, 1957.

DURAND-REVILLE, LUC:

"Le Bilan Economique de l'A.E.F. pour 1952," *Marchés Coloniaux*, May 16, 1953.

"Les Forestiers du Gabon Désirent une Valorisation de leurs Ressources," *Marchés Coloniaux*, Feb. 5, 1955.

"Le Problème Cotonnier en AEF," *Marchés Coloniaux*, Mar. 24, 1951.

"Les Problèmes de l'Industrialisation des Territoires d'Outre-Mer," *Le Monde Non Chrétien*, January–March 1950.

DYBOWSKI, JEAN:

Le Congo Méconnu, Paris, 1912.

La Route du Tchad; du Loango au Chari, Paris, 1893.

EBOUÉ, ADOLPHE FÉLIX SYLVESTRE:

L'A.E.F. et la Guerre, Brazzaville, 1943.

Circulaire Générale sur la Politique Indigène en Afrique Equatoriale Française, Brazzaville, 1941.

Les Peuples de l'Oubangui-Chari, Paris, 1933.

Encyclopédie Mensuelle d'Outre-Mer, Paris. (Monthly. Formerly entitled *Encyclopédie Coloniale et Maritime*. Suspended publication April 1957.)

EHRHARD, JEAN, *Le Destin du Colonialisme*, Paris, 1957.

D'ESMENARD, JEAN:

Afrique Equatoriale, Paris, 1931.

Les Défricheurs d'Empire, Paris, 1937.

ETIENNE, EUGÈNE:

Les Compagnies de Colonisation, Paris, 1897.

"Le Congo Français," *Grande Revue*, vol. 50, Paris, 1908.

Les Etudiants Noirs Parlent, Paris, 1953.

L'Evolution de l'Enseignement Technique Public dans les Territoires Français d'Outre-Mer de 1946 à 1953 (La Documentation Française), Paris, Oct. 15, 1954.

"Expansion de l'AEF," *L'Exportateur Français*, June 1955.

EYDOUX, H. P., *Savorgnan de Brazza, le Conquérant Pacifique*, Paris, 1932.

FABUNMI, L. A., "Egypt and Africa," *West Africa*, Dec. 21, 1957; Jan. 4, 1958.

FARSON, NEGLEY, *Behind God's Back*, New York, 1941.

FAVROD, CHARLES-HENRI, *Le Poids de l'Afrique*, Paris, 1958.

FERRANDI, JEAN, *Le Centre-Africain Français*, Paris, 1930.

FIEVET, JEANNETTE, *L'Enfant Blanc de l'Afrique Noire*, Paris, 1957.

FOLLIET, JOSEPH, *Le Travail Forcé aux Colonies*, Paris (1934).

FONTAINE, PIERRE, *La Mort Mystérieuse du Gouverneur-Général Renard*, Paris, 1943.

FOURNEAU, ALFRED, *Au Vieux Congo*, Paris, 1932.

France-Equateur, Brazzaville. (Daily.)

France in Africa (special number of *Current History*), New York, February 1958.

FRANZINI, ANGE, "La Forêt," *Afrique Equatoriale Française*, Paris, 1950.

French Colonial Policy in Africa (special number of *Free France*), New York, September 1944.

FRENCH GOVERNMENT, *Journal Officiel* (*Débats de l'Assemblée Constituante, Débats de l'Assemblée Nationale, Débats de l'Assemblée de l'Union Française*, and *Débats du Conseil de la République*).

———— CONSEIL ECONOMIQUE:
Bulletin.
Avis et Rapports.
Etudes et Travaux.

———— MINISTÈRE DES COLONIES, *La France d'Outre-Mer dans la Guerre*, Paris, 1945.

———— MINISTÈRE DE LA FRANCE D'OUTRE-MER:
Annuaire Statistique de l'Union Française.
L'Equipement des Territoires Français d'Outre-Mer, 1951.
Le Gabon et le Moyen-Congo, 1953.

———— MINISTÈRE DE L'INTÉRIEUR, *Les Elections Législatives du 17 Juin 1951* (La Documentation Française), 1953.

———— PRÉSIDENCE DU CONSEIL (LA DOCUMENTATION FRANÇAISE):
L'A.E.F. (*Carnets d'Outre-Mer*).
Notes et Etudes Documentaires.

FREY, ROGER, *Brazzaville* (special number of *Encyclopédie Mensuelle d'Outre-Mer*, August–September 1954), Paris, 1954.

FROIDEVAUX, HENRI, "La Politique Indigène au Congo Français," *Questions Diplomatiques et Coloniales*, vol. 21, Paris, 1906.

GABON, TERRITOIRE DU, *Débats de l'Assemblée Territoriale*, 1947–58.

GAIDE, M., "Situation Rizicole dans le Casier A, Nord-Bongor" (mimeographed), Fort Lamy, October 1958.

GAMACHE, PIERRE, *Géographie et Histoire de l'Afrique Equatoriale Française*, Paris, 1949.

GAUD, FERNAND, *Les Mandja*, Brussels, 1911.

GAUTIER, JULIEN:
"L'Avion Cargo Permet la Mise en Valeur Complète du Territoire du Tchad," *Marchés Coloniaux*, Feb. 7, 1953.
"Le Développement de la Production dans les Bassins du Tchad et de la Haute-Bénoué," *Marchés Coloniaux*, July 16, 23, 1949.
"Il Faut Repenser Notre Politique Agricole en A.E.F.," *Marchés Coloniaux*, June 30, July 7, 1951.
"L'Industrialisation Agricole de l'A.E.F.," *Marchés Coloniaux*, Dec. 20, 1947.
"Notable Contribution Possible des Zones Cotonnières de l'A.E.F. à la Production des Huiles Végétales," *Marchés Coloniaux*, Sept. 25, 1948.

GAUZE, R., *Guide Touristique de l'Oubangui-Chari*, Caen, 1958.

GENTIL, EMILE, *La Chute de l'Empire de Rabah*, Paris, 1902.

GENTIL, PIERRE, *Confins Libyens, Lac Tchad, Fleuve Niger*, Paris, 1946.

GENTY, PAUL, "Chambres de Commerce, d'Agriculture, et d'Industrie," *Afrique Equatoriale Française*, Paris, 1950.

GIDE, ANDRÉ:
  Retour du Tchad, Paris, 1928.
  Voyage au Congo, Paris, 1927.
GOCHET, JEAN-BAPTISTE, *Le Congo Français Illustré*, Liége, 1890.
GONDJOUT, PAUL, "Autour du Manganèse du Gabon, *Marchés Coloniaux*, Oct. 17, 1953.
GOSSET, PIERRE and RENÉE, *L'Afrique, les Africains: France-Afrique, le Mythe qui Prend Corps*, Paris, 1958.
GOULVEN, J. G. A., *Etude sur l'Evolution Administrative, Judiciaire, et Financière de l'Afrique Equatoriale Française*, Paris, 1911.
GOURAUD, H. J. E., *Zinder Tchad; Souvenirs d'un Africain*, Paris, 1945.
GOUSSET, MARCEL, *En Brousse, A. E. F.*, Paris, 1943.
GRANDIDIER, GUILLAUME (editor), *Atlas des Colonies Françaises, Protectorats et Territoires sous Mandat de la France*, Paris, 1934.
GRÉBERT, F., *Au Gabon*, Paris, 1948.
GROSSARD, Lt. Col., *Mission de Délimitation de l'Afrique Equatoriale Française et du Soudan Anglo-Egyptien*, Paris, 1925.
GUIRAL, LÉON, *Le Congo Français, du Gabon à Brazzaville*, Paris, 1889.
GUIRRIEC, ARTHUR, *Brazza, ses Premières Explorations*, Cairo, 1944.
GUNTHER, JOHN, *Inside Africa*, New York, 1953.
HAILEY, Lord W. M.:
  An African Survey, London, 1938.
  An African Survey—Revised 1956, London, 1957.
HARDY, GEORGES, "Origines et Formation de l'Afrique Equatoriale Française," *Afrique Equatoriale Française*, Paris, 1950.
HODGKIN, THOMAS:
  "Arab Africa and West Africa," *West Africa*, Aug. 24–Oct. 26, 1957.
  Nationalism in Colonial Africa, London, 1956.
HOMET, MARCEL:
  Afrique Noire, Terre Inquiète, Paris, 1938.
  Congo, Terre de Souffrances, Paris, 1934.
HORNER, NORMAN A., "The Development of an Indigenous Presbyterian Church in the French Cameroun during the Decade 1938–48" (M.A. thesis, typescript, Hartford Theological Seminary, 1950).
HOWE, RUSSELL WARREN, *Theirs the Darkness*, London, 1956.
HUGOT, P., "Tchad et Soudan," *L'Afrique et l'Asie*, No. 37, 1957.
HUMBERT, CH., "L'Oeuvre de M. Merlin dans l'Afrique Equatoriale Française," *Grande Revue*, vol. 66, Paris, 1911.
INSTITUT D'ETUDES CENTRAFRICAINES, *Bulletins, Mémoires*, and *Rapports*.
JONCHAY, I. DU, *L'Industrialisation de l'Afrique*, Paris, 1953.
JOSET, P. E., *Les Sociétés Secrètes des Hommes-Léopards en Afrique Noire*, Paris, 1955.
KINGSLEY, MARY H., *Travels in West Africa; Congo Français, Corsico, and Cameroons*, London, 1904.
KITCHEN, HELEN, *The Press in Africa*, Washington, D.C., 1956.

Le Kouilou (special number of *Industries et Travaux d'Outre-Mer*, No. 58), Paris, September 1958.

LABORDE, H., and X. PAOLI, "Organisation Judiciaire," *Afrique Equatoriale Française*, Paris, 1950.

LABOURET, HENRI:
"L'A.E.F., 1937," *Afrique Française*, March 1937.
Histoire des Noirs d'Afrique (Collection Que Sais-je?), Paris, 1946.

LAGUERRE, ANDRÉ, *Free French Africa*, London, 1942.

LAPIE, P. O.:
Les Déserts de l'Action, Paris, 1946.
Mes Tournées au Tchad, London, 1943.
Le Tchad Fait la Guerre, London, 1945.

LARRIEU, PIERRE:
"Le Commerce," *Afrique Equatoriale Française*, Paris, 1950.
"Les Grandes Régions Economiques," *Afrique Equatoriale Française*, Paris, 1950.

LARTÉGUY, JEAN, *Les Clefs de l'Afrique*, Paris, 1957.

LATTRE, JEAN-MICHEL DE, "Mékambo et la Sidérurgie Atlantique," *Marchés Tropicaux*, May 3, 1958.

LAURAINT, ANDRÉ:
"Le Plan Décennal de Développement Economique et Social," *Afrique Equatoriale Française*, Paris, 1950.
Les Problèmes de Transport de l'Afrique Equatoriale Française, Brazzaville, 1945.

LAURE, RENÉ, *Le Continent Africain au Milieu du Siècle*, Paris, 1952.

LAVIGNOTTE, HENRI, *Ces Hommes Ont Peur*, Valence, 1957.

LEBEUF, JEAN-PAUL:
Bangui, Paris, 1952.
La Civilisation du Tchad (with A. MASSON-DETOURBET), Paris, 1950.
Du Cameroun au Tchad (with A. MASSON-DETOURBET), Paris, 1954.
Fort-Lamy, Paris (no date).

LE COMTE, CH., and J.-S. BOUCHAUD, "Les Missions Catholiques," *Afrique Equatoriale Française*, Paris, 1950.

LEDUC, GASTON:
L'Economie de l'Union Française, Paris, 1952.
"La Situation Actuelle et l'Avenir du Marché de l'Okoumé," *Chroniques d'Outre-Mer*, February 1957.

LEENHARDT, R. H., and P. OSCHWALD, "Les Missions Protestantes," *Afrique Equatoriale Française*, Paris, 1950.

LEFEBURE, JULES, *Le Régime des Concessions au Congo*, Paris, 1904.

LE GRIP, A.:
"L'Avenir de l'Islam en Afrique Noire," *L'Afrique et l'Asie*, No. 10, 1950.
"Le Mahdisme en Afrique Noire," *L'Afrique et l'Asie*, No. 18, 1952.

LEIRIS, MICHEL, *L'Afrique Fantôme*, Paris, 1934.

LEMASSON, J., "Les Travaux sur la Pêche dans le Bassin du Logone–Chari–Lac Tchad" (mimeographed), Fort Lamy, December 1957.

LENFANT, EUGÈNE ARMAND, *La Grande Route du Tchad*, Paris, 1905.

LEROI-GOURHAN, ANDRÉ, and JEAN POIRIER, *Ethnologie de l'Union Française*, vol. 1, Paris, 1953.

LE VACHER, CHRISTIAN, *Le Congo, Fleuve International et les Régions Riveraines*, Rennes, 1902.

LONDRES, ALBERT, *Terre d'Ebène*, Paris, 1929.

LOUSTALET, LÉON, "Propriété Foncière," *Afrique Equatoriale Française*, Paris, 1950.

MAIGNAN, Capt., "Etudes sur le Pays Pahouin," *Bulletin de la Société des Recherches Congolaises*, No. 14, 1931.

MAIGRET, JULIEN, *Afrique Equatoriale Française*, Paris, 1931.

MAISEL, ALBERT Q., *Africa, Facts and Forecasts*, New York, 1943.

MANOT, MICHEL R. O., *L'Aventure de l'Or et du Congo-Océan*, Paris, 1946.

MARAN, RENÉ:

    Afrique Equatoriale Française, Terres et Races d'Avenir, Paris, 1937.

    Batouala, Paris, 1921.

    Brazza et la Fondation de l'A.E.F., Paris, 1941.

    Légendes et Coutumes Nègres de l'Oubangui-Chari, Paris, 1933.

    Savorgnan de Brazza, Paris, 1951.

    Le Tchad de Sable et d'Or, Paris, 1931.

"Les Marchés d'Afrique Noire," *Vente et Publicité*, July–August 1954.

Marchés Coloniaux, Paris. (Weekly. After September 1956, entitled *Marchés Tropicaux*.)

MARELLE, A., "L'Industrie Minière," *Afrique Equatoriale Française*, Paris, 1950.

MARIE-GERMAINE, Sister, *Le Christ au Gabon*, Louvain, 1931.

MATIP, BENJAMIN, *Afrique, Nous t'Ignorons*, Paris, 1956.

MAUBLANC, H. DE, "Electrification," *Afrique Equatoriale Française*, Paris, 1950.

MAURETTE, FERNAND, "La France en Afrique Equatoriale," *Revue de Paris*, Année 27, Paris, 1920.

MAURICE, ALBERT, *Félix Eboué, sa Vie et son Oeuvre*, Brussels, 1954.

MEGGLÉ, ARMAND, *Afrique Equatoriale Française* (Collection des Terres Françaises), Paris, 1931.

MÉJAN, FRANÇOIS, *Le Vatican contre la France d'Outre-Mer?*, Paris, 1957.

MERCIER, ANDRÉ, "L'Industrie," *Afrique Equatoriale Française*, Paris, 1950.

MICHELIN, PIERRE, *Un Défricheur d'Empire et un Apôtre, Monseigneur Augouard*, Paris, 1943.

MILLE, PIERRE:

    Au Congo Belge: avec des Notes et des Documents Récents Relatifs au Congo Français, Paris, 1899.

    Les Deux Congo devant la Belgique et devant la France, Paris, 1906.

"La Mise en Valeur de l'AEF," *L'Exportateur Français*, December 1953.

LA MISE EN VALEUR DE L'AEF (special number of *Réalités Africaines*), Casablanca, 1956.

MISSION HUGUES LE ROUX:

    Gabon, Paris, 1919.

    Moyen-Congo, Paris, 1918.

Mission Hugues le Roux (contd.):
  Niger et Tchad, Paris, 1918.
  Oubangui-Chari, Paris, 1919.
Monmarson, Raoul:
  L'Afrique Franco-Africaine, Paris, 1956.
  L'Afrique Noire et son Destin, Paris, 1950.
Moran, Denise, Tchad, Paris, 1934.
Morel, Edmund D., The British Case in French Congo, London, 1903.
Mougin, L., "La Monnaie et le Crédit," Afrique Equatoriale Française, Paris, 1950.
Moussa, Pierre, Les Chances Economiques de la Communauté Franco-Africaine, Paris, 1957.
Moyen-Congo, Territoire du, Débats de l'Assemblée Territoriale, 1947–58.
Mullender, J., "Le Marché des Tissus et de l'Habillement en A.E.F.,"Marchés Coloniaux, Mar. 1, 1952.
Murdock, George Peter, Africa: Its Peoples and Their Culture History, New York, 1959.
Nassau, Robert Hamill, My Ogowe, New York, 1914.
Neuville, D., and Ch. Bréard, Les Voyages de Savorgnan de Brazza, Paris, 1884.
Nicault, J.:
  "Panorama de la Prospection Minière en AEF et Perspectives d'Exploitation," Chroniques d'Outre-Mer, November 1953.
  "Les Ressources Minérales de l'Afrique Equatoriale Française," Cahiers Encyclopédiques d'Outre-Mer, No. 1, Paris, no date.
Nord, Pierre, L'Eurafrique, Notre Dernière Chance, Paris, 1955.
Normand, J.-Y., and Ch.-J. Barbarin, "Urbanisme," Afrique Equatoriale Française, Paris, 1950.
L'Organisation Judiciaire en AOF, en AEF, au Cameroun et au Togo (La Documentation Française, Notes et Etudes Documentaires, No. 1947), Paris, Nov. 12, 1954.
L'Oubangui-Chari, Territoire de, Débats de l'Assemblée Territoriale, 1947–58.
Padmore, George, "Subjects and Citizens in French Africa," Crisis, No. 3, March 1940.
Paraf, Pierre:
  L'Ascension des Peuples Noirs, Paris, 1958.
  Rendez-vous Africains, Paris, 1952.
Pargoire, J., "La Vallée du Niari," Encyclopédie Mensuelle d'Outre-Mer, January 1955.
Paulin, Honoré, Afrique Equatoriale Française, Paris, 1924.
Pauvert, J. Cl.:
  "Notes sur la Coopérative Pilote du Woleu-N'tem," Institut d'Etudes Centrafricaines, Rapport, 1951.
  "La Notion de Travail en Afrique Noire," Le Travail en Afrique Noire (Présence Africaine, No. 13), Paris, 1952.
  "Les Villages Gabonais" (with G. Balandier), Institut d'Etudes Centrafricaines, Mémoires, No. 5, 1952.

Percher, J. H. (alias Harry Alis), *A la Conquête du Tchad*, Paris, 1891.

Picard, E., *L'Enseignement Technique en Afrique Equatoriale Française*, Lyon, 1927.

"Les Pionniers de la Forêt Vierge," *Paris-Match*, Aug. 25, 1951.

Poirier, Léon, *Brazza; ou, l'Epopée du Congo*, Tours, 1940.

Poquin, Jean-Jacques, *Les Relations Economiques Extérieures des Pays d'Afrique Noire de l'Union Française 1925–1955*, Paris, 1957.

Pouquet, Jean, *L'Afrique Equatoriale Française et le Cameroun* (Collection Que Sais-je?), Paris, 1954.

Preclin, L., C. Brisson, and M. Reymond, "Les Voies de Communication," *Afrique Equatoriale Française*, Paris, 1950.

Le Premier Congrès International des Ecrivains et Artistes Noirs (*Présence Africaine*, numéro spécial), Paris, 1956.

"La Presse en Afrique Noire," *Vente et Publicité*, Paris, July–August 1954.

"La Propagande Soviétique en Afrique," *Afrique Française*, March–April 1956.

Puech, Georges, "Régime Douanier," *Afrique Equatoriale Française*, Paris, 1950.

Raynal, Médecin-Général, "Pathologie Humaine et Armature Médico-Sociale de la Santé Publique," *Afrique Equatoriale Française*, Paris, 1950.

Receveur, Pierre, "L'Elevage," *Afrique Equatoriale Française*, Paris, 1950.

Redier, Georges, "L'Afrique Equatoriale Française," Société de Géographie de Lille, *Bulletin*, 1912.

Renard, Capt. E.:
La Colonisation au Congo Français, Paris, 1900.
"Lettres du Congo," *Revue des Deux Mondes*, tome 28, Paris, 1935.

Renouard, G., *L'Ouest Africain et les Missions Catholiques. Congo et Oubanghi*, Paris, 1904.

Reste, J. F.:
A l'Ombre de la Grande Fôret, Paris, 1943.
"Brazzaville, la Grande Cité Equatoriale," *Encyclopédie Mensuelle d'Outre-Mer, Bulletin Périodique*, No. 5, April 1955.

Riedinger, Marcel, "Organisation Administrative—Politique Indigène," *Afrique Equatoriale Française*, Paris, 1950.

Roberts, S. H., *History of French Colonial Policy*, 2 vols., London, 1929.

Roche, Jean de la, *Le Gouverneur-Général Félix Eboué, 1884–1944*, Paris, 1957.

Romieu, Jean, *Les Mouvements Coopératifs en Afrique Noire*, Montpellier, 1953.

Rondet-Saint, Maurice, *L'Afrique Equatoriale Française*, Paris, 1911.

Rosenfeld, Oreste, "Le Problème de la Main-d'Oeuvre en A.E.F.," *Marchés Coloniaux*, Feb. 24, 1951.

Rouget, Fernand, *L'Expansion Coloniale au Congo Français*, Paris, 1906.

Roure, Gil, "Le Tibesti, Bastion de Notre Afrique Noire," *L'Illustration*, Apr. 1, 1939.

Roussignol, Ch., "Le Bois," *France Outre-Mer*, August 1956.

Roux, Charles, "La Pêche," *Afrique Equatoriale Française*, Paris, 1950.

Rouys, Governor, "Rapport Présenté à la Session Avril–Mai 1956 de l'Assemblée Territoriale du Moyen-Congo" (mimeographed), Brazzaville, 1956.

SALVIATI, CESARE, *Italia e Francia nel Sahara Orientale*, Milan, 1929.

SANMARCO, LOUIS, "Harmonisation et Stabilisation entre l'AEF et la Métropole," *L'Exportateur Français*, December 1953.

SAUTTER, GILLES:
"Le Cacao dans l'Economie Rurale du Woleu N'Tem," Institut des Etudes Centrafricaines, *Bulletin*, nouv. série, No. 1, 1950.
"De l'Economie de Subsistance à l'Economie du Marché," *France Outre-Mer*, August 1956.
"Les Paysans Noirs du Gabon Septentrional," *Cahiers d'Outre-Mer*, April–June 1951.
"La Population," *Afrique Equatoriale Française*, Paris, 1950.

SAUVAGE, MARCEL, *Sous le Feu de l'Equateur: Les Secrets de l'Afrique Noire*, Paris, 1947.

SAVORGNAN DE BRAZZA, PIERRE, *Conférences et Lettres*, Paris, 1887.

SCHWEITZER, ALBERT, *A l'Orée de la Fôret Vierge*, Paris, 1952.

La Semaine de l'AEF, Brazzaville. (Weekly.)

SERVEL, ANDRÉ, *Etude sur l'Organisation Administrative et Financière de l'Afrique Equatoriale Française*, Paris, 1912.

SICÉ, Médecin-Général A., *L'AEF et le Cameroun au Service de la France*, Paris, 1946.

SIRIEX, P.-H., and J.-M. HERTRICH, *L'Empire au Combat*, Paris, 1945.

La Situation Economique de l'Afrique Equatoriale Française, Paris, Aug. 30, 1955.

SOCIÉTÉ DES RECHERCHES CONGOLAISES, *Bulletin*, 1922—.

SOLER, G., "La Riziculture au Tchad," *Marchés Coloniaux*, Dec. 27, 1952.

SORET, MARCEL, *Démographie et Problèmes Urbains en A.E.F.: Poto-Poto, Bacongo, Dolisie*, Montpellier, 1954.

SOUSATTE, RENÉ-PAUL, *L'Ame Africaine*, Brazzaville, 1945.

STEVELINCK, W., "Le Développement du Coton dans la Zone: Mayo-Kebbi, Logone, Moyen-Chari," *Marchés Coloniaux*, July 4, 11, 1953.

SURET-CANALE, JEAN, *Afrique Noire: Occidentale et Centrale*, Paris, 1958.

SUSSET, RAYMOND, *La Vérité sur le Cameroun et l'Afrique Equatoriale Française*, Paris, 1934.

TCHAD, TERRITOIRE DU, *Débats de l'Assemblée Territoriale*, 1947–58.

TEMPELS, PLACIDE, *La Philosophie Bantoue*, Paris, 1949.

TERRAIL, GABRIEL, *La Chronique de l'An 1911*, Paris, 1912.

TERRIER, AUGUSTE:
Afrique Equatoriale Française (vol. 4 of *Histoire des Colonies Françaises*, G. Hanotaux and A. Martineau, editors), Paris, 1931.
"La Réorganisation du Congo Français et la Mission Lenfant," *Questions Diplomatiques et Coloniales*, Année 8, Paris, 1904.

TERVER, P., "Le Nouveau Régime Forestier en AEF et au Cameroun," *Marchés Coloniaux*, June 22, 1946.

TEULIÈRES, ANDRÉ, *L'Oubangui Face à l'Avenir*, Paris, 1953.

TEVOEDJRE, ALBERT, *L'Afrique Révoltée*, Paris, 1958.

THIELLEMENT, ANDRÉ, *Azawar*, St. Vaast-la-Hougues, 1949.

THOMAS, JEAN, *A Travers l'Afrique Equatoriale Sauvage*, Paris, 1934.

THOUIN, MARCEL, *Etude sur la Délimitation de Frontière du Congo-Cameroun,* Paris, 1911.

TILHO, A. J. M., *Le Tchad et la Capture du Logone par le Niger,* Paris, 1947.

TISSERANT, CH., *Ce que J'ai Connu de l'Esclavage en Oubangui-Chari,* Paris, 1955.

TRAUTMANN, RENÉ, *Au Pays de "Batouala,"* Paris, 1922.

Le Travail en Afrique Noire, Paris, 1952.

TRÉZENEM, E., and B. LEMBEZAT, *La France Equatoriale,* Paris, 1950.

TRILLES, H.:

    Les Pygmées de la Fôret Equatoriale, Paris, 1932.

    Quinze Ans au Pays Fan, Paris, 1912.

TROCHAIN, JEAN, "Institut d'Etudes Centrafricaines," *Afrique Equatoriale Française,* Paris, 1950.

TRYSTRAN, J.-P., "Rapport sur le Régime Foncier des Ouaddis du Kanem" (mimeographed), Office de la Recherche Scientifique et Technique d'Outre-Mer, Fort Lamy, Apr. 25, 1958.

Union Française, 1953 (also *1954, 1955, 1956, 1957*), Paris.

URVOY, YVES, *Histoire de l'Empire du Bornou,* Paris, 1949.

VASSAL, GABRIELLE M., *Mon Séjour au Congo Français,* Paris, 1925.

VEISTROFFER, A., *Vingt Ans dans la Brousse Africaine,* Lille, 1931.

La Vie Française, Paris. (Weekly.)

VIVIER DE STREEL, E. DU, "L'Evolution du Congo Français," *Revue Politique et Parlementaire,* vol. 50, Paris, 1906.

WEULERESSE, JACQUES, *L'Afrique Noire,* Paris, 1934.

WITTE, Baron JEHAN DE, *Les Deux Congo,* Paris, 1913.

ZIEGLÉ, HENRI, *Afrique Equatoriale Française,* Paris, 1952.

ZWILLING, ERNST, *Jungle Fever,* London, 1956.

Index

Africanization of government, 31, 49, 66–71, 107, 394–402 *passim*; *see also* Civil service

Agriculture: Credit, loans, and subsidies, 118–23 *passim*, 170f, 216, 231, 334, 505; *see also* CCOM

—Export crops: AEF, 162–73 *passim*, 211; Gabon, 358, 364; Ou.-Chari, 397, 403, 406; Tchad, 442, 459; M.-Congo, 517; *see also* Duties: export; Exports; *and specific commodities*

—Government role in: historical, 11, 27, 30f, 109, 113; under ten-year plan, 162–78 *passim*; specific commodities, 179–96 *passim*; Gabon, 366ff; Ou.-Chari, 398ff, 448, 454–62 *passim*; M.-Congo, 481, 493, 499–502, 506, 510f

—Methods, indigenous, 161ff, 172–77 *passim*, 185, 190, 193, 202, 324; Ou.-Chari, 399, 415, 417; Tchad, 454, 501

—Subsistence crops, 4, 17, 20; research and new techniques, 162–65 *passim*, 168; policy abuses and reforms, 171ff, 177ff; labor problems, 255f, 260f, 275; missionary influence, 302; diet, 329ff; Gabon, 364f, 368f; Ou.-Chari, 406f; Tchad, 453–62 *passim*; M.-Congo, 502; *see also* Corn; Manioc; Millet; Peanuts; Rice

—Training, 23; new techniques, 162ff, 168, 176f; results, 184; in the schools, 278f; by missionaries, 304f; Gabon, 367; Ou.-Chari, 400, 411, 415, 422; Tchad, 454ff, 460; M.-Congo, 481

Airfields and air transport, 98, 103, 153–56; military, 88f; food shipment, 200f, 207, 330, 366; Ou.-Chari, 387, 399; Tchad, 22, 443, 449f, 467f, 470, 473; M.-Congo, 513

Alcoholic beverages, 4, 119; taxes, 128–32 *passim*, 213, 403, 447; alcoholism, 326f, 331; in Gabon, 337; in Tchad, 469; in M.-Congo, 524

Algeria, 9, 91, 96–104 *passim*, 382; *see also* North Africa

Angola, *see* Portuguese African territories

Animal husbandry: introduction of, 4; AEF, 27, 30f; Belgian influences, 106; private investment in, 117; introduction by missionaries, 301; in Gabon, 348, 374f; in Ou.-Chari, 417ff; in Tchad, 426f, 430, 436, 441–48 *passim*, 455f, 464–69; in M.-Congo, 500f, 508, 512ff; *see also* Meat and livestock; Hides-and-skins trade; Nomads; Water supply

Animism, *see* Fetishism

Artisans, *see* Labor: artisan

Aubame, J., 46, 49f, 64, 348–58 *passim*, 395, 438

Augouard, Father, 301f

Bakongo, viii; religion, 5, 301, 305–13 *passim*; tribal cohesion, 51, 93, 107, 323; in M.-Congo, 476–82 *passim*, 487f, 490f, 525; *see also* Balali

Balali: political movements, 44; education, 284, 292; religion, 301, 305, 310, 314; tribal identity, 323; in M.-Congo, 477, 479ff, 484f, 490

Bananas: AEF, 165, 167, 206; Gabon, 370; Ou.-Chari, 406; M.-Congo, 499–504 *passim*, 516

Banking, 117–23 *passim*, 203; *see also* CCOM; Housing; Monetary system

Baptiste, J., 430n, 433, 435f

Batéké, 3ff, 7, 225, 260, 323, 477, 484

Bayrou, M., 41, 44, 86, 247, 262, 351, 354, 482f

Berbérati affair, 40n, 82, 303n, 338, 392f

BET region (Borkou - Ennedi - Tibesti):